The FILM CRITICISM of OTIS FERGUSON

THE FILM CRITICISM *of* OTIS FERGUSON

Edited and with a
Preface by
ROBERT WILSON

Foreword by
ANDREW SARRIS

Temple University Press
PHILADELPHIA

5 0703 00016736 9

EVERETT LIBRARY QUEENS COLLEGE
CHARLOTTE, NORTH CAROLINA

791.437

F 3812f

Temple University Press, Philadelphia 19122
©1971 by Temple University. All rights reserved
Published 1971
Printed in the United States of America

International Standard Book Number: 0-87722-005-0
Library of Congress Catalog Card Number: 72-174660

To Dorothy Chamberlain

and to Sue Young and Kevin Wilson

3/25/74

E.B.S.

Contents

Foreword

The long-overdue republication of Otis Ferguson's movie reviews within a single binding should help correct much of the nonsense written elsewhere about the period from 1934 through 1941. There is no better film chronicle of this era anywhere, but try selling this proposition to most publishers. *We* don't want just another collection of faded clippings, they cry in unison. What *we* want is an authoritative history written especially for us by a recognized film scholar, and we have just the man for the job: Wolfgang Krockhaus of the Altamira Academy of Cinematic Art. As it happens, Herr Krockhaus has seen only nineteen movies in his life, but he has accumulated secondary reference material on nineteen thousand more. At the drop of a footnote, he can quote you what Vachel Lindsay wrote about Mae Marsh in 1916, but he himself has not had an original insight into acting since *Birth of a Nation.* What makes Krockhaus such a renowned authority is his sociological certitude even in the face of contrary aesthetic evidence. As Eric Sevareid has said of the persuasive man in the Pentagon with the blackboard and pointer, Krockhaus may be in error, but he is never in doubt. Nor is he ever afflicted with the specialist's ambivalence toward his subject. Official film historians cannot afford to be either specialists or particularists, but must pose instead as generalists par excellence so as to present publishers with the illusion of unity in a field in which unity is impossible. However, when the need arises for even random specificity, Krockhaus is clever enough to have access to every word Otis Ferguson ever wrote, and thus is free to render clumsy paraphrases of Ferguson's opinions as his very own.

If I seem to have spent an inordinate amount of space exposing poor, harmless old Krockhaus, it is simply to prepare the reader for the possibility of encountering echoes from forgotten readings and conversations in Otis Ferguson's critical prose, a bit like the old lady in Henry Fielding's *Tom Jones* with her complaint about Shakespeare's being made up of old quotations. I had that same sensation reading Ferguson on *Modern Times* to the effect that Chaplin had borrowed the assembly line from René Clair's *À Nous la Liberté* four years earlier. A very knowledgeable and knowing young lady dispensed that little tidbit back in my high-school days in the forties, and I was very impressed, but, looking back, I think she must have gotten her scholarly insight (and many more like it) from Ferguson, perhaps subliminally from the pulpy but otherwise politically fashionable pages of the *The New Republic.*

To my knowledge, reprints of Ferguson's movie pieces have popped up only in Alistair Cooke's *Garbo and the Night Watchmen* (Jonathan Cape, 1937) along with criticism by Cecelia Ager, Cooke himself, Robert Forsythe, Graham Greene, Don Herold, Robert Herring, Meyer Levin, and John Marks, all very good critics indeed. And I would add to their number the eminently seminal Gilbert Seldes and the unfairly neglected Patterson Murphy. Still, taking into account Ferguson's distinguished contemporaries mentioned above, and such distinguished predecessors as Vachel Lindsay, Hugo Munsterberg, and Robert E. Sherwood, and such distinguished successors as James Agee, Manny Farber, and Robert Warshow, I think a strong claim can be made for Ferguson as the writer of the best and most subtly influential film criticism ever turned out in America.

If Agee's criticism reflects a passion for poetry, and Farber's a passion for painting, Ferguson's reflects a passion for music. No other film critic has come as close as Ferguson to x-raying the connective tissue—physical, visual, soniferous, psychological—that binds isolated images into an organic narrative on the screen. He managed on more than one occasion the difficult stylistic feat of describing the tedium of movie-making without being tedious himself. His hilarious blast at the boredom of Dziga Vertov's *Three Songs about Lenin* in 1934 consisted mainly of an improvised mock montage à la Ferguson, and like all first-rate parodies it really isn't too far from the real thing.

Ferguson was very much in tune with the technocratic spirit of the thirties, and very much in sympathy with the working stiffs who were both the subjects and the labor force of so many movies. His instinctive populism, however, never degenerated into crudity, vulgarity, or philistinism. And he was deadly serious about the craft of film criticism even when he was poking fun at its pedantic excesses. In fact, Ferguson was one of the few professional reviewers of his time with more than a rudimentary interest in the history of the medium, and film research in those days was a far more strenuous proposition than it is today.

Why then has Ferguson not been more widely recognized as the trail-blazing beacon of film criticism that he was? The most obvious reason is that no critic can address any meaningful portion of posterity except between the covers of a book. As it happened, James Agee not only followed Ferguson; he completely supplanted him on the cultural scene. Agee was blessed with the kind of bookish credentials that enabled the trolls and Trillings of the literary establishment to hail him as the one and only compleat film critick. Ferguson's enormous influence on Agee (and Farber) was never mentioned even by people who had been reading *The New Republic* since the year one, and the new breed of American Bazinians and Cahierists (to which this reviewer belongs) never paused to consider the possibility that Ferguson might have anticipated many of Bazin's ideas on film history from an entirely different vantage point. Indeed I can think of no higher tribute to pay Ferguson than to say that he is the one American movie critic who most closely resembles Bazin.

Even today, however, an appreciation of Ferguson depends largely upon an appreciation of movies. Ferguson reads even better when you know what he's writing about than when you don't. His style is often more ritualistically judgmental than novelistically descriptive, and he never got around to editing out flabby adjectives like "swell" and "terrific." But then, unlike Agee, he was more often pointing than preening. Ferguson understood movies too well to attempt to duplicate the sensuous sweep of their detail, and he was civilized enough to stand relatively mute before their ultimate magic and mystery.

Ferguson had no idea at the time that he was witnessing the final flowering of the classical tradition of movie-making. Like any reviewer worth his salt, he took each movie as it came along, shook out its inevitable puerilities and pretensions, measured whatever conscience and craftsmanship were left, and seldom missed the slightest semblance of style, whether of a Humphrey Bogart in his early gangster period or of a Fritz Lang in his back-to-the-wall exile. He could appreciate the finer points of W. C. Fields, Charles Laughton, and the Marx Brothers without overlooking how sloppy and undisciplined they could be without half trying. Actually, his outstanding surgical specialty was the funny-bone, and no one else of his time or since has so perceptively appreciated the comic genius of the early sound film, that most mindlessly abused of all periods of production. There was in Ferguson none of the numbing nostalgia for the "Golden Age of Comedy" celebrated in Agee's elegant essay. Agee was, of course, emotionally driven by memories of laughing uproariously with his father at Chaplin's antics in the midst of a softly focused childhood in Arcadia. Ferguson's childhood seemed to have been somewhat harsher and less protected than Agee's, and his view of childhood was more Dead End Kids and less sweetness and light than Agee's. Similarly, Ferguson's theory of comedy was more devil-may-care and less angelic than Agee's, and it follows that Ferguson barely noticed the loss of the stylized clown personae of Chaplin, Keaton, Lloyd, Langdon, et al. in the rush of a mob of bit players full of roaring realism and bustling individuality. And it is at this point that Ferguson and Bazin intersect most strikingly, Ferguson more through intuition perhaps and Bazin more through theory, but both arriving at the unfashionable conclusion that the coming of sound had not only been commercially inevitable but also aesthetically desirable as an extension of realism. Actually, the breadth of Ferguson's sympathies provided him with a European sensibility tempered with American skepticism, a tough mixture that was never soured either by

European knowingness or American know-nothingness. Hence, his critical vision could grow through the evidence of his senses, and not congeal in the molds of preconception.

I cannot pretend or presume to measure the full meaning of Ferguson's life as a man on this planet, especially a life of thirty-six years snuffed out prematurely in 1943 on a cargo ship in the Bay of Salerno. Alfred Kazin has written eloquently of Ferguson's tough-minded iconoclasm in the literary-political memoir *Starting Out in the Thirties*. Kazin knew where Ferguson lived and worked, but surprisingly little of what he was about as a film critic. To read Kazin one would think that Ferguson wrote about films merely to spite the literary aristocracy. Nothing could be further from the truth. Ferguson may have started movie reviewing as a lark, but once he plunged in he dedicated himself with a fervor that is still exciting to read thirty years later. His Hollywood articles alone are worth the price of admission to this testament of intellectual faith in a mass medium, and his articles on *Citizen Kane,* the first Louis-Schmeling fight, *It Happened One Night,* and a couple of hundred other film-related subjects rank so close to the top of American journalism that it isn't worth measuring the difference. The important thing to remember is that Ferguson, like Agee after him, was not merely a disconnected stylist writing about nothing in particular. He was writing about something very important, something that went beyond the screen to the furthest reaches of art and life, but without ever completely by-passing the screen. Ferguson plus Film equals the best of autobiography and the best of aesthetics.

ANDREW SARRIS

Preface

Manny Farber once remarked that "Americans seem to have a special aptitude for allowing History to bury the toughest, most authentic native talents." Otis Ferguson, who has been dead and largely unremembered for almost thirty years, was on Farber's list of forgotten men of art. He is among the last to be rediscovered.

It is to the credit of Farber, Andrew Sarris, and very few others that Ferguson's name has been kept alive in film history through the years of neglect. James Agee was collected early, and after Agee, Pauline Kael, Sarris, and almost as an afterthought, Farber—critics who form an unbroken chain of relevant American film criticism. But first there was Ferguson, who influenced and taught them all.

Because of Ferguson's importance as a critic and informal historian of an era, an unusually large percentage—roughly 80 percent—of his film writing has been preserved in this volume. An attempt was made to cut only those pieces in which Ferguson's reaction was lukewarm, space-filling (this happens to even the best of weekly reviewers), or in which the film itself brought down the level of keen perceptiveness that marked Ferguson's response to all but the dullest of thirties features. Regrettably, Ferguson did not begin to expand his insights into longer, theoretical essays until the last years of his life. The three articles of this type that he has left us are grouped together under the title "The Promise of the Movie in America." In 1941 Ferguson was sent to Hollywood by *The New Republic;* his marvelous reportage on this trip comprises the final section of the book, "To the Promissory Land."

It's been many years since the reference to Otis Ferguson in Farber's 1957 article "Underground Films" led me to the yellow and brittle pages of *The New Republic.* Now that those pages are falling to dust, it's a pleasure to know that this collection will restore a great critic to the mainstream of American thought and writing.

ROBERT WILSON

xiii

Biographical Note

Otis Ferguson was born in 1907 in Worcester, Massachusetts. When he was about fifteen, he started working, so he could stay in high school. At seventeen, he enlisted in the Navy; he was paid off, four years later, as Seaman First Class. With his $1,000 Navy pay, money from odd jobs and scholarships, he was able to finish high school and obtain, in three years, an A.B. degree from Clark University. During his college years, he ghosted a history thesis that earned a master's degree (for someone else) and began to learn his future profession by writing theater criticism, articles, fiction, and poetry for the *Clark Quarterly*. In 1932, his entry "Gaush!" won *The New Republic*'s college contest. He went to New York after his graduation in 1933 and for a while met expenses by reviewing books. His first film criticism for *The New Republic* was published in January 1934. He joined the magazine's staff the following summer and later became an assistant editor. Besides his movie and book reviews, he wrote about jazz and the theater for *The New Republic* and contributed to other publications.

Soon after Pearl Harbor, he went into the Merchant Marine as an able-bodied seaman. In February 1942 he signed on his first ship, which took almost a year to deliver its cargo to Archangel and return to home port. He shipped out again in 1943, this time bound for North Africa, Sicily, and Italy. He was killed when his ship was bombed in the Bay of Salerno.

1

THE PROMISE
OF THE MOVIE
IN AMERICA

Life Goes to the Pictures

There are the categories in art of realism and naturalism, but for the most part they have remained conveniences of designation. The truly natural and unforced, especially as applied to the ways of common life, are hardly possible in such forms of expression as music, painting, writing, because the long and uncommon discipline of these crafts has made the men in them a different breed: they are easy and at home in their job only when the job is the unnatural one of creation. Although the majority of playwrights are only second-class writers at best, and the majority of actors ham it even when they are asleep and snoring, the stage is much nearer to the actual look and push of things, if only because its people, particularly its minor people, are, after all, people.

The movies, however, are today the nearest thing ever imagined to the unaffected and unconscious process of life, as expressed in art. That takes a lot of qualification, and will be hooted at in some quarters anyway, because it is the fashion to judge movies by their worst excrescence, and I suppose much more fun that way. In theory, I imagine this distinctive quality owes most to the fact that the films combine both immediacy and an almost boundless range as to time, place, and fancy. But much of it comes directly and without forethought from their origins and audience, their rank growth as a new art. We will be at that presently.

First, there is the matter of a tradition in art as it affects its practitioners. Take writing, the most familiar of the arts today: writers are above the blind aping of tradition that becomes so ridiculous in opera singers and the vaudeville Abe and Irish. At the same time writers are marked by the occupational disease of intellectualism. If they came from the working class, it is a good bet they were odd nuts even while they were working—tolerated and even liked perhaps, but outsiders, strange with books and questioning. If they had a privileged background, they are outside the main part of the world anyway: their sympathy may be acute and wide, but has to be objective. In either event, their urge to

3

express the world about them has had a good long soaking in the accumulation of styles that makes up the literary tradition.

We have learned, every man jack of us, only a tiny fraction of life from our personal experience. The main body of knowledge is handed down by word of mouth and, on the higher levels, by words in print (otherwise how would we know that tomatoes aren't poisonous and the world isn't flat?). And more subtly, our estimate of what is natural shifts with each new stylization of it. Milt Gross once had the last word in transcription of joosh dialack; then come people like Odets, Irwin Shaw, Jerome Weidman—and what happens? O. Henry was once the whole seamy side in neat bundles, and then comes Damon Runyon, and you can have them both. Jack London was once the strenuous life stripped to the bone, but who would follow him after Hemingway? The point which I will not labor another minute is that in all fields of presentation the world is seen through somebody else's glasses—which have been ground into a cunning instrument just as the good oculist would grind at his work: partly by inspiration, partly by relentless application, but mostly by the best use of the best tools and precepts developed in his own guarded craft.

In their forty-odd years, the movies have developed their high craftsmen, and gradually out of the craftsman's effects, an art. But forty years is nothing in art, especially such a hole-and-corner art. The movies were upon us before anyone had time to grow up and become a professor in them. They literally grew out of the people, the hundreds and thousands of people who jumped in to produce, distribute, exhibit, direct, write for, or act in a popular commodity; and the millions and millions whose demand for some kind of excitement or relaxation as available and easy as the funnies, has made the whole sky-high fantasy not only real but inevitable. The legend has it that any businessman, or even college man, can jump in, learn the ropes, and become a producer with some bold or clever stroke. The legend is that any grip on the set with ideas can substitute for an assistant cameraman someday and become Darryl Zanuck. The legend is that a director spies some handsome filling-station boy, readies him in a few pictures, and a star is born.

Legend is usually a good part hogwash, but there is justice here. For the intellectual classes, the earlier nickelodeons were houses of shame: directors, producers, exhibitors had to be recruited from the vulgar. As films gained prestige, actors, directors, and writers went over to them. If they went to Hollywood, though, there was still the feeling of cultural betrayal. It was all right to be a foreign director or cameraman, or an established name like Chaplin or Griffith. But even while someone like Edmund Wilson was awesomely mistaking an uncut travelogue for a modern epic, he was (and still is) sternly deploring the desertion of any first-rate literary hack who got the chance to hit for the Beverly Hills.

It is still true that movie people come from among just people, bringing their unconscious shabby baggage of popular life along with them. Some of them go so rapidly and so far upstage, or commercial, as to get clean out of sight. And there are very few wholly conscious of a purpose. But there is also an in-between belt of nice people who bring to the screen only their natural selves and the simple things they know. They may be technicians, or dialogue writers, or advisors, or "character" players. They may be very much in the background, and they still may be the most important aid to truth—for there was never a more relentless eye and ear for petty fraud and the easy glozing over of truth than the modern camera and sound-track.

As Lewis Jacobs reminds us in his recent history of the movies, the films of the earliest period, hundreds upon hundreds of them, turned on incidents in the commonest of common life. But what you do not get from reading such titles as *A Plumber's Plight* is that the treatment itself is as far from life as any black-face Al Jolson is from cotton. It was only with the full flexibility of the camera and the added latitude of sound that they really had time and scope for the hundred and one details that, observed in the film's motion without checking it, take an action out of stylized presentation (however effective) and make it completely natural.

Along with the growth of naturalism there has gone an influence that is wide and unmeasurable—the old question of, Which held the mirror first, art or life? Even within our generation, some sources of our knowledge of the world have been taken over from the knowledgeable class, especially in all the more vivid departments of presentation and document in pictures. Knowledge today is so lost in a maze of simple environment that we may catch ourselves criticizing the "likelihood" of one submarine picture by a wisdom of underwater techniques that could not possibly have been gained from experience. (As a matter of confessional fact, I can't today distinguish between the antiquated type of T-boat I have actually been down in, and *Submarine D-1* and *U-Boat 29.*)

Turn on yourself and ask quickly if you ever saw a tiger in the jungle. You get an image though, correct? (Any sensible tiger would probably laugh at the image you get, but that's not the point here.) Ever since the first Tarzan epics and on down through the Fox Magic Carpet of Movietone and the Armand Denis's, we have been as familiar with wild animals as Hemingway. And this goes over into character. As Alistair Cooke pointed out a couple of years ago, Churchill and Chamberlain are mere cartoon figures: the British Empire is C. Aubrey Smith. It is as familiar as tigers.

And to go even farther afield, take the common-variety American in his occupation. He is Pat O'Brien, or something like that. I remember *Here Comes the Navy*, in which O'Brien was a chief-petty-officer, for the purpose of mortifying James Cagney, seaman-second-class. He lined his company up and walked it down the dock and came front and center in a medium shot and I nearly talked out loud in the theater: "Tague (chief signalman), you sonofabitch!" (Just an old wound, gentlemen.) And then from the opposite angle, I remember being on a banana boat and watching them repair a winch, and then the second engineer knocked off and went forward, looking vaguely sardonic—and he was John Carradine to the teeth.

When I was a kid, my old man worked a starveling New England farm in a section where every other name was Lubitzcki and there was deep snow, winters, and when King Vidor made *The Wedding Night,* I liked all those hulking Polacks I had known, for the first time in my life. I worked in a bowling alley two years and my boss was a very second-rate Edward Arnold. I even did a little robbing once with a slow Dutchman and a very special-edition little Italian, and I see them occasionally even in the most faky gangster films.

This isn't a jag on autobiography, and I haven't been a fan since the days of William S. Hart, I guess. I am trying to get at a point about movies, especially as made in America. On the surface and often below it they have a magnificent realism. Their men and women, from both sides of the camera, were in so many instances a part of common life just yesterday that they haven't had time to forget it, dress it up, and bury it. Too much talk has been wasted on the tendency of the movies to type people. They do, they do. But this is the new method and here to stay, for with so many levels of life to be covered, faster and faster, they simply can't wait to develop the old-type character actor with his bag of tricks and crepe hair.

I know for a fact that Cagney can coax or shove a director until a scene from a dreamy script becomes a scene from life as Cagney remembered it. I'm sure that hundreds of lesser people—in a picture where they are well cast and let alone—dredge up out of memory, way back beyond Beverly Hills, the natural phrase and gesture which let the same life in, in spite of the director.

In such a mixture of chance, collaboration, and hurry, the real thing is often smothered by surrounding irreality, to be sure. But often—and most often—the element of clear and simple truth as it is distilled for the screen is the work of some kingpin in the organization. A director like King Vidor under a producer like Goldwyn (*The Wedding Night*). A czar-director like Alfred Hitchcock, who still has them wondering how he can openly take what is usually passed off as melodrama and get excitement out of every character along the way—his open secret, which cannot be copied, is that in spite of the requirements of speed and tension, he can stop and figure out why a person would do this if he were somebody you might meet, and if he were that real, how would he go about it? A writer-director like Rowland Brown, whether he is his own director or not, remembers so vividly his experience of childhood *as a child* that he could never make a *Wizard of Oz* or *Road to Life* (which is simply Louisa May Alcott on a collective farm, which is to say, childhood through the wrong end of a telescope). I won't forget Brown's *The Devil Is a Sissy,* but I remembered its intangibles better when I tried to set them down in review:

". . . at the time Gig's father is going to the chair, and there is that day at school and that night when nobody can sleep, Buck standing with Gig under the streetlight snapping his knuckles and nothing else to say, except in apology for his own blunderbuss of a father: 'The old man, he . . . Wull, he means all right.' This part, in the authentic schoolroom, flats and streets, was done with what struck me as straightforward and absolutely unpretentious beauty. And shrewdness too: Gig's sudden brief shift from awe and bereavement to bragging next morning was very shrewd." The stuff was there—the human relations as well as the truck-hopping, apple-swiping, and a hundred deft activities—because it was written in and allowed to come out as felt. If you throw out the moral slops of the ending, this would be the first of a perfect trilogy on low and high life in big American cities—the other two being *Public Enemy* and *The Roaring Twenties.*

In analysis, our belief in any kind of life on the screen is dependent on many things, animate or inanimate, the people seen and the people unseen who planted the line or rolled the camera or set the whole motion in tempo. A picture can thus be pure hokum and still be very true in parts, or it can be the Great Social Document of the age and never really stick for a minute. Further, I realize that this subtle combination of many forces often plays tricks on us: we think it is the actor who is fine or the director who is shrewd, when it is really that and something else too. (This should be little of our concern, but I'd like a dime for every quote I could bring in, even from established critics, praising the fine "photography" of a picture whose beauty was purely a matter of natural scenery or fine set-building.) So when you go to the vivid feeling of life to be got from a picture like *Come and Get It* (if you remember), you will find that those loggers and lumber kings were natural partly because of the magnificent documentary sequences of big-scale logging—with which they had nothing to do—and the construction of such sets as the one for the big-town saloon. All I have to do is thumb back through some old clippings to be reminded of this constant element beyond both story and character as such: "What the screen really makes out of *Ah, Wilderness* is a first-class atmosphere piece. It calls up more matters than it knows of by its sure reconstruction of the day-to-day life of the New England country in a time that is as dead but vivid in the general memory as the smell of leaves burning in piles along the gravel walks. . . . Not only the sets of stiff cluttered rooms, lawns, gas buggies, picnics, but the incidental life of the place."

Or, *"Rhodes of Africa* progresses unevenly, shirks some duties, and ends in a ponderous fussiness. The outdoor photography in Africa—the plains, hills, mines, and such mob effects as the trek north, the attack of the Matabele—is the best of the production values, being handled by a separate director, Geoffrey Barkas." (And for that matter, the work of Otto Brower and Osmond Borradaile has lightened many an African epic that otherwise falls with its own weight.)

So when we say that a film is a good picture of men working (as we often can), we recognize the understanding and talent of many people outside the actual men at work in the story. I just wanted to get that straightened out, because there are not words enough yet for the different ways in which movies affect us. If I were to pick the Hollywood film *Black Fury* over *Kameradschaft* for "Realism" or even "Naturalism," half my readers would get black in the face. Of course Pabst's film is a monumental sketch of men working shoulder to shoulder, and way ahead of its time in a film sense. But *Black Fury* was made in another, more familiar tradition, at another time: piece by piece it is nearer to our life if only in that the life of its characters was dramatized until we actually participated in it. The film got a blast from all labor sympathizers, and in a tactical sense deserved it (if you recall, the story was a true enough story about a certain kind of union activity, but by that part-for-the-whole business of presentation seemed to stand for all union activity). However, it said more about miners and their miserable lot than anything else we've had. When those men were working, or chewing the fat, or drinking their pitiful nickels away in the bar, they were no strangers to you. Rough men and awesome, yes. But so cleverly worked into a story-pattern of cause and result, environment and hopes, that they were neither symbols nor foreigners, but people you knew and hoped the best of. You knew their work and their dinner table, their mean streets and threadbare pleasures; and everything about it was simple and just-so, through the medium of the most complex and expensive art on earth.

And then there was *Fury,* Fritz Lang's picture of a lynching, a wonderful picture through the first two-thirds. The boy was just homely and hopeless enough, saying goodbye to his girl and trying to keep his brothers out of mischief—for these were poor people, and no doubt about it. In the story he saved up enough to buy a piece of a small gas station and a cheap car, and go to fetch his girl, who had a teaching job. And all this quiet and decent life (the simple pleasures, etc.) was blown to glory in the best study of mob stupidity anyone ever saw. The audience knew who this man was, and then saw—detail after detail—the growing antagonism and mass hysteria of the small-town types who didn't know and didn't care. (Not a lot of mugging faces in close-up or fancy cutting, either.) That thing built into terrific drama, but from the ground up.

And another film, not so well known but one of John Ford's: *Prisoner of Shark Island.* I remember that above almost any "historical" film (it was the case of Dr. Mudd), if only because it got clear of period and costumes; it became to its audience a common carrier. I know nothing of Dry Tortugas, except the general climate; but I do know barrack routine and never saw it so well used to heighten illusion and tension. The bugles, rifle racks, relief of the guard, etc., were only a part of it, though. The main thing was the sweating men in that end-of-the-earth shambles, what they did and what was done to them. You got *involved* in that picture, and I believe that was brought about by such a shrewd care for the pitch and speed of every move, every detail, that there was no need for suspension of belief. Except for a few tank shots, it was one of those things that come down off the screen and pull up a chair.

It is a certain thing John Ford gets into his pictures—it is more than pure skill in the medium, for it releases the imagination of all the people working on the set. Even a hoopla Western like *Stagecoach,* admittedly made as such, packs its scenes with the same kind of likelihood; and a picture like *Submarine Patrol* is a story of the Splinter Fleet that would be accepted by veterans. In this case it isn't that Ford recaptures those gray belting north seas in winter, which job can wait for Robert Flaherty. Again, as before, it is the recreation of day-to-day relations—life in action and at mess and horsing around.

(Here we come to what the printers call Insert A, the occasion being the happy appearance of Mr. Ford's *Grapes of Wrath* before this article had got further than galley form. The film is just what such a piece was waiting for, and indeed could stand as its single illustration, for in addition to its true-as-life study of people, jalopies, Okie camps, and the roads, it had a superb job of writing, direction, and camera, and a subject worthy of the best capacities of the medium. And when that malignant clown Martin Quigley attacked the truth of the story, *Boxoffice* was able to run—in addition to other supporting documents—a remarkable juxtaposition in two columns of photographs—one of actual cars and people and Okie villages, one of stills from the picture. And on a different scale there has been that running-mate by proximity if nothing else, Milestone's version of *Of Mice and Men*— see below—another study and another proof that the truth of films can be more vivid than the truth of fiction, and still as true.)

Don't worry; this is not going to fall off into directors-I-too-have-watched-with-interest. But Lewis Milestone is another to contribute to the naturalism of the Talking Thirties by this same aptitude for letting characters talk for themselves, or making them, and covering all loose joints with details from life. *All Quiet on the Western Front* is certainly the pioneer in this period, head and shoulders. But I'd like to bring back a screwball Milestone film of 1934 that never got much play: *The Captain Hates the Sea.* Its comedy was delicious; its human content was absurdly high for such a piece of gentle spoofing; and better than anything there was that feeling about it that everybody read the script and said This is going to be fun, and they made it so. In spite of comedy, it was just in everything, from the captain on his bridge to the fly bartender, and the only true steamer orchestra I ever saw except on a steamer. But the film is a hobby of mine, a cruise story to end cruises forever, and perhaps it is best I get off here.

Generally, you remember films by their total effect, so that if you are thinking "sea," you think of *Captains Courageous* or *Mutiny on the Bounty.*

That is why directors get such a big play, as having been responsible throughout. But there are many other things to consider in this realism of life on all levels. I'll bet few remember a melodrama called *Wharf Angel,* and I wouldn't myself if it hadn't had some shots in a stokehold that were so dark, hot, and real they hurt. Of the memorable stuff in *It Happened One Night,* anyone properly conditioned to long bus-hops will have a certain nostalgia for the sequence around the Gr-yh--nd terminal and the bus itself. Anyone who has been a machinist's apprentice will remember the groundwork sequences for *Black Legion,* which wasn't an awfully well-made affair as a whole. And some will recall newspaper and magazine offices—one especially in that fast-talk piece that was ripping beyond its time, *The Front Page,* another in *Friends of Mr. Sweeney*—both hokum, of course. And so on.

As I said before, set-building for atmosphere is a responsible part of all this, but if it were the whole of it, we would have to give over to the French, who when they are good are the best in the world (take *The Lower Depths* for one, or take the René Clair carnival in *Quatorze Juillet* or the sets in *Crime and Punishment*). And for realism as such we could never put a finger on such films of the latter Soviet period as *Peasants,* where you could damn near smell the pigs and the cow-shed—in fact, nothing has ever been done so close to the elemental dirt, drudgery, and delight of farm life. No, this faster and more flexible camera eye we're considering picks up half-finished lines, personal habits, street noise, shades of daylight, and a hundred familiar things, and when done with imagination and feeling—and only then—can become as near and eloquent as the room you're in. The environment with all its familiar nuisances and pleasures, and the people in it, with all theirs. Doctor, lawyer, merchant, chief, etc.

You could stop right here and make a thesis for Hollywood as the mirror to low life, if you had to make a thesis; for its shakiest reenactments are in general those of Presidents, Morgan Partners, Supreme Court Justices, Diplomats, and such rarefied fields of the intellect as may also be spelled upper case. Colleges, for example—with the one recent exception of *Vivacious Lady,* college has had an absolute hex on producers, who have approached it with a singular mixture of trembling and football. Writing and painting, of course. (*Rembrandt* would be my exception here; *Zola* wouldn't.) And strangest of all, the ordinary run of musicians—who litter every set, every day. A danceband is still a studio blind spot: the iron rule is that everybody wears a funny hat in rehearsal or in bed; if a musician forgets and acts naturally, they have to retake the scene because that isn't the way musicians act; and a few months ago there was a producer spotting talent in New York who wouldn't listen to Bobby Hackett's cornet because, hell, he played it *down,* whereas everybody knows a cornet is played straight up in the air, balanced on the nose.

Truck drivers, linesmen, floorwalkers, train dispatchers, fighters and promoters, and the working press—the movies wade right into them. Doctors and nurses and district attorneys too. But art and thought are something special, you know, like in De Mille on the flossy. Well, let it go at that. Certainly there is everywhere in pictures a tendency to fakery and Dick Powell that has disgraced enough walks of common life to make a bookful of articles by anyone with a typewriter (and believe me it has already made several). My concern and pleasure are in movies when they are good, and rather than go nagging along with a thousand more modern instances, I will remind you of a film called *Ceiling Zero,* which I couple with *Grand Illusion* whenever I think of the best expression of men in their calling, whether at odds or together.

As what the movies recognize as a "team" I believe James Cagney and Pat O'Brien have done more than any other combination to search out and show in theater terms the obscure tie that exists between men who share the same danger, privations, and sack of Bull Durham. Often they have been cast for a simple Quirt-Flagg type of surface thing. But occasionally, working together, they have got more into it than was there to be read. And in *Ceiling Zero* they were able to let go—it was the kind of thing which was high and fascinating to audiences, dealing with the romance of flight, and which was true too, dealing with the conflict between men who only want to do the job and men who want to make money on it; with the self-destruction of one of nature's incurable wise-guys; with the life of nice people.

The picture had that quality of mutual experience and trust, mutual affection and exasperation, of a profound but tacit dedication to getting the work out, through hell and high water, that becomes the kind of bond and shared belief that is usually known only by the men sticking it out on the job. In some form or other its possibilities have been exploited in pictures, from *Beau Geste* to *Lives of a Bengal Lancer,* and it is as romantic as any straight romance. In the easy life, buckled-on routine, casual patter, and terrific high tension of this story of planes making their appointed round or crashing on it, there was something that has often been felt by men thrown together in peril or hardship, something that has always been beautiful and almost never expressed.

It was the story as much as Howard Hawks' direction; it was both as much as it was Cagney and O'Brien and all the other good people. But it was the movie-in-America even more—it was the setup to make such a thing possible and vivid, and to afford the chance to people who still remembered something of life as it appears to those who merely live it, to get in there pitching before they had become a critic or Robert Mantell, and make it live again. Like the novel, the fiction film is wide open to anyone who can use it to advantage. Unlike the novel (which please compare in its year-to-year output), and through all its silly and vicious blunders, it has taken all of actual life to be its province. And in the part of life in which the majority of people—only shadowed up to now by George Eliot and Stendhal, Millet, and Dickens and the last-gasp proletarian writers of today—are the principal characters, it has an open slate still to write on. That is the promise of the movie in America, and if there were not some token of its fulfillment, of things having been written on such a slate before this, we would not be going to movies, and talking about them.

Films, Spring 1940

The Camera Way Is the Hard Way

It is hard to realize what tedious and backbreaking work goes into the actual shooting of any Class A picture—six or eight weeks' time is more the rule than the exception, and each of those working weeks has six days, each of the days has at least eight solid hours, nine to six (often earlier to later), with a breathing spell only for lunch. The picture runs a mere hour and a half when they have finished with it, and you wonder where all the time goes. It would seem easy to get at least twenty minutes of dialogue and action into a day of hard work with cameras and stuff. And there you are: all the shooting washed up in a week, with a day to spare for retakes and special odds and ends.

Standing around on one foot and then on the other for an afternoon, dodging grips, gaffers, and the constantly shifting equipment on any set, would probably give you some idea, certainly leave you dead tired, and possibly still leave doubts. All this going over and over the same few lines, the shifting of half a ton of apparatus in a long wait, the going over again—isn't this waste motion? Not in the picture of any good director, not much of it even in the technique of movies as we have them today.

That a scene is taken several times before the thing you actually see afterward is selected is a fact merely corresponding with the rehearsal before performance in plays or music. That two or three takes of everything are printed is merely acknowledgment of the fact that the camera does not show what the eye shows ever, and even the experienced have to guess. And that many scenes are shot first from one side, then from another, then from above, etc., is the elemental fact needed for the camera to keep shifting to its highest point of emphasis and interest, while the normal and rightly placed voices of all those taking part must remain steady on the film's sound-track as the camera looks away or over them.

Take an afternoon on the set where William Wyler was starting off *The Little Foxes*—more interesting than many because of the complexity of the setup, the size and fine design of the set itself, and the imminence of a good director's picture (don't try to catch a director's "genius" when he is working: it is in his head if he has it, and in his puttees or accent if he hasn't). The big stage is filled clear up to the parallels by three sides of a square of two-story buildings, with a lawn and driveway, bushes and flowers, trees spreading their branches over everything and going up out of sight (see stage plan). It is also filled with people, everybody with something to do, usually something mysterious.

The afternoon is only a detail in the completed picture, running off before your eyes in less than a minute, but it carries on the story. It isn't even the whole of the detail, which started with trying out effective angles and maybe the first line or two in the morning. It is almost at the start of the picture as we see it now, where Zan is getting out of the buggy at her Aunt Birdie's house in the morning, her aunt coming to the upstairs window. If you look down at the set from above, this window would be at the extreme left in the back, the carriage at the extreme right. The only actual changes in position are Zan's moving three steps toward the left as the carriage drives off, then to the center, and the aunt's first coming to the window and leaving it on the last line.

I will give the lines of this scene as nearly as I can remember them, then the positions of camera covering each (see fig. 1). Then all you have to do is to see the picture and figure it out. You will be on your own, and you will not want to be a movie director again.

Zan: Good-morning, Aunt Birdie, is your headache gone?

Birdie: Oh yes, it's all gone, thank you.

Queenie: Good-morning, Miss Birdie.

Birdie: Good-morning, Queenie.

Zan: You go along, Queenie, I want to talk to Aunt Birdie a minute.

Queenie: You better hurry, because your mother's waiting and she ain't *no* person to be kept waiting. (Drives off.)

Zan (moving left): Guess where we went this morning, Aunt Birdie.

Birdie: To—Lyonnet! Oh darling, was it beautiful? I know it was, it was always beautiful this time of year. I can see the house shining in a new coat of paint, and the flowers blooming in the gardens, and —

Zan (moving to center, speaking to overlap the last of this): Oh Aunt Birdie, I've learned the Schubert piece, all of it, except the middle part—Auntie, couldn't we play it without the middle? Mr. Chalmers would never know.

Birdie: Indeed we can *not.* It's so easy, I'll come right down and play it through with you. Now you wait, darling. (She retreats from window; cut.)

Now for this they had a camera on a crane, an enormous affair that looks something like a derrick, carrying the camera and its attendants up and down and right and left, forward or back on the wheels of the base; and the usual camera on the ground. The first setup was the crane at the far left (see I), on a level with and close up to Birdie's window (up among the trees too: they had the devil of a time with the trees and would now and then have to take off a branch

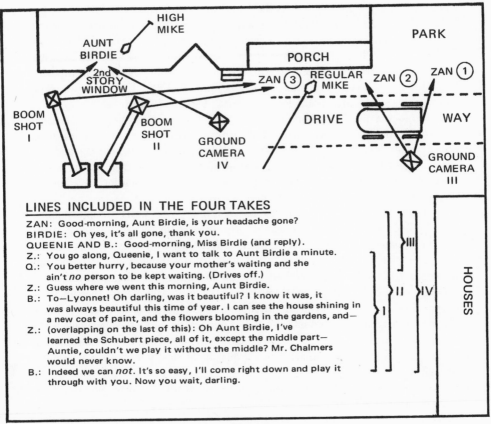

LINES INCLUDED IN THE FOUR TAKES

ZAN: Good-morning, Aunt Birdie, is your headache gone?
BIRDIE: Oh yes, it's all gone, thank you.
QUEENIE AND B.: Good-morning, Miss Birdie (and reply).
Z.: You go along, Queenie, I want to talk to Aunt Birdie a minute.
Q.: You better hurry, because your mother's waiting and she
ain't *no* person to be kept waiting. (Drives off.)
Z.: Guess where we went this morning, Aunt Birdie.
B.: To—Lyonnet! Oh darling, was it beautiful? I know it was, it
was always beautiful this time of year. I can see the house shining in
a new coat of paint, and the flowers blooming in the gardens, and—
Z.: (overlapping on the last of this): Oh Aunt Birdie, I've
learned the Schubert piece, all of it, except the middle part—
Auntie, couldn't we play it without the middle? Mr. Chalmers
would never know.
B.: Indeed we can *not*. It's so easy, I'll come right down and play it
through with you. Now you wait, darling.

Figure 1

and put it somewhere else). Second, the crane was moved a little and the camera panned to where it could look down at Zan and the carriage (see II). Third, the ground camera was far left (see III), closing on Queenie in the carriage. Fourth, it was center (see IV), looking up at Aunt Birdie as Zan would look up.

The same microphone on its mobile boom covered all the speeches except those of Birdie, who had a high microphone for herself.

Now if you will refer back to the few lines of speech, with their minimum of action, and keep in mind about where the people are as the camera changes: in the first position (see I), the close-up of Birdie in her second-story window, they shot everything from Queenie's exit speech down to the end. (And all through here the fact that the camera is turning means that everyone involved, whether he can be seen or not, is there and speaking in his place, the place his voice should come from. Everybody, the company.) From the second position (see II), the crane shifted a little, camera turning to look from the distance of Birdie's window down in long-shot at the carriage group, they went through the whole business from beginning to end. (Director's voice in patient interruption: "Miss Collinge, wasn't that line 'Now you wait, darling.' This time you said, 'Wait right there.' " Miss Collinge: "I'm sorry." Director: "Again, please.")

From the third position (see III), down on the ground near the carriage, they make the scene only as far as Queenie's exit. Then an interim of great bustle as all traces of the boom and paraphernalia are lugged away and the camera is got back to center, looking up at Birdie across the front of the house. Then they run through the whole scene again, every line, including the sound of the carriage being hauled out on the gravel drive.

Each different take was run over several times, with waits for adjustments, with actors getting weary enough of the hundredth "Good-morning, Aunt Birdie," to stumble a little as they went on from there—usually on what was to have been the final one. Each different shift of anything at all, let alone the whole camera, involved a hundred adjustments down the line, with all those batteries of great and small lights on their shaky, grotesque stands dragging their tangle of cables behind, with the microphone equipment and its tangles, screens and flats and scrims and broads and dobos enough to start a new language, with carpenters tacking on a board to cover and painters putting on a touch to bring up an outline. If you can imagine just a quarter of this, you will see where the time goes.

But this business of repetition, changes, repetition, changes: you don't see it in the picture, but they were not just playing leapfrog. In fact, the very reason you don't see it is its own justification: you are not conscious of camera or effects, for the little bit flickers past in the final version and you are conscious only that a story is starting as you follow. Only! One of the first things in making a word effective is in showing its effect on someone—so after the cutting room has got through, we see Birdie as Zan is speaking to her, Zan as she hears Birdie. But *the* first thing is established: the audience must know where it is, who is talking to whom—even what is the mood of the morning and the place. So as we see Zan looking up, we instinctively raise our eyes to see that it is Birdie in the window (that's just what we think: that was Gregg Toland looking up). We see Queenie starting to preach the law and are not conscious that as her law keeps laying down we have fallen back to see the whole group, the house and the morning light and the carriage in the drive (and the horse).

To carry us this way without many strips of film to intercut is a thing technically impossible to plan: a mosaic is a simple thing in comparison, for it is not made (except by Montgomery Ward) from the starting point of: "We will take 22 reds, 14 purples, 8 greens, a yellow, and whatever is left at the bottom of the kettle, and make an American eagle." It hasn't the rhythm in motion which pictures have and which music has. The director, like the composer, plans what he wants, he hears the idea in his head; the director, like the composer, needs still to try it out on his piano.

But this was not what you could hear on *The Little Foxes* set along toward six that hot day. They were bringing in the camera and the nests of lights into the downstairs room of the house for the next immediate following line, as Birdie comes down to run through the middle of the Schubert. It wasn't only their busy endurance that killed me, it was my feet; and the last line I heard on the set was "Can you for God's sake knock some of the heat off that 5000 so these white piano keys won't look like they was biting her hand off?"

National Board of Review Magazine, October 1941

While We Were Laughing

The status of film comedy in America has suffered from two things. The first may be called Hollywood apathy. The second and more important is the low-rating of Hollywood, the breast-beating, the abject apology for the near and native that has been the occupation of our intellectual classes and the standby of what leaders they may have in the critics. This last attitude has its importance as attitude, though of all the arts today the movie is the least affected by what thinking people find to think about it.

When I got the Chair of Films in a journal seven years ago, there were two things you could be outside of (1) a trade-critic, whose job is to report on comparative values and box-office chances, and (2) Gilbert Seldes, whose enthusiasms for the vulgar arts were designedly and successfully flash. You were on the dailies as an ex-legman or press-agent with broken wind and a liquid yearning eye on the dramah page; or you went upper-case on the weeklies and monthlies, seeing what played at the arty shoebox houses and speaking sternly in tongues such as the French (*régisseur*) to confound your readers, who felt elevated by the experience and then sneaked off twice a week to see the feature at Loew's.

In those days there were two names operative in American film comedy, and you used them in constant allusion: Chaplin and Disney. Enough authoritative and erroneous articles had been published so that you could mention the Selig and Keystone lots for a historical footnote. Otherwise you stayed abroad, where in Russian films the characters spoke Russian.

I bring this up only because, getting started at that time, I was in at the birth of another institution in American movie humor and was still reading carefully to find out what a critic ought to criticize. And I can report that you could have read the critics' circle until it squared without ever having guessed that within a year of its modest opening *It Happened One Night* would have become an absolutely gilt-edged source of reference for lowbrow and highbrow alike. The film came in as another comedy—oh, quite harmless and amusing if

18

you like that sort of thing. But it stuck so well that—with Capra now gone off the deep end apparently for good, hunting the wild platitude in Shangri-La and all that—his name is spelled in some of the biggest letters that ever went up on a marquee.

And what made him? The critics? Baby talk. The critics have given wilder raves to pictures they couldn't remember the director of to save their space-rates today. Capra had already made a few pictures, his *Lady for a Day* and *The Bitter Tea of General Yen* being clearly recalled by a small but intense following. What made him on this comedy was the public, which went back to *It Happened One Night,* and went back again. They talked it up, and it kept replaying dates all year and became an outstanding example of what the trade calls word-of-mouth build-up. It made history while the historians were asleep. The pay-off was that, while it was just a picture at the beginning of the year and was only in third place in the fall when five hundred national movie reviewers were rounded up in the *Film Daily* poll, it swept the field of awards by Christmas.

So Capra was a genius, yet was in print; it was enough to say of any other director that he wasn't Capra. In some fonts of type it was only necessary to remark that Hollywood had a director who was *presque régisseur* and to add his name to those of Disney and Charlot (as we lovingly call him) for a perfect three-point landing.

But this sort of thing cuts two ways. A certain universal acceptance and delight will put a director's name up in lights, and reviewers just have to go down the line. But once the people who are all the time talking and writing have got a thing accepted as a topic of polite literary allusion, the bird with the big director's name can throw the weight of his prestige around in either direction. He can make the world's best features and get away with it. Or he can make the world's worst, and for all you can read anywhere he is still getting away with it. And that is where the intellectuals come in, with the sub-intellectuals on the popular magazines and feature-sections following with their tongues hanging down like red neckties. All the talk, talk, talk gives a man a rating. It's the simple human assumption that where there is smoke someone must be burning.

This is where we come to the subject of film comedy in America. It is really a tradition, with the great anonymous backlog of all the people who have worked something out, or set a standard, or patterned a custom, that has to be in anything before it can be a tradition. It isn't just the two or ten names you can remember because they have been spattered all over the place in boldface. Just ask yourself: who made *The Front Page? The Gilded Lily? My Man Godfrey? The Milky Way? Sing and Like It? The Captain Hates the Sea? Forsaking All Others? Stage Door? The Shop Around the Corner? Stand In? Twentieth Century? Design for Living? The Gay Divorcée? Jimmie the Gent? Something to Sing About? I Met Him in Paris? Swing High Swing Low? The Beachcomber? The Thin Man? Desire? Vivacious Lady? Bachelor Mother?*

All right—you remember some of the titles, what the stories were about, and who played the leads. But who was responsible for a story's being done the way you remember it? Of course any given picture includes a range of talents and many lucky combinations—with this story but a different cast, or treatment, etc., with this director but a different producer or budget, etc. (If you try to go past who was responsible for anything *as credited* to who was actually responsible, you will go crazy—let it alone.) The point is that we have in the best pictures a comedy expression that is peculiar to the films. Many men in the American studios worked this funny thing out by hand and at great labor—yet who of those laughing knew what men they were, or cared?

While we were laughing, were we paying attention? Do we realize even today that there is a form in comedy as native as the air we breathe, that it has been developed partly in writing and on the stage but finds its most individual expression in the quick shadows of the screen? I doubt it.

Like any true thing ever achieved, this form owes many debts to other things and times and places. Its kingpin, Chaplin, got his training in the music-halls of England; its more subtle directors have learned a good deal from Lubitsch and René Clair; it is endlessly dependent on what in the Western world is funny and what isn't. But it has used these many old things to make a new thing, and it has been jabbed along to much faster and funnier effects than the old stage ever achieved, *per minute,* by the original demand of films for speed and variety.

This new comedy form, without the presence of flesh-and-blood performers and in the early years without music and voices, placed a severe demand on the department of visual contrasts and upsets. There was no room for gradual development, for the labored, tedious exposition of stage shows, for the stagnant patter of vaudeville turns and minstrel endmen. Something had to be happening all the time, and it couldn't be the same thing. After the first few years, even camera and cutting tricks were old stuff unless they kept being new stuff or were used differently.

Against these challenges to the inventive mind, the men of the old Mack Sennett productions worked day and night. It is too easy to remember that the pies thrown were invariably coconut-custard and five inches deep. It is not so easy to identify such elemental confectionary with comedy as we know it today. But what they were working on was the outline of it: the fast and furious, the surprise through a new kind of motion developed in the camera eye and the cutting room. Since something had to be happening every minute, new effects were devised on location, and pioneers in the technical department kept on developing ways to make them more visible—learning that there is an angle and an instant at which the true point of any motion may be caught, figuring distances and planes and cutting possibilities toward this end. Although the main formula for early comedy, as still remembered by its ever-bawdy and succinct practitioners, was "a kick in the ass and cut to chase," the way of capturing this for the screen was vastly complicated and became not only more so but a governing factor in the business of making comedy and still getting a laugh.

Now it is ironic but provable that before Capra the one man to make best uses of the screen art as it had been developed in the old days by Keystone was René Clair, whose early sound pictures have never been surpassed for what I call the old domino play. That is, you take one incident good enough in itself to set off a laugh, and then use it to explode another, and before anybody has recovered from the first, let alone the second, you apply both to setting off a third. It goes like string-firecrackers. The first gets you off-balance, the second knocks you over altogether, and the third jumps up and down on your chest. At ninety feet of film per minute, the process only runs about twenty or thirty feet, but it always takes you the next five hundred to recover.

Here a parenthesis to say that this is no jingo piece: Clair took the best available things in film technique when he was ready to use them; it didn't matter a hole in the snow where they had been developed; it mattered everything what he was able to make out of them, which was the first truly modern film comedy. Whatever he got was in the manner of treatment, not secondhand ideas for things to treat—which, I am sorry to say, was exactly the thing got from his *À Nous la Liberté* by our beloved Charlot for the conveyor-belt sequence in *Modern Times*.

The parenthesis should, in fact, be extended to French films in general, for the Frenchmen are the only producers who have approached comedy on our level. (The Russians have done some fine real-life comedy, but mostly in pictures where comedy was strictly in passing, no more than relief.) A distinction not frequently enough made is that the most French thing about most French movies is that there are Frenchmen in them. Actually, the effects are achieved by players recruited from the Parisian stage, which ranks with that of Moscow as one of the greatest theater reservoirs ever heard of. And by those familiar with the French habit of literature. When comedy in the French manner is good, it is terrific, droll, and lovely at once. But this should not blind us to the fact that what there is in it of actual screen art is something the Hollywood men have worked out and taken for granted years before—and to the fact that French pictures often seem to have been taken in somebody's cellar with a pocket Kodak.

The French are droll. O.K. Making pictures in an offhand way at something like a nickel a throw, they do not have a big and stifling mass-production business around their necks. They can dare to fool around with the more charming aspects of life as people live it. O.K.

But, to end the parenthesis, what we are talking about is the development of screen comedy as a department of art in itself, owing goodness knows what to the stage, the original burlesque idea, the vaudeville blackout, and the comic postcard—but assimilating all of them and still remaining unique.

In the jumping invention of American movie comedies there was a general drying-up after the crazy, cuff-shooting Mack Sennett days, with their near-perfection of the balanced plank, the pratfall, the pie, the teeter, the ubiquitous chase. We gradually got over into the comedy with the star in it. Whereas you could once hang a sign in front of the theater with just the word Keystone, it got to be, for years, a Buster Keaton picture, a Harold Lloyd picture, a Ham Hamilton short, a W. C. Fields short, an Our Gang short. Or it was the legitimate-stage type of drawing-room ruckus, advertised as a Wallace Reid or Douglas Fairbanks or Adolphe Menjou picture. Even the cartoons didn't keep their identity: people went to see a Mickey Mouse, knowing the guy behind it was Disney, to be sure—but how long do you think the [Max] Fleischer studios have been working, and would you be able to say even today who produces Popeye and who Betty Boop and whether either or both ever had anything to do with the "Out of the Inkwell" series? Comedy in the twenties became pretty dull and copycat, I am afraid, and a thing like the Broadway stage, where it is abundantly known that nobody cares what the book is like if Ed Wynn is playing it.

The big change and new impetus came with the introduction of sound and the addition of ripping dialogue to the original bedlam of the visual gagmen. Sound was an expensive and rather horrible trick at first; but after 1930 comedy really began to take over. Sound opened up the field for the voice of Jimmy Durante, with its overtones of someone making a prison break through a set of iron bars; for such madmen as the Marx Brothers; for a list of minor and major roles you can make as long as your arm. The movies began to approach naturalism—and that seems their dedicated goal.

And as they approached naturalism, emphasis was thrown more to character, not as played by some renegade from the Broadway tradition of saying "Morning, Zeke" as though eating a pork chop, but as devised in the script and worked into some place in the overall framework. They were American characters—what else could they have been? They came from every kind of place and tried out for all kinds of parts. The old stock roles of City Slicker, Cranky Spinster, Deacon, and Uncle Tom were being chased off the set simply because they had become cartoons and cartoons don't talk. The movies had the means and the press-agent flamboyance to screen-test anything that could get out of bed and walk. They didn't have to develop a school of acting. They accumulated, from all the fields of entertainment, including real life, a gallery of natural types such as was never seen on the face of the earth.

This applies to Hollywood in general, but particularly to comedy. The majority of the people you see on any screen today were people before they were actors, and it is hard for them to forget it. Under bad direction and their own worst compulsions they are typed without mercy. But given leeway or tricked into being natural, there they stand and talk and breathe at you, the whole amazing lot of them, busboys and hotel clerks and court clerks and plug-uglies and C. Aubrey Smith, but from life.

Hollywood at its best is as near to American humor at its best as you will get, purely because Hollywood has the fabulous wealth and appeal to get everybody from anywhere, professional or not. W. C. Fields, say, is a veteran trouper, operating the perpetual shell-game by which he once undoubtedly paid the rent. They have him. Frank Albertson, say, was so recently cutting out of high school for a quick butt between classes that he couldn't possibly make a Barrymore out of the situation even if his uncle's name were Drew. They have him.

In having these people to work with, to nurse along or hold back, the director has come back into his own—at least as much as the producer will let him. He has them and he has his story: when both are right and he is right, he makes pictures that have a styling, a speed and lightness and frequency of absurd surprise that combines sight, sound, motion, and recognition into something like music. When there is such styling, with its inevitable base in the life all around, there is a good approximation of what is most typical and good in American humor, which is fast and salty, a bit sentimental and a bit frantic, tough and gay and sweet.

Of course there may not be any such thing as American humor. All I know is I keep laughing every now and then.

If you will think back to *It Happened One Night,* you will remember that it wasn't the plot, which was corny, or the dialogue, which was of the sort to snap the brim of a very old hat very smartly. It was a trick of building a whole thing out of little ordinary things, all caught in the shifting eye of the camera and picked out as clearly within the cross-country bus with its ranged seats and mission through the night as over the countryside and in the cabins later; and all joined to make a pattern of life as we all know it, with the unfailing tough surface and the grace beneath that we at least hope to find. It had the direction of a man who had a special talent for the mixed absurdity and loveliness of little things. But, more important, it had a man with the whole range of a medium at his back—a medium that had long studied and finally developed a way to bring up the constant and perfectly focused detail until it became the main thing by sheer force of numbers and their light progression; and common people and common things became real, and eloquent.

Though the movies had already produced fast, nifty pieces like *The Front Page* and *Design for Living,* 1934 was a calendar year for American pictures in more ways than that *It Happened One Night* introduced it. Three or four months later we had *The Thin Man,* which kept romance on a modified scale and added crime-detection and had people laughing and holding their breaths until the time more than two years later when it was called in to make way for the sequel. *Twentieth Century* came about the same time and managed some ripping comedy before it got down to the shrill and rather made-up business of the original stage play. And toward the end of the year, the Astaire-Rogers' *Gay Divorcée* just about rounded everything out, with music, dancing, and a balance of high-frequency comedy that hasn't been equaled by anything in the class since, or before.

It wasn't that something new had been given the world, but merely that the movies had arrived at a new ease and maturity in form, a form that became most distinguishable in that it had tempered all effects from wipe-dissolves to Clark Gable into a steady line of clear motion. The funny character with or without the funny pants, the funny incidents, the gag and the breakaway and the washtub full of cake-dough, were assimilated into the progression of a main effect—namely, the whole story and the whole show. Since understatement had become possible through the new fluidity of camera eye and cutting scissors, the thumps and mugging of unrelated clowning were out. To a master of this new art, it was possible for the first time in any art to make the sentiment and absurdity of life as natural on a black-and-white screen as getting up from a good breakfast in a sunny room, kissing your wife a hurried bye-dear-back-at-six, and discovering it was your mother-in-law or somebody with a mustache like her.

With *My Man Godfrey* in the middle of 1936, the discovery of the word screwball by those who had to have some words to say helped build the thesis of an absolutely new style in comedy. Actually a movie released two and a half years before was not only consistently funnier but more screwball as well—only nobody knows what it is. The film, *Sing and Like It,* hangs very near the main entrance of the Ferguson gallery. And a half year before that they got out another prominent Ferguson acquisition called *The Milky Way*, which was just as fine and crazy as anything that had ever been called by a new name for pure dumb lack of knowing the venerable branch of the family it honored.

In the five years or so since, there have been a thousand tries and dismal misses. But there have been *The Captain Hates the Sea, Stage Door, Bachelor Mother, Ninotchka,* etc. Comedy may get something new and better someday, but it hasn't yet; and when it is good in its tradition, it is still tops so far as we know. The argument isn't, of course, that, once you have such a tradition of speed, relevance, and gaiety, you can just go out and knock off laughs as with a cookie cutter. It is rather that this tradition is forever there as a means to production for use and for laughter. The form is ready to hand and a ferryboat to glory for the man who has the talent to find it out and use it. It is complex, but it may be made as bright and warm as sunshine; and among all the things men can do, it is a thing inimitable.

2

TAKING
THEM
ONE BY ONE

1934

From Ozep to *Dealers in Death*

Ozep and Walt Disney

Recently I have been sidling into several picture houses, though with some hesitation. So many movies come to the arty places now, dressed gravely up in a reputation for being studies in something or other—montage, for example—that a person gets a little scared.

Mirages de Paris, a French film now dialogued in English, carries some such recommendation, and purports to be dangerously satirical to boot. But don't be afraid: go see it if the chance affords. It is a lively, fetching sort of thing. You will laugh; you will want to whistle with the orchestra; you may even (how old are you?) get tricked into believing the striking camera work to be fine art. Some of it really is fine, I think, though there is a certain tendency on the part of the director, Fedor Ozep, to play with the medium, to be taking his shirt off so you can see him bunch up his muscle. On the average he is alert, can suggest variously, and in general make you feel that you are feeling what he intends you to—anyway, that is the idea.

I wish I could say that he captures Paris, but I have not been to Paris. He captures something, say the city. Well, he captures this city and then he throws down over it one of the shaggiest old plots you ever saw, and crowds crowd, and dangerous people break into places, and police blow whistles and fall over their flat feet considerably, and in the end round up the wrong types, and there are many other things. You see some rather antique shots of traffic and electric signs and garret windows, and some rather lovely play upon streets in the rain. You get good punctuation in the way of sound—especially a chorus of newsboys, very catchy, rollicking.

The plot itself brings an escaped boarding-school girl to the city, where she stores up enough trouble for herself to last the piece out by mistaking a smooth young theatrical chap for Tonnerre (the mighty actor, the voice of the hour). She becomes implicated in a robbery, in her own death by drowning, and lastly

All of the reviews in this section are from *The New Republic,* 1934–42.

27

in a sinister hotel, where some true naturals take to her very kindly and propose to avenge her desertion by the imaginary Tonnerre. To this end they make several comical lunges in the direction of the real Tonnerre, and wind up coming to the theater and pelting him with refuse just as he is bowing and smirking in fatty pomp. Ultimately Tonnerre is arrested for the murder of the girl, who in turn is arrested for robbery—and when the smoke clears she fills the smooth chap's arms in the middle of a whopping stage-set arranged to indicate her final triumph and the happy close.

Actually it is better than that, but no deeper, no more purposeful. The director has been content to let his wit and sensibility frisk it through an entertainment piece which is so well designed, so skillfully composite, that the whole runs off with a patter as smart as the language of its production. Rumors as to the presence in it of a recondite meaning probably arise from a tendency somewhere to confuse satire with incidental burlesque, and certainly apply to it no more truly than they would, say, to a Silly Symphony.

Mr. Walt Disney has had a dozen of his pictures rounded up for performance at Carnegie Hall (cf. *Silly Symphony*), where I sat through a group of seven and then in a manner forgot to get up and leave before sitting through two or three of them again. The charm which makes this possible, considering the rush people are in, is the main thing to be considered here; and yet so much unnecessary emphasis has been given to it recently as to make one draw back. It is such a simple thing. It is merely the charm of an imagination that can perceive all sorts of fantastic attitudes and action in things so common, so near to anyone's hand, that the sudden contrast of what they might be with what they certainly are not is universally droll, and not to be resisted. Add an uncanny eye for characteristic detail. Add a limitless invention, a happy choice of what seems the best medium for Mr. Disney's peculiar talents, its present perfection and the combination of it with sound. But his gifts, like a speaker I heard of once, need no introduction, having already endeared themselves to children and associate professors. They are restricted gifts, I suppose: what is astonishing about the man is that he can make an endlessly amusing operetta out of some old razor blades, a needle and a thread, and perhaps a few soft-shell crabs.

10 January 1934

Histories and a Travelogue

Of Miss Garbo's performance in *Queen Christina* (now in its fourth week at the Astor Theatre in New York City) I can only venture that she seems to do well enough considering what she has to do. When she is the queen before her ministers, she sustains the illusion of royalty, drawing upon herself for a strength and grace without which the regal attitude would be absurd. When she begins to swell with all the inflated emotions which have been pumped into the play in invitation to the popular tear, she commands herself remarkably, manages still to be a presence, but becomes an empty and a futile one. The vehicle of her appearance, that is, affords her a certain easy triumph; it also makes her silly. Taking the subject of Christina, enlightened despot, Lesbian, free-lance adventuress, it substitutes for all the strange facts bearing upon her reign and exile the considerably mildewed fictions of the Graustark cycle. To be sure, it borrows enough facts to make a setting; it indicates the Swedish court, and makes itself pleasant with glamor while it may. But then come the big scenes, the Od's-wounds-milady-'tis-but-a-scratch. In the end, it reduces the complex circumstances surrounding the abdication of a homosexual queen to a quick and wholesome elopement with the Gentleman from Spain. And here it reaps no profit from the fact that under the ambassadorial mustachios you can perceive the lineaments of Mr. John Gilbert, made up like the devil in a musical comedy and loving to beat anything. So the whole play falls down, echoing falsely. Its essential crumbling, of course, has come about not because it is poor history but because it has nothing satisfactory to give in history's place.

The Acme Theatre in New York City offers still another new historical venture in *Enemies of the People,* a Russian film not too adequately translated. Here, as you might guess, the setting is more recent: Annenkov and the Allies are in Siberia, are making themselves dangerous and unpleasant, are finally driven out by the incoming Red army. The thing is suggestive, striking. I enjoy it, for I am easily taken with hoarse exhortations, scourges of God, men marching, nips with the enemy, and other excitements. But hardly taken in. Filling itself out with a deal of inconsequential by-play, the piece at bottom is little more than a huddle of dramatic incidents, and escapes from melodrama only by virtue of a crowning seriousness. I cannot think of its many significances without being incongruously put in mind of the early Miracles, somehow. Everything represents something else, and the assumption is that the crude and hasty symbols will not only be accepted, but that you will be instantly in sympathy with them. The play does not have its own life and movement: it becomes eventually the dumbshow of a set of tenets.

But there is something else at the Acme, unadvertised, without precedent. In a little Fox travelogue you are taken 'way, 'way up the Yangtze River. Oh see the little people. See the town of Chunking. The streets here are steps, the title says. Here, it says, the foreign residents go forth in sedan chairs. Then, actually, the camera is put in a chair, and you can see the heavy crosspiece cutting into the back and shoulders of a coolie weighing perhaps ninety pounds, weaving and stumbling up the steps which are this very strange street, preceded by other chairs, and (it is to be assumed) other foreign residents, and underneath other coolies, weaving, stumbling, half-naked, half-dead. (This is the way they ride about, ride about, ride about.) Chunking is near the river gorges, and so naturally there now follow many quaint views of the junks working upstream with coolies on their sweeps. And suddenly you are right in among the frantic heaving lot of them—the shoulders, arms, the harsh faces, a bare foot, very dirty, slipping in sweat on the planks. The current is swift and you expect to hear backs crack, but you cannot hear anything: when they lean to the sweeps the coolies sing out EY-OH, but you cannot hear that. In some parts there is such a push of water that the many little men get off and spread up the bank, each with a warping-line over his shoulder, all clawing for footholds and bent clear to the ground and moving only by inches on the steep bank. As they strain out fanwise, the warping-lines make a fantastic web from the shore to the junk, which hangs sullenly there in the gorge without motion. (The quaint little fellows.) Of course the river here is very dangerous, the title says. Some time back, possibly for contrast, you have been shown a Standard Oil boat with a slick white officer on its bridge, steaming merrily along on the dangerous river. . . . Well, I am not very sure, but if true propaganda may be described as that which truly incites to rage and pity, then some Fox cameraman has, wittingly or no, pieced out the first bit of true propaganda that has come my way. It is smooth, ineluctable, damning. There is no bellowed moral: there is only the comment implicit in any travelogue, "But how engaging, how very picturesque!"

31 January 1934

Doing Good by Catherine

If the personal lives of queens and seneschals continue to flit across the screen at the present rate, it will get so a person can sit before any given one and call his shots—here an eye-dimming address to the mob before the balcony, there a bugle point and the guard stomps through, and always somewhere around the corner a good ringing allusion to the tillers of earth. In the main, I have come to infer, a ruler divides his time between wondering whom to go to bed with and whether the peasants have got enough hay to eat.

Catherine the Great, the latest of the royalty spectacles, wears all the decorations of the order. (It is still at the Astor Theatre in New York City.)

What is more important about it, however, is that while it rumples the skirts of history in the usual embarrassing way, it still has a credible plot to show for itself. To make a tremulous virginal creature out of Catherine II, who even before coming to power had run through something like 17 percent of the male population, is a sanitary measure which might cause a twitter in the lecture halls. But to develop an adoring bride through humiliation and despair into a woman of action, a responsible leader, is an undertaking which—shorn of its inevitable fustian—I am able to respect. If the continuity succeeds, though, it is not because of the direction, which seems hackneyed enough, but because of the solid support of Douglas Fairbanks, Jr., Flora Robson, and Elizabeth Bergner (the Grand Duke, the Old Empress, and Catherine).

About Miss Bergner, I am made hesitant by the fact of her stage reputation abroad (especially as reported in the correspondence of Charles Morgan), and by the recent cooperation of all concerned in tossing her name to the clouds. Certainly she does an impressive job of work here; but just as certainly she falls quite short of magnificence, or anything like it. She is a little too much a virtuoso of the eyes for one thing, tending toward a dilation of pupil which concentrates attention unpleasantly; she has overstated her final scene, for another, and has seemed occasionally careless of her carriage. There are some things—some states of mind or spirit—in which she is superb, and I remember her most gratefully for a wedding scene in which every facial and bodily line conveyed a mixture of shy pride and wonder, hesitation and eagerness, which must approximate creative purity. Then, too, there is the later banquet episode, where she pokes at her food in the clearest statement of dignity in scared humiliation that I have ever seen. But the excellence is restricted to certain moods, and her accomplishment in this one film calls up a corrective to critics in the way of ragtime epitaph of happy (if obscure) memory: "Now, I'm not the best, though it's well understood, Ev'thing that I do, I sure do good. . . ."

Mr. Fairbanks does a surprisingly effective interpretation of Peter III. Whether from shrewd casting, whether from his own intelligent conception of the character, he is able to veer between petulant imperiousness and hysteria, insensibility and cunning, in a manner which convinces and even wrings a drop of sympathy from an essentially unsympathetic role. That he sticks to his guns here rather than attempting the Great Lover has caused concern in some quarters, but should go far to cancel such lack of personal dignity as still shows through. I can give the heartiest praise to Miss Robson, whose tottering, shrieky, sensual Elizabeth filled me with a sense of a living body—something not often experienced on the screen, somehow. Working within the limits of a subsidiary part, she yet managed to give the clearest and least exceptionable performance of the picture.

On the whole, I am thankful for *Catherine the Great*. Whatever its shortcomings, it represents genuine entertainment compared with Hollywood's choices in the past weeks—*Moulin Rouge,* for example, or *Nana,* introducing Anna Sten's full-blown personality and emotional incompetence. The only saddening thing is that the hope that springs is considerably dampened by the fact that it is not a Hollywood but a British product.

7 March 1934

Genesis, 19:8

I am shocked and somewhat delighted by the strange mixture of fact and fancy which is *Lot in Sodom*. Although it is almost two months now that this two-reel film has been showing in New York City (where you can still see it at the Acme Theatre), it has been either so ignored by reviewers or so learnedly obscured with generalities that nobody seems to gather the least idea what it is about, or why. Obviously it retells the Biblical fable of the fall of Sodom. And surely it is a lolloping stride toward some technical end of grave import. But incidentally and to speak plain truth, it also gets good and bawdy before it has done. Whatever the main intent of the directors, there is just enough concern for realism in the matter of how Sodom took its pleasure (Lot offering his daughter as an incentive to the Natural Life, and the boys indignant; the angel of the Lord arriving and they making what are called passes at him), and there is just enough of the uncalled for in the conception and birth interlude, to suggest something of an exercise in seeing how much you can get away with.

But if I hint that there have been several tongues in several cheeks during the film's execution, it is nothing against the serious artistry of the non-professional group which, headed by Messrs. J. Sibley Watson, Jr., and Melville Webber, has made it possible. The directors have made great headway in the evolution of a style, of a manner of statement peculiar to their own medium: what is more important, they have something to use it for, something to say. But speaking in symbols, they essay to walk too far and fast, and stumble. They seem to have forgotten that symbolic art-forms—poetry, painting, the like—require a leisure for reexamination that is denied the stage. Because the life of the stage is a life in time, actual in one moment and committed to experience in the next, its movements must be clear and memorable. And any complexity thrown into the inexorable tempo of the present movie must fail to take the observer all the way with it.

Essentially, though, the desired impression is got across, and that is much. You know that in this city you would be afraid. Not with the simple terror bred of war-whoops and maelstroms: you would be afraid of what the directors have captured here—possibly the Spirit of Evil. By casting types whose feminine bent is made only more sinister through its superimposition upon a brutal masculinity; by the manipulation of focus toward the end of distortion, dismemberment, inversion, and grotesque movement—by these varied means and with the incidental aid of fire, smoke, lightning, and modern orchestration, the directors go beyond the fact of Sodom to their special feeling for it. Despite the pleasing absence of moral purpose, and the beauty that attends much of its unrolling, the story makes sin very sinful, heartily repellent. A person could say, in fact: For God's sake go see *Lot in Sodom,* and be literally justified.

The only fine thing noticeable in Pathé-Natan's *Ariane* is that in knocking the sense out of Claude Anet's fine novel of that name, it creates a part through which Elizabeth Bergner can move without a trace of strain. You would not know from her work in *Catherine* that this slight creature could so consistently take your breath away with the clear grace and intelligence of her style. Here, shorn of the pretentious, she is a lovely spirit, and enough to make even this silly film a pleasure to watch. . . . One other waste of celluloid that has been made pleasant by an unspoiled character is *Palooka,* a prizefight story not quite able to contain Mr. James (Schnozzle) Durante, who—in his own uncontainable and somewhat muggish way—is lovely too, though I doubt he ever would admit it.

21 March 1934

Worth Seeing

It is a little late in the day for mention of *It Happened One Night,* but since the picture is still floating around the little houses and since it would be a pity to miss it, I should like to plump for it here, and strongly. Considering its subject, it is better than it has any right to be—better acted, better directed, better written. The plot has to do with a girl who escapes the rigors of life on her father's yacht and takes a long-distance bus for New York, where she proposes to join a villain she has just married. She runs into a fired newspaperman who at first is rather hard on her but soon turns out to be a very number-one sort of chap indeed, and everything runs along nicely until the two have surmounted about everything and are nearly home. But then, everybody being in love with everybody else in pleasantly conclusive fashion, there enters more confusion as to who loves whom and why than might be expected of a Molière comedy. Barring the incidents of the bus ride, the outlines of the story have a deadly enough familiarity all through anyway. What the picture as a whole shows is that by changing such types as the usual pooh-bah father and city editor into people with some wit and feeling, by consistently preferring the light touch to the heavy, and by casting actors who are thoroughly up to the work of acting, you can make some rather comely and greenish grasses grow where there was only alkali dust before. The cast was particularly sound from top to bottom. Claudette Colbert sensed what was required of her, and did it very well, though I do not care for her much as a person—not as much in fact as for Walter

Connolly, who was delightful. Clark Gable was the outstanding feature, managing to be a rowdy and a perfect gentleman and a newspaperman and a young lover, all in the same breath and the most breezy and convincing manner imaginable. And now having adjudicated and discriminated and in a word defined the picture with proper regard for this and that, I am reminded that such a picture cannot be defined at all until we find a way of describing whatever it is that makes first-rate entertainment what it is.

But there are comedies and there are comedies, and the new Tarzan film—though possibly without intention—is certainly one of the funniest things you'll ever see. [Johnny] Weissmuller and Miss [Maureen] O'Sullivan do their triple somersaults and back salmons through the air and under the water and into the arms of their friends the apes as though there were nothing in the world to do but that, and yodel; and every minute or so someone douches the scene with buckets of blood, this last development owing mostly to the writer's having got his stage cluttered with more than a thousand superfluous lions, natives, and extras, and having to shoot his way out. At the curtain, though, everything has been cleared away, including the white men who had considered stealing Tarzan's ivory and wife, Tarzan has killed in single combat or ridden no-hands everything but the West African steamship line, and now goes thoughtfully back to his flying trapeze, having just previously been shot through the head. The picture is studded with high points (as witness a battle with a rubber crocodile lasting about five uproarious and thrashing minutes), is consistently hair-raising with ambuscades, tom-toms, and near escapes, and lasts for something like twelve reels.

Of a much quieter (and, from a natural point of view, more fascinating) nature is Frank Buck's *Wild Cargo,* being the pictorial record of an expedition into the jungle for the purpose of capturing alive whatever may live there. Some of its dramatic passages I suspect to be made out of whole cloth; but the absorbing part of such a piece of work lies not in the drama but in the authentic background, the movement of wild life—especially the almost incredible lightness and grace of the scene where the monkeys are first sighted, and the whole business of the harnessing of elephants to catch elephants. Even in the case of such phony conquests as the snake episodes, the picture is absorbing enough, though possibly repetitious of *Bring 'Em Back Alive,* which I haven't seen. Whatever may be said of Mr. Buck's qualities as a hunter, he is to be thanked here for his sure and good taste as a showman.

I'll Tell the World is not much to see unless you have a special appreciation of Lee Tracy, who is bright and flip and on the whole agreeable when left to himself, which he is not here. Together with Roger Pryor, he is given a little leeway, but gets almost nowhere before it is necessary to return to a romance-with-royalty plot that gets just about as dull and impossible as could be expected.

9 May 1934

It's Up to the Kiddies

My modest system of cataloguing has got to be extended, I see, because it is impossible to sit through a film like *Stand Up and Cheer* and then just file it away in the ordinary drawer labeled Stinkers. This one is extra, it is super, and more, it butters itself very thickly with the most obvious sort of topical significance. In body it is half on the vaudeville side and half in the lap of whatever maternal instinct it is that responds with little cries to the spectacle of diapers in art. But like all musicals it also has a story, and that is where the significance comes in. From the story "suggested" by Will Rogers and Philip Klein it seems there was once a depression, no matter where. Well, the President of the country where this depression was heard about it and decided not to have any. So he called to him and appointed as Secretary of Amusement some flash promoter from the Broadway district, the idea being that any people as ruggedly fibered as that country's citizens could laugh off a depression if they just got to feeling snickery about it. So the promoter (Warner Baxter) appointed an office building and divided his time among his Director of the Kiddies' Hour (Miss Madge Evans), wholesale auditions, and a coast-to-coast trunk line: Yeah, yeah. Twenty male choirs and a gross of trombones. Yeah. . . . Then you begin to see the country singing—sweatshop women, cops, kiddies, brakemen, typists—all singing something about "If I can smile, why can't you?" So pretty soon everybody was smiling and everything. But some bankers and reformers didn't like this smiling promoter, and started a whispering campaign to disconcert him. However, he kept ordering trombones and stroking Miss Evans and then, flash, he quit, and then, flash, he didn't quit after all, and then, flush, he decided to purge the system of such extravagances as Departments of Kiddies' Hours—and then, pitter patter of little feet, what should come but word that the kiddies had made the country laugh and the depression was over. And the way this last was made clear to the reapers and the sowers, to the drivers of trucks and sweatshop help, was by a horseman larruping along at an altitude of about 2,000 feet, looking from his mount and coattails like George Washington and from his aerial Americanism like Charles A. Lindbergh, but from his face, which showed finally in the close-up, exceedingly like a waffle—tearing up the sky until, in a state of complete suspension, he led all the country (which had by now assembled in columns of fours directly underneath) in a community song composed expressly for the occasion with all three of its notes entirely new and different. "We're

Out of the Red," the song with notes, is the work of the man who composed "Brother, Can You Spare a Dime. . . ." And as this later effort seemed to relieve the people of that country immensely, I suggest that those several million Americans to whom its fine optimism is directed be if possible a little ruggeder, and hock their relief tickets or panhandle some dimes, and go stand up and hear it.

16 May 1934

Credit for Comedy

Dealing out credit for the fine swinging comedy Hollywood makes of the Hecht-MacArthur play *Twentieth Century* is an involved business. Into the role of Jaffe, the impresario whose tantrums make the story, John Barrymore fits as wholly and smoothly as a banana in a skin; and appropriate metaphors should also be devised for Walter Connolly, Carole Lombard, and Roscoe Karns. But for the various other pictorial elements, major commendation must go to Howard Hawks' flexible and integrating direction. Also the major reproach. For, so long as the movie remained a movie, it traveled in a fast even line; but when it cramped itself into the actual setting of the stage play (it had already swept through most of the play's material), it became redundant, stationary, faintly boring. In that respect it was disappointing; but as evidence of a tough new life already emerging from the sedate husks of the American stage, it was a heartening thing even after its spontaneity had been checked.

The only thing to be said for *You're Telling Me* as a film is that it stars W. C. Fields—which is quite enough. Because Fields is not only a funny man with a fair bag of tricks; he creates a type. Nature's nobleman, let us say, considerably beery and with a strong touch of the sideshow barker. A blend of Jiggs the impenitent household man, and a promoter of itinerant shell games. But his manner of getting these things into stage terms is not so easily reducible to words. He is not a star playing a buffoon, but is completely within the role; he is his own hero and his own dupe and must accept this, to make the best of it. And when there is no best to make, why, you must be sad for him—because he is so earnest, because he moves with such absurd gravity and concentration. Even in such a vapid piece of plot, casting, and direction as this he leaves a residue of something more real, more touching than the froth and fizzle of wit alone.

Another good man, not too well recognized as such, is James Cagney, whose latest, *He Was Her Man,* is not the right medium for him and lags terribly. His *Jimmy the Gent* (still around) is the fast, hard-hitting sort of thing for his dynamic talent; and this slight though soundly built story of a racketeer he fills to overflowing, imperturbable, flip, colloquial to the point of unintelligibility. It shows him a lively, graceful, and endearing vulgarian, and is enough by itself to place him with Fields, Durante, Mae West, and their like in humor—that is, with the best and most honest Americans I know.

6 June 1934

Pudovkin and the Little Men

It is a pity that the New York Acme Theatre will be one of the very few in this country (if there are any others) to show such a securely front-rank film as *1905,* made from Gorky's *Mother* by the Soviet director [Vsevolod] Pudovkin some years ago, and only now permitted to be shown here by the censors. Because it is so good and because it is so true. Because it is at once a work of art and a statement of the heroic conflict, not of armed knights or empire builders or Colonel Charles A. Lindbergh, but of those whose heroism is forever obscured by terms relating to the stink of their breath or the state of their finances: hoodlums, loafers, malcontents, and bums. And this will not, I hope, be interpreted as praise of the film on grounds of its daring (small daring necessary for Russians to support the ruling class in Russia certainly); praise goes to a new, sound conception of values that were themselves always sound.

The story is that of the abortive rising of the Russian workers in 1905, and though its progress is focused in the individual characters of the son, who is jailed for his activities as an organizer, and the mother, whose energies are from that time diverted into revolutionary channels, it is a story of masses. And these shifting crowds—dynamic bulks, typical of hell let loose—Pudovkin handles with special genius, filling the flat dimensions of his screen with quick and brawling motion.

Although sound effects and a running commentary in English have been added, the picture was originally silent; it was to speak only in terms of its camera, which seems at times uncanny in its clear recording of both the fact and the comment upon it. For the extremely effective filming and cutting of such bits as the rhythmic patterns of the factory and the courthouse, and the escape of the prisoners; for the casting of such brawny figures as give the action its crude strength; more, for the intangible matter of breathing life into this whole continuity of shadows upon a screen—for all these Pudovkin seems to have made himself responsible. Vera Baranovskaya and Nikolai Batalov had the principal roles, and made them sharp with meaning, to be sure; but for the most part character development is at a minimum in the play, which aims to make up in collective power what it must lose in individual depth.

As to the flaws, they are several: a tendency toward black and white, an unwillingness on the part of the director to let go a sequence once he has got his teeth into it, and most of all a spotty print, not geared to modern projection machines and giving rise to the jerky and frequently absurd acceleration peculiar to the old newsreels. And yet the picture as a whole shakes off these handicaps as a dog would drops of water, to stand squarely on its merits, a shaggy giant of a thing. It provides an experience that should open a few rather sleepy eyes to the artistic possibilities more and more being realized in this medium.

It is a stiff jump from *1905* to the screen version of *Little Man, What Now?* To some the latter also will seem to have significant social content, and to others it will seem nothing more than a rental-library approach to the business of earning a living; and prominent among the second group you will find your present correspondent, who can stand just so much inversion of Horatio Alger in the interests of modern romance, and no more. A great deal of Mr. [Frank] Borzage's setting was effective, and I guess you could call Margaret Sullavan's sensitive carriage through the part of the young wife rather lovely. But for Douglass Montgomery as the Little Man, the only logical comment is, So what—which comment may as well be enlarged to include the whole lagging story.

I do not suppose that there is much to be said about *Now I'll Tell* at this time, or indeed any other. It is Mrs. Arnold Rothstein's version of Mr. Arnold Rothstein, with its situations wonderfully familiar and the case for Mrs. Rothstein wonderfully strange. The story of a gambler who could be nothing else, and died therefore in sin, though bravely, is aided by Spencer Tracy over some tall obstacles, but not enough of them. In spite of the breezy sequences with which it starts, the picture quickly gets improbable and goes from bad to maudlin.

Also a brief and tardy mention for *Little Miss Marker,* to which my reactions are pretty negative. A little girl falls into the power of a ring of touts and bookies, eventually making cleaner and better people of them by her innocence. I liked [Adolphe] Menjou, doing more than his usual bit, but owing to what may be an alarming atrophy of the maternal instinct, I like cute toddlers like Shirley Temple only in their little cribs, or whatever receptacle it is they should be kept in—not that of several thousand feet of film, surely.

The bottom of any list is the exact spot for the Nazi film *S. A. Mann Brand*—not so much because it is bad propaganda in a bad cause as because it is shabbily and obviously put together, a cheap, boot-licking sort of thing. Showing the rise to power of the Swastika Boys (their I.Q. levels off unmistakably here at something like Hi-Y pitch), it is anti-Semitic and anti-labor, and as such might be considered a menace if it were not the ridiculous performance it is.

20 June 1934

Mysteries and Medicals

If there is any one thing that the movie people seem to have learned in the last few years, it is the art of taking some material—any material, it may be sound, it may be junky—and working it up until the final result is smooth, fast-moving, effortless. Hollywood may have to go elsewhere for its central idea. Outside of the work of such screen writers as Ben Hecht it usually prefers to. But once it has got the idea it goes ahead with cameras and gag-writers, jazz bands, and (most of all) directors, and works up something totally its own, a picture. Those who take their pleasure in observing facts will trace the similarities of plot between, say, the novel and the movie, and stand forth with a report on Faithful Renditions; but the truth is that whoever started the thing in the first place, Hollywood has it now, and Hollywood speaks a different language.

Because it has a book with good dialogue and sprightly movement to lean on, *The Thin Man* leans frankly on Hammett's novel for its effects. But *The Thin Man* also makes a very neat movie of itself. From the off-center shots of the dance band to the killing on the front doorstep and the symbol of the thin man, it is full of the special touches that can come from nowhere but the studio, that really make the feet a movie walks on. Up until the time it found itself faced with the need for becoming a detective story at last, it had used the murder element only to keep up suspense and provide an excuse for all the urbane and charming business going on between Myrna Loy and William Powell on the one hand, and an assortment of thugs and police and citizens on the other. But finally there was a large dinner at which the murderer had to be pulled out of the hat, all rather heavy and slightly silly; and that, I suppose, is the price you have to pay for being a detective story. There was as well a little too much of one thing and another at times, and William Powell seems to need watching, lest he be too gay. But on the whole it was thoroughly well conceived and carried out—a strange mixture of excitement, quips, and hard-boiled (but clear and touching) sentiment. It is a good movie and should not be missed.

Men in White is another fairly smooth picture that Metro has lifted from elsewhere. The film is less smooth, however, goes deeper, and is somewhat of a disappointment. Despite the realistic problem of an interne faced with the choice between medicine and marriage, and the trappings of up-to-the-minute hospital equipment, the actual story is pretty familiar and in spots not altogether probable. Young chap truly loves but slips once with nurse; nurse pregnant, hopes blasted, nurse dies, ushering in Understanding. But all this aside from the actual piecing together of the movie, which spared no expense to make the hospital background real and immediate. Those who saw *Once to Every Woman* will need no introduction to the fact that an operating-room scene can be almost intolerable with its sharp statement of isolation and terror—the ether, the knives, the heat, the glaring lights, the ether. . . . *Men in White* does not give so much emphasis to such matters, but enough to make itself exciting. Clark Gable and Myrna Loy, nice people in any situation, didn't get very strong parts: honors for acting must go to Jean Hersholt, whose Dr. Hochberg gave the whole thing centralization and sympathy. He pulled it, that is, out of the red, because Hollywood had in this case been a bit too literal about some rather flimsy material.

There are other Mysteries and Medicals abroad, all of which are less success-ful, between two of which—*Murder on the Blackboard* and *Murder in Trinidad*—there are several contrasts to be drawn. The former, like *The Thin Man*, makes its detective content palatable by building the detectives up as central characters and taking time out for a great deal of byplay. While this seems a more advanced method of procedure, it stumbles about a good deal here for lack of decision whether it is to be mainly genial or mainly macabre. The idea is to have a rather horsey teacher poke about with virginity and an umbrella, solving the murder of another teacher in the school while her friend the gumshoe tramps on the wrong toes in a very official way and is humorously harsh with her. ("Ree-lax, Hildegarde, ree-lax.") As a detective story the thing is only 60 percent as probable as a *Herald Tribune* report of a strike; there is much mumbo-jumbo in the cellar, a foolish solution, and no end of completely irrelevant clue-finding and thickening of the plot. But there is this business of good-natured romping around on the part of Edna May Oliver and James Gleason, a superior (though too much overdone) sort of slapstick that is entertaining whatever you think about the corpse. *Murder in Trinidad* is the other type of thing, less concerned with gag-lines, building up a faster story, but turning for romance to a secondary and cluttery theme of young love. A ring of Trinidad smugglers, with quarters in a nearby swamp and friends in Government House, are rooted out and hunted down by a shambling oh-hum kind of fellow; and this much of it was worked out with many excitements and given likelihood by the well built character Nigel Bruce made as the detective. But so much was Not Enough, and so what must be stirred in like spoons of syrup but Heather Angel and Victor Jory, kissing and yearning and so painfully present as to spoil the whole brew.

As to the other films centering on the problems of the medical profession, there is *Once to Every Woman* (Fay Wray, Walter Connolly, Ralph Bellamy) which is rather old now, and quite fair though foolish; and *Dr. Monica*, which is recent and not quite fair. Woman doctor steals man from friend, wants baby and can't have. Other lady already has baby on way, doesn't want, wants man, can't have. From which tragic state of affairs we may as well turn to the brief observation that when Entertainment is forsaken for Appeal ("You women who long for the touch of baby fingers," says the Strand Theatre program; "You men to whom a wife has cried, 'Life Owes Me a Baby!' ") there gets woven a tangle of plot that is bound to trip up the more calloused observers. Hollywood can make good pictures out of good material, but it can also make as big a donkey out of itself as anything anywhere.

4 July 1934

Both Fine and Foolish

In a way it is too bad that the picture John Cromwell has made from Maugham's *Of Human Bondage* is so closely tied up with the book. It comes, like the famous son of the famous father, well recommended to our attention; but at the same time it stands enough in the shadow of a finer thing to blur the fact of its being a very fine thing in its own right. Its screen story is pretty much a story of Philip and three women, with his periods of artistic and economic bankruptcy no more than indicated, his childhood and successive intellectual adjustments cut away completely. It becomes a little happier and (more regrettably) cleaner, but gains in quickening of speed, in unity of impression. And it moves beautifully, being one of the best examples of pure directing craft to be found. Leslie Howard and Bette Davis have the main parts, and while the one seemed at times to lack the flavor of earth you might expect (a little too much soul, perhaps) and the other simply hadn't in her what the highest scenes required, both leave you finally with the sense of a happy and right choice. Intelligence, spirit, all that. As a matter of fact there was a whole troop of good people in it: Kay Johnson, Reginalds Owen and Denny, Alan Hale, Frances Dee. Whether or not the picture can properly be divested of the book's overtones, it is easily one of the best screenplays of the year.

The place is filling up with funny movies again, of which my choice for the craziest is *Sing and Like It*. I count the thing a prize, though not doubting it has some awful things wrong. I lost track. I would like to be a good critic and keep a severe check on whether Values are realized and all, but I kept falling out of my seat, and so the best I can say about *Sing and Like It* is, It's probably a lousy picture but you fall out of your seat. Well, it seems Nat Pendleton stumbled into an amateur dramatic rehearsal on the way home from cracking a safe with the boys, and was moved to tears by a song ZaSu Pitts was singing, something about Your Mother. "Monicker?" said Nat, which demand being interpreted and the name of the girl being given, Nat decided to put it in lights. Which he proceeded to do, Ned Sparks translating for him at sight all words above five letters and the boys sticking rods into producers (Edward Everett Horton), ticket choppers, and finally into the *Herald Tribune* critic, who was thus persuaded into a four-star falsetto that misled everybody, including the other critics, and the play that had been built up around the Mother song left them in the aisles. Miss Pitts, having risen to fame, was prepared to make the Supreme Sacrifice for her art, but this Nat couldn't see, his dear mother having just got out of stir and wouldn't they all come over to her party quick before she went under the table. It is just as well that everybody overdid everything and that the play as a whole had little edge to it, because a thing like this might become a danger to health.

Then there is *Strictly Dynamite,* also comic though hampered by too many angles on too many people. One of those affairs where, things beginning to clog, they tossed in a little talent and then, things thereby being clogged completely, they hit upon the remedy of throwing in a little talent. Jimmy Durante can be a small uproar by himself, but finds no strength in numbers, and gets lost in the hybrid confusion of Lupe Velez, Norman Foster, William Gargan, Marion Nixon, Sterling Holloway, Minna Gombell, Jackie Searl and I could go on, not overlooking the Mills Brothers. Durante is a radio ace here (though still my baby, I like to think) and is shown getting poems for his act by the expedient of (is he mortified: the last of the Durantes) buying them legally.

The Affairs of Cellini is a humorous extravaganza that flops, partly because of what it tries to do and partly because of who does it. Frank Morgan makes delightful work of the sanguinary though somewhat muddled Duke of Florence, but is only a finger in the leaky dyke of Fredric March, who assumed at the outset that Cellini was John Gilbert, and would not be quelled. The humor is quite subordinated to plot complications that, for all their trappings of goldsmiths and the long ago, run on a formula that will seem familiar to some, being in effect, Are we in love or are we in love. . . . In *The Circus Clown* Joe E. Brown had one very good scene, hiccuping around among elephants; otherwise I am sorry to have brought the picture up. Do better next time.

18 July 1934

Mostly Unfunny

Just now is a pretty rocky time for pictures, what with purity leagues beating the mental age down and everybody looking toward Hollywood with an expression of pity-the-poor-sailors-on-a-night-like-this; and I suppose we should be very gentle with movies for a while, as they are a sick man. But after moving in and out of theaters for upward of two weeks and drawing almost nothing but blanks (and this is to include the revival of such elaborate lollypops as *Cavalcade*), a person can end up feeling savage. Same old story of waste and slapdash. Scattered through a dozen nullities there was enough of wit and feeling and hard cash to make two or three first-rate films; but the two or three weren't made; there is no provision for that. The trade would bear a dozen, so here we are.

Fortunately, Warners have managed to throw two rather good ones into the breach, *Here Comes the Navy* being the first. In it James Cagney enlists in the navy in order to get even with one of its petty officers, Pat O'Brien, and does not really get even after all, falling in love with his sister (I mean O'Brien's), and heaping coals of fire instead. Essentially, the old boys' school plot, rewritten for battleships. So far as fidelity to background is concerned, it is an ambitious and ballyhooed sort of fidelity, the kind in which Hollywood is never fortunate. The routine of the service is very well conveyed, but those old library shots of maneuvers might as well have been painted on glass. And the battle-practice scenes—people standing around a powder bag that has caught fire wondering if it is going to catch fire; and the first-cruise seaman being made a warrant officer (warrant officers are made in heaven); and the official benevolence—"The navy wants to make men, not break them." Well well, I heard it different, but let all that go as being too technical. The saving business of the picture is the give-and-take as between Cagney and O'Brien, who do not so much act parts as make them. Cagney especially is a very good man for the films, he is all over the place, expressive from head to foot, and catholic of appeal—though I do not know whether the freshness of all this will go on forever. His latest movie is not his best, but has a lot of bright quirks and is worth going to.

Friends of Mr. Sweeney (at the Mayfair in New York) is comedy with a stiffening of rather aimless satire, made over from an Elmer Davis novel. About Charles Ruggles, once a wild wildcat and now becoming a stuffed one from long association with his boss, the owner-editor of a liberal weekly. (Hear.) In the end, he breaks away one night, and spins around with Ann Dvorak upsetting people, getting tight, catching crooks, politicians, and the owner himself with pants not quite all the way up. Some (not all) of the satire is pretty far-fetched, but the lines are good and situations funny—there is even smooth dramatic irony where irony usually comes out at you wrapped up in custard pies. The cast is hand-picked from top to bottom, with Eugene Pallette, Berton Churchill, and Harry Tyler standing out pleasantly. Ruggles and the director (Edward Ludwig) seem to hold key positions, one with intelligence and character sense, the other with an eye to the whole, that each piece should fall into place quietly, with a neat forward motion.

In the matter of constructing these two comedies, the basic purpose of the play came first, the humorous slant afterward. We are now about to enter upon a whole string of pictures that start building from the roof down, that begin their fun and frolic before they have written their play. *Private Scandal* does this, and escapes the junkyard only by virtue of a few good sequences and quite a bit of good work from Ned Sparks, ZaSu Pitts, and others. Mr. Sparks pecks around, a gloomy and cynical bantam (too much rope given him here though), trying to find the murderer of the boss while the office force gets in his hair and Miss Pitts tries to find her way into or out of the W.C. The story moves along somehow, but is foolish, and thus fails to shore up the comic element, which thus falls to pieces. . . . *Ladies Should Listen* goes the same way, only much more definitely, on account of Cary Grant and the sad Alfred Savoir comedy from which it was made. . . . *She Learned About Sailors* mixes Lew Ayres, Alice Faye, Frank Mitchell, and Jack Durant all up in a pretty terrible brew of misunderstanding, clean relations, and acrobatics as of the Keith Circuit; while *Cockeyed Cavaliers* is just one happy ragbag of [Bert] Wheeler and [Robert] Woolsey jokes, and perhaps I should say so-called.

But to pass from helter-skelter entertainment to a more intellectual, drawing-room sort of comedy, there has been brought from England a picture that manages a most peculiar unity of tone. It is called *For Love or Money* and it stars Robert Donat and Wendy Barrie, and it carries on every inch of celluloid its trademark, which is the word ham. I had not expected to see anything so steadily unfunny again for quite a space, but was immediately corrected by what is almost a companion piece, *The Lady Is Willing.* This Hollywood version of a French comedy has Leslie Howard popping in and out of places with false whiskers and an intellectual playfulness that is enough to make you feel embarrassed for all concerned, including the projectionist. Like the British film, it is, part by part, neither very bad nor very good; where both are notable is that when all the parts become one unrelieved entity, it is hard to imagine comedy more dull and witless and flat on its feet.

In the way of melodrama, there are two more pieces that should be given a wide berth: *Blind Date,* an extremely old and homey triangle story, and *Wild Gold,* a tale about mines and love and how the dam broke. *Find the Woman,* which shows a cub reporter among thieves, places a notch higher; it is stupid, but also fast, and will at least keep you awake.

15 August 1934

Some Films That Failed

I wish I had seen a good picture somewhere, or even a significantly bad one, because criticism when it becomes yawning and noncommittal and safe (Oh, you might have a look at this if you've a taste for that sort of thing) is a poor crutch to go on. Conviction, one way or the other, will almost write a review by itself. And it is hard to be convinced of anything where, as in the present crop, the most interesting things are the interesting failures.

Our Daily Bread is the picture Mr. King Vidor has been making independently of Hollywood, doing his own writing, directing, cutting, and financing the venture by mortgaging (it is said) his shirt. What with Hollywood's aversion to social content, and Mr. Vidor's preoccupation with it, and the bars being thus down and all, there has been quite some interest in the result. Excepting several strong and good scenes, however, the result could hardly be distinguished from Frank Borzage in all the panoply of his glory and with the bars firmly up. Its only real social comment lies in the state of unemployment of a score or so of people brought haphazardly together by a farming venture in which, docile under the leadership of the hero (Tom Keene: Y.M.C.A. rough-rider), they labor and share the fruits communally. There is a drought, all waver, hero flies coop with stray tart. Meeting water three miles off, hero comes back to lead the boys in climactic excavation of a ditch. The central idea of men working together is good, some of the soil element fresh, and the outcome stirring. But there in the main foreground is the most obvious sort of boy-girl-siren triangle, and wouldn't you guess that the minute someone got a free hand in plot construction he would hang the whole story on the back of such an old love nag as even Hollywood might be ashamed to take out for a canter. The trouble is that Mr. Vidor, however independent, still seems to be governed by the industry's idea of box-office requirements, which in turn still governs the industry. If you are going to subscribe to the first, of course there is no use trying to be free of the second.

Another film made with no Hollywood restrictions is *The House of Greed* (a Russian-language film at the New York Acme). But here the story is so fumbled in getting into screen terms, and the technique so poor (the photography was good, but its effect hamstrung by cutting, sound, and lighting), that the satire on landholders in Old Russia never really gets through. There is the suggestion of an art form that is new and unsteady on its feet in the handling of the material, but the material itself lacks the rough strength often associated with such a form. The minor characters are striking types, but stylized. [V. R.] Gardin in the main part is a sort of cross between Tartuffe and Harpagon—the praying usurer who gloated and inherited at his brother's death, drove his mother to her grave, his son to Siberia, one of his nieces to incest and both to suicide; who oppressed his tenants and sent his bastards to orphan asylums. Gardin is mostly hampered by a makeshift plot, but near the end takes on a crazy sinister dignity of his own, moving off in that half-light in a way to suggest judgments and dooms not implicit in the facts. The picture is an advance over The Rover Comrades on a revolution sort of thing but is still in the pantomimic stage of the old half-formed silents.

Whoever has seen Will Rogers has seen *Handy Andy,* in which there is a little homely humor and so much goodness and horse sense (as of the family man) that you had better stay clear of this dull evening, too. *The World Moves On* is so sleazy with sentiment and striving for big effect that I could not last it out. It has a World War story, Madeleine Carroll, and Franchot Tone, who is becoming ubiquitous—a wet charge of powder if there ever was one. . . . Up to the time of writing, the best bet in movies seems to be *The Man with Two Faces,* an inconsequential murder piece, but sustained in tone and cleverly put together. It is a little old now, but has the virtue of being neither tiresome nor irritating.

29 August 1934

Screen Versions

I do not suppose we will ever get this matter of the relation between books and movies straightened out, for there are too many angles. The manner of production alone can make a bad film of a good novel, and a good film of a bad novel, and all the grades in between. Then there is the matter of whether the material was adapted to the screen in the first place. This nobody seems to know: if a book is on the best-seller lists, it is famous, it is enough. Being bought, it is either forgotten or put into production, and fun (if it was in no way a funny book) then commences. An established best-seller is of course too well known to allow a great deal of tampering, because there is always a large section of the public to keep a stern eye on whether it was the same in the pitcher how he leaves the old man, etc. So instead of making it over for studio purposes, they keep to the story and scratch around trying to give it more punch by cutting out motivation and heightening conflict, which should be as between heroes and villains throughout.

Under these circumstances the cards are stacked against Hollywood and the result is awful to see, and people who do not quite guess what it is all about will see it and say Ha, giving a bitter laugh. Having missed half a dozen good ones they will rouse themselves and go see what Hollywood has done to *The Fountain,* and it is just as they thought sure enough.

As a book *The Fountain* was a fine book, but had a great deal to do with certain inward processes that must slip out here. The pattern of two men in love with Ann Harding and she loving back through a mist of tears does not of course make any sense. Character strength and the unnatural stone quiet of Enkendaal are not caught by the camera, which otherwise finds little else to do with itself; and so there is nothing for it but to work up the pretty intrigues, patriotic differences, and meaningless amours of people who live in a castle with a secret staircase and a harpsichord. Barring the presence in it of Brian Aherne, *The Fountain* is nothing more than a very apt vehicle for Miss Harding, being as it is long and solemn and wonderfully empty.

The Barretts of Wimpole Street is the same sort of thing, only much more of it. Sidney Franklin apparently directed straight from the stage version, which in terms of celluloid occupied exactly ten reels and three sets. And the result is that while there have no doubt been sillier plots than that showing Fredric March squirting around among father and daughter and Flush, I don't recall seeing a movie more in the position of sitting around with its jaw hanging while the last train pulled out of the station. Norma Shearer was all right if not Elizabeth Barrett, and Maureen O'Sullivan did a rather fresh interpretation of the younger sister. Otherwise The Old Wampus of Wimpole Street was ready for burial before it started, and then went on forever.

A story that offered no subtleties and all sorts of high adventure was realized in *Treasure Island,* which makes a picture so good in some ways that any but the most determined can see what fresh possibilities in the way of beauty and free movement lie in this new art of the screen. The frank swagger of the story was caught from the first, and somewhere near the first there was a fine sequence of the ship getting under weigh, one of the most lovely I have seen. Until this picture, everyone will perhaps have forgotten how shrewdly Stevenson worked in all the rich incidents of a time when, instead of organizing a strike—which is not fine and dashing, but the work of vicious malcontents—people took their damn ship away and struck for booty. The story and the good work of most of those in it were sadly enough spoiled at the end by the extended sentimentality that was allowed to spring up between Wallace Beery and Jackie Cooper; but the first three-quarters of it was still so lively and well established in its mood as to make the whole quite worth going to.

The movie version of Lockhart's *British Agent* brings up a question going a step beyond that of Hollywood's translation of materials. As the stuff of a great popular art it is inevitable that such material should mirror the ruling-class ideals of its time. But what is often confused is that in making use of it the movies are consciously trying to meet with, rather than mold, popular taste. If there is glamor in battleships or the business of the Rothschilds, then they will splash around in it, doing, like the ladies of the Norfolk waterfront, anything to please. There's no denying the social viciousness of the result; what one gets rather sick of is the criticism that finds the munitions trust or the Chase Bank directly behind all this. Big Money may influence this or that aspect of the trade, but the actual truth is that Big Money is not bright enough to conceive all the wicked designs attributed to it. This is pretty well borne out by Paramount's *British Agent,* which taps the glamor of a new and powerful theme, the Russian Revolution. That it stylizes its materials as usual, making the large drama a mere setting for the romance of an Oxford chap (Leslie Howard) and Lenin's secretary (Kay Francis), is beside the point. The encouraging thing about it is that sympathies are not too unequally divided, that the Allies are shown selling their silly idealists down the river, and that for moments at a time the movie public is allowed to glimpse, not dirty unshaven treachery, but ideals of a nature that Mr. Mark (Bombom) Sullivan could only describe as Russian. The picture itself is a spectacle and only fair. Whatever indictment it carries is very soft and there is much nonsense about going down for one's flag and all that. But for anybody with a grain of imagination there is also the suggestion of a great brave shaking of the world underlying the whole, and I am glad to see it.

12 September 1934

A Few Films from Many

Although there have been several of greater pretensions, I think the picture for this month must be *Crime without Passion*—more for what is behind it than for what is in it, though its story of a criminal lawyer who was all brain in the courts and all something else in love makes good enough stuff for the films. The author-producers are Ben Hecht and Charles MacArthur, two men who took what Hollywood might call high foreheads out to Hollywood and made a success of it. They have learned how films should be made and accepted all the terms, and they are now out to make films on their own.

Their first release is a frank thriller, mostly. Claude Rains as the legal mind prepares elaborate and cruel devices for getting rid of a dancing girl whose affection has become repulsive; there is a scuffle and the girl is shot by mistake, and the legal mind (now most unfortunately symbolized by a sort of continuous insert of Mr. Rains, cautioning himself, directing) prepares elaborate devices for baffling detection. Follows the usual routine of alibis, close calls, and a final breakdown that answers the need for an ending, but little else. In the long run the thing does not stand up properly because action came first, motives, problems, and the like being thrown in gratis. What makes it interesting is that the authors have brought wit and wisdom to a medium rather deficient in the latter at least, that there is a meaning to some of the situations and an edge to some of the dialogue not found in the usual run of scripts.

Claude Rains seems to be an essentially right man for the part, but there is too much of him by far, and the part itself is neither sympathetic nor well worked out: Ben Hecht has always been ready to fall into a flash sort of display, and Mr. Rains now seems prepared at such points to see him and raise him one, getting hold of an idea and then plugging it to death. The film is helped most by Margo, a girl recruited from the night clubs who sings her song with guitar and acts the part of the jilted dancer with such naturalness and human quality, with such lovely restraint of feeling and voice, that you will come away thinking her beautiful, which in plain daylight she is not. Paula Trueman also does a nice bit of work. Lee Garmes, Hal Rosson, and Slavko Vorkapitch have been brought from Hollywood for camera work and technical advice, and reports are that responsibility is all in a jumble out in Long Island where the picture was made. But the fact remains that *Crime without Passion* is worth seeing for Margo alone, and also for other reasons, one of them being that the whole venture seems to take a long stride forward for the movies, with promises of more to follow.

One Night of Love is an innovation of another color, an attempt to deal with Great Music. There are some good swelling notes in the last sixteenth of it, and moments of humor here and there between Tullio Carminati and Luis Alberni; but in the main it turns out to be a gawp-show. Most of it is taken up with a very wearing story: the maestro, the prima donna, temperaments, Italy, romance. All leading up to a few shots of the proscenium at the Metropolitan and the Diamond Horseshoe (there, implication has it, sit those who will know great music when they see it and register the same on shining faces); and all bearing the words, done in splendid grease paint: This is how it is with the Artist. Ah Life. Ah Art. There is no denying that something fine might come of such an initial idea, but it will never come on these creaking wheels, and it will never walk with these silly genuflections toward a picture-man's version of what music must be like. Even if there were not all this vulgar bowing and scraping, there would still be those long stretches of Grace Moore, who has a voice, but beyond certain wooden pantomimics, no acting grace whatever.

There is more honesty if not talent in the native product *She Loves Me Not*, in which Bing Crosby sings pleasantly and even acts a bit. A pretty bad and raucous but lively story of how a night-club girl (Miriam Hopkins) fled for refuge to Princeton—where, one gathers, everything is collegiate, everybody's father is president of something, and heroines have *just* got back from Paris. The picture has a plug for Chase National (Chase has got Paramount where it wants it), and a plug for Paramount itself, but also some quite amusing satire on the making of a newsreel, a couple of pretty songs and spots of group singing that are effective. It does, in short, what it knows how to do, which always seems to make the bad spots of any picture more endurable.

To these few pictures, chosen rather arbitrarily from among many, add for balance: *Side Streets* and *Straight Is the Way*, slight drama but worth the time for their good handling and reality; *Bulldog Drummond Strikes Back*, slight comedy but hardly funny; *Hide-Out*, to be avoided; *The Scarlet Empress*, to be shunned.

26 September 1934

Foreign Movies: Not to Praise

According to the stories, British films are going to be pushed much harder in this country, not only by a widening of their distribution, but by designing them more consciously for what some fancy to be the American Psychology. This is news of mixed goodness. Outside of *The Constant Nymph, I Was a Spy,* and *Catherine*—the few special exceptions good enough to be distributed on their own merits anyway—the pictures sent over by English companies this year have not been such as to whet the appetite for more. They are so earnest and inept, they apply Hollywood gags to the wrong situations three years later with such an air of trying, that to sit through one is a peculiar experience. You are not amused, you are not angered, you are embarrassed merely.

In the field of writing, Englishmen had a tradition going back so far you couldn't see it, and if Americans didn't like a book, they could pick up their swaddling clothes and go home, no one had asked them in the first place and what did they know about tradition. In the movies, fortunately for our self-respect, it is different. When something English is particularly boring or particularly thick, one can speak stiffly and with confidence, saying: We were cracking this joke ten years ago, and it wasn't very funny. And when program pieces like *Friday the 13th, It's a Boy!, For Love or Money* (that is, the routine product of the industry) are made more available and frequent over here, more and more of the less polite of us will be saying: Yah.

The latest importations include *The Bride of the Lake,* which may have been stepped up to the American tempo, but is still a soggy and obvious sort of thing. It has a background of Irish countryside and a plot of heroes, villains, and the family nag saving the family fortunes: a Tom Mix Western with the advantage of scenery and tunes. *Little Friend* is not quite so definitely British as others. It is notable chiefly for its sentimental fingering of a "problem": How can the little girl reconcile her estranged parents? By morbidity leading to attempted suicide? Yes. Nova Pilbeam, the child, is sensitive and rather sweet, but not able to hold such a story together. Hollywood's *Little Miss Marker* had the same false weepiness, but also a partial shine and vigor that leave no comparison.

But all this in no spirit of hatred for the English: only to say they would do well to keep their average films at home. I don't suppose it would have been brought up even now if it weren't for another picture, one of the kind the English seem to handle as well as could be expected. It is an operetta, *Chu Chin Chow,* and manages to swing successfully between fantasy and a humorous kind of realism. All about Ali Baba, the Forty Thieves, plots, riches, and blood (of which last three you will not have seen so much in years). There are dull spots sprinkled throughout, but in general it gets the objective, tongue-in-cheek treatment the theme demands. The settings (especially the streets of the town) are well worked out, the effects nicely accented by an intelligent musical score. George Robey and Fritz Kortner are funny and human looking, but ride their parts too hard. The movie is flawed and may require a certain mood of acceptance, but it is foolish and delightful, and I like it.

There are importations of a different nature from the Soviet Union, which has also been turning out a run of disappointing films this year. *Petersburg Nights* (from two of the lesser Dostoevsky stories) is about the best, and a long way from being splendid. I think no disservice would be done the downtrodden millions of the world if one were to come out and say that whatever has been done in the past, the Soviet product is getting pretty shoddy. Yet you might think Amkino was the King, and could release no wrong, the way people circle the point. There is certainly nothing in movies today so immediate and real as the premise from which the Soviet artists start, nothing so intrinsically powerful as these sudden dark faces, thick arms, and swaying mobs. The music is big and competent, and then there is that vast and thrilling country, with its history, to draw upon. They have got all this and they are facing in the right direction; but they do not move forward. *Petersburg Nights* (the Acme Theatre) is the story of an artist who drew his music from the masses, refused to lick boots, failed in the salons, and won the lean final victory of hearing his song in the throats of strikers, headed out for Siberia. All this in a procession of fragments, some of them banal, some (the marching sequences, the wind on the steppes) striking, but all of them lacking in sureness, fitted into no compact and moving whole. It is confused, jerky. Even if all the sequences were as brilliantly conceived and photographed as some, there would still be this uncontinuous procession of attitudes, simple but not clear. It is as though the pages of several novels were shuffled together, good with bad, and then bound up to look like a book.

Mass Struggle has the same faults and virtues, but less of both. The Ukrainian peasants moving against the Poles, winning, being sold out, some few of them knowing the issue and paying the price of being born before their time. A good theme, some fine, unintegrated touches, but otherwise inconclusive and poor. And that being the case, we might as well say so. The Soviet industry has turned out some thundering fine pictures, and one will do these no great honor by cheapening their praise on every patchwork that comes along.

10 October 1934

Stars and Garters

Occasionally the question comes up, in connection with the art of the screen, whether much attention should be paid to its actors. There is of course no doubt on this score in the fan magazines or the daily press. There is not really cause for much doubt anyway. But because of the peculiar thoroughness of publicity in this country (where surely more people could be found with a knowledge of the likes and dislikes of Mr. Gary Cooper than with the simplest idea of the main precepts of, say, Jesus Christ), there are those who get so sick of drinking Gary Cooper with their morning coffee that they will turn about and say, If you're going to chat about the stars, you're no kind of critic and to hell with you.

In their reaction against the nationwide puffing of Hollywood favorites these stern friends certainly have a case: it is an awful thing not to be able to go into a theater without the fear that it may be Fredric March again. But in denying the part that a cast plays in any given film, they are merely being silly. Because the most immediate and touching thing about any fiction is the sense of character it manages to build up and because, in the movies, the combination of actor and director is the final means of giving expression to this. Such a sense of real people is not written into the average script; it is never conjured out of a camera. It may be aided or marred by cutting, title writing, technical manipulation one way or another. But in the end it comes across to us from the people whose illusory life is taking place on the screen. A film story without people is like a novel without a character, music without a sound. And all you need for proof is a criticism of *Belle of the Nineties* without mention of Mae West.

Miss West, as a matter of fact, makes her own personality such a focus for a whole picture that its merits become to some extent its defects as well. Her latest film has very few good things outside her, its story is poor, it comes to nothing. Miss West, who is credited with having written it, evidently felt that there was no need of its coming to anything, so long as it gave her a setting, which it does. It is about how the Belle fell out with her slugger and fell in with the bad man of old New Orleans. Plots, double-crossings, and revenge, with Mae West sailing along, as tall and handsome as a ship, serene, full-rigged, setting off broadsides of wisecracks with fine timing and authority. She blows them all down. She sings a song about Her Old Flame and what an experience *he* was (she can't quite remember his name), and the treatment she and Duke Ellington's band (fine accompanists) give the "St. Louis Blues" is the strongest and most appropriate I've heard. As always, she shows a fine grasp of the American idiom and some sense of tradition; her film has some delightful flashes of hoofers in checkerboard suits and a Floradora chorus that would average at least 187 pounds. She has all these things and a great deal more that can't be described:

charm, a fine sense of what will be appropriate to her. She not only gives more and better publicity to the chief erogenous zones than any five Godwin authors: she has moments in this picture of clear loveliness. She has the most honest and outrageous and lovable vulgarity that ever was seen on the screen (where, incidentally, she is not the archetype of American womanhood on the make, or the archetype of anything else but Mae West), and enough other qualities so that she can get by with it. They made her change this picture all around, but they have probably found since that if you want to censor Miss West, you have got to lock her in a plaster cast.

But in Mae West we have the case of a performer who is her own manager, knows what is her own good and how to bring it out. Not everyone in the business is so fortunate, and so we have a whole hinterland of people whom a story or a bad director can make foolish, who are cast in lead roles regardless of their aptitudes. They are made over into someone's idea of what would be a money-making type, perhaps, or tweezed and painted until they have the superficial resemblance of some type that has already proved to be a money-maker.

You could take for one fairly good example Anna Sten, who certainly did not build her Continental reputation on the empty creampuff sort of thing she was made to appear in *Nana*. Now, in *We Live Again,* she is actually brought back to life as a person—partly by casting, no doubt: she still seems incompetent in the higher ranges of acting, but she is a good healthy peasant type, and capable of the reactions you might expect. The story of the picture has revolutionary implications, but all in a remote sort of way: the best parts of it as pure film are the prison scenes and Easter services at the church, where there is a great deal of movement and atmosphere. Miss Sten, a servant in old Russia, is betrayed by her young master, leaves the estate, and goes from bad to worse in Moscow, while the boy forgets his early humanitarianism and becomes a hardshell Cossack. The girl, deported on a quibble, eventually brings him to a realization, first that he has wronged her and, through this, that he and his class have been wronging her class all along, and that this is not right. So the picture closes on the renunciation of his birthright and his going with her to Siberia: musical chords, an obvious-looking boundary marker, a mellow and happy defeat.

The Count of Monte Cristo, to continue on the subject of whether the stars make the picture or the picture breaks the stars, is the sort of thing that represents partial victory for both sides. It is the old Dumas story of how Edmond Dantes was buried alive in a dungeon through malice, and how his revenge was slow but complete—an action story, that is, but given a meaning by the purpose and fortitude of its principal character. Robert Donat is an appropriate and solid choice but no great histrionic shakes in the part, which returns the compliment by carrying him along skillfully from climax to climax, but letting him down at the end, where a great deal of unexplained veering about confuses the main issue and detracts from it. The picture would have been much stronger if both the story and the whole company had been better: as it is, I cannot think of faults without remembering that while the thing was going forward I was sitting up in my seat hoping for him to soak them plenty.

24 October 1934

Rock and Water

Mr. Robert Flaherty, one of the few directors who can sign his name in lights and still not make money for somebody, has been two years on his latest picture. It is being distributed by Gaumont-British as *Man of Aran* and was taken on the Aran Islands, where there is little besides rock and water and the wind, and where these three combine to make one of the most dangerous—certainly the most mighty and beautiful—seas in the world. The only plot is the natural one of people struggling to keep alive—in this case a man, a woman, and a boy, all islanders themselves. They go out to fish in boats and come back if God wills; they scrape up enough soil to grow spuds in; they bend down and straighten up and keep an eye on the weather. And their struggle, open or implied, is vivid enough to carry the more documentary parts of the film.

Technically, I found *Man of Aran* rather wonderful, never having seen such a boil and thunder of surf as takes up a third of the footage. Mr. Flaherty himself is responsible for the camera work, which is really very fine all the way through: there is good feeling of the part the elements play—even in clear weather on shore—in the way people stand against a tall background of sky and in the way wind is almost made visible in this monotony of low tableland and the sea far out. One of the most authentic things is the talk of the people, sometimes unintelligible, sometimes with a word or phrase standing clear, a command passed along in the quick thoughtful way of men whose whole concentration is on the action it calls for (Hold what you've got, Hold hard now, Steady now), several voices speaking at once, grunts, murmurs. No one speaks into the camera, there are no soliloquies: speech is a natural thing rather than the means of exposition it has become on the stage. The effect is one of good accompaniment, and should be copied.

But *Man of Aran,* however real, would have made better truth if it had been handled with more of the art of fiction. In the first place, I do not think that for all the roughness of their clothes, their labor, and good stout speech, Mr. Flaherty's people have one-quarter as much of what it is really like as Synge's in

Riders to the Sea. Here the material is so concentrated on the more vivid episodes of island life that the result is more idyllic than actual: there is no full conception of the long round of bitter days making up the less picturesque side. How you could remedy this and still make it dramatic is hard to know: there is small precedent in the movies. But certainly the film could with advantage be more varied than it is. There are only four or five phases of life touched on, if you exclude such incidents as the patching of the boat, and in working these out (especially the seaweed carrying, the putting of those at sea in relief against those on shore) repetition is too much favored over selection.

There is always a tendency to ridicule fiction in the movies, many confusing the easy, empty, he-she-it stuff with sound creation, which relates people with whom we can associate ourselves to the fact we are supposed to be assimilating, making it more memorable and vivid. Mr. Flaherty, for example, has inevitably adopted many of the means of storytelling in stating his fact: his storm is little but water until men have to beat in through it; his way of bringing in many things is the casual one of letting you discover for yourself (not a title: This is the way they wear their shoes; but a close-up, while the man is engaged in something else, of the shoe on his foot). But, although he started with good material, in understanding, varying, and selecting it he should have gone further. His picture is beautiful but occasionally dull and almost altogether too happy, and still beautiful, better than anything else around.

Proper selection and variation, two important adjuncts of fictional truth, are too frequently dismissed under some such glib term as Hollywood slickness anyway; and those who could sit at the feet of the best slickers are many. In running the camera letter by letter from A to Z to show that the character is eating alphabet soup, the Soviet directors are the worst offenders, above all in their documentary films. I still remember two rather old products: *A Day in Moscow* and *The Soviets Greet New Turkey.* These, stretching material for about one reel out into forever, were pretty terrible, and not in a quibbling art-for-art sense. The most important thing about any creation, certainly, is the general effect it has on the observer; and how can he be coaxed to like even a good thing if you keep rubbing his nose in it? Hollywood seems to have learned better than anyone that in making a picture you are not writing a book, that because the observer can catch in a visual moment or two what would require five pages of print, a film has got to be kept moving and shifting if its material is to be developed rather than worn to death. And what is Hollywood doing with this special knowledge at present, lest we should load the dice too much in its favor? It is displaying in full and advertised view such big-time pieces as *Madame du Barry, Caravan, The Last Gentleman, Peck's Bad Boy, The Barretts,* etc.—all practically fatal. You might try to be partial to Hollywood, and might in the case of such lively pictures as *The Merry Widow* (of which more later) succeed for a time; but in the long run Hollywood will knock that on the head all by itself, never fear.

7 November 1934

Artists among the Flickers

In Vertov's *Three Songs about Lenin* the Soviets come forward to bury the great leader in Westminster Abbey, with something of the atmosphere of Patriots' Day. Objectively, it is an attempt to idolize, not so much a man as his concepts; it is thus rather limited in appeal. Washington in boats with his ragged army, Lincoln freeing the slaves—these things could be dramatized in some fashion. But when Lenin tots up a column of figures to give some of the Eastern peoples economic freedom, what are you going to do about it in terms of pictures? Near the end of the film there is a moving section of Lenin's Russia today, with men working, tractors, forges, the dams, etc.; but on the whole it seems poorly melted newsreel material with a poetic cast. I would not have brought it up except that it has gone the way of many foreign films in its reception here, and got its most honorable citation on the grounds of its being pure cinema.

And this suggests the subject of film criticism in general, which is really the subject of this piece. The appreciation of pictures is much like all other forms; but there is the sad fact of its having thus far got so little intelligent consideration that intelligence, when it appears, tends to become the high priest guarding marvels. Everyone goes to the movies, to laugh or to delight his heart; they are a part of common experience—and very common at that, usually. Now and then one is good, but in thinking of it we do not think of art. It's just a movie; we only went for the fun. So when someone comes along and says down his nose, Art in the cinema is largely in the hands of artists in cinematographic experimentation, we think, Mm, fancy such a thing, I wonder what *that* is like. When someone, almost holding his breath, says, Well, there is surely no better *montage* (or *régisseur*) than this *montage* (or *régisseur*), we are apt to be discouraged: Oh damn, I missed it again, all I saw was a story with people and action. And when someone says of *Three Songs about Lenin,* This is pure cinema, implying that you couldn't say more for it, we think, Well, well, can't miss that surely.

The pay-off is that *régisseurs* are in ordinary life directors, that *montage* is simply the day-in-day-out (in Hollywood) business of cutting: all you need, except for the higher technical reaches, is a pair of shears and a good sense of timing. As for pure cinema, we would not praise a novel (in which field by this time you must, to be intelligent, be intelligible, or perish) by saying merely that it was pure *roman.* I do not wish to pull rabbits out of the hat, but here is a fact: you too can make pure cinema.

Given the proper facilities and scientific advice, anyone can, me for instance. Out of my window I can see a rather mean-looking tenement. Doors, windows, a sidewalk. Just above it, rising over it, is a tall very recent building, elevator apts. electrolux, 1, 2, 3, 4, 5 rooms, etc., but wait, we'll not open there.

We will catch the meanness of the mean street by opening on pages 18-19 of *The New York Times* for last week, dirty and blowing along the mean sidewalk in the morning wind. Dust, desolation. The paper blowing and on the sound-track a high piccolo note—wheeeeeeee—and the street empty, deserted, it is morning. Now (take the shots separately; cut and paste them together afterward): the sky (gray), the house (sleeping), the paper, the sky, the house, the paper (whee). Follow the paper down to, suddenly, the wheel of a milk truck (Ha! truck—life, the city stirs; throw in a tympani under the piccolo for the city stirring) which goes down to the mean house, stops, the driver gets out: follow him with one bottle of Grade B up three flights of mean stairs to a mean door where—stop.

Down in the street the driver comes out, yawns. Up the house front slowly to a top-floor window where a man, touseled, yawns. As the truck drives off its wheels turn, gain speed, and suddenly there are other wheels (the city awakes): trucks pounding down the Concourse, the subway, the "El," streetcars and the trucks pounding, the "Els," the subways, and now (on the sound-track, the piccolo goes a fifth higher) you cut in the big dynamo wheels, all the wheels, all the power houses, wheels and wheels. Rah, *montage.* Then from the dynamo out (space, motion, speed) to—what do you think? An electric grill in the big stinking apartment house, with a colored servant in white, frying bacon and looking at the dumbwaiter. Title: WHERE ALL IS THAT MILKMAN NOHOW. Now down to the milkman, taking in a bottle of heavy cream (flash: SERVANTS' ENTRANCE) to the dumbwaiter; now back to the poor house, and out over the city and up over the high, proud bulge of the apartment house to the high gray clouds, over the city, over the rich and poor getting up, getting their separate service from the milkman. And on into a great dither of wheels, clouds, gaping windows, yawns, men walking—into plush elevators, on the hard, mean sidewalk, faster, faster, everybody getting into motion, the same city, the same sky, the two remote worlds rich and poor. For special effect, let us say, a kid coming out of the door of the mean house, with pennies for a loaf of whole-wheat, and running past the feet and in front of the wheels, and tripping on the broken cement, falling, smack. Close-up of the head showing a splash of blood spreading on the mean stones, and flash to the apartment house, up, up, to a window, in through the window to the cream being poured into the coffee, being drunk in bed, in silk pyjamas, spilling, a splash of coffee spreading on the silk pyjamas.

Any good? I'm afraid not. But it is pure cinema. Pure cinema can be anything: the important thing always is whether it is done well, whether you can pile one thing on another in a clear beautiful moving line. The wonderful and humbling thing about the movies in general is the skill and sure judgment behind this mechanical transfer of images to strips of celluloid, of a certain number of feet of celluloid into a moving series of images that will have a certain effect on those who watch. It doesn't matter whether the result is a story of a Significant

Experiment: what we have got to single out is the difference between a picture that catches you up in its own movement, and a picture that stammers, stands doubtfully, hammers at a few obvious meanings, and leaves you with a feeling of all the mechanism used to capture emotion, without the emotion. *Three Songs about Lenin* may have been attacked with a new attack, may be an awesome experiment. My point is that it is not a good picture, and my quarrel with movie criticism is simply that if it was, those who thought so have not done one thing to show why, in so many simple honest words.

5 December 1934

It Happened Once More

Frank Capra is not the genius of the age, but he is a careful, talented director who has made a Hollywood success and earned an office of his own, and still not been taken in by blobs of gilt. Thus far he has used his prerogatives as a sure-fire money-maker to hold out on one important thing: it will either be good comedy before he is through with it, or he won't be through with it.

His latest production for Columbia is *Broadway Bill,* the story of a young man who got stifled by the smell of his in-laws' money, and went back to horse racing, and got overtaken by a good many disasters, but finally won the Derby, bringing all to their senses and himself to an appreciation of the rebel kid sister and so forth. If you look at it that way, there is little there. It is nice to see someone stand on his own legs and abuse the filthy rich, and the horse race is pretty exciting: but anyone can do that. Where the film stands out is for its incidental human warmth and naturalness; and more than anything, for its continuous sideshow brightness. There is a crazy tie-up between the race horse and the rooster, with the latter crowing at odd moments and the former chewing around on its tail feathers; there is a drinking scene, and one of the neatest con-games you'd care to watch, and a break away from an unpaid meal that is so well worked out as to be a model for all directors in what, if we were speaking of music, we would be sure to call phrasing—everyone going on enough to deafen you, a perfectly atrocious hubbub, and yet every detail coming clear, so that you follow in each case why he is yelling, and what.

Where the film stands out, really, is for what Mr. Capra has to give it in the way of painstaking supervision (there is a certain individual stamp on dialogue, incident, and smoothness of technical attack); and for what he can get out of all the people in it, which is a great deal when the people are as good as they are here. Anyone familiar with Warner Baxter's sad succession of recent duds might suspect the hand of God in his present transformation; those who saw Clark Gable in *It Happened One Night* will recognize, in Baxter's quick, breezy, off-hand naturalness, the hand of Mr. Capra. The cast is fine from top to bottom, including Walter Connolly, Raymond Walburn, Lynne Overman, Clarence Muse, Harry Todd. As for Myrna Loy, I have never seen her so fresh and touching and really lovable; but the hand here is her own, one feels, sensitive and firm. Mr. Capra has the wisdom of being able to mold them or leave them alone, as the case requires.

And where Mr. Capra himself stands out, after you have granted him intelligence, technical skill, a sense of character, is for his mastery of two of the most vital factors in comedy: timing and accent. There is no need to be too intellectual on this: it is merely the old difference between the man who can, and the man who can't, tell a joke—extended from the point in a two-line gag to the interwoven points of a sequence, and from the innumerable separate parts of a picture to their relative duration, the way they run into one another and carry along the mood without spilling a drop. And it is largely this precision and instinct for where the swing of the words or of the body should be, that makes everything so natural and irresistible here. (The René Clair pictures show the same thing, more complex, more highly developed.) *Broadway Bill* has faults, there's no denying that—an almost unbelievably false uplift in the end, a song about the split-pea soup and the succotash that is given too much extension, and Mr. Capra tends to repeat things out of his old pictures. In substance it is a little thing. But we can finish with it quickly and definitely by saying that it will be a long day before we see so little made into so much: it is gay and charming and will make you happy, and I am sorry to say I do not know recommendations much higher.

19 December 1934

The Movies Go to War

The appearance of several new war films suggests a point that has not had much attention, namely, muckraking in the movies. It is true that pictures, even more than other art forms, reflect the ruling ideals of their social system. But, in a loose sort of democracy such as ours, it is also true that they do so in a haphazard manner. Movie scripts are not written in the vaults of certain holding banks, all underground and sinister: they are written for sale to the public. The public, having been born with the tin spoon of rugged individualism in its mouth, usually clamors for what it ought to clamor for. But when it gets a perverted taste for something hardly favorable to the ruling interests, do the producers know any better? They do not, as a rule: they have been taught to make things they can sell for a tidy profit (for the owners), and they go ahead making them if they're able.

The Warner exposés (*Massacre, Cabin in the Cotton,* etc.) and such rare pieces as *British Agent,* which was actually hospitable to the Russian Revolution, have already appeared to worry the black-and-white boys, who must have all their categories imperative. The radicalism of such pictures was isolated and safe, but still there: they were undeniable deviations. The new war pictures represent something else again, and go farther. Not, certainly, Laurence Stallings' *The First World War,* which is as diffuse in its emphasis on stuffed shirts and as jingoistic in its treatment of "brave British lads" and the fearful Huns, as could be expected. And not Leon Garganof's French production, *The Battle,* which is very well done melodrama, waving its flag incidentally but without shame. Where the muckraking comes is in the first film to capitalize on such munitions exposures as (notably) the several recent books, the article in *Fortune,* and the Senate Report: *Dealers in Death,* now playing at the Criterion Theatre, New York City. This picture was made, quite frankly, by a few independent movie people, and made solely for the purpose of selling it. It veers between an illustrated lecture on the international war profiteers and a carefully pieced together historical collection of war and other films. It sensationalizes, that is, the basic scandal of war profits, and works up through the mock peace treaties to the war that is brewing today, with new guns and new gases, planes, ships, and always profits. In deference to possible censorship (it gets a great deal by the censors as it is), it does not mention by name those behind the profit lines in this country: otherwise it minces no words. It is as true and effective a document as you could ask for.

But the question comes up: is it really dangerous from the point of view of war industries? The history of its production is rather strange, but informative. The makers (Messrs. Hershey, Shaff, Kusell) found immediately that shots of modern steel and munitions plants were not to be had under any pretext. And their first inquiries were followed almost immediately by a visit from Mystery Man number one, who wondered what the boys wanted film for, and hoped they would remember their old friends Bethlehem and U.S. Steel, to deal with them gently. The boys covered up. That night their new office was torn up; but the script of the film was elsewhere, nothing was taken. Who can know what to say of this? When the film had been made there came Mystery Man number two, with no definite connections, but hints that a Certain Organization would like to see the film, perhaps buy it. The organization had nothing to do with the movie industry. The boys said they were making the film for release. Not interested in chicken feed. The man wondered if they could call $50,000 chicken feed, and left. Mystery Man number three had somewhat the same proposition, and, like the other, he may have represented breakfast foods or he may have represented the steel interests, but he represented somebody.

But the important point is that, once the film was being shown around at private screenings, the mystery men saw it somehow and were suddenly satisfied to let the matter drop. The film was frank and denounced the steel and munitions people, but at the same time, the emotion it would arouse in the people was one of panic: a war is inevitable and terrible: the whole world is arming, and we must have protection. The munitions makers sell protection.

Dealers in Death, therefore, is a muckraking film; but it is hardly an exception to the fundamental rule of support to the most powerful. (*War Is a Racket,* which was slapped together in an attempt to beat *Dealers in Death* to the screen and shows it, hardly needs mention.) Where we get to the subject of subversive films in earnest is in Walter Wanger's *The President Vanishes,* which coats a strong pill with melodrama.

This picture shows a group of conspirators sitting around, plotting to get the country into a European war. The oil interests, the banking interests, the press, steel, munitions, an ex-justice, a crack lobbyist. In a war they can clean up a million a day, and what did the last war cost? A mere 50,000 dead. Gentlemen, what are we waiting for? They need a slogan: Remember the Maine was one; Make the World Safe was another. Something about Our National Honor now, perhaps? This is decided on: the publisher will put it in eight-column heads, the radio will gargle appropriately. They'll get speakers and the oil man knows something about this new national organization of Gray Shirts: if the boobs won't fall, they will be pushed. And how about Congress, can this be arranged? It apparently can. The only one not in the line-up is the President, who shortly turns out a very good fellow, almost the hero. He is against war but helpless, and will probably be impeached. The rest of the story turns about the supposed abduction of the President, the inevitable frenzy of the country, the return of the President in such a manner as to frame the Gray Shirts (they have been carrying on in great shape, beating up haranguers of the workers, objectors, everybody), and the presidential address to all good Americans—rather paternal, but ringing.

Whatever may be said for the story, which is at once naïve, oversimplified, and well carried out for all that, the basic line-up is shrewdly conceived. These forces, when they get to work, will not be headed off by any business of kidnaping: but they will be the forces at the bottom of the thing, and they will work in just about this way, ostensibly for God and actually for profits, with all this ballyhoo of press and radio and shirtings. According to most of the hard and fast rules we know about movie production, therefore, a picture getting after such sacred trumpery in earnest could not be made, or at least could not be shown to the nation. But according to the setup of the picture industry, it can be made if there is a demand for it, and it has been made, and is getting a national release through Paramount no less, and it will be shown as widely as the box-office figures justify. Reports at present are that it is doing less business than was expected, but even at that it will prove a more healthy influence on the national susceptibility to war scares than any propaganda we have seen. If, as even this picture might suggest to the more cynical, any peacetime influence on the national susceptibility can be healthy enough to matter anyway.

26 December 1934

1935

From *Don Juan* to *Show Them No Mercy*

Two Camera Pieces

With such ebb-tide movies still fresh in mind as *Bright Eyes* (for mothers) and Gene Fowler's sluggish *The Mighty Barnum,* there is little use my talking about the current Hollywood output. As far as film making is concerned, *The Little Minister* is not very noteworthy either, though the very special radiance with which Miss [Katharine] Hepburn fills it is enough to set this picture aside for some later comment. The films most interesting to me just at present are several non-Hollywood productions, notably Alexander Korda's *Private Life of Don Juan,* and G. W. Pabst's English version of his film *Don Quixote.*

The Don Juan story, starring Douglas Fairbanks, spoofs the subject of the Great Lover, and makes fair entertainment. Don Juan, no longer young, skips out on creditors and assignations, allowing Spain to think him dead. In the country he rests: good food, sleep every night, no worries. A romantic book is got out about him; his legend grows (one thinks of D. H. Lawrence). At length, planning to reappear in a blaze of open arms, he reappears. Nothing. The legend has already passed human proportions: how could any mere man be Don Juan? His famous powers, in actual practice, don't get him to first base; he is ridiculed, thought mad, and so finally driven into the bosom of his loving wife, whom he had really never noticed. Too busy.

All of which is fairly well done, though often mishandled (transitions too abrupt, the satiric edge too often dulled, etc.). But the story is not the important thing here, one sequence in the first part alone making the picture worth seeing. A funeral in Spain, with the black figures milling slowly in all that unearthly white light. The rough stones in the walls and statues pile up into the sky, and the sky is framed boldly. Everything has a curious buoyancy and is carried along on the music, with its thin oboe figures and choir of voices, having both volume and restraint. Even a bigger aid to the illusion—though I am not sure why this should be so—is the light touch used throughout: Don Juan, moving through the

63

crowd to watch his own funeral, and the women weeping because they had never seen him, and he dead. One shot in particular—women in black hoods are moving diagonally up the steps, and the white stone cuts into a vivid dark sky, and everything swings along upward with the choir voices—this one flash has enough sweep and clear beauty in it to set the tone of a whole film. The film as a whole tapers off somewhat afterward, but those responsible for the best parts of it seem to be Georges Perinal (formerly Clair's cameraman), Michael Spoliansky (music), Director Korda—and also Mr. Fairbanks, for whatever you think of his calisthenics, the man has a certain rank swagger and grace: with a cape and go-to-hell hat and a clear hip line, he is fine costume material. Here he fits nicely into a picture that suggests a phenomenon peculiar to the medium, namely that of a background's coming to life, coming to mean something, getting its own mood into the audience. Whether intentionally or not, the film is not nearly so striking for theme and story as for the atmosphere in which these are established.

In *Don Quixote* the visual effect is also one of beauty always (photography by Nicholas Farkas); but as far as such central matters as the dominant idea and its execution are concerned, the picture is a pretty straight flop. A few attitudes, a few big tableaux, and no flowing of one small thing into another. As for the central character, you could forgive the inattention to the original Quixote, who was often shrewd and never completely pitiful; but what you can't overlook is the lack of any single conception of what the knight should be, in movies. And so you get Feodor Chaliapin, a fine deep-voiced tragic figure of a man, being indiscriminately a tragic figure, a clown, and a baritone out of Verdi, popping his b's and t's all over the place and in short mugging almost every line. Let's forget the famous name for a minute and realize that here is an actor with no governing idea and a tradition that stems from opera, where true acting has no point whatever. In direction, the film veers between a period play and a stooge-act, mixing courtly address with outdated American slang; and it isn't that mirth is a foil for sadness, or vice versa. It is simply that Pabst is never sure whether he is operating a tragedy or a bawdy house, but will fumble around for what he can get out of both, which is not much.

And still the picture is beautiful in its last part, with the camera looking over the grain fields to the sky, and the men coming through, partly visible with their heavy sacks, and Don Quixote riding into his windmill, getting pinned to and swept up with it. There is a high, strange quality of motion in that grave sweep of the arm, seen from below, with the poor fool dying and the soundtrack subdued to the creaking of the mill and the wind in the sails. And say this for Chaliapin: in the last scenes the requirement is tragedy, and he stands up under it, in his own sure right at last. So, almost by accident, *Don Quixote* gets a few great moments to add to its scenic realism and beauty, and to set it apart from the run of ill made film duds it otherwise resembles.

By way of a footnote, I think now is as good a time as any other to point out that when names are mentioned in connection with these or other movies, credit can be given only in a loose sort of way. Production is such a complicated and overlapping process that no one who was not actually on the set can hope to be accurate in saying whether or not the cameraman had his finger in the direction, or the director had his finger on the camera, or the writer of *Don Quixote* (Paul Morand) was to blame for its clumsy movement. The best that one can do is to trace matters to their own department, and take a chance that its titular head had the authority to be as good or bad as he seemed. In the case of exceptional work, at least, someone ought to take the bow.

9 January 1935

Movies: Arms and Men

I can see at the start that this film, *Lives of a Bengal Lancer,* is going to cause me a lot of grief, first, because from a social point of view it is execrable, second, because it is a dashing sweat-and-leather sort of thing and I like it. The story is one of men in a frontier division of lancers, and does what *The Lost Patrol* did more strongly last year, substituting for the customary emotional pull of boy and girl the emotions of the service. Kipling stuff. We're in it and it's pretty hot, but we'll take it off neat if it kills us, going down like men. (That is, like Englishmen, because, in fiction at least, a Britisher who catches himself being a man invariably figures that qualities so unusual must be home products.) The colonel's raw cub of a son is brought out to India straight from military school, to carry on the family traditions, and he can't keep his diapers on and eventually gets popped into a bag by the natives (this, you feel, is a fine young squirt for grown men to chase after and lose their lives for). In the end he is shielded by surviving friends, so that it won't break old armorplate's heart, and there is a lot of stuff about this handful of iron men holding up the millions of India and the like. Every attempt to give it mouthfuls of meaning is either silly or a fine glorification of empire and the wars of empire; but somehow these drawbacks don't get in the way as much as it would seem.

The good part of the picture comes in its subsidiary business. There are stock situations, of course, such as rubbing a little nut oil on the face and passing for a native, the imminent Union of the Tribes, etc. There is the business of cavalry drills and formations, really done with great flourish and dash, and there are the life in quarters, the long file riding up to the fort, and the well-managed skirmish scenes, with machine guns spattering around and all. But occupying the best part of the footage is the main situation of men living together and getting in each other's hair, tied together by the strange bond of work and discipline, by the common pride of doing the job.

The execution of all this is what makes it effective. Franchot Tone and Gary Cooper make a convincing relationship by the solid types they build up, with their horseplay and nagging and rough loyalty. You would not have conceived how well they show up when there is no longer need for them to be draped around Miss [Norma] Shearer's gown for sequence 28, night shot. The scene, for example, where one of them grubs a cigarette from the other, after both have just got through with having burning splinters driven under their nails, their hands fumbling and grotesque, is really strong enough not to be in pictures. The dialogue is laconic and good (when it is not in one of its declamatory moods), and Sir Guy Standing does a good version of the colonel, and C. Aubrey Smith is a fine man for these parts: he has a wide deliberate voice, and presence, and a face appropriately like an old army boot. The direction (Henry Hathaway) seems to show a high amount of skill, for there are not only difficult matters handled very well, but a lot of minor points where missing the beat would have soured whole stretches of the film.

And so I am taken by the show, imperialism and all. After all this fustian of Hollywood romance, I may be a pushover for scenes from the lives of men who live and work together, but I imagine that the glamor will get over generally, and I suspect we can't any more combat by detracting the dangers of having such stuff around than we could save the victims of a handsome woman by tipping them off that she was ugly as sin. And anyway, the important point here is not the glorification of the army *per se.* You see the same thing in shops and in a city room and on farms—men with their minds not on the money, like merchants, nor on just what interests they are serving, like Senators, but on hitting a good lick, on the rough satisfaction of combining finely with all the others to make the thing work, go off smoothly. And in a thing like this the real emotional pinch is not what ideal the men are going down for, but in the suggestion of how men do the impossible sometimes, doing and enduring in common.

Otherwise we seem to be in a low-pressure area for movies these last two weeks. Owing somewhat to Miss Anne Shirley's performance, *Anne of Green Gables* is just about the best treatment the theme could get. Essentially the film is made-up and monotonous—tragedy having its breakfast in bed. And *The Unfinished Symphony,* an English version of Schubert and his more romantic troubles, is kept pleasant if not exciting mostly by the competent work of Hans Jaray and Marta Eggerth, and the Viennese Symphony orchestra. *Charlie Chan in Paris* is a very modest thriller. *It's a Gift* might have been written by Chic Sale and taken in somebody's cellar with a pocket Kodak. (If it weren't for Fields, who can always do something to keep life bright, I don't think they would get their money back at that.) *The Right to Live* is one of those pictures that is worth going to considerable trouble to avoid.

23 January 1935

Movies: Pay No Attention

I have been trying to get a picture that is worth reviewing, for the last two weeks, and hereby throw in the towel. What, for instance, is there to say about *David Copperfield*? The producers have made all the details of it—the famous names, the awful expense, the insurmountable surmounted—so familiar to everyone, including the reviewers, that there is really only one thing left to mention in review: *David Copperfield* presents as many characters and situations as possible out of a novel that is very long, very inclusive, very famous, and very bad; it runs for well over two hours, and is a pretty straight bore. *The Good Fairy* is much better stuff, having quite a lot of honest pleasure in it. I could wish that the true comic capacities of Frank Morgan and Reginald Owen were not so often overlaid with bogus histrionics (partly writing, partly direction), and that Herbert Marshall were not restricted to being so sheerly well bred (Oh I *am* so soddy). But Margaret Sullavan is, most of the time, entirely lovely, and if she isn't an actress I wouldn't know it, that is the way things are between Margaret Sullavan and me. In the end the picture suffers mainly from good fairyism: it is a bold and technically successful screen adaptation, but look at what they had to adapt.

Alexander Korda's *The Scarlet Pimpernel* isn't so bad either. It certainly puts the French Revolution in a bad light, what with Leslie Howard tying knots in the French Ambassador and simply baffling him by a tendency to vanish up chimneys. But although the film tends to defeat itself by poor continuity and unintentional burlesque, Mr. Howard and Merle Oberon are attractive figures. With a clear-headed, drastic screen adaptation, something might have been made of this, for the theme is exciting and the production is in general well managed, especially in the photography.

If these two are bearable but not worth turning aside for, then what can be said about *The Enchanted April, Wings in the Dark, Clive of India, Bordertown*? The first is typical Ann Harding; the second is a sky opera with good air photography and terrible emptiness; the third is dilly-dally biography with elephants and Ronald Colman; and *Bordertown* is a complete dud, barring the presence of Bette Davis and Eugene Pallette. These films could be talked about for hours, and who would listen?

But this will very shortly get us all down, and we had better turn for a minute to something interesting, such as *Variety*'s mid-year boxscore for true critics, just out. Every quarter *Variety* lines up the leading daily reviewers and gives them their report cards, having kept a careful check on how the critic seemed to like a picture as against whether the picture seemed to make money. By this standard his review is either "right" or "wrong." If the critic saw thirty pictures and liked thirty pictures, and ten of them were box-office headaches, all he can bat with *Variety* is .666, *Variety* is sorry. If the thirty he saw and liked were winners, he would do 1.000, but don't worry: the highest average listed is only .824 (awarded, by an odd stroke of fate, to *Variety* itself: nice going).

So there they all are, *Variety,* the nine New York critics, and the four Chicago critics, all in black and white, and their relative worth carried out to three decimal places. And all one of them has to do if he wants to find out whether he is a good critic is look himself up in the list. Incidentally, all he has to do if he wants to *be* a good critic is keep his ear to the ground for rumors, his eye peeled for double-truck advance ads, and his nose out for the way films are going financially before they break in New York—as reported weekly in *Variety.* It is absolutely wonderful. Of course, there is no provision for registering such subtle shades as whether a winning film in which the critic has detected immortal tragedy turns out to have a Max Fleischer short or the trailer for *Babes in Toyland.* But it is still wonderful.

And this is not in any spirit of mean derision either: the whole thing must be quite an incentive to good work, to say nothing of heightened interest all around, and if I thought for a minute that *Variety* had heard of *The New Republic* I'd write in like a shot and no stopping me: Dear *Variety,* How'm I doing, signed Anxious. In the general excitement I am even betrayed into nervously throwing around a few prizes myself. The first, to be known as the Great Ivory Prize, will be pinned on the following exhibit from *Variety*'s own calendar of current movie releases, now in its second appearance and about due for a third: *"Babbitt"* (*Variety* says, describing the movie) is from "Upton Sinclair's *Main Street.*" Prize is awarded for most boners in fewest words. Score: words, 5; bones, 4.

I'm afraid this review is going to get inconsequential before long, but I tried to find a good movie—I must have seen twenty-seven. *Devil Dogs of the Air* was the main disappointment. It is not only mildly harmful as an incentive to combat by sea and air, but silly and dull, completely wide of reality. The underlying suggestion is that a Marine is a cross between Strangler Lewis and the perfect knight. But Marines, outside of a tendency to shine their brass buttons, are people, and there are no people here. Everything is subordinated to the usual Hollywood version of fleet and air maneuvers—including the friendly enemies of the piece, James Cagney and Pat O'Brien, who deserve something a great deal better. The doings of the animals in *Baboona* (a pretty dull film) really have more of both sense and interest.

20 February 1935

The Pictures in Motion

King Vidor's new picture for Samuel Goldwyn, *The Wedding Night,* is the firmest bit of drama to come from the picture studios for quite a while. A good picture, never really powerful but constantly fresh and right, it can be touching for minutes at a time without paying for it by directly going maudlin. Except, that is, in the several spots where can be discovered the boot tracks of Mr. Sam Goldwyn, stepping in with his cigar and the determination to have a pitcher with some art in it, damn the cost—witness that last fade-in of Miss Sten's ghost.

We have seen the story before, of course. This time it has Gary Cooper as a broken-down novelist who retires to the ancestral property in Connecticut and meets Anna Sten as the daughter of the Polish-American farmer, falling in love with her during that winter and writing his first good book around the pattern of her family life. The resolution—his wife's return to him from the city and the girl's accidental death in the row with her bumpkin bridegroom on the wedding night—hardly makes tragedy of it, but in no way glosses over the grief inevitable in such matters. Lines, for example, like those of the wife in stating the case for wives—"With you he's got nothing more than he had with me before it wore off, but what he and I have now, after these five years is . . . well after all, five years"—these are enough to give it an air of truth we don't usually expect in films. And this is not merely an occasional factor in the picture. The parts of the novel the writer was writing are lush and empty enough for snickers, but in general things are expressed in such natural terms as to be a pleasure to witness. Nor only are the roles given Gary Cooper, Anna Sten, and Helen Vinson well carried out, but even the bit parts are shrewdly cast and played. Take the business of the Jap muttering over his fire, the part of the depotmaster, or such accurate bits of dialogue as Siegfried Rumann's: "Better you don't talk to me," he will say, getting hoarse with anger. And all the little character touches, such as Cooper's confession of what he used the bedspread for: counting the patches at night, fifty red and twenty-six black—these, I suppose, all go back to Vidor's own preoccupation with natural things like Polish families at dinner or at a wedding, work in the tobacco fields (a little out place as it happened), farmyards and stove-dampers and country roads.

All of which leads up to another and more central consideration, namely that while we may have seen the story we have not seen the picture before. So much goes into a decently made film besides the story that the usual literary standards are largely invalid. By nature of its brevity and its need to translate all things into terms of moving images, a picture cannot hope to do the same work as a novel: it does both more and less. It may start with a plot that will hold only as much water as a large bath towel, and yet may surround it with a new sort of glamor. By resort to its own peculiar devices it can at times get effects as strong as those of a full novel. And a picture must be judged while these devices are in full play, while it is in motion. Once it has stopped and someone recounts the mere story, some of the most vital things are lost: the color of its setting, its speed and lightness, the play of relations as between the various people.

It would give an able writer a good deal of effort to make up a character with the warmth and feeling of solidity that one gets from Mr. Cooper before his part is played out; and any woman so fresh and sensitive and strong as Anna Sten in the part of Manya must always remain the despair of writers. Miss Sten is awkwardly clothed and lighted in some stretches of the film, and when great conviction is necessary she still seems not to be up to it; but her presence usually goes so far beyond the mere part itself that you can watch her put such mawkish questions as "I wonder what you were when you were a little boy?" and be touched that she should say that. Acting, especially in the films, is to a considerable degree improvisation, and in the same way that a cast such as this picks its reality almost out of the air, a talented director can bring the people and background before his cameras, regulate their movement and cut nicely from parallel to contrasting moods, from spoken lines to choir voices, and in short release the genii from the empty bottle.

Well, the picture is no world-beater, and perhaps I am puffing it up out of shape by so much attention to matters that must hold generally true for any example of good film making. *The Wedding Night* has more natural coloring than most good films, that is all. And I was glad to see it, not only for the usual pleasures of participation, but because it is heartening to see another token that pictures can have so healthy a basis in actual experience. Whether or not it is thought successful enough to be copied by the trade, any similar good work, in such an imitative and repetitious art as Hollywood's, is never completely lost: every picture we see today, good or bad, has the advantage of the whole traditional range preceding it. And what I wish sometimes were more clearly understood is that this silly silver screen, with all its tendency to spew forth a thousand and one quick shoddy imitations of anything that strikes pay dirt, is gathering all the time and right under our noses a tradition that is alive and doing well, going forward steadily, with a good foundation in the lives of those who may be fooled all the time and wrong most of the time, but yet the final body of reference for the simple reason that they are the world we live in. I have a feeling that any step in the advance of such an art is rather worth considering now, with just as little condescension as possible, before the whole business has become a stamping ground for those high spirits whose most reverent hope is to uncover a first cause or a quaint folkway, to fondle it intellectually fifty years after the sap has gone out of it altogether.

3 April 1935

Not So Deep as a Well . . .

Private Worlds is a surprisingly good thing for Hollywood to be making from a novel like Phyllis Bottome's, which is much too inward to be picked up by the cameras, and which might therefore have been replaced by some such convenient pattern as that of passions practiced between, say, Fredric March and Norma Shearer, the theme tune being, Private Worlds, I Love You. The original story has been simplified, heightened as to coloring, and made more compact; but it has been turned into a movie that runs off with less of flash than of dignity and honest intelligence.

Here and there in the film matters go noticeably wrong. The part of the matron is plugged too hard, and there are several spots where a patient is restored to calm in too much of a jiffy for total credence. Joel McCrea is miscast, and though Claudette Colbert is one of the few young women who could even be considered for the part, with brains and a good style of her own, she confuses a few basic meanings by sticking too close to herself—here she is to be found reading lines that would indicate a cold, controlled personality, and yet simply radiating her own charming come-ons from start to finish.

These things do not seem to be right, but in general the management is so good as to cover up the fact that such a story—a combination of brash exterior action with extensive clinical explorations—is simply too complicated for the screen to handle properly. The action in the movie culminates in the young wife's accident, and therefore has to taper off shortly thereafter, making the end a little unreal. Nevertheless this whole way of doing it seems to have been about the shrewdest, given the book, because at such a point it can be carried off on the backwash of the scene where the girl, having all along harbored a morbid fascination for the parallel existing between her case and that of poor Carrie Flint, goes out of her head one stormy night, hears voices, and jumps from the stairs.

We can only imagine what a headache a scene like this must be by taking it from the point of view of director [Gregory] La Cava, holding the mere script and wondering what the hell to do with everybody. Shall the girl go up the stairs, sweeping along like Ann Harding, and take the header clutching at her bodice? Shall she roll her eyes and paint furrows in her cheeks and clutch rabidly at banisters, as in a Boris Karloff? Or shall we just have her standing at the top, tragic like Kay Francis, and cut to her lying with tragic grace at the bottom in a completely new and different creation by Adrian?

In the actual picture this scene starts ordinarily enough, with the young wife (Joan Bennett) alone in the house, and the library recording for thunder-outside on the sound-track. Then she goes to the window, hearing a voice call her by name, Sally, Sally, in key with the music, which has started up; and although this musical twist is not at first convincing, as she starts for the stairs the whole thing is made completely eerie by distortion of sound, echoes, and overtones, and there are heard directly several lines from a former scene with the crazy girl—"I'm Carrie Flint, I've come to tea, I'm Carrie Flint"—blurring and echoing, the music rising. Through here the camera is twisted on its axis through several different planes: the girl gets to the top of the stairs in this shifting, unstable state, and jumps finally toward the voice, going down and out of the camera, which remains on the empty landing until the fall is over, and the next sequence elsewhere is cut in. This bit is the most effective thing in the picture; but it is more important as an illustration of something very necessary to any consideration of pictures as a whole: namely, that the superficial realism of photography and sound recording can be extended just as infinitely into the irreality of illusion as the medium of any other art.

All of which leaves little space for mention of the clear line of action into which the separate parts of the picture were fitted, and of the restrained naturalism with which these separate parts, especially the background scenes of dementia, were put on. Or for the central figure of the whole production, Charles Boyer—a man with not only unmistakable personal force, but sufficient artistic command to turn it into almost any part as a strong and convincing current. And Helen Vinson, as the rather odd sister, shows a capability that might well have earned her a bigger role. It is clear that she is not playing a type part, but one she has thought out for herself, studying what details of motion, under what central control, will build her own personal qualities into a character in a story, for whom certain actions have been devised, to whom has been left the responsibility for squaring these actions with some believable, separate personality. This care and intelligent foresight are more or less characteristic of the picture as a whole—it is a good, grown-up job on a difficult theme, and thus in the long run a more cheering spectacle than most of the picutres that have come out this year, though there have been several of more drive and beauty. And with such family films as R.K.O.'s *Laddie* trembling somewhere under the release-horizon, it is quite welcome as a corrective to certain unescapable though temporary presentiments that we are growing into, rather than out of, diapers.

17 April 1935

Men Working

This last Warner picture, *Black Fury*, has not got the subject of strikes reduced to final terms (in fact its strike is a phony, its villains are not the actual owners at all), but still it is the most powerful strike picture that has yet been made—so far as I am aware, and I am aware of the better known Soviet jobs in the field. [Vsevolod] Pudovkin has produced the most massive and beautiful works of this kind; but even his best film, *Mother,* was lacking in the suppleness of personal development, the direct and hard-hitting action where action is needed, that are required to give a picture its air of easy, continuous motion and real life, and to sway its audiences.

Black Fury has this motion and this air of life, whatever we may think of its social content (and from the row being kicked up on several sides, we may think some very thoughtful things indeed). As to story, *Black Fury* goes into a mining patch, below-ground into the mines where the men are working, and it sets up most of its drama in the Hunky character of Joe Radek (Paul Muni), who is tumbled out of his great boisterous content with the world by his girl's desertion and then tricked into bringing on trouble within his union, fumbling along, leading the men into a strike that is a setup for the strike-breaking agency behind it. Scabs, beatings, evictions, all of the men turning against Radek. To say that the whole matter is settled by Radek's getting off a hospital bed and shutting himself up in the mine with dynamite enough to blow it to pieces does not do justice to what the picture has been broadening into all this time—something more than an action piece, something more than a spectacle, something powerful and, by virtue of the contagious excitements peculiar to its form, very strange.

It may not be taken as the study of a typical strike: it does not show why strikes are generally made, or even how. It is a story of the suffering in the life of a single man—his betrayals, the battering of his poor muddy wits, the unquenchability of his vigor and loyalties. To this story certain conditions of life in a striking town are essential; it derives its force and persuasion from the fine tangible way in which these conditions are built up around plot situations and brought to bear on the central figure. And because this central figure is made dominant and real, laying a strong hand on his audience, including it in his humiliations and rough and tumble victories, all these incidents will be seen through his eyes and taken at his valuation.

I have not space for the various elements that actively contribute to the general effect of this picture—Muni gets into his part a mixture of brawn and puzzlement and fury that is grand to see. And the whole line of direction is vivid—I mean to say that violence in this picture is not a rubber-stamp symbol; it is a thing that shrieks along a man's nerves and settles in his stomach. The word great is certainly one to be sparing of in pictures, but if it may be lavished on any half-chewed jumble of stills that comes in from abroad, then I am in favor of loosening up with it on the home product. Director Michael Curtiz and whatever combination (writers, actors, camera and sound men) working with him is responsible for the fight in the mine, the terrible slugging to death of little John Qualen, the strike meetings and the work below-ground, the bar scenes and such interludes as that of Radek, drunk and jolly and already betrayed by his friend, piling up to the girl's house and calling out for her before remembering her desertion—if we must talk of greatness it is about time the men responsible for a picture like this were given the inside rail, particularly since the best work in pictures anywhere in the world just now is going forward out there on the West Coast of this country, and has been for these two years or more.

24 April 1935

Mostly Clinical

Concerning the making of pictures, there is always in the air a question that comes to have the proportions of a pebble in a shoe, namely, When is direction, and has mortal man ever seen one? We might ordinarily assume that the direction (or production) of a picture is simply the making of the picture, out of things, events, people. Yet these matters are often spoken of with an air of technical distinctions too fine for the lay eye, the critic seeming to say, There is something going on here that doesn't escape me; it is direction and happy I am to find it—although I daresay you mugs won't appreciate anything out of the ordinary. As a sort of case study along these lines, there is *The Man Who Knew Too Much*, a recent British thriller that, if reports are to be believed, is directed to a point that would make a person gasp.

In the first place, we will not be forgetting that there may be in a film two principal matters not to be credited to its management: a strong cast, a strong story idea. And there is a certain edge and novelty to the situation of the couple who, their child having vanished below the innocent surface of very evil waters, move toward the confusion of an international murder plot. The actual story is full of unlikely holes, but the idea is mostly exciting and comes to a good focus in the figure of Peter Lorre—wickedness personified and made terrible by the contrast of a benign, jolly exterior.

Episode by episode, however, this goes poorly. It may progress from beginning to end, and with a certain pace; but surely this is true of any quickie. As to handling of its cast, it fuddles. People who should be sympathetic appear quite otherwise: certainly the child, Nova Pilbeam, need not have been made into a grimacing little pest, and Leslie Banks should have been advised of why, for example, he was humorously sending his friend on to take the rap—in the dentist's office, in the church—so that he could make the motivations faintly credible. And if four men sitting on a bench are to indicate the presence of sinister types, it is not wise to cut baldly to a line-up of mugs reminiscent of the Marx Brothers posing for a still. Furthermore, there is a strong tendency earlier in the film to make matters go neatly by introducing raffish little exchanges among the people, and this is carried off with such a genius for coming down with arch clumps on the up-beat as to throw everything out of key.

As to the handling of incidents, the modulations as between one and another—all the little cares that have to be expended on static things if they are to create a general forward movement—there is a came-the-dawn ineptitude approaching burlesque. To illustrate: the shot of a ski-jumper registering horror in mid-air; the stiff business of holding up a whole succession of Swiss travel books to indicate we will presently open in Switzerland; the fingers pointing in neat geometry at a bullet hole in glass, to indicate of all things a bullet hole in glass. Then later, the ludicrous battle in the church, everybody picking up chairs and smashing them on the floor with the unconvinced and lackadaisical precision of a Busby Berkeley production number; and after that the sequence where the heavy, holding up his evil business on the roof, freezes there so we will not miss the fact that this is truly serious.

But where most admiration has been expressed, some of it slightly hysterical, is for the sequence in the dentist's office, and that in the Albert Hall (both centrally fruitful ideas, but hardly the director's). In the first, the situation is tense, but the struggle is simply too steep, and the motivations are too confused to be believable. (Why, in such desperate circumstances, should they go about it in this silly way, of all ways?) And in the second, there is much clumsiness. At a certain double forte in the music, a gunman is going to get a diplomat, and so how we work up suspense is to cut six times (by actual count) to the assassin's dark box—now the curtain bulges, as with elephants at play, now a gun sticks out so far as to scare the life out of Edna Best, rods away. We cut to Edna Best, torn between duty and maternal concern and showing this with considerable facial play. We cut to the dreadful box, to the orchestra, to Miss Best's emotions, to the diplomatic gent, moved by the music in the worst manner; to the box, to the woman, to the stage, to the gent—and after all this has been going on long enough to become a game, there come the scream and the shot, nicely anticlimactic. Whatever the director had to work with—the story, Peter Lorre—his touch in all these innumerable places is heavy and unimaginative, if not ham.

There can at least be said for *The Youth of Maxim* (the latest Soviet job; life in reactionary Russia and on the whole pretty ineffectual) that it is out in front for a type of management in which the Soviet men have always excelled—namely an original and strong composition of separate parts. It has not only the contrivance of the factory scenes, the burial, the workers' dead march, but the development of more personal episodes: Maxim's interviews with the inspector and the little squirt on the log, and the singing in prison. Matters such as these, if they are to come through clearly and well, require craftsmanship; they must be taken in the right stride and from just the right level. Their director couldn't get his whole story over for apples; but he had something on the ball here, and anybody can see it.

And then, to show perhaps more concretely what an illuminating thing direction may be if it is good, there is a touch I saw recently in a film that is otherwise boring and sterile, *The Unwelcome Stranger.*

Here the story is going to treat mainly of horse racing and the addiction to it of an orphan with a crippled leg; and so at the start there is a shot of horses running, the camera wheeling along just in advance and tending to focus where the knees are pounding up so proudly and high, and then just in the swing of all this there is a cut to the smother in some sandlot, all dust and the ragged knees of the boys tearing along toward the goal posts with the ball, a jerking crippled leg well in the foreground. This is only the old parallel-action device, and over in the briefest of moments; but its main point, for present purposes, lies in the beautiful ease with which it sets up the main themes of the story, hints at its interacting moods. Surely direction of a picture, if it is to be worthy of any special mention at all, should be something like this rather than the opposite, something that translates a given fact into its own terms of visual motion, by some means unpredictable and fine.

1 May 1935

Cops and Robbers

There is of course nothing much worse in movie criticism than the practice of reviewing pictures by reading their scripts carefully through one's spectacles; but there is also such a thing as a competently made picture failing to come off properly because of difficulties that got their start before the film even went into work, and several of the new shows seem made just to illustrate this. Take Warners' *G Men,* well enough made, well enough invested in the characters of James Cagney, Edward Pawley, Robert Armstrong, etc., yet falling considerably below the pace for excitement set by its more frank predecessors among the gangster shows.

That the production is breaking the doors down at its first New York showings (at the time of writing, the Strand Theatre is dark only three hours out of the twenty-four) seems to indicate that the public has been dying for a little dish of crime—but not so fast there, public. The keepers of national morals have long since put their flat feet down on any attempt to show crime truthfully as an actual, if exciting, phenomenon. And so the writers of G Men had to wriggle around and show the underworld from the top looking down, dissolving finally on the hint that old Joe Crime, he dies herewith. And so we get Cagney in the well worn service situation, with few changes. He joins the federal agents to revenge a pal, and whom does he butt his tough head directly into but an old back-breaker of a training officer, and what is the officer equipped with but (steady now: surprise) a neat little bit of sister. Brother and sister would rather die than come near Cagney of course, though really loving him dearly all along; and that is the plot. Most of the time they stick to it, the driving urge behind the war against crime waves being largely Cagney's desire (1) for personal revenge, (2) to get even with toughy, (3) to get next toughy's sister. Rising out of all this lah-dee-dah, the massacre at Union Station, the acting out of the historic surprise of Dillinger and the boys, and the various other holdups and counterplots borrowed from recent gangster history—this more serious business, though handled with straight and ripping realism, comes with diminished intensity.

The big-time gangster as a sort of inverted public hero (not enemy), a lonely, possessed, and terrible figure burning himself inevitably out at inhuman speeds, is not shown here. In G Men he is simply a dangerous bad man who would have gone on nefariously forever if the government had not come along and, with the aid of love and that delightful man Cagney, put a stop to him for good. All gone now, all better. It not only makes a flabby evasion of the rather cruel truth, but it makes a flabby picture, and a disappointment.

In blaming the slowness of Les Misérables on the story (here, incidentally, is another variation on the cops-and-robbers theme), I do not wish to misprise the screen writers, who have made one of the most compact scenarios imaginable out of this infinitely rambling work. But whatever is wrong cannot be laid to the way the story was made into a picture. Fredric March carries the part of Valjean through the years of respectability and flight well enough; Charles Laughton continues to be a baffling figure, impressive even in his inevitable overplaying. And although the early business in the galleys is too artificial to be powerful, the action scenes in general—mobs and carriage rides, challenges, armed turbulence, movement in the streets—are carried off boldly and well.

The structural fault (and one seems to sense some such thing vaguely rather than to spot it at once) lies in a certain sweet irreality introduced by the relations between Valjean and his rather insipid ward, and by the whole pappy love affair between the ward and Mr. John Beal—who should really have been remanded to the Boy Scouts some time back. Richard Boleslawski's genius as a director lies more in the coordination of complex matters than in attention to character, but it is becoming an axiom in films that anyone who can make something more than a silly paper bag out of Fredric March can handle actors and no mistake. I mean to say the director cannot be blamed for the uneven and loose texture that keeps *Les Misérables* from being a first-rate film. The silly and slow parts are traceable to the story, and they leave the picture just good enough so that it should have been better.

And then along the same line, there is the Ben Hecht-Charles MacArthur production *The Scoundrel,* starring Noel Coward. Hecht and MacArthur are the literary boys who have found out enough about making movies so that you needn't worry over whether their show will move with vigor and effect. But even as literary writers, one will recall, they were sometimes so bright as to shine in their own eyes. And much the same goes for this picture.

Noel Coward is a publisher completely without scruple, seducing anything with skirts and letting her know beforehand that there will be no dashed nonsense; slick, cynical, supremely bored—got everybody's number but too ghastly much work to call them up or down, you know really. And this part is done with a fine sharp point, the literary types being traced in with just enough acid to show to a fraction how many cocktail parties Mr. Hecht has weathered. Epigrams sprouting like a crop of wheat, etc. But when the turning point has been reached and it is necessary to go below the hard surface for some ending that will knock their eye out, the boys get heels over bandbox in the hardly new situation of the man without a soul who cannot rest in death until he has felt pity, touched a human heart ("He prayeth best who loveth best," etc., of all the ancient albatrosses). By a judicious use of music, sea shots, Noel Coward, and a certain common-sense attitude toward the macabre, they carry off this end of the story with less of bathos than might be imagined. But the film in general is so fastidious in skirting the homely dumbness of average Hollywood productions that it does not create figures and situations that will enlist people's hearts. And the striking elements it substitutes for more accustomed emotions prove to be different, but not convincing.

There are other pictures abroad: *Baby Face Harrington* and *Star of Midnight,* both swaggery and amusing; and for musicals *Naughty Marietta,* which is good Victor Herbert; *Mississippi,* with Fields, Crosby, and atmosphere (silly but bearable); and *George White's Scandals*—poor but with some bright moments in song and situation. For a chiller there is *Mark of the Vampire;* for an average detective there is *The Casino Murder Case;* for rough and spotty comedy there is *Hold 'Em Yale;* and for staying away from there are *Reckless* and *Strangers All.* This is not the whole list, but it is enough.

15 May 1935

Two Films

Out of the several pictures with great possibilities that have come along in a month, it is oddly enough *The Bride of Frankenstein* that puts up the best show. Advertised as a chiller, this film turns out to be something else, having a lot of jollification, nice fancy, elegant mounting—there is, in short, beauty as well as the beast.

James Whale's whole method of production has been one of going as easily as possible on the supernatural. The everyday note is stressed continually—as in the petty bombast of the chief burgher after the monster's capture, as in the pathetic business of having the Thing burn his hand and, with every man's horror turned against him, find a friend in the blind hermit. And for macabre good humor, there is the role of the scientist who uses his power over the monster to get Frankenstein's collaboration on a mate for the poor brute. With the good assistance of Boris Karloff, the producers have made their wild story rather human, and the audience gets it.

In background, atmosphere, dramatic invention, *The Bride of Franken-stein* will stand up as one of the best of the year. The episode of the electric storm is an astonishing bit of well-sustained imaginative play. There are traces of *Caligari,* particularly in the stylized woods and crag of the first chase sequence (a quite breathless and eerie sort of affair), but the point is that in such matters *Caligari* is gone one better, cardboard backdrops not being here quite so much an end in themselves. In short, a great deal of art has gone into the planning and taking of whole portions of this film, but it is the kind of art that gives the healthy feeling of men with their sleeves rolled up and working, worrying only about how to put the thing over in the best manner of the medium—no time for nonsense and attitudes and long hair.

The picture that John Ford has made out of Liam O'Flaherty's *The Informer* opens a lot of new possibilities for Hollywood, tackles something that is really fine, and manages several memorable scenes. But because it deals with the sort of thing that must be handled adequately if it is to go over, its persistent inadequacies make it more disappointing than many pictures with less to recommend them.

The story gets off to a beautiful start, riding along on the unfamiliar color and excitement of the period when the Terror was in Ireland, tightening on the country and walking through its streets in armed squads. And it carries well through the early part of that evening when Frankie McPhillip (Wallace Ford is excellent in this part) came in from the hills, to slip home in the fog and be sold to his death, with the Tans piling out of their lorries to surround the house, and Gypo Nolan, the betrayer, watching the clock at headquarters in a cold sweat. For dramatic vigor and beauty of composition there have been few sequences to compare with the one that ends with the camera looking from behind Frankie down into the court where the Tans look up with their machine gun.

So far, the atmosphere and the sense of a tragic character have been well built. But shortly after Gypo has stumbled out with his blood money, there begins a train of happenings many of which hang fire altogether—the result partly of faulty casting, partly of bad plot treatment. Margot Grahame has a weak part as Gypo's girl, and fits it; Heather Angel is a personal nonentity; the rebel leader (Preston Foster) is hollow and his chief aide spoils a fine likely face by pantomiming with it, while Una O'Connor as the mother is a constant irritation. These people all play inevitably into the story, and are abetted by the director, who must needs drive every nail down three inches below the surface: hence whole organic stretches are made flabby or (as is the case with the last episode in church, the intercession of Katy) actually distressing. What is more, there is constant reliance on symbolic fade-ins and ghostly voices, on an elaborately cued and infirm musical score, and on the device of squeezing the last drop of meaning or sentiment out of a ten-minute sequence by hanging onto it for a quarter of an hour. It hardly seems that the man responsible for these cheap shifts could be the one who schemed the earlier episodes, the extended revelry of the middle parts, and the final trial scene.

But any one of the ham touches would be negligible—all of them taken together might even be discounted—if the central part had been sure of conception and if [Victor] McLaglen had been all the way up to it. I kept feeling that he lacked the final subtlety requisite to making the crude lines of this character wholly true. In attitudes he is at times superb, but he simply does not carry the thing along. Partly because of this, partly because of the direction, the doom Gypo Nolan is preparing for himself does not seem inevitable, and one gets the feeling of impatience that always comes when what should be a natural downfall seems to be turning into a dramatic pushover.

Hollywood deserves a lot of credit for tackling such a job, and thereby opening a new field for pictures; but I do not feel that the film itself does right by a story so powerful and moving as that of a man who was driven by hunger and suspicion into the tragic foolishness of turning informer in the Irish Terror.

29 May 1935

New Wine and Old Bottles

Although wishing to give his new color process every chance and set it forth with a high-class story and cast, Robert Edmond Jones has gone the usual way in *Becky Sharp* and made color the big thing—with the result that the story, already sketchy, doesn't seem to mean much. The weak (sentimental) part of Thackeray has been retained; his strong polite prose, social bite, and portrayal have been left behind in *Vanity Fair*. The best dramatic meat here is in the personalities: Miriam Hopkins as Becky, Nigel Bruce (Jos), Alison Skipworth, Alan Mowbray, Cedric Hardwicke. And in the hands of that misdirector, that splash in pictures, Rouben Mamoulian, even this natural talent is overlaid with staginess.

The picture is the first feature film in color, and therefore a sort of presage of the strong chance that some such process will someday not only replace the present halftone prints entirely but affect the technique of pictures—though to a naturally lesser degree than the introduction of sound. But the trouble with all the color films so far is that the producer becomes a kid in candy land; he has still to get sufficiently used to color to keep it in its place, a means, not an end. The colors in *Becky Sharp* are nearly natural, but terribly gaudy, partly because of the hard, garish light under which shots were taken, partly because Mr. Jones as designer cannot cry quits to a set until that last bit of wall is covered with a tasty blue curtain, until everybody is dressed in blue, or red, and when Mr. Jones says red he means red. Yellow on white comes through well, and there are some rich browns—including the faces of the cast, which looks like a boatload of tennis players from the Canal Zone. Otherwise it is all very wonderful and amazing and as pleasing to the eye as a fresh-fruit sundae, but not much more. It will take time, we must be patient.

It begins to appear, from the G-men films that have followed the release of *G Men* (which, being the first, was cautious and sluggish), as though we are back in the gangster cycle. The same safety device is employed in all of these films, but the observance becomes more and more perfunctory. The routine is as follows. There is a jail break and a dangerous criminal is at large, burning up the countryside with his mob of pretty lads. Of this Washington hears, without liking it. Clues pass through the laboratories for detection, the inexorable law studies its road map and buckles on its roscoe. Pity the poor scofflaws on a night like this. And now, the build-up for a quick end to evil completed, we cut back to the mob again, being only in the third reel. The mob appears to be doing quite well, sitting in a hideout, wearing hats and rods and talking big.

And from this point on the federal men may do whatever is to their pleasure—such as spring empty traps, look inexorable, and cooperate with the love interest—but one thing is sure, and this is that they will not take anybody. It takes from 7,200 to 7,500 feet of film for them to get worked up to that point, and even then someone has to jump conveniently into their lap and turn rat for them. Led to the hideout they riddle it with lead and the hero goes in to get the leader single-handed and he's down, he's up, he's all over the place, he's lost his gun, he's down again, and so on until there is no hope for the single-handed hero, except that in the next two minutes the gangster's gun has failed to go off in his face and right has triumphed. Fade on right triumphing, also love.

This federal stuff is all so many gooseberries of course; the show is really about the gangster. In *Let 'Em Have It* he was a chauffeur and hated the rich. His mobs came to be in more banks than the Morgans; he wouldn't stop until he got independent for life; then the money got too hot, and he had to stop, but couldn't. He is Bruce Cabot and convincing in the part, which is well built up, especially in the scenes of Public Enemy No. 1 at home with all the little public enemies.

In *Public Hero No. 1* the public villain is Joseph Calleia, a strong, dark, close-mouthed fellow; he is in prison, sitting with his mouth shut, and comes to trust Chester Morris, who is loud with protest against the prison treatment and suggests a break. So when they've made their break, Calleia finds shelter for them both with his gang, because this man is his friend, see, and he trusts him. Chester Morris then reports to his chief, having been Public Hero No. 1 all along, though feeling no compunction. But when the girl turns out to be the gangster's sister, then our Hawkshaw is torn mightily, he is really torn. Even then, the only thing he ultimately balks at is betraying his girl into betraying her brother, and his chief doesn't balk at his doing that—in fact threatens to disgrace him if he doesn't. Very fine people.

But in spite of this unfortunate side, *Public Hero No. 1* is the best picture on criminal life I've seen (and that includes *Public Enemy,* which had a franker truth but now dates in tempo and power). The producers have profited from the recent trend in detective pictures; they keep their action clear, but work in a natural and breezy romance (thanks here to Jean Arthur) and quite a bit of tough, pertinent humor through the character of the gang's dipso surgeon (Lionel Barrymore and eminent in the part). And they have brought to bear on their subject matter of violence and sudden death a wonderful combination of strong cutting, sound, and delicate camera adjustment. Not just automatic realism either, as can be seen from a shot like that of the two prisoners marching across the court, covering their guard with concealed guns, and trying to step naturally in all that bare, hostile space, the camera looking down on this from up in the guard tower, from behind a loosely held machine gun that in some of the art we have been told about might even be found to be a Symbol. Then there is all the usual stuff raised to a high degree: the usual attack and running battle, the terrible hail of bullets on the gang's last stand, registered in splintering wood and crumbling plaster, in the particularly shrewd device of having a bar in the line of fire here, with all its shelves of bottles and that methodical holocaust of flying glass and liquid.

These films give the highest dramatic expression to things that are no less a social truth because you can read them in your paper; they are not only intense melodrama, they have something to them, of pity and terror. The story, brutality on a treadmill and its own death sentence, is not safely classic and may not be intended for social comment and all that; but as far as putting a thing into terms of its medium is concerned, the movies are really fine. There is a false thing at the bottom of them, to plague their best friends, but what it would take to make them wholly straight could be supplied by any literary mug. With their feeling for oppressive truth, their explosive timing and genius for significant details, art could go anywhere. But art could not get to first base with what their story lacks.

26 June 1935

Love Me Some Other Time

Serious music has had quite a career in the movies already, apart from its frequent use for purposes of accompaniment. There have been such awful things as the short subjects depicting the sad love life of Tchaikowsky, Liszt, *et al.;* an occasional recording of fragmentary symphonic performances; the more effective full-length works such as the recent *Unfinished Symphony* and the still supreme *Constant Nymph.* And now in this same highbrow field comes Miss Grace Moore, bringing art to those who faint by the wayside for the lack thereof, and furnishing the text for today.

Grace Moore films—first *One Night of Love,* now *Love Me Forever,* and practically endless future possibilities: *Two Loves in One Night; How Lovely, Lovey; Love Me Tomorrow; Love Me on Friday,* etc.—these films threaten to become a tradition, and therefore cannot be turned aside lightly, but may be studied with profit. They have, so far at least, these significant elements in common: (1) a great deal of care for the mechanics of music, that the sound shall be recorded clear as a bell; (2) one original theme song and the balance Puccini; (3) a story that has seen better if not more romantic days; (4) a comic relief in the person of Luis Alberni; (5) a smash ending in the Metropolitan itself (the old house ringing with merry sound and the old art-lovers in boiled shirts loving it to the point of epilepsy); and (6) the continued presence and histrionic splendor of Miss Grace Moore, one-time auxiliary of the New York Opera (I mean *the* opera).

The show, in fact, is built entirely around Miss Moore, who shapes up as follows: A trained voice, cool, thin, mechanically perfect but without much color, beautifully recorded. A youthful figure; a face not lovely but with enough regularity of planes to be called pretty, if you like—somewhat reminiscent of that other national darling, Miss Mary Pickford, and best expressive of a certain arch emptiness. In carriage rather moosey, by which I mean no offense but simply that she has neither graceful motion nor a natural disposition of members in repose, always giving the impression (without quite doing it) of standing pigeon-toed or crossing space at a gallop. She is not an actress, but acts the part of an actress, a sad cross between the best schools of elocution (not to forget gesture) and the worst Wagner. Failing as an actress, she might well fall back on a natural dignity of her own—but no, she must be vivacious, irrepressible, girlish; she will only be herself in so far as a well-marked tendency for flouncing and stiff mummery is herself. She must give it this, she must give it that; she must talk on the tonsil.

Analysis of anything so complex as a personality is always difficult and usually unfair, because when everything is said you either like a person's type or you don't like it at all; but I imagine even the best friends of this gorgeous creature would admit that when it comes to stage genius and stage presence there are scores of little girls in Hollywood who can run wide circles round her. Miss Moore is here solely for her music. And her music in *Love Me Forever* adds up to one chorus of the theme song, two arias from *La Bohème*, a few rounds of *Funiculi, Funicula; Il Bacio*, and a participation in the *Rigoletto* quartet (computations based on *Variety*, which is wise in many matters).

In actual running time, that is, her use to the picture is very small. Yet the whole story has to be tailored to her; she is its star, she must have dramatic moments, playful moments, cozy, homelike moments, close-ups, medium shots, long shots, follow shots—the works, in short. And every time she begins to vibrate in the vocal cords, the effect is supposed to slay whole roomfuls of people and you sit there and watch them slain, and no mistake. Leo Carrillo (low gambler and high flier and good in a stock interpretation) is also slain and gives up all for her; and that makes the story, which in turn makes up the picture, which thus gets to be makeshift, unoriginal, and (particularly in the part of Miss Moore) quite ham.

Everything in *Love Me Forever* is jettisoned in favor of the elaborate production and recording of the big punch numbers. But here at last in these numbers, descending in the vestments of art on the American movie, we have something, have we not? There must surely be something here, at long last? Briefly, what we have in these big numbers is a first-rate and literal copy of an eighth-rate (and outdated) treatment of distinctly third-rate music. And that is about all.

Such purely popular musicals as Warners' new *In Caliente* are built along the same lines—except that their popular music does not, like that of Puccini, represent some of the best and most enduring of their time and place. Their story is equally foolish and sketchy (in the latest, it revolves about the troubles of a dancer in falling in love with a critic who once panned her); their emphasis is also placed on lavish production numbers—of which, for a welcome change, there is only one really big one here. But *In Caliente* has a lot of good spots in the relations between Pat O'Brien, Edward Everett Horton, and (aptly enough) Leo Carrillo, and in Dolores Del Rio it has the presence of a woman ripe with charms and a constant pleasure to the eye. And in all the musicals, however bad, there is an absence of this stuffy insistence on Art, an absence of this self-conscious strain that is invariably in evidence when the movies—so astonishingly at home in newspaper offices or stokeholds, in hospitals, on the ranch, at police headquarters, in the Foreign Legion, anywhere—get completely out of their water into the rare and awful air of artistic creation, as pronounced upper case.

Average musicals are pretty dull, but so are these Moore pieces pretty dull, and what is worse they have a holy smell of uplift about them. And all this (at last) through a medium in which, to mention only the native achievement, Walt Disney, not three months ago and with very little acclaim, blended music with his pictured story in such a bit of sheer genius as *The Band Concert;* in which, about the same time, there was performed offhandedly a little stretch of cartoon called *The Kids in the Shoe;* in which Duke Ellington has fixed up an arrangement of "The St. Louis Blues"; and before the cameras of which Louis Armstrong has performed upon his brash and lovely horn. What the hell, I say, love us some other time can't you, Grace; we can hardly be bothered.

24 July 1935

Extra Added Attractions

Because Walt Disney has always had his eye on his business and no time for fooling around, the wind raised by those responsible for the dither about him as a Significant Subject has passed over in an interesting way. The air clears and he becomes what he was in the first place: common and everyday, not inaccessible, not in a foreign language, not suppressed or sponsored or anything. Just Disney, making another to go into all the big gaudy houses and little tank-town houses all over the country, under Extra Added Attractions. And so he can be seen at work again and it can be seen whether he is any good after all.

There was a time when the Disney outfit seemed to be stalled in the rather pretentious dead-end alley of *The Three Little Pigs,* and practically everything it touched turned to lollypops for the kiddies. But now, certainly *The Band Concert* and *Who Killed Cock Robin?* are not only Disney at his absolute best, but represent two of the most nearly perfect film bits I have seen anywhere (the first of these is already out of immediate circulation, the other just getting into the second-run houses).

The Band Concert is a good reminder that whether these cartoons are overtly Silly Symphonies or not, the musical staff at work on them always seems to be well out in front of other musical staffs in the industry. I do not mean for the mere synchronization and recording of sound, but for making sound a natural and basic part of the production, for originating scores and putting them over with good orchestral swing and nice handling of the vocal work—trios, choruses, or whatever. The music is light, but often fetching and always adequate, its function well understood.

But aside from reminders, *The Band Concert* was a really marvelous little bit of nonsense, with a fine, tempered edge and the consistent ability to carry the fancy on, not letting the old dog die. The situation was that of a few musicians from the animal kingdom playing a job in some open-air stand—led, as I remember, by the mouse gent, who was most terribly baffled by a sleeve that flopped down over his baton in the *sforzando* passages, and by the tendency of his band to leave off following the beat and join in with a wandering duck, who was getting "Turkey in the Straw" out of a tin fife at a signal strength of about forty, beating it out with his foot, and not to be quelled either. I don't recall all the details now, but the main number was the "William Tell" overture, which was assisted by the elements, there coming up a fierce twister of wind along in the more dramatic passages, the band getting carried up in the air completely, scattering individually through the air but still playing music like the devil and on the beat, and finally coming down one by one into the coda, which wound up in a glory of sound and wreckage.

The thing in main outline would be very little, if it weren't for the way every incident, every foot of film, is given a solid basis in observation, so that natural action is caught and fixed in a typical gesture, rendered laughable through exaggeration or through transference into the unfamiliar; and for the swift way all the incidents pile up on one another. No one ever saw a band so busy, proud, and full of troubles as this, from the virtuoso swapping of hands in the flute duet to the hard-pressed air of the brass section; but the point is, no one ever saw a band that did not have all these things logically in solution, once he looks back on it. As one who has wasted the better part of a lifetime following the bass drum and wondering whether to be a great trombonist, with all that sweep of brass, or famous in the lower registers, to blow thunder into a tuba, I can say that in *The Band Concert* one of the final comments on the public playing of instruments everywhere has been commented.

Who Killed Cock Robin? sounds like one of these colored-candy things, but nothing of the kind. It is one of the most cynical of the Disneys, and even for those who attend comedy not to laugh, but sheerly to gaze down their noses at it for traces of Content, Social Meaning, and the like, it may prove beneficial if not funny. It has a combination of takeoff on Hollywood personalities and burlesque of the ways of justice (a rather pat ending, however).

The opening stretch shows Cock Robin, nominally a bird, but giving out a serenade that is surely in the accents of Mr. Bing Crosby, falling afoul of himself in his best manner by trying to do it sweet but also hot. The female lead is likewise feathered, but by virtue of certain astonishing developments in the upper regions, forward, and by a routine of sundry bumflips, you-impress-me's, etc., turns out a dead ringer for Miss Mae West, complete with voice and picture hat. Some vague sinister shape cannot stand all this from Bing and puts an arrow through him; and this brings on other business: the wagon coming up, the coppers jumping out, rounding up bystanders and clubbing them plenty, and eventually the trial for murder.

The courtroom (and main) sequence has an owl for judge, giving out the theme in a voice like the low pedal point on the Music Hall organ, and for prosecuting attorney a likely and damn suspicious parrot, with coattails and hands under them. Also a jury, which supplies a neatly pattered chorus where appropriate; the usual police, who are busy; and a suspected toughy with the phenomenal bass vocal cords of Poly McClintock out of Waring's band, telling the coppers "Lay off, lay off."

Burlesque slants on the courtroom are old material, but this one is surely one of the most completely ingenious that has been done—all by means of a few forms of wildlife, the most painstaking original care for design and animation, and a practically inexhaustible genius for locating the familiar in the strange. Bright with both sound and motion, it works in the solemn institutions of the bar, the pen, etc., to the delight of all, with the judge doing double kicks, the prosecuting attorney trying to outface Joe Mayhem as defendant, and the McClintock voice coming over: "All right, so what. I rubbed him out, so what," with the police slugging everybody in sight and Mae West parading it right up to the jury, looking to avenge her man.

But there is no use talking along forever about anything so vivid and quickly over as this silly operetta. In twenty or thirty years, pokers in film archives will be pointing to pieces like *The Band Concert* and *Who Killed Cock Robin?* saying with authority that this was a fine thing for American pictures to be doing, and we will read all about it in the right places, if still around. For the present it may be just as well there is no need for these solemnities, the main thing being that there is something very good to see here.

7 August 1935

The Great McGonigle

To see the contour and splendid coloring of his nose, one would naturally assume that the worst enemy of W. C. Fields was himself. And this would be borne out by his reputation of some two years ago, which was that of a man who had not only lost his drawing power, but proved so testy and difficult to handle as to have washed himself up with movies for good. At one of the lowest of his low spots he even went to the RKO lot and offered, for no pay at all, absolutely on spec, to conceive, write, dialogue, direct, and act in a series of two reelers; and RKO thereupon said, speaking personally to Mr. W. C. Fields, otherwise The Great McGonigle, Nuts.

Since then, of course, Fields has not only got back into pictures, but with a wallop, becoming one of Paramount's top-drawing male stars. And since then, especially during the past year, it has become a tossup whether honors for worst enemy should go to him or his producers. He was given a walk-on in *Mrs. Wiggs of the Cabbage Patch* and his name was dishonestly starred on the marquee to float that whole lighter of garbage. In *It's a Gift,* his presence dignified a magic-lantern show that as it stood could not, without the grace of block booking, have ever made the grade of being double billed into the neighborhood houses of Canarsie. He got considerably smothered in the costumed fakery of *David Copperfield;* he was practically all the bright moments in *Mississippi;* and now he is used as the sole come-on for one of the world's weariest: *The Man on the Flying Trapeze* (written, according to rumor, by the old boy himself).

Now the great, the one and only Fields' picture could like as not be called *The Man on the Flying Trapeze* (in the present case the title has nothing to do with the film, which is about a memory expert and his family troubles). Fields is a setup for the Big Top type of story—posing in striped tights and promoting a roll-the-ball game on the side, incurable in hokum but always secure in a foolish sort of dignity, alibi-ing and aside-ing down his tremendous nose even when most tangled up in the spaghetti; a stander-upper and perfect snide, loud with boasting, sophisticated in all the arts of the dodge, a barfly and stout man of the world; but married, and one step ahead of the constabulary, master of every house but his own. He is supreme in all these things in this stock part—so much so that in his hands slapstick and stock parts become as naturally fresh as they were in their original intention, before automatic handling made them the blurred things they are. We would get one of the highlights in pictures if there could be found writers and a director who would take all this hokum for what is behind it, rediscovering the material.

But we will get precious little so long as Fields continues in his present rut, and so long as Paramount, having rebuilt the Fields name, continues to squander it by casting him as bit-player and shock-trooper for the smellers. Most stars can make or break, and who should worry. But Fields is more like a national resource: he should be got into his one ace picture before his time is out, because there is a certain savor still lacking in the national salt, there is a show about show business still to make.

No one can have drifted normally through the county fairs, chautauquas, coney islands, the carnival midways, circuses and stock companies trouping the whistle-stops of this country, without having some very definite feeling for its most fascinating business, which is show business. No one with any imagination can help being engaged by the idea of this society in miniature, more important to us than all the other kindred societies because it is in closer contact with all of us, its secret wisdom being that of bringing gawps to wonder and city slickers to be amused, by tricks and wiles and ballyhoo, at so much the copy all over the nation. And W. C. Fields, by virtue of his accessibility and talents, is one of the chief emissaries of this state—almost, so far as we are concerned, its first citizen. The branches of show business in which he moves with the most conviction are not the whole of the business, and his generation of showmen is passing away. He is not an actor in the universal sense: he has not built up a variety of parts, been a lot of people. But he has, without the assistance of any writer, made himself a single role that he can carry off with infinite variations, that will include a large chunk of our experience of a large chunk of America.

For humor in dialogue, I can remember better than anything else the scene with him bowling across the grounds of an awesome estate in a Model T full of family and out of control, shattering a seven-foot statue on the lawn and then explaining the whole thing with amazement and instant vindication, to his wife: "Why the man ran right in front of my car!"; for humor in any routine, his jugglery of balls and cigar-boxes in *The Old Fashioned Way;* for implication by action, his leadership of the troupe down Main Street, in the same picture, drum-majoring with his silk hat and cane, and sidestepping horse-droppings with the greatest of ease and no conscious attention whatever. He is a funny man, and also a perfect showman, in that his stage presence is never jarred. But he is something more, and has got to be something more before he is worth much time. In his representations there are reflected experiences outside himself, there is a focus of many things that go back to the somehow basic point of the place you were born in and learned to see and get around in. He is not only a funny man, he is a familiar and endearing figure, to be seen with mirth and remembered with special affection; a minor Jack Falstaff on the sawdust of the twentieth century.

21 August 1935

Two Show Figures

Alice Adams is a picture that will be remembered longer than it deserves, and all because it is designed not so much as a show as for purposes of elevation. It is the kind of picture that takes up a subject. What is more, it takes up a subject that a lot of people are very close to, because a lot of people have had doors slammed in their faces, usually when they were too young to know how to put their feet in them; and because they have practiced in private all these pitiful little artifices, now made public.

The Adams girl lived on the wrong side of town. She didn't get to parties, pretended that she simply couldn't stand going; she pretended that holes in stockings were a perfectly delightful eccentricity, that she was having a perfectly ducky time. And she was completely miserable.

Now such painful subjects demand a great deal of delicacy and restraint in the treatment. And quite apart from delicacy of any sort, *Alice Adams* goes about slugging its points home by means of an assortment of devices that are only described with the beautiful economy of one word, which word is hokum. Take the dinner scene, where she has the boy in to meet the folks on a sweltering night: detail piling on detail, everything going wrong in the most stock manner, until the audience is all set for the shot where the old man's galluses drop his dress trousers down clear to the floor, revealing a pair of bright polka-dot drawers. The actual treatment, that is, seems a cross between harrowing tragedy and the honeymoon-breakfast routine in a Charley Chase.

Miss Katharine Hepburn, as the heroine of this romantic business (the screen, as a matter of fact, has chosen to keep the bitter-sweet edge of the thing, but rewrite it into a happy ending), has a curiously unsympathetic role, when you consider it. She tries to make a spread, she is terribly filled with cheap aspirations, and she makes poor Fred Stone—the part of the father, played with a good rough edge but an eye tending to slide off to the camera crew to see how they're taking it—she makes him miserable. She poses, she acts a spurious part, she cheats. All of which is human, well we know it; but it is not the nicest type of human. Miss Hepburn gets some real stuff out through all this—as when she steps out of the part she is playing into her own right, into these little breathless things, like the place where the boy says, meaning it now after the whole picture, I love you, and she says, in a soft-focus close-up, Gee *whiz*, she says.

And even in the midst of the faults to be found with her work, no one can doubt for a minute that Katharine Hepburn is one of the rare quick spirits to be seen anywhere, being in the last analysis one of those who can influence somewhat the world's conception of beauty in a woman. There has been exploitation before of this business of a boy's hips, the dress falling from them in a white clean line; and of this fine and evident carving in the bones of the head; and of these easy shifts of mood—tremulous, storming, suddenly lovely, etc. But Miss Hepburn has worked such qualities and mannerisms into a style, into something of her own that she herself has built and is true to. The trouble, particularly in this picture, is that the style is a restricted one, demanding certain special conditions for its best expression; and that anyway it is not a thickset style, but one that wearies quickly from overwork.

The Little Minister was a silly picture, made up from a silly Barrie play; but I had one feeling all the way through, and that was a feeling of being thrown in touch with something beautiful, like springwater. *Spitfire* was completely cockeyed as a story, and yet the part of the mountain girl as played by Miss Hepburn was so resilient, direct, and near to some natural center as to be a strange and rather lovely thing to watch. In *Alice Adams,* though, Miss Hepburn

is repeating the part-within-a part routine of *Morning Glory,* giving too much to
a role that was lean to start with, being studied, overaccented, too girlishly
much. All this hushed wonder and elfin verve of hers, used not as one means of
expressing something felt but as a whole conscious method in itself—the tacit
assumption being that this is enough for all purposes and may without regard be
put to all purposes—this becomes in time a palpable set of habits, no more.

Miss Hepburn couldn't have made a good picture out of *Alice Adams;* but
she shouldn't have made her performance in it simply a smudged copy of
something that in time leaves open to easy jeers qualities that are essentially
enough to take an ordinary person's breath away.

I meant to say of *Doubting Thomas* at the time it appeared that though its
rewrite of *The Torch Bearers* seemed a terribly old pack of cards, there had been
more aces shuffled into the comedy as a whole, in the way of people and high
management, than might seem possible. It had a consistently better type of
visual humor than I've seen for a long time, some of its pratfalls being as good as
the slapstick of René Clair; it featured people like Sterling Holloway and Alison
Skipworth; and it had a part for Will Rogers that was rather incidental and
stodgy but nevertheless one of his best. And that is my reason for bringing it up
at this time, to say a few words, intended before but delayed too long, about
Will Rogers.

There was always a tendency to confuse Rogers with the national boobies
to whom his frequent social pronouncements linked him. But he was in the first
place a show figure; even in his worst things one could not help recognizing him
as a very good one. And where his political views gained their weight with the
populace of this country was from the character he had created of a typical
American—a man in suspenders and stocking feet, unpretending, kind, bashful,
not knowing about all these here newfangled customs and ideas, but (and here is
where he became the ideal of the type rather than the type) disposing of them
with native shrewdness, moving toward a final triumph over everything that was
new or fancy or politically not right. Too homey and dependent on the old gags
of faith in a simple world for comfort, there was still a certain common-man
homeliness and goodness about him that everyone could see at once, a
wholesome impatience with frippery and a running mumble of irony against it.
In this created character he was a valuable property, just as he would be in real
life, on a farm say, heckling the cows and squinting at the tarnal weather. He was
one of the naturals of show business, and it is not pleasant to lose him.

4 September 1935

From the New World

Peasants, still at the New York Cameo Theatre, is a film that it would do anybody good to see. It is solid and slow, but with enough shift of motion to keep it alive. Friedrich Ermler, though not among the great experimenters, has been shrewd enough in picking and choosing among such treatments as have been developed, to give his story the depth and body-warmth he was after.

The picture is simple, unaffected, and full of natural juices, flavors, smells. The setting is a collective pig farm, as a consequence of which you can't go anywhere in the picture without falling over the pigs, and the pigs can't go anywhere without scaring the feathers off a brood of hens, the silly, solemn things always shrieking off in preposterously wrong directions, and there can't be a tangle of human affairs so hectic that we may not be brought up short by cutting suddenly to the cow—placid, full of reflections and cud, forbearing in her wisdom to speak out on the vanity of all vanities and yet with just a trace of being the most supremely foolish animal that ever fell through her own manure trap and got drowned from the sheer surprise of it.

This is not as good a still-picture of farm life as *The Old and the New,* but it has something that film greatly lacked: it has a clear line of development and a good dramatic strain. The idea was to show the danger to collective farming in the U.S.S.R. of kulakism; but Ermler has got far enough away from the didactic bones of an idea in his preoccupation with showing its sidelights, tragic or humorous, with making a good moving story out of the lives and troubles of these people, so that the idea becomes subconscious and implicit with him.

The plot, in essence, might be the story of reform on the ranch, the hands brought around to the side of the new boss, the rustlers scotched (and yet there is something more here, something real to hope for in the rough spots). There is a villain, a murder thereby, a detection thereof (and yet it was his girl he killed; he wasn't a villain out of sheer badness and choice, it broke his heart). And the chief has not only got a dominant role, he commands the picture in his own right—Nikolai Bogolyubov, a fine figure of a man, strong in a flannel shirt, resourceful and brainy, but worried into scratching his head, into walloping the table and saying goddamn.

But there are several others in this company who are more than sufficient in their parts: the girl, her lover, her brother, the old peasant who gets his beard snipped finally, on account of their succeeding in getting a bath built and him into it. And there is quite a range of strong effects, as in, for one thing, the love scenes, gay, vital, beautifully awkward; as in, for another, that business of the dinner, with everybody sweating *pirojki* out by the quart and still stuffing, or cheating about it, scared of giving in first. And as in the action which dominates the picture, namely that leading up to and away from the murder, with the man terrified out of his mind, trying to cover it up as suicide by hanging the dead girl from a limb, desperate with his private fear, yet cherishing that bright body, staying to clear the foot of a wisp of straw caught, unsightly, between the toes.

These things are difficult to attempt and harder to accomplish, and there are noticeable detractions. There is still a little heavy slugging of the moral, there is still an unclearness of sequence, and there is still too much reliance on printed titles (Came October, etc.), too much time given to phony and unhelpful camera work. And the picture could stand cutting.

But there is something shoring such a picture up against all objections, from underneath. There is all this business of living as it is lived, natural, human, not pretty, but great to see. A man with a sudden itch, say; a man sneezing into his beer, making sly with his girl or badgering with his pig, confidential and off his guard. These gestures from life, quite apart from whatever delight we may take in them as such, serve a very real purpose. They further the illusion, they heighten drama immeasurably. If this man is a real man and if he has kicked his wife in an unfortunate spot, and is broken up over it, why you are sorry for him, you bleed. If people, with their dirt and earnestness and sniffling noses, are real people, and a man speaks, over a dead friend, words strong enough and beautiful and simple enough to move them to real tears, then it is enough to move anyone to furtive wipings.

And there is something more in this treatment of characters in a play, something partly responsible for and partly released by its naturalism of procedure. The makers of a film like this manage to pervade the whole, finally, with one dominant characteristic—the compassion and tolerance and fierce love, the absolute tenderness they have for these people. The peasants are exasperating, of course, they are fractious, easily befuddled, sly in the wrong dodges, and they smell to heaven. But they are ours (this is how it works), our people, to be helped rather than sold something, to be understood and appreciated and spanked into the best way, with firmness and loving care.

Purely in terms of film making, there have been no great Soviet pictures since *Storm over Asia* and *The Mother,* but in terms of the humanities there is something here, a tendency and broad feeling, that will surely be released someday into a work second to nothing whatever, a sort of wonder of the modern world.

18 September 1935

Words and Music

In pictures, it would be natural to expect that the best thing this country could turn out would be the musicals. We have a first-class body of popular song writers, the best jazz bands (marvelous enough in themselves), literally millions to squander on choruses, singers, hoofers, and people like Busby Berkeley and Hermes Pan, who live apparently for nothing else but to turn these things into production numbers. And in Hollywood we have a tradition of flash comedy that isn't to be equaled.

But what comes of all this? Something like *Roberta* or *Flying Down to Rio;* something that is colorful or vibrant in this or that part, but as a whole pretty vacuous and dull. So that when a picture like *Broadway Melody of 1936* happens along, with a consistent brightness about it, the show is so much more than was expected as to seem enough. And when there is a picture that is splendid with the presence of Mr. Fred Astaire, people will get violent and say to stop grousing—what do you expect from a musical anyway?

And that is the main trouble: you can't expect anything. A musical rarely attempts to be more than a ragbag of various show tricks; and even when it does, there is no relation between its comedy, which is mostly wisecracks, and its songs, which are mostly sugar. As for possible plots, there are two in use: the Hymie-the-Hoofer type, where the boy makes the grade with his act; the My-Gal-Daisy-She-Durrives-Me-Crazy type, where the boy makes the girl. These are naturally followed with no conviction, the chief problem in any given picture being, how to bring in the first number. Somehow, before the film has gone many feet, somebody has got to take off from perfectly normal conversation into full voice, something about he won't take the train he'll walk in the rain (there is suddenly a twenty-piece band in the room), leaving everybody else in the piece to look attentive and as though they liked it, and as though such a business were the most normal of procedures.

From this first number it is customary to push on to the second. The boy, for instance, refuses to meet the girl, who refuses to meet him. So they fall in love. Singing together in close harmony for the first time without knowing it, they sing:

> How sweet to meet
> My pet unmet
> I kiss your feet
> Madame.

And the band has got five more pieces, including marimba and steel guitar, and a chorus of forty voices resolves one of the spare seventh chords downward, *piano, pianissimo:*

> We kiss your feet'n fite'n fotum. We
> kiss. We—e—e kissyourfeetmadame—

and the line spills out into formations that would cover a four-acre lot.

In short, the second number. Having reached this point, anybody can ad-lib the rest, there being nothing to do now but keep the girl from falling into the boy's lap, by many ingenious devices—such, for example, as having him misremember where he put it. If the picture is R.K.O., the chances are the lap will have been mislaid in the butler's pantry, which is the clue for some good and funny business with Eric Blore; and just as you go out of the room, there is E. E. Horton, a nervous wreck; and there can possibly be another touch of comedy before the girl slaps his face and takes off for Lucerne, thus introducing the lonesome, or I-Yearn-for-Lucerne, number.

This business of the comedy element in musical comedy, incidentally, is a ticklish business, because often there seems to be none. *The Gay Divorcée* was a musical built and directed primarily as comedy. *Top Hat*, an attempt to repeat on it, throws in practically the same stock company (Horton, Blore, Erik Rhodes, etc.); but it goes back to the old hit-or-miss method of letting the cast get as many laughs as it can and throwing in a two-line gag whenever anybody thinks about it. *Broadway Melody of 1936* is more in the tradition of the stage revue, and by far the funniest show around. It has, for example, made a place for such charming and individual drollery as that of Robert Wildhack, professor of soft-palate calisthenics, or the snore—austerely scientific in procedure and powers of research, rich with illustration, *e.g.*, the varieties of the labial, or ah-pooh, type, the thin or blonde snore, and the various expirational classes: the whistle, the wow, the straight plop, etc. This is an absolutely star performance and worth the price of the show by itself, although the story derives a lot of meaning from the parts of Jack Benny and Sid Silvers, and some brightness from the tap dancing of Buddy Ebsen and Eleanor Powell. As music, its numbers are flat and stereotyped, lacking even the tailored verve of the several pieces Mr. Berlin wrote for *Top Hat*.

But when we come to the subject of music in the musicals, we come to the first consistent expression of popular songs and rhythms that this medium has seen, namely Fred Astaire. From the crowds he draws, I should say that Astaire must mean many things to many people—as, for example, glamor to married ladies in for the day from Mamaroneck, real elegance to telephone girls whose boys suck their teeth and wear pinstripe suits, etc. But one thing he manages above all others, and that is the best visual expression that has been generally seen in this country, of what is called the jazz. As an actor he is too much of a dancer, tending toward pantomime; and as a dancer he is occasionally too ball-roomy. But as a man who can create figures, intricate, unpredictable, constantly varied and yet simple, seemingly effortless, on such occasions as those when the band gathers together its brasses and rhythm section and begins to beat it out—in this capacity he is not to be equaled anywhere: he brings the strange high quality of genius to one of the baser and more common arts. Some of the aspects of jazz—its husky sadness, its occasional brawling strength—do not appear in Astaire; but its best points are sharp in such of his steps as those of the soft-shoe sandman number and in the number where the lights go down, just before the line of men, with top hats and sticks, swings up the steps, over the rim of the stage. Fred Astaire, whatever he may do in whatever picture he is in, has the beat, the swing, the debonair and damn-your-eyes violence of rhythm, all the gay contradiction and irresponsibility, of the best thing this country can contribute to musical history, which is the best American jazz.

2 October 1935

Editorial: *Red Salute*

Those who report on fascism in the movies tend to overdo it, frequently calling up a picture of some group of big bankers sitting around behind closed doors and turning out film scripts by the crate. But it would surely be overdoing it in the other direction to say of *Red Salute,* opening shortly in New York City, that its jingoism is merely misplaced fervor, its anti-labor elements purely the spontaneous expression of small and dim and muddy minds. Produced by Reliance Pictures for release through United Artists, this film is unmistakably a made-to-order attack on radicalism in the colleges. It opens on the American flag, floating over a quite phony demonstration on some campus, and it reaches an emotional climax when an American soldier of the cleanest cut bares to the multitudes his forearm, prominently tattooed with Old Glory in full color. In between there are at least three places where someone wishes they'd start another war, hasn't had any fun since the last one. There is talk about Reds, aliens, loyalty, the minds of our youth, and what not. There is evidence that the chief student agitator is a paid propagandist, not to say a sybarite and nasty fellow. There are shots of thirty-year-old college boys with tough black mugs, and shots of silly intellectuals, hungry looking, pimply, behind glasses. And the dialogue throughout suggests nothing so much as the triumph and angry clucking of five bridge-tables of D.A.R. delegates, reading antiphonally or in unison the week's crop of scareheads from their respective local branches of the Hearst press.

As to story, the film is about so-so, being in its major portion a rather dim copy of the *It Happened One Night* formula (the soldier having stolen a military car for her sake tries to dissuade the spoiled rich girl from getting back to Washington for her fiancé's May Day address—spats, sudden tenderness, car wrecks, escapes, humor, etc.). And while this story is not enough in itself to put the film over with large audiences, the dangerous elements of any such business should not be minimized. Whoever is ripe to be fooled will be fooled to the hilt when it becomes a question of wrapping frauds up in celluloid, because of the immanence, vividness, and persuasive tangibility of the American picture as a form. The one happy element about this film is that it is too palpable and jerrybuilt to carry conviction with a considerable part of the present movie audience. It will be boycotted in some places; and exhibitors, who are businessmen and don't want trouble on one side of the line or the other, will find it both too weak and too hot to handle with the highest profit. *Red Salute* seems strangely out of place for this time: it belongs with the special gullibility of some more frenzied period, such as that of a war. For the present, the most effective propaganda for the status quo is made by those who are too naïve or sluggish to be conscious of it as such.

2 October 1935

Shakespeare in Hollywood

Opening at an $11 top, running well over two hours, costing more than a million and (to ensure getting this back) press-agented for months ahead as the greatest marriage that was ever married between (among) William Shakespeare, Max Reinhardt, William *(Fog over Frisco)* Dieterle, Felix Mendelssohn, Bronislava Nijinska, James Cagney, and a good sprinkling of Warners' best California baked hams—being all this, the film *A Midsummer Night's Dream* demands a certain attention that will never be justified in terms of pure entertainment. At its many screenings there will be no lack of Ah's and Oh's, culture clubs will have discussions, newspaper critics will put on their Sunday adjectives; but the picture is fairly tedious, being twice the average running time, and there is going to be a powerful minority of American husbands who will get one load of the elves and pixies, and feel betrayed away from their stocking feet and sports page, and say as much, violently.

Apart from such unconscious and partly philistine criticism, there is to be said about this version of the Shakespeare extravaganza that it is topheavy with the weight of its art departments. (You can just see the camera and property and boom men standing around and scratching themselves, balancing the impulse to guffaw against the uneasy wonder whether there may be something deep in these here Nijinska, what do you call them, esthetic dances.) Its worst contradiction, in fact, lies in the way Warners first ordered up a whole batch of foreign and high-sounding names to handle music, dances, general production—and then turned around and handed them such empty vessels as Dick Powell, Jean Muir, Victor Jory, for actors. A second major contradiction appears in the way the whole thing is approached. For a while the producers will stand outside Shakespeare, handling each line literally, with marvelment and awe. Then suddenly they will either forget the book altogether and go Hollywood, or else get inside it, improvising on it as familiarly (and justifiably) as they would with any mortal working script.

Where they have arranged to forget the original is principally in the supernatural doings of the midsummer night, where there are fairies singly and in Music Hall troops, Titania, Oberon, and Puck (Mickey Rooney, too ill instructed and raucous to be given such prominence). Here situations are elaborated for all they are worth, regardless of the main play, like so many independent sideshows on a midway. Oberon's ensemble departure, for example, must take up all of ten minutes, and yet right in the middle of it is inserted, for no earthly reason, the detailed seduction of a white nymph by a black sprite, she finally on his shoulder and disappearing down a black distance, weaving away at a fire symbol with her hands, wrists, and forearms—in short, a dancer with a specialty in a long vanish shot. The necessity for some such figuration in a play of this type is obvious; but there is also a need for distinguishing between fantasy and *Flying Down to Rio*.

The idea of the goblin orchestra—grotesque little figures in masks—is by way of contrast a touch of what is needed. Introduced only occasionally, this effect is fresh, pleasing; it represents the imagination at work and is worth all the brute mechanics, however elaborate, of settings, costumes, parades, and spangled gauze shots.

But where the film really goes along with Shakespeare is in all that play-within-a-play business of hempen homespuns, the weavers, tinkers, cobblers of the city. Here the lines are surrounded with enough business to give them a bright and plausible reality. As Bottom, Cagney is out of character but still able to give it something; and his associates in earnest buffoonery—Joe E. Brown, Hugh Herbert, etc.—are the best cast figures in the production. With their various interpolations and properties, they are made into something that can be laughed at because it is real and funny, rather than a classic thing to laugh at.

The principal difficulty is that the stage of Shakesperean comedy is not the stage today, that this business of groaning, sighing, jiggling couplets, spouting passion, and still mistaking your grandmother for the girl friend for three acts straight—this tradition in humor is a diaper that we have put away for good. The humor that really comes out in Hollywood's *Midsummer Night's Dream* is based, like the best of Shakespeare, on people; the formal comedy element is false to us and must be toned down with more subtlety than the producers of this film can muster. They could have done it far better by taking the whole less solemnly, by using people who (like Olivia de Havilland) might read the lines with some comprehension of what they were about. But they would have done still better by taking another play than this particular play, the product of a poet's exuberance and youth. Its phrases still ring like bells, there is an easy strong vigor and charmed air to the whole. But owing to circumstances and the matter of a few centuries in time, its words are beautiful as words in a book, not in the mouths of fools.

16 October 1935

Sad But (Otherwise) True

La Maternelle, the latest French film to be released in New York, can hardly be called a first-rate picture for several basic reasons. But there are many fine things about it, and in particular there is a good tip as to what may be done with camera art, to give it a home of its own and a difference from the other arts, so that it will not always be something like their poor relation.

It is not so much that *La Maternelle* has anything to contribute in camera work as we now know it, in angles, perspective, design—in the way of photographing a thing, that is. Some of its photography is good and some (the trick dissolve shots or that seedy sequence of the kid throwing pebbles at an image in the water, and finally jumping in) ought to have been left on the cutting-room floor. Its departure is rather in the choice and use of the things photographed: it is one of those rare films where the camera has gone out into the world, instead of having the world come before it, and pose.

Jean Benoit-Levy, who directed with Marie Epstein, had the job of filming a story laid in a school for young children. He could of course have rigged up a school set and flooded it with little Shirley Temples, Nova Pilbeams, Our Gangers, and other stage-hardened prodigies. Again, he could have gone into an actual school and scared the pants half off the kids by trucking up with his cameras and saying: "Now, Johnny, you just speak this line, carefully adapted for the part by Joseph Mankiewicz, and don't be afraid"; walked through it a couple of times, and then taken a picture of kids trying very bravely not to be kids and not to look as though they had any idea where the camera was. In short, he could have got either the usual adult's idea of what a kid would do, or what passes for "unaffectedness" among the usual documentary films.

But he had time, he had patience. So he went into an actual school and worked around with the children till they were so used to him and his strange machinery that they could apparently go on with their play and work, grave and oblivious in their own strange world. There was a minimum of actual necessary business for them to go through consciously, and when he approached this, he seems to have given the barest stipulations, letting the kids play around with it until they felt it, answered, and reacted spontaneously.

Out of what they were able to get in this way, the directors (to give their high naturalism a meaning) have selected and put together just the right elements to make a setting that is germane and completely charming. What they load this setting with is another and sadder matter. A lover of children, a general maid in the school, has taken particularly under her wing little Paulette Flambert, a girl of definitely psychopathic jealousy and emotional hunger, deserted by her mother, who is a tart. There are several supporting plot movements; the pathos of everything is established by cutting upward of forty times to Paulette, her face and body twisted with the agony of it (variation here is so meager that one ten-foot clip could just as well have been used for half her work in the picture); the kid finally wanders off and attempts suicide because her idol has been proposed to by the good and wooden doctor; and in the end there is achieved a happy marriage and the New Understanding.

All this is possible but the story is slight, the child moons around until the unsympathetic nature of such a character is raised almost to burlesque, and as to the business of Rose's romance, the causes and consequences thereof are rather obscure, Madeleine Renaud having produced (whatever her creative talents) a figure that is a cross between several splints of kindling wood and a glass of milk. Development is at a minimum and made terribly stiff and unreal by repetitious and prolonged and inconsequential close-ups. As far as the main story is concerned, it is a frank tear-jerker, handled as such with obviousness and a ponderous lack of resource. In short, this part of it, which is right in the dead center of it, I can't even take seriously. I guess I'm just not the eternal mother.

But where the sentiment is true, where it is managed as it should be, with open sincerity and the right delicate restraint, the film becomes lovely indeed. I don't now remember anything on the screen that is quite so engaging as the part of Mme. Paulin, played by Madi Berri—such a mixture of natural roughages and low comedy, quiet busyness, tenderness, and homely beauty. Alice Tissot gives the stock matron part a fine, intelligent reading. And no one will remember anything like the children, filing out of the school, squabbling solemnly on the playground, uneasy in their school cantata with scratching for lice, singing and asking and taking their dose of salts as they're told with the remote, careless unconsciousness that is as natural to them as it is to puppy dogs. And this is the thing, this finely arranged composite of little, overlooked details, that the cameras may go out and catch and give a fresh meaning to, so that the screen will hold up the mirror to life, not as lived on phony studio sets, in books, in paintings, on the stage, but as lived. The difference is as sharp and refreshing as the difference between the woods of New England, now in the fall, and an expensive landscaping job in Westchester.

30 October 1935

In a Dry Month

So far in the fall picture season, about the only cheery news is that dug out and decoded from the trade journals, where "Boss" 17 G, BIG IN CINCY, or CRAWFORD BIG $21,000, BALTO, will tell disbelievers that a theater in Cincinnati claims to have taken $17,000 away from the people in seven days' run of that weak sister in pictures, *She Married Her Boss,* and that in Baltimore they report having shaken twenty-one thousand depression dollars out of a week of Joan Crawford in *I Live My Life.*

Otherwise, Hollywood has had a rather sad, solemn look for quite a while. Much of its fall offensive seems to have been massed along the front of old and weighty matters—Shakespeare, for example, the Crusades, the blowout at Pompeii, the Opera—where the movies are a trout in a dustbin, busy, goggle-eyed, but somewhat at a loss. And even when Hollywood has been working in its own element there has been a noticeable spirit of boredom. So that now we have a good picture again, it is a cheerful sight.

Hands across the Table is the new Paramount picture, a smooth but natural job, a happy mixture of brainwork and horseplay and a reminder that when intelligence goes for a walk among even the oldest props, the props may come to life. The plot here is Group A, Subtype 11-C: (A) he falls for her at the start yet remains in a state of falling all through the picture, suspended in midair like the floating-hat trick; (11-C) he is a rich young scion and she is a poor young shoot. Add complications AX2 and BOP: he has to marry the society page, she is loved by kindly gent with a million, who would take her under the wing of his yacht for life. Originally a story by Viña Delmar.

But the film people have somehow beveled and canted and trued it up at just the right places until it is a natural, airy structure, mostly well founded. The girl was hardboiled, suspected this business of love (where did it get her mother?); the boy was the son of big money but did not have any ("Maybe you, uh, heard about the Big Crash? Well that was, uh, us") and was also hardboiled, out to make a living and marry it. They met, decided they were of no use to each other, and proceeded to hang around together for a while, having fun. And most of the picture develops out of that, moving along from give-and-take to tenderness at an easy, smart clip. And without plugging sentiment too hard or taking too seriously the thesis of love triumphant in spite of itself, it is able to wind up still doing nothing in particular, very plausibly.

The trouble and the danger with light comedy as a rule is that it is self-conscious over its lack of weight and either leaves reality altogether in an attempt to be capricious and unexpected about everything, or fastens on each excuse for feeling with a hollow and forced semblance of deep emotion. That *Hands across the Table* keeps the delicate and hard balance between these two courses of procedure is partly the work of direction, cutting, dialogue writing; but considerably the work of Carole Lombard and Fred MacMurray.

In this picture these two make an all-time copybook example of how to play a movie for what it is worth, with subtlety, much resource in the matter of visual expression, and the open, sustained kind of charm that can be projected through the shadows of a mile of celluloid. They are, after all, the deciding factor in whether the whole business of dinner for two, with hiccups, the evening with its last lap in the taxi, shall end up as a collection of comedy ideas or as smooth development of the situation, a successful piece of fancy; and whether the faked call from Bermuda shall be a mere crutch for the plot or straight comedy in itself; and whether roofs, stars, etc. are mere stage properties or what makes the world go around.

But it would be unfortunate if we got too much stress on acting here, because *Hands across the Table* is a first-rate piece of film management. Some stretches are handled pretty much as vaudeville blackouts (especially the part where MacMurray answers the girl's door in his drawers and scares the dumb gentleman friend out of his candy and plenty else, the whole ending in a merry pratfall down the stairs), there is an occasional heavy touch, and the whole idea of getting Ralph Bellamy in to sound his hollow changes on the role of old Mr. Sweetly-kindly is about as germane as a saucerful of warm milk in a glass of beer.

But these are instances merely; in the run of the film there is a shrewd genius for effect through understatement—all sorts of touches like the action when MacMurray leaves the apartment after a sleepless night and you see him stop to look after the milk wagon on the block, the camera looking down through the morning air from over the girl's shoulder. No comment, no superfluous footage. But the hint has been planted, and will later underline the scene where he says he is going to get a job if it kills him, he could deliver milk, couldn't he. Or take the summing-up of that first night, when they had hiccups at dinner, such a lovely time only it had to be the last, and she sits on the edge of the bed after it is all over, all played out, catches suddenly on a hiccup in her throat, and breaks down crying like a kid.

These things taken by themselves are not much, but they indicate a wisdom of procedure that it is good to find in pictures, where careless use of camera devices, the didactic cutting in of wheels, clocks, calendar leaves and what not, and all march-of-timing and Eisensteining in general, are often confused with intelligent and true exploitation of the medium. And the picture itself is not much (builds no Dnieperstroys), except that it is a good one, a rain in a dry month, and incidentally a certain advance in film treatment. Whatever its label may indicate in the way of old stuff to those who count on reading the label, it is encouraging to remember that anything which is delightful is never old in any real sense of the term, because delight is a fragile and immediate thing, and new always.

In newness as such, the latest thing is *The New Gulliver,* a sort of tridimensional animated cartoon. Its makers were more concerned with mechanical problems than with its persuasive motion as a picture; the plot is thin and hasty, the satire of the kind that will say Pie-face, Pie-face, Pie-face, Pie-face, until the words lose meaning. I liked the tinny bustle and Rube Goldberg complications of the eating scene; also the monstrous machines in the factory, the police cars, pompous marches, etc. The puppets are marvels of invention, but an invention that stops with the still photograph. Taken as an experiment it is valuable; taken as a high-water mark in films it gets a bit absurd—the Duller Gulliver, the New Hullabaloo.

13 November 1935

The Picture of the *Bounty*

Mutiny on the Bounty is one of the best pictures that have been made, and this is largely due to the facts it was made from. More than most violent acts, a mutiny is a striking thing, requiring strong causes and breeding strong results. And more than most mutinies, that of H.M.S. *Bounty* was part of an incredible chain of events, logical developments and illogical strokes of chance, ill winds, bitter privations, the sweet land breezes off islands—and all anchored to a few powerful characters; heroes who were villains and villains who turned great.

The zest and careful research of Charles Nordhoff and James Norman Hall are responsible for the present version of the story: without their books Hollywood would never have come near this gold mine. But Nordhoff and Hall were not shrewd creators of fiction—their *Mutiny on the Bounty* was sometimes dull and frequently ineffectual, when you came to separate their handling of the story from the story itself, and their best passages were those where they were transcribing testimony, quoting from logs. It remained for the movies to give the thing a strong line of action and a fictional body.

The picture that Frank Lloyd has made wastes little time on preparations in England—the pressing of the crew, the signing on of Byam, etc.—and uses this time to best advantage in setting up the main currents of the story. They come over the side of H.M.S. *Bounty* and there is all the packed confusion and bustle of a ship, at the dead center of it the captain in his thundercloud; and before they leave there is a man flogged through the fleet, the flesh stripped from his bones in accordance with the printed word of Article XXI; and when they do leave there is a certain coordination of cameras, sound recordings, and cutting that makes something strange and beautiful out of an old hulk the movies bought up and glued their properties to.

The whole tone of the picture, in fact, is set by this beauty they have found in ships and described with the true care and knowledge of the craftsman. The picture really gets under way when the ship gets under way, with everybody piling ashore and the captain's gig coming in, with matter-of-fact, routine yet portentous commands, and with the top-men letting go the canvas, the sails cracking and filling in the offshore breeze, and the helmsman spoking his big wheel over—"Steady as she goes, sir." And then with all the scurrying of men, up in her rigging and pelting down the decks, the ship slowly spreads her canvas and steadies on her course and becomes, slowly, a moving, live thing, handsome and intricate, sighing with the wind and creaking in her timbers from the swell, standing up from her maindeck in a tower of sticks, sheets, halyards—damnation to manage and working a man's heart out. The details are right from start to finish, even the Turk's heads worked on the stanchions, the thin bos'n's pipes and chanteys. But all this life and commotion is principally a background: in the center of it is the camera's picture of the whole ship, looking up from the water's edge as she passes, swinging slowly from her foot up over rigging and away, so that there is a great circular motion to the whole as the music blares up in bands and chanteys and complaining gear, so that you sit in a crowded theater and feel His Majesty's armed ship *Bounty* grow and gather herself in a great circle over the horizon.

This is the start, and as the ship goes down around Africa and up into the southern Pacific, weeks and weeks, you begin to see life develop in the relations among the men. As the food rots and the water gets low and monotony grows and the men grumble with it, they are flogged, keel-hauled, knocked about, and the sense of Bligh as a cruel, inexorable force grows well. They make port and there is an interlude before they put out again, but within two or three days of departure so much insult has been added to so much injustice that the explosion comes, set off by chance, on the April morning when the chief officer takes over the ship.

From here on the actual story sprawls all over the ocean, but by virtue of such vivid action as the mutiny itself, the sequence of Bligh and his hard-bitten survivors, the device of having Bligh himself bring the *Pandora* back to the island as the mutineers leave in the mist, and the hurrying-up of the trial scene in England, the picture manages to hold it together. While the native Tahitian stuff is convincing enough to have its own kind of truth—the girls are fine, the drums are fine, the island is misty and lush, fine with trees and all that—it is pretty heavy stuff for a picture that runs over two hours. It might just as well have been cut to a length proportional with the trial scene, the wreck of the *Pandora,* the landing on Pitcairn, the cruise of the *Bounty'*s launch—all of which could have been longer, but gain marvelously from the way in which their high points have been selected and put together.

The putting together of static fragments into a live story is what is most wonderful about this picture anyway. Just as the most striking aspects of ships getting under way and standing out in a line are sifted out and worked into a motion that is something more than the motion of vessels through water, so the details of various actions are made up into patterns and carried on from one to another. The action of the mutiny in particular has a brawling motion possible to no other art, with men pitched screaming out of the shrouds, blown down companionways, pinned to bulkheads, and just plain battered in a frenzy of released hatred. And the incidents leading up to the violent overthrow are made vivid in terms of the medium—the swish and pistol crack of the lash, the sweating, lean bodies, the terrible labor, and the ominous judgment from the quarterdeck. The ship and the ship's life open out here, but the film becomes grand by virtue of something more than quarterdecks and hurlyburly. It is the reworking of a large tragedy—men not only against the sea but against their own forces, both universal and particular.

Even if there were no other human touch in the picture, Charles Laughton in the part of Bligh would be enough to hold it together. He is able to lead the show, as a leader of men and as a man hounded by his own frenzy, in the face of whatever the show provides in the way of high adventure. He makes a foundation that stays solid even under the most towering passions and against the most violent sidethrusts of personal madness. He is genius itself and in an exacting part; he has never played a role of such devious subtleties and frank power and neither has anybody else in the movies. For his soundness of instinct, the range of his talent and perception, it should be enough to say that no man can really wear the shoes of a great character without, in his own way, fitting them. There is too much of a spread between his character and that of Fletcher Christian—whom Clark Gable nevertheless goes beyond his ordinary self to make a pretty believable figure, a plain good fellow with powerful voice and physique. And together with the empty uplift of the end, this confusion of issues is about the only thing in the picture that anyone could really quarrel with.

As Byam the spectator, Franchot Tone is up to what is asked of him, without giving the part any more. The native chief wears his lack of clothes with a fine, simple dignity; and the crew is as fine a collection of tag-end types as you will see anywhere—Dudley Digges as the sawbones, Herbert Mundin, Donald Crisp, etc.—and it occurs to me that while we have seen these people before, there is something about the make-up and the fine spirit of the thing that takes them beyond their usual capacities—and makes them for these minutes on the screen the bullyboys and hearts-of-oak that the great country of England, with her great tall ships, has used for mean labor and battles, and cheered very handsomely some time after the battles and mean labor had worn them down to the bones, and committed these bones to the several (see Freedom of) seas.

27 November 1935

The Marxian Epileptic

In terms of rhyme, reason, good taste and formal plot structure, *A Night at the Opera* is a sieve, a leaky ship, and caulked to the guards with hokum. It has three of the Marx Brothers and absolutely no pride. It seems thrown together, made up just as they went along out of everybody else's own head—it steals sequences from René Clair, it drives off with whole wagonloads of the Keystone lot without so much as putting the fence back up; it has more familiar faces in the way of gags and situations than a college reunion—it has even got a harp-and-piano specialty, which it goes through with dead solemnity for about fifteen minutes. In short, *A Night at the Opera* is a night with the Marx Brothers, who have a zest for clowning and a need to be cockeyed that are either genius or just about enough to fit them all out with numbers and a strait jacket, and who troop through this impossible hour and a half of picture with such speed and clatter as to pin up a record for one of the most hilarious collections of bad jokes I've laughed myself nearly sick over.

The film could have been grand satire on Lawrence Tibbett in *Metropolitan* or Grace Moore in the love-me-love-my-tonsil cycle; but satire, like the cherrystone clam in the colonel's slipper, was too much. It has a pretty idea and starts off with a fine edge—the Italians are a singing race, so open on Italy singing. And then the Marx Brothers, in the onward march of their stealing everything in sight (you couldn't have kept a camera or a chorus girl on that set ten minutes running), steal the idea and the edge. The romance is handled straight, the love and singing scenes being cut out like slabs of mince pie. And the picture has no line or continuous pitch of its own at all.

Yet many of the individual scenes show much sure generalship in the way of galloping through it, one, two, three and putting over the big punch before you can get your breath, and keeping the boys in focus, all the boys all the way (try this sometime—that terrific walk of Groucho's would get out of focus like a clay pigeon). In the good spots the action is kept swift and disentangled, evenly spaced and in clear relief. Groucho has just squeezed into a third-class stateroom with a trunk big enough to hold two brothers and a tenor, who pop out of it as soon as the door is wedged shut, and then people begin to pile in—manicurists, cleaning maids, retired majors, stewards with trays, the engineer's assistant, the engineer looking for him. They begin to get about seven deep and the laws of physics are insulted right and left, Groucho still the host, sarcastic and regal with a cigar, the other two still swarming up the chambermaids, everything still piling up and bulging the walls until just the second when the rich matron, never so outraged but blackmailed into it, sweeps along to her assignation with Groucho and arrives square in front of the door, which breaks out like a shot and they all spill out clear across the ship, like a tubful of blueberries.

Or take the opening night at the Metropolitan. The issues at stake here are too many to recount, but the impresario is lashed in his closet upstairs, Groucho is wearing his tails and addressing the throng from the rich matron's box, and the others have slipped sheets of popular music under the second page of the overture score. Everything is in place, the horseshoe, the music-lovers, the maestro's wee baton (ha!); the orchestra is just rising into one of those ripe overture chords, the second-chair men snaking the page over desperately, and down comes a full brass choir on "Take Me Out to the Ball Game," and Harpo has got hold of a baseball and is passing it clear across the pit to Chico, and the hubbub keeps warming up and the ball passing until one of them snatches what must have been a violin but looks like a cello and lines it clear out of sight into the wings, and Groucho is dropping his top hat excitedly off the box into the orchestra, whistling with his fingers to get it back up—Hey Shorty, he says to the music-lover in a stiff shirt, Hey! Hey Shorty.

This is wonderful while it lasts but it gets anticlimactic as it extends through all the scenes of the opera; and that is the way the picture as a whole goes. There will be stretches of dull clowning, of the boy getting next to the girl; and then there will be something like that perfectly irrelevant four feet of film where the set has three cots and two Marx Brothers asleep, and the third cot has right in the middle of it an alarm clock. One, two, three—you just get time to count the cots and the alarm clock explodes and Harpo automatically raises a twenty-pound mallet and comes down, whango, right through the works of the clock with his eyes still closed, and that is all. That is the way it goes with the picture as a whole, a breakneck crazy business, made violent and living by the presence in it of some impenitently ham and delightful bad boys.

The Marx Brothers' type of humor is frequently not their own; but what is never anyone else's is their ability, when they have got a laugh, to put it over the plate and halfway through the catcher's glove. Having no controlling idea, they cannot make their comedy stick—*i.e.,* you realize even while wiping your eyes well into the second handkerchief that it is nothing so much as a hodgepodge of skylarking, and soon over. Their picture is done the minute it fades on the screen. But the boys themselves are still with us, and I estimate an average period of ten days to three weeks, as the picture gets around, before the American public will be able to open its garbage can in the morning and not duck involuntarily, anticipating that a Marx Brother will pop up and clout it over the head with a sackful of tomatoes.

This fact and the exuberant antic that carries it along will remain for a while as a vague monument, in something more than wax, to a colossal burning energy spent on anything and nothing. With the definite exception of Groucho, who would be funny in still photographs, the Marx Brothers are an uninventive, stupid bunch. They are very much like somebody exploding a blown-up paper bag—all bang and no taste; but they are also irrepressible clowns with a great sense of the ridiculous. They tear into it by guess and by god, they rush through it as though it were meat and they starving; their assurance, appetite, and vitality are supreme; they are both great and awful.

11 December 1935

To Act One's Age

In putting *Ah, Wilderness* on the screen Hollywood has done some beautiful work. Also it has done some very shoddy work, partly owing to Eugene O'Neill's original play. There might be adolescents like the hero here (I have never seen one), but even granting that, there would be nothing so very fine about them. Such cases of acute callowness may be made the object of serious study, just as you could take for study the tapeworm (*cestoda:* a family of Platyhelminthes). But they cannot be taken with any seriousness when they are put forward as the hero, as Youth Eternal, spouting its Swinburne, joining its Christian Endeavor to save the world, and at the same time pompous, pulpy, mean, and eternally damp of diaper.

This play, centering all the regrettable features of adolescence in one character and then implying that this is the essence of a soul on fire, is false at bottom; it is designed for the patronage of those who like to forget, gloss over, not understand, and generally think well of themselves, looking back. I am sorry to mention it here, but the nearest thing to O'Neill's hero that I can remember, from living as a kid in those New England towns, is a group of upstanding youths that my folks once forced me to travel clear across the town to strike up a comradeship with, instead of hanging out with the scum of our own neighborhood. The lads across town had honor stars from the First Congregational Church of Ware, Massachusetts, they were clean and orderly sons of good Christian people with money in the bank, and at the age of thirteen they concealed a mixture of incest, exhibitionism, and betrayal of their sisters to neighboring honor-star lads (also of the Eagle Patrol) that surprised me considerably.

Well, well, boys will be boys; but the point to keep in mind for all aging idealizers of puppy attributes is that children are also people, however difficult and inept, and that adolescence is a stage of life, not never-never land. O'Neill's play pivots around some young squirt who graduates from high school with a violent and empty yen for revolution and for a slip of a daughter whose father is very mean and disapproves of everything, including the squirt. His own father is kindly and quizzical in curbing the radicalism of the wayward boy (who for climax gets drunk, quotes Oscar Wilde, repents, and gets the girl), and tells him straightforward facts about Life, Society, and, hm, well, a certain kind of, hm, Woman. Stage and screen can play around with this as they like, developing characters and creating business, but this is the basic thought that Mr. O'Neill thought.

Some genius on the stage might make something reasonable and real out of the boy. But that this would have to be done largely without benefit of the playwright is very well illustrated in the picture, where Hollywood has cast for the part some earnest soul who will read the lines for what they look like and raise unlikely banality to its highest degree. The fault here, that is to say, is brought into clearer relief by the more naïve and literal method of the movies. The virtues are some of them undermined because of poor acting (*e.g.,* Wallace Beery, all-time Muggenheim Fellow), and some of them made vivid by the screen's flexibility as a medium.

What the screen really makes out of *Ah, Wilderness* is a first-class atmosphere piece. It calls up more matters than it knows of by its sure reconstruction of the day-to-day life of the New England country in a time (1906) that is as dead but as vivid in the general memory as the smell of leaves burning in piles along the gravel walks, this fall or when you were a kid. Practically all of it that is good is background, in the way of local color. Not only the sets of stiff cluttered rooms, lawns, gas buggies, picnics, but the incidental life of the place. Take the high-school graduation, shifting rapidly from the audience of proud parents to the speakers, quartets ("Asleep in the Deep"), the valedictorian, and the serious young chit in pigtails, fighting a very sick clarinet with a wild roving eye of reproach for her accompanist. Or the barroom scene (the fast baby here was perfectly fine); or the scenes at table, or on the morning of the Fourth (a little overdone), or at the school sociable. And at times, what with the genius that often goes into Metro production—cameras, set crews, and particularly the musical arranging of Herbert Stothart, always appropriate and frequently an inspired counterpoint to the action—at times the picture is beautiful, as in the spooning at night on the Common, with the trees quiet and dark over the grass, framing a white Georgian church as sweet as music. Much of the film is silly, but *Ah, Wilderness* remains a job of picture making, in craftsmanship and feeling, that is wonderful to see.

Show Them No Mercy is a picture that comes nearer to acting its age, in the sense both of timeliness and of maturity. It is a gangster film, with the boys hiding out in an old house in the country, having kidnaped parents and child and got away with thousands in ransom. The baby squalls, a woodpecker drives Edward Brophy practically insane, one of the boys wants to delete the family by means of gunfire—and this growing turbulence among themselves, leading to wild moves, stupid blunders, and betrayal, makes the picture. The story is built logically and with dramatic pressure on every square inch, and there are cast as the outlaws Cesar Romero, Bruce Cabot, Warren Hymer, and Edward Brophy, good solid performers all. The forces of good, represented by the mother, father, cooing baby, chief of detectives, etc., are incidental here, the payoff being that although Will (Sniffer) Hays held up the purity seal until the original title, *Snatched,* was changed, he subsequently solemnly affixed same to a show that pictures virtue as being dull as dirt and villainy predominant and fine.

There are unfortunate lapses—Romero, brain guy, becoming a babe in arms and letting Cabot get him; Hymer overplaying the contribution-box theme; the close-up of Cabot, machine-gun slugs showing in catsup marks on his chest like four dots on your typewriter, etc.—but these faults are shoved aside by the sheer violence of the story as a whole. Such a scene as that where the two are running from the stalled car in the meadow, wild, awkward shadows picked out by a spotlight, one of them brought down in the machine-gun fire, sets the pace for the show, which is conceived and managed so as to be direct, surely dramatic, inevitable, and full of terror. It is a credible story of men; it has a wilderness, but no Ah.

25 December 1935

1936

From *A Tale of Two Cities* to *Rembrandt*

Take a Fireside Classic

The movie version of Dickens' *Tale of Two Cities* is a bore, notable for its mob scenes and for the attention it will receive, and it illustrates a movie tendency that is getting to be almost a fixed course of procedure, especially on the Metro lot. Take a fireside classic (take a mental age from one to ten), find out how many well-known names will be available to set forth the quaint characters; and then while some director with a famous touch is mismaking the first sequences, let the publicity department busy itself with rumors about the well-known names, the famous touch, the expense, the expanse, the difficulty, the elaborate care. Spend a million, make it a million and a quarter in round numbers, what the hell. The more bread cast on the waters the better; the gravy will come back.

But a picture like this needs a little more than the expenses, names, etc. It needs some kind of sentiment and continuity, and both of these in *A Tale of Two Cities* are strong enough. The Defarge wine shop, the Evrémondes and the Manette household are cued in at the start and quickly followed by the trial scene at the Old Bailey, thus introducing the Crunchers, Carton, and Stryver, and leaving the forces of melodrama and proper sentiment free to go their joint way, with everybody saving everybody else and Carton saving all by means of a far, far better thing, etc.

The best of Dickens is pretty well lost here. The Crunchers are more prominent and infinitely better in the book; the same for the Old Bailey action, the Defarges and their Jacquerie. But the worst of Dickens—the bathos, smug morality, and provincial missionary spirit—is not only retained but made the bulk of the film. Even the best part of it, where mobs of people fill the streets and pour along in natural turbulence toward the Bastille, where they converge in one tatterdemalion army, attack and retreat, line the passage of the tumbrils, surround the guillotine, etc.—even these fine things are somewhat canceled by a quite determined playing down of the French Revolution, which is resolved by the special help of printed titles into lawlessness, injustice, unkempt frenzy, and little else.

The movies could make a good film out of *A Tale of Two Cities,* but they could not make it as one of the fireside-classic cycle, and they could not use this staff, which has put together a fairly good example of how not to make a show with cameras.

Like all instruments that are easy to play with, such as the marimba or tenor saxophone, the cameras in a motion picture must be handled with severe restraint, their strips of impressions delicately timed and fitted together. Here, when the effect of something is to be shown on somebody, he is cut in with a thud and then cut out. This goes on with steady uninventiveness; and the unfortunate part of it is that almost every time this happens, there is Donald Woods, there is Elizabeth Allan, there is Claude Gillingwater, or Henry B. Walthall, or Edna May Oliver, or Blanche Yurka, or Tully Marshall—or else there is one from among the most hollow and posey set of extras that the Central Casting Bureau ever rounded up. I never again expect to see so much ham crowded into one smokehouse—but the point at present is the monotony with which the film is put together: a three-foot clip (one, pause, two) if the character is just to look; a five-foot clip (one, pause, two, pause, three) if he is to speak a line (if Miss Allan or Mr. Woods is to emote a Dickens emotion, though, either of them will burn up half a reel). The camera comes to them one after the other, and they throw out most of the lines in the picture as though they were hollering up an empty steam boiler, to try out the echo.

Even if it had everything else, this production would still need picture-making imagination. In the assassination sequence, for example, the director starts with Evrémonde going to bed and marches step by step through having the Marquis fancy seeing a face at the window, the valet go to the window, the camera go outside the window, showing first the valet looking out, then the assassin flattening back against the inner balcony. Then back to the room—nothing there, my lord—the lights put out, all leaving; and then immediately to the window, the man coming in, creeping over, planting the message (close-up of the message), stabbing, mugging, creeping off. You have been allowed to see everything except the spout of blood; but in another sense, the dramatic sense, you have not been made to see anything.

More simplicity would come nearer to giving terrorism some slight aspect of terror. For instance, let the camera remain inside as the valet goes to the high, closed window, turning to follow him and showing it dark and empty, following him back. The master shrugs and settles under the covers; the attendants snuff the candles and tiptoe out. And the camera swings back to the window, staying for emphasis just a little too long on the window, still dark and empty, the scene fading slowly on that with the wind coming up outside. If there is any further build-up necessary it may be made here, where there is need for a time-break anyway, by showing, say, the effect in the servants' quarters of the master's hallucination—or was it?—of the way the wind is yelling outside, of the sullen resentment of the people. After some such break, you can go back to the same camera position and the same window, now broken wide open, its curtains streaming in the morning wind. A servant comes in, rushes to the window, turns; the camera follows him to the bed and trucks up to the Marquis, still quiet under the fine covers, the message from Jacques nailed in his side. Some such simple method of suggestion would at least not belie violence by plodding through it with painful literalness and no conviction at all.

Ronald Colman, Reginald Owen, Basil Rathbone, and the trial judge stand out from this stupendous assemblage as being both true to themselves and believable as someone else. But they and the other sparse good things in the picture are not enough to save it from the burning. If you are interested in movies, you can forgive a fairly bad one for its several good points, or a thoroughly bad one for its lesson in what a blessing mere competence is after all. But any film doing so little so poorly, running into seven figures on the cost sheet and assured of getting several more figures back, appealing to the worst popular taste and that with certain naïve overtones of propagating the classics and the splendor of art—such a film is a public waste and a stultifying influence on the industry, and deserves about as much tolerance as you would give to a reversal of the sewage and drinking-water systems, under the name of The David Copperfield Project.

8 January 1936

Best Neglected Film

Now while the general excitement of picking the one, the ten, the how-many-hundred best pictures is still hot upon us, I wish to urge the case of the absolutely best neglected picture of two years, *The Captain Hates the Sea.* After having made it boldly, the film's producers (Columbia) lost heart very early, the rumor got around that it was a flop before the print arrived, the bookers booked half-heartedly, the exhibitors exhibited even less so, the press quite naturally assumed that nothing so modestly presented could be at all funny, and that was that. The best reports made it show so poorly that I never bothered with it until it was too old for review, over which I have been uneasy ever since and in expiation of which I hereby establish something like Malcolm Cowley's conscience fund for book reviewers.

As to details, Wallace Smith wrote the story, Lewis Milestone directed, and they had the longest list of comedy players I remember seeing: John Gilbert, Walter Connolly, Fred Keating, Alison Skipworth, Victor McLaglen, Helen

Vinson, Leon Errol, Walter Catlett, Donald Meek, Luis Alberni, Akim Tamiroff, Arthur Treacher—they had practically everything but the Bronx telephone directory and Lady Gregory. But in spite of its being packed with talent the film was weak in big-drawing stars—and it had a worse weakness from the point of view of popular appeal: it lacked a definite story.

In pictures there seem to have been two main types of successful comedy: one where the plot is more or less subordinate to or transcended by the performer (W. C. Fields, the Marx Brothers, Mae West, Jimmy Durante, etc.); and one where comedy interest is nominally subordinate to some other interest, either that of action (*The Thin Man*) or of sentiment (from the Capra films to such weak stuff as *Ruggles of Red Gap*). But let a producer once get off these beaten tracks, get a little satirical, or hard-boiled, or flippant with the wrong things, and out in the country they will not be amused. In fact some of a person's best friends in comedy—*Twentieth Century, Sing and Like It,* the Hecht-Lubitsch *Design for Living*—have gone out in the country and met up with the great national blank pan. It is very sad. And then along comes *The Captain Hates the Sea,* not only a departure from the safe cycles but a picture without a plot, an informal, nonhomey, so-what sort of picture. Sadder.

The picture starts with John Gilbert leaving his girl to get on a ship and clear of Hollywood, to sober up and write a novel; it ends with his coming down the gangway, still handsome and still high, to fall into the girl's car in New York. This rather delightful comment on human intentions is not enough to make a picture: the picture is made by what goes on between these terminal points—incidents, entanglements, hails and farewells—all coming somehow through the atmosphere of John Gilbert's quiet bun, hazy, mellow, unreal but not to be surprised at.

Walter Connolly as captain gets the picture off on its proper foot immediately: "I *detest* the sea," he says in exasperation to a bunch of reporters. He detests also the whole mess of gabble-gabble passengers, and if the old crate doesn't hold together for the trip he won't be surprised and it might interest them to know he won't be sorry for it. Like to see any damnfool women and children beat him into a lifeboat, he'd break them in two with his own hands—slack off on your forward lines, mister—and what is more—two-thirds ahead both engines—and what is more where is the damnfool steward. Leon Errol is the steward, and he owns a terrific bugle bird and the captain can't find out from him what's going on in his own ship, even a fire. McLaglen is aboard from a private agency, to put handcuffs on Fred Keating, who would steal your socks though politely, and whose accomplice is Helen Vinson, who literally steals McLaglen's. Alison Skipworth is always sitting at her corner table and foiling the bartender horribly by eating the lemon peel out of her horse's neck; and practically everybody is one of the boys—except Donald Meek, who rouses in the captain a lust, hidden since boyhood, to get a man with a beard leaning over his soup on one elbow, and knock the elbow out from under (his old man ate soup with a beard and it's why Walter is at sea); and the English major, who has a terrific lust to hit the bass drum in one of the most weary and delicious steamer orchestras ever seen (Jerry and Moe Howard, and Larry Fine).

The people are natural, the situations they get into proceed naturally from them and from each other, and are carried out with an ease of direction that is as simple and right as the principle of cantilever, so that everything matches with the dominant mood of good temper, gentle mockery, droll high spirits, and edge. Practically everything, that is: there is in the picture's disfavor a queer confusion that shows from time to time, and strikes a particularly jarring note in the firing-squad business, the pitiful case of a man's having married below him and going practically crazy.

Well, it is past recalling now, or at least—in the event that neighborhood exhibitors could be persuaded to revive it sometime—it has gone underground. But in support of its right to a better life I submit that, after more than a year, I can recall with affection and recite to the extreme irritation of friends entire sequences, almost by the dozen, about the captain and the steward and the bird and the whiskers, the flatfoot, the smooth gentleman, the whiskey-sodas and pretty moll.

But about comedy. I saw this one in company once with a small-town audience, once with a rather selected New York audience; and both times the audience not only laughed but laughed pretty constantly, in the right places and from the right region, which I believe is the diaphragm (cf. belly-laugh, gut-bucket, etc.). Those audiences were not fooling, they were practically in the aisles. But did the film get any word-of-mouth build-up? It patently did not, and I think I can tell you why: it had no elevation. No readings from the classics, no moral from life. In fact, nothing at all. And so the critics and plain people went away with a weak back from laughing, and feeling good—but also feeling deprecatory. And so we must conclude that in spite of a definite genius for laughter, we like the English are really ashamed of falling for anything that is nothing but fine, free, and funny, that makes you laugh and makes you feel good but does not balance an ounce of open fun with a pound of betterment. We want to eat our cake and have it certified as oatmeal too, and what I say is: out upon any such pack of mental percivals—and more particularly out upon the general run of its critics, those knaves and solemn humbugs, duly appointed certifiers by virtue of God knows what.

22 January 1936

Movies: When They Are Good

Unless the movie industry surprises everybody, including itself, *Ceiling Zero* will be one of the best pictures of 1936. In a sense this film is the kind of thing the movies do best; in another sense it is the sort of thing they seldom do at all. It has dash, vigor, the fascination of strange, deep, and meaningful devices; but it carries a sting, it has several things to say about the lives of men, without benefit of a happy ending. The story is about a group of fliers, sticking together since the war, now in the airmail business. One is already broken, feeble in the head from having flown through a tree. One is Stuart Erwin as Texas, a veteran flier, plodding, good-hearted, the comedy interest. One is the chief of the airport, Pat O'Brien. ("Get them feet moving—what are we flying, a lot of box-kites?") The fourth is James Cagney as Dizzy Davis, a brash lovable fool and crack pilot, romantic as anything, and the women can't leave him alone until, sooner or later in each case, he takes care of that matter for them.

The mere situation always has a strong and instant appeal: devil-may-care and shoulder-to-shoulder, and the life of danger we all would plunge into gladly, if we could get off our tails long enough and if it weren't so pesky dangerous. But although the early scenes—scrapes, reunions, the frictions and jollities of life at the airport—proceed lightly, with sly and witty competence and nice sentiment, there is soon indication that life is not all horseplay and kisses. Dizzy seems to have got tangled up with too many people's women, and with too many easy commitments. His friend Texas, duped into taking Dizzy's run, crashes; the Washington inspector lifts Dizzy's license for good, and he gets told off bitterly from several quarters. His friends and his flying have been his life, which now falls about his ears completely; and so he sneaks his last plane off the ground in suicide weather.

Outside of a few too-mellow lines on the life of action, none of this is wrong either as a whole or in details. The story moves along at a good clean pace, there is much snap to the lines and plenty of authentic color. Some of the scenes build up a high dramatic pressure, thanks partly to the story, partly to its background of curious instruments and procedures; but mostly to its acting and direction. There is an intricate art by which the line of feeling is kept uppermost and rising in the midst of a staccato din of commands, interjections, screams, speakers, plane-motors, tickers, sometimes as many as five or six voices going all the time, so that the crash of Erwin, coming in too low in the fog and blowing up on the wires, careening across the field on fire and smashing into the glass windows of the hangar, is a terrific bit of action. And there is a good simplicity and rightness to the last sequence—Dizzy, with the ice too thick on his wings and going into a spin, speaking a word for his chief and beloved friend, still ordering him profanely back to the field: "Don't be mad at me, baby," he says just before he hits; and O'Brien goes dully back to his routine, ordering out the crash truck, etc., listening to the monotone of the loudspeaker: "Temperature, 30 degrees, wind, etc., etc.; visibility, zero; ceiling, zero."

The dramatic high points of this story are mostly in the air and would be melodrama if it were not for their effect on those below, an effect made solid particularly by the work of Cagney and O'Brien. Cagney especially plays his best part here with fine feeling and wisdom, at last given a chance to fill out his own screen character—which is as tough and bright and endearing as life—with the other half of the story, which is the effect these irresistible happy-go-luckies invariably have on those who get left with the bag, and how, if they are true, decent chaps, it catches up with them in the end; and he does it beautifully.

But this is not all Hollywood's doing: outside of a few vivid seconds of fire, speed, and explosion, a few conventional shots of planes in the fog, fliers at the stick, people at the phone, the film is still a stage play with one main and two subsidiary sets. The fliers, the chief, the big shot, the salesman, the mechanics, together with their wives, girls, and other troubles, have to bring their lines and their crises into the control room, either personally, by radio, or by phone. It speaks very highly for the original stage play that the lack of diversity is not felt, that the whole thing was built right, constructed and tested under pressure at the start, so that it makes one of the very rare pieces to be transferred bodily to the screen as a good movie.

The Story of Louis Pasteur is a picture which holds one—with the insistence of its theme, with the dignity and competence of the title role (Paul Muni) and of many small parts and situations—but which continually disappoints with a wasting of its substance, with a transmission of the feeling that whatever has been gained, too much has been lost, that what should be vital and arresting has been made hollow and dull, that we hereby are tendered something that is bright and stagey for something out of life.

The first criticism is that the story is undramatic, that Pasteur's conflict is either against intangible, nonscreenable forces, or against the solemn beards of the academy, who are too overdrawn, dull, and fatuous for a good fight. And the second criticism is one of overdrawing in general: Pasteur is too good and meek, his wife is too patient and sugary; Donald Woods as the assistant is Donald Woods, which is to say, damn; and the decent sentiment of the family scenes is so invariable as to be tiresome.

Most of the fault, that is, seems to lie in the story and dialogue, plus the way story and dialogue were in several instances invested in weak screen characters, plus the way William Dieterle as director did little to repair this. Dieterle's genius shows in the nimble (slightly formalized) arrangement of the introductory scenes and the details of his scenic construction, which is sometimes sweeping and lovely. Where he seems to be at a loss is in the handling of people, of tempering even a bad line with some special flair for pace and modulation—so that riding in a carriage and opening the front door, announcing a miracle or saying "I am at your service, sir," all come through stiffly, with all the best intentions in the world but just that lack of illusion which makes the difference between good and moving theater (*cf.* the movie *Arrowsmith*) and your daily paper. Coming from the same company that made *Ceiling Zero* and the newer *Petrified Forest* (another beautiful transfer from stage to screen, of which more later), the Pasteur film is an apt reminder that if the movies are good, this is enough, and it doesn't matter much where they got it.

5 February 1936

Hallelujah, Bum Again

Modern Times is about the last thing they should have called the Chaplin picture, which has had one of the most amazing build-ups of interest and advance speculation on record. Its times were modern when the movies were younger and screen motion was a little faster and more jerky than life, and sequence came in 40-foot spurts, cut off by titles (two direct quotes here are "Alone and Hungry" and "Dawn"); when no one, least of all an officer of the law, could pass a day without getting a foot in the slack of his pants, when people walked into doorjambs on every dignified exit, stubbed toes everywhere on the straightway, and took most of their edibles full in the face; when tables and chairs were breakaways, comedy was whiskers, and heroes maneuvered serenely for minutes on abysses that were only too visible to the audience. It is in short a silent film, with pantomime, printed dialogue, and such sound effects as were formerly supplied by the pit band and would now be done by dubbing, except for Chaplin's song at the end. And not only that: it is a feature picture made up of several one- or two-reel shorts, proposed titles being *The Shop, The Jailbird, The Watchman, The Singing Waiter.*

Part of this old-time atmosphere can be credited to the sets. The factory layout is elaborate and stylized, but not in the modern way or with the modern vividness of light and shadow; the department store might have been Wanamaker's in its heyday; the "dance" music is a cross between Vienna and a small-town brass band, twenty years old at least; the costumes are generally previous; and as to faces and types, Chaplin has kept a lot of old friends with him, types from days when a heavy was a heavy and Chester Conklin's moustache obscured his chin (still does). Above everything, of course, is the fact that the methods of silent days built up their tradition in group management and acting—in the first, a more formal explicitness, so that crowds gather jerkily from nowhere, emphasized players move stiffly front and center, the camera does less shifting; in the second, actors tend to underline their parts heavily and with copious motion (see the irate diner, see the hoity-toity wife of the parson, see Big Bill and the rest).

Modern Times has several new angles, principally those of the factory and the occasional off-stage reports of strikes and misery (the girl's father was shot in a demonstration). But they are incidental. Even in taking René Clair's conveyor-belt idea, for example, you can almost hear Chaplin, where Clair directed a complex hubbub, saying to one of his old trusties: You drop the wrench, I kick you in the pants, you take it big, and we cut to chase, got it? It has the thread of a story: Chaplin's meeting up with the orphan girl, very wild and sweet, and their career together. For the rest it is disconnected comedy stuff: the embarrassing situation, the embroilment and chase, and the specialty number, *e.g.,* the roller skates, the completely wonderful song-and-dance bit, the Chaplin idyll of a cottage and an automatic cow, beautiful with humor and sentiment. These things and the minor business all along the way—in jails, cafeterias, with oil cans, trays, swinging doors, refractory machinery—are duplicates, they take you back.

But such matters would not call for discussion if all together they did not set up a definite mood, a disturbing sense of the quaint. Chaplin himself is not dated, never will be; he is a reservoir of humor, master of an infinite array of dodges, agile in both mind and body; he is not only a character but a complex character, with the perfect ability to make evident all the shades of his odd and charming feelings; not only a touching character, but a first-class buffoon and I guess the master of our time in dumb show. But this does not make him a first-class picture maker. He may personally surmount his period, but as director-producer he can't carry his whole show with him, and I'll take bets that if he keeps on refusing to learn any more than he learned when the movies themselves were just learning, each successive picture he makes will seem, on release, to fall short of what went before. The general reaction to this one anyway is the wonder that these primitive formulas can be so genuinely comic and endearing.

There has been a furor here and there in the press about the social content of *Modern Times,* and this could be skipped easily if Chaplin himself were not somehow confused (see his introduction to the film) over its worth as corrective comment. Well, the truth is that Chaplin is a comedian; he may start off with an idea, but almost directly he is back to type again, the happy hobo and blithe unregenerate, a little sad, a little droll. Whatever happens to him happens by virtue of his own naïve bewilderment, prankishness, absurd ineptitude, and the constant support of very surprising coincidence. He couldn't keep a job or out of jail anywhere in the world, including the Soviet Union—that is, if he is to be true to the Chaplin character.

And Chaplin is still the same jaunty wistful figure, pinning his tatters about a queer dignity of person, perpetually embarked on an elaborate fraud, transparent to the world but never very much so to himself. He brings the rites and dignities of Park Avenue to the gutters of Avenue A, and he keeps it up unsmilingly until it is time to heave the pie, to kick the props out, to mock with gestures and scuttle off, more motion than headway, all shoes, hat, stick, and chase. With him it is all a continuous performance, played with the gravity, innocence, and wonder of childhood, but with ancient wisdom in the matters of sniping cigar butts and tripping coppers into the garbage pile. He is pathetic with the unhappiness of never, never succeeding—either in crossing a hotel lobby without at least one header into the spittoon or in eating the steaks, chops, and ham and eggs that are forever in his dreams; and yet he somehow cancels this or plays it down: when the ludicrous and debasing occurs, he picks himself up with serenity and self-respect, and when it is time for heartbreaks he has only a wry face, a shrug, some indication of that fall-to-rise-again philosophy that has made hoboing and destitution such harmless fun for his own special audience, the people of America. His life on the screen is material for tragedy, ordinarily. But on the screen he is only partly a citizen of this world: he lives mostly in that unreal happy land—you see the little figure walking off down the road toward it always into the fade-out—where kicks, thumps, injustice, and nowhere to sleep are no more than a teasing and a jolly dream (Oh, with a little pang perhaps, a gentle Woollcott tear) and the stuff a paying public's cherished happy endings are made of.

19 February 1936

The Milkman Rings the Bell

Unlike Chaplin's one-man show, the new Harold Lloyd comedy (Paramount's *Milky Way*) is up-to-the-minute in construction, the work of many hands, all laid on expertly. Lloyd is the milkman who was a little slow but loved his horse, and got wrongly notorious for dropping the middleweight champion in a brawl—it almost finished the champ's manager until he got the idea of building up Lloyd as a fighter by crooked bouts, and then having the champ beat him for fair. Enter from several sides love, the reporters, the police, freaks of chance, etc.

The parts and people playing them are rich with possibilities: Adolphe Menjou as the promoter and nonstop talker, tough and dapper, an ace of a study; Veree Teasdale, who lives around with him, complete mistress of the bored, acid rib; Lionel Stander, the deadly ape, croaking murder and wearing a face that is a romping ground for mental adventures, calling up somehow the picture of a two-weeks puppy with a garden hose; and Lloyd himself, with a certain charm and candor—always as though he believed it and liked doing it—the agility of a clown and the sense not to try stealing the show.

The material is a strictly hokum proposition, but it is worked out and put across with the best use of the screen's varied resources. Take for one illustration Lloyd's proud athletic leap over the hedge, where the camera gets him coming over and lowers to the water beneath just in time for that terrific header. The idea as such is a gramper, palsied with honorable service; but like many old ideas it can't be topped when they handle it naturally, keeping it fresh and unexpected, the ludicrous in a flash. And then for more complex matters, the hot-and-heavy or one-two-three method, there is the bit after Lloyd's first knockout, with Lloyd saying a word of wonder to the folks: "You know I'd have sworn I missed him" (one); and Menjou jumping into the breach, talking fast to cover up while Lloyd, as previously coached, clears in one gay bound all the ropes but the top one, on which he gets fouled like a squab on a spit (two), Menjou still covering up at the microphone—"I tell you folks he's a great fighter and a great little kidder, just look at him now, he's"—and turning from looking at him to find they'd walked away with the mike some time back (three), and the cut. All the way through there is a fine tendency to spike it with fragments of understated business, not shoved down your throat but planted off center—and you find them for yourself.

The film works up to such a fast even pace through the whole middle section, in fact, that it tapers off at the end. Anticlimax is still anticlimax and a real dramatic ailment, not just a word thought up for intellectuals to play boogie-boogie with. The remedy here would have been to keep the end in view from the start, cut down on complications, bring up a few independent laugh-getters from the first part, and bring the end on faster. And a little doctoring on a film like this is worthwhile, because by and large it is very near the top for screen comedy. Which is to say it is not pompous, dull, or strained (*cf.* Ben Hecht's *Soak the Rich,* René Clair's *The Ghost Goes West,* Metro's *Rose Marie*); the laughs are there, and spontaneous, and with no aftertaste.

26 February 1936

Mr. Baxter and Mr. Ford

Good pictures are for once really piling up too thick to be reviewed, imagine the embarrassment of a reviewer. I am already behindhand with one first-rate film (*The Petrified Forest*), one middling good film (*Next Time We Love*), two partly good musicals (*Follow the Fleet* and *King of Burlesque*), and with *The Trail of the Lonesome Pine,* done in color and a bath of tears, but good enough and bad enough to make good target practice for a column and a half, ordinarily. But there is a picture abroad that takes precedence over these others: *The Prisoner of Shark Island,* a natural, one of the best. The story is about Dr. Samuel A. Mudd, who innocently repaired Booth's leg after the shooting of Lincoln, and was made a national scapegoat for it, sent to the Dry Tortugas for life. It is a good story for the screen, its action being direct and plentiful, and far enough removed in time and implication so that injustice can be handled straight, with no need for temporizing and prettification. It still could have been made stiff and dull—who has not seen this done? The main credit for the show, that is, goes to the various factors of its production.

In the beginning was Nunnally Johnson's script, a bit of screen writing that—although a little too unpretentious and right to come in for awards at the end of the year—will certainly stand up among the year's best. A good ring to the dialogue, a steady, smooth flow of continuity, and everywhere an unassuming assurance, maturity, native good sense. It passes over the usual snares for unwary overwriters—the comedy on the stage, Mudd's address to the court or to the Negro soldiers, Lincoln's balcony speech, verdicts, commands, the language of mutineers and court-martial boards—as though they weren't there; it has what is rarely found in the movies or on the stage, the soundness of a workmanlike book.

As far as the expense of putting this on goes, they do not seem to have spared the horses, the background being as logical and persuasive with atmosphere in the 1865 countryside as in the prison on the Dry Tortugas, in Ford's Theatre as in the doctor's home. And they apparently got the right man to work on these materials, director John Ford, whose genius shows in the management not only of the action, but of the actors in it, so that the routine parts of Ernest Whitman, John Carradine, Claude Gillingwater, Harry Carey, O. P. Heggie, and even the child Joyce Kay mean something and come to something, slip into the story with a complete absence of all the usual business of entrances, takes, scenery-chewing.

There is a guiding hand visible in the rejuvenation of such stock situations as that where the fiery Southern colonel is introduced, haranguing from the head of a table in all oratorical splendor before an audience that is revealed—the camera opening back on the fine imposing room—as the colonel's little granddaughter, barely able to reach up to the hominy grits on her plate; and in the part where the colonel's blood is at a final boil and he digs up his good sword, flourishing it tremendously as he walks out, saying it's pure Toledo and if it don't fetch what it's worth, egad, he'll run the man through.

Ford is the one who is responsible for the way the action moves from the establishment of the period to the assassination and getaway, the resetting of Booth's leg and subsequent apprehension of Mudd, the trial (there was some very clever work here, although the execution scenes might have been telescoped), Mudd's prison life and near-escape and final service during the plague. The escape sequence is among the most vivid and somber that have been made—Warner Baxter (as Mudd) loose somewhere inside the heavy sultry walls, suspicion rising, the guard being broken out, and the angle shots of Baxter climbing desperately up and over the stones toward the moat, where he is finally silhouetted clearly in the rifle sights. The oppressive hysterical atmosphere of the yellow-jack siege is felt in the audience; and the whole business of the prison is made terrible with authentic detail—stilted quick-time of the guard, the dead murderous heat and its effect on the men, the thick walls, the surf off-stage, the empty iron routine of the guard room, even the bugles sounding, the rifles locked properly in their racks. The mechanical sharks and some of the water scenes provide a slight jarring of reality; but mostly the picture is complete and sound in its illusion.

It would not, however, have been possible in its present strength without the main figure of Warner Baxter, who rises out of his former halfway pictures (or worse) into an absolutely first-class piece of acting. The story of this country doctor caught in the machinery of large matters is wide and complex and he is in the center of it—tender, furious, bitter, suffering, plain tired, whatever is needed. He carries the demands of the part with solid strength and subtlety of shading, and it should also be remembered that he is under the handicap of a dialect part here, managing it shrewdly, holding himself down to the indication of difference by certain easy but consistent verbal habits, rather than trying to ape the whole impossible range of rhythms and vowel music that such a part entails.

But too much taking to pieces may very well obscure the real effect of the assembled whole. *The Prisoner of Shark Island* is a powerful film, rarely false or slow, maintaining the relentless cumulative pressure, the logical fitting of one thing into another, until the audience is included in the movement and carried along with it in some definite emotional life that is peculiar to the art of motion pictures at its best.

King of Burlesque is about the best musical since *The Gay Divorcée,* which has never been equaled. And this is for reasons connected mostly with the story. The music is nothing special (the house-band swings out with some pretty good background stuff, though); the dancing is even less. But they handle the old synthetic situations somehow as though they believed them a little, they have Warner Baxter and they have Jack Oakie, who if given enough rope could hang everyone in the cast. Oakie is one of the fine fellows of the screen, and with such national busts around as Mr. Jolson, or Mr. Jessel, or Mr. Cantor, it is something of a pity that a man who can play a part with such good-fellowship, rough charm, and out-and-out, sure-fire comedy should be so complacently passed over by audiences who never fail, while in the theater, to be amused and obviously captivated by him.

4 March 1936

Something Attempted, Also Done

Empire-building seems to make capital stuff for motion pictures, whenever a director can keep from tripping over costumes, the unfamiliar, the absurdly epic, etc.; and more's the pity that the countries who can handle this sort of thing best are still empires themselves and therefore have to be justified. The Gaumont-British *Rhodes,* however, is a film dealing with forces pretty much as they shaped up at the time—dimly realized, inexorably felt, serving best those shrewd and hardcase spirits who guessed and rode the wind of them. Its covering up is done by natural omission and a perfunctory scattering of titles; mostly it sticks to its business—the life of Cecil Rhodes as set out in Sarah Millin's biography.

The picture is guilty of double-dealing in some of its favorable lighting of Rhodes, and when it goes into the effect of all this imperialism on the Blacks it steps around like a high-class undertaker on a plush carpet. But there is a really tragic scene where the old chief, high above going back on his word even when he finally realizes what a word can be taken to mean, knows at last that he has sold his land and people down the river. And for comment on the Englishman's sacred burden there is the old Dutchman, the fine, stolid ox, sitting there among his peaceful Boer farmers, mighty in his immobility and eloquent with monosyllables. "Murderers," he says, "there have always been thieves and murderers. But I will make no bargain with them"—and his voice seems to come up from the ground under his feet. As an "exposé" of imperialism the film would have to show the Dutchman's background as well (what after all was *he* doing there), and it would have to have a better mouthpiece than the lady novelist whom, though sympathetically drawn, you would have kicked out of the office yourself, if there had been work to do. But it is not an exposé, does not need to be. *Rhodes* stays on the surface, but this is a surface of great and stirring matters, enough to fill any one picture.

There is no special brilliance in the shaping and pacing of the thing as a movie. *Rhodes* progresses unevenly, runs through whole blocks of exposition at a standstill, shirks some duties with titles and makeshift transition shots, and ends in a ponderous fussiness (including the secondhand passions of a professional off-stage reader) where it would have been enough, and beautiful at that, simply to let the camera go up, through the dissolve on Rhodes's deathbed as used in the picture, to those high bare rocks where he is to be buried, and pan slowly into the fade-out, looking from that hill off over the land. As it is, the outdoor photography in Africa—the plains, hills, mines, and such mob effects as the trek north, the attack of the Matabele—is the best of the production values, being handled by a separate director, Geoffrey Barkas. Berthold Viertel as the main director knew what his story and his actors were about, but shows awkwardness all through, as in speakers who crop up 1, 2, 3, in turn and deliver different sections of the same sentence. And besides the sound is punk, not only as to native chants and drums, but as to effects in general—and if any shoestring Hollywood producer were told that on the big-time in England they thought they could get rifles and machine guns out of a drunken snare-drummer and someone tearing old linen at the microphone, he would die laughing.

When everything is said, the best asset of this screen story is its cast, the people who carry it out. Walter Huston is in the main part, studying the character of such a strange man as Rhodes must have been to be what he was, making it tough and human, forfeiting flash for sustained fire. As the Boer President, Oscar Homolka is the outstanding character, unhurried, regal, impossible to budge him, but nevertheless a character part—by this spare business of a pipe, a great Bible, a terrible chin-whisker, a wife bustling with coffee through the stern house, you shall know him. It is one of the best parts I've seen, but still a special part, and the sort of thing that, if it had to stand alone in the center of a picture, could not have been played that way. Huston's role has the most severe demands, requiring that a man shall grow with his troubles and victories, and grow old, and win some more, and grow old, and lose—it has large range and little relief, and to give it life without falsity is a first-class achievement. Of the smaller parts, that of Ndanisa Kumalo, doing only a bit as King Lobengula, is charming for its natural mixture of dignity, naïveté, and simple homeliness; and the rest are good troupers. It is the vivid sense of the lives of these people that bridges pictorial gaps, makes speed and fireworks unnecessary, and leaves you after the show—whatever its weaknesses as listed or overlooked here—with the feeling of something rather large attempted, something definitely done.

18 March 1936

Guest Artist

Joris Ivens is a name that is practically unknown over here, although moderately famous in Europe. It is the name of a young man who helped start an amateur film league in Holland some years ago and who has since been making independent pictures in that country and others. He arrived here recently, bringing some of his work with him. It turns out to be very good work.

Ivens started out doing technical films for a university, then began fooling around by himself. The earliest piece represented here is *Rain,* which is about nothing but a shower coming up and passing over and the sun showing again, and really lovely. It is consistent with the ability to touch just what ordinary thing it is that gives us our impression of sunlight and lassitude, sunlight with a suggestion of darkening, then a cloud and more clouds, a gusty sky and all hurrying, the darkness and first wet of rain and then the rain itself, working up to its monotonous pitch on housetops and canals and the business section, the water busy in eavestroughs, etc. And then the easing up and first clear sky, with everyone mirrored in sidewalk pools and the nickel-work of parked autos, the sun coming back on the water and the cyclists into the streets.

Well, as Ivens says, there you are, rain. There seem to be, ah, other matters. So he went on to other matters—but in a direction that might be guessed from his preoccupation, even in this lyric stretch of film, with the machinery of living, with kitchen floors and buses and people getting wet or driving the buses. I haven't space now for all of the subsequent Ivens pictures shown here (*Industrial Symphony*, made for a Dutch radio firm; *Borinage*, made in a Belgian mining town; *Song of Heroes*, made in the USSR). All the Ivens films are documentary in type; some are one-reelers, some three. His characteristics show most clearly and best in a film I like better than the others, the one called *New Earth*.

New Earth shows how they dammed the Zuyder Zee and pumped four great sections of it dry, for growing wheat—12,000 men working in two shifts for ten years. The picture deals in fascination from the start: what they would have to do and where to begin, men making great rafts of trussed saplings, floating the rafts at high tide and towing them out (three tugs in line with the tow-ropes straining in a fine pattern), anchoring them at a certain imaginary point (the sky gray, the sea gray and enormous, the smoke from the tugs drifting), then sinking them under scow-loads of rock. After that, the foundation for the dike proper, clay dredged from the sea bottom and brought by scores of lighters—everybody busy, the tugs, lighters, engineers' launches swarming around, the dredges scooping and puffing away. Tons of machinery, but always with men running it: Ivens not only gets a poetic line out of the revolving structure of cranes and mixers, he gets the men working them, tripping the bucket or heaving around at the winches—in particular one shot of a barge going out at noontime and a figure, great in pantaloons, appearing from below through the hatch and standing there with a bowl in his hands in the middle of a busy day, eating his necessary soup against the horizon.

And in the midst of this enormous bustle of each man with a job, the dike is getting base and height, rising out of the sea, being reinforced with sand, faced with rock, slowly becoming a geographical fact, with a familiar form and car tracks. You could stand and watch a job like this for weeks (12,000 men, two shifts, ten years) and what little might seem to happen would be monotonous. To make a truly moving picture of it demands imagination (what to show and how to take it, by what light at what angle, so that your personal feeling for the motion may be caught in a camera box); also experimenting and brute work; also skill in cutting. Above all, the cutting.

There is a point in this record, this nonfictional account, where by virtue of its management the tide of conflict sets so powerfully that at the final resolution the audience breaks into involuntary handclaps. It seems that, as the two ends of the dike approached the middle, the whole power of the dammed water would be thrown against the narrowing gap, tearing at the clay as fast as they could dump it, like a river in flood. In the picture you can see the lighters nosed up to that opening by their tugs, sweeping through like catboats and dumping the clay as they pass. You see finally the shovels working, tugs and lighters all around, first one shovel and then one on each side, getting a bite on their loads, swinging around (there is some beautiful play here of the two high patterns of steel framework moving against each other), dropping their sodden tons into the current, swinging back. The shovel bites in, locks, starts up and away, and you are cut to the control house with its levers and singing cable, you swing with the framework and stop short where the throttle goes down; the operator steps forward and kicks the trip, and you are cut back to the shovel, swaying and then letting go with a great slipping out and muddy splash.

The whole machine, its purpose and guiding force are made graphic in a natural flowing line; and as the work goes on the thing is stepped up so skillfully that when the last dumping of clay rises successfully above the surface and the waters separate into two calm bodies, there is a feeling in the audience, applause or no applause, of release from labor, whoo what a job, knock off now and take a blow. And as the film goes on to the next step of the work, the image is very apt: three or four men scrubbing at their hands and sloshing their knobby faces under a faucet—and the dike is built and the locks are set and here is something of a miracle, damming the ocean with sand, etc.; but here also, to come back to earth, are the common men who did the work and worked the miracle, and now call it a day like any other, and slosh their faces.

The artistry of all this—this reduction of the rambling facts of living and working to their most immediate denominator, to the shortest and finest line between the two points of a start and a finish—is so evident as to set the key of the picture, making the explicit irony and social criticism of the end only incidental. In the end, after the land is drained and wheat grown on the fertile soil and the first harvest ready, there is just no place to sell the wheat, so they burn it in piles or dump it, thousands of bushels of wheat, back into the sea. The plan was wrong, but the work was true, and it is the work that this picture is about. Like the rest of Ivens' films (being shown around by the New Film Alliance), it is more exciting than rapid fiction, and twice as beautiful.

15 April 1936

Mr. Capra Goes to Town

Frank Capra's new movie, *Mr. Deeds Goes to Town,* is every bit as good as its logical predecessor, *It Happened One Night,* possibly better. But I doubt if this will be accepted so very generally, mainly because of what may be called the growth of legend in art. *It Happened One Night* had a peculiar and interesting career. It was not so much the first thing of its kind as the best thing of its kind then made. But it opened simply as a movie and how is such a thing to be recognized at the time of release? No splurge, no spectacular press-agenting. It was rated just another comedy and quite good if you like that sort of thing. Then it began to build. People who saw it told other people, and people who saw other people who had seen it said, Didn't you just *love* the part where he, etc. And people who had truly enjoyed it but would, in the course of two normal months, have forgotten the title said, Yes and do you remember the part where, etc. It built up strongly in repeat engagements. It became a classic. And so after more than a year, with everybody keeping Capra's memory green and talking classics and all, there hastened in some really grave beards from the critical world to announce it was certainly certifiable as a classic. And so now it is a certified classic, too bad.

It is too bad because now, just when *Mr. Deeds* is ready for showing, the *Happened One Night* legend makes it difficult to remember that the story of the earlier film, as originally seen, was really so much dishwater, and leaked through here and there in spite of a beautiful film treatment. The myth and hullabaloo have overshadowed the real lesson (also found in *Mr. Deeds*) this picture might have taught, namely that it is purely foolish to consider films in terms of what their story would look like on paper. And that a movie can be made out of anything or nothing so long as it is in the hands of the best picture makers—which is to say, those with the best feeling for life and for the intricate possibilities and effects of films.

What any director can do is pretty much limited by what he is given to work on and how far he is allowed to go with it. But Capra, by luck, persistence, and (mostly) ability, has got to a place where he can keep by him his familiar in the writings of scripts (Robert Riskin) and be choosy over what he works on and with whom. He takes a plot with as few restrictions as possible (it has the necessary sentimental angle and forward motion but is fairly empty of anything else) and proceeds to fill it up with situations and characters from life—working the situations into some direct line with wonderful care both for their speed and clarity as parts and for their associative values, their cumulative effect in the whole story; working over the casting and combined performance of the best actors he can get hold of; making his own show with genius and humble labor from start to finish. His type of comedy differs from that of Clair in minor respects (with the possible exception of Lubitsch, there have been no others so far who can keep up with him); but the two have in common the same basic drollery, good spirits, and human sympathy, the same quick perception and whatever magic it is that can keep several irons in the fire all the time, and the fire blowing bright. Capra hasn't the hard universal brilliance of Clair at his best (some years ago now) and his prize effects happen in twos rather than in Clair's one-two-three formation; but he is more homey, less apt to make his sentiment slush, closer to the lives of his audience, enlisting more of their belief and sympathy.

Mr. Deeds is simply about a corn-tossel poet (Gary Cooper) who inherits millions and goes to the city, where everyone upsets his naïve faith and honest good-fellowship by ridiculing or trying to swindle him, from the directors of the opera to the girl, who starts out by playing him for a boob and ends up breaking her heart over it. Gary Cooper is not the I-swan stooge of tradition but a solid character, shrewd and not to be trifled with, sincere, gay, charming, the girls will want to muss his hair. And Jean Arthur is well set off, smart, a little husky, with good emotions in reserve. And then Lionel Stander, press-agenting his way with vowels like iron filings, and Douglas Dumbrille, the legal snake from Cedar, Cedar, Cedar and Budington. Everywhere you go in this picture there is someone who is a natural in the part—Raymond Walburn, Warren Hymer, Walter Catlett, George Bancroft, Ruth Donnelly, H. B. Warner, Gene Morgan, there is no end to them.

And everywhere the picture goes, from the endearing to the absurd, the accompanying business is carried through with perfect zip and relish. The entourage tracks down the new heir and there he is, polite but abstracted, getting a round, clear E-flat out of his tuba to help him think. Budington, he says, funny I can't think of a rhyme for Budington. They are at the station waiting for him, Lionel Stander's hair still on end from the thought of poetry and where is he now? The town band is playing, the train is coming in, and no heir—or leastwise not until the camera closes on the band and finally on the new millionaire in the middle of it, working over the stock arrangement bass part to "Auld Lang Syne" on his tuba and proud as all get out. The film has some prime examples of the spoken gag ("What's that, who said that?" the boss says, his staff filing out after a terrific dressing down; and the chap says, "Uh, I was saying you got dirty plaster") and it has prime examples of purely visual comedy—precisely timed kicks in the pants, banister glides, headers over garbage cans, etc. It has this and it has that, and I begin to realize about here that it is the kind of thing there is no use talking on about. It is a humdinger and a beauty, but—like anything so conceived and expressed in terms of motion—literally too much for words, more to be seen than heard about.

22 April 1936

More Things in Heaven and Earth . . .

Up from fairyland for consideration at this time are two breathtakers, the films *Things to Come* and *The Great Ziegfeld*. The year has already had half a dozen better and more truly founded pictures than either, but for pure splash and splurge and trade excitement, both steal the spotlight. Thanks mostly to the increasing opulence of picture companies, their rapid advance toward technical perfection, and the gradual enlargement in the receptivity of their audiences, each represents something in production that has never been seen before.

In *Things to Come,* H. G. Wells and Alexander Korda's movie staff (William Menzies directing, Georges Perinal on camera, etc.) come to a view of civilization much more sweeping than is usual in films, taking in everything except what may be called the life of man. Wells sees the coming war as a universal explosion, lasting thirty years and driving civilization back six hundred (in which he may possibly be right). He sees a group of airmen surviving as civilized, replanning the world for peace but using force if necessary. By 2036, such is the progress of science, friction in the world has ceased, cities are built under glass, hygienic and with beautiful sweep and space, leisurely reasonableness is the order, classical attire the dress (which—as acted out here by very clean blonde types, all wishing to be the first to sacrifice themselves for the ideal of interplanetary traffic—is either quite wrong or saddening to think of).

The filming of such a story is a large order in any event; and they go about it in an impressive way, with delicacy and something over a million dollars. Wherever ingenious camera work and design (except possibly in the costumes) can create the illusion, the producers overcome difficulties handsomely, making enormous machines in miniature and world chaos in fragments, getting their never-never land as solid and polished as an MGM ballroom set, and in general achieving success where you would not expect it—as in the explosion of the space gun, managed by showing first the barrel itself, standing like Rockefeller Center; then the control room and inside of the lowered shell, all shining with intricate devices; then the switch being thrown and the explosion itself, mainly felt in the clouds of gas and smoke which fill the screen, swirling off upward in the blast.

But it is the living material we must consider—the stuff, unfortunately, that good little boys, girls, and movies are made of. The first part of the story is best, and good comment too: how war is declared and the boobs rush off to it, all nations pushing on to a victorious peace through the bombing of cities, the gas and senseless killing of men by other men, until towns are brick ruins and communications are forgotten and men have no shoes and no tools for making them or anything else. In this part the inexorable tragic machine is shown by the trick-photography inserts of men and tanks and guns and the shadows of these things on different levels, marching in converging lines to the same end, best of all the shot of planes over Gibraltar, out of the cloud and into the distance, the thousands of them.

The middle section—Everytown in its early-feudal state after the war, fighting the plague under a warlord, trying vainly to get a couple of crates in the air and push on to final victory—has convincing characters and events, particularly the figure of Ralph Richardson as petty dictator. And when the extremely international and decent airmen get the world in hand, there are many arresting matters—terrific machines blasting away the hills, foundries turning out great walls of building-glass, cranes picking up practically everything, and the singing of monster dynamos everywhere. The completed version of Everytown is a great piece of fascination in itself, with stories rising endlessly in the clear air and everything white (camera note: all this glass and light make for blurred focus and a strain on the eyes), and the quiet hum of engineering devices, perfectly slick and baffling.

But when plot comes in through all this business of world construction, it makes an evident fool of itself, vague and full of wind. The new progress, it finally seems, is unconstitutional and too fast, so the villain in sweeping robes harangues the people by television, saying: Destroy the symbol of this vicious progress, smash the new space gun. So they start for the space gun, but just in time the blonde types enter the space bullet and are fired in it off toward the moon to the everlasting glory of something. And the end is a speech that goes on and on.

The picture, in fine, is supreme in its mechanical invention and camera magic; but when it goes beyond the machines of the future world (no more extreme, incidentally, than the drawings from patents in any of the popular-science magazines) to the people in it, it demonstrates that no convincing good will come of fooling around with a next world until you have some understanding of the complexities of this one, what will come of it, and in what way—no lessons to be learned playing hooky into the future. I imagine lots of people will share my interest in the unfathomable gimmicks and doodads of *Things to Come;* but I doubt if many will be either emotionally lifted or intellectually improved by its rather unrelieved prophecy (Jules Verne in celluloid) of the world as a pure-food restaurant. . . . *The Great Ziegfeld,* that other spectacle mentioned in this review, will have to wait until later: it being exploited as a two-a-day roadshow, there will be plenty of time before it gets around very generally.

29 April 1936

The Dead and the Living

The Great Ziegfeld is about how Flo the Showman started as the son of a respectable musician, barking for a muscle-man act on the World's Fair midway, how he went from a shoestring to dazzlements in the Broadway theater, and back to the shoestring, and back again to greater dazzlements, making stars and marrying women; how he got old and broke and died that way, leaving over the street a legend that is brighter than the lights. We have had romanticized biographies of show people before, but this is apart from them in scale if nothing else: three solid hours of tunes, girls, specialty numbers, and all the bustle of people and events in the lean and fat years of a national figure. The movie is fantastic, yet curiously appropriate, its atmosphere matching the topsy-turvy reality of all this blare and tinsel. Too glib for real life, it is persuasive for all that—possibly just because of that.

To take Ziegfeld as legend, as he was felt across the footlights and known to stars in ascendancy, the picture would properly be something like this, full of glamorous types, color, brash spectacularism. The only other way to do such a figure—why and how he did it, what it took from the country and what it left—would be to do a book, to be more sober and thorough and first-causey—and inevitably to lose the principal radiance identified with the name. Of one whose energies dazzled the eyes and ears of an immediate (also fleeting) moment, it would be rather barren to write a book: the truth would be truer and more precisely gauged, but to those who had known the blandishments it would be partly false, the statistics of moonshine without its magic, and who cares anyhow.

The Great Ziegfeld is full of many matters, too many for recounting and certainly too many for its own good. Even if it didn't run on forever, there is no excuse for the lag in the first part, the long-drawn-out death, the stage-spectacle material in the last half, etc. And since it does run on, everything should have been tightened—not in the tremendous job of cutting those miles of negative, but in boiling down the script, saving a line here, combining two scenes into one there.

The best acting part is that of Luise Rainer, whose Anna Held is gay, touching, and just about right, though probably not Anna Held. William Powell is a plausible Ziegfeld, dressy, flashy, mostly surface; and for solid support there are Fannie Brice, Frank Morgan, Reginald Owen, Ernest Cossart, etc. The story has nice fun and sentiment, but its setting and numbers are even more important to its effect, one bit of gorgeous flummery standing out above all: the "Pretty Girl" number, serving as a first-act curtain and also as an example of the best to be done anywhere—a revolving stage, surmounted by a great spiral staircase that sweeps up, covered with girls, as the circular curtain rises and the spiral turns, the spectacle spreading to a climax. In the end it is this general atmosphere of hysterical lavishness and aimless splendor that stands out from *The Great Ziegfeld*—the unreal made actual by our knowledge that such things *did* happen here, and that there is a like fever of aimless glitter and lavishness still in the world—people building the pyramids for a night, the Hanging Gardens for a finale, Ziegfeld's ghost having apparently gone west.

Footnote to the foregoing and supplement to a previous piece on Joris Ivens.—All we see of the three-reel film Ivens was commissioned to make by a Dutch radio factory *(Industrial Symphony)* is a reel of excerpts. Which means that we lose not only the complete conception, but also continuity; and yet it is a beautiful piece of imaginative photography, demonstrating with simple eloquence how a single camera, with some definite genius behind it, can find in the coverage of everyday facts more shining wonders than all those prodigious sets and mobs could put before the cameras of *Ziegfeld* and *Things to Come.*

At the start of *Industrial Symphony* there is an effective contrast: the massive steel forms of automatic blowers over against the new glass, bright and delicate in bubbles, taking shape, moving off down conveyor slots. Then as the mysterious processes of making and assembling a radio tube go on in the factory, the inexorable movement of these traveling belts and tireless human grotesques of machines begins to be felt as a weight bearing down on the people at their work, intent to desperation. And the thousands and thousands of parts flow or soberly pirouette along, and finally the camera swings over the lines of glassware racks, geometric, precise, finished, and beyond counting, almost an explosion of intricately refracted light.

The final sequence is where Ivens shows most clearly that base on which he can safely build whatever beauties of abstract design may suit his purpose: his highly developed feeling for the way work is shaped by and felt in those doing it. The major qualities of love, death, fear, hatred, etc., do not register in this film, having no place in it; but the major attitude of men to their work is rendered finely when we come to the glass blowers. Everything about them is brought out by the camera's shifting from the man against the background to the braced bones, the flex of muscles, the hands almost a caress on the whirling blowpipe, the facial expression and sweat of the man himself. Ivens said the other day he wouldn't think of photographing work with a crowbar until he had gone through the action himself, to find where the strain came and where a picture of it would sum up the whole movement. And you can see how this materializes in the final sequence, where is shown the dean and basso profundo of all glass blowers, puffing and moving back in an epic trance of concentration and evident anxiety, his cheeks filling out like basketballs, his eyes straining for a sign from the great glass bubble, which grows with the blowing and rounds smoothly as the pipe whirls; and finally the job is done and this hulking man looks it over, his face still carved with fierce care and effort, his body molded with sweat.

Ivens' films are beautifully photographed and joined, but documentary as they are, they are also alive with a feeling for people. Not people done in the weird realism of snapshots seen in the papers—somebody walking, running, falling in an attitude the eye never registered—they are as real and meaningful as created characters. And so his factory, with the men and machines and miracle of their industry in it, becomes fascinating and rather terrible, touched with meanings that go beyond statistics and blueprints, and even (granting you put one part of imagination with the part supplied in these fragmentary hints) beyond the books it would take to express them in concrete words.

13 May 1936

Legends from Kronstadt

Having heard from several quarters that *We Are from Kronstadt* was a great film, I directly went back to see it a second time, this time trying very hard. But while I found more things to like, all I can say is that if this is high art in films, I shouldn't like to be the boy who had to go to bat and say why.

The story is that of the Kronstadt sailors in the Russian Revolution, how they were a rebellious and unkempt bunch until their commissar led them into the proper way, how a contingent of them was practically wiped out but how the hero escaped and brought the fleet to where the Red infantry was itself about to be wiped out. The commissar died but the colors of his teaching rode high through the battle, which was won. Outside of minor business the story is as simple as this—so simple, in fact, that it becomes a series of tableaux illustrating certain phases of the Civil War in Russia. And this simplicity is the beginning of the end, for the director (Efim Dzigan) has grander pretensions: he wants to be Eisenstein and so follows the crudities of *Potemkin* without having the conscious technique—the labor of cutting, the running comment of contrasts and symbols, the camera of [Edouard] Tissé—that made such a film possible. He also wants to be Cecil B. DeMille and work in magnitudes, but he is without DeMille's material resources and patient literalness; he wants to use the humor and life-colors that *Chapayev* showed to be possible in Russian pictures—but the pressure of this is incidental rather than steady and cumulative. The end effect is confused if not fake.

The theme in any such picture is grand beyond a doubt; the line of its development here impeccable. The relations among the characters are quite sound from a human point of view and shrewdly devised to give life to what would otherwise be a diagram. Artem the sailor, a fine solid chunk of a fellow, stays in the center of the picture and develops his feud with the infantryman, his seaman's suspicion of the commissar, his roving eye for the chippie (stunning creature: I wonder if she has a phone number) who turns out to be a Party member and, what is more tragic, the wife of an infantry officer. His friend Bezprozvanny and the guitar are a good touch, both for humor and poignancy; and there are some incidental types. When these people are doing their various bits, there is nothing more fetching and lifelike in any theater (the prize line for many a day, in fact, is that spoken by Artem when he is escaping disguised as a woman, and some White Guard with four-inch mustachios tries to make him and follows him into a house—from which come first silence, then a low thud and moan, then Artem, very mad and wiping his knife: "Infantry bastard," he says spitting, and starts to walk off. He stops, scratching his head: "Hm-m," he says to himself, "and a White Guard, what is more").

Life on the ships and in camp is a meager quantity in this picture, but there is one very beautifully conceived night scene in quarters—just before the alarm the children come out and clamber around, quite innocent in wonderment and play, gazing and touching in the middle of all this weariness and hunger and the instruments of death. These things I liked, and also some of the excitement of the fight scenes, but they are subsidiary and lose their best luster by not being in the position of contributing to, and taking life from, the main line of development.

All through the picture Dzigan stands in no awe of his facts, throwing them in for what the spectacle is worth and when it is time for consequences, stepping out from under and moving off to the next set. There will be such a striking scene as that where the tank comes tremendous over the hill; and then the effect thins out into the trick it is when, as the director walks abstractedly away, we see there are no other tanks, no supporting line; just one of the most priceless pieces in the arsenal wandering lonesomely around looking for an owner.

Likewise the effect of those terrible waves of enemy troops coming down from that same hilltop thins out somewhat when, in the interests of building suspense, those inevitable waves seem to be crossing the same fifty yards for half an hour. "I wrote this scenario," to quote from the few words Vishnevsky has been prevailed on to say to the folks, "refuting many cinema traditions, blazing new trails. I came out against parlor realism, against a conventionally symbolical cinema." Well, his trail-blazing is that of one who would attempt to drive down the Bronx River Parkway and up the Post Road at the same time, landing up in something of a mess, but his realism is what gets most in your teeth by the end. One sequence will illustrate this unfortunate cross between the fish of symbolic attitudes and the flesh of everyday reactions: the place where the Whites don't shoot the captives because it would waste ammunition (logical) and then instead of using bayonets spend half a day lashing rocks to their necks and pushing them into the sea after appropriate speeches from each (applesauce); and where one captive smuggles a knife, cuts the lashings, and swims ashore and, getting his breath, decides on further rescue (right); and then carefully drops the knife and plunges in with his soggy greatcoat on (odd), dives and comes up with the commissar, with whom, plus the weight in rock which sank all the other hearties, he then swims to shore (impossible) and buries without testing for death or trying resuscitation (foolish).

But in spite of all such typical matters, the film seems to excite many, and I should attribute this largely to its origin and still unfamiliar sales ballyhoo were it not for one good mind whose enthusiasm is not induced this way. It thrills him, he says, as a legend they have been working on for years, a great myth.

Well, well. So maybe I should forget the trouper who played "The Star-Spangled Banner" and saved the act, and forget all about my grandfather, with his fierce daft eyes and brows, and the scheme that got to be so dear to his heart, in those last years, of making hens lay hymnbooks. It was all to the glory of God—and there he would be, walking out day or night, Sunday stick in one hand and in the other his private chamber pot, so as to make it a real long friendly call on the feathered friends. He was busy for years on that scheme; but I recall clearly that the old gentleman died in his bed one night, babbling about flaxpits and the living Jesus; that our hens went right on laying eggs as they always had; and that neither they nor the old gentleman, bless all their foolish hearts, had the least thing to do with the fine and complex art of moving pictures.

27 May 1936

Hollywood's Half a Loaf

The boys in Hollywood must get bewildered if they turn to the right sort of left criticism occasionally. In the day-to-day course of their business they've developed an art of screen fiction that is equaled nowhere; but the comment on this is the prevalent formula: Hollywood slickness. They learned first and learned for keeps that camera .spectacularism is more of a hindrance to a picture's motion than the mantle of art itself; but the comment here is the dark question: Ah, where is the camera of the exiled Pflugg, of Pirojok or Pissé, or of the superb Pckzy, who has eliminated motion and whose amazing study of decomposition may be seen tonight through individual stereopticons at the New Museum of Social Modernes? And so on.

The boys get their worst drubbing on the score of content—and even more so when they attempt to include some they have long been reviled for not including. When they made *Black Fury* they made it as good a strike picture as they knew how, but localized the issue and otherwise pulled teeth to the end of selling it here and abroad. So when the social-hopers got hold of this picture, which made the idea and need of strikes more understandable and real to more people than any picture ever released, they went angrily on, reducing their own principles to the final absurdity of the proposition that anything not a whole loaf is necessarily an antiloaf, or rat-biscuits.

The two sides don't get together. Movie people tend to understand things in surface terms rather than basic principles. But their command of surfaces is supreme, so that when in their best stride they show a thing, there is no need for thumbing back through Marx to find if it is safe to believe, let alone laudable: the thing exists by itself for its moment on the screen, unquestionable. Whereas the professional content-sifters have all the correct principles in their little black bag, but small comprehension of how a story is set in motion or of its possible effect on audiences.

MGM's picture *Fury* is a powerful and documented piece of fiction about a lynching for half its length, and for the remaining half a desperate attempt to make love, lynching, and the Hays office come out even. But I doubt if those who see it will carry the whitewash part of it so long in their minds as the straight action of the introduction and middle. The boy (in the person of Spencer Tracy a homely human boy, a little old and clumsy and hulking) sees his girl off on the train and goes back to his two kid brothers, whom he is trying to keep out of dangerous mischief in their unemployment, and to the routine of his job where he is scraping pennies toward his marriage. The three chaps get a gas station and make it go; the boy buys a cheap car; and finally he starts out to get his girl, after months and years with his dull pain of wanting her.

But a small-town force picks him up for a kidnaper: a mistaken identity that will clear up in a minute—but doesn't clear up. And then the mob begins to work and we get about the finest exposition of ferment in motion that has ever been done. The gossips, the troublemakers, the stout citizens. Gatherings in bars, easy talk, the dynamite of outraged womanhood and other standard American (*i.e.,* easy and dithering) ideals, and the spark to set it off. And then the crowds gathering—only a few active ones, the rest coming to gawp and joining in—the mounting hysteria and march on the jail, and suddenly the jailhouse, the object, giving pause. The sheriff with his lean figure and white hair standing out on the steps, trying weak reason and invective, invoking state troops and rallying his scared deputies. And in the middle of this stupid growing fury, with such fine submental types as Bruce Cabot in the foreground, this picture has the true creative genius of including little things not germane to the concept but, once you see them, the spit and image of life itself—as witness the kid hanging on to one of the vantage points attainable by kids, and during a lull in the crowd's roar giving out a fair imitation of Dave Fleischer's theme line: "I'm Popeye the sailor man (*wheat wheat*)." It goes beyond the thick noise and action of mob fury as a concept, to the macabre sidelights—the kids, the hurled tomato, the women's taunts—that make it not only more likely but more terrible.

Anyway, failing to get him, they fire the jail, and his cell window is framed, small and high and desperate, when his girl finally arrives to witness what they are doing to him with fire and smoke and mob frenzy—only they had to dynamite the burning jail to cover up their guilt before the troops arrived, blasting the place open and allowing him to make a secret getaway, burning his side off. Then we go on to the trial, which is tense, especially in the introduction of newsreel action and stop-action shots of riot, but marred by a nance of a district attorney and by confusing plot trends. By now they are trying to change a lynching picture into a love and personal-vengeance story.

Even in its powerful moments this is not the story of a typical lynching—there is no race angle, there is a dimly implied class angle, there is no multilation, and the man escapes. And then minor discrepancies: the sheriff has a strange sense of justice and, insulted and stoned by his townspeople, stands like Jesus Christ with a rifle, I mean he won't shoot; but after being slugged and thrown out of his own jail he perjures himself to conceal the identity of even those rabble-leaders already shown to be public enemies and thorns in his side. The Governor is justice incarnate (the evil genius is some unnamed political boss); and that strike-riot squad sometimes referred to as the National Guard is shown here as a national guard. But even if these facts cannot be considered canceled by such incidental edges as the comment on the newsreel, on the radio announcer, the editorial bit about how we are always hanging our own community troubles on foreigners, etc., they have bearing only on how typical and agitationally useful the story is, not how true it is to the strange facts and contradictions that may be called either the exceptions to historical rule, or the actual stuff it is made from.

For those who already have all the dope on lynchings, *Fury* will have nothing to say, and will not say all of that; for those whose business it is, it will prove meaty matter for angry discussion. But, if you will be patient with me in a crusading moment, who in God's name is to be educated around here anyway? That handful of liberals and last-gaspers who have known all the answers these many years? The people to get to are those who don't even know the questions yet, and on these little will be lost by a movie company's trying to eat its cake and sell it to the chains too, so long as on the one subject they treat, however obliquely, terror is made true and the truth terrible.

10 June 1936

Wings over Nothing

Secret Agent is a Gaumont-British film on the old formula of love and spies and wartime. But it is the work of Alfred Hitchcock—which makes all the difference. The rapid development of this genius in the form—his eternal inventive sense, wit and good taste and flair for swift, open movement—is already making some big names look rather lower-case. Mainly against him so far is his material (easier to concentrate on good effects if you don't have to make your story come out even). In *The Man Who Knew Too Much* the story about the people shown was so unlikely and maudlin as to spoil the picture for me—even if there hadn't been an amateurishness about much of the direction that can only be explained now by crediting Hitchcock with the rare quality of developing his strong points to the exclusion of all else. *The 39 Steps* went far beyond this: it was a delightful film, really a miracle of speed and light. But its story was hokum, you had to accept that at the start and keep on accepting.

And now in *Secret Agent* there are still a lot of holes—the hero's squeamishness, unlikely in wartime; the general reluctance of deadly enemies to kill anybody who would interfere with plot development; the British War Office's cueing in feminine interest by sending some silly society girl out to ball up deadly missions and practically lose the war. But in general there is a lot of sounder stuff—still on the surface, but present at least and with motivations. Madeleine Carroll makes fine capital of her first breakdown and subsequent near-hysteria. And John Gielgud is right for the character of one of those backbones of empire, brave and decent enough to get into a horrible spot of conflicting loyalties (Dash it, man, and all that).

Best of all is Peter Lorre's study of the assassin as artist. As satyr, humorist, and lethal snake, he shows, here as always, a complete feeling for the real juice of situations and the best way of distilling this through voice, carriage, motion. He is one of the true characters of the theater, having mastered loose oddities and disfigurements until the total is a style, childlike, beautiful, unfathomably wicked, always hinting at things it would not be good to know.

His style is most happily luminous in the intense focus and supple motion of movie cameras, for the keynote of any scene can be made visual through him. In close-ups, it is through the subtle shifts of eyes, scalp, mouth lines, the intricate relations of head to shoulders and shoulders to body. In medium-shots of groups, it is through his entire motion as a sort of supreme punctuation mark and underlineation. A harmless statement is thrown off in a low voice, and it is felt like the cut of a razor in Lorre, immediately in motion—the eyes in his head and the head on his shoulders and that breathless caged walk raising a period to double exclamation points. Or the wrong question is asked, and the whole figure freezes, dead stop, and then the eventual flowering of false warmth, the ice within it.

And Alfred Hitchcock is the kind of director who can make the finest use of such character effects, neither exploiting nor restricting. The vital imagination behind almost every detail shows in the fleet economy of the opening sequence: the false funeral, the Chief, the mission. It seems hardly three minutes before everything is known, and the scene gathers itself into premonition merely through the wide, dark flight of stairs being seen from that angle, with the men at the top. Then the scream, the horrified servant girl running up, then back to the door and Secret Agent Peter Lorre in hot and sly pursuit—a perfect entrance.

All the usual expository sediment of a play, that is, runs off in solution like brook water here; and presently we are in Switzerland, spy meets girl-spy with some fetching and varnished byplay, and here is Lorre again, barking like a spaniel, breathless with the devastation brought about in him by sight of anything wearing pants that don't show, and already established as a major and mysterious force. And then the absolutely stunning sequence in the church. The organist being their agent, they come in, light the candle signal, wait and wait, and there is no answer but the sustained organ chord of minor thirds, which swells and becomes tremendous as they creep up on the organist, to find him strangled across his keys. There follows the flight to the belfry and that beautiful shot looking down from there—the space and dwarfed perspective, the twisted form sprawled on the stones and the pulling of the bell rope.

After this comes one of the finest suspense foundations I know of: their singling out the wrong man and hoaxing him up the mountain to his certain death. The hard intention is set off against the humor on the surface, the act against the result. The mountain, Gielgud's revulsion and quitting of the expedition to watch through a telescope, the house back home with the wife complacent in her German conversation class but anxious over the husband's dog, who worries the door and whines—and the visual bridge between these in Madeleine Carroll. And finally the three scenes merge in one as the act is framed in the telescope, a terrible moment of space and falling and cloud-shadows over the snow, the dog's howl rising over the picture above and bringing the camera back to the quiet, terrified home scene below.

There is no space for going into the manner in which superimposed images, throwbacks in character, blended contrasts and camera positions and well-paced cutting, constantly heighten effects. Or for any analysis of just how Hitchcock and his camera can load the simple entry of a building with suspense and terror. But something should be said of the use of sound, which is not equaled anywhere else: the music in the church, the howl of the dog, the disembodied voice in the rhythm of the train wheels (he mustn't, he mustn't, he mustn't), the deafening factory and steeple-bell noises, etc. Then there is the growing discord of the peasant-dance scene, after the murder, where the voices go from sweet to wild and the accompaniment becomes the metallic scream of coins whirling in bowls.

In all matters of treatment, the director of this film hardly has a rival. And whatever may be said for the boys who start out with a conviction and philosophical good-will large enough to cancel out all the unimaginative heaviness of their execution, I still think Hitchcock should be rated among the best if only for what he can teach them. In a latter-day fashion, he is a pioneer of the movie, increasing the range of its plasticity and power: he can take something that is practically nothing and make it seem like music and give it wings.

24 June 1936

All the World Loves a Winnah

There is nothing on the screen this week, there is nothing anywhere this week, that for implications and sheer electric excitement can come up to the pictures of the Joe Louis-Max Schmeling fight, run off at the Yankee Stadium in New York, the night of 19 June as a foregone conclusion and box-office flop. People had stayed away in droves—from what turned out to be one of the fights of the century. But in any event it is here now in pictures. They had cameras well placed, both on a special elevated stand and just below the ring looking up; they had sound equipment to catch the crowd's roar outside in the dark and the abrupt, pregnant explosion of the major blows inside this unnatural square of light; they got all of it and have edited the several prints so that both the flow of action and its crucial points are developed on the screen, until tension is heavy in the audience and the illusion of attending the actual thing is complete.

The picture tells a more accurate story than could be got from even the first row of ringside seats: the camera eye is not subject to human excitement and fluctuations (if a handler leaps up in imprecation or horror it does not stray off), and what is more it is a collection of eyes seeing several sides, from right or left, close or far, capable through editing of registering the most significant.

In the picture you can see the biding restraint and driving power of arms and shoulders, the bodies weaving, surging, braced. You can see in perfect focus the deadly precision of Joe Louis, weighing 198 pounds and moving like 140, also his one-two-three routine—a left to the body followed through, by some powerful flex of shoulder, into a left hook to the head, and the right coming in through the opening, bam. You can see in slow motion every step and blow following the first blow to stagger this fighting turret, the long-range salvo against the bones forward of his left ear which sent the Brown Bomber scuttling off backward in queer little half-circles on his heels; and Schmeling moving up on him in a fury of attack and Louis melting under those blows like butter, seeking cover where there was none, blown wide open with a left and seeming in the slow motion to hang there for seconds as the right came in like a train of cars, bouncing him on the canvas.

In the camera record you can see the several low blows struck by Louis subsequently, and along with the worst of them the somehow touching picture of his remorse and mute reassurance to Max (one doesn't talk through a clenched mouthpiece) by throwing arms over his shoulders with futile pats of the glove. And you can see the kill as clear as crystal—Louis coming out wavering but still to be reckoned with as usual, his being driven back around the ring, knocked silly with the final direct hit, toddling like a baby under the pelting gloves, and then the last completely safe powerhouse sending him halfway around and down like a brick chimney.

These pictures of the fight must be among the best ever made; they are a night with the gladiators, a round trip to Mars, they are practically everything. And yet there is missing from their flat black-and-white motion across the screen something vital—whatever it took to make the fight a fight and the air charged with uncertainty, everybody there with his nerves strung like a harp. Without the crowds and smoke and sharp cries growing through the preliminaries, the atmosphere becoming heavy as the fighters climb through the ropes in their bathrobes, the color and rough tangibility and spirit of the place, the recorded action becomes more like a waxworks, however true to life—a little ghoulish, like the acting out of a murder.

For one thing, the picture has been cut down so subtly that you would not know it if there were not the fact of its running time (33 minutes as against almost 40 of actual fighting, let alone introductions, throwbacks in slow motion, credit titles, and shots taken between gongs); and in cutting they have somehow deleted the suspense we felt in the stadium, those interminable seconds of the first few minutes, where lightning might strike with the next move and few moves were made, the fighters feeling out and testing and blocking, many people yelling and the question silent in the air, When will it come?

For another thing, we know the outcome now; we are here only to see the bloody flux of its execution. The Brown Bomber having, as a matter of record, been practically grounded in the fourth round, we have no terror of him now. Joe Louis, as seen after the event, appears merely as a stubborn, doomed hulk, going through the motions and postponing the end, pitiful or ludicrous as the case may be.

Well it wasn't that way with us in the Stadium, where the idea of Joe Louis as the invincible torpedo died hard. We had been told. This Negro heavyweight is a sensation—young, purposeful, on the up-grade, backing weight with speed, and speed with dynamite in both shoulders (speed and weight without that special slugger's leverage in the muscles of the shoulder and back are no good), and rounding it all off with an unflustered command of all the blows and their combinations and the angles from which they may be swung.

And what is more, Louis is a killer, always has been a killer, sullen and cruelly efficient and heavy of eye. He doesn't grin, slap backs; doesn't have to.

Whereas Max Schmeling is thirty now, pretty old for a fighter. He has been The Champ but is champ no longer, and was never very glorious. What has he got? A right, a clumsy technique, and lead in his pants. So the sportswriters have a lot of fun with him. Well, well, one more day before they lay Maxie in his pine box. Der Big Max will come in like a lion and go out like a light they say, and laugh. Spare a laugh for poor old Max, with one doubtful right arm and one foot in the grave.

And so it took quite a long time for the idea to sink in that the newspaper boys must have been talking about somebody else. And still the tension held, for even after the seventh round the fight was no certainty, there were no wise guys at the time who jumped up and announced that the fight was in the bag. That man was still worth watching, and when he flicked a shoulder you could see Schmeling's head go back, hard. Louis was instinctively game and a living danger so long as the feet held up under him, and even in the last round managed to throw in a long right that would have mowed the whole working-press section down like a row of wooden soldiers. But not Max, he couldn't get Max down, and so as the people gradually caught on that Louis might be the Brown Bomber but old Max was outfighting and outlasting and gradually knocking the heart out of him, they began to shift, until Joe Louis as the peepul's favorite was lost sight of, during the last two or three rounds, by all except the Negroes in the audience, who were silent and seemed dazed.

The people weren't very decent about this fight. You wonder what they go for. You go yourself and are nervous as a chicken, more scared of Joe Louis than anybody who faced him in the ring. You watch the fight and don't know if it's Friday evening or San Francisco. And if you have a taste for imagination you imagine how the world of these two has shrunk to a right glove and a left glove and a tough weaving head above them, the yelling night air of the place falling away to a stillness of inhuman exertion and inner counsel (watch his right, watch his right, back a little and shift, watch, watch . . . just over the cheekbone, just below the ribs), to an almost visual chart of moves to make or block, and then the false move and the rain of blows, the giddy lights and whirling universe and gloves as big as boxcars (get clear, get clear now, stay up, clinch for cover and stay up). And then the gradual shift to blackness, a nightmare of circling and blocking and striking out automatically, the body no longer under control as such, the remote movements of arms and legs coming as a dim surprise but as of no moment, the iron gloves in front and a painful brief rest in the seconds' corner with acid restoratives and rubs and slaps and out again. And then a heavy jar (get back, get away out, stay off) and then the big guns and a fall through space, thousands of faces through the ropes, a convulsion (*three, four, five*—the count, get up, knees up—*seven, eight*—knees up, try, move, get up) and the knees giving like jelly and the floor coming up and the body gone into it, nothing but distant noises, lights, and rest with a bad throbbing.

But do people feel it this way, is there some such feeling for the tragedy of a man's being pounded groggy and the senses practically blown out of his body, some kind of awe or pity or something? It must be there in some, but it is certainly not vocal. Max Schmeling hasn't a chance, so they come in yelling for Joe Louis (here and there a rebel voice going counter to the crowd); then in the theater they know Louis was beaten raw, and so come in yelling for Max (slug him, Maxie, oh, it's murder, oh, slug him). And for that pitiful figure of a man wobbling around out of his senses with the head being blasted off his shoulders, for that proud two hundred pounds of fighting power and skill, tottering and fumbling and shooting its weak lefts at the moon, there is no more compassion evident than shows itself in the laughter to see him bounce grotesquely on the floorboards, the hoots for his rubber knees, the final anxious clapping and rooting for the kill.

Of course the boys are fighters in a prize ring, it's their job, they are paid for it: no use getting soft on the subject. But all this turning of coats to be on the winning side, all this mirth and high spirits in the face of a man's ambition and body being broken under spotlights—this is callous, knavish, the presence of it in this theater disheartening, somehow obscene. It would seem that the main part of our boasted interest in boxing as an art and sport is simply a desire to see blood let and tissue bruised. And as to another one of our pet national qualities, may we not put it that we are always cheering for the underdog just so long as we can find an underdog who is a ten-to-one shot to come home ahead and on top—the winnah.

8 July 1936

They, the People

The film *Anthony Adverse* being on the edge of release to an impatient public, there are facts that might be of interest. For example, the trouble they must have had making it: the picture is a historical-dramatical-spectacular-swashbuckler, which means all the business of movie rights and treatments and stars and costumes, headaches for the research department and the devil to pay for special-effects and set-building help. And the final print makes the course in two hours, nineteen minutes. (It seems strangely like more. In the heat wave it seems like the Seven Lean Years in person.) Then there is the matter of the film as entertainment.

Anthony Adverse is just about at the center of that low-pressure area reserved to big pictures from long books. No life, no flow of story. It tries to dramatize as many of the book's episodes as possible; but in the dramatizing there is shown no relish or conviction. Only a retentive memory for all the old clothes of show business: the gauze shots of lovers' meetings, signals and sweet partings in the bazoom of nature; saint-days in Italy and the very droll Italians (including Luis Alberni), the court of France, the pitching of villains over the cliff, the quaint steeple bells, the babe in the casket, the house of this-a, the honor of that-a. All exhumed, held up to sight, and (as part of the job) put brusquely back in mothballs almost before the cameras have stopped rolling—for all the world as though the simple holding aloft of such relics were enough by itself. With characters like printed signs (FAITHFUL RETAINER, SCHEMING STEPMOTHER, SIMPLE PRIEST), and printed signs and titles all over the place to illuminate the "action," it isn't, as I may have suggested, much of a picture. There is a nice fresh bit in the Cuban sequence, where Akim Tamiroff carries his stock part with an air, bringing everything to life with a few good lines well driven down. Otherwise it is so stagey, skimpy in care, invention, plausibility that you wonder why anyone should want to make it.

You wonder, that is, right up to the point where it suddenly becomes clear that just this empty razzle-dazzle is what is needed. What *Anthony Adverse* may be considered from this or that impeccable point of view falls rather sharply away before the thought of how it is going down with the people of the nation, and what meanings there are to read from this. People *want* to see the funny Italian mans, the darkness of Africa, youth triumphant and love in bloom, titled bitchery, ups, downs, swords in a tavern, ride Harry ride, and the damsel is mine sirrah. It doesn't matter whether these things are worked into the best movie in the world or into what we have here. The producers here aren't onto their jobs by half; but they know their public, they know that better than most of the wise heads who will tell us just what a public *ought* to want.

There is too much talk about what we are going to do about public taste, and how we could improve it if the movies wouldn't debase it. Public taste is simply there, like an appetite for pie, and doesn't really change after all. And at times one gets a glimpse of it like the moon through clouds, riding along as remote, fixed, and unimpugnable as that, neither to be scandalized nor boasted about and certainly not to be claimed as a special pet and puppy by any of the ideologies in any of the major leagues. Showmen, who have to live by it rather than by talking about it, know what it looks like: the people either come or they stay away.

People want a little laugh, a little strangeness, and are quite partial to the idea of riding down the Native Tribes fiercely by day and, of an evening, conversing airily with desirable members of both sexes in select plush atmospheres they personally will never live to breathe; they want their hearts in their throats, tears in their eyes, to be excited, dazzled, flattered, full of power by proxy and abandoning themselves to the great love that has either gone out of their lives or never was there. Boy meets girl—did anybody think that was only a gag? And in this popular desire for a good lift easily bought there is not much finicky choosing: if a thing is there, it is there; and so long as its clothes have the cut of the day's fashion the subject is closed.

So we can go on talking about deep art and high drama. Meanwhile *Anthony Adverse* goes out to the public displaying certain sure-fire elements in their crudest forms; and one look ought to convince anyone that given the necessary shifts in scene, angle, time, he could repeat them for people and make a success of it till doomsday. And if it is lousy art and an insult to the masses, who says so or thinks so but a few handfuls of us, standing around and shouting this or that, forgiving ourselves today the mistakes we made yesterday and pretending to find in these shifts from one hot spot to another the motion of change in the public taste itself? The boy met the girl and the girl met the boy right back, and whether we like this or not we can hardly legislate, to call it right or wrong, because 100,000,000 Americans can't very well be either.

There's no doubt the people will go for fine things. But their immutable demands must be understood and met first; the thing must be put over on them, and that is the job, the true test of good faith and skill—that, not empty words. Look at the case of the Resettlement Administration's film about the Great Dustbowl, *The Plow That Broke the Plains*. It was a grand subject and the treatment had good ideas and scattered brilliance. But the film was definitely ticketed for the experimental-amateur audience, which is numerically lean pickings. Yet when the big distributors turned it down there were charges and yelling: the people were denied something which was good for them and for which, what is more, they were crying out. But were they? Was the picture really *made* as their oyster? Those who exhibit to the people saw at once it had no exploitation angle, to pull them in off the sidewalks; it had no real punch once you'd got them in by other means; and it was a three-reeler, *i.e.*, of a length that is the showman's bane. Nevertheless Arthur Mayer (an independent exhibitor— which means he can show what he chooses but must choose what the chains don't want) sneaked the film into his New York Rialto Theatre program, to catch the audience reaction anyway—and rejected it when his audience went to sleep. Then some critic came out saying the film wasn't shown because no one *dared*. So Mr. Mayer, still short of product and liking a bit of a fight on principle, got *The Plow* back and bolstered it up with the ready-made ballyhoo ("See the picture no one DARED show"). He got a small audience of the curious, had a little fun losing a little money, and detected no sinister pressure, before, during, or after. Subsequently the film (which had been available right along) was booked by at least two small New York exhibitors who worked the "no-one-dared" angle (plus a certain snob-appeal) for what could be got out of it.

The point is that whether or not there are ogres abroad in the land, this film could never be the test case of it, not having what it takes. And we might put a little time into studying why not and how to correct this—if in fuming about the popular good we are indeed sincere at all. If not, we can I suppose go right on proving irrefutably how the public still cries piteously for the bread of beauty and truth, and is tossed instead a million-dollar Hollywood bone.

5 August 1936

Pretty as a Picture

Mary of Scotland owes a good part of its success in the movie version to Katharine Hepburn, as a personality and moving force. A good deal is also owed its production, direction, screen treatment, etc.—but since the anti-Hepburn leaguers are going to yell murder at the whole business anyway, we might as well dispose of such complaints as are justifiable at the outset. It is Maxwell Anderson's stage play, which means that it will have some good dramatic flash, no clear direction, and a lot of what I shall laughingly call high poetry. Preparing it for the screen, Dudley Nichols tightened up the script, broadened out the action, and (bully boy) heaved Mr. Anderson's iambics in the ashcan. Even so, it is clear that in following history they muff their climax, and that in working to keep it climactic and fast (also clean) they muff their history. The result is a picture that is always in between, or among, something, succeeding more by chance than by plan.

In the large it must be regarded as the work of John Ford, who is partial to underlighting (art, no doubt) and to a lush overscoring of music; who has always had one wooden foot, which he puts forward here in the English sequences. These are unconvincing and weakest in the character of Elizabeth, in creating which it is forgotten that royalty may be hollow and ordinary anywhere but those places (such as the stage) where there is no royalty until it is established—where illusion must substitute for coronation, that is. There are several points at which Mr. Ford's conception shows as a mere striving for effect, not worked into the film's motion at all. And the picture is overboard in length—made painfully so by the simple-narrative pedestrianism of its last half-hour, where events are walked through as though they were rooms in a museum, and closing time at that.

So much for these things—which amount to little more than the copybook exercises of criticism. It is more difficult, and more essential, to give an account of the picture's success, to discover where the heart and virtue of it lie. *Mary of Scotland* is mainly good as superior and handsome melodrama, I think; or call it the triumph of histrionics over history—which in this case serves only as a romantic storehouse from which may be requisitioned the necessary matters of state, love, action, what not. Yet there is something in this borrowing from history that is stronger than melodrama. There is the knowledge or at least belief—the faint but sure excitement tugging insistently—that these people had their time in the world, coupling and swarming and busy with envious plans, their needs and actions large before themselves and men, their disturbances elevated (by chance or sheer magnitude) into a matter of record, into something to roll back the stones of the tomb with. And while accounting for the trick of this romantic distortion is simple enough, making effective use of it never is, because the Heroic Time of past events has its revenges. It is about as difficult (if not so desirable) to make a thing seem what it wasn't as to make it appear what it was, for without the semblance of life—never mind whose, when, where—in the present of the theater, everything will be fakery, there will be no mood of belief and participation established in the audience. And thanks to its business of kilts and castles and stout insolence, thanks to the people expressing it, this is a picture that borrows the glamorous costumes of history without seriously sidestepping the real need to provide, out of its own resources, the frame and flesh to wear them on.

The actual story is more fast than deep. Plots, alarms, the gathering of the clans, and a girl just back from France, with graces and an Italian secretary, to keep the throne of Scotland against the great lords there—all damned villains naturally. Daggers, Knox's hellfire, the English ambassador, Darnley dead, Riccio dead, and the ride on horseback to Bothwell's black castle. And above everything—the accumulating incidents and their settings against the huge rooms, council tables, flights of stairs, and (in particular) one stunning fireplace—there is the galvanic effect of Bothwell's bagpipes, as seen swinging into the square at his back or off with him into exile, and as heard rising on the sound-track in the measured defiance and pride of their wild sad music. They are a beautiful touch, they half-make the picture, and even after it has gone to sleep in England their brief ghostly echo in the air is enough to put the life and meaning back in it for a while.

Fredric March is surprising and fine, but the topmost influence in humanizing all these deeds and speeches is Katharine Hepburn. In her best moments (and this is one of her best) Miss Hepburn has and projects over to her audience a high measure of spirit—both in the meaning of essence and in the meaning of vitality, mortal spark, and force. We may stand off and scrutinize and come at length to the conclusion that this is not stage creation in the accustomed manner of ladies who have developed baritone voices and rolling r's and many interesting ways of plunging a rubber poignard into their bosoms, all with that special majesty which can blow a brace of Alexandrines up into two cubic minutes by the clock. We can say that Miss Hepburn is acting Miss Hepburn, too—and God knows how such a venerable pillar of platitude is to be cracked. But we can hardly fail to see that there is something else here, still inwardly untouched; that this screen is made bright and deep for us with the life of a character, it does not matter whose so long as it is not that of an actress with an entrance.

For when the spotlights and scenic effects have faded, there still remains the fact that for all her digressions into mannerism and poor type parts as of the past, for all her naïve reliance on her own resources and befuddled trying, this girl, with the curious wide mouth and eyes and flesh tight over her facial bones, is an artist in our theater by virtue of combining personal strength and fire with the grace of giving those out to the people. Her work is not in mimicry or in a sedulous building of many parts, but it is creative in itself, a sort of bright emanation; and to say it does not go beyond this is about as helpful as saying that music is music and only music, therefore it may not be served up hot for breakfast.

In any event the magic works in *Mary of Scotland*. Produced generally with an open hand and much sense and taste, the picture still builds itself about a central figure, and is not let down when the figure turns out to be real and exciting not as Mary Tudor but only as Miss Hepburn. After all, the field of past and present world drama should be big enough to hold the special talents of both these girls.

19 August 1936

Young Love, etc.

On *Romeo and Juliet* in the screen version I can only report that if you like the play as it stands and do not require something far and indefinable and somehow beyond, you will like it; if not, not. The picture is done well, but seems little more than that—and may no more be regarded as a commission of nuisance on the precincts of Shakespeare than it may be hailed as Hollywood's admission ticket to the rare pasturelands of art itself. (Shakespeare having sustained worse soilments, movies having known higher pastures in their own right.)

Leaving production values till later and taking the play as the thing, what would the story look like if it had been written last summer for production in the fall? How quick the criticism, how clear the analysis as you would read about it in the proper places. Love as between two young people and against the obstacle of their deep family feud (old stuff but dramatically vital, having both the motive power and necessary element of conflict implicit in it—what is more, there is a chance for hinting at themes of larger amplitudes: invocations to the stars, the quality of mercy, the workers' state, or whatever else is current). But the love story isn't very well worked out—from within the characters and their situation, that is—because the chief dramatic instrument is not a motivation but a device, the ruse of a potion that will create the appearance of death, thus permitting escape and clearing the slate of both human and dramatic needs (this was known to the Greeks but is still effective, because the potion is the little brother of death himself, lending awe all around).

These matters are at the bottom of it, but there are others, especially in the beginning. There are good characters for the purposes of humor, armed turbulence, loyalty and disloyalty, and for the forward passes incidental to the action. And there is the shrewd employment of pageantry—the great families and the Duke in the square, the masque of the Capulets, etc.—to hold the eye while the plot machinery is set up and in motion. And though once we arrive at the main objective of the potion sequence these matters fall away, like so many tugs as the ship straightens on her course, they have served well. There is also good support by incident and coincidence—coincidence particularly and throughout, because without the chance failure of one messenger, the chance success of another, the rash expedition of the young man at the tomb, nothing would have come of it in the end: the lovers would either have been miserably married or spanked and parted again, Juliet becoming a lady poet, I like to fancy, Romeo signing up, say, in the navy (do him good, too).

But this begins to get over into the fact that the conventions acceptable as simple truth to one age are the hokum of another. Our stage has young lovers as brash and silly as Shakespeare's, but not in the same way, their foolishness being more guarded, their sighs and avowals less opulent. They are called Dick Powell or Jean Muir or something, and that is different. Love is still treated as a convention, but the convention has been brought considerably nearer to life, and for the most part we are spared the embarrassment of watching our Dick Powells die in blank verse, their agonies being little ones. I should say that the incidental people here (the true Shakespeare genius in character showing through) aren't enough to change the basic form, which seems hardly more than a gorgeous valentine—overlarge to the point of boredom at that.

These are rather mathematical considerations, and take no account of the play's mood—hard to feel now. And they leave out the poetry, which is at the heart of it, still vibrant after plot trappings have raveled and faded, and no harder to feel than the heritage of sunlight, for no one who can speak the words of our language with relish may fail at it. A little rich for our blood perhaps, and certainly (in a landscape of gray little poets, biting off important thoughts with a thin sound of effort and champing) a present discouragement. That time was simply an easier time for poetry, in which stars were near and familiar, and the ocean a wild brave thing to conjure with, and morning just walked in on them over the dew of hilltops; in which great matters could be made into such little words, and the little words so gallant; and there was nothing amiss if small conceits were blown up till a biological necessity like sleep became the death of the day's life, a weaver at the sleeve of care, a balm, a scarf, and all such things in color, set in rash bold enamel or inlay, made to leap, ring, and tumble before the eyes in those great strutting periods or slight traceries, as of the breath on windowpanes. But enough of that. We are too wise now to be so simple again; such poetry is a bit too carelessly rapturous for our uses, and the attempt to recapture it on the stage seems to emphasize this, not alter it. Whatever devices the actor brings into play to reconcile the common feeling expressed with the uncommon quality of the expression, the fact still remains that through whole pages of *Romeo and Juliet* the character is no more than a peg to hang fine poetry on: if he can turn the words finely, well and good, but for us he has stepped out of character to declaim; and if he is a mere loudspeaker, then so much the worse.

So *Romeo and Juliet* must be accepted (and will be widely) as the framing of an old picture rather than the execution of a new one. But the framing has been done with admirable taste and earnest care. Shakespeare has been so studied and held in awe that where exigency demands extra music, the producers go to *Twelfth Night* for a song, and where the action of one scene requires more explanation they have taken a speech to fit the purpose from another. In casting they have got as good a group of small-part players as could be demanded: C. Aubrey Smith as the most solidly believable of all; Edna May Oliver as a good Nurse, but occasionally as an old warhorse smelling the sawdust; also Reginald Denny, Basil Rathbone, Andy Devine, etc. As to the leads, Norma Shearer is rather unappetizingly made up, but neither bad nor good and (surprisingly enough) usually content with just being in there trying; Leslie Howard has grace, intelligence, and a flair for lines but the sophomorics of Romeo are too much for him, and there are times when that sensitive horse's face of his, wrapped in these disguises, must lead to unfortunate giggles. But as Mercutio, John Barrymore is the real study. I hardly know what to say about it, but am sure there will never be seen on the boards so much scenery-chewing and rubber-face trickery until the day they put *Lear* into the Billy Minsky houses.

2 September 1936

Odets Takes a Holiday

It is quite sad about *The General Died at Dawn*—not so much for what is there as for what should have been there, and isn't. It was directed by Lewis Milestone from a script written by no less than Clifford Odets. And while I never could join the hallelujah chorus over Mr. Odets as the new gift to world drama, I did feel he had brains and talent; I did suspect that having bought him as a name Hollywood might be awed into giving him latitude in the exercise of these endowments; and I did know that Gary Cooper could be relied on for a fine part, that Madeleine Carroll could be a honey, that one is rarely let down by such troupers as Akim Tamiroff (really a star here), Dudley Digges, William Frawley, Porter Hall, J. M. Kerrigan, etc. And Lewis Milestone of course, from *All Quiet* to *The Captain Hates the Sea,* has been right up with the top directors here. I simply figured these people plus the routine competence of Hollywood itself would be just the balance wheel to gear all this promise to some actual performance; that we could be assured of a tidy job in the first place and might even expect the splendid addition of such sharp points of truth as are rarely driven home to audiences so universal as those of pictures.

But no matter for that now. What seems to have happened is that Mr. Odets was given a free hand, and then instead of using it to whip a weak story into shape, spent his time writing in dramatic fireworks. Care was given the production, which has glitter and a bang-bang sort of interest, many good clear strokes of character and incident, and a fairly high content of wise and salty dialogue (partly because the actors are able to put over what would otherwise remain Charlie Chanese; partly because of bold conception and nice quirks, like Chang's relish of the word "etcetera"). But so far as the plot goes—as a matter of plain fact the plot doesn't go anywhere but to pieces, like a cigar-box Eiffel Tower in a wind. And so you have an embarrassing mixture of the hastiest melodrama with the gravest of sentiments, Mr. Odets having stuffed his lines with a kind of ready-made and surface reference to important matters that seems even more spurious now that he hasn't got his gang with him.

This is the story of the American O'Hara, smuggling gold in the cause of the people of China; and of how he was betrayed by personal weakness into the hands of Chang, a dictator with a black heart who needed the gold to buy arms with and had the best of it up to the last minute, when he was stabbed by accident and tricked into ordering the self-annihilation of his whole crew, letting the main characters go free. In performance it is better than I am able to say, with a high pitch of interest and many bright surfaces to catch the eye of human sympathy. Fact is, I saw it through twice with enjoyment. Nevertheless, there is a mounting sense (especially in retrospect) of good things attempted in bad faith and taste, like a meat-tea in a charnel house, the Lord's Prayer under the barn.

I realize it is much too easy to sit back and say what might have been done; but the truth is that something *should* have. Maybe the general could have been allowed to triumph anyway, leaving O'Hara with his life and the girl but the heavy conscience of his self-defeat, strong only in the prophecy that this same power that has broken the two of them as it has all the millions before, is still doomed; because even in this failure there is implied something new, something attempted and in the bare attempt an omen of forces which are too large and deep for personal weakness and gusts of chance. Since there is a symbolic (effective, too) prelude to the picture, maybe there could have been introduced some fade-out like the tremendous finale to *Storm over Asia,* which had no pat speeches, no pretty allusions, but only a great wind gathering over the land, carrying with it first grass and leaves, then sticks, clods, roofs, and finally rolling up the advancing regiments and mounted chiefs, with the men scuttling or sprawled on the ground, the horses riderless, and all blacking out in that great scouring blast over Asia—or over the world.

But we shouldn't even need to be epic about it, so long as the story were somehow given a leg of meaning to stand on. I should be less confident in suggesting that there were several possible major operations that might have done this, if there were less evidence that even in minor details of the story as it stands, precious little thought has been given truth and plausibility. The first sequence goes off all right, though with too much reliance on talk; and the second is very effective, what with dark action, whispers, the partial lighting of the billiard room, Pete's cough, etc. But on the train the trouble begins. Speeches for the sake of speeches. Fireworks for the same reason. And in the interview with Chang you are made uncomfortable with the growing conviction that people simply don't do that, there is no need for it, or time for it, or room for it within the characters. Then (leaving that awful end out altogether) on to Shanghai with Judy, Wu, Pete, Fats, and Brighton, all tangling in one place, and then O'Hara and then Chang, everybody coming into the same room with a loaded gun until we are in a mood for more—come on, now, where are the Marx Brothers, where is Man Mountain Dean?

But I like to think of another story about another brigand general in China, who had to take an American girl into his safekeeping (the story had opened with neat irony on the mission where she had just arrived as a bride). Conventional enough, for the general fell in love; the cost to him of undermining the girl's smugness and glib mission standards proved just what his life was worth; and it closed on the renegade cynic and adviser saying that if there *were* some queer Chinese place where such a man went, why he guessed when *his* time came . . . and the girl saying she would too, yes, Oh she would. But in all it proved up as good metal with a damning edge, having rather more to do with life and folks and rather less with death, dawn, destiny, and similar poetics. Just for the sake of the record, the number-one story about China was done as a picture and some years ago and in Hollywood at that, almost without modern plumbing and without benefit of the Significant Word, by Frank Capra, whose picture was called *The Bitter Tea of General Yen.*

16 September 1936

They Are a Funny Race

In *La Kermesse Héroïque* the French have sent us a charming costume comedy and a good film. One hardly expected it. Over there they speak French nicely, which no doubt gives them quite an edge, but for some time now they haven't seemed very bright about making pictures—always excepting René Clair. They have employed fine solid actors and put difficult, un-Hollywood stories into production, but out of the last two years I can't recall much beyond *Crime et Châtiment*, which had true (if uneven) power and dramatic tone, and *La Maternelle*, which was clumsy and foolish as a movie but beautiful for its camera study of child life. This new Jacques Feyder picture is an entirely different matter, a mixture of gay absurdity and shrewd comment, selecting its own pitch and holding it—comedy, as you might say, self-contained. It is never so fast and furious as our best comedies, but it has less of that centrifugal tendency to go flying to pieces any minute which comes of too much speeding up, as by additional gags and specialty numbers. Its qualities are all of one piece; it is almost a comfortable thing.

More than by anything else, it is probably held together by its period and the settings that go into establishing the feeling of this. I haven't much of an eye for anachronisms, so I can only say that the seventeenth-century background seemed reasonably impeccable. But accuracy is a mathematical virtue, and there is a proper mood and natural air to the life here, lovely and quaint in a sort of kidding way, that is literally beyond physics. Not only in the solidity of the hundred seemingly careless details but in the large exteriors, the occasional camera sweep over the flat, thrifty husbandry of the landscape; not only in the wary burghers hiding firearms in loaves of bread at the ovens but in the whole conception of the good chaplain and priest of the Inquisition ("And what damned traffic will you be up to with the prose of this heretic?" he asks terribly as the dwarf piles bound volumes of Erasmus on the chair to bring him to the table's edge; and climbing down later, the dwarf: "*Hm, que ce sale Erasmus m'a brisé le cul!* "). The costumes are really the thing through, merciless reproductions and always looking not only as though they had been lived in (as I think somebody has already said) but when need arises as though they hadn't been changed for at least forty-eight hours (and when the butcher is jogged awake in the early morning it is something you can almost smell).

The action covers some twenty hours in the bustling tidy life of the town of Boom in Flanders, where the burgomaster and aldermen were surely as splendid, fat, and stuffy as mayors and aldermen get to be, and naturally married. It was the day of a special carnival (*la Kermesse*); but all it took was a hell-for-leather messenger to say the Spanish duke was on his way through with a squad of drums and a few pikes, and the fine merchants were practically under the bed, leaving the women in charge, what fun. The men had planned to fake the death of the burgomaster, all of them mourning him under the bed, thus saving the town from pillage and rape. But the women, having their own sense of honor, went out to meet the duke with their own plans and best clothes, giving him the key to the town and making clear that if he and his lads didn't see what they wanted they should ask for it. So the town was saved from pillage all right.

There are many other matters, such as the inconsequential romance of the burgomaster's daughter and the town artist, but no need of going on with that. And while the soldiers of Spain were no pretty joke in the Dutch countries of 1616, the dark, brawling packs of them, the story has nothing to do with history and the Treaty of Westphalia: time and setting are no more than the use of dim distance to rob facts of responsibility and actions of consequences, so that everything will be good harmless fun. Its purpose and outcome are farcical, but it is hardly a farce by treatment—more genuine and simply human. The burghers are extravagantly pompous and unequal to occasions, but the main study is that of Françoise Rosay as the burgomaster's wife, quite excellent and true. Wife and mother and busy mistress over the ramifications of household, the equal of any necessary husband, the fierce guardian of her growing girls; moving through the house with shrugs, tart speech, and impulsive maternity—so he loves my pretty, eh, now go wipe your nose and no nonsense. And then when the duke comes she is just the perfect tremulous ninny of second girlhood, cutting out the town beauties like a veteran and the next minute sighing archly for life in Venice—ah! how Venice calls to her, with its leaning tower and all. . . .

Louis Jouvet's priest is one of the most perfect solemn and risible characters I remember, thought out and carried through, in every line of bearing and spoken or unspoken dialogue, with true and unique style—very hard to put a finger on, much less describe: Buster Keaton, shall we say, infinitely projected into depths of philosophy, benevolence, inviolable and holy composure.

The comedy is not one of continuous bright dialogue and it hasn't the wonderful cumulative slapstick of René Clair (the touches of the crashing bed canopy, the proud lady's pratfall, the headers down staircases, are good but not hilarious or in any way magic): it is rather a comedy of main characters in a single situation. It is all conceived and carried out very much like the part of the burgomaster, which is a fine study in how to get the ridiculous out of observed traits and human giveaways—burlesque, perhaps, but using a slapstick of the spirit. There is nothing in the picture that will have audiences actually in the aisles, but there is an open good-will, a sort of invitation to share, which gets people feeling mellow and feeling that these are matters which might happen to everybody, all very droll, genial, and common, with the enchantment (necessary though imperceptible) of one remove.

All of which reminds me that we should not overlook several Hollywood films of the last few months: *We Went to College, Yours for the Asking* (though with George-on-a Raft), *Sing, Baby, Sing, Rhythm on the Range,* and *My Man*

Godfrey. These comedies were in old forms, without too much distinction, yet pretty good fun and in places brilliant—*My Man Godfrey* being the best to come East since *Mr. Deeds*.

14 October 1936

Huck Finn in Hell's Kitchen

The Devil Is a Sissy is a picture about kids, and a fine reassurance to those of us who like to think all is not authentic childhood that says Da. There is a lot to it in the way of idea, execution, insight, and genuine warmth; and there is also a certain break with convention. We have always shown so little understanding of or desire to know the child's strange world, and such an anthropomorphic determination that it shall be nothing but our own world in cute miniature, that picture makers have naturally taken the easier way of keeping a Shirley Temple always moving around for us in her exquisite goldfish bowl, while such actual children as those of *The Innocent Voyage* stay where they belong, safe from the aroused mothers of the nation. The tradition of infancy is almost as bad a stereotype as the vaudeville Sandy McTavish.

And then too the fact is that a good story of childhood is difficult to make in dramatic form. It is easy to start it and set up a believable conflict, but what are you going to do for an end? Childhood is only a way-station, admitting no lasting achievement and none of the finality that provides satisfaction in drama. And the hopes, aims, and fearsome adventures of this period cancel out before the fact that the one eternal consequence of childhood—known in the audience, impossible to escape it—is that of its growing up into something else. Suppose the lad does become a policeman or neighborhood hotshot, what then? This may sound like the quibble of pure theory, but you will not be able to think of a production of this nature that didn't dodge the issue one way or another. The good films from abroad (*Mädchen, Poil de Carotte,* etc.) worked the combination of a psychopathic case and an attempted suicide. Others have followed the idea behind all the Eagle Patrol and Dare or Rover Boys series, namely that of making the lads so many junior grownups, with responsibilities, mature motives, the capacity to win the war or save the city (the Soviet *Broken Shoes* picture, for example, was merely the theme of the revolution worked out in diapers; and *The Road to Life* very little more in the end than Louisa May Alcott on a collective farm). The most common way out dramatically is that of letting the boys and girls be boys and girls, and relying for the plot proper on the older people with whom they have to do. To be added to these is a certain hybrid, especially prominent in this country, a mixture of child-as-adult and child's-influence-on-adult, which gets particularly in the hair. Here are the poor little tots, trying so obviously not to be their age; here opposite them are our patient veterans of stage and screen, inwardly fuming and outwardly Peter Rabbit.

I am sorry for the long delay in getting to the point, but some statement of the problem is necessary in speaking of *The Devil Is a Sissy,* simply because the story and treatment here go a long way toward solving it. Kids in New York, pretty tough kids and too low for any kind of social register, so they make their own. The well-brought-up English percival, whose wish to be one of the gang shapes the story, moves to the neighborhood at the time Gig Stevens' father is going to the chair, and there is that day at school and that night when nobody can sleep, Buck standing with Gig under the streetlight snapping his knuckles and nothing else to say, except in apologizing for his own blunderbuss of a father: "The old man, he. . . . Wull he means all right." This part, in the authentic schoolrooms, flats, and streets, was done with what struck me as straightforward and absolutely unpretentious beauty. And shrewdness too, Gig's sudden brief shift from awe and bereavement to bragging next morning was very shrewd: It took them seven jolts to burn him, jeez, seven jolts.

The story goes on, sometimes regulation but progressing naturally and well, with the kids very serious and wise about hopping trucks and ducking coppers, little percival getting the usual razz but working out of it by sheer determination. They let him come to the hangout, and his progress is illustrated in the very neat scene where the boys just walk past the Greek's as innocent as you could ask and come up a block later with everything but the peanut roaster. They pinch spare tires too, and are well on their way to a life of crime before the moral element enters. They are caught in a second-story job and brought into children's court and then God save us all if the judge isn't just a regular fellow, soaping them up with a Y.M.C.A. fairy-tale about how it takes a *real* guy to go straight and the devil is really a sissy after all.

Head and shoulders above anything of its kind so far, the film now begins to slide downhill on its need for ethics. The boys blackball Reggy because while his little honor-bright play in court saved them from reform school, their iron law says that he ratted; and when he tries to prevent them (getting up out of a sickbed) from running away to escape probation, they push him in the water. There is a climax in their capture by gangsters, their getaway thanks to percival's palaver, and the predictable finish. The last third of the picture is partly saved by the good foundation already laid down, partly by touches of action and character—particularly in the knife-edge given to the part of Gene Lockhart as the Legionnaire father.

It is hard to say what the public will take but there is certainly a chance that on this picture they would have taken a logical conclusion. If people will be satisfied with the purely implicit morality of *Public Enemy,* there is a chance this picture could have been made to stop where *Public Enemy* starts, letting its boys go on from little jobs to bigger, letting it end, say, on their break out of reform school and hard-bitten assurance that they would never get caught in any such short-pants game again, closing on the good fun of their cemented threesome (say they've hooked onto a fruit truck, the three apprentice public enemies bumping along toward the fade-out with their faces screwed up eating green apples), their doom as firmly set upon them as it was on Gig's father.

And to suggest another ending for *The Devil Is a Sissy* is not just to make a hollow noise, for if there was ever an image of the boy's life as boys live it, this is it. It has several good people, especially Mickey Rooney, Jackie Cooper, Gene Lockhart, and Freddie Bartholomew; but it is the more special work of Rowland Brown, who did the story and the best part of the direction. In spite of the structural faults already suggested, the picture in its good parts is as sweet and clear as Tom Sawyer's whistle, and I'll go bond that the exact like of it, nudging us so intimately with the thought that we were young once, has not been seen in any art or form.

21 October 1936

Musical Note

Whether we will ever be able to put music in a picture and still have any picture left remains a question, but Hollywood is getting a little quicker with answers and the true solution may come someday. I'm afraid that *The Gay Desperado* is stiff and slow and wears pretty thin. But it has the right idea—the comic-opera idea with its face lifted, brought near enough to life so that it is not merely making fun but poking it, at the intolerable solemnities and at itself a little.

The picture opens with the gunplay and stunted speech of the underworld (shots, fast cars, the death-dealers saying "So you won't talk, eh?" to the prisoner in the back seat) so seriously that the audience isn't sure its leg is being pulled until the camera moves back to show all this as passing across the screen of a Mexican neighborhood house, where Leo Carrillo and his trusty bandit lads are taking it all in along with the rest of the audience, and admiring greatly. Very pretty, Leo thinks. Iss how he, Leo, should operating it. The movie works up to a free-for-all fight, getting more open in its takeoff (the same toughies are still saying "So you won't talk, eh? " to the same prisoner in the back seat, who is now shown, however, with a gag in his mouth) until someone tells Leo to pipe down, starting a free-for-all in the audience. And they are tearing the place to pieces before the manager can throw in the travelogue, something about Mexico the Beautiful, and a singer comes to stand by the screen, raising a dominant tenor voice in one of the songs that are sung to the guitars of that country. The singer is Nino Martini and Leo the Lionhearted proves just a sissy about music. So the day is saved and (incidentally) a legitimate musical has got under way without reference to the Metropolitan.

The story of *The Gay Desperado* from this point is the story of how Leo took Nino off with him and got him a radio debut at the point of his bandit rifles and, still under the American gangster influence, went through with a snatch of the American girl, but was brought to realize that the tradition of the best Mexican bandit families was still good enough when it became evident that Nino and the girl had fallen in love, thereby making it essential that they be released for a happy and legal married life.

The movie version of it is the work of Wallace Smith (he did both book and screenplay of *The Captain Hates the Sea*) and has a lot of fine ideas: the stick-up of the broadcasting studio; the refreshing foolishness of the lovemaking scene where Nino and the girl fire ovenware all over the place; Mischa Auer as the sour-pan Indian henchman whose mute attendance and serene dignity (in his filthy blanket or riding a Ford mudguard) act as the final critical acid on these newfangled alloys. And the ending is a good effect, with Nino singing in full voice as the boys ride off in a smother of dust and beautiful horseflesh against the sky.

But while some of the show is fetching, the ideas mostly miss fire and the spell, as a whole and as upon audiences, is fitful and unsure. Nino Martini is little more than a voice, of course. I liked his regulation opera-tenor parts and was grateful for the variation when these were relieved by native music; but there is a certain wild drive and swing and heat of the blood to music reaching us from Spain via Mexico that he cannot be expected to imitate or be praised for trying. And in general there seems to be lacking the kind of direction necessary to make this material plausible or in any way smash.

Mr. Rouben Mamoulian's finished show favors effects over effectiveness and cardboard over character. The girl's fiancé, apart from being a pest by type, is nothing more than a few hasty lines; Harold Huber, usually a very good type, is miscast as the Leo Carrillo of *Viva Villa;* Leo Carrillo himself is more sketchy and unconvincing than I recall seeing him; and anybody who gives Ida Lupino this much rope deserves the consequences. The show cries out for more care, in handling actors and in planning situations; it seems the right sort of thing but is definitely under the wrong auspices. And I should be more reluctant to hang this on Mr. Mamoulian if it weren't for his performance in movies so far. He is no doubt an artist at something, but one picture after another shows him as having no flair for the medium, so that among all active film makers he stands apart, definitely in the company of those intellectual types who are always standing on the outside looking elsewhere, who can talk art right out of the movies into cinematographics as quick as look at you, and wouldn't know a good picture if somebody came along with one and set it off under them like a bonfire.

It's a relief to turn to Paramount's *Big Broadcast of 1937,* which does not have the Archbishop of Canterbury (Paramount talent-scouts: there's a joker here somewhere, better skip it) but gets along quite well with what it has. Jack Benny as a radio official. Martha (Bazoomba) Raye as a scat singer. Bob (Bazooka) Burns as the perennial puncher without his hoss—also on occasion as a wanderer in the waistland, for one of the prime gags of the show comes when Bob has got a holt of Gracie Allen and appears to be chewing her neck and she is of course screaming for George Burns, George, George, and when he shows up, the rescuing husband taking his sweet time, her relief is so vocal and George, she says, George hold his hat. So Burns and Allen are there as program sponsors of the Platt Golfball Hour; some new girl as a singer; Ray Milland as the agent and boy friend. And Leopold Stokowski. And Benny Goodman (also responsible for a magnificent orchestra but feeling no need for a plastic laying on of hands before it). And Gene Krupa, riding along above the band on the most terrific set of drums that has ever been captured for the cameras—the high spot of the show for many of us. There is also a sumptuous rumba numba and in addition, a spin around the New York night spots (Leon and Eddie's, the Onyx Club, and those) brings in snatches of additional talent. Hail, hail, et cetera.

The picture is really just a glorified vaudeville program, but while it has been done before it has never been done so well. The radio angle gives it a chance for a lot of good-natured burlesque on air personalities and practices; and Jack Benny manages pretty well at holding together all the tangents of personal appearances, two-line gags, three-minute blackouts, etc. It isn't a comedy and it isn't a musical, but it has a lot of laughs, the best in several types of music, and I don't know where in the world you will see anything like it. After something like this, the deluge or something.

28 October 1936

Hail but Dead End

Having gone up to see *The Thin Man* once again before Metro called it in to clear the way for the sequel, I can report that in spite of a tattered print this is still an ace picture, beautifully timed and executed, shrewdly invested in character, and with its conflict, meanings, and sentiments seeming to have been photographed in a bowl of light, so easy and lucid is all its motion. But the reason for looking it up now is that in the two and a half years since its release this picture has been playing around almost steadily, has somehow been more in the public eye than other films just as good, and has become a myth.

So I am afraid that when Metro comes along with its new *After the Thin Man,* figuring that you can take a list of the same key names, dial them out like a telephone number, and have immortality on the wire, people are going to be disappointed. Not only because there is no formula by which a true natural can be duplicated, but because *The Thin Man* itself has already passed out of flawed reality into the awe and perfection of legend.

But before they put it in mothballs for good, a few remarks on this picture might be read into the record. In the first place, it is the best of its type but the type has limitations. I have just read the book for the first time and find that Albert Hackett and Frances Goodrich did a wonderful job of reshaping the story, softening it up considerably but humanizing it even more, giving a local habitation, etc.—in fact, their treatment, with its inserts of gaiety and underlineation of dramatic points, definitely overshadows the original source. Nevertheless they had to deal with the problem of all detective novels: the need at the end to unravel for the audience all the strands of plot they have been weaving together with such care for the audience's mystification all along. And so there is a banquet scene in which all the motives and the culprit have to be revealed, and in a hurry, to the inevitable detriment of plausible human values and straight logic. It should go without saying that if so many emotional lives are to arrive at a simultaneous crisis believably, the whole story must lead up to such a climax, not around and away from it.

But while it is also true that stories depending for success on a surprise twist at the end must forfeit, when the end is already known, the long-term values of a second reading (thus daisies and reviewers of murder-mysteries won't tell), *The Thin Man* is still good, seen for the second or third time. It is not only a handsome piece of craftsmanship, it has appeal and a cocky good humor. Recall Miss Loy's grand entrance, Christmas morning on the air-rifle range, the life and doings of Asta the terrier, and that expansive party, packed with types and droll situations and lines—*e.g.*, the conference in the bathroom ("That's all right, we're only chatting"), William Powell saying why nonsense he used to bounce her on his knee and the lush following him around with happy hope, "Which one, can I touch it?" And the predominant sentiment, being the tanned leather of an equable married life rather than the friskier calf of boy-chases-girl, was a fine and refreshing change.

Yet from being tender and being gay the film was never permitted to go soft or forget that it was a pretty tough case, with murders and stool pigeons, the law working its victims over and Edward Brophy giving off that classic address: "That'd be very smart. . . . Me that a police captain's been in a hospital three weeks on account we had an argument. The boys would *like* me to come in and ask 'em questions. Yuh. They'd like it right down to the end of their blackjacks." Add the fearful visit to Wynant's shop, Wynant with his hawk face rising in the elevator, and his shadow, as the Thin Man, projecting all across the picture. So there was the drama and the fun too, one being the flesh, the other the hard necessary bone, neither conflicting. All in all it was a miracle of coordinated talents—writing, casting, acting, W. S. Van Dyke's direction and the staff men under him, on cameras and in the recording and cutting rooms, who assisted in catching the spirit of every scene, from cocktails and jazz pianos to gunfire.

It was a miracle but also a dead end: it can hardly be bettered and there is no constructive use in imitating it. In the way of light pictures, the best body of work so far (outside of Chaplin and Capra and such unclassifiables as *Sing and Like It, The Milky Way*) is the Paramount comedy cycle. I mean the MacMurray-Colbert-Lombard type of pictures, which hit the top two years ago in Wesley Ruggles's *Gilded Lily.* The line has since gone to seed—*Hands across the Table* (next best), *The Bride Comes Home, The Princess Comes Across,* etc.—but is potentially good stock and surely worth more deliberate care than something which has reached its limit.

Libeled Lady is Metro's best and latest entry in this field, a frothy thing like all the rest, with touches of feeling, little stagnation, and considerable laughter. The plot is one of the chestnuts of romance: William Powell and Myrna Loy are really meant for each other but are slower in finding it out than the audience, because he is the fixer for a metropolitan paper, trying to frame her into dropping a libel suit that runs to millions. Spencer Tracy is the managing editor, Walter Connolly is the millionaire father, Jean Harlow is the bride who never quite gets married, a little stormier than her part but none the less doing valiantly on the barricades, or should it be breastworks?

The situations step right along, first with fireworks between Powell and Tracy, next between Powell and Loy, and finally among all five principals. There is a tendency to work out one incident at a time for its own sake, but everything hangs together nicely and we all leave the theater in a fine humor, feeling that newspapermen and rich daughters may be pretty tough nuts, but love is the thing that will crack them—and if the same is not demonstrable by facts, who cares? Also everybody is telling everybody else, Did you get the part where he was saying, Why, don't you worry about *him,* he's just like my brother, and Jean Harlow came back at him, Maybe so, but he's not *my* brother; and what was this she said to the taxi driver when he told her I can go faster lady but the cab can't, and a dozen others—the snapper-answer method here prevailing over sustained flights of dialogue. It is too long for its story, holding off with needless complications and then resolving too glibly; and it is a bit mean to some of its characters. But it moves and sparkles, has some good-natured swipes at things, and may be remembered with some affection. Given the genius spent on *The Thin Man* it might still be no more stunning; but given more it should be better and—because it runs in a straighter channel to start with—true comedy.

25 November 1936

Laughton of the Movies

The vote for best screen citizen must certainly go at times to Charles Laughton; without him there is no knowing what would have happened to Alexander Korda's new version of Rembrandt. For *Rembrandt* as a picture is massive rather than neat on its feet, being heavy of motion and Old Testament in accent. But with Laughton standing up under it in the make-up of his several ages, dominant in his constant mobility and command of lines, filling in the written part with his own character and conception of character, there is no doubt that the picture is good, at times pretty grand.

Outside of Gertrude Lawrence (a fine example of divination and strong style), Elsa Lanchester, and the beggar, the support is that degree of adequate which escapes particular notice. And outside of certain necessary considerations, the production angle never stands out as what makes the film good. The interior sets are solid and have a good air, and while some of the outdoors has that fixed, flat, backdrop feeling, there is an appropriate swimming of things in clear space and enough of the tidy quaint atmosphere of another time and place to keep this from being disturbing. (Partly because Georges Perinal was at the camera, no doubt, finding beauty all along the way in a bridge, a kitchen corner, an angled roof, windows.)

The main points of attraction are Laughton and the idea of Rembrandt. Once someone is found who will make the character credible and big, much has been done to support the story with meaning and excitement. I can't pretend to legislate on what was or was not in the private life of the painter, but certainly a likely and satisfying figure is built up here—granting the inevitable distortion both of the theatrical précis and of the man's being made purer than life, less jealous, wrong, selfish. The story takes Rembrandt just as he is losing Saskia, and leaves him in the final stages. Its emphasis is divided between his experience of the delights and buffets of the world, and the study of a man gifted above and driven beyond his fellows and still needing their love and respect sorely.

The story serves its purpose, but beyond that there is a reliance on and reading of the Hebrew poets that gives a strange air of fitting majesty in places. And here is where Laughton goes beyond carriage, make-up, expression. He has a beautiful sense for reading poetry, rolling out these great deep rhythms of the Old Testament as fine as ever was heard. He is learned in all the devices of voice and attack—in particular he is good at floating a period by starting it with a full resonant beat, so that the rest carries along after it with the solemnity and ponderous sustained rolling of the night freight—but he goes farther than devices: he comes to poetry in the right way. That is, he comes with the true appreciation for the subtle taste of its words and with a wide reverence for its dignity, neither to deny its frank inflections nor to vulgarize its complexities of pitch and stress with some recitation in singsong with gestures. No apology, no emendation as by actor's business. The emotion is there, but it is felt in terms of reserves not called upon, central and under control. And so he can apply his method—long bold phrases, their internal monotony and fall heightening the variety of pitch among them, the overtones blending with the whole—and make the old words live with simple belief and fall into music that is usually heard only in the mind. "And it came to pass, when men began to multiply on the face of the earth, and daughters were born unto them, That the sons of God saw the daughters of men that they were fair. . . ."

But this is no mere exercise. The poetry is a part of the character and part of the story, through the initial architecture. In Laughton's first long speech (going on mightily about women) there is evidence enough that in the writing Karl Zuckmayer did wisely in forsaking ad-libbed high points for scriptural quotation and paraphrase. But the stuff has been quarried and used so well that there could have been nothing more appropriate for Rembrandt's moments of triumph, despair, exhortation, or prophecy than his measure from the Psalms, his parables and story of Saul and reading from the great Bible at his father's table, finally, his old voice rising great through the laughter of the young: "I have seen all the works that are done under the sun; and, behold, all is vanity and vexation of spirit" (and the picture fades on that loose massive face, wise in the mirror of another self-portraiture, and the words fading) "Vanity of vanities, all. . . ."

Establishing valid moments in a life, these periods give it continuity and a meaning. Laughton starts as the young idol, flown with the insolence and wine of success; losing his wife and his public he hears the first mutterings and confronts them with grandeur and insolence still; he becomes more alone and bitter with purpose, strikes up with his neat housekeeper but cannot follow her pattern of economic respectability; he becomes more hard and reckless in the pride of his art and goes home, but that simple life cannot be recaptured and he leaves in just one more humiliation and defeat; returning to the city, always older and more wise, he falls in love with a servant girl and lives with her, his great house gone, in an Indian summer of their poverty and love and her failing health. There is little after her death but the years which pass over and the growing carelessness of destitution. The last phase may have a bit too much of twinkle and senility—but when the merrymakers find that this genial old cadge is Rembrandt van Rijn and start back, perhaps with the name already ringing awe in their careless ears, he thanks them for their wine with a very human sweetness, standing with true dignity in his rags, his face flabby from age and full living and winking after the girls, but still suggesting a final anchorage of the spirit in the wisdom of the cynic: "While the sun, or the light, or the moon, or the stars be not darkened, nor the clouds return after the rain. . . ."

Whatever brevity and abruptness are imposed on this by the writing, facts, production, there remains the fact that Charles Laughton and Scripture and the latitude given both have rounded it out, so that we have some idea of how the rough busy world might look to such a queer type as a great Dutch painter, and see the mortal weaknesses tied up with a driving, immortal talent.

The Yellow Cruise (Fifty-fifth Street Playhouse in New York) is ninety-two minutes of the pictures taken on the great Citroën expedition from Syria over the Himalayas and North China to Peking. Poorly edited but an amazing thing—not only for the long perils of the trek itself, but for the rich documentary stuff on unknown people, their country, customs, and practically impossible life.

16 December 1936

1937

From *Black Legion* to *The Night Mail*

The Truth in Fiction

Black Legion takes a stand against the hooded terrorism and senseless boogie-boogie of the organization it deals with. It just about stops with the specific, of course, not going into the many uses of such instruments, into their origin, backing, place in history. But I must be excused from the game of basing a whole review on what isn't there, because of a certain queer idea I have, namely, that even half a loaf on the national stomach is at least nourishment taken in, and as such worth fifty pood of pie in some ideological sky.

The conflict here starts with rivalries for promotion in a machine shop, and mounts as Humphrey Bogart's anger and disappointment are played on by the boys: he learns that he is an American (a studious Pole got "his" job), that there are others, that something ought to be done, etc. So he joins the boys—a chap from the shop, a druggist, many other types. There is the business of initiation hocus-pocus, a night raid to chase the Pole out of town, more raids, the growing neighborhood suspicion and Bogart's attempt to get clear of the whole business, the raid on his good friend Ed who had learned too much through trying to help him, his apprehension for the murder of Ed—and finally the trial, where threats against his wife and child make him cover up for the Legion until he sees that the defense is such as to kill his wife with shame anyway, and breaks through to denounce the Legion men (rather too conveniently in the courtroom). The story ends on a harangue in favor of democracy by the judge and sentence of life for all concerned, with the picture fading on the wife as she watches her husband file out for his long lesson with the boys.

On the screen we see a typical group of people, their background and responses; outside of one short sequence (a Legion head is revealed as boosting the idea for what he can make out of selling the members hoods and guns) the general pattern of violence and injustice shows only by implication. Any awakened mind can see that the wisdom teeth have been pulled, so where is the bite? You might settle part of the question just by listening to the remarks of wonderment and new conviction in a typical audience: "Was this all supposed to happen somewhere?"—"So *that's* what this Black Legion stuff is all about"; but it is a question of more things than agitational orthodoxy. For one thing it suggests the business of possibilities and limitations in popular fiction. What can you put in a story and still have a story?

In the Soviet Union the finding was recently brought in that a film story, like a tree, should grow and be visible to folks, not just be banged up out of dialectical lumber. And indeed in this country it has long been a known fact that movies don't go over with the popular audience unless they are built to move and enlist people's belief by means of characters sustained through their make-believe problems, conflicts, joys, what-not. So much of a film's production is taken up with building these qualities tightly in, that when you have to turn about and spend most of the time sketching a wide historic or economic background—well, trouble: and generally nothing much in the total but bits of obscure action, intercut with parades and mass hoopla, intercut with printed titles, intercut with short strips of mugging to register half a hundred cases of fear, lust, agony, virtue, etc. Even a good actor is in a bad way here; even the most delightful, likely types are splendid only in patches, never having been made organs of the story to begin with. Sad it is and a loss to the race that the lads who know by the yard just how to hop over these obstacles continue to prove it irrefutably on paper and it is almost certain their secret will die with, or possibly on, them. For it is a pretty sure thing that those who actually sweat to make films haven't worked it out yet and, on the subject of whether they think they will, keep their mouths buttoned.

Now *Black Legion* is both this and that. Being a Hollywood film, it is a story; being an exposé piece, it has a tough problem of coverage. In the ordinary picture sense it is well made without having the genius in the form that *Fury* showed. The casting is good; the use made of its possibilities by director and actors is thorough (from Humphrey Bogart to the chap who did the small bit of being recruited in the shop washroom). Each incident as it comes up is gone through skillfully, with a dexterous economy of relation and point. It has excitement, reality; and its seeds of truth are assured of being sown nationally.

But from the angle of mass appeal (*i.e.,* box office; *i.e.,* the final index of educational value) it shows strains and weaknesses. It has a general dramatic indecisiveness, ending not only in gloom but without much clear satisfaction either way. And this is probably traceable to the more general fact that it is fiction under difficulties, so conscientious in coverage that it moves by jerks. Flashes of life in the shop; domestic flashes in the neighborhood; back to the shop; back to the houses; then to the drugstore, the Legion meeting, the first raid, the shop, a street corner, and so on. Each one of these is essential, mind; each a lesson in speed and focus. But there are too many of them crowding too fast; no one of them can stay long enough on the screen to become an accepted part of our dramatic experience—and the same is partly true of the people involved. To have grafted together all the people and properties and random branches cut from the tree of current history, so that the didactic edges would have disappeared in a finally growing whole, would actually have taken four times the present footage. Which would absolutely bore the pants off anything but a Eugene O'Neill audience in the pink of training.

It is a pity to make general points at the expense of an honest job of film work and one of the most direct social pieces released from Hollywood. But the picture is a very good illustration of what is possible and what is too much for the time limit and need for explicitness of all films. It is an encouraging sign, but also a warning signal: to stop demanding a ten-reel feature on the Rise of Western Imperialism and look around to see what *can* be done with pictures.

17 February 1937

The Earth, the Egg, etc.

When Hollywood bought *The Good Earth* many of our better people must have had their quiet laugh. The rigors, constant striving, and humdrum satisfactions of peasant life haven't been among the things that fit into Hollywood's light and fast routine. And anyone knows that in the movies, China is Charlie Chan, whereas this is a story of a simple farmer and his wife, their industry and devastation by the famine, their chance luck in the city, wealth, near-disaster, and return to the ways of their farming ancestors. It would certainly be an easy thing to improvise a Joan Crawford mission for the screen treatment, have Clark Gable bobbing up as a coincidence off the *Empress of Asia,* and then throw in all the rest for background—such background to consist of a few library shots of the Bund at Shanghai, several Willie Fungs padding around through a studio rice field saying "Me velly solly," etc. And yet the treatment of the book's large simplicities runs across the screen for nearly two hours and a half and turns out to be among the grandest things done in picturization.

To let highlights wait upon the dimmer regions, the story is occasionally disjointed or telescoped (negligence in the transitions from poverty to wealth, from the simple to the sybaritic and back again, are excusable in the light of the vast territory to be covered: the ideal treatment must simply cut away some of this ground altogether); and the emphasis on main characters should have been more evenly distributed—the uncle to be cut way down, the wife to be cut a little in repetitious moods, the friend to be built up somewhat. As to the central theme, it is trite without being a general truth, for although chance and industry may make this salvation through the soil a fact for hundreds, there are larger things (manifest, for example, in the revolution here serving as plot mechanics) governing the millions, for whom industry must prove vain and their good earth bitter, the present receptacle of their futile bones.

But the picture. It works its characters into the illusion of life, the life into the place and social state of their background, with a serene constancy of pitch that is surprising in a form so easily shifting from scene to scene, so quick and brilliant where the subject before its cameras is so even, dull, and geared to oxen. A good deal of the mood comes from a miracle of solid patience and skill in the way of creating fields, implements, houses and everything in them, so that the smell and thickness of air in the Chinese household is all but in the theater—the worn door frames would be smooth to the touch, the vital crops outside are almost tangible in their growth and meaning. Photography of exteriors is in keeping and frequently beautiful, what with grain in the wind and the wind over famine acres, clouds rolling up, and the countryside under its careful husbandry. And all edited as a movie should be—flexibly, unobtrusively clarifying the story, joining multiple sequences, and bridging over gaps in time or sense by intercuts and the dissolving fragments that serve so well here.

One of the most delicate problems was met rather well, though it will never be solved—I mean the problem of casting and making up actors, both white and yellow, to play Chinese lower-class people. The smaller parts soon become passably natural (Charles Grapewin, Walter Connolly, the people in the Great House, Tilly Losch, the friend Ching), and the main parts pass almost without question. Paul Muni is a fine talent and he builds the character of the husband; but there are qualities here which remain outside the range of the style he has chosen, so that he seems to dull his mind into character before he has penetrated the character. Thus as the clod he often seems to know what a clod is supposed to be, playing with the uneasiness and stiff emphasis of a peasant in a charade. His genius in character is felt again in the more difficult registers of despair, rage, tenderness, the triumph of will; and in the end it isn't that someone else could have filled the assignment better, but that Paul Muni (remember his magnificent Hunkie in *Black Fury*) ought to have made it better himself.

The personification of beauty and strength in *The Good Earth* is left to Miss Rainer, who enters the part of the slave-girl wife as humbly as she enters her man's household in the story, choosing to be plain, small, quiet, the little figure awkward in its cares and heavy clothes. There is weight to be carried and work to be done; there is an even steadfastness to be maintained above all things; and if there is to be any attainment of loveliness, it must be through the acceptance of these stern duties, not in spite of them, or around them, or in time off from them. Retiring, shy, and so very grave, her place becomes the center of the story; speaking few lines and those halting, her eyes, head, shoulders, and subtle cast of face are presently the clearest expression an audience finds of what grim forces and simple faiths are involved before it. No one could fall naturally into such a part without study; no study would be enough without the clear genius to dissolve it in the expression; and even then there would be little without personal radiance and the constant flow of feeling—not too even in tenor for the relief of tears once, a fine flash of anger once, and often a new wonder, or tenderness, or a smile that is secret and obedient, but wiser than her lord. The Chinese wife is a powerful job of creation, but all below the surface, which remains wide, serene, and fine.

Any testimonial to the excellence of these things in the production is in some measure a credit to the skill and good taste of Director Sidney Franklin; but in addition to these and the general run of the action there should be special mention for the superb effect of the locust sequence, where the lighting and sounds and mêlée of people built up a rare tension and held it for minutes. I don't know how they got it—the locusts come over the hill on the wind in a shifting awful cloud, and when they sift into the wheat the millions of them make a noise like a great fire, they pile up in ditches and move on across and nothing can stop them, the field is black and crawling with them, microscopic flashes showing the horrible avidity of their dense career—but I do know that it was not by simple chance and mechanics, for the whole thing is coordinated into one majestic movement of rise, climax, and fall. What with the slow sweep of the general doom and the intense struggle and motion within it, I don't know when I have seen anything so lucid and terrifying.

But a good film is not to be made by spectacular touches alone, as can be seen from *The Lost Horizon,* which appears to be Mr. Hilton's rewrite of *She* with a little reverse English and something of a special screwball in the way of cosmic thought. Frank Capra made it with evident care and faith, and Frank Capra has made living screen fiction out of nothing at all and a few bent hairpins with such steady ease that we have come to expect seeing him walk on the waters any minute now. But something has happened. The picture has its spots of charm, some really big adventure moments in Tibet, and the good work of Ronald Colman and Edward Everett Horton. It is a big, expensive job and perhaps the capital letters and blast of horns with which it is being opened on the two-a-day time can be interpreted as happy days for it and lots of money. None the less it strikes me as little more than moxie and noodles, being in total mawkish, muffed, and as mixed up as the only figures by which you could describe the general effect—*e.g.,* by saying in one breath that the Master's hand was not steady on the throttle because in diving off the deep end he had landed on the horns of a dilemma and laid a pretty terrific egg.

Among films that should have got a play while this column was absent from its duties are *The Plough and the Stars,* an exceptional production of

O'Casey's play; *The Eternal Mask*—really the new *Caligari*, very intense and strange; *The Man Who Could Work Miracles; The Plainsman*, an elegant Western more reminiscent of movie history than of the pioneer background borrowed for its cowboy-and-Indian fiction; and *Camille*, which is still wonderful enough for future discussion.

17 March 1937

Camille: Rebirth in Pictures

The present movie season is not only good but in unexpected ways. As to *Camille*, the surprise is to find a story that should by rights be old hat coming to such insistent life on the day's screen. On the screen, of course, there is no such easy thing as material's just "coming" to life: the life has to be put there, and lived in make-believe, all of which takes understanding, faith, and craftsmanship. The story of a farm girl whose loveliness and adaptable wisdom had promoted her into a nineteenth-century Paris figure, exquisite, obtainable, and expensive as to surface, but inwardly consumed with a certain sickness and spiritual uncertainty; her surrender to and partly wasted sacrifice for simple love—this could have been made into many things: the perfunctory observance of a theater classic, a costume piece, a vehicle for some heedless star. But although George Cukor's direction has seemed to be on the consciously classic side previously, his work here with the cast, material (treatment credited to Zoë Akins, Frances Marion, James Hilton), and technical staff (the top MGM crew: Herbert Stothart, William Daniels and Karl Freund, Cedric Gibbons, etc.) is a firm and straight-out piece of film work.

The life of the times grows up unobtrusively around the people as they take their dramatic position in the story, so that the complexities of an unfamiliar code of living and way of life become the simple background. This has flaws (some of the outdoors is needlessly artificial), but the point is that it serves functionally rather than as a separate effect in itself. In the same way the people become part of the life there. The work of Henry Daniell as the Baron in particular is a grand, subtle study of a man bred to pride and cynicism and scorn at war with the human immediacies of impulse; there is also Rex O'Malley, foolish and true; also Lenore Ulric, properly too shrill and venomous; and Laura Hope Crews, just flighty enough and perfectly the bitch to be infuriating; and Jessie Ralph. Robert Taylor himself is about what the part calls for, not too cold or complex or bright, canceling pretty-boy looks with candor and loyalty and the impulse of laughter.

And all of this frank, sensitive reanimation of a thing that time and change and indifference had almost made into a dramatic platitude is all the more generous of Hollywood and unexpected because it is the setting for a personality that truly requires none, being beauty in itself and its own excuse for being. For this is the Camille of Greta Garbo, the screen's first lady and dramatic phenomenon of our time—and phenomenon it is, because not wealth or her legend or the adulation of millions seems to jar her pure constancy; because in spite of a private dignity that has moved to envious jokes the whole army of those whose profession it is to fawn, pry, and peddle gossip, she is still high in her place, an abiding name in this nation; because she continues in a form that still distresses the high of brow, with a power and unfailing beauty that are undeniable to all brow levels by the million.

The picture opens with lights, gaiety, and the coarse swirl of life; but if its end is to grow naturally from these first scenes, the mood must be set now. Camille must contrive from the start to be radiant in the tricky strange light of a figure with the late sun behind it, the outlines on fire and a lengthening shadow at the center. And she must be—nothing so obvious and easy as the lily defiled, the stinkweed transformed, but a plant that grows in these low places, both part of and lovely above them. And some such presence is felt from the earliest scenes at the auction rooms and music-hall, by no more outward signs than the slight cough (it is nothing), the straight glance and word for Young Handsome, the delight in flowers, the shrug for her friends' scheming prattle or the Baron's propositions. The emotional charge becomes heavier as conflicts develop, until we have the superb duet between Camille and the Baron at the piano, the mortal eloquence of the love passages, the renunciation, forced quarrel, last words, etc. But the gauge of Miss Garbo as this or any other figure may be taken from her command of the screen in her first tranquility, before an explicit relation with the audience has been built up or the action has provided for revelation by word or gesture. It is more than the distant shimmer of beauty, or a resonant husky voice, or a personal dignity wide enough for the demands of both humility and arrogance. It is more than can be measured in any of the dimensions through which we receive it, because sound waves and planes of light are only a medium of reflection for the regions of the spirit concerned here. Greta Garbo has the power of projecting not only the acting moods of a play but the complete image of her own person; and seeing her here, one realizes that this is more than there are words for, that it is simply the most absolutely beautiful thing of a generation.

24 March 1937

Flaherty and the Films

As his pictures get no better and his reputation grows, it becomes more difficult to place Robert Flaherty's film work. He has been a free-lance and restless spirit; he was grown gray in the honorable service of following his personal ideal and damning the eyes of all commercial movie comers. He has completed, usually against backbreaking odds, at least four feature-length pictures that any reading person could name off without hesitation (try this on one of your favorite directors). But in the case of his new *Elephant Boy*, I think *Variety* had the simplest and most lucid approach. Animal picture, *Variety* said.

Now animal pictures and travelogues are fascinating stuff when their material is strange or exciting as it should be. But with such ventures the act of creation (I think we may use a few art terms here occasionally) largely amounts to whatever it takes to promote the money, push into these outlands, shoot the giant panda with the right lens, etc. The creative process used in writing songs or a book only enters here when the material is arranged in some dramatic pattern—after the fact, as in the abridgement, contrast, emphasis of cutting; before the fact, as when natural people are made unnatural ham actors in the interests of the "candid" camera. And since to make anything in the way of a picture you must have a scheme of arrangement and sequence, the value of work like Flaherty's depends upon the natural art with which such artifices are concealed and still made to serve their purpose. For whenever we come to trust the camera eye as a peephole through which we may see wild or human life unobserved, the first hint that the deadly python is Goodyear rubber or the first trace of self-conscious mugging in Intimate Native Moments becomes much more devastating than it would be in pure fiction, frankly accepted as such. Robert Flaherty has always relied on some of the devices (both before and after the fact) of fiction; his main weakness is always that he will jar truth with faking and at the same time scorn to learn how it is done by the Great Fakirs (by which I mean the brightest artists in the screen story, by which I mean Hollywood).

Apparently a story he didn't care for was forced on him for his film of India; and worse than that, they called in for the "treatment" an evident veterinary. A huge damned villain is created, to beat the elephant until it runs amok; Toomai steals off on the elephant to save its life; the tame beast is apparently drawn by the wild herd, also apparently not; and the overdone triumph of the end is made to come when Toomai brings in a couple-hundred tusks for Sahib High-class Englishman. So the screen story was weak to start with. But whether any story becomes fine or foolish in the end depends greatly on (1) the people who act it out, (2) the way they are managed and fitted into a final pattern. And Flaherty was not blessed in his actors.

The boy Sabu was a natural find, assured in his command of the ponderous tricky livestock of the story, standing before the cameras with the candor and grace God gave him. A Little Major in eloquence too, with the required hurts and glees and solemn ambition. And smart's a whip. As to the rest, they are something between a class in elocution and the endmen of a minstrel show that died on the road and passed into some ghastly everlasting of blackface and jokes they couldn't remember, something in a turban and the best Oxford English—but this group of Hamlets has to be seen.

But even with such a story and such people, there are still ways of coaxing and forcing and fooling and bearing down with the cutting scissors. The well-tempered film director should be able to do what others have done before him: size up the situation and say, "Now Farnsworth, we're going to junk the surprise here, that's out; we open on you standing here and you're looking off at the mountain, you simply keep your eye on that mountain, see"; and then kick the cameraman in the shins to start them rolling, quietly blow up a paper bag and then POWIE, just out of the camera but two feet from Farnsworth's ear. Etc., etc.—for if you can spend days getting a shot of the three-toed leopard, certainly no price is too high for any similar achievement in the natural history of the wild actor.

As to technique, I noticed that almost all the transitions were managed by an unvarying overlap-dissolve, that the close-ups were so constant as to become awkward—and indeed young Sabu was frequently centered in a background that did nothing but recall the time some photographer got my Uncle Rob fixed for eternity in the family album, astride the crescent moon with a derby hat. Then there is a definite poverty in variation—big scenes built up by two or three shots running over and over; some strips (the elephants trumpeting or dancing or waving a trunk) brought in so often you begin to call them by name.

In fact, it is better to ignore everything about the film but its record of a trip to the elephant country. There is the great cat, hungry and smelling the breeze and bringing terror delicately right up to the camera; also the native boy; also a batlike small thing with eyes as wild and liquid with fear as anything ever seen; and then the elephants, in all the slow mighty grace that has made them an object of awe and delight from Ceylon to circus parades. In Osmond Borradaile's camera they walk, lope, charge, wallow in the river; there is the biggest one in captivity and a baby about two feet high that has my money over Shirley Temple any day, always worried, and falling behind, and trying to make a noise like an elephant. There is a wild herd and the business of its capture, beaters scaring the stupid lovelies with torches and rattles until they fall against each other like apartment blocks; and the business of building a corral to hold the captives. The work of the sound crew adds to the excitement, and the great ones bugle or rumble with that terrific organ pedal-point they have—all in all a fine din, with a heightening note I never heard before, a sort of slurred trumpet third, very wild.

And that is what is valuable here—too bad you have to go through so much to get to it. Robert Flaherty is eager and serious in his work, but he is really more interested in poking in the ends of the earth than in creative film work (or he would have done a better job); to this end and this extent only is he a rebel (or he wouldn't scorn Class-A Hollywood just to work on such Class-C fiddle-faddle). Yet the more we clarify his position, the more we are indebted for the stuffs he brings back from the wanderings of his desire. His interests are wider than those of the usual travelers and animal-picture showmen, deeper with meaning. Even with the false truck of his latest pack, there are a shine and mood to it that set it apart. He is still the Grand Old Pedlar of the moving pictures.

21 April 1937

But Is It Art?

Looking at pictures and studying what is said about them, one occasionally gets the feeling of men working along out there in Hollywood, shaping the mechanisms of a complex art delicately and getting no more reward (outside the trade, that is) for their labor and vigilance and aspirations than a blundering, imprecise praise or the customary blanket dismissal of all their works. The men make their way in the industry of course, earning titles and fat bonuses and a chicken in every garage; but while that ought to be enough for anybody, I am wondering about the good film makers who must know very well that the same rewards would flow, and often twice as fast, if they made pictures atrociously. It must make them rather cynical to see that about the only way a director can become recognized as a good artist, among the very people who give out the loudest yells on the need for improvement in Hollywood, is to get out of Hollywood altogether: either go abroad and grow an accent or stay at home and join a Group.

Mitchell Leisen makes good comedies; indeed there is enough concentrated filmcraft in his current *Swing High, Swing Low* to fit out half a dozen of these gentlemen who are always dashing around in an independent capacity making just the greatest piece of cinema ever. The picture will play the big-time and there will be press raves and an audience of millions; but one doesn't begin to speak of art until a picture becomes unavailable because of an unfamiliar language or a lumbering scowlike motion that tickets it for the 600-seater houses. Take the new imported version of *The Golem,* which is an example of art as nobody could deny. It has the great Harry Baur and it manages a fine atmosphere of the Ghetto and sixteenth-century Prague and it tells a good yarn. But outside of a surface approach to sociology it isn't a patch on the creative effects of *The Bride of Frankenstein.* James Whale's *Frankenstein* played into the New York Roxy, though, and the Roxy seats around 6,000; it was more thrilling in practically the same way, but since it didn't have to be played up in a shoebox theater as art, it was played down in the normal circuit as a thriller. And that was all.

Swing High, Swing Low is romantic comedy shading into tragic effects, the story of a happy-go-lucky Canal Zone soldier who plays the trumpet without knowing how good he is, and falls in love with the lady without knowing how deep a responsibility *that* sort of thing is. It is all fine until an agent books him into New York and he begins to live high and forget about everything, or put everything off. Misunderstandings, too many bars, and presently he is a down-and-outer, and presently (for the happy end) he isn't. The reasons for the failure of this story as truth are various and as follows: (1) the shift from comedy to near-tragedy is thin and difficult ice here as anywhere, (2) coincidence is made to explain turns of the story that should really have proceeded from the weakness of character just as it stood, (3) the trumpet music is so thin and colorless that it is a drag on the story rather than the buoyant influence it should have been.

The faults are easy to catalogue; the virtues are those of good film comedy and about as easy to describe as running water, having the same continuous flow and play of light and change without effort and joy to the senses. Not just dialogue; not just the people who put it over; not just the situations they are put in; not just the clear development and right focus of everything in the cameras. It is a little of each of these and a lot of something else, some sunny genius for the total effect.

You can pick out a spot like the complex visual play of the sequence where Carole Lombard is busy building a fire in the oven and Messrs. Butterworth and MacMurray are busy rousting a six-foot bed through a three-foot door, and it goes on and on (not the bed, however) and everybody talking and saying What? and dropping the bed—I thought I'd die. Or take the little duel where the rival chippie starts out to freeze Carole by announcing her contract with the El Greco in New York, "Which naturally everybody has heard of the El Greco," she says. "Yes, dearie, but has the El Greco heard of you?" Carole says from off-stage where she is changing a dress or something. "Oh of course, sugar," the chippie says, "they must just know me by reputation"—and Carole comes out fastening a strap as demure as sin itself: "Yes, dearie, I'm afraid everybody must know that" and goes into some feminine business or other before the girl can get her breath, "My *angel,* isn't that a stunning hat—is that a *feather?*" and gets away. Or take the way they mount the scene where MacMurray is trying to put on an airy good-bye and the camera frames both her against the door and him going down and starting back up the steps, the contrast of plane and position of each helping to bring out the unspoken juxtaposition of their private worlds. Or you could mention the auxiliaries to comedy: Charles Butterworth, Jean Dixon, the gamecock, the flair for the unexpected but completely human that shows in the lines. You could go on and mention each thing in turn, but that wouldn't be the half of it because one thing merely leads to another, just as in life, and this leading-on motion (or continuity) becomes a sort of fourth dimension to the whole, in all its intangible, persuasive charm.

5 May 1937

The New and the Old

A Star Is Born is a good picture and the first color job that gets close to what screen color must eventually come to: it keeps the thing in its place, underlining the mood and situation of the story rather than dimming everything else out in an iridescent razzle-dazzle. The boarding house is drab and the sanitarium is severe and quiet, and when it comes to the splendors of Hollywood money the sets have a rich but subdued luster (done, I suspect, by featuring natural-wood finishes and dull metals and by having a pretty good taste in browns and pastels). And if the outdoors looks a little parky, that is not a fault but Beverly Hills—though it is still true that where outdoors is not landscaped, the color cameras still need adjustment to make up for the sensitive compensating apparatus of the human retina: they are still too bold and brilliant.

On interiors, technicians are learning fast that colors must be softened down a few shades from what you would see in actual life, if they are to seem like it. The floodlighting necessary to bring out all details for an audience will create a gorgeous unreality that the movies can't pass off as the stage does—by telling people it is Illusion, Pure Theater, what not, and making them like it. To illustrate what they're up against, take a room in your house, clean it all up, flood it with about 10,000 watts of arc lamps, and then look in at it through the window. Why it isn't livable, never happened, Hollywood tinsel, etc. Then in addition, what we call "natural" color is only a part of what is always there; when an exact mechanical register picks up all the things we don't see or cancel out in the phenomenon of perspective or pass over in the unconscious shifting of focus, it becomes unnatural. There is no tail to the camera eye; within the frame everything is seen and nothing is half-seen; and if this is a difficulty in ordinary film, in color it is the very devil.

Anyway, Janet Gaynor (well cast as Flossie from the Farm) makes her way star-struck to the Coast, almost starves, and then catches the eye of Fredric March, the reigning favorite on a bender. As you expected, she becomes his wife and America's sweetheart overnight; as you did not, he begins at this point to die at the box office, and it shifts to the rather grim picture of a man going to pieces, sinking fast as the fair-weather rats desert in boatloads, and nothing left for him but to be Mr. Janet Gaynor and hit the bottle a little harder, if possible. He might for love of his wife pulled out of it after they'd taken the bottle away and locked him up; but he got worse again, and when she got him out of police court one night he sobered up for good and walked out to sea.

For about the first time, the mechanics of the industry are worked in with thorough coverage: fan-magazine gossips, preemeers, the struggle of extras, the splendid pampered way of stars, the shot-in-the-dark making of a star with cosmetics and lighting and gowning and naming and shameless press agents. And all done with a sense of the actual hardness and fabulous confusion—as for example in the mild burlesque of the screen-test scene, which is a little orchestra of strange hustling sounds and motions in itself. But this is more in the way of the story's atmosphere than of its point. Hollywood only forms the background for the familiar picture of a man on the skids—not demoralized by anything peculiar to the industry, but by himself and a public captiousness and careless cruelty that is as old as old. With the exception of Lionel Stander, who is made to carry all the personal opprobrium, everybody has a heart of gold.

The main part of the film is written (original by Director William Wellman; adaptation, Dorothy Parker) with such edge, charity, old knowledge, feeling; the support is so dependable (Menjou, Stander, Andy Devine, Edgar Kennedy) and the direction so firm through comedy and pathos, that the whole body can turn some pretty ancient corners and climb several very rocky hills of difficult emotion and stridency, and not leave the ground or jar loose or falter in its momentum. That goes for the main part, where Mr. March studies and commands the characteristics of a figure whose weakness shows in the midst of his time of charm and phony glory, and whose broken humiliation in the last stages yet manages some of the dignity and strength that mortality will sometimes find even in humiliation and the fruits of weakness, and fly like a banner—Fredric March carried that part beautifully.

The beginning and end seem tacked on, simply vague and poor writing: the story really starts when Miss Gaynor arrives at Grauman's Chinese and ends where Mr. March turns at the door before going for his "swim" and says again the line planted way back in the bright beginning, "Do you mind if I . . . take one more look?" Let the camera follow him through the door toward the water for half a minute, then dissolve to the open sea and hold that as the music comes up. If it must be driven home, let the water shot fade slowly and just come back to Miss Gaynor, arriving at another preemeer in smart mourning, and her knees buckle suddenly as she catches sight of the first marvel she saw there, the name and the imprint in the cement of the walk: Fredric March. With the people gaping and crushing and the autograph collectors all around in their weird frenzy, I daresay you could write End of Picture then and not lose a drop of what meaning was already there.

The Last Night is a fine picture, though in an established groove. It concerns a whole Russian family, called to the Red colors in the fall days of 1917. There is the *Kronstadt* sailor-and-commissar relationship; there is a family of Whites from a source we might call Passim.; there is the fighting mother from *1905* (a beautiful part here, played with the quality of endearment which comes from the joined qualities of laughter and tears); and there are snatches of character and speech that come straight from the delightful source material of Zostchenko—especially the salesman, who is a fat triumph of humor, and the father, who is human and funny and grand. The mass movement is thrilling stuff, but more or less secondary to the human element—in searching out and presenting which the Russians are second to no one on earth. For just one example, take the awkward, touching beauty of that fade-out, where the troops are pounding off out of the square and the little mother of them all is hurrying to catch up, all hustle, fire, petticoats, and poor tired old feet. The sound-track, lighting, and development harass eye and ear with an inadequacy that is almost a tradition; the title-writing is the best job I recall seeing; and the story of the Revolutionary Passion is as clear and fresh again as though it had never been told.

19 May 1937

Montgomery in the Movies

Thanks to its original in Emlyn Williams' wild, subtle stage play, and in spite of the fact (seen in retrospect) that because of original restrictions a great deal of the motion still comes out in dialogue and from practically the same set, the picture *Night Must Fall* is one of the most vivid and powerful effects the films have managed. It has unity without any waste or flaws and a gathering momentum as exact, clear, fascinating as a ball of crystal on a black felt incline, under lights. (Hunt Stromberg produced; Richard Thorpe directed.)

The story is complex in conception only; in outline it is direct and simple. Its effects of horror and suspense come from no outer mechanisms of vampires, werewolves, etc. It develops wholly from within three people: the page boy, the girl, the old woman, in that order of importance. And its method is that of an intellectual scalpel, bright and delicate and laying back the tissues with almost unbearable steady precision—almost with the surgeon's healing function as well, because those who would appear in headlines simply as fiends or fools reveal themselves gradually here in impulses common to all humanity, but warped into the unspeakable by simple inner and outward pressures, as of some bedeviling bone against the brain or of some stored-up wrong, old envy, hatred, frustration. So they are to be understood and, even when most pitiless and terrible, pitied.

There is an old woman living off in the forest, demanding and venomous from behind her money and pretended invalidism; there is a niece in the house who is something of a sensitive nature and the butt of the old lady's spleen; and there comes to answer for the condition of one of the kitchen girls a lout of a page boy from the hotel in the village, carrying off a supreme insolence with blarney, and all women with his bold charm. Also there's been a foul murder nearby in the forest but never mind that: the youth manages to take the old girl into camp straightway, and he comes into the house as her special servant. He is a slick one; he is so brash and male and infuriating to the niece in some wild way that she begins to, well, in a way hate him of course but, well, when will he come out and cross the room again? Having some wild blood of her own and being about him the way she is getting to be, she sees more and guesses more than anyone and in that close house things get about as tense as ever will be seen, for she can neither stay nor leave, nor sleep from the rushing of her blood; she knows the young bucko is forever playing a part, hiding something, never to be touched in the world of his own ego. . . . There is no use going on to the end with the mounting story—the girl released, the boy trapped, the old lady paid off in the hard coin of her own mean foolishness.

It isn't a story that can be "told" anyway. The words are there but the truth behind them is only released through the contrast, comment, and continuity of moments visualized in the camera—so that the awful hatbox may be openly referred to in three scenes and still dominate twenty, and the serene and private black Persian may cross the frame as silent as a symbol forever and yet be the final strand in the pattern as night falls, and things seen by the character may be denied the audience through the camera's focus, or the opposite of that; and a spoken line may take on some essential eerie quality by reason of the speaker's invisibility. And the acting in this picture is of the clearest water, with the depths of meaning visible and no alien sediment (as of personal pose or inflection) to refract the main light. Rosalind Russell is so much the creator of her part that the unspoken lines go beyond those written into the play, until a complex and ordinarily opaque character becomes as clear as air. Dame May Whitty lays down a groundwork for her last frenzy that raises into pure terror a scene that would have been the comic death of all the many who can do a good stock part labeled Crotchety Old Lady. And the maidservants had the touch of life (the two from the play) and the Scotland Yard man was quietly Scotland Yard, and I liked everybody and the way they were handled in the scenes where the English guide with an umbrella led the gawps to the scene of the crime.

In spite of all that went into it, the outstanding factor in this picture is the job of creation Robert Montgomery does in the main part. It is a role within a role actually, for he must be one thing to each of the characters and another thing to the all-seeing eyes in his audience; and it is dangerous not only because of the difficulties of moving convincingly along two different planes of technique (audiences must see him act for others without losing the illusion that for them he is not acting, he is real life), but because the part as written is so far beyond general experience that its improbabilities must be seated in some person whose movements we can follow with trust, yet whose first false move will tip the whole boat into ridicule. And Robert Montgomery does it, with his hint of brogue in the right spots of emphasis, his open swagger and terrible inner seclusion, the chuckles, the boyish honey, the horrors, hooded vengeance, and all. And he plays it like a good pianist, whom you will see leaning back from his instrument at ease, negligent, and almost contemptuous in his sure command, yet always with loving care and the gift of beauty on him.

Bob Montgomery, the playboy type. Wisecracks in penthouses. Quite good as such. Make a million for somebody all right, and if he doesn't like the type part, he knows what he can do with it. Well, it is also the fact that he is president of the Screen Actors' Guild, and there are rumors that when he asked for a chance at this different part his company saw the boomerang qualities and said, So let him have it, let him have it right in the neck—teach *him* to agitate around here. In any event, it seems Montgomery has temporarily hurt himself at the box office, and that there are some who do not find this unamusing.

But leaving these folk to their little laugh, it is an important thing that he has done in breaking through here, and I should be happy to have it stand as a signal to others in the industry, so that they would take heart a little, and get up on their hind legs a little, and not give up in the battle against the chumps. Good work has got to be done by individual directors, writers, actors, and specifically those who have already proved they can produce the goods, and I don't mean slightly hungry fellows hollering manifestoes down a rain barrel. And what they are up against is no such easy entity as the "crass stupidity of capitalist Hollywood"; they are up against the fat torpor of the companies *and* the reviewers, chatterboxes, intellectuals, and our very good friend the public. When by breaking their stout backs to make a good film they turn out a superior job in spite of everything (see above), why you can paste it in your hat that something genuine has been added to the cultural history of this country—and crept up on most of us while we were dozing at that.

And the Actors' Guild (so long as it keeps out of the hands of little schemers) should be one of the best ways of getting such things done. It is a fine thing not only for cracking down on the sweating of extras and all the bitcheries of contract lawyers and racket magazines, but for making it easier and safer for good people to do good work—now while the iron is hot and the professor sleepeth—in an art we will all someday have to be proud of. For the most beautiful thing about the movies is that they are still so close to their public that good work is usually appreciated on the spot, which was as true of Mack Sennett and Thomas H. Ince and Chaplin and Disney before the Museum of Modern Art had ever thrown down on the Cinema with its earnest monocle as it was of Frank Capra when he released a little film called *It Happened One Night. Night Must Fall* ran into crosscurrents at the box office; but it shouldn't actually lose money and its effect shouldn't be lost. Although subject to correction as being far from the scene, let's say that I am near enough to it in hope and faith to lead a cheer for Mr. Robert Montgomery of the Screen Actors' Guild, and for what he stands for in the movies.

2 June 1937

These Three to See

There is a building tradition of screen comedy on the Paramount lot that may be worth discovering someday, but for the present it is enough to go see *I Met Him in Paris* (Wesley Ruggles' direction again; Claudette Colbert's opposition this time divided between Melvyn Douglas and Robert Young, cast in the lark of their lives; screenplay by Claude Binyon). It plays down sentiment more than the others and goes out for laughs in a droll, brilliant sort of way. On the whole, nothing funnier has been seen since *The Milky Way*. It starts with an American girl feeling rather low on her trip to Paris, moves on to the Swiss Alps with the girl and two rather frightening boy friends, and ends with three boy friends and the girl in Paris, getting funnier in a cumulative sort of way until it is a good thing for your ribs that they stopped it.

The film combines a lot of absolutely fresh devising with the good old action-comedy tradition of pratfalls (of which there are some beauties), the man being sent into a spasm with his mouth full of liquid, etc. Take Robert Young's line as he starts a love scene, "Ah, I can't talk in the daytime, I keep seeing the tip of my nose"; take the terrible Swiss desk clerk, the eyes on the French train guard, the waiter on skates. Take the next to last sequence, where Young and Douglas kidnap the goof into the bar; take the whole business in winter sports, with dignity and the grand passion wobbling around on skates, skis, bobsleds, and with that weird bevy of Swiss always tearing around a corner with fierce competence and yodels, missing Robert Young by a hair. (There is nice space and scenery, too.) But there is no use taking anything if you don't see the picture. At least half of the footage is a perfect scream and if you miss it you are an old sobersides, and who cares.

Kid Galahad is the best prize-ring film I've seen—both for the explosive pace of its fight scenes and for the edge to its realism. Its germane dramatics include as a matter of fact the practices of a gunman promoter, the rigging of fights, the making or breaking of fighters, etc. The story is about a clean-living bruiser from the tall corn who got into the preliminaries thanks to chance and to the sharp promoting talents of Edward G. Robinson, who is in the middle of a feud with the Humphrey Bogart mob. The good heart and caution and pity have to come from Robinson's mistress (and how are *you*, Mr. Hays?) and Harry Carey, still around and still wonderful. Bette Davis (as the mistress) falls in love with the innocent palooka—who is almost at the top when Robinson catches him trying to marry his kid sister. And the blow-off comes at the championship fight where there is sudden death but no promise of purity for the fight game, no clinch; only Miss Davis walking alone out through the dim, dirty alley—after another of her distinctive screen portrayals, incidentally.

And in closing would state: That Robinson and Bogart are swell enough types at this sort of thing to write their own parts almost. That the writing was still good, fast, and commendably lean on overstatement. That Michael Curtiz kept the direction clean, particularly in scenes about the locker rooms and ringside, where there was some of the most bloody realism and mauling ever made up for cameras.

There will be time enough to see *Captains Courageous* when it gets out of the roadshow class and into the moderate prices. Though dragged out and often weepy, it is a corking yarn (direction by Victor Fleming). The center of the story is Freddie Bartholomew, the unbearable little percival who fell off a liner into the Gloucester fishing fleet on the Grand Banks, got a little decency rubbed into him, and fell in love with Manuel, the great Portugee dory man. The movies seem to have developed the best crop of child actors ever seen: Bartholomew here is not only clever and endearing but sensitive, controlled, as wise as any grownup in the cast (which is all good, incidentally); he has a delicate little style of his own, working the audience steadily around from a yelp of delight to see him clopped across the fishpile, to esteem and tears. Mickey Rooney is another bright genius and present here, though in a small part.

The largest figure is that of Spencer Tracy as Manuel, simple, boisterous, rich in his powers, speaking to God and the little fishes direct. He is felt in the story long after he has gone under in a tangle of wreckage; and for once the imposition of his happy image over the action at the end is not felt as a trick. His adopted accent was too much for him all the way through and was given a backbreaker about heaven to speak near the middle; but the point is that he finally comes through all such obstacles like a bull through a picket fence.

With Freddie's three-month regeneration as the main theme and the secondary business of skipper L. Barrymore's rivalry and tragic race to lead the fleet home, the great part of the footage is sea stuff, and it is no secret that these cameras perform a constant miracle of walking on the waters (photography by Harold Rosson). Much of the action had to be taken indoors and processed, of course, and the cutter and the dialogue writers weren't seamen. But even the tank shots show an uncanny genius for the shipshape, that inimitable seaman's order in a cramped confusion of halyards, rope ends, buckets, pins and tackle, hatches and capstans and standing gear. The procedure at sea is good—*e.g.,* getting the dories overside with way on, clearing the wreckage in that stunning carry-away of the mast; sometimes a documentary delight. To those with salt in their hair, the scenes of that stout little fleet, lying morning and afternoon with its boats out, slipping off ship by ship in the early mists, will be worth waiting through any two-hour movie for. And I believe that the running picture of the *We're Here* is more beautiful and strange than anything that has been recorded of ships, showing her snugged down and heading home or breathless within a calm horizon, spanking along on her actual beam-ends, heaving literally two-thirds of her length out of water and smacking down into it again, or slipping out of a fog bank or with sails black against the clouded sky at suppertime.

Franz Waxman scored the music, which struck me as adequate and often delightful. Not only the accompaniment but the general position of music in the picture—for the touching business of Tracy and his honest baritone over the hand organ; for the several bits of chanties and the working song, "Oh—What a Terrible Man!" made up for that crew to sing. Indeed the whole MGM staff has treated this film with so much respect and shrewd artistry that the treatment seems almost unsatisfied, as if it were mutely in search of some bigger theme.

16 June 1937

In Mournful Numbers

It's wonderful how the movies can make available such priceless antics as the Marx Brothers'; but it is getting clearer that the use of an entire film to frame a few splitting comedy sequences is simply a road to nowhere. Out of *A Day at the Races* I got some ripe laughs, but they were a long time in coming and when there wasn't a laugh there was nothing—ham dialogue, a ham plot and cast, no belief or interest anywhere. The W. C. Fields-Mae West-Jimmy Durante-etc. type of film has been going the same way for a long time. I'd run a mile to see any one of these people in a walk-on, but when as performers they become more important than the script, direction, and film total, they defeat the film and themselves in it.

The idea in this latest picture is good—Groucho as the horse doctor called in to save the sanitarium and finally engineering success on the racetrack—but the picture treatment shows just about as little imagination as you can have and live. The stuff with Groucho as head surgeon and overworked lover is fine, and all three boys go through a fantastic sequence in the examination room and high jinks at the racetracks that no one else in the world is capable of. Otherwise there was a little scattered fun (Groucho's rhumba I remember well), and pouf pouf. Only the box office and time, apparently, can teach them that the same harp act, the same doubtful piano from Chico will never be missed; that a sequence of which the high comic point is pronouncing the name Hackenbusch "Hack-in-a-puss" may get a nervous laugh response from small towns on a tryout but hardly adds to the world's humor; and that a wastebasket of show tricks perched on such a rickety pretense at plot construction is not a picture and gets less so every day. The dizzy pace of the Marxes at their peak might never be held in any story or treatment, but I wish to God they would for once cast around for a good comedy director and some crazy writing team who might in time cook up something really worth their terrific energy and talent.

In matching *The Road Back* against *All Quiet on the Western Front*—related books by the same author, filmed by the same company (Universal)—a whole volume could be written on the subject of the rare peaks and awful valleys of the country called Hollywood, and how they exist side by side or hindside-before in time, and how those who are angry with the movies will never lack for ammunition (for the bad shows are truly frightful, though fortunately they pass quickly away), and how those who like to fire a hat up into the sky now and then will have their ammunition too (for the notable ones are the good ones, and will be with us a while). But on *The Road Back* there will be no volume written here. Too dispiriting.

All Quiet was a better subject for camera treatment, of course, the drama of it unmistakable and mounting—whereas the drama of the sequel is inward and widely social, thus difficult. And certainly anyone given this cast of near-ciphers (excepting Slim Summerville and Andy Devine, who shouldn't have been there anyway) has got two strikes on him before he even gets to the park. Yet Lewis Milestone finished that first picture over seven years ago, when sound was still a novelty and Hollywood a babe in arms at those foreign scenes where there is now a tradition of easy illusion; and you can see it today and marvel at the way that film, battered print and all, was built into a unit with all its devices showing a prophetic genius in their clear establishment of the mood called for, its elements of humor and terror and mortal trial perceived and laid down with the surety of foundations. But that was Lewis Milestone, just about the first of the modern film men.

The director-producer of *The Road Back* is James Whale, who can do both good work and bad. About the story, the moral, the meaning, I hardly know what to say. At first there is a bit of war, the soldiers with such clean faces, their parts learned so earnestly, their enunciation so cuh-lear. Then presently the Armistice is signed and this Road Back might as well be the path of a unit on the Chautauqua time, a little of everything and something for all. What with hollow speeches, quaint types, mob-scene choruses by The Company, a shabby burlesque of the German people's rebellion, tears as thick as buttermilk, and Louise Fazenda and all, I do not know when confusion has been so confounded, the tremendous so tinny.

There are some funny moments, some drama is still evident in a few scenes, but there is so little story left, so much pulling back and forth between lines from the book and somebody's ad-libbed idea of a neat blackout, such a lack of direction to the whole and climax to the end, that I don't think even the Class audience they make a play for by roadshowing the film will be taken in. Just for the record and an even perspective, I haven't been so bored and put out by such an extended treatment of a major theme since Broadway produced *Bury the Dead* and (before that) the old Acme imported *Hell on Earth.*

The Harry C. Pearsons' *African Holiday* is one of the genuine camera explorations, this time in the magic land of East Africa. There is less slaughter and animal melodrama than usual; the Pearsons offer peaceful studies of the wildebeest, giraffe, hippo, alligator, lion, and many other fascinations, including the rare okapi, the Masai, and several such things never photographed before—which you are never allowed to forget for a second (while Mr. Pearson does the commentary with clarity and restraint, his voice becomes tedious in its ubiquity and occasional complaisance). But dim photography and editing and the substitution of a faint musical score for living sound effects remind you all over again that even the Honest Truth itself can be pretty tasteless stuff beside some of the better effects in pictorial illusion. On the same bill, for example (at the Filmarte in New York), there is a handsome job of exploring nearer home: RKO's short on the New York waterfront. The human element was left pretty much to a chance flip comment; but all the docks and ships and bridges, the contrasts, the magnificent and monstrous flow of life and commerce—all these things move on the screen and in the motion of their joined fragments convey a clear and total idea. And finally on the same bill there is perhaps ten minutes of *Easy Street,* which represents Charlie Chaplin's explorations in the field of visual comedy—still quite fresh somehow, for that is the strangest region of all, always present for all to see, but never charted. It is the Marxes' land too, but they waste it now, sprinkling it in handfuls to the twelve-reel winds.

30 June 1937

New Film in a Dry Month

What with all we know of Hollywood idiocy, capitalism, plagiarism, fearsome-fascism (read all about it), we ought to have a neat pigeonhole for the cycle of pictures with social teeth to them that the Warners have been releasing. If we are wise we won't, though: I never saw a good mouthful of dialectic yet that didn't prove any such thing impossible—they cannot be, hence they aren't, never were. And yet here currently is another, made from Ward Greene's novel on a case study of mob violence in the Deep South, directed and produced by Mervyn LeRoy, called *They Won't Forget.* Whatever is behind it, the fact is that in content and uncompromising treatment this film is just the blood-and-guts sort of thing we've been hollering for. I suspect it's more fun to demand when there is a pretty good assurance you won't get it, and so I imagine there will be a certain embarrassment at finding that here it is, and in the guise of nothing more than a pretty good movie. Pshaw.

In any event, nothing has been left out of this picture of small-change humanity in a small city, the individual characters demonstrating how the simplest of mortal decencies may be brutalized into tragic and imbecile horrors by the workings of circumstance and inbred hostilities, of frustration and that universal muddy numbness of skull which almost begs these flip reporters and ham politicians to step in and play hell with it. A girl is murdered after hours in the business school; among other ephemera of evidence, the janitor and the Yankee teacher are observed at the building that afternoon; and the rest (the conviction and lynching of the Yankee) is done by the papers and a snide D.A. The D.A. is allowed some pretty plain words, saying that hanging the nigra would be a pushover, what he wants is a big-time trial; and when the leading citizens get panicky at the furor rising in both North and South, he takes them back to their part in all this and rubs their noses in it. The popular Governor is shown being broken by his own simple uprightness. And the whole thing is worked out so fairly that the brothers of the dead girl can serve as a focus of the hatred alive in that region, and still not be villains—for their lives had not been those of movie heroes, it had got so that slip of a girl was all they had to come home to at night, the way she had with her laughing, she was the prett'est little theng, etc. It happens to be the South but for once you can infer that it might be anywhere, shift the superficials and the basic stuff is still universal.

The film has an awful opening—six Civil War veterans lined up on a bench and speaking on cue for all the world like a Vitaphone short of Shep Fields and His Rippling Confederate Rhythm—but this is surely canceled by the handling of suspense in the schoolhouse; the powerful understatement in the fading out of the lynching sequence, where the camera doesn't follow the group away from the train but, as the other express comes through, raises the focus until the main object is the mail sack hanging from its patent gallows, seen for moments and then jerked out like a shot as the mail car passes, etc. For the most part, though, the story is told straightforwardly, the school, the home, the streets, the jail, first this, then that, one, two, three. And the general effect of day-by-day honesty is somehow helped out by a cast of unfamiliar faces, competent actors and not distinguished, altogether managing about the right air of candor, bewilderment, the good intentions and undistinguished state of actual life. The reporter was about the best; the Negro janitor sounded too much like a cantor with a cold for my taste; and of course Claude Rains's approach to a part is always to grab it by the throat—which happens to be just in character here. So the thing happens, slowly, before your eyes. Since nothing seems to have been omitted (the solution of the mystery can safely be left to William Powell films, I think), nothing had to be added. This is one of the cases where news made its own drama, complete with rise and fall, but where those who would reconstruct it (main credit still goes to Mr. Greene) must walk with even greater care than usual, for fear of making simple things too simple, the complex of causes and effects too pat, and thus robbing the story of life and its end of power.

This isn't one of the pinnacles of art; we aren't talking of that here. But those who remember the heightening of fascination and awe that Fritz Lang achieved by the magic of his craft in *Fury* will also remember that his story never squared itself with its ending. There are many different levels of creation and recreation, but what we will principally find in *They Won't Forget* is that the plain statement may tell more and remain longer than fragmentary eloquence, however high and handsome.

It may seem incongruous that Edmund Wilson's piece of last week* should appear in the same paper carrying these movie comments of mine—though it should not seem unnatural that a Journal of Opinion should be open to writers having some. Along with a couple of people in the office, Wilson himself suggested with a mean twinkle in his eye that I might want to "answer" his good licks of invective. Well, well, I've got my idea and I know Wilson has his and what's more would keep it if Jesus Christ, Karl Marx, Chaucer, and Pushkin walked right out of the screen at him, holding hands and all in Technicolor. And I've observed that when people with ideas start throwing them at each other like spitballs in print, nothing comes of it except a slight rise in circulation. I know how Wilson feels because I felt precisely the same way myself some years ago. The way I felt was a very unimportant and unprofitable way, of course, and so when I got a chance to do some actual writing, even if only film criticism, I snapped at it. Upon which, perhaps unfortunately for my state of mental balance, I had to learn about pictures, see them and see them plenty. Having to know about pictures before sounding off on them was a good thing for me, I still think, but anyway the result is in *The New Republic* files of the last three-odd years. If there is a Question, the curious can find the Answer in the long, cumulative, sweated-out record of this column—over 100,000 words already, my God! And if you want to examine it, you will find that hot or cold it has been pretty seriously dedicated to the appreciation of a new, vast, and popular art, uncharted and exciting and naturally often foul. And you will also see that what with its natural bent and limitations of space, there can't be very much room in it ever for things that have so precious little bearing on the actual making and function, the meaning and style and living effect of pictures today.

28 July 1937

*"It's Terrible! It's Ghastly! It Stinks!" is included in Edmund Wilson's collection *The Shores of Light*.

Bring Them Back Alive

The Life of Emile Zola is one more of the mature jobs Hollywood has turned out, pretty much against the best expectations. Along with *Louis Pasteur* (same company, director, star) it ought to start a new category: the Warners' crusading films, costume division. Of the two, *Zola* is nearer to being a well-made picture. But both suffer from a difficulty peculiar to their type of story: they must stretch the play to include all the historical facts possible, thus forestalling cranks and throwing a bone to all proud literates (indeed, discussion of the value of such pictures almost always centers on the, shall we say, fidelity frequency); yet the facts themselves are often such obstacles to dramatic structure as to require the best part of a film's energy merely in circumventing them. Even here, where history has provided such fine natural drama, the continuity is in some ways scattered and bumpy, some of the interrelations stretching a bit thin. The sloppy manipulation of history is never excusable, but neither does a good picture inevitably result from photographing happenings just because they happened. Once the solid human truth is grasped, the play should become the thing.

At any rate, *The Life of Emile Zola* is important above other things as being a further incorporation of pretty solid home truths into the frivolous movie, and it is certainly good to see Hollywood discovering that it can make the actual people of history as exciting in a general way as their costumes. Though they probably would not have splurged on Zola if they have not had the Dreyfus case for their real drama, the using of this national conflict as the expression of one man's career was as full of technical difficulty as it was rewarding in the end.

Zola is certainly no easy subject to tackle for any purpose, being one of those cases where none can say at what point the writer left off and the campaigning public figure began, being at once a force in his own time and a prophetic voice beyond it. For dramatic purposes the problem is even stiffer. The actual business of writing is a slow, concealed process that has always laughed at plotsmiths, for no matter how seasoned and literate the authors, stage or screen, when a writer is to be shown writing they begin to bog down in a mixture of self-consciousness, awed mumbo-jumbo, and anticipation of what the public thinks a writer ought to look like (yes, but where did the public get it from?).

Zola handles the problem in an unpretentious and pretty good way, sketching in the author's special background and leanings at the start, later showing him as he absorbs the life around him at three or four points, showing him as he comes upon the story of *Nana,* as he comes upon the General Staff, the bureaucracy of France. The personal side is in it too, and the working out of his first success is as touching and lovely as it should be. Much later there is the shrewd device for putting over "J'Accuse"—he has just finished the tract and brought it before his friends at the publisher's office; it represents a dangerous decision and involves powerful forces, and he is still full of it and mad as hell, and why shouldn't he read it out word for word and make the paragraphs blast, for it is dynamite and he is glad of it. And toward the end I think you get the effect of things never seen by the eye, this burning spirit and onward drive of the work, we have only just begun to fight, etc.

This picture treats its material with honest dignity and restraint, having seen its duty and done it. From what can be observed of its few imaginative flights—the device of book following book onto the table, the close-up on newspaper headlines that is simply today's heir to yesterday's came-the-dawn title mat—it appears just as well they stuck to business. There are directors and cutters who could have made a more fluid and striking job of it—Zola walking the streets in that first part, hands in his pockets and the shrewd eyes in his head, just walking through a series of backgrounds against the wind or in the shade, at morning and night, and what he saw would not be the planted incidents of this treatment but the unobtrusive life of another city like New York as he walked down Delancey and up Lenox Avenue and across Fifty-second and up and down the ferry, the mere rhythm of this pacing motion building up into its own effect as it is intercut with the progressive scenes of the story. And the ending might have been done so well (Paris, Paris, the city he loved, all through the story, yet they couldn't take the tip), with funeral services and the sound of bells gradually shutting out the words of tribute and prophecy, and up to the place where the bells are and slowly out over the city from there, Paris, the eternal scene fading as naturally as the land from a ship's departure. (And don't say the muggs won't get it: the muggs have and will again, the real muggs being those who figure it would be something tasty to run five hundred feet beyond the end with ceremonies and talk, while audiences fidget.)

There must have been a thousand headaches in getting up the material and manner of treatment, but the final impression is one of boldness and triumph. The story sails right through the early troubles and later successes and, when this much has been established, makes no bones about breaking off and starting over with the affairs of the General Staff (the transition device is good, the camera receding over the licks of flame in the fireplace as Zola is comfortable with speculation on the mischance abroad in the land, and advancing again on a man at a door, the name on the brass nameplate: ESTERHAZY). Zola goes to the background while the story of Dreyfus is told; then Dreyfus in turn becomes merely a Case, and must be kept in the story by an occasional far-fetching shot of him aging on Devil's Island. It makes dangerous dramatics, and it is a wonder they bring it off at all, let alone keep the suspense high and the central idea mounting. Actions gather together and the Zola trial is held, and as justice is raped and truth lies bleeding the issues get over to the audience pretty hard. Trial scenes are naturals for the movies, and while this one is not handled in the staccato emphasis of the best styles, it carries along on a slow powerful swell—not just the personalities and the mob outside but the whole weight of machinery and fustian and snide incompetence—having so much behind it that Paul Muni can stand up at the end and read off a speech, choosing his words and pauses, that would have been top-heavy almost anywhere else, but is here just what the audience ordered.

In addition to all the rest that went into it—William Dieterle's direction, the screenplay, research, set construction, etc.—the film is happy in its actors, solid character people like Donald Crisp, Henry O'Neill, Joseph Schildkraut (particularly), and many more I don't know. As Zola, Muni is in one of his best parts. That final speech, not to mention the other extended readings from the Master, calls for the utmost in the way of actor's business if it is going to become more than printed rhetoric; but beyond technique and the studied idiosyncrasies of character there is the feeling he has maintained through the picture of assurance and worth, dignity and depth and large feeling, so that there is never the question: Will he put it over? and never the distraction from essential emotions of wondering if that anger isn't just a shade rant, that confidence bluster.

It isn't this business of stopping to be Someone and becoming Someone Else; we didn't know Zola anyway. The point is that he goes beyond the lines to create, work up, ad-lib a figure of a man large enough to hold whatever kind of man Zola is in our imaginations and was in life. And something like that act of free creation should be the aim of the story as a whole: to get the main facts from history and from there on put everything into the construction of something that moves under its own power, and may have been what happened because it happens plausibly now before your eyes.

18 August 1937

"And There Were Giants on the Earth"

Top place in importance for the week goes to the set of pictures *[Spanish Earth]* Joris Ivens brought back from the Madrid area and has finally got edited, scored for music, and ready to go. His camera was in the fields, the rocking streets of the city, behind redoubts and with the tanks, sometimes in the advancing front line. He got as much of it as he could under such difficulties, sizing up not only perspective, sufficiency of lighting, the best points of shelter and focus, sizing up as well how each thing would fit with his idea. Then he took what he had and worked out his idea through it.

There are two simple themes: the suffering and dogged purposefulness of war for the cause; and the bulk and onward motion of the cause itself—the earth and its rightful function and what the chance to use and irrigate it will bring forth for men to eat, and how they will not be denied now at last even if they have to die for it. The film opens on the husbandry of the countryside, the look and meaning of the land. A spoken comment rushes in here to assume the unestablished, its faulty cuing presently demonstrated by the ease with which the film brings about the contrast in its own terms. Over the loaves of bread from the ovens, the war posters look down, and over the ordered fields and fruit trees the sound of firing comes to end the first sequence, the explosions growing louder, still unseen.

Then the defense of Madrid, the ravages within the city, the fighting itself, rifle and machine-gun fire from the gaunt shells of buildings, field-pieces in the orchard, citizens lined up to drill and become soldiers, soldiers lined up for attack or for soup, scattered in sleep or sniping positions or over newspapers. In the trenches as in the city life goes on, precarious but familiar, a strange world of death and strenuous doing, yet somehow the same, people clinging to their songs and houses, and in the fields there is yeoman work on the ditches and rude aqueducts: much of the old machine is down or silent but the life processes go on and a new machinery must be set up. And over all this, the strangeness itself becomes a part of routine, the heightened tempo of trucks hammering up with soldiers, the big planes out of the cloud somewhere, and the air full of plaster dust, stretchers, and ambulances by the door.

Though the camera never seems to get near enough the business end of things to catch the fearful symbol of the enemy or telltale thinning of the line (one figure falls; for the rest we get a particular group, the scream of a shell on the sound-track, and cut to a stock explosion), the picture is definitely on the side of the harsh truth, for there are plenty of close-ups of violent death after the fact, and the comment is beautifully explicit on the price men will pay—that advance in echelons of six, the six becoming five and the four three, and this is the way they go into action, not with trumpets. Yet one of the most convincing things about it is its abstention from bombast and sloganism.

Much of the carrying power in understatement should be credited to Ernest Hemingway's commentary. His voice doesn't come over too well, and what with his suggestion of some overrehearsed WNEW announcer in an embarrassment it isn't vintage Hemingway; but with his knowledge and quiet statement of the odds against survival, that feeling for the people of Spain which comes from his heart, the combination of experience and intuition directing your attention quietly to the mortal truth you might well have missed in the frame, there could hardly be a better choice.

But the rest of the credit goes to Ivens and his unquenchable feeling for the life of people, at war or at work. He might have found a way around the sort of scene where "natural" people are not natural at all but stiff and uneasy, and he skimped a little. But what he has brought back is convincing as the real thing, sparing neither cause nor effect, talking straightly as a man should talk. There are beautiful shots of ruin against the sky, and of the rise of native hills under it. There are no razzmatazz of angles, trick dissolves, symbols as such. He has saved for the last the advance that took the bridge and the running comment of symbol-in-fact represented by the completion of the business that loosed the water over the parched waiting land—but the whole film has been built up toward these two things, not just around them as spectacle. And though it is not a great film, it has been made so that somehow the power and meaning of its subject matter are there to feed the imagination of those who have any.

It isn't so much in the outward drama of the attack, the rattling trucks and tanks, breastworks and machine-gun placements and range-finders. These things are here but subordinated to a purpose, which is recorded in this camera simply because it is there in Ivens' and Hemingway's people—the serene grim cast of feature or carriage of the body, the fine figure of a man who comes up to address his brigade or parliamentary body. Men for the most part whose clouds of doubt and petty worry have burned off before a confident power imposing its symmetry from within. Relaxed, haggard, or plain dirty, one after another is seen on the screen going through his heavy job as though in very token of the fact that a million or ten thousand or even fifty such cannot be wrong. There is no need for vilification and babble of glory here; showing the Spanish land and the people related to it, the film does not have to raise its voice to be undeniable, its report a plain testimonial to the way men can be lifted clear beyond themselves by the conception of and full response to the epic demand of their time.

Another important picture for today is *Dead End,* as scrupulous and handsome a production as you could ask (William Wyler working for Samuel Goldwyn again). Having been made from a stage play it lies open to all sorts of tricky discussion and hitting of pro over the head with con; but for the main part it is a vivid movie with a drive of truth and groupings of street kids (from the Broadway cast) that will take your breath away. Its theme is the effect of environment on character and career; its story has the poor youth find the way to his true love, trouble building in the neighborhood, the public enemy trapped. But the best values are the sidelights on life in the city and on the various human elements represented by the children, Sylvia Sidney, Humphrey Bogart, parents, policemen, etc. The lines are good—humorous or grim but always racy—and the people give life to them, the continuity and direction are straightforward and clear. And outside some too obvious contrasts and unreal background processing it follows *Ceiling Zero, Night Must Fall,* etc. in the class of screen adaptations sound enough in wind and limb to run by themselves.

It is true of these productions that the ranging energy and mobile freedom of the screen story are put on the short tether of the original restricted form; it is true that Hollywood was not the nurturing ground for their material and thus that they are part of picture development only by chance, and not organic. But their importance should never be obscured with quibbling over Derivation and Pure Form. One after another these films raise the artistic level of films in general; their success widens the cultural expectations and capacity of an audience of millions and (even more important) of the producers themselves, willy-nilly, breaking down superstition and giving the good craftsmen confidence and some comfort.

1 September 1937

From the Original French

The French film production of Gorky's *Lower Depths* should help nobly in taking away the taste of all the clumsy pretentious miles of celluloid that have been coming in from abroad these last years (with isolated exceptions, of course). The quality of the print, development, camera equipment, and lighting will still take you back ten years or so but the main power of this film makes it one of the grand ones.

Jean Renoir's version is no landmark in the technique of handling film stories. It is a case where the material is so terrific, the cast so naturally wide of capability, that the severest demand on the producer must be that of holding onto what is there, and not botching. For to be anything besides exotic slummery or Marie Dressler in *Min and Bill,* the swift fantastic turns of a story like this must be held to their solid background; and to be more than picturesque the background itself must reach beyond atmosphere and the life-types natural to it, into implications of some governing moral. In shifting the story to get the tighter continuity necessary in pictures, they have also shifted the moral axes. The vise of environment is still an iron one but the glimmer of redemption through love is made to play on love as an individual affair; the loving-kindness expressed by Luka is removed to the background. The man and the girl get clear in the end, and the characters almost inevitably have more freshness and charm than a Gorky original. But the relief an audience may feel over one case of deliverance is just one more token of its participation in the tragic hopelessness of life on those levels. And in general the play is served well, sense being read into the senseless topsy-turvy world of creatures that once were men without the nonsense that would lie in either overplaying its tragedy or making the tragedy suddenly all better.

But take the moral however you will, and in whatever sequence of scenes, Gorky's magnificent talent for absorbing life and for dramatic violence will be just so many words in a theater sense until the actual place is fixed and actual people set moving in it. In the conception and building of sets I can't think of a picture more successful than this. The gray, tumbledown general outlines of squalor are fairly easy: the real test of genius is in the delicate obtrusion of one out of the thousands of mean and unobtrusive details that swarm in such a culture by the millions, their mass giving it these characteristics of sluggishness and thick odor and refraction of all light. The rug in a room, as seen through an off-center door, properly laid and the hole in it visible only by scuffed-up edges, but in its lack of any life and pattern the suggestion of a musty smell. The axle-and-wheels thing in an angle of the court, so natural to that place and inscrutable as to its original purpose that it might have been moldering there half a lifetime. The junk in the kitchen, a useless profusion yet out of the way of household activities; the ironware mess of the pantry mostly cut off by the angle of the door. And any chance view of the court, the general dormitory, the rooms of the house, does not reveal the artificially shaky and decaying but only an original cheapness of joining and materials that has been worn smooth and chinked with filth until it is a monument to cheapness, native and timeless. The camera never has to focus on lice and waterbugs and roaches, for this woodwork is the official hotel of their obscene national convention.

In creative background I am sure the Frenchmen stand first. Both the Germans and the Russians have done beautiful things, but in Germany there has always been a national tendency toward stylization and kraut, and the Soviet artists have known all along that in registering Bad Smell anything less than four close-up angles on a dungheap is escapism and betrayal of the worker. Hollywood has played along and incorporated everything, often with a fine perception of the flawed excesses of the original, usually with the increased facilities of its millions and superb technicians, but always with too much awe for the general design and art layout, or too many absolutely authentic items photographed under too much high light. The British have followed every lead hopefully, but usually in the wrong suit.

But you can never truly separate a stage-setting from the costuming and carriage of the people moving across it; and surely Vladimir Sokolov as the pious fence is no less suggestively indigenous than the bugs in the ticking. The narrow hairy face, the bodily suggestion of scuttling in fear and creeping up with venom. Repulsive, subhuman, fascinating; the spider. All this comes through and adds immeasurably, though there can hardly be any doubt that Sokolov is a character actor with a part, which he milks in the best tradition (incidentally, the best tradition is being dealt a rather low blow in the movies, where situation is subordinate to continuity and where even the highest-class chewing of scenery cannot be tolerated because the scenery, like everything else, is vital in the total effect). Louis Jouvet (the Baron) makes a fine study of his part, for he is among the blessed of histrionic types—an arresting awkward figure, infinitely capable of shaping all odd motions into a grotesque central dignity that becomes beautiful as it mounts—from the goggling eye, the elevation and slow arc of the chin, the splayed walk or antic gestures in repose—until the mere figure as of the story is overshadowed by the complexity and premonition of the figure itself. Less prominent but more essential to the film's texture is Jean Gabin, the hardened picklock and lover in spite of himself. He has a fine strong head for the role and a trick of suggesting strength behind silence, sense and passion behind a guarded calm. This person or that incident may bulge in your mind afterward, but you may be sure that as the story was being released through the camera, the main cohesive was the part played by Jean Gabin, who gave no less and asked no more than the role stipulated. The girls Junie Astor and Jany Holt and Suzy Prim were about what women under those circumstances should be, and indeed the sister who loved Pepel was as much a rose among natural thorns as anyone could wish. It is the natural presence of these people, in this natural solid picturing of one of the world's most exciting pieces of dramatic creation, that sets this film above the general film level for eminence and power—without the director's ever showing a flash of the genius in the form peculiar to *(e.g.)* Capra, Clair, Ford, Milestone, Lubitsch, Lang, Pudovkin. It would seem that merely to sense what is enough, even in pictures, can be enough.

Mayerling (also from France) is another good film, but unreal even in pictures, where romance is so long and the facts of life so brief. The Archduke Rudolph is curbed and spied upon by the guardians of The State, which supposedly he personifies. If he finds pleasure in liberal-intellectual company, then pouf, the company is disposed of; if he falls in love, why nonsense, union can only be with some titled battle-ax, all reasons of state and no fun. If he gets out of line anywhere, they begin to rattle the royal chains, and the only thing he can do which won't be unseemly of a royal heir is go drinking and whoring around the capital, which he does. The problem is Charles Boyer's; the blaze of light in his somber life is Danielle Darrieux (a new lovely for screen parts); and so the thing is almost near and real as it is being acted out against its impeccable mounting. I can't remember when romance was more romancy, as a matter of fact, or hearts more true—but haven't we been through this proxied trouble before? And didn't we decide there was little to do but wring our hands and try to forget? Is it possible that even in the never-never land of movies we have come to demand that we be enlisted in struggles more closely allied to today or to the eternal fate of the race?

The Prisoner of Zenda is another thing again: it has the youth of royalty, to be sure, but its adventure is more outward and more ingeniously worked out through blades and black villains, moats, swordplay, escapes, and a young Englishman with a heart to lose. Certainly it is one of the best things in its class. They throw in everything but the War of the Roses and elephants, and if you were to question the producers on the probability of any one scene they would take you for someone from the Department of Internal Revenue; yet once the story is accepted, you can see how they have worked at it with sincerity and scrupulous care, treating its hokum almost with dignity. Ronald Colman in the main double role is one reason why the scenes are built into credibility; and Madeleine Carroll as Flavia is another reason, though it is unfortunate that anyone so lovely should occasionally suggest Ann Harding; Douglas Fairbanks, Jr., makes a good ornamental rogue; and C. Aubrey Smith is there for background. (Raymond Massey, if I were running the show, would speak all his lines with his back to the camera, through an interpreter.) So the young king is saved from himself and his brother, love is renounced and the national welfare invoked, and Zenda lives again, if any.

15 September 1937

The Breath of Life

In the recent group of pictures brought into the little houses, there is one more that deserves a report here, the Soviet *Baltic Deputy*. There is a power of truth in it, and it is in its way a beautiful thing. The revolution this time is only background for skirmishes and dangers on the field of scientific thought—some testy old coot of a professor, creaking around in his library and lecture halls with as young a fighting heart as the best of them. The story is based on a case in history, but the documents seem to have been pretty sparse so far as the thought content and narrative qualities are concerned. The man of thought publishes his book; sways the militant ranks with the idea that he is merely an extension of their advancing line, fighting their identical battle on the front of natural science; loses the respect and friendship of his rightful class; and is elected a political deputy by the Baltic sailors.

This, of course, is another case where the visual arts get into the difficulty of having thought processes for protagonists. But here, instead of even trying to symbolize the mental conflict, they cover up with attitudes fundamentally apart from it. The scientist's whole function is represented by no more than pledges of allegiance and a couple of library sets: what he was doing we have no better idea than the sailor had in all his gruff, charming naïveté, clearing the path with loyalty and fierce awe and drowning out all question or challenge with thunder: "Nichevo! He talked with Newton"; and even the printed congratulation from Lenin, on the completed masterwork in natural science, is no help: "I liked your remarks about the bourgeoisie." The wife, the nervous pupil-assistant, the chunky sailor in charge provide the incidents; the continuity as written and filmed by the two directors has neither shape nor pace; it just happens.

But the slow miracle of the life in its happening is what counts here, as is often the case with films made in this tradition. The miracle seems to bemuse us, and even the sternest of us will sometimes say: It was very real and good, therefore a good job of picture making, cinema indeed. So sometimes it is worth a little carping analysis to demonstrate that while you can knock these things into a cocked hat but can't stop them from living, the reason for this lies in a national genius for acting out and building up the truth of life in all its homeliness of detail and splendor; that the genius would show in any presentational art and that this is precisely why its presence should be no more characteristic of films than of puppetry. And so while this month's two additions to the 200-odd absolutely great Soviet directors probably couldn't hold script for a good producer of average Westerns, there is quite another thing in their traditional knowledge of character and how to let it speak through scenes and sets and camera.

The main thing here is not the story but the shrewd solid masonry in Nikolai Cherkassov's study of the professor, which continues to be a moving principle when the other characters come in to support it and when script and direction contrive such a sequence, both humor and heartbreak, as that where the old boy pits his valiance against the empty chairs of his birthday party. And where the continuity lies inertly in lumps like a hodful of coal, there still comes out this feeling that life is beautiful, all over again, and though we have not known or ever heard of this man who scorned wearing rubbers and made his crotchets the law of the house and did not know what to say in all this smell of sailors' sweat and herrings, and yet said it, softening craggy grandeur with the endearing small grass of human weakness, the figure is committed to our memory more vividly than any history. The greatness to be stated is not thrust upon us, but left to be discovered as we should come upon it in life, standing out of a massed confusion of details by some special immobility or gesture or statement of yes or no.

The foibles and busy purpose of this bent figure with its pinned shawl, gruff kindness, wrath and irony and frosty twinkle, are a magnificent piece of actor's business. But these and all the general creative business worked out within the sequence only serve to surround and support the bigger thing, the actor's sheer conception and will. Both actors and those working with them must see very deep into natural humanity to portray figures so solid. And here the things seen are projected with such authority, craft, and simple faith that the portrait itself becomes almost a substitute for drama, that other, connective thing with its tensions and clear gathering progression from cause to consequence. It is still a parable at heart; it is also one of the loveliest samplings of life ever taken by the camera.

29 September 1937

Cagney: Great Guy

It was just four years ago, when I hadn't been going to the movies very much, that I stopped around to see *Footlight Parade* and made the happy discovery of James Cagney. He had been known to almost everybody else before that in heavier roles (*Public Enemy*, for instance), and before he was well known at all he had been doing bits in pictures. But in this one he happened to be cast as the original Cagney, the hoofer and general vaudeville knockabout. The story had him drilling a line of girls, stomping out the routines and cracking around like the end of a whip, and even the presence of Dick Powell could not dim that vitality and flow of motion, and a grace before the camera that puts him in the company of the few who seem born for pictures.

It was a sunny introduction: seeing him you couldn't help feeling better about the industry—or the state of the nation for that matter. Because through this countrywide medium and in spite of whatever its story was about, this half-pint of East Side Irish somehow managed to be a lot of what a typical American might be, nobody's fool and nobody's clever ape, quick and cocky but not too wise for his own goodness, frankly vulgar in the best sense, with the dignity of the genuine worn as easily as his skin.

Since that time it has come out plainly that his character was no delusion of the flickers, that there was conscious purpose behind it. Once he was a star, Cagney used a star's privilege to tell them what was in character and what wasn't—gently, though, and with tactful stratagems, for he is no sea-lawyer (you will remember from the screen his trick of speaking more softly the more violent he gets). They wanted him to enounce with measure and dignity, now that he's got to be a star on them; so he had to explain that the characters he was portraying never knew anything about this enounce, measure, etc.; and an actor should be in character, shouldn't he? So they finally had to skip that. For *Jimmy the Gent* he got his head shaved and reported for work. The director was scared to death of shooting him that way (Ah, he kept saying with a slight accent, my main love interest should open with a head like a pig's knuckle?); and lord knows what the office would do. But Cagney gentled them and squared it with everybody—and anyway they couldn't hold up work while his hair grew—and managed to bring out a story about a thug who chased ambulances or sneaked up on dead horses or something, giving it the works. And if this wasn't the fastest little whirlwind of true life on the raw fringe, then I missed the other. When the picture *Here Comes the Navy* came out, the New York heavy lads naturally placed it for an incentive to imperialist war—Cagney had been so neat on his feet that only the common citizens got the obvious point of this bantamweight taking his blithe falls out of the stooge tradition of the United States Navy itself.

In such seemingly little ways he has managed to ad-lib, shift emphasis, and bring out his own relief. But behind that is the basic appeal he has for the audience as a person—under all that tough surface and fast talk people glimpse a sweet clarity of nature, a fellow feeling and rightness and transparent personal honesty. It makes all the difference in the world, and when he rips out a statement you sense without stopping to question that it is the living truth spoken through him, and not a line rehearsed and spoken on the set any longer. His screen life is not a natural autobiography, not something he just fell into. He is not a mug but one of the intelligent few; he isn't a perpetual handspring but a man with a troubling illness; his conversation is more a subdued questioning than a bright explosion of syllables; and while he swings all the punches in his stories he has been taking plenty on the chin in all these actual years, from down-under to up-on-top (no one can help wondering if the ship isn't sinking when Jimmie Fiddler creeps over ratguards to write a patronizing Open Letter from awfully safe ground). Don't think because he didn't produce *Hamlet* on Broadway last year that Cagney is automatically himself; and therefore no actor. His art is in an intense projection of those qualities within himself which he feels to be honestly representative of something, and in the fact that while all that rapid fire and assurance and open charm are enough to take the audience anywhere he wants to go, he has a guiding notion of where he's going.

Since blowing up on the Warners more than a year ago, he has made two modest semi-independent pictures. *Great Guy* was all right, but all right for a Class-B picture only, and it is hard to think of Cagney except on top. The new one, *Something to Sing About* is a different thing and about the happiest experience we've got in the last few months, what with all the lavish splashes and worthy wordage.

It's just about Cagney as a performing band leader who goes to the Coast on contract for one film. If I told the whole story I'm sure anyone could stop me because he'd heard it—they don't dare tell the boy how good he is, which he only finds out when the girl he's left behind him comes out for a honeymoon, and then his marriage has to be covered up for publicity purposes, which leads to domestic misery and a final happy finale with the band back home. But this story is less story than business, and the business is subtle, pointed, and meaty. For the producer and press agent (respectively) they have a couple of my favorite seasoned troupers, Gene Lockhart and William Frawley, who either catch the spirit of the thing or had the spirit bred in their bones. There are also the director, who is able to act like a director, the three fates from the department of elocution, make-up, and tailoring, and the Jap valet who speaks better English than any of us and originally had the acting ambition, now hidden behind a prop accent (Sank you, please).

The romance element is not helped by the girl Jimmie is supposed to go for like pups for biscuit, played by Evelyn Daw, a "find" who would be a mild sensation as typist on a WPA project but is fazed by the camera (not that she is afraid of it: there are times when she seems about to chew the hood), with a cute twitter of walking knock-kneed and a jaw always there ahead of her, the little-girl's voice pinched up under her nose, etc. (oh, it isn't her fault, poor girl, but neither is it ours). But in the way the rest of it is worked out there is enough snap and good fun about the movies to make it go.

It is likely that Cagney was responsible for a lot of the spoofing ("I've heard all I want to about Robert Taylor") and someone with union experience was certainly behind that comeback to the four-weeks-vacation offer: "Four weeks *successively?*"—and the Goldwyn producer answers with majesty, "Successively and positively." The fight is one of his favorite subjects: how to set the camera and throw a punch that will miss by millimeters, the precautions to take with green actors. Then his line about, Do these heavies understand this swing-to-miss stuff? You know him—Johnny Come Lately; he just doesn't want to be the only one around there playing house. And the business of the Hollywood double-take, the triple-take, the triple-take with a slow burn and the one-eye fadeaway, is brilliant.

Except for the scenes of the gang around the camera and boom, the actor on the set, the jam in the cutting room—the most quietly natural I've seen—and for bits like the cut in rhythm from the rushing minor thirds of the band to the westbound limited, the direction was run-of-the-mill and sometimes ham—Victor Schertzinger being still punch-drunk no doubt from the film he did with the great Grace ("Moo-Moo") Moore. The good time comes from the feeling that they had a good time making it, that Cagney said, Let's put this in and everybody said, Why not, and they worked it out, a black eye for authority here, a bit of fun at their own expense there. The independence and small budget gives them more leeway and genial leisure, and perhaps we ought to have more of the same (though it is true that Cagney's best film was made in the mass-production pattern: *Ceiling Zero,* still one of the finest).

I think much can be done by good people who break away and bring the industry up short by independent accomplishment. But when all is said and wherever he is, Jim Cagney is bound to shape up as a regular great guy you'd like to have around the house or on any job you're doing. Would anyone argue that in the sacred fields of art there is no room for such?

13 October 1937

Through the Looking Glass

I don't know where you will find so much delight and unspoiled entertainment as in the RKO picture *Stage Door*. The title, which they have scrupulously kept intact, once belonged to a chore Edna Ferber and George Kaufman did for Broadway. The play had some stage people for characters and a moral about how, for a *real* actress, Hollywood was a fate worse than death. It had quite a run and so the movies were happy to buy it. Then apparently they read it, and some smart producer put Morrie Ryskind and Anthony Veiller to work writing a picture around the title and Gregory La Cava to work directing the finished script. And the result is one of those miracles in celluloid.

The outline is simple: a school for girls with a theatrical boarding-house background. There is the little hoyden with the stout warm heart; there are the girl with a sensitive talent on the downgrade and the girl with the rich poppa riding her high horse; there are comradeship, cat fights, and the subsidiary play of gossip, rivalry, boy friends, meals, openings for work—in short the process of life going on. In the relationships of four or five of the girls and the producer, the main story is carried forward simply to the point where the one who should have the big part goes weak and deranged from hunger and walks through the window on opening night, and the smug one who actually got the part makes her entrance through a sudden knowledge of her own wooden deficiency and the sight behind her eyes of that wronged, crumpled figure lying in the alleyway.

The story as written belongs in the department of the true and trite; but I think most of us are agreed by now that the difference between the bound book and the experience is precisely the vital stuff the theater is made of, that even the simplest story can be so presented by actors and direction and living background that the emotional experience of those who follow could not be duplicated by anything short of some great long novel. As the girls sit around in the boarding-house parlor, swapping thrust and riposte and grousing about the stew, their lines and habit of living are undoubtedly both more brilliant and more warmly generous than life. But these reservations are not a part of the theater experience. All that counts is that while this picture is being reeled off it is humanly lovely, bright and sad and true, that any overdose of either brilliance or easy simplicity is carried off in the happy stream of the thing before your eyes. It is temperate with wisdom or perfectly ripping, at its own discretion.

What with Katharine Hepburn, Ginger Rogers, Andrea Leeds, Constance Collier, Gail Patrick, Lucille Ball, and all the others, it is a long time since we have seen so much feminine talent so deftly handled. When you think of Miss Rogers' former song-and-dance appearances, it seems as though this is the first chance she has had to be something more than a camera object and stand forth in her own right, pert and charming and just plain nice, her personality flexible in the actor's expression.

Andrea Leeds as the girl who starves has an arriving talent and a persistent gentle sweetness that puts the story much in her debt; and all around, from Constance Collier's veteran job on the elocutionary biddie to the singing housemaid and the dancing partner with the comeback and the little unsung heroine who marries men from Seattle, and Grady Sutton, and Adolphe Menjou, who drives the meaning and effect of the Broadway-producer part right down through the wood, countersunk.

About Katharine Hepburn, it has been recently fashionable to wink, pull a face, and *poor* Kitty and tsk, tsk, tsk, Hollywood has ruined her and of course she never was more than a couple of mannerisms and a hank of hair to start with, poor *Kate*. As the spoiled rich girl she comes into this story cold, playing across the grain of audience sympathy. But she is the girl of that awful first night, and there is felt through her as she comes on that tension of the inexorable rising curtain and first cue, when the actor is isolated within the range of his own devices and inner terror. And the effect in the audience is one of difficulties falling way in a command, faith, and purity of feeling that leave no room for a doubt or question anywhere.

The point of the story (oh wide and subtle revenge on tailormade wisecrackers) is the bias, cruel ignorance, and commercialism working behind stage productions, as it works in any art. But mainly it is just happy in its story and boarding-house routine—the girl with the cat, for example, wearing it draped around her neck and telling it (when the Perfect Lady shows up in a gorgeous fur): "Get a load of that, Henry; that's where *you'll* wind up," or (at the dinner bell): "Let's go in to the stew, Henry; you might find a mouse in it." And the direction is sometimes inspired, for even leaving out scenes of climax, you get a really first-class play of motion in such scenes as the one where the two girls are at each other's throats in the producer's penthouse, and he trying to square it with each of them, and poor Franklin Pangborn in and out and across corners like a bobbin, doors slammed in his face and harsh words spoken, the most baffling moment of his career. But although memory plays around the words and scenes of these minutes in the theater like blue flames around a Christmas pudding, quotation in example is misleading, the bare words of a report robbing the natural freshness of the actual thing in its context and film pace.

The people in action are the living matter of this piece; yet the idea and fulfillment of it, the direction, camera, and cutting had to come first. And however we analyze, the sum of its parts is one of those things we have to catalogue under the term Miracle, so little we know of it. The miracle happens when everybody concerned seems in sympathy with everybody else's intention and gives it play, each gaining in personal achievement from the common inspiration. Between its extremes of making you laugh and tearing your heart out and altogether beside what meaning it has, this picture is in touch with its audience at every point, it seems to grow along with them and they with it. And in this easy proximity the mechanical voice and flat halftone screen drop away like the dimensions in a stereopticon; and an audience of millions leaves its private life to take part in this hour or so of life recreated, passing as though through the looking glass.

27 October 1937

Old Man River

The film men who work for the Farm Security Administration are just now releasing a picture about soil erosion and flood control that is very strange and exciting, in all its departments a honey of a picture: *The River*. Pare Lorentz had an organization that would stagger even Hollywood: assistants, second assistants and third auxiliaries, advance men and supply men and sound experts, camera crews scattering out over the country, cutters working on what they brought back. But there was one man directing all of them and shaping the film, to bring these miles of stuff into the focus of a half-hour on the screen.

The picture starts with the Mississippi, with where it came from and where it went to and how it ran through American history—the drip of each season's melting snow gathering into trickles and the trickles into brooks, the brooks into branches, creeks, young rivers, small tributaries into bigger and all gathering volume ("The Mississippi River runs to the Gulf").

Then the story of men pushing across the river and spreading out to exploit its territory—cotton in the South, timber in the hills; the Civil War and its resultant clean sweep for the industrial big-time. With the soil harried to death and the timberland down, the despoiled land has its inexorable revenge. Down from the first thaw the waters converge to cover dry acres with inland seas and pestilence and floating rubbish. And now in our time the levee is built higher for a thousand miles and still the waters rise and thousands of families are swept before them. Sandbags are useless against this swollen power, and so there dawns (as easily as morning) the idea of control at the source, a whole network of dams and locks and spillways.

This is no sales talk, you have been conscious of no special pleading. The bulk of the picture is in the tragic stated problem, the floods and the parched soil and the hillsides cut to the quick and burned over, a continent as the mute playground for reckless spoilers, biding the time of its terrible revenge. And the last section develops as simply from that, as the resolution of any drama: what may and must be done, and the modern epic of our start on the Tennessee Valley ("You cannot plan for water unless you plan for land. . . . You cannot plan for water and land unless you plan for people"), dams and power plants in all their monstrous beauty, and shrewd crop rotation and homes for people and the significant planting of little trees. The picture as propaganda doesn't even have to try, because whatever it started out to do it has tapped a national dramatic source that has more potential splendor and vital energy than any number of quaint covered wagons or "births" of a nation. Crime and punishment, death and renascence ("And a generation growing up with no new land in the West—no new continent to build—a generation whose people knew King's mountain. And Shiloh. . . . ").

Outside of a Hollywood shot of riverboats and overage from *Come and Get It,* this film was all photographed by FSA men out in the country, under the three main camera supervisors, Stacey Woodard, Floyd Crosby, and Willard Van Dyke. What they brought back, over and above the spoiled negative, the repetitions, etc., is as good as anything that has been done. During the filming they had heartbreaks by the bushel basket, and after they thought they were all through (in January of this year), that old devil river raged over into the headlines, and so they went into the flood area in boats and over it in planes, and got some of the most exciting stuff of the picture. But quite apart from the flash element, some of the most beautiful stuff was framed in the course of duty—the sharecropper sequence on the one hand, the stump country and its angry growth of waters on the other.

The camera is alive, but you can't miss Pare Lorentz's part in mounting, in devising the whole picture and setting its pace. Because Pare Lorentz wrote the narration (I have never heard a film commentary with so much eloquence and restrained good taste as Mr. Thomas Chalmers sustains throughout his reading), and the narration makes both sense and poetry. The poetry of simple facts and names, the beauty of geography and national experience rising through the picture. You must see the small brooks everywhere running to waterfalls and slow bends and final open rivers before you get the sweet, haunting flavor of the words as they fall: "Down from the turkey ridges of the Alleghenies. . . . Down the Yellowstone, the Milk, the White and Cheyenne; the Cannonball, the Musselshell, the James and the Sioux . . . down the Miami, the Wabash, the Licking and the Green, the Cumberland, the Kentucky, and the Tennessee." And this is a theme, woven in at intervals—first it is the river as we found it, and then as we fought it, and then again as it has taken a swollen vengeance: "Down the Judith, the Grand, the Osage and the Platte, the Skunk, the Salt, the Black and Minnesota. . . . " There are other themes. First as the camera swings over great heads of timber, then as the double-blade axes bite in and loosen chips, then as the camera swings over a desolation of stumps and mean shrubs, with the rain falling and a sad mist hanging in the rear hollows as though to cover the path of this blind savagery (one of the loveliest things ever taken): "Black spruce and Norway pine; Douglas fir and red cedar; Scarlet oak and shagbark hickory; Hemlock and aspen. . . ."

These are not words for words' sake, but rather for what they can tell.

"Corn and oats down the Missouri, tobacco and whiskey down the Ohio; down from Pittsburgh, down from St. Louis. Hemp and potatoes; pork and flour; we sent our commerce to the sea." And the names of places, hanging on the edge of fond recollection, albeit we've never seen them: "New Orleans to Baton Rouge; Baton Rouge to Natchez; Natchez to Vicksburg; Vicksburg to Memphis; Memphis to Cairo—we built a dyke a thousand miles long." With the eye of the camera of these cotton fields, sawmills, wharves, levees, the words take on a majesty and meaning that move people as no history book will ever move them ("For fifty years we dug for cotton and moved west when the land gave out"); and teach them as they could never be taught ("For a quarter of a century we have been forcing more and more farmers into tenancy . . . no home, no land of their own, aimless, footloose, and impoverished"). It is like the truth of facts set to music (Virgil Thomson's actual score, thoughtful and indigenous as it is, forms only a constituent part of the total effect; which seems to have used the best of everything). And that is the way to do it always, so that people will see it not out of duty, but with pleasure.

10 November 1937

A Lick and a Promise

The funniest picture of the season is called *The Awful Truth.* (*It's Love I'm After* is supposed to be its twin for rollicking, but what with relentless overemphasis and crude hangfire direction I did not find it so, except for the part and person of Eric Blore.) Leo McCarey's version of one of the oldest theatrical hats—the divorced pair who come to realize that marriage was nice work after all, if you could get it back—seems to be a true director's triumph. Take this story and any actors, and you could so easily get something that would serve you right; take these actors (Cary Grant, Irene Dunne, Ralph Bellamy) in any story, and you could get the same results or worse. But that is only speculation; what we actually have is thorough comedy, a whole pattern that is neither actor's vehicle nor technician's holiday. It is quite grown-up, and even the hotter passions are endured with consideration and suavity; at the same time it has an innocent zest for the homely that makes you think back to Capra again.

Miss Dunne is getting a divorce from Cary Grant at the beginning, she can't *stand* that man, and presently she is taking up with Ralph Bellamy, who apparently plays a perfect Good-Time Charley from the long timber without realizing it much. She keeps running into Mr. Grant, who is killingly polite about everything, even Charley and his mother—much more helpful than is necessary, and perhaps a shade too apt in showing up at the wrong times. That keeps going on, and there is a nance music teacher who make a lot of trouble for his size and talent, a sour aunt, and something about some motorcycle cops. I can't remember very clearly what they did because I was laughing, and everybody was laughing, and it kept going on like that.

The dialogue is good, clever, or uproarious; but dialogue fades so quickly in the air, and here there is the necessary visual play to complement it. For one example from a whole picture, take the closing sequence, with the weakly latched door between their private rooms, his coaxing the rising breeze through the window to blow it open, stealthily adding the weight of his fingers, finally getting down to peer under it for obstructions and (from the other side) the girl lying awake and listening, suddenly the cat getting up and walking off in her private way, letting the door open on him kneeling there in the most ludicrous flannel nightgown. All this without a word, all clear and (in its small way) exquisitely final.

It is simply that way all through, gay and ridiculous but too serenely founded in the commonplace of actual life to be confused with the more irritated humorous intention of those who rack their brains for gags, falls, punch lines, and the cake-dough blackout. It is a foolishness that doesn't go wrong or strained, and for this the script men must be partly responsible. In the general taste, motion, and final pictorial result, above all in a sense of timing that is as delicate and steady as a metronome, you can see the hand of a man who is sufficiently an artist in movies so that he can make one out of almost anything, with almost anybody.

There are lots of pictures, some of which I promise to go into when we get some space around here: *Stand-In,* which is just as good as *The Awful Truth* and the sharpest comedy on Hollywood low-life yet; *Conquest,* which is a handsome job on love and Napoleon; *The Hurricane,* which seems to contain a hurricane and bits of goona-goona; *The Return of Maxim,* which is second in a trilogy, quite strong in spots, also pedantic and talky. Add musicals: *A Damsel in Distress* is absolutely the saddest of the Astaire pictures, which have been getting no better; *52nd Street* is the ripest turkey since they wired Ted Lewis for sound; on a clear morning you can smell it from here.

1 December 1937

Home Truths from Abroad

Paul Rotha, the English film man, has done a lot to solve the problem of independent film making. With John Grierson and others he has got several units under way in England, making documentary, "realistic" two- and three-reelers for whoever will back them. I have just seen several of the more successful ones, of which some are beautiful, some striking, and some just true.

There are difficulties, for these short nonfiction films develop most easily when the subject itself is in motion and presents rudimentary conflict. All there is to do in *Housing Problems* (directed for the gas industry by Arthur Elton and Edgar Anstey) is to show the old rickety houses and the lives within them, crowded and filthy, crawling with vermin, full of the air of decay and back-stairs privies; then set this off against modern developments, built reasonably enough so that the same people can move into them, and get clean for the first time, and sit looking at the four-star luxury of a bath with running water. So this is what they do, a moderate workmanlike job which wouldn't be exciting if it weren't for the people, and the trick of interviewing them with sound-truck and camera.

And these are absolutely the most genuine people I ever saw on the screen, speaking right up in their own words and habits of phrase and no nonsense about it. There is no suggestion of pose; there is above everything a shrewd dignity that keeps them both from whining and from the pathetic little makeshifts with which men and women usually try to hide their poor condition. They are fair sick of the cramping and dirt and stink, they have fought it and never won out and it's not their fault, and they let you have it with both barrels; with cynicism and the eloquence of disgust.

Getting people like this is never accidental and the genius behind this is apparently Ruby Grierson, who got to these people and earned their confidence, smoothed away embarrassment and suspicion, singled out those with a direct voice and a natural twist of word, and worked them over until they would as soon talk to a camera as to Mrs. Flibbity on the next stoop. And that is what makes it really fine.

Children at School was also made for the gas industry, but simply does not come off. The old and the new again, a competent statement of a problem, but no life, no fire—even the kids are stiff. *We Live in Two Worlds* (directed by Alberto Cavalcanti for the Post Office Film Unit) falls in the same category eventually, though it has some very fine pictures of life in Switzerland, and an imaginative treatment of the boundary walls of nationalism.

My favorite among social films is Rotha's production, for the National Council of Social Service, *Today We Live* (direction credited to R. I. Grierson and R. Bond). It opens on the dead mining and industrial region in Wales and (I think) Yorkshire, a perfectly stunning sequence of still wheels and tipples, chimneys with no smoke, no motion except the advance of rust and rot. This is the true wasteland, for nothing will grow in it except people, who grow sparely. So the camera goes to the people living listless and cheap, their rough strong hands bewildered with idleness. In their homes, into their pubs, into their doled pennies.

But the idea of this film was to show how the Council is serving England socially, and of course the Council felt that its work in rehabilitation through community life was enough solution to guarantee a happy ending, the people *were* being made happy, weren't they? The producers said "Yeah"; but to themselves. It is the implicit irony of their last section that brings it under the wire (and it was a long struggle of conferences to do that), making it serve both the truth and the very distributing facilities that would alone make such truth available. One town gets a social center; the other a center where things can be made and mended. The people work and sing again—and supposedly the chap who keeps hanging back and objecting is just a typical sea-lawyer. But in the end, as the camera shifts from activity to the great mills and mines again, gutted and silent, this chap gets the last word, the word of truth. He agrees it's better than nothing. "But *this* isn't our work," he says; "not the work we want"—and your eyes go involuntarily to the bulge in his coatsleeves and his hands, gnarled from their training, strong and good and useless.

Of all the six I saw (there was a Len Lye color oddity that was quite free and new), the one most naturally effective was *The Night Mail.* You can see the possibilities at once: The Postal Special (Basil Wright and Harry Watt did this for the Post Office) leaves London and tears along up through England all night, coming into Glasgow in the morning. All the business of wheels and steam and the counties of England, the whistle for the crossing, the far sound coming nearer, the rush of iron and fire and the mailbag ripped from its patent hanger, and they're out of the sleeping town again, off up the line. The junction, engines shifted and trucks rattling to load and unload letters by the ton, men shouting and heaving and jumping around to beat the schedule. The London crew goes off here and the Glasgow shift takes over, swinging on with familiar banter. Inside the cars there is a steady business of dumping, sorting, resacking, always to beat the schedule—when they pass the first bridge, and then the second bridge, and count the beats of the 95 rail-ends, then the sack for that town has to be ready and strapped, tied to its patent davit and swung out; there is a sound like a shot, the davit swings in empty, and *that* town has had its mail delivered in its sleep.

The exposition covers a hundred fascinating details, the knots used, the method of sorting, the stationmaster's telephone, the struggle with faulty addressing—the romance of the ordinary, "the world is so full of a number of things," etc. But there is more than the mechanics of the job; the men work as men actually do work, with deftness here, a bit of puzzlement there, with an economy of phrase and an occasional grunt, always with a little ragging, done with a nudge, a look, a knowing word. And as the crews shift and they get farther into the North, the accents thicken. Well, the mail gets to Glasgow, the post office sells us (painlessly) its bill of goods, and we have got more interest and excitement than if the Postal Special had been wrecked, robbed, and reported by Bette Davis.

Paul Rotha is trying to get something like his and Grierson's multiple-unit system working over here; and this is interesting enough to be gone into later, when I have seen the rest of the films which Rotha is now showing through the Museum of Modern Art, and which you could start setting up a yell for locally.

15 December 1937

1938

From *Snow White* to *The Beachcomber*

Walt Disney's Grimm Reality

To say of *Snow White and the Seven Dwarfs* that it is among the genuine artistic achievements of this country takes no great daring. In fact, outside of Chaplin, Disney's is the one Hollywood name that any corn doctor of art and culture dare mention without fear of losing face, or on the other hand of having to know too much about the subject. There is this to be said of Disney, however: he is appreciated by all ages, but he is granted the license and simplification of those who tell tales for children, because that is his elected medium to start with. It is not easy to do amusing things for children, but the more complex field of adult relations is far severer in its demands.

Snow White is a fairy-tale, surely the most vivid and gay and sweet in the world; it is done in color, photographed on different planes to give depth, and it runs almost an hour and a half. Some of the short cartoons have been more of a riot, some have been more tender even. But this is sustained fantasy, the animated cartoon grown up. The fairy-tale princess is just what you would have her; the witch is a perfect ringer for Lionel Barrymore (not by accident, I take it); and the seven dwarfs have been perfectly humanized by somewhat the same technique, though each is more a composite of types, not quite identifiable. The animals of course are as uncannily studied and set in motion as they have always been.

The Disney artists and animators are practically zoological, nearer to the actual life of animals than any who have endowed it with human traits for purposes of fable. Take the young deer in the little scene where the forest life first gathers around Snow White: shy but sniffing forward, then as she starts to pat it, the head going down, ears back, the body shrinking and tense, ready to bound clear; then reassurance, body and head coming up and forward to push against the hand—half a dozen motions shrewdly carried over from the common cat. Or take the way (later) the same deer moves awkward and unsteady on its long pins in the crush of animals milling about, as it should, but presently is graceful in flight, out in front like a flash. Disney has animals that are played up for comedy, like the turtle here, the lecherous vultures, the baby bird whose musical attempts are a source of alternate pride and embarrassment to his parents (on a finale he will get as high as eight inches straight up from the limb); but even in these cases, the exaggeration is based on typical form and trait.

The story is familiar in its simple fantasy. The castle, the stepmother with her black arts, Snow White escaping in the forest and keeping house for the little men; the witch seeking her out with the apple of living death; finally the young prince coming to break the charm. But all of Disney's fantasy starts out with a simple frame of story: the main body of the thing is incident. And the incidents start from a firm base in the realism of the everyday, serving to steady the fantastic (dwarfs, witches, alchemy) either by complementing it with the matter-of-fact, or by becoming fantastic through a seemingly logical progression from their common shape and function. Thus the fairy-tale dwarfs, in their diamond mine and home, go about their business in a highly natural manner, digging, appraising, grading, leaving the dirty dishes and going to bed. And thus the birds and animals, invading the empty house with the shy fits and starts appropriate to them as real birds and animals, fall to helping the girl clean up with highly unnatural abilities (the squirrel's tail for a bottle brush, other tails for brooms and dusters; the birds winding up cobwebs, flying with sheets).

I was disappointed to see the comedy faltering at times here. Such things as running into doors and trees on the dignified exit, the jumbled consonant (bood goy, I mean goob doy, I mean . . .), headers into various liquids, etc., are short of good Disney. For the most part, the thing is as ingenious as ever, the idiosyncrasies of each dwarf quickly established and made capital of—Grumpy, Dopey, and Sneezy in particular—the flow of comedy through animism still on that level at which Disney's men have never been equaled. Witness the organ pipes in that wonderful music-hour sequence, made of penguins, the vent holes being choked off with little clappers, Grumpy frequently losing patience with his stop and whacking them shut by hand.

It is not all comic and quaint. The imaginative transformation of the stepmother, her mission, flight, and death (the vultures banking slowly down in the dark air), make a suspense and chase interval that will put your heart back a few seconds; and there is something not mawkish but gentle and nice about the little girl, her face and singing and adventures in friendliness with every living thing. Something beautiful about all of it, I think, because it does not try to be wise about fairy-tales, or fairy-talish about its birds, rabbits, people. And all of it, the whole feature-length true motion picture, is nothing but a hundred-odd thousand colored drawings, photographed, and set to music.

The art work is fine, particularly the castle at night, the scenes in the woods, the march home of the little men. The color is the best ever, though it is true that its pastels would be up against more difficulty in a film less deliberately imaginative. And music is as much a part of the picture as it always is in the Disney scorings, with nice songs and a rollicking chant and swell background stuff for the moods of the story.

Disney gives credit to his directors, animators, musicians in a way that is heartening to see and a list as long as your arm; but while it is true that his pictures are built on the conference method, good ideas being kicked around until they suggest others, there is the fact that he apparently has known how to pick his men, train them, and give them free rein to contribute their individual best. A film is a collective enterprise anyway and should be made that way; but in general there are too few men of talent at the top who have the leadership and patience, the exaltation of job over ego, to do it. Walt Disney is a pioneer in more things than his conception of and tireless experiment with the animated cartoon as a reflection of life. Now that the best picture of 1937 has been adjudicated, awarded, etc., the best and most important picture for 1938 is called *Snow White and the Seven Dwarfs.*

26 January 1938

Time Steals a March

The boys at the March of Time are pretty gleeful these days, for their re-lease on Nazi Germany has kicked up more dust than anything in films for a long while, and Dorothy Thompson has come through with a column. The question of controversial subjects in the movies has been broken wide open, because the reel is controversial with a bang, yet quite the opposite of keeping people away, it has even topped the business done by the *Hindenburg* newsreel at the Key Embassy theatre. As for out-of-town business, the report last week was that competitors of theaters on the Warner chain (from which Harry Warner has banned the film on rather questionable and certainly amusing grounds) are scrambling to book it themselves, which is to spit in the Warner exhibitors' eye, and is relayed quickly back to the main office. Proving merely this: that if you do a job well, you can do about anything in films as elsewhere, and people will pay to see it.

However, the March of Time has had favoring winds for this venture. They do not book in Germany. The American Nazis are numerically a minor national group; no large interests are touched; a big and determined Jewish group is on the other hand benefited. And the Hays office with its stooge decency legions should not be opposed (at the time this went to press Will himself was still presumably in the woodwork and that end of Hollywood's horse known as Martin P. Quigley had not trumpeted the attack). A film like *The River* isn't so lucky.

In answer to those wooden-wits who have insisted on reviewing the film as an exposé, crying, Where is the hydra? Where are the hobgoblins? Where is the rotting flesh and do you mean to say that Nazis don't have tails? the editors have run in a little note saying that this is merely an objective pictorial record. This gets them off on the wrong foot, because the pictures could be duplicated almost exactly with shots of life in the USSR itself: the cutting and the commentary give them their direction. The film is really an editorial with pictures, an editorial for democracy and against suppression, militant nationalism, and shoving people around. Balanced, fairly complete, decisive, it is a more likely statement of Germany today than many of the editorials we have seen printed, for that matter. (Where do you think the people who protest get their idea of a ground covered with dragons and an air full of darkness and *New Masses* cartoons anyway?)

The March of Time starts with travel posters and Berlin as the showcase of Germany today, good food, the normal pleasure throng, etc. You wouldn't guess from the surface that underneath are these facts: The population is squeezed to pay for it. The working-man has got a job, yes, but the government says when, where, what and ten dollars a week (average). He eats, yes, but on something like war rations. He saves scraps. He accepts as minor prosperity what we would call being on relief—why? Here the film goes into the propaganda machine of Mr. Göbbels: pageantry, slogans over and over in the papers and on the air, every thought and action under rigid control. Make Germany self-sufficient (produce much, use little), mighty (the best work of the population going into munitions, military roads, tanks, ships, etc.), and nationally pure (down with Jews, swastikas over churches, endless steeping in the national legend). Get them early, and keep at them, primitive schools, compulsory military service, work camps, the frenzy and superb spectacle of mass meetings and parades. So they give and give and endure in a sort of glory—why? Because the machine is infinite and psychologically simple, and it kills off the inquiring intellect that we had thought separated men from oxen, even if heads must be lopped off along with it.

The camera covers all this; the editors have cleverly intercut shots of Hitler and the boys, and kept the scene shifting. Beatings, concentration camps, undercover opposition are not shown. These things are missed, but as frescoes on the main idea—like lynching in a democracy. Toward the end, the film jumps over to the United States for the activities of Fritz Kuhn's *Bund* and the resounding slap he got from the Southbury burghers. It underlines Ambassador Dodd's message on the threat to peace in Europe and goes back to the funny and terrible pomp of Duce-meets-Führer, and closes on a marching Germany, oiled, armored, and belligerent ("democracy talks, fascism acts"), the Frankenstein's Thing of the Western world.

For a while I had a sneaking idea that it might be just as well not to encourage anything so rickety in social theory as Luce Enterprises to go in for open crusading, this being the kind of gun as likely to blow its breech out as produce a true salvo. But that is a consideration for the future, which already seems to be in the proper hands. For the present it is heartening to see good young blood making a field-day of the creaky superstitions of the movie trade. The best reassurance in the case of Time's *Inside Nazi Germany, 1938* grows out of the report that around the office in the feverish days before deadline, never had hard work (this was their first entire release on a single subject) seemed easier. Working under Louis de Rochemont (a veteran film man) on the shots Julien Bryan brought back from Germany, the majority of this staff seems to have been working on something it believed in. And in making any good thing, belief tells in the end. Even if the heat were put on Luce Enterprises and the liberal element were tossed out, where could you gather replacements of talent who might throw punches with the same conviction for the side of darkness (look at *The American Mercury*)? The larger fuss of smaller talents often obscures the fact that, working quietly in the creative arts, some of our best people are radicals.

9 February 1938

Gone Are the Days

David O. Selznick's colored-candy version of *The Adventures of Tom Sawyer* should make Mark Twain circulate in his grave like a trout in a creel—sentimentalist though the old boy was, partial though he was to the black-and-white, the character bromide. Twain used a rather crude story, but mainly to hold together all the details of remembered boyhood, the houses, back fences, the church and schoolroom and busy kitchens at suppertime, in the little town on the great river. Swimming and pirates and glassies, fish hooks, hoptoads, bare feet and Saturday chores, and behind-the-ears inspection, and walking past Her house—all the fearful adventures and penalties of that lost country restored to the mind with a sort of perfection in miniature. And since the outward form of that boyhood has passed as surely away as the busy quiet town on the old Mississippi (its main form has shifted even in our own time), the book has above its own endearments the quaint charm of history.

Well, Messrs. David O. Selznick and Norman Taurog are busy men in a million-dollar venture. They got a book here, a classic; they got a script for it even; a production date, a location. So make a picture. But high class. All right, they comb the country for ideal actors; they build sets, beautiful sets, every last detail cross-checked for historical accuracy; they figure angles and costumes and how to get every precious happening (it's a classic, ain't it?) into the story. All precautions have to be tripled because the film is done in color. They work with all the energy and skill at their command week after week, a small army of them, a small city of the arts—and what do they get?

The Film Library of the Museum of Modern Art has built its "Making of a Movie" exhibit around this picture, showing from script revisions and location diagrams to costumes, sets, and sneak previews the amazing resource and patience that were behind its millions of things and dollars. But the Film Library exhibit gives the tip-off. In one panel there are specimens of correspondence with Joe (Seal) Breen and with the British office, all about making this film safe for English exhibitors, Catholics, and kiddies. Selznick, however, is so imbued with the classicism of this story that in one place he goes so far as to say that if the British censor laws rule out his main scene in the church, then to hell with the British—he'll make it anyway and provide an alternate sequence for England. He agrees to go light on kids swimming naked, the whipping of Tom, Injun Joe's violence and death; words that might Give Offense ("Lord" is one) are to be deleted; and in one place there is a rather quaint note of protest against required excision: "The Biblical quotations you [this to old Watch and Ward Breen himself] drew our attention to, such as 'Spare the rod and spoil the child,' 'Virtue is its own reward,' are not actual Biblical quotations"—on account of they come from Shakespeare and Browning, who were only poets. Thus it goes, and the real point of pre-censorship is still only implicit, because there exists from the start a *pre*-pre-censorship attitude on the part of all worried producers, a nervous watchfulness lest any real flavor get in to degrade the mix of Dignity and Good Taste appropriate to classics. The Film Library exhibit shows the vast and intricate workings of the movie industry. But it has nothing to say about the actual *making* of a movie: there is no word expressed here of the real mood and meaning of the thing—scads of research about what Huck Finn might have worn; of his immortal figure, nothing.

As to the picture itself, the infancy of color photography provides the exact comment: that painted sky, that punkin-moonshine moon, that road-show-opera version of gypsyish rags and tatters—what more of life and feeling can they describe than the sentiments of a picture postcard? The story of the original is shoddy melodrama at best—it isn't for the *story* that Tom Sawyer lives in memory. But with unerring touch these people follow the story, parading its episodes stiffly, squeezing each character and episode for more emotional pulp than Twain himself ever conceived. As to the casting, the final choice led inevitably to the well-smoked-ham type (*vide* May Robson's Aunt Polly) or to youngsters so cute and colorless and eager that inveterate mugging could be taught them in two easy lessons.

In motion the picture is so pretty and futile that there would be no need to mention it at all if it were not for the finger it points. In spite of the unconscious gaiety and tiny evil of the kids in things like *La Maternelle* and the newer French ones about to be shown here (*Merlusse* and *Generals without Buttons*), in spite of the fine and more advanced child psychology of *Mädchen* and *Captains Courageous* and *Poil de Carotte* and *The Devil Is a Sissy* and *Boy of the Streets*—in spite of all that has been done for and accepted as truth by the people, it is still assumed that in the case of one of the stories dearest to the popular heart, the people want a chocolate-marshmallow sundae, with nuts, and have elected as expressions of their will the Messrs. Hays, Breen, Quigley, and their whole auxiliary of dull but militant battle-axes. I prefer to give the people a better break. Stupid they are, yes; but more than that, they are inert. Busy as they are on their own precarious business of staying alive and liking it, their combined quiescence and innate gullibility give franchise on lesser matters to a prime collection of time-servers, ego-preeners, and out-and-out political quacks, the like of which has rarely been seen.

Young men of faith, ability, and a purpose will constantly arise to confound any such self-constituted authority. But these attempts so far are sporadic, too occupied with the working of an art itself to cope with the log-rolling organization set up to stifle it. Someday a shrewd fellow is going to rally the American people against the minority strivers who have put a ring in their nose; and he is probably going to achieve this by dark and bloody ways. It will be very regrettable—but it will be poetically just. Mr. Hays, Mr. Breen, Mr. Quigley, and their kind are a little too stupid to see that their course of restriction cannot be tolerated by the slow inevitable growth of such a healthy popular art. A *David Copperfield* is made, and makes money; a *Tom Sawyer* is made and *it* makes money. But rising behind these successes, encouraged by the life and meaning of pictures less classic and more satisfying, there is a potential source of strength. May not the ship desert sinking rats? Arise, folks, and spit in their eye.

2 March 1938

Film-Goers' Grab Bag

In view of the heavy thought that has recently gone into the question Is Humor Best for Us? I am happy to report that *Bringing Up Baby* is funny from the word go, that it has no other meaning to recommend it, nor therapeutic qualities, and that I wouldn't swap it for practically any three things of the current season. For comedy to be really good, of course, there is required something more in the way of total design than any random collection of hilarities. There must be point—not *a* point to be *made,* which is the easy goal of any literary tortoise, but a point from which to start, as implicit throughout as the center of a circle. *Bringing Up Baby* has something of the sort. The actual story goes into the troubles of a paleontologist who first offends a prospective angel for his museum, then his fiancée, and then gets into the wild-goose affairs of a girl and her leopard and terrier and other family members, ending up in jail and of course in love. That could be done in two reels. What puts the dramatic spirit into it is the character of the harebrained young thing who gets him mixed up in all this.

Katharine Hepburn builds the part from the ground, breathless, sensitive, headstrong, triumphant in illogic, and serene in that bounding brassy nerve possible only to the very very well bred. Without the intelligence and mercury of such a study, the callous scheming of this bit of fluff would have left all in confusion and the audience howling for her blood. As it is, we merely accept and humor her, as one would a wife. Cary Grant does a nice job of underlining the situation; there is good support from Barry Fitzgerald, Walter Catlett, May Robson (the leopard was better than any of them, but is it art?). The film holds together by virtue of constant invention and surprise in the situations; and Howard Hawks' direction, though it could have been less heavy and more supple, is essentially that of film comedy. All of which could be elaborated, techniques analyzed, points cited, etc. But why? *Bringing Up Baby* is hardly a departure; it settles nothing; it is full of an easy inviting humor. So do you want to go or don't you.

There are several current films that I suppose ought to be mentioned in the comedy department, either because they try to be funny or because they try not. *The Goldwyn Follies*—folly all right, in color, with Adolphe Menjou, Andrea Leeds, the Ritz Brothers, and few else I want to remember—is some of it quite amusing and some of it awful. . . . *Marco Polo* is a fantastic bit of candy and something went wrong. It has Gary Cooper playing straight, Ernest Truex apparently playing a comic, the rest of the Hollywood natives playing subjects of the Khan. To make the rousing adventure its subject suggests, they should have junked most of the elaborate background and used some sense. . . . And there has been an idea going around that *A Slight Case of Murder* is a comedy (which it may be if comedy means a story of farce complexion with laughs coming at you from way down the track like a freight in a nightmare). The idea of a beer racketeer (Edward G. Robinson) going straight and getting innocently tied up with four cadavers and an affair between his daughter and a cop, still shows enough of the irresponsibly fantastic to have made the highest flight in humor. But it was directed by a truck driver, and if the mere sweating intention of its tired clatter has any life on the screen, then there is something of life I miss in the following image: Picture four grown men seriously occupied for fully two minutes in going through spasms of gagging, spitting, and retching to establish the climactic and hilarious point that the beer, of which each has had one swallow, is not good-tasting beer. That's all.

Though hampered a little by a satirical point that is eccentric to the story, *Generals without Buttons* is a picture you could truly call sweet. At the Filmarte in New York—French with dialogue titles. The story (if not its awful prologue) goes in a breath: Two French villages are ancient enemies, one praying for the rain to grow its cabbages, the other for sun on its grapes. The new girl teacher finds the children fighting in gangs, and with the help of the neighboring mayor (young, naturally) brings about peace among them. The joint *fête* ends in an adult brawl with the kids looking on wisely, but fearing that when they grow up, even they may be just as foolish. It is simple, but pervaded with the take-your-time air around these tiny clusters of houses, hidden from the progress of time in their lovely countryside. And it simply runs over with the life of children, seen completely in the eternal double-existence of their secret world, in which there is so much more time and fervor for codes, ritual, high deeds.

There is a little play in the schoolroom and homes, but this story is occupied with councils of war, and skirmishes under a strategic leader. Capture by the enemy means the humiliation of having all your buttons cut off and how would you like that, let alone your parents? They try to fight naked, then get a scheme for hoarding all the buttons in the village—the girls, sending off their heroes as is the custom, will sew them on and they will be impregnable. The war is practically won when they take the enemy chief's pants off altogether, but the large matter of good pants lost in a poor village brings the elders in.

The kids are fine, so grave, wily, and determined that the story keeps its suspense effortlessly. The director, Jacques Daroy, apparently had the talent to see that since his story depended on boys, the will to follow was a boy's will, and the thing to do was accept the children's code of values as perfectly natural until they were unself-conscious and interested, and then say, "All right, we're going to have a war for a bit," and start the cameras. The leading young ones have talent of course, but it is the just talent of expression through themselves, as opposed to the customary hobbling process of seeing a thing as they see their elders seeing them see it.

So the film does nicely, carrying its mild preachment along on a sort of natural delight. Outside of the envious squealer all of them are more brave and kind than might be found in life. But that is the solidarity of danger I suppose, and any suggestion of the goody-goody should be dispelled by the picture of the rearguard valiant up a tree, the enemy surrounding and stoning him and trying to beat him into saying the catchphrase of surrender, and he is saying everything else. For a climax he is stuck. *Et puis,* he screams at them, defiant and furious and blubbering openly, *et puis—et puis, merde!*

16 March 1938

Movies: The Fat with the Lean

Bluebeard's Eighth Wife suffers from trying so hard. Of course Ernst Lubitsch directed it and of course it has all sorts of apt comedy talent—Gary Cooper, Claudette Colbert, David Niven, Franklin Pangborn, Herman Bing, Edward Everett Horton. And when its situations are funny, which is often the case, it is very funny. But the Alfred Savoir plot was rancid from the start.

Gary Cooper, as the big financier with seven divorces behind him (a slight miscast in one eye here), falls in love with Claudette, and vice versa. Fine. It might happen to you. But though the last hope of a titled family practically on relief, Claudette has a mind of her own—proud as Lucifer, to coin a phrase worthy of the situation. So they get married, but little recks he. *She* is not going to be tossed aside like an old sock; his haughty whatsis must be broken. So a good part of the story turns around the two of them wildly in love and honeymooning all over Europe, and spring at that, and she won't let him touch her, absolutely no dice. Yes I know, but that is what it says. Months go by and fie sir not I sir she simply will not take off her things and stay a minute. Yes I know again, but according to the story he doesn't.

So finally to prove she is the kind of girl worth waiting for, she drives him into a nervous breakdown and divorce and he sees (here is another hot off the mint) the error of his ways. If they had come out with the story of the Indian squaw and the broken glass, or if the couple had been Grace Moore and Charlie McCarthy, we could at least have swallowed the yarn up to the point where he was taken off to the sanitarium, just a bundle of splinters and well out of it at that. But otherwise the whole idea is so (1) absurdly fake, or (2) inherently morbid, or (3) both, that laughter at antics becomes more uneasy, strained, and flat as the thing runs on. In the end it is hard to remember laughing even when the comedy was most bright and clever.

Merlusse, a contrast from France, is curiously successful in making a short story into about an hour of feature picture. There are many things Marcel Pagnol does not know about setting the pace of a film story, and in a way this quiet ignorance works in his favor. He has a sure touch for certain human and dramatic values, and the main test anyway is whether a man can bring the thing off, which he does. The story is a sort of Christmas-Carol affair, and if the obstacles to any kind of success aren't apparent at first, just imagine a standard program picture going into the subject of the gruff schoolmaster who finally betrays his sensitive love for children (Lionel Barrymore, Jane Withers, and Our Gang), and try not to laugh.

In the drab atmosphere of a nearly deserted boarding school at Christmas, the film is immaculate. Surely there is nothing more desolate in the back of your memory than the bare scuffed corridors and boxed rooms, the fixed, unfriendly lighting, desks and chairs, the air of a hostile and inscrutable discipline as heavy in the air as the mixed smells of ink and chalk dust and cedar pencil shavings, old books and paper, wet shoes and girls' hair—all that from the schoolroom after hours heightened by the contrast with the home festival of all but this handful of little misfits and toughies who either had no home for Christmas or weren't wanted at it. (The spirit of all this is beautifully underlined in the shot of the long dining hall, with the handful of them at supper deep at the end of that long hall of tables, the high shadows of the line of boys marching, etc.)

The story element is in abeyance through most of the film. We merely see the kids and the routine of their Christmas Eve under the ogre with the glass eye, whom they call Merlusse, the old dried codfish. Exercise, study period, dinner, and finally to their beds in the cold dormitory. The only real action, in fact, is the surprise twist of the kids getting up in the morning to find, in each of the shoes left under their beds, some toy or favor or prize of boyhood. It was old one-eye—someone peeked and caught him at it during the night. So while he is still out washing they get up their personal treasures and pile them on his bed, being touched as they should be, sensing the desperate bluff of his former defenses as well as we can from the action which follows. (The final bit ties up a thread running in the background of the story, of Old Merlusse's unpopularity and his possible failure of advancement.) Really a *tour de force* and turned quickly, it is still done with such delicate true sentiment, such a fireside warmth of what we forever hope to find in human nature and with steady disappointment, that it throws a glow back over the whole picture, giving it the total illusion of truth (and let who will be clever).

And Besides. – The New School for Social Research, taking advantage of the current interest in factual-fiction films from life, has embarked on an interesting if shaky experiment in presenting a course on the documentary film. Worst lecture so far: Terry Ramsaye, who was entertaining enough in a strange informal manner that combined the oracular sneer with a petulant down-at-the-heel nihilism. If there was anything good as art in the movies, that was "our" mistake, meaning the mistake of Mr. Ramsaye and other big movie men. As a matter of fact Mr. Ramsaye has followed the industry since magic-lantern days but as an amanuensis rather than a magnate: he is still a follower and his feet hurt. His talk, illustrating the "documentary" content of fictional films, was as far off the track as the exhibit—which consisted of dramatic moments from such nondocuments as the inevitable *Covered Wagon*.

Best lecture so far: Jean Lenauer, who had Cavalcanti's *Rien que les Heures* (1923); Ruttmann's *Melody of the World* (about the first sound film in Europe); and Ivens' *New Earth* to talk about. Only a theater exhibitor, and more at home in other languages than in English at that, Lenauer spoke with a quiet cogency that threw more light on comparative techniques and progress, gave more idea what creative filming might be about, and cluttered the mind with less high nonsense, than a majority of the people you can read or listen to. Ruttmann's sound effects came through as more imaginatively mature than we are now, ten years later, but the best film of the evening was *New Earth,* even in a sad, chewed-up print. For the record be it said that there has been no projection and amplification equipment more shamefully inadequate than that of the New School since they used to run off Lyman Howe in the Ware, Mass., Town Hall.

6 April 1938

Movies: Add One, Carry Two

The saddest thing is when the boys in pictures get everything in their hands—a cast, material, narrative skill—then after tossing it back and forth a while, throw it away in several directions at once. That in the end is the ticket for *Crime School,* Warner Brothers' attempt to repeat on *Dead End.* (Well, they had the *Dead End* kids and Humphrey Bogart under contract, didn't they?) But though the writers openly cribbed several turns from the former play, there is no need to waste time on comparisons. Their failure is one of hollow carpentry throughout, slapping up any old false front of lath and clapboard to make it come out even and happy.

Six of the toughest kids in the world go from idle if almost frightening chatter on the doorsteps of the city to their set business of bringing in looted bicycles, bathtubs, spares, and auto accessories for payoff night at Junkie the Fence's. This is fine, sharp stuff, the pace and setting are just right, and those boys are more authentic in gesture and living speech (grade-A low-Manhattan) than you'd believe. And the juvenile-court scene is good—a little heavy on law and order, but wide open about the educational nature of reform schools, and the lives of slum kids, and what it is that twists and drives them. The picture is still going well through the sequence of first night in the reform school, with Frankie's fight, wild break through the rain, and flogging.

But if the compound lesion, fissure, and buckling of intentions from here on could somehow be made visible, Metro would grab the negative for earthquake scenes in its next *San Francisco.* The bad warden is fired by a social-settlement gentleman, who falls in love with Frankie's big sister, who mistakes him for a perfect rotter. Frankie continues to get twice as desperately tough with the nice man as anybody could be and hold together, but presently turns around and takes the Scout Oath. Then, owing to the curious workings of an Evil Scheme, he becomes *three* times as desperate and would have shot the nice man if it hadn't been for the complicated godsend of a breathless climax, after which the whole gang is sprung, and the Bad Dannies have gone beyond *Little Men* into the Eagle Patrol for keeps.

There are lots of keen or funny things in this last part, but they drift around on the surface. There is no chance of anchorage because (1) the universal problem recognized at the start is ducked by an individual chance solution; (2) character and motivation have been booted around and completely out of shape in the sole and evident interest of a show having equal parts of excitement, happy ending, love interest, humor. Go to see Billy Halop, Leo Gorcey, Bobby Jordan, Huntz Hall, Bernard Punsley, Gabriel Dell—the kids—and Humphrey Bogart, the man against odds. Go to see, and stay to wonder.

Sacha Guitry's *Pearls of the Crown* is an extremely venturesome job—action, philosophy, didactic narration, three different languages, five different centuries, ten different countries at least, all bound round with the history of a string of pearls. And there are occasional settings, actors, and excitements which are delightful, seeming to come from life. Surely these are things worth something. Still, the continuity is such a discontinuous juggling of historical fragments, embalmed epigrams, wigs, words, and waxworks; the acting is so frequently ham in thin slices and the meaning so missing, that I don't know what a plain reviewer is to make of his boredom.

Grant that the trilingual experiment is of value to the history of film expression. Grant the episode with the Ethiopian Queen to be priceless, the Anne Boleyn French lesson good, Pope Clement VII good, and Mme. Guitry something you'd like to have around. Still, Sacha Guitry's idea of film cutting is feeding a lot of stock strips into an electric fan, his idea of unity in motion something like taking a deck of cards (well shuffled and thumbed and for pinochle at that) and dealing them solemnly out, face up, jack, ace, king, ten, queen, queen, queen, saying over and over in a drilled trilingual elocution "Lwee Quator'zuh, Hanry dee Ate, noh? O baby che malo I say et spiritu sanctu O K boss." With just that feeling, meaning, and sense. I am wondering what anyone would find to say if Monogram Pictures should suddenly dig up a lantern-slide amateur, leave him in the studios a week alone with a pair of scissors and the customs-house personnel, then print and distribute the result (taking the sole precaution to see it didn't run backward) as a motion picture or anything else.

To which pretentious busts I somehow prefer *Lady in the Morgue*, a routine Crime Club job on a Jonathan Latimer novel, and manufactured out of Universal's shoestring at that. It is about how Preston Foster and Frank Jenks held the New York homicide squad practically in its tracks while they unraveled matters too complicated to catch up with at the time or tell about after. It has humor and action and keeps moving busily along; and if it isn't so much, you at least aren't pestered by its trying to be. Humor and action and moves busily along—and that, if you will think back to Ince and the Keystone lot, was why movies were born in the first place.

25 May 1938

Spanish Omelette, with Ham

Although it is always possible that the right company could make a good fiction-picture out of current affairs in Spain, the odds against it are too infinite to monkey with. The dramatic arts have a special access to people's imaginations and nerve centers. And of all the arts, the movies play on the feelings of the most millions. Anything in films touching on things remote in space and time is fairly safe: anything that deals with matters of present hard feeling is just so much broken glass in an angry wound. If you made a true and good picture about Spain, the busy Catholics would be at their screaming and hopping around again; and if it were possible to dramatize the frank Catholic view, the easy going millions of our democracy would rise out of their engrossing petty worries to give a great and awful yell. The movies aren't going to stir up any such trouble. And if they make a film on anything like Spain, they have to make it mostly hokum or just in fun.

All of which never stopped Walter (Wonderboy) Wanger. Casting around for something different and already seeing himself as quite a hot rock on matters of cosmos, Mr. Wanger hears about Spain (one will get you five Clifford Odets tipped him off), and decides that a picture showing the romance and drama of it all would be sensational, positively. So, writers, cameramen, a director; Madeleine Carroll and Henry Fonda, Leo Carrillo for laughs, Vladimir Sokolov for acting—Mr. Wanger will spare no expense except maybe on exteriors: why go on location for half your footage when it can be easy painted on glass? So there are romance, truth, drama, difference, and humor, all in one picture, released under the title *Blockade*.

The story is the familiar one of the beautiful female spy (against her will, of course) and the young man of burning faith from the other (or right) side, who falls in love with her and indeed vice versa. It is a fact of screen record that Madeleine Carroll is among the most lovely of women; and Henry Fonda opposite her does very well at coming through silly rubbish to establish himself as a good man, an honest, troubled but steady spirit in his country's service. The enemy (designation carefully unknown) has got Miss Carroll and her weak father in their power: the Right (likewise undesignated) is rising up to fight for its homes and sheep and vineyards. Good stuff here: the mere quiet statement is enough. Then we get into the besieged town with Miss Carroll operating to destroy rescuing food-ships, and hating it. Then plot and counterplot from down under to high up, the ship comes in on a ruse, all are saved, and Mr. Fonda speaks some ringing deep lines for the rights of man, the right to work in and breathe freely the air of his own land, worth fighting for.

These last lines and the intent hunger-worn faces of the people as they watch for the ship (unusually fine types, though passed too mechanically through the cutting machine) are what the whole thing should have been, and wasn't. It could have been carried on some such sort of story perhaps; but in the case of Walter Wanger's production of William Dieterle's direction of John Howard Lawson's script, there is achieved a deadly numb level of shameless hokum out of which anything true or decent rises for a second only to confound itself. When it comes to what *Blockade* has to say for Spain to the common bewildered man, identification has been so smoothly rubbed out that to protest its content, as some of our hair-trigger Catholic friends are already naïvely doing, is to give away the fact of a deep and abounding ignorance, or of a stinking guilty conscience, and very probably of both.

29 June 1938

The Soldier and the Lady

The Shopworn Angel isn't the kind of film you'd expect much of, especially in this fearful night of the Hollywood spirit wherein red figures cover the land and any expense is too great, and absolutely everybody must tighten his belt except girths over forty-eight, and nothing must be ventured, absolutely. It is a remake of the 1929 screen version of a Dana Burnet war romance in *The Saturday Evening Post* of 1918, and it tells the story of a Texas rookie from Yaphank who focused the girl of his dreams in a Broadway actress, who was rather weary but really in love with another, to a knowledge of which she was revitalized by the doughboy's faith and living sweetness. So she married him just to keep his dream real until such time as it took them to blow him loose from his identification disc.

The other man hung around during the time of this regeneration and sacrifice and it is all very bloody delicate to start with. But the point is that somehow they did it, Director H. C. Potter working out Waldo Salt's screenplay at just the time when 1918 seems less quaint and more prophetic than it has at any time since.

It is a queer thing and a true thing that while the movies will bungle a good deep novel more times than not, they can turn around and take some story of flash surfaces and give it the depth of reality. The reason should be clear, but I'm afraid it is not. (The practicing literary gentry, who have such matters in keeping, always seem to get irritated when things get clear on them. Sometimes I figure it won't take more than a generation for us to learn that very few plays can be read and very few books can be played, so obvious is this truism of difference. Sometimes I see this misconception stretching to eternity and to hell with it.) Anyway, most of our deep novels are so lacking in the quality of interest and exciting movement that an average large public demands that when you skim them for their few actual bits of dramatic motion, you get a specious, talky melodrama. While stories constructed for this color and constant motion and nothing else make such natural material that the truth and character a writer may have neglected can be filled in during production—because the director and camera may become their own philosophy at will, and the characters are already full grown in the actors, bringing to every story their foibles, strength, mannerisms, and undeniable humanity.

The human quality here is owing partly to the schooled restraint of writing and direction, but even more to the unaffected appeal and warmth of Margaret Sullavan, James Stewart, and Walter Pidgeon (Hattie McDaniel, Sam Levene, and Nat Pendleton are also there, but it is strictly a triangle picture). For if you said, writing for *The Saturday Evening Post*, that the girl was knowing and tired, pert with her small mouth, stem of a torso, and low whispering voice, yet fresh with some wonder of dew still held in the inner leaves—you would have just those words and no more. The same if you said the boy was a nice simple chap with a hand for milking and one word to the minute, yet with the true grace of mind and spirit, the dreams and slow certain wisdom. Whereas in the moving shadows of the screen Margaret Sullavan is there to bring this poet's tracery of a girl into the motion of life; and James Stewart—rapidly perfecting a technique of saying the thing by planting it in the unsaid territory of false starts, half words, and general confusion—is deep slow yokel because he has created the illusion of a personal hurt and belief. Walter Pidgeon holds up a living mask for his difficult and (toward the end) shadowy part as the offside hero, having subtlety in strength. It is really our acceptance of and association with these people that makes the story actual in its time and place, actual and poignant.

In short I think you will enjoy the picture. The direction is clean, competent (and montage effects by Slavko Vorkapitch). The abundant talk is carried nicely by spacing and focus of interest. As to atmosphere, the period is carried out with a certain thorough attention to details way above the head of the current audience (the wartime barracks, the upright phones, the furnishings, the flag over every act, and even the songs), though I'd like to protest a tendency that is all too general: the research department will break its neck to authenticate a thing, and then the efficiency department will turn around and use a glass shot, a canvas background, a process shot, which will make the picture funnier by next year than any historical lapse.

People around New York City should take note of the new policy being followed by the Apollo Theatre (Forty-second Street, west of Broadway); and people through the country should take note of the way this policy is going over. The Apollo is booking the outstanding foreign films of the past, on what *Variety* would call a grind basis (continuous from 8 A.M. to 2 A.M., 10 cents till noon; 15 cents till 6 P.M., 25 cents thereafter) and it is cleaning up on it. When films of this kind make their way at popular (*i.e.,* nonsnob) prices, I begin to feel better. The revivals may be good, they may be bad, but the full-house attendance figures suggest one thing above all others: people are becoming conscious of the vast fund the moving pictures have been continually depositing in their name—not by the superficial processes of formal education, but through seeing and enjoying, through filtering into theaters of their own volition, sifting out the good from the bad with a certain lasting shrewdness.

20 July 1938

Algiers

Algiers is one of those naturals in pictures, having action, romance, strange places and predicaments, and the peg of character to hang it on. It is the story of Pépé le Moko, a Parisian jewel thief who for safety dug himself into the fantastic, tortured native quarter of Algiers. Part of the story is taken up with the foolish incursions of the French police, who should have known better, and the rest with the coming to Pépé le Moko of (but maybe you guessed it) love. What you wouldn't guess is that right in the middle of these secret exits, sighs, and pistols there is a pretty good study of a man trapped in his own fastness, sick of the smell and the ways of people there, hungry for the beloved common things of his home town, Paris. The girl when she comes is as much a nostalgia as a love affair (thanks to John Howard Lawson or some other author, one of the climaxes of passion is when he tells her she is not only Paris to him, but even the subway); and when he walks out of the Quarter to his certain fate, it is partly the girl and partly the familiar clean air of home (though to tell the truth if a thing was that way between you and the girl Hedy Lamarr, I don't see what the devil France would have to do with it).

But what makes it a natural is the action—and of course the glamor over it: the strange city, which grows very convincingly, and the enigmatic presence of Charles Boyer, who moves freely through and holds his court in it. He has a strange assortment of men who assemble quietly to guard all doors in the best fashion; he has an amiable if contemptuous understanding with the native inspector of police, sworn to get him; he has a stool pigeon and a woman to betray him. Above all, though, he has that mixture of grace, assurance, and brute male command that the story needs, for seeing him in it you could not doubt its actuality any longer. Boyer is one of the rare actors with a personal depth and sophistication that will suggest anything according to context—which tells you from one picture to another whether the smile, cigarette, and slow, careful word are the surface of beneficence or of wide evil. Here he is infinitely above enemies and friends in poise and guile, and the audience snickers to see him call the turn. But he is human, alas, and not above foolish grief and falling in love, and so the audience hopes for him and sorrows with him and shudders to look down over his shoulder at the innocent open streets that are not his domain but his death.

Now that you speak of it, the film's action is more that of character than of jostling events, for the police action, the betrayed friend, the motion of intramural life would be slight of interest without the suggested past and imminent future of Pépé le Moko and those surrounding him in the story: Hedy Lamarr, Sigrid Gurie, Joseph Calleia, Gene Lockhart, Alan Hale, etc. And all the more credit to them in that this looks like one of those productions where it is every actor for himself, those few minor characters who felt the need to ham it being given a shamelessly free rein.

But of course actors are nothing without something to be, say, and do, and the writing ought to come in for a bit of applause. After the first talky, nonfilm sequence it keeps development simmering right along, some very neat humor just around the corner, and a general level of mature dignity that is all the more welcome as it is not demanded by this type of story. Much of John Cromwell's direction is first-rate stuff—good conception of timing, placing the action, riding the crest of interest, and particularly an Alfred Hitchcock use of the homely unexpected and of sound and of the significant hinting camera. Parts of it—witness the unquelled elocutionists, the manipulated beginning and climax— are curious lapses into mummery, but the general tone is that of the decent artistry we must demand of and enjoy in pictures, which should someday be as respectable as books, only more near and vivid.

When I think of *Algiers* as contrasted with John Ford's *Four Men and a Prayer* (this is in the nature of a flashback: the film is still around though I missed its first run), I have to laugh. Not meanly, I hope. John Ford has made superlatively good ones and also bad ones, by which I should judge that he can be hogtied by his story. But a few years ago he made *The Informer* and the critical rumpus over that made him the little Jesus and ace of spades over all directors, at least for a while. Well, I won't trouble you with my own guilty doubts whether I underplayed that yarn at the time (it was a yarn all right, but not having had an Irish rebellion here we fall for the purity of Irish rebellions like a brick house); but what I imagine you'll see when you wait say another two years and see it in revival is that the story is an easy success and that the direction was partly good and partly not. *Four Men and a Prayer* is just another flop so far as going to see pictures is concerned, but if you'd like to see what I'm talking about, then go catch it somewhere and try to discover a director. The story itself is a turkey, and this might happen to anybody. But outside of the firing-squad sequence, where the weaknesses and absurdities of the human figure are raised to the tragic level of life and death, the thing just in film terms is confused, silly, dispirited, and dull. The actors are there to hand (David Niven is always good and Loretta Young can be handled, as witness the two of them in the nice little comedy *Three Blind Mice,* still around); and the chances to make a strong flashing play from a weak hand. But no. Without a story having the kind of message to his liking (and without his writing partner, Dudley Nichols, apparently) John Ford hasn't the patient skill in his own trade to place among the first ten or a dozen. This weakness is what I thought showed through *The Informer,* though I can confuse you even more by saying that John Ford's *Arrowsmith* was not only made in the dark early thirties, but belongs among the masterpieces.

3 August 1938

The Natural in Movies

When I said last time that *Algiers* was a natural in pictures, I'm afraid I left the idea undeveloped. For pictures not only have a method of appeal peculiar to the magic half-darkness of the movie house, but in the thousands of movie houses, and millions of people flowing through them like the tides, they have at once the lowest and greatest common denominator ever appealed to. Generally, pictures require above other forms the constant push of excitement and the romance which may come from love in June (see moon), or from strange doings, or from things remote in time or place. *Algiers* had a combination of all these things before it even started.

I never have the space or clairvoyance to go into the eternal phenomenon of box-office appeal as a finality in itself—into how a film that is the weary jape of anyone who has read a book or seen a play or heard music can still prove itself the balm and beauty of a million living men and women, who leave its howling absurdities with their eyes wet (or completely vice versa). Nobody has mapped that country, and the only true and unforgivable chump is the intellectual who will assume for his purpose either of the two following absolutes: (a) that the masses of people do not appreciate the best art; (b) that these masses will not equally relish what appears to be the worst. And so while *Algiers* appeals to many of us as a good story well done and we are thus permitted to hope that its great majority audience sees and applauds for the same reasons, we should remember that its almost formulaic ingredients have been demonstrated as foolproof in the scores of stories whose merciless fakery in treatment has brought the very same box-office results.

I bring the subject up all over again only because of another picture that suggests the same questions, another and even brighter natural, *The Amazing Doctor Clitterhouse*. The elements of the strange and exciting are here, but there is a happy absence of that literal, unfilmic treatment which blunted and dragged down *A Slight Case of Murder* (you might have thought the crime-comedy style of *The Thin Man* would have taught a lesson on the difference between literary intentions and actual picture flow to the most literal bodies; but alas not yet). The story is ingenious, but Anatole Litvak and his producing-acting crew have so thoroughly kept the larky mood of it while setting up the necessary undercurrent of interest and suspense that it is hard to see where conception leaves off and the shaping of it into motion begins.

The Amazing Doctor is interested in crime, no doubt in a purely scientific way at first; and the problems of original research are so great that there is but one answer: the only way to chart the reactions of a criminal on the job is to go out and pull a few jobs yourself. Curious people, criminals. Very. When the Doctor decides it is time to get out before crime as an intoxicant gets stronger than the pure fire of research, he finds a certain party isn't going to play it that way but tag him for endless blackmail instead; and when he kills the party he discovers that the police have some curious practices too.

The characters for all this are about the pick of the Warner stock company. Edward G. Robinson even when chewing the props right off the set has some magnetic kind of film personality; here for once he is allowed (or forced) to break the type, and his study of the Doctor is not only lively but a well-founded job. Humphrey Bogart is probably the most subtle bad man (genus American) the films have produced; he is here, and practically horrid. Claire Trevor, Allen Jenkins, Irving Bacon, Henry O'Neill, Donald Crisp, Maxie Rosenbloom, Bert Hanlon, Vladimir Sokoloff—you can't begin to list them, because even the walk-ons are favorites and the action that much broadened in likeliness and appeal.

In making use of both his actors and the situations of the story the director has a fine organizational talent for keeping it good and clear in motion—for a good line, like a good idea for a sequence, is only half the battle, and the rest is planting it. Take Allen Jenkins' offside business: University? He had a brother in one, sure, it was his kid brother—what did they call the place . . . Harvard, that was it. Sure. What do you mean, how was he doing? It was legitimate, they had him in alcohol right there. He had two heads. Or the case of the Law whose name turned out to be Ethelbert. Then there was the neat idea of rigging up the mobsters as the Hudson River String Quartet and quartering them in the Carnegie Hall apartments, developed with many touches like that of having a Mozart serenade as background for talk about the split, the ice, and get this, mugs. And the reversal of usual trial stuff by throwing the decisive word to the human and baffled jury foreman—a fine sequence all around. But more than *Algiers,* this film shows evidence of our widening exploitation of the camera medium over here. Some of the pioneering in Alfred Hitchcock's approach seems to show through the dramatic irony of the gems in the doctor's bag, later under the pretzels, in the restrained burlesque of that complete and effortless opening sequence, in the inverted, telescope device of the dying gangster, in the shrewd use of music and sound as contrapuntal emphasis.

Many will enjoy the film without stopping to ask what makes the story run so lightly with such vivid effect—which is unfortunate as far as credits go but not wholly uncheerful: art is often most healthy when it does not stick out all over everything like a bagful of nails.

10 August 1938

Doldrum Weather

Variety used to maintain that it was impossible to review a film justly without seeing it in the theater with an audience, but I notice lately it is breaking its own house-rule and I don't blame it. The way film audiences are tossed around in New York and everywhere else is something that sours my disposition just to think of. I won't go into the fantastic spectacle of people herded and roped up and down the block in the hot summer noontime, waiting to see *Alexander's Ragtime Band* before it goes into places half as expensive and twice as convenient. That is partly a phenomenon of pictures but mostly a repetition of the patterns of get-your-news-hot and the stand-in-line patience of the human race.

What I'm talking about is the whole conception of how to see a picture—which is cockeyed. Granting that the meanest movie house is miles above the stuffy discomfort of the legitimate theater (more room, more ventilation, more visibility), there is still the fact that the exhibitor's ideal is to keep every seat occupied by as many different people during the day as the traffic will stand. Can't blame him. But since the show is continuous, people are continuously streaming across, in front of and upon other people. This is uncomfortable, and so are buses; but the main thing is that it adds a certain element of mystery as to what the thing you paid to see is about. The Radio City Music Hall is probably the most comfortable and rigorously manned large commercial theater in the world, yet in whole blocks of seats on either side there walk between spectator and spectacle file upon file of spectators either going out or to the million-dollar jakes half a mile below.

To present its single square of light and shadow, the Music Hall spreads and rises to accommodate some 6,000 ($1.65 top) customers. As in all such structures, the birds who get in last (and at certain times of the day most convenient for seeing a show, everybody seems to get in last) are perched about a quarter of a mile from the screen, and from the speakers that are the voice to its image. No magic conquest of the laws of optics and acoustics can keep both sound and picture from distortion somewhere along the line even here—and when you get to older palaces like the Paramount you can sit in seats at such an angle that you wouldn't know your own wife on the screen (not a bad idea but the trope holds good); and you can sit so far away that even above the buzz and bustle of the thousands between, you can hear enough of the sound to realize that it is coming somewhat later than the motion (bands on the stage sometimes seem to be putting away their instruments during the climax of their music).

While the democracy of this is really fine, the edge must be taken off any enjoyment of the beautiful when, if you are to see it, you must move up upon it by a constant stalking vigilance and a series of lunges for the seat five rows up before it gets cool. (Be sure if you remain resolutely where you are, content with half-glimpses, you'll still be moving against traffic, for the tide of half the theater is moving up, past, across, and over you.)

I suppose it is this democratic franchise that makes such poor audiences of movie audiences. It is a careless and good-natured rudeness, as distinct from the smugly traditional ill manners of the regular theater audience (the late-comers, my-worders, social ceremonialists, etc.); but it cuts into a good picture horribly. Women of course have a monopoly on rudeness, and where they hunt in packs (matinées particularly and the Music Hall all the time), sight and sound seem to act as almost obscene releases on the reservoirs of chatter. And there is no idea of responsibility to others—you stand in front of them for moments, wavering over a choice of seats or absorbed in what is still passing across the screen. You tramp across eight people in one row and then across four in another to move up twenty feet. You read printed matter out loud unconsciously. Since those who shove make out best, you shove too.

It may seem a sad mess to the numerical few who wouldn't pay any attention to a picture unless it were worth their full attention, and who believe deeply that pictures are worth attention. But the mix of humanity is the same as it is anywhere else. It's all a matter of the tradition. From what I have seen of people looking at something or listening to something anywhere, I should say that the natural response to anything is half response to that thing and half a continuation of the rhythm of personal life—Oh, I just remembered: Joe told me to tell you that Herman . . . or, Doesn't that remind you of, now *who* was it that. . . . But in Symphony and Carnegie Halls, do you understand, the personal half of it is agreed upon as poor taste, definitely. The yap who suddenly remembers the light in the bathroom is by common and almost gleeful consent the center of some very fancy black looks and the target of conclusive hisses. Why? Because he doesn't like the music, because he is the boor implied? No.

Because one simply doesn't. Open and shut—and that is the real meaning of audience tradition.

I'm convinced that the audience of movies has a fresher interest and more understanding of the performance than audiences in all the arts where prestige, tradition, social prominence, etc., have entered to confuse the issue. People go because they want to, and not because they must or ought. But here the human weakness is unconfined. And here, more than in any other art, there is much more that is not worth attention by sheer crushing volume.

I don't know what we're going to do about it, or rather I know as usual we'll do nothing but wait for things to change. Things *are* changing slightly, as witness the success of *Cue* and its assumption that there is an awakening audience which wants to go to *a* movie as opposed to just going to the movies; and the fact that three Metropolitan dailies now list the starting time of the principal feature pictures each night. Some take their movie art seriously, and while I hope they won't presently get stuffy about it, I do hope even more that they will impress upon themselves and their exhibitors that dignity and responsibility which are just as necessary on the part of those who watch as they are on that of those who make and show. There has been a lot of bushwa tossed around about how moving pictures aren't worthy of their audience. I say the two go together, and that since the producer-exhibitor's business ear is attuned to the faint whispering rub of one loose penny against another in anybody's pocket, it is up to the owners of the pennies to indicate which way they are most pleased to spend them.

And everything being in the summer doldrums, I will now report briefly the few films it has seemed worth chasing after in the last couple of weeks.

Marie Antoinette is one of the historical-colossals where the pageant is actually secondary to a rather fresh story of love and personal tragedy, tied to history mainly through the costumes and sets. Robert Morley makes a grand figure of the slow and tortured Louis XVI; Norma Shearer carries the main pattern; Joseph Schildkraut and John Barrymore are good in their separate ways; Tyrone Power is in it.

Sing You Sinners, one of those I half-saw in the theater, would probably be a good Wesley Ruggles comedy if you could get it out and see it quietly somewhere. I thought the action stuff a little tortured and wished that Elizabeth Patterson were too; but the main thing was the character of Bing Crosby, who can sing and also be a swell feller. Might be worth seeing, when it cools off.

Alexander's Ragtime Band will have to be seen by all who can recapture those dead years through hearing the Irving Berlin tunes which marked them—it is a top-flight job of working music into a story, though the business of telling a true story of music is bungled as absurdly as always. As a picture it isn't much—what shall be done with Tyrone Power and Don Ameche? please don't write—but as a tribute to a genius rising from Tin Pan Alley to cover the land with the memory of music, it can't be beat.

South Riding is so good probably because the English studios had no bright ideas about making it better. It is exact and ponderous and thus tells the story of class disintegration the best way. It's an old story but new in regional color and in this kind of treatment in pictures, and the best word is that of my friend Jim, who points out it's good in spite of itself. A minor must, I suppose you could call it.

31 August 1938

Pictures from England

The time comes to report on the British again and on what happens when they set out to make a film. In the past funny things have happened, though not in comedies; and it could be said that outside of Alfred Hitchcock the most consistent filmic thing the empire on which the sun never sets did was lay an egg. This season's *Storm in a Teacup* and *The Divorce of Lady X* showed that the talent for making those pathetically sweating little farces had not waned; *Troopship,* as one of the more solid ventures, proved that clumsy dialogue and a sort of heavy pouncing treatment can still fuddle anything—even the good idea and fine mass scenes they had here. But recently it seems like a different day. After Hitchcock's *A Girl Was Young* there was *To the Victor,* among the best of the year. Then there were *Three on a Week-End* and *South Riding*—both of them difficult effects to bring off.

I got to *Three on a Week-End* only recently and thus very late, but it is one of those films good to see for their hold on the familiar, on the intricate, unimportant, homely, and sweet ways of life. The story can't quite make it: a nurse is troubled all through a bank-holiday excursion with her boy friend by pictures of the chap whose wife just died in childbirth on her hands. As uneasiness turns to certain premonition she returns to the city in time to prevent suicide, while the boy friend discovers (by what in charity should be called a lucky coincidence) a little girl just as sweet and not so busy.

The story is certainly a writer's shot in the dark, but it still does not arise to trouble you until the very end. The heart of the picture is really the city, the poor tired, sticky, determined city moving into trains and onto buses and taking its high birthrate out for this jaunty and pitiful fling at sun and water and air. There is a wonderful family man all through, there are two bloody blades in uniform, an ugly duckling in high cockney, there are about forty million people in a resort that is a cut above Coney but still beneath Mr. Moses, a beauty contest, a flea circus—later a really beautiful small-town police chief.

But none of these are thrown in as "effects": everything simply seems to grow there. Carol Reed must have seen that emphasis on the story as written would founder all and turned the cameras on the inevitable human sideshow for all they were worth. And the result, deliberate or not, is what you could call documentary: the city of people goes out and comes back again, as absurd, incorrigible, noisy, and touching as it ever was.

The new picture from England (at the Fifty-fifth Street Playhouse in New York City) is something to remind you of Flaherty's *Man of Aran,* being about the life and gradual extinction of the hardy men and women clinging to the rocks against the sea, living (but just barely) on one of the islands off the coast of Scotland. Comparisons will tangle us all up, but at least you can see that while there is no such dull fussing here as there was in the unenlivened portions of *Aran,* there is no comparable mighty effect of wind and sea and a waste horizon to burn your eye. Michael Powell heard how the last hatful of people had left their homes on St. Kilda in the Hebrides, and saw a story in it. So he went to the similar island of Foula, carrying the usual amount of etcetera referred to in press releases, and spent the usual amount of etcetera (according to the release, six months and 200,000 feet of film), and he worked out a story.

The main point is that the island is played out, what with the peat thinning and trawlers sweeping out the fish; and the little community is split into a faction for getting away and starting over, and the die-hards who can think of nothing but that they were born there, and the generations before them. There are a boy and girl, one in each camp of course, and the sort of complications that often materialize out of such situations (alack). The boy returns rather too patly in time to get the baby to a mainland doctor; the community packs up to leave the homeland; and old sobersides, for no particular reason outside of plot convenience, "goes over" the cliff.

But here again, and much more deliberately, the story serves only as a window on a kind of life. It enlivens the facts to be presented but at the same time it diverts attention from their simple verity whenever its forced structure shows through (and strangely enough, the simpler the tale the more chances it seems to have of looking Simple Simon). Principally we are worried by and excited over the way things go in the island: the stout homespun sermon, the village parliament, the trawlers rolling and scavenging out there, the seamed but strangely peaceful faces looking away into the weather (all but the principals were recruited from Foula).

Recalling Flaherty's picture of Aran, I can see that many more essential details of life were brought before its cameras complete. Still it seems to move more easily this way, the worries of people actually giving point to the tight, frugal little houses and paths, sheep-pens, and cliff faces, making the harsh elements and clear air nearer to the senses as one realizes their doom and elusive promise. *The Edge of the World* is a sort of halfway mark between fiction pictures and those semi-fictions we call documentary in our unguarded moments (P.S., most of our moments are unguarded anyway; documentaries have to have a story to be more than family albums, and some of them have stories pretty well developed).

14 September 1938

Boys of All Ages

Still the films about slum children come along—forget sordid matters of finance for a minute and you can close your eyes and see Hollywood with one burning reform project and plan for world redemption: getting the young toughies off the streets and giving them a nice glass of milk. There probably hasn't been so much compassion for and understanding of the offspring of the masses since the Sermon on the Mount, but the comment on picture making goes beyond that. Childhood is one of the few remaining fields where you can base a picture on a known fact and not find yourself in the middle between the Legion of Decency howling down from one side and various other political or social or racial trash blowing up from the other.

They used to get something out of the Fallen Woman until old Sniffer Hayes came along and said if she was fallen she must have been pushed, and you couldn't let her up because it all must be part of a moral lesson, not fun. They used to hold a deadly fast pace with gangster stories until nice people arose in groups and passed the ball to J. Edgar Hoover, a prominent author, under whose guidance it was presently arranged that Humphrey Bogart should join the Boy Scouts. You can and always could make a film with a kick in it, but it becomes increasingly necessary to make it so good in the first place that it will get by in spite of truth.

The average film maker can't risk his job on the possibility that any little wettypants who can organize fifteen clubwomen will set up a noticeable fuss and cawing. So he falls back into the groove where romance is the ballroom at Versailles, beds are strictly for comedy falls, and motherhood is sacred but you'd better not have a baby until it's at least three years old and fully dressed. Well, isn't that what they want, the people who sleep in the beds and have the children? Not exactly. It is what they are told they want by the unhappy, never resting crew of spellbinders whom they elect, trust, flock to, and patiently suffer, and thus I suppose deserve. Anyway, the thing must pass for what people want out where the product is put up in the kind of package they will buy.

It must have been a source of surprise and delight in some quarters (in addition to that of the audience) when the stories of Rowland Brown and the realism of the *Dead End* youngsters showed Hollywood that children could be more than an extra $2,000 production cost of shooting around how and why they were born, or Little Goldilocks and the Three Brown Barrymores. A writer could go ahead with the streets and houses and condition of life he knew; if people were poor and conditions bad he could say so without calling Joe Breen; if there was trouble, robbery, shooting, he didn't have to worry about the Department of Justice. The ending of course had to have a note of hope like forty iron bells, but the processes of life up to that could be as true as life itself. A field day.

The latest venture is *Boys' Town,* which turns on the activities of Father Flanagan of Nebraska (Norman Taurog directed for MGM, John Meehan, Dore Schary, Eleanor Griffin did the writing and Slavko Vorkapich the quietly effective special effects). After the usual build-up of environment, gang spirit, "reform" schools, it goes into the business of the good father and his growing brood, and how he expanded out from the city onto the land, and built a town, to be lived in and worked for and run by his growing hundreds of boys. For conflict there is Mickey Rooney, who came to the settlement almost too late and was so tough he was constantly bouncing back in his own eye.

In general the story is sound and soundly carried out, though rounding some of its sharp corners awfully fast (for example, I still don't know how the three gunmen were taken like so many lollypops at the end). And many of the scenes are managed with first-class aid to their effectiveness (the petering out of the singing in that first pitiful Christmas; the hot-and-cold game of the candy and the priest and Peewee, leading to its quiet heightening of effect in the later sequence). I suppose no real thing ever happens with such unalloyed goodness and happy coincidence, and I know that Father Flanagan's boys resemble the pattern of *Little Men;* but that is not much of a worry while the thing is happening.

They had a lot of good kids for the parts; and of course Mickey Rooney is developing an acting genius that should soon be its own monitor over such weaknesses as the overly tough style he is encouraged to follow here. But mainly the story keeps its balance in Spencer Tracy, a man with the true actor's gift of projection without the true actor's awfullest error, which is that of complacency in your art, letting your self-satisfaction show through in struttings, mouthings, and stage bounce. So here he is as the kindly priest but nobody's football, redeeming what is in danger of becoming sentimental or silly by standing through it as simply natural as a tree. For all his homely face and lack of surface charm, he is about the finest figure of a man you'll meet, and I'm happy that he has finally got a part here to show it off.

It may be disappointment that any Frank Capra comedy should be heavy and overdone which makes *You Can't Take It with You* seem such a dud. It has its play of interest, its bright scenes, its James Stewart, Edward Arnold, Jean Arthur, Mischa Auer (from Omsk). As for the original material (the Old Folks at Home crossed with a Keystone two-reeler on a Night in the Nuthouse), Capra and Riskin have made a good show out of a weak sister before. Yet there is little throughout to suggest the felicity in his own medium which has been the Capra hallmark all the way from *The Bitter Tea of General Yen* to *Mr. Deeds.*

Mr. Deeds seems to have given writer and director an idea of themselves as social philosophers which does them no good. There is an embarrassing amount of space here given over to the spiritual poverty of riches, the wealth of the simple heart, the glory and pity of it all. The comedy of falls and upsets seems perfunctory though dogged (more, any actor who wants it is given enough rope), as though the main business in hand were to make platitude boom like truth. As a picture I suppose it is better than average. As for Mr. Capra, I believe he has not returned from Tibet, where last seen; and *You Can't Take It with You* is simply Shangri-La in a frame house.

21 September 1938

War and Other Pieces

Of all the war films there has been up to now only one which was made with something like the dignity and terror the subject demands, and it was made eight years ago in Hollywood by Lewis Milestone, from the book *All Quiet on the Western Front.* Now there is one to put beside it, a nearly prophetic story for these days made by Jean Renoir and showing in New York at the Filmarte Theatre: *Grand Illusion.* There are't any trenches in it, for it is a story like *The Enormous Room,* more serious-seeming if not so beautiful. It is about what happens to people—three French captives in particular, and the German commandant, and later the young German widow—in country behind the German lines; finally of the escape of two of the men.

And while this war drags on there are echoes through the story of another, in the relationships among the commandant of the fort and three Frenchmen: gentleman, bourgeois, and Jew. The German is more stiff in his courteous contempt; the French gentleman seems to have no bitterness against the democratic idea but maintains as a part of nature the reserve that baffles his comrades. And when he dies (he created the diversion that allowed the other two to escape) he represents for this story the end of a world, the only "escape" possible for his class.

The picture is filled out with these complexities, which lie between the crude black-and-white of enemy and friend, between simple ideals and difficult reality. Soldiers and sick to death of it, they come up with delight to the lifting roll of men marching in formation. Safe for the first time and knowing that "freedom" means going back to be shot at, they scheme, dig, and suffer for it, to regain their dignity and hear people talk like home folks. There is nothing to live for any longer, except to live—which becomes the main business of a strange, twisted world.

In all this there is a rare compassion shown—for the broken commandant in his gloomy stone fort and for the men in their degrees of hopelessness and dirt. Surely one of the most moving expositions in the film is the flare-up between Gabin and the Jew, the blunt words and misery, and the bond of common suffering still too strong to break; and then the idyll in the German cottage, so easy a thing to go astray on, but done beautifully with little scraps of French and German, a cow, and oddments of food. The acting is as fine as the picture deserves: Erich von Stroheim, Jean Gabin, Pierre Fresnay, Dalio, the first two especially giving the thing its basis in believable life, but all contributing: in a fairly extensive supporting cast I cannot recall even a walk-on that was not easy and right. The only weak points are in its structure as a film.

Renoir has not learned how to indicate shifts in time, and the result is that you jump from sickness to health, from today to tomorrow to Christmas, even, with the abrupt jar of scenes in a play but without so much as a curtain fall. Its moments of feeling are never squeezed limp, but there is a rhythm to be discovered in any kind of feeling and Renoir doesn't always have it. He is apt to leave an emotion before you have finished with it—sometimes where even a casual dissolve would have allowed the last three beats, four, five, six, to raise it to the proper intensity. Or he will cut flatly from one level of emotion to another without that transitional strip as necessary as the modulation between keys in the line of music.

Nobody wants a good thing muddied up with the heavy symbolism of special-effects men; and the length of the film is about right as it is. But the way could have been made smoother at the expense of some of those bits that a moment's reflection will show to have been tossed in without thought for true dramatic purpose. The man suffocating in the tunnel was effective but perfunctory; the rifle shot after the two had crossed the border was false suspense; the effect of the soldier in woman's clothes was pertinent but unskillfully done. Perhaps a few others.

If such considerations were pure fussy arithmetic we could laugh at them. But the truth is that in the special liquid form of pictures, an audience confused even for a moment (where are they now? how long has this been going on?) is an audience losing altitude and that much heavier to get back up. A little more art (always as opposed to artifice or the arty) could have heightened the beauty and truth of this film, which already has as much as we've seen anywhere this year.

The Lady Vanishes is a typical work of that genius in the art of motion pictures, Alfred Hitchcock, the overstuffed and delightful gentleman from London.

But Hitchcock chooses to use his genius where it will do the least harm to the most effect, and so while everything he does has such speed and clarity it's a pleasure to sit there over and over and watch him work, he works frankly in surface motion. There are human interest and sympathy because his people are always right; but the action is violent, the need for it somehow unreal, and emotion does not mature.

This new one reworks the idea of the young lady whose mother vanished right in the middle of Paris (the explanation was cholera; this time it is just spy activities), getting all its characters into one Continental express train. The story is almost unimportant: boy and girl find lady, have to shoot their way out, saving the nation and getting married. But it's just the thing for Hitchcock, who has more fun with the people on that train than a barrel of monkeys—the fun more liberally interjected than usual into throttled guitar players, false compartments, drugs, guns, and evil. It's as much comedy as straight plot, in fact, and some of the exploration of the English mind is as neat as you'll see, done with relish and droll good humor, planted not only in dialogue and perfect delivery but in the concept of type and situation.

The acting here, too, is all of a piece with the mood of the thing; but more than any of the English-speaking film men, Hitchcock is a one-man show, getting every detail straight in his head and the way he wants it before the first camera starts rolling. He is almost an academy, too, because no one can study the deceptive effortlessness with which one thing leads to another without learning where the true beauty of this medium is to be mined.

Sacha Guitry is also a one-man show, but though a witty and audacious fellow, his main idea of a film is that you set up a camera and photograph something, preferably Sacha Guitry talking. He brings a new angle in his *Story of a Cheat,* and makes a nice evening's entertainment—oh, much more subtle than movies usually have to offer. But, you see, there is nothing beautiful either in what he says or the way of saying it; his evening—a lecture with lantern-slide tricks—is a nice evening and speedily forgotten.

19 October 1938

Hollywood Hangover

It is ironic but perhaps not strange that in these past months when the air has been shaking with the barrage about Motion Pictures' Greatest Year, Hollywood has been supplying the nation's first-run theaters with a steadier run of out-and-out turkeys than has been seen since 1930. The whole place out there seems to have the financial jitters, what with reorganizations, government investigation, the European market blowing up in their faces, and so many pressure groups burning around getting insulted that the only thing they aren't scared of their lives of casting for a stooge comedy part is Elmer, the trained seal. The result is that a producer would be afraid to look in his own bureau drawer for a pair of socks without a search warrant; they won't try anything, they won't let anybody else try anything, and picture after picture comes out of the grinder as a mix of only the most safely venerable gags and situations—the result of which is something like locking the barn after the horse is dead, and not a matter of days at that.

Even the men who have come through with fine work in the past are putting their stuff on the line this year, one after another, and the best you can say for it is it must originally have been something they et. And when it comes to a team like Leigh Jason and P. J. Wolfson (an ex-writer who has quite a hot lip for Left ideals but I notice has cut himself out a producership), and they bring out for RKO a bit of class-A production called *The Mad Miss Manton* that is booked into the Radio City Music Hall, which has almost a pick of the product—I quit. Not everything that moves is a motion picture, as your doctor will tell you, but this one moves anyway. And in a sense it holds the interest—as indeed it might well, for it picks the brains if not the teeth of half the smart fellows who ever borrowed a sure-fire line or incident from a smarter fellow who had seen it in the original plagiarism, dimly and long ago.

Its idea for a story frame is to have a crew of Park Avenue girls solve a shocking lot of murders in a larky way and Park Avenue is I suppose what is new about it. Henry Fonda, Sam Levene, and a few other nice people are held strictly to nonsense and supported by Barbara Stanwyck and the rest of a plaster cast—but this isn't a review or even a summary of the fortnight. This is just me throwing in the towel, and why. This is the last picture I saw in Motion Pictures' Greatest Year, and walking out of motion pictures' greatest first-run showcase, loaded to the guards with customers still nickering and wheezing at this strip of old and stolen tricks, it certainly did seem to me a little as though this was also the motion-picture audience's darkest day. (It isn't one picture, or even one class-A audience in one city gone silly in one night, but the low average that permits this low bottom: it's the hammer, hammer, hammer.) Outside the Hall, of course, there was Sixth Avenue perpetually torn all to hell with a mythical subway, and it was raining. I don't know what that's got to do with it, but that's the way it looked.

That it can't rain forever may be a hope justified when Columbia releases John Brahm's newest picture, *Girls' School.* It is one of those fugitive works—not too splendid but still honestly and decently and quietly made—that we are usually given when the shoestring companies like Grand National, Monogram, Universal, etc., get hold of a good man and give him a chance. But while Columbia can by courtesy be called a major picture company, it is by pure chance that John Brahm (an ex-German with only four Hollywood pictures to his credit in all) drew a producer who wouldn't meddle. So in this case he took a Tess Slesinger novel and made a picture out of it sound enough to look like a pretty breeze in such a doldrums. There are dramatic properties in it, as there must be in anything dramatic; and there are parts where probability is passed over rather hastily. But in general there is the feeling of sincerity, of belief in your material and concern with the best way of expressing it. And I don't suppose anybody will ever make a really good thing until he believes what he's doing, and worries about it.

The story has the simple main pattern of a poor girl in a rich girl's finishing school—eager, sweet of spirit, but put-upon by the snobbery of girls and faculty alike. As a picture of youth's troubles it is about as true as any and touching at moments, and its subtleties at the expense of the gloved hand of wealth deserve a better ending. But principally (take the student-government meeting, the charm lecture, the informal camera at the prom) it looks like the good clean work of someone who has a job to do, and likes it.

For the first time since I've been reviewing movies it is true that the sound and interesting picture jobs, over a period of months, have come mainly from outside Hollywood—whether from studios abroad or from little packing-case outfits wherever they may be set up. Alexander Korda's *Drums,* for example, was done better in Hollywood years ago but is not being done anything like so well this year. A Technicolor story of an incident in England's cleanup of the bad Indian tribes, it is a bang-up adventure job though particularly anachronistic for this time and pregnant with Raymond Massey and other bad jokes in blackface (Osmond Borradaile and Georges Perinal are responsible for the frequently beautiful camera work). I've mentioned most of the other interesting ones in this column, but there remains one of a different type, the travel film called *Dark Rapture* (by some horrible stretch of the imagination). This is the one about the Denis-Roosevelt camera exploration of the African interior, generally agreed to be the best of its numerous kind.

Other films have packed in more strange thrills: this trip was good for the spirit it seems to have been made in. Being stuck in Africa with expensive equipment means looking sharp for stuff that won't be a waste of negative. These people missed the elephant hunt the first season, but instead of pitching little live rabbits at a boa who would obviously be curled up somewhere with a good book, they looked around at native life, which they appear to have both understood and liked. The film ends on a terrific fire that all but got them; the elephant hunt is as exciting as anything; the intricate patient work of the grapevine bridge makes a wonderful sequence. But the feeling that remains is one of serious investigation and good-will, and is restful after all the tourism, shock hunting, and goona-goona of this general type.

2 November 1938

Whether to Laugh or Cry

I suppose Walt Disney's *Ferdinand the Bull* should lead off for this pre-Christmas season, though the cartoon is very short and made for kiddies. The fabulous success of the Leaf-Lawson book is impossible to explain unless we grant such a slight thing the rare quality of being a new fairy-tale, something in which the idea is different yet so simple that you can put it in a sentence, as: once there was a bull who wouldn't fight but liked to smell the pretty flowers; and remember it by its main characteristics, as: Jack and the Beanstalk, Beauty and the Beast, or Minnie the Moocher (if it's of any interest I'll still take Minnie and the King of Sweden, he gave her some things that she was needen). This general popularity in any event made the Disney men keep pretty close to the original. A commentator tells the story in the right fairy-tale way, in a voice you might call deliberately wide-eyed; and the rest is Disney sound effect and detail—though there is not so much scope for these as in the best ones. I remember the little bulls butting each other automatically, the Spanish cow with her bell in tango time, the arrival of the men in funny hats; and in general the effect is charming, good fun, and of course clean (there was definitely no feeding time for the little bulls and I couldn't see whether, in deference to Decency Legions, the boys had taken a hint from the apocryphal but best of Ferdinand stories, the one about his carrying a glove across the pasture to a group of cows to see, as he confessed when questioned, if any of those ladies over there had lost her brassière).

The Cowboy and the Lady is also clean fun and simple enough to be put in a sentence: the cowboy didn't want a lady who was rich like this one and so after an hour and a half of misunderstandings they lived happily forever and ever until Sam Goldwyn can team them up for another picture. Some of the writing is bright and there is romance, and what with Merle Oberon, Gary Cooper, Patsy Kelly, Walter Brennan, Mabel Todd, and Fuzzy Knight in and out of the doings, you couldn't help having some good laughs. But the laughter dies in your throat soon enough, for the story is just a lot of chestnuts pulled out of other people's dead fires and the director is no aid to its embarrassment, for his idea of light treatment seems to be that of lifting heavy weights clear from the ground. Not even Gary Cooper has enough human appeal to hold this together, so in general the big money is wasted and love is lost.

Just for contrast, consider *Spring Madness,* a silly but gay little piece, much helped by its unpretentiousness and sensible comedy writing. (Much helped also by the fact that when you throw a line to subordinate players like Sterling Holloway and Frank Albertson, you will not throw a line away.) Briefly, Lew Ayres is in love and poor, but serious about going to Russia for a couple of years to study the natives; and Maureen O'Sullivan no like. For the purposes of the story everybody is in college, and while campus complications pile up more than would be seemly even in Princeton, there is more naturalness to the film's absurdities than I've seen before. (College to Hollywood is usually some sort of mysterious Gothic elaboration produced by Billy Rose but opening out of town—who the hell ever *caught* the show, tell me?) And I do believe the young-and-worried-love scene in the gymnasium is straight and fresh. And though I usually like to keep Burgess Meredith at arm's length, his part and he in it have just the right goofy charm and spontaneity to quicken everything round about—a man with practically no Tor at all. It is sometimes too broad and sometimes too shallow, but it's another good score for the decent, small-budget type of picture.

Professor Mamlock came right off the top of the news (it is closer to events than the latest March of Time, which goes into the training of diplomatic career men if not into what just now they are doing with it). It is a pity that its statement of the Nazi uprising in Germany will play only to the few thousands of the foreign-theater audience who know the statement by heart, because while even general movie audiences today join in the sport of Hitler-hissing, they could stand a lot more education than they'll ever get about what they are hating and why. Mamlock, the head of a clinic, wished only to serve humanity, believed the papers, and eventually forbade his son to continue Communist activities. Already he was treating "industrial wounds" and he didn't like it. His son kept on, meetings, leaflets, addresses to the workmen. The shirts came in and the little band had to go underground, while Mamlock was hounded out of his clinic, and like more and more of the complacent learned what had been happening when it was all over.

The changing relations in the hospital staff, the Party activity, the growing hardship of the poor, and the precision of the Nazi machine are well handled. It is true that the main figure has none of the marvelous humanity of the scientist in *Baltic Deputy,* that character drawing is hasty, and that there is little dramatic pull to get an audience behind it. But the main weakness is in the patient didacticism with which they approached the subject, as people who will say, this happened and you should know it, and now since you know it you must feel it. Whereas the whole principle of organizing material into a form of art is to make an audience feel it so that they may know it.

Mamlock will not play to the millions who need it because it doesn't go after them in the first place. Of course the wheeze about the best mousetrap and the automatic path to your door won't work in a society under pressure, because suppose the Hays office won't okay your mousetrap and Martin Q. Pigglywiggly and other odd bits of cheese begin to send up a smell and picket such a trap as being beneath a good Catholic, as sacrilegious, demoralizing, and a plain violation of the American constipation? But there is still the possibility of making just a clever trap that will still get by. Soviet pictures telling their own audience how happy it is usually prove too slow and heavy and foreign for our different tastes. There is left a chance for a picture from outside the Hollywood distribution channels that is supremely good, or for a regular entertainment picture just good enough in itself to carry a little social wallop. This time of all times seems to indicate a wide audience in this country for a thoroughly dramatic job about these thick sluggers and blood-bathers and envious sneaks, about how innocent slogans and fat promises could be made to serve their wide and crafty plan, until decent people found themselves overrun, and their part of the world with them, by a minority group of riffraff suddenly elevated to uniforms and motorcycles and guns, a whole trampling arm of blond zombies.

14 December 1938

The Good with the Bad

Movies are such common and lowly stuff that in intellectual circles we often find ourselves leaping, like trout for flies, after something in a new offering that promises to set it off from the average run, something of special interest or fame, in short any branch of art certified to have nothing to do with that of making pictures. If Jean Cocteau (ah fame!) should make a little job that ran backward, all in black, and no hands or cameras (ah soul!), you give me a good publicity department and I'll give you a good press for it, and a certain discerning audience.

This leads up to the new movie made from a Shaw play with the permission and active connivance of old twinkle-eye himself: *Pygmalion.* The film is going down very handsomely with many more types than would find interest in a Shaw play, which is suggestion enough that they managed to make an interesting movie out of it: in addition to a fresh idea it has humor, gadgets, romance, and edges of comment. A brilliant phonetician takes over the job of passing off a flower girl as the best English blood, and makes her so lovely and so involves his heart in the process that the joke is off and he can't live without her. Many of the lines are good, and the dustman part is both full and sly. But extending all through the length of a feature picture is just what it takes to give it away: in the end their main problem neither had much to do with phonetics nor was solved: the natural ease and grace on which success mostly depended can never be taught and rarely aped and at any rate weren't expressed here. If we are going to bring high intellect to the benighted movies, what I say is let's have an intellect that won't go around taking absurd pratfalls on its own back stairs.

Pygmalion has none of that sense of spring you get when comedy seems to leave the humdrum of its manufacture naturally and with its own crazy grace. Here it is always somehow calculated and self-conscious—not only in the general sweep but in each detail, as when an effect has to be registered and the camera goes smack to a close-up of SURPRISE, RAISED-EYEBROWS, and all the rest, or to a posed group of hopeful extras; as when an interlude of symbolic shots follows too fast from too many trick angles; as when a scene is held beyond its measure or a small device repeated like a headache. And there has been no balder makeshift in modern theatricals than the introduction of Major Whosis as confidant and commentator.

This is all tied up in my mind with Leslie Howard as the star and co-director. A sensitive actor on his own plane, he tackles comedy with a serious vim that would be impossible to describe if Stark Young hadn't described it already, saying of Howard's carriage in a similar part that he went at it like an undertaker with a sense of humor. He is at once too stiff, too delicate, and too damned resolved to throw himself out of joint; and he is naturally embarrassed by the part itself, which is unsympathetic and humanly unlikely. In spite of the overdone rows of the first part (leading the way to higher planes in pictures, Shaw introduces a terror-of-water and bathtub wheeze), Wendy Hiller makes a lovely gutter girl and gradually fine lady, and her it-was-my-belief-they-done-her-in scene is the one high-comedy touch in the film. But generally it runs on and on like old Mis' Beamish in to borrow a cup of cookin' butter on a busy morning, and I swan to Betsy if I haven't forgot what 'twas I come for.

If you want a good picture and fun too, you can go see *The Beachcomber*. Erich Pommer made the picture from Maugham's "Vessel of Wrath"; and while Charles Laughton, Elsa Lanchester, Robert Newton, and Tyrone Guthrie dominate the visual play by filling out its characters, this is a show where the camera, the framing and handling of scenes, the music (by Richard Addinsell), and the writing, all brought their special skill to the total effect. Especially the writing, because that is where the whole good idea comes from; the English stewbum on one of the more obscure Dutch East Indies who keeps up his brazen-furtive league with the Controleur against the two Church-of-England missionaries between jail sentences, and winds up regenerating the missionaries and himself too. B. Van Thal's adaptation is part of it, for there is good balance in the scenes and continuity along a straight line, and the waste-not-want-not sententiousness of the missionary brother and sister is used to the best effect in hilarity throughout.

A thing like this, beachcombers to end beachcombing, soul-savers at the height of caricature, gin and jungle and sweat and blacks, could so easily have got out of hand that it is a wonder they made it so delicately, both in the nearly imperceptible sentiment and in the frank and joyous semi-bawdy. The brother waves nervously about in the breeze, a cross between a homo and the Holy

Ghost; the sister is a mixture of your high-school algebra teacher, Florence Nightingale, the original thousand virgins, and unfolding womanhood (too late); and Laughton himself gets into his part with such relish you can nearly smell him. And yet with all this seeming excess there is such restraint in emphasis all around that the most comic situation or utterance seems the only natural outcome of such a character under such circumstances, so that there is something touching in the ridiculous and vice versa.

For loveliness catching you unawares, you have the scene where Laughton has got his black girl and is drinking and dreaming and telling her how you can see your breath in the air and how your shoes ring in the snow like bells, back home, in England. And for the funniest entrance contrived anywhere this year you have the brother, who has huffed himself off into his room and been forgotten about in the following news of epidemic, bouncing back in to drape around his sister's neck: Martha, I apologize, and the look on their several faces. To a fair degree it is Charles Laughton's picture, and he is all through it grand. But the timing and motion of the more complex parts, not only the shift of body or camera but the holding back of the unexpected until the right split second for its explosion, the swift completion of the appointed round, are a lesson for all to study in the difference between hitting the nail on the head and hitting your head on the nail.

Of course part of the blessing of this film is its unbound appreciation of some joys of life to which the movies are making us rapidly unaccustomed. But in a larger way it is a reassurance that true comedy lives as it always has had to live, full of people and motion and the things we know, exaggerated to make us laugh, surely, but never so narrow or meanly cerebral as to leave us with a dry throat or a bad taste in it: comedy should be near enough to us in honest familiar warmth to make us in some way happy.

The movies, which were after Mr. Bernard Shaw's time, left Mr. Bernard Shaw building houses out of alphabet blocks, but not in his first childhood.

28 December 1938

From *Gunga Din* to *The Roaring Twenties*

It's Criminal

The movie *Gunga Din* is to me a sad marker of the decline Hollywood has gone into since the days a few years ago when it could bang out *Lives of a Bengal Lancer,* a film that was Kipling without the credit title and such a good show that (we were saving the world then too, you recall, or more so) the right people were perfectly furious about the wrong things while the show generally played right on. At this time we haven't got Kipling or anything else but indecision and a lavish splash.

It is not only the blithe roof-jumping of the younger Fairbanks in *Gunga Din* that reminds you of such fast ones as *The Mark of Zorro;* the action throughout is ripping in the forgotten manner of the silent days, when a director didn't have to worry over whether Herbert Marshall was lighted right for the great renunciation speech, and would just say: "Hell, make it: if they want a continuity too we can work that out after." The fighting has terrific motion, the elephant is fine, the battalion parade with bagpipes is always good for a lift, and the only thing lacking from the temple rites is Bela Lugosi. But the fact is that they can neither believe their own hokum nor leave it alone. They play up the undying beauties of comradeship, and then have two of the buddies scheming to wreck completely the honeymoon plans of the third; they assume everyone should pant to die for England if he's really alive at all, and then have men risking all the lives in the Indian empire for some prank to further the plot; they get a nice idea in the elephant's breaking the prison window and then go barging on into something which would have been thrown out of *King Kong.*

Cary Grant, Douglas Fairbanks, Jr., and Victor McLaglen do nicely in spite of everything, though I regret to say that Sam Jaffe was persuaded to play Gunga Din, a part to which he brings everything, including the apparent belief that East is South and that Little Eva was the natural son of Uncle Tom. But the whole mood is irresponsible and wrong, as though there were nothing left in the world to do but try on other men's hats by pulling them down over your ankles. It is not so much that they'll stop at nothing here as that they'll start with nothing and keep on till it bleeds. Outside of a few quoted lines, there is no more of Kipling than there is of *Daily Worker.* Kipling stuck to the bright side of

service life but never made it silly; he was what you wish, a tub-thumper or a
fascist; but part of his marvelous power of projection was his affectionate
knowledge of these constant dopes in their sweaty uniforms or dress whites,
doing and dying because the bugle played to quarters or something and knowing
no more than that, saving their obscene cockney humor. The harm done by his
special type of glorification is another thing; and if this *Gunga Din* had been
made with the right tongues in the right cheeks it might have passed as a fine
burlesque of all this. But it remains a miscomprehending lark, and over the finish
of it you can almost hear one of Kipling's rear sergeants: "A bloody lark, my
you-know-bloody-what!"

They Made Me a Criminal is a rather obvious piece and routine in many
ways (incidentally the time approaches when the boys from the *Dead End* cast
must be graduated from reform school and matriculated at CCNY). But its
hokum is all of a piece and its interest is correspondingly higher. John (*né* Jules)
Garfield is a ring champ who gets implicated in a murder and blows town. Still
traveling under his original assumption that anyone who does anything out of
kindness or decency is a sucker, he shows up on a sort of *Boys' Town* date ranch
in the West. Once you know that there is a gal on the ranch who has all the little
toughies nailed to an honor-bright basis and hates evil like anything, you can see
the rest of it—except that the proof of regeneration comes out for all to see
when the sluggaroo himself takes a terrific beating from some barnstorming
gorilla in order to lift the mortgage (and except for Helen Westley, who is
apparently unshaken in the belief that no matter what the picture, you can play
the witch part from *Snow White* for laughs, and get them).

So: fast talk and action, plus conversion to the better life, plus a
near-tragic lucky finish. But Garfield and the kids and the gal, the director and
those who worried the script into shape—and even Claude Rains as the broken
but hopeful flatfoot—these people manage to salvage enough truth out of it to
make most of the business convincing and pleasant. Generally, the film holds
together enough to make nice fast watching, solving one of the old old problems
in one of the old old ways.

The movies have made their idea of the Broadway production of *Idiot's
Delight,* and in their awed literal way have emphasized its weakness without
living up to its strength. It has got known as an antiwar play: actually it is no
more than an adventure-musical with certain antiwar sentiments lashed in here
and there. The main interest centers in the sort of unconscious romance between
a rough-and-ready chap from the American vaudeville time and a wistful admirer
from an aerial act on the same bill. They met once and then the show broke, and
in the years that followed, the chap got on a European tour with some chorus
beauties. When they met again the girl was traveling with a Zaharoff type and all

the characters were stranded in a hotel overlooking a lethal airbase. War declared, girl deserted, chap to the rescue, and so forth.

Obviously this business between boy and girl was done well enough to carry the play: in the movie it boils down to Clark Gable in some bright moments and Norma Shearer in many awfully extended starring scenes in which a carefully learned "accent" only shows that nice little girls should be made to stay at home. The antiwar stuff is straight and genuine (the Hays office apparently manages to look the other way when objectionable lines have been produced on Broadway and passed around for the applause of the nation); and there are fragments of real feeling. But the mood of the whole thing is forced and cheap—the coming world war staged by Maurice Chevalier. The film has a brisker motion than the play, but is full enough of Norma Shearer, phony accents, and heavy bombers that swoop down across the windows like seagulls, to spoil its own fun. The fact that movie-house audiences applaud some of the more ringing speeches makes the picture valuable in its way. But the general idea is essentially no more antiwar than a few squads of well-meaning and offended citizens, pelting a nasty old caterpillar tank with chocolate éclairs.

22 February 1939

The Best of Class B

For his Rialto Theatre recently, Arthur Mayer had something just his meat, and I don't blame him for being enthusiastic about it. (Arthur runs what he calls a male-audience house, action and horror pictures mostly; he rues the drawing-room in films and rather enjoys being a target for the daily men, who escape monotony by figuring up cracks about the newest Rialto opening. The best so far was Frank Nugent's remark in January that the last one of 1938 wound up the year with a perfect score for Arthur: "No hits, no runs; all terrors.") The picture is *Boy Slaves,* a class-B production made for RKO by P. J. Wolfson out of an original script by Albert Bein, and it goes back to what the Warners did in *Cabin in the Cotton, Massacre, Fury,* etc., and what major companies have not been doing for a long time—however ripe and gorgeous the stinkaroos of this last empty season.

I have been thinking that the only present hope for true screen originality—outside of sending every Hollywood executive drawing more than $100,000 to Congress—is the chance that lies with the producers of small-budget pictures, independent or otherwise. When you can make a feature film and get out for little more than what it cost to feed the elephants in *Gunga Din,* nobody is going to worry so much if you happen to get a good idea of your own. There is a company making films over in Astoria for Paramount release, and we'll see about that later. But thus far there hasn't been enough screen talent going into the inexpensive jobs—which naturally get kicked around into obscure and distant corners of the lot and come to the public through the back door like the iceman.

Boy Slaves is not really a first-class picture, though it's got more pull to it than you might find in some of the films belonging in that category. It is about several poor kids who form a vagrant company to get something to eat in the world, and get caught in the lethal grind of a Southern turpentine camp. Through the endless wheel of the company store, extended indenture, overwork, cruelty, and slops for their meager food, they are driven to a desperate attempt at escape and finally to violence with guns—at which point the outside law steps in. They might have been shipped back for good, what with the scandal and all; actually they struck upon an upright judge whom the scandal only moved to compassion and anger . . . land of the free . . . leave no stone unturned, etc.

It can be claimed that the ending is somewhat lollipop even if likely; but a story after all does have to have an end. It is nice to hope always, and people usually won't go for pictures in which kids are just sent back to misery and early death without some promise of retribution. In the case of such individual histories, the closing note of Change the System! would be even more empty of anything save rhetoric than usual: what little we are able to do to improve matters will not help these American sons, or their sons after them if they have any. It is all very dispiriting as the truth often is; but it won't hurt anyone except where he damn well needs it; and ending or no ending the story has already done its work of exposition and exposure. Any film that persuades people of even an isolated truth, in its own terms and by its power over their imagination, is worth ten to twenty pictures that were made to state the whole outline according to the book, and then seen principally by friends and relatives of the producing group.

Boy Slaves has the necessary dramatic punch to make its picture of conditions real. The turpentine camp looks actual and ominous enough. The kids are fine; their characters (from Toughie through Tubbie to the gentler boy fighting a general suspicion of squealing) are conceived so as to keep the facts in view and the story of their progress mounting. A good standard of plot-making and human observation, the illusion of participating in something with real and troubled people—these must be present if fiction pictures are to get over as pictures at all, and they are here to the point of leaving an audience moved and really mad. It isn't so much that this film tackled a problem as that it tackled well, on the one hand. On the other, it is not so accurate to call *Boy Slaves* a film that failed (which in a larger way it did), as to recognize it for doing something too seldom attempted at all.

8 March 1939

A Picture

Though having released nothing of true interest since motion pictures generally came of age, Sergei Eisenstein has somehow managed to keep the memory of his importance green, and so his new film, regarded from one angle, is an event.

Alexander Nevsky is a straight historical picture—apart from occasional strains of what I believe used to be called jingoism, or saber-rattling. Thirteenth-century Russia. From the ill-organized and war-torn country, now being invaded by Teutonic bands, a leader comes to marshal armed forces and even peasants in a battle that is decisive, a complete rout. The situation and feudal period are established and the battle is drawn; the balance of the film is taken up with the rivalry in love of two military oafs and occasional references to the sententious but valiant armorer, the fighting orphan girl, etc.

That is all the story, and though comparatively simple it is long in the telling, because each attitude, point, and symbol hangs on like a drowning man. As to how the thing is done, I can't report justly so long as it is possible that shortage of material and technicians is responsible for this wheezy sound and this cheesecloth scenery (I can however make a better galloping horse with a pair of chopsticks on a pincushion, and guarantee that if the best close-up you can get of a knight on horseback is by putting a man in a rocking chair with a champagne bucket over his head, you would do best to skip the close-up). The mass action is exciting, if confused and clumsily intercut; the Prokofiev background music is impressive; but the actors are either not capable of making or not encouraged to make the character interest much higher than zero.

Except for two or three spots where the motion broke clear of its awkward wits and unconvincing rubber-ax work, and ran like water or poetry—the troops going up a rise of ground, horsemen converging below the camera and streaming across its focus—the few outstanding things of this film could have been done in stills: Tissé's dark composition, the details and implements, the faces. Far from being the thumping great film people come to expect of a thumping name, *Alexander Nevsky* is way behind the good Soviet (and how many other) films of the last five years, in conception, story, pace, and vital meaning. Its effect is something like that of Max Reinhardt making *Adrift on an Icepan* in the Hippodrome.

12 April 1939

For a Picture . . .

The movie *Wuthering Heights* came just in time. The film year has been about the leanest in seven—and Sam Goldwyn's version of the novel turns out to be among the best pictures made anywhere. Our sleepyheads in the prints and the industry itself have been apologizing and deprecating and rolling sheep's eyes at the legitimate stage for so long that the habit of playing down movies is ingrained, while even in mildly good theater there seems to be nothing but sky for a limit to critical hurrah. I have enjoyed quite a few of this season's plays, yet most of them don't make more that a good patch on *Wuthering Heights,* for truth, vigor, and thorough expression in the form. Just watch the words go by, however, and count how many times this picture is very respectfully restricted to being, oh quite fine—for a picture.

Pictures made from novels, especially novels everyone is supposed to have read, are usually desperate ventures; but in this case the script writers were both sober and skillful enough to get a film story out of the book; it was impossible they should not lose some of the solid effect, but on the other hand they have delivered the action from that heavy weight of words. The production was given the best in everything except music, and the best in this case included a free rein to sincere workmanship. From then on it was up to William Wyler's direction, cameras, and cast.

Wyler has many adult jobs to his credit, but more than usual was required of him here, a sustained mood of bleakness and sullen passions. Part of this is achieved in the film by remarks in character, and part by the setting on the Yorkshire moors (some artificiality shows through, reminding you of the superior natural effects of a film like *South Riding*). But the closeness with which the story holds together is ultimately the result of the way director, photographer, and cutters have used what should be called the moving camera, the part of photography that goes beyond a register of things to the position from which they are seen, moved up to, led away from, to the value in tempo and coloring of each strip of film with relation to that of all preceding and following strips—the camera telling a story.

It is a very intricate and wonderful art, and William Wyler's staff have achieved one of its best examples. Without the distraction of trick effects, however stunning, they have taken a story anchored to three main points and with most of its action interior, and given it a pattern of constant forward motion, with overtones maintained throughout the rise of interest and suspense. The art serves its true purpose unobtrusively, and for that reason will not be fully appreciated unless you start asking yourself afterward how else in the world you would have gone about it.

Laurence Olivier makes a fine cryptic and dominant job of Heathcliff, and Merle Oberon opposite him gets over the difficulties of being beautiful, wild, and sweet all at once very well. The only fault with the picture as a whole, though, is that these people are not in themselves twisted enough to make their actions and end inevitable: they are able to give credence to a scene once they are in it, but they have not by intrinsic nature prepared you for the revelation of such dark obsessions. David Niven triumphs over a weak and unhappy part as he always does, by a controlling sensitivity and intelligence that go beyond simple trouping. For the rest, the cast was as near perfection as you could ask: Donald Crisp, Leo G. Carroll (a pity he had so little, with that dry and infinite capacity of his), Flora Robson, and all the others right down to the Great Danes.

The production was done with such dignity and grace as to remind us again that the chances of artistic purity in such a vastly complex business are at least a hundred to one (good director, mean producer; good cast, weak script; good subject, sloppy treatment; good start, meddlesome bankers; and so on indefinitely). But for all the funny jokes about Sam Goldfish, for all the self-hugging that goes on when American Flag meets Hammernsickle along Broadway with sufficient vitality to draw a few thousands, I am reminded again by a picture like *Wuthering Heights* that art should be high and valid enough, maybe once in a century, to slip out of the custodianship of a jealous and self-conscious culture club, spilling its effect into the lives of our eternal millions.

Add Notes from a Ten-O'Clock Scholar. —*Huckleberry Finn* is probably the hardest picture in the world to make, for the story is as much a part of all of us as our childhood, and as difficult to recapture. The current MGM version is fairly well done, and its shortcomings are canceled out by the presence of Mickey Rooney, who is my Huckleberry against all comers. When you see such good veterans as Walter Connolly and William Frawley being allowed (or made) to play as though they were endmen for some insolvent minstrel show, and see Mickey breaking through in spite of everything, you get some idea of the vigor and finish of this young talent. (Mickey is getting to be a big boy now, but we are not going to send him to CCNY, as he is reserved for Lord Jeffrey Amherst and the immortals.)

The action of the picture is carried out about as well as its abrupt simplicity permits; I liked the atmosphere, the quiet home, the raft, the riverboats, and the river; and once you discount the general hollowness of the supporting cast, you can excuse all excess sentiment on the grounds of faithfulness to the original. But it is Mickey Rooney's picture as it should be, the story of a tarnal nuisance but ideal American kid, living out his small pleasures, miseries, and rebellions along the great river.

26 April 1939

They're Down! They're Up!

The Warners' *Confessions of a Nazi Spy* is one of the most sensational movie jobs on record, workmanlike in every respect and spang across the headlines. Its specific outline is the work of the FBI in rounding up Nazi agents here; but so thorough is its coverage that the effect is much more than one of simple crime detection: it is the most vivid, matter-of-fact, unescapable induction into Nazi principles and practices that the majority of people have ever been given outside a concentration camp.

They are smooth as silk about it, starting off without credit titles of any kind, on the words of a "news" commentator who leads directly into the action in March of Time fashion. The illusion is freshened from time to time by reversion to comment plus rapidly intercut news shots and animated maps. But instead of the brief, self-conscious "enactments" of the news-film type, characters here build with the story, understood and projected with the natural truth of good theater illusion—indeed Francis Lederer's part is a thorough study of small and shifty megalomania by itself.

Scores of people come into the story, temporarily or to stay, but you find yourself not identifying them as actors at all: everyone seems carried beyond his usual attitudes either by the excitement of truth or Anatole Litvak's direction or both. Edward G. Robinson is more effective and subdued than ever, and Paul Lukas has the part of his life as the rising career man in propaganda. The German-English is maintained with a wonderful absence of the usual strain after dialect; the officers, small fry, dupes, and thugs natural to such a worldwide blood cult have been rounded up in a nearly flawless collection of types for every occasion. Yet in spite of this attention to character, fact, and detail, the pace never lets down for a minute. They have discovered the story for a natural and let it have its head without trying for plot, romance, heroism. The result is terrific.

A little too terrific, perhaps. The film is a hate-breeder if there ever was one, and when even our playboy intellectuals are charging around proclaiming the duty to go into battle of somebody else, any aid to national hatred is dynamite. The picture is specific about the thousands of good non-Nazi German-Americans, but the old human tendency to mass identification is bound to make trouble there. Also it overstresses the theme of a Nazi America and the importance of swiping military secrets for that or any other end—which is a dangerous piece of naïveté. Still and all, who's doing all this in the world, us? Did we make it up? Our people never can learn from all the talk of ideologies and political theory, or from scare-heads in *The Daily Mirror,* just how repulsive and impossible in a decent life this whole combination of a blood-gorge and horsefeathers actually is. This is no *Beast of Berlin,* but a statement of sober, inevitable facts, so brilliantly realized that no one can hide from it; it happens before his eyes.

Now, as you were. There is nothing like a good million-dollar sales campaign to make a million-dollar picture seem like an important picture. But by Thanksgiving, when reviews, page-ads, and other fireworks have left the sky, Warner Brothers' *Juarez* (juar-ez) should begin to tower as one of the really memorable turkeys. The story of Maximilian in Mexico is a tragic story; but they have simply made it look like a million dollars' worth of ballroom sets, regimentals, gauze shots, and whiskers. The story of Benito Juarez is a national epic from a period of turbulence and desperate growth; but even when this story is not subordinate to the lachrymose affairs of the Maximilian family, it is bogged down in close-ups and two-shots and medium shots of people talking at great length. The end is quickly foreseen and forever in coming, not only in the story as a whole but in so many of its parts, especially the absurd stretches of the wife at the shrine, the off-stage singer of "La Paloma," the partings, baby kissings, family groups.

It could have been a good and true picture. It announces with dignity and intelligence the principles of freedom from oppression, and Paul Muni's arraignment of nineteenth-century European diplomacy is as massive an effect of this kind as you could hope for. They stuck by history at the expense of action, happy ending, and romance; and their statement of democracy *v.* dictatorship is better education than textbooks. (At the same time, it is primer stuff and too smug: American democracy hasn't done away with injustice and oppression, and has taken Mexico for plenty itself; and you would think the Catholic Church in Mexico was just kindly padres and scenes with soft music.)

Still, intentions are not results. Bette Davis has a good mad scene but is generally held down by sentimentality and some of the most banal dialogue-writing to be found. The cast is as long as your arm, seven of them starring players in their own right; but William Dieterle was unable to bring out their natural talent: they are all right but seem scattered effects as people, uneasy in their lines and make-up. Dieterle directed some whirling action bits and fine companies of soldiers and crowds, and his blackout of the crazy empress fluttering off into darkness will be remembered. Otherwise no, and no. As a picture it does not move in any sense of the word: it's a road-company Passion Play.

Paul Muni dominates a scene when he is given one, with force and dignity. But Juarez and the story of his country, in all that two hours of spectacle, seem to play hardly more than background music for the sweet and slow sorrows of Mr. Brian Aherne's Maximilian, his court, his family and honor-bright helplessness, his dignity and facial hairdo—a sort of interminable bath in sesame and warm molasses.

The Warners' publicity department has *Juarez* billed as the film showing "how great the screen can be"; a few doors down Broadway the Warners' *Confessions of a Nazi Spy* is being run as a topical shocker. And just recently a little comedy piece passed through unobtrusively—though no one concerned with screen art could miss the beautiful assurance in the form with which its old statements, clichés of situation and attitude were lifted almost beyond recognition by a morning freshness of eye for each small thing around, and a way of expression as natural as singing in the shower. The movie (RKO) was *Love Affair,* still on view.

With Donald Ogden Stewart on the script, Charles Boyer and Irene Dunne for principals, Leo McCarey managed a happy command both of the complexities of his job and of the absurd, homely, garish, and touching things in ordinary life. The plot isn't worth recitation and so those interested in how art may be talked about even though cinematic, may skip it. Those excited over the mastery of form already achieved in pictures, and over what the screen can be, will like to follow this demonstration of the qualities of technique and imagination the films must always have and keep on recruiting to their service.

10 May 1939

Goodbye Please

I might have spotted *Goodbye, Mr. Chips* as a good weep for Woollcott; but as for the rest of the big hats MGM's publicity men have been able to get thrown over the roof, I can't find out from the picture what all the shootin's fer. It is the story of a shy chap teaching in the same English public school through some fifty years, his early unpopularity and failure with the boys, his absurd romance in middle age and the success that followed his marriage, the death of his wife, and the later years as a beloved fixture in the school. The picture runs two hours.

It is a simple story but it is not simply told—I believe the only direct-narrative sequence in it is the holiday love affair. For the rest there is a brief bit of action here, a long speech there, a snatch of dialogue picked up to show what year we are in. Since boys are always growing up and masters changing, Mr. Chips has to be the whole thing. And as a character he does not change much, except for make-up and the difference between success and failure.

Beyond our interest in what happens next, we have to rely on the business in the school, whether funny or sad or educational. And I think the business all through is handled with a minimum of talent for the natural and right effect. Care has been spent on authenticity and costuming and general good mounting (it was produced in England for MGM). But director Sam Wood is a heavy man against a tiller: when he wants a tear he ships bucketfuls of water, and when he wants a laugh he rocks the boat. Ties or no ties, his school is no school that was ever gone to, and the difference in any language can be seen from *The Devil Is a Sissy* to *Merlusse*, from *Decline and Fall* to *What a Life*.

Goodbye, Mr. Chips will appeal to others more than to me, for while there is no run and life to it as a movie and a general air of stagnant sentiment, there are certain qualities of kindness and wisdom, loneliness and enduring faith in the figure of this spry and gentle soul. (Robert Donat does wonderfully well against the handicap of having to be a young actor in an octogeneric wig and twinkle; but even so the part as written for him is actually pretty straight type, and monotonous in incident.) I thought the emphasis given in writing and direction to the old-school stuff made it less recreative of an attitude than silly. And I know that two hours of episodic speeches, proclamations, entreaties, and obituaries can be a pretty wispy bore. Mr. Woollcott and even his principal, the original James Chipso Hilton himself, feel the picture keeps pure faith with the book, but I'll probably never know that. So goodbye, Mr. Chips, goodbye please.

Howard Hawks has had an uneven if successful career, but he directed the best of all airplane pictures, *Ceiling Zero,* and so it is too bad he and an above-average cast had to be wasted on the story of *Only Angels Have Wings.* With a good story, the swift suspense so naturally brought out in movies of pilots and their job would have become a terrific thing under its own power. But this was done in the run-of-the-mill Hollywood way: get something that will wow them, gag it up, bring the girls in, bring everything else in. And so Cary Grant's troubles with a mail schedule in South America, with a girl that drops in, pilots that lose their eyesight or take chances, with the coward who is making good, etc.—this stuff soon gets out of hand because there is too much of it to fit in any line of meaning, so to keep it going the writers then throw in more stuff—the less they know the more they speak. Added to the dangers of this torturing of coincidence, there comes the slowing down necessary to fix half a dozen different things so they can work out happily for the end.

Power dives are always ripping across a theater screen somewhere: but in this case more could have been done. The atmosphere was right to start with, the give and take among the men, the hard-pressed finances of the outfit, the dangers known and unknown, and the good likely people: Cary Grant, Jean Arthur, Thomas Mitchell, Richard Barthelmess, Allyn Joslyn, Siegfried Rumann. In the minor things, where the ridiculous or the stereotype didn't intrude, there was a swell realization of their personalities, of friendship and banter and weariness and trouble. Howard Hawks can be faultless in a sense of how to speed up a situation, or make it flexible and easy with the right emphasis, grouping, understatement. In fact, all these people did the best they could with what they were given—but look at it. The battle with mechanics and the elements, in this as in other air films, provides suspense all right; but so does hanging.

It's a Wonderful World is, despite the title, one of the few genuinely comic pieces in a dog's age (direction of W. S. Van Dyke). It occasionally gets too loud and raucous for my taste, but it has a lot of funny people and funny situations, and it clips right along. Much as I do not admire Mr. Ben Hecht, I must insist that he is one of the most brilliant writers in pictures—even among the few who know what pictures are all about he is at the top—and has been proving it for years. His script, like that of the aviation movie, is frankly designed for box-office success. The difference is that it's all of a piece; it hangs together and moves smartly without confusion. It is the familiar compound of the romantic comedy and the detective thriller. Beyond the fact that it brings a shady private detective and a caricatured lady poet unwillingly (at first) together as fellow fugitives and at the same time investigators of some excessively criminal manipulations, the plot is too complex and unimportant to go into. Its virtue is that it does not make you think of plot: suspense holds like a cable, the interest keeps jumping, and there's a pretty good laugh around every corner. (Hecht knows slapstick, but he has a lively imagination that has gone to schools more subtle than Keystone Academy, and he is none the worse for either.)

James Stewart, Claudette Colbert, Nat Pendleton, Guy Kibbe, Edgar Kennedy. They're all good people in the right place, and they have it here. There is a delicious edge to the satire on the flatfoot element; but I take it as farce comedy only, and I find that sometimes my remarks on this form of endeavor are misconstrued, and embitter friends. For all those serious but admirable people who don't mind a good laugh so long as you telegraph it to them, but really prefer, in these changing times, something they can get their teeth into, and factually—hell, I mean, Dear Malcolm Cowley: Save your money and stay away from the present comedy manifesto.

31 May 1939

Abe

Young Mr. Lincoln is another of the strangely honest movies that this year has produced, without producing much else: most of them have been unspectacular, though two have had real brilliance (*Wuthering Heights* and *Nazi Spy*). This one is good but, opening without expense or explosion, it may slip past all but its audiences without much notice. Outside of being better constructed than the year's Lincoln play, and less dependent on the business of make-up and excerpted speeches, it requires no comparison. It starts with Lincoln in his home town, not sure of what he would do but already attracted to book learning and politics. It hangs most of the action around an early law case and the general life of fair-day in a frontier town—referring back lightly to Nancy Hanks and Ann Rutledge, suggesting the future parts of Stephen Douglas and

Mary Todd—and just about leaves it at that. I couldn't say whether this is the historical spit and image of Nancy's boy Abe, but it looks pretty likely and it looks pretty good.

John Ford deliberately used a slow drawling tempo to fit the subject. And where Lincoln himself is not concerned, this has a clogging effect. With any ordinary trick actor the pauses, jew's-harping, and untangling of feet would have become a pure bore. But John Ford didn't have trick acting, and when he takes his time he never throws it away. The long sequence of fair-day in town is a fine example of the way he can make use of period color and scene and incident to give life to the story; he is a spendthrift with actual air and trees and water throughout. The trial scene is the big dramatic part, and comes over well as such; the best Ford manner shows in the dark and breathless struggle in the clearing at night; but the best things as a whole are the solid rightness of each thing used, and the shrewd way the main theme was given its head.

Henry Fonda shares top credit. He has played so many young-romantic parts as to be known everywhere in his own character; the part here is that death-trap to actors of the man whose later days became a national legend and stone statue; and the story demanded a genuinely rustic clumsiness covered with the constant implicit dignity that an "impersonation" like Mr. Donat's Mr. Chips would simply ruin. Well, he did it. His delivery was good, his carriage was good, his dance steps at the ball were wonderful. But he did it mainly on some rare and unshakable belief in what he was doing and in himself which goes beyond the most brilliant or veteran technique. In the way this shambling mixture of bewilderment, sweetness, tarnal humor, and gall is held together, the character does not have to be an exact Abe, being something Abe himself wouldn't be ashamed of.

As a movie it might have been made stronger. It surely could have been shortened, toughened up in its weak parts (the anxious mother and all). And the symbolic mess of the ending could have been so easily wiped out by simply letting the "Battle Hymn" music come up on the sound track and the camera go up the trail as Abe says he guesses he won't go back just yet; he'll just walk on, far as the top of that hill. But as it stands, the movie carries out its difficult job without raising its voice, moving people more than it probably thought to. Its simple good faith and understanding are an expression of the country's best life that says as much as forty epics.

21 June 1939

Breathing Spell

What with the theater and all, I have been out of control when some of the worthy pictures that are still bobbing around through *Cue* were first released. I missed *The Hound of the Baskervilles* by a few hundred miles, for example. I have always missed the hound, having been busy with Young and Old King Brady and The Dare Boys at an age when everybody else was taking this on. But by pure coincidence I came across it in a ship's library last winter, and read it at last. My impression was that I should have got to it earlier if I was going to get to it at all.

As you probably know by this time, they got their effects with Basil Rathbone, Nigel Bruce, and a dog the size of a colt. Also pretty realistic moor scenery, mist and rocks, etc. Where the story wouldn't fit into pictures they changed it, but otherwise they kept soberly to the business of the novel, clearing away its ornate impassages of writing and succeeding marvelously in making real characters of both Holmes and Watson. I thought the hound should have been heard from more, and I suppose the SPCA kept them from setting him on fire with turpentine to get a terrifying silhouette in the dark. I don't imagine anybody's blood was refrigerated much below room temperature, but it is a self-respecting job and as good an excuse as any to spend an air-cooled hour or so one of these evenings.

I was sorry to miss up on *Man of Conquest,* too. Its story of Sam Houston and the grabbing off of Texas is perhaps less prettied up than is true of the run of screen epics, but its importance to the trade is that it was made by one of the "small" companies. Republic is of course getting larger, but there is always the dazzling hope that someday some outfit too small to tremble with such mighty fears as shake Metro will take a subject that is not good movie taste, and do it up brown. *Man of Conquest* is done brown enough—it scandalizes history with the best of them.

Dark Victory is another film that I neglected to report, and shouldn't have (week before this it played eighteen houses in Manhattan alone). Looking back over the course of the last five years I realize suddenly one reason may have been that a picture like this is not news any more. I don't mean that a finely rounded job of film making isn't important in any season, especially the present; it's simply that we have come naturally to expect, when a movie is good, that it will be good all the way; made with and by the right people, it stands complete in itself, and fumbles with its cap before no other art whatsoever. *Dark Victory* is the my-days-are-numbered type of story, this time operative on an impetuous young thing who learns responsibility, and true love, too, through an affliction of brain and eyesight. And Bette Davis is the very genius of the screen. You might say that Miss Davis was restricted in range in that she couldn't play Katharine Cornell, but by me that would prove only that there is a happy freedom to be gained in restriction: in her capacity she is not equaled by anyone, and in developing this special capacity—always the suggestion of almost evil and certainly unhealthy subsurfaces—she has achieved results in general intensity that are exceeded by few. *Dark Victory* as a play ran in one theater on Broadway; as a picture it is running out over the world like quicksilver, for all people to see and to some extent adjust their expectations of art by. I said eighteen houses in Manhattan alone. I said in one week.

To get up closer to the day's work, there is a film that has just left the first run in New York, *Clouds over Europe*. It's a picture all right: it is printed on celluloid and moves before your eyes and people talk just like real and everything. In its story, which it takes seriously, it seems that some Teutonic cheps are up to no good with reference to a new super-charger developed for the exclusive use of some English cheps in the flying service. The trial-flight planes are brought down at sea by a powerful ray with annoying efficiency, and since no one thinks to lay a course anywhere but directly over the death-ray ship, the process would be going on yet if it hadn't been for Ralph Richardson—who is a swell enough actor to be the life of any party—and a young lovely whose veteran skill in scooping all other reporters of any sex has given her a certain nose for the deepest intrigue of nations and a charming manner of coming to the point: "Oh look here, you know, a jubb's a jubb." Aided by these two, and a unit of His Majesty's fleet. Laurence Olivier is finally able to keep the supercharger, the girl, and the jubb too.

The film was made (by Columbia) in England, where there is a general lack of the technique for smoothing over high events and small talk. Where Alfred Hitchcock can use a fast-action formula to hang character and comedy on, in addition to every ounce of suspense the traffic will bear, these people have used a Hollywood-Hitchcock formula to hang themselves on. They see perfectly that there should be a laugh here, a bucket of blood there, and then get so anxious to telephone you that there it is, it's coming down the track, that they miss the train altogether. They are learning though, and there are a few laughs and thrills in the picture. I prefer going to *The Lady Vanishes* (Hitchcock) for the second time, and *I Met Him in Paris* (Wesley Ruggles) for the third. The world is so full of a number of things that I see no more reason why you should get the latest movie smell up your nose than you should abstain from reading a good book in a weak publishing season. The movies are always wonderful, but don't say I sent you.

5 July 1939

Movies: One Here, One There

The special style of comedy in *Bachelor Mother* is not easy to mark off. Its formula is worn enough—rich-man-poor-girl, etcetera—but perhaps what distinguishes it is a certain appealing belief in its own simplicities, a keeping of faith with its people, making their troubles felt as troubles and never letting them down into meanness or absurdity just for a laugh. The laughs are there all right, and so is sentiment; but there is maintained an almost colloidal balance between decent feeling and the tough, ready wit of people who know their way around.

The story just shows what can happen if you can't prove it isn't your baby even though you are Ginger Rogers, and if a store like Altman's had David Niven for the son of the firm, and Christian responsibility as its moving ideal. (All together now, girls from Notions, Handbags, Hose: *Yah!*) As for the details of it, we can leave them to the picture, where they belong.

Garson Kanin made the film for RKO, and the way he can fill out a sequence with visual comedy is something to put in your notebook. There are so many neat lines and ideas that a lot of credit goes to the writing; but no line is ever good until it is planted. I think the whole Cinderella-at-the-ball sequence is a piece of genius, from the entrance all through the play of dancing and dinners and pidgin-Swedish to the hilarious breakdown exit. And for instruction, you wouldn't do badly to analyze the timing and motion of the scene where father and son come together at lunch, both red in the face and horribly short-circuited by the busy servant. It is a rare trick to be able to set cameras so that people will see what you wish them to see without being slapped across the eye with it.

The landlady is too good to be true; the shopgirl never comes home to soak her feet after standing all day on them in a street-floor Christmas rush; and no one ever saw a baby so dry from head to foot. These aren't complaints in the name of realism, because the picture already is real. But there is still room in the magic of pictures for more of life than we see lived there, and it is up to the people who make good pictures to exploit such a rich human vein.

Hollywood has become very adept in getting around the charted obstacles in the way of a straight story. However prettified, I can forgive this picture's lapses in department-store biography for its neat comment on such types as floor-walkers, and for the explosive sequence where Niven in disguise tries to exchange something in his own store (the girls have a word for "exchange" and the word, pronounced behind the hand, is Hoh-hoh). And while everybody's moral waterline is actually above reproach, they certainly had Joe Breen looking at the little birdie when they took this one: Ginger Rogers is not an unmarried mother, but is accepted as such in the picture's best circles.

The characters are squarely written into the story and are there only for their use to it. But there are so many slips between script and lip movement on the screen that any director is lucky to have such a thorough troupe. Ginger

Rogers is certainly one of the most talented and still human lovelies that have come down the road, ease without pose, comedy talent without brass, and a wonderful kind of understanding that carries her over tough places she could have had no formal training for. David Niven is another of my favorites, a quiet mild chap, sharp as a razor. Add Frank Albertson, who for several years now has been the ideal post-adolescent American with all the answers. And Charles Coburn is a wise and veteran actor for any situation, with a subtlety that triumphs over typing. There is besides a feeling you get from a movie only occasionally, that the company had a good time making it together, that it was one of those happy things from start to finish. Maybe it wasn't that way on the lot, but that is the way it is on the screen when you see it—and that's what you're there for.

The Fifth Avenue Playhouse is making a nice summer business out of its second "international festival" of movies, and though the fifty-three films have to be selected more by audience appeal, availability, and print condition than by actual merit, it gives you a fine chance to enlarge or revise your film perspective (you will get little perspective on American films, but what have you been living here all you life for?). The best service the Playhouse has done this year is in dragging out G. W. Pabst's *Kameradschaft* again. I have worked out three loose categories for old movies as seen today: (1) historically important; (2) originally important as snob appeal; (3) enduring merit. *Kameradschaft* belongs squarely in the third group—along with Milestone's *All Quiet*, it is among the few early sound films that still travel on their own power.

Its theme is that men do not know they are brothers until there is some kind of disaster or war. Its subject is an actual incident in the mines along the Franco-German frontier, when fire and water and terrific weight of earth broke through onto the entire French day shift, and the German miners coming off forgot the stored hostilities and suspicions of life in boundary towns, and went lolloping over temporal barriers and down the endless black shaft to stand shoulder to shoulder against the only true enemy of men anywhere—outside of themselves, that is. There are few things that time and circumstance have made more poignant than the end of this story, worked out at the time with such truth and faith in a country where today the real truth of life and faith in people are twisted or made a mock of. They are the same good people and hearts of oak beneath, still capable of herosim and universal friendship, but stirred to one thing or another because while they work with their hands and feel with their hearts, their heads are an open bowl of chowder.

About the picture itself: Pabst got a wonderful impression of living people. Despite occasional superimposed love and interest angles and a certain inevitable muddiness in translation, his choice of types and latitude in giving them free play keep the movie away from the pitfall of the impersonal diagram. The fire and cave-ins are unbelievably vivid for the resources of eight to ten years ago, but even they would be little more than meaningless spectacularism if the men down there were not true theater properties, their lunch period or changing of clothes or cabaret of an evening as carefully devised as an explosion. And so the dark mine corridors, the poor spot of light thrown across them by the single lamp of the man stumbling there, the rising water and the buckling walls, the smoke and crash and bottomless dark of the elevator shafts—these catch at the lungs in the air-cooled audience because of a human meaning that has been put into the film. Even today, with today's patronizing attitude toward the first fits and starts of yesterday, it is impossible to see without feeling. *Kameradschaft* is a film like the Pudovkin films, rising above time or language to hold any audience by its command of theater illusion.

19 July 1939

No Visible Means of Support

I remember the lusty belt I got from the first *Beau Geste* picture, and how everybody straightway forgot about being the Sea Wolf or Zorro or William S. Hart, and thought nothing better than to get out in the sand with a bottle of absinthe. And so Paramount's 1939 *Beau Geste* is like meeting up with an old schoolmate who has become the town idiot. This isn't because of the framework of the story, which is still good for handsome adventure. It isn't because of rapidly shifting times and attitudes—going back to *Lives of a Bengal Lancer* almost five years afterward, you will find it just as politically incorrect and marvelous as ever. It isn't even because the movies and I have grown up, a little. The weakness here has something to do with the heart's having gone out of a thing—characters being booted around like old tomato cans, every dramatic effect being thrown bodily into your face, and no time or concern being left for such minor things as plausible motives or reason.

It's the same story treatment: the wonderful idea of the silent fort with its dead garrison, the cut-back to the three Geste brothers as kids, the business of the missing jewel and wild horses shall not make them tell; then the three indigestions popping up one by one in the middle of the desert, the horrid sergeant, cafard, battle, death, etcetera. Of course such a piece of whole-cloth romance can be made ridiculous in the telling—and that is precisely what they did for it.

Unless his good films of the past were pure luck or two other guys, I don't know what William Wellman was doing here as director. And though Gary Cooper is the same flagpole of strength and taciturn humor he always is, there is nothing much he can make out of these strange lines and situations. The rest of the cast are near enough the general production level not to stand out one way or the other—except for Albert Dekker, who apparently had a dream that he was Sam Jaffe and is still trying to wake up from it, but violently.

The Alexander Korda film, *Four Feathers,* is a piece of thorough absurdity as far as the story is concerned, but worth mention (if not attendance) for some very fine production values. It is about a young English officer whose upper lip wasn't stiff enough when his regiment was called out to Egypt, to send the Fuzzy-Wuzzies away from where they came from. So his three friends and his fiancée each handed him a white feather. Gad sir, a cad sir. So he discovered to himself that his pacifist talk had been mere cowardice. So he went to Egypt and fought the war practically single-handed, gave back the white feathers, and everybody liked him again. And as far as principal motives go, it is done just about like that.

But the boats on the Nile, the camps breaking up and camels getting under way, the riding and fighting in the desert, are fine stuff—the best of their kind, I believe. There are some amazing large actions, but the atmosphere is best served by the way the camera delights in all kinds of details—in fact, some of the studies of native life are so thorough as to suggest that maybe the working crew was only too glad to stay away from the story as long as possible. Sound is used very shrewdly too—especially the incidental sound that builds up reality in a scene; and for once the "natives" don't seem to be all grease paint and the better class of spoken English. There are sudden shots that point up an effect—the vultures, for example, or that wonderful explosion of birds near the water; and there is a good use of the "narrative" camera in the scene of rescue in the desert. All being done in color, this was more difficult than is usually the case; and more the pity that anything so handsome should be thrown away on such naïve hokum.

Each Dawn I Die gains somewhat the same effect of serving up the seamy side in milk and mush, but I found it a little easier to sit through—partly because of the prominence in it of James Cagney, George Raft, Stanley Ridges, Maxie Rosenbloom, George Bancroft, and half the Warner lot. The people and the violence of their action were given as much scope as the story would allow; but the story is of the kind that you would have to see to disbelieve. Cagney is a by-line newspaperman who burns to clean up the world (hoo-hoo), and is framed by one of Warners' most evil District Attorneys. In jail he teams up with George Raft, which of course means with a very criminal sort of criminal (bang bang). Cagney helps Raft get away, and in consequence submits to a third-degree that breaks him up completely; but in consequence of something the script writers thought up, Raft then sits playing cards in a hideaway and saying "eh-h-h shet ap!" and forgetting his pledge and pal. The writers do some involved thinking all through here, in fact, and the story doesn't start up again until Raft decides that the way to spring his innocent friend is to get back inside himself (yo ho ho) in time to join in the prisoners' uprising (and a bucket of blood), in which he dies nobly.

The action, the treadmill background, the incidental relations of the men, are brought over with the kind of vividness we expect of pictures. But the writing is as fantastic and out of joint as the muddy poetics of its title (one of a feverish cycle, so stand by for *Look Homeward, Angelface* any day). Like *Four Feathers,* it is good in the particular. But either of them could be run with their reels in reverse order: you'd be little wiser, and probably less sad.

The really big laugh of this present season is a deadly earnest piece of comedy called *Winter Carnival.* It probably would never have seen the darkness of a New York movie at all if it hadn't been made by Walter Wanger, who has promoted an A.B. degree into one of the fanciest shell games even this industry has seen. With the businessman-gambler sense of any producer, he flushes enough money to get a picture ready for distribution; then he calls in a few ex-legmen and says for release, "Boys, I can't help it if I'm a courageous rebel: I went to *college!*" Well it may sound funny but it certainly gets him around, striking awe into the hearts of Hollywood and (subsequently) *The New Masses* and (finally, but hold tight) the college itself, which asked him to inaugurate a course in motion pictures.

Winter Carnival, in fact, is Wanger's tribute to Hoof and dear old Dartmouth. It was changed over from a Corey Ford satire to a straight-face story of young love and disappointment during the carnival high-jinks. Maybe it will be required seeing where the ivy twines (though it is released square in the middle of the vacation, possibly through oversight), but I don't know when I've seen so many unaccomplished actors in so many embarrassing complications. Scattered here and there are shots of skiing and skating and campus buildings—all taken on the spot and then put there. The story is a disgrace to freshman composition and the direction keeps its development on a level with the action in Charley Chase shorts. I suppose there is enough atmosphere to give a twinge to some fond alumni and enough fake-quaint buildings to keep a few unprivileged gazing in wonder at the strange sight of education. The rest of us can either stay away or go and snicker at the joke that was played on so many people the day Walter Wanger got off the train at Hanover.

9 August 1939

Pick of the Pictures

The pick of the pictures just now is *Stanley and Livingstone,* which avoids some of the traps set for the usual splash of epic and uplift—possibly because producer Darryl F. Zanuck looked some other way while his assistant Kenneth Macgowan did the work; but more probably because the main acting assignment is left to Spencer Tracy. The acting is a genuine help all through, with fine support from Walter Brennan, Sir Cedric Hardwicke, Charles Coburn, Henry Travers, the natives, even Nancy Kelly. Henry Hull, I regret to say, assumed that the publisher of *The New York Herald* should be Robert Mantell as Coriolanus, but he was not given much footage to chew. And the African background stuff is solid and sometimes thrilling (managed by Otto Brower in spite of Mrs. Martin Johnson, who was encouraged to flounce around on the safari unit for the value of her name). But isolated merits will add up to little—as the recent cycle of epics can remind us—unless the story makes a sense of its own. I think this one does.

Stanley goes out to get his story as newsmen sometimes do even when working for papers, a hard-case cynic but still (and here is the value of the actor) a decent fellow and sweet spirit underneath. Skip various complications: he finds Livingstone when he is almost a case for a search party himself, and finds to his amazement that the man is there because he *wants* to be, that it is his dedicated work. Gradually admiration mounts over disbelief, and he becomes almost a disciple—at least on the explorer side of Livingstone's missionary activities. Back in England, he tells off the piddling geographers, and returns to work in Africa.

It is the story of a good and not too important man, who found something to work for; as such it is well done. Spencer Tracy is there, to make anything believable; but he is given support in some very crackling lines, in direct and logical continuity. And Henry King's direction knew how to take advantage of certain writer's touches (screenplay by Philip Dunne and Julien Josephson), to make little human things meaningful and even lovely, as the bit where Tracy hesitantly leaves the tin mirror as a parting gift to the black man he had kicked around for stealing it when he first arrived; or the morning choir rehearsal, where the black converts are swinging the hell out of a hymn and Livingstone is roaring and jabbing at them and—he, Sir Cedric Hardwicke—almost skipping. It is one of the few safari pictures that has realized the fact that the truth of common life can be as dramatic as the magnificent sequences of the attacking tribe rolling down over the hill. But whatever the talent of the production, Tracy should be a picture maker's holiday, for character and its development, action and its consequences, can be built upon him as on a concrete gun emplacement.

Not to overpraise the film, it is certainly slow in some portions, rather painful in the final "trial" scene; it could have done its business in less space, and is not blessed in the footage given to the decent sentiments of Richard Greene. But while it does not pretend to chart the course for a New Africa, it is a good statement for human understanding and responsibility, and a good picture; and I got more all-of-a-piece enjoyment from it than from anything else I've seen in quite a while, quite a while.

I hesitate to put down anything in criticism of the new French picture, *Harvest,* because just now it is under the droopy cloud of the New York State Board of Censors. In the interest of public morality the Board has refused to license this picture for showing in the State of New York, the home of *The Journal American,* Bernarr Macfadden and the Minsky brothers. Members of such censor boards have to pass a rigid examination in whether they are able to read or write and possibly both, I believe, though I know this only from hearsay; but on such subtle distinctions as whether a film is good, fair, or foul, they usually prefer to throw in their hand and wait for Moses to come down off the mountain with the home edition of *The Morning Tablet.* Therefore they are sure to pounce on any weak voice protesting that the cutting was probably done by the original man with the hoe, and say, You see? Ain't even artistic!

But *Harvest* is good enough and harmless enough so that it looks as though the censors have bitten off more this time than the people are going to stomach. The funny thing is that, being nowhere so good or prize-laden as *La Kermesse Héroïque,* which got the okay for the whole range of its broadly hinted bawdry, it didn't scare these Albany wetty-beds so much; by its lack of front they were emboldened to come down with a terrific thud on something which is actually reverential, almost to the point of immaculate conception. Its handicap with the censor board is that in the story the marriage is a common-law affair and that when the wife gets pregnant she says so.

Its handicap as a film lies in a pretty complete innocence of the motion of pictures. The actual screen credits do not list Maurice Pagnol as director, though the program notes do. But whoever may be responsible for this unimaginative and chunky surrender in the face of modern film requirements, the scenario itself is originally responsible for the diminished effect (M. Pagnol also gets credit for the scenario). Characters appear from nowhere and you are supposed to guess why they act as they do—and then for the most part they don't act at all. Yet Fernandel, who is only a minor stage device, is given thousands of valuable feet for overpantomimic comedy. Emphasis and means of transition are so out of whack (and surely emphasis is almost the art of storytelling itself) that at times the characters might as well all be Chinamen.

In spite of its faults, *Harvest* is a film that somehow establishes a mood rarely found in pictures. With almost no story content at all, it manages the story of a girl fairly on the loose and no better than she should be, her chance meeting with the last, half-wild peasant in a deserted Provençal village, and their mutual regeneration. It is a fable really; but while fables are rarely true, there is something about their hope and fantasy that always falls beautifully on the ear. She is no heroine and he is an unreclaimed hulk, but their half-articulate aspirations make a prettier case for industry and domestic concord than has been seen in a long time. It should have been rounded out with more detail and more touches like the single lovely incident of the bread—but possibly part of its effect is gained by just this slow, awkward simplicity. Sometimes there is a touch more surely communicative in the fumbling pat on your shoulder than in any of the intricate holds of Masonry or jiu-jitsu.

23 August 1939

It's Not the Humidity . . .

Directors and writers change, sometimes even the story changes; but a picture with Ginger Rogers in it is simply a Ginger Rogers picture. This time the title is *Fifth Avenue Girl*, and the main support is Walter Connolly, which is all to the good; Gregory La Cava (producer-director) has done pictures like *Stage Door*, but also is occasionally found with one foot on top of the other. And everyone is at the mercy of a weak script, the unrolling of which I shall not attempt to trace here. It's enough to say that Miss Rogers is put in a false position (but clean) by a rich man who employs her to bring a straying and wacky family back to their senses; and it's a little rough on the feelings of everybody.

There are the pleasant comedy stretches we expect of a GR film—the seals at feeding time, the night-club sequence, etc. There are the wicked verbal jabs that Miss Rogers can trade with anybody in the world; there is the funny butler. It fails to be a *Bachelor Mother* because it will get raucous and mean to people to get a laugh—which like as not sounds hollow when it comes. In the brief bit of the labor-union conference it gives a fair idea of what contract negotiations must look like to an employer; but in the deliberate characterizing of the class-conscious chauffeur, it gives the weirdest version of radicalism ever seen outside of *Soak the Rich*. Useless to get worked up over it, unless that is your profession, for it is so stupid and wide of the mark as to suggest the pitcher who got beaned with his own outcurve: those who laugh at this slapstick agitation are those irreclaimables who still grin and dribble at the cartoon with the bomb and the whiskers. This is not important in the picture, but it is important as an example of how desperately the picture tries to get together with itself. In this crooked mile Ginger Rogers plays a straight part, and everyone is familiar with her peculiar and happy grace by now. I couldn't say it was a bad picture. I won't say it is a good picture. I'm not talking, see?

Manhattan-to-Hollywood Transfer.—I think probably the movies have made something more solid out of *The Women,* a play of bright though depressing bitchery. But the picture runs two hours and a quarter, which is inexcusable in itself, and it features Norma Shearer in some of the most incessant weeping and renunciation since Ann Harding—which may not be inexcusable but is no fun for me. It is a holiday from Hays all right: there is more wicked wit than Hollywood has been allowed since *The Front Page,* and half the girls practically live in Reno (where the other half send them). There is a general tolerance of overplaying and a drippy, glucose quality to some of the scenes which suggest better direction could have made it tighter and dryer; but when things are going they really go—which is in general all through the venomous parts. The script keeps a logic of its own in spite of sprawling; the dialogue crackles; the cast is very expensive and pretty good. Whether you go or not depends on whether you can stand Miss Shearer with tears flooding steadily in two directions at once, and such an endless damn back-fence of cats.

The Old Maid is a pretty dated stage play done over carefully and expensively for the movies. It is better than average and sticks heroically to its problem, forsaking all delights and filling a whole laundry bag with wet and twisted handkerchiefs. The idea is to have Miriam Hopkins and Bette Davis fight over an old love affair until an illegitimate daughter has grown up and been safely married, at what sacrifice we don't have to guess. It is well produced, and could possibly have achieved its purpose of tearing our hearts out if the writing had been less overemphasized and undernourished. As it stands, its two real contributions to gaiety don't have to be seen to be appreciated. One is the way the Hays office doesn't object to a girl's being put in the way if a very big producer explains that it was only a little-little baby (though by context it wasn't even love but a sort of absent-minded quick one). The other is the blowing up into a deep and tragic theme of an old song that agreed with the girl's name all right (Clementine), but that will never be heard without its peculiar lyric color—"In a cabin in the canyon, excavating for a mine"—"Light she was and as a fairy, and her shoes were number nine," etc.

Odd-End Department.—*In Name Only* gives handsome and serious attention to the problem of the scheming wife and how to get shut of her, with nice Carole Lombard-Cary Grant comedy bits along the way, which nevertheless seems a long way. Possibly Hollywood is allowed such mentions of divorce and illegitimacy because Hollywood as a good child shows its heart in the right place by going to the extent of making Joseph Calleia a kindly priest—that is to say, to any extent—in a picture like *Full Confession,* the whole point of which seems to be a proof that there is nothing more religious than religion, especially Legion-of-Decency religion. Victor McLaglen makes a good study of the sub-mental; honors divide up about evenly between medium shots of albs and altars and close-ups of a face that looks like something the floodwaters have receded from. And if it isn't a good picture, why that is not what they were trying to make anyway.

Change-in-the-Weather Department. – I hadn't really enjoyed a picture, in spite of assorted merits, until I came to *Jamaica Inn*—which has assorted defects. It represents Alfred Hitchcock and Charles Laughton laboring under story difficulties and Charles Laughton—who is too large for a Hitchcock type. It is not at all in the brilliant plausibility of Hitchcock unlikelihood: Laughton as the impoverished squire, living magnificently by running a gang of ship-wreckers and murderers, with the Inn, the pirates, the sailing ships, and treasure all out of Stevenson. But in spite of some creaky motivation, it is true enough in general outline and in the part of Laughton absolutely genuine, meaningful beyond Stevenson (and probably the book itself). It has suspense and a good run of motion. It has a fine tone—the Inn and the doings there, the coaches and night roads, the English types Hitchcock knows so well how to keep both vivid and credible. (The squire's house is too magnificent for anything short of an Earl.) What it is above everything else is true to its form, without pretensions but without fawning. Better movies can be made, and have been; more ambitious movies are being made all over the place without half the honest picture skill, consequently without half the audience satisfaction and freedom from pose.

6 September 1939

There are Wizards and Wizards

The Wizard of Oz was intended to hit the same audience as *Snow White,* and won't fail for lack of trying. It has dwarfs, music, Technicolor, freak characters, and Judy Garland. It can't be expected to have a sense of humor as well—and as for the light touch of fantasy, it weighs like a pound of fruitcake soaking wet. Children will not object to it, especially as it is a thing of many interesting gadgets; but it will be delightful for children mostly to their mothers, and any kid tall enough to reach up to a ticket window will be found at the Tarzan film down the street. The story of course has some lovely and wild ideas—men of straw and tin, a cowardly lion, a wizard who isn't a very good wizard—but the picture doesn't know what to do with them, except to be painfully literal and elaborate about everything—Cecil B. DeMille and the Seven Thousand Dwarfs by Actual Count.

The things I liked the best were the design for a witches' castle, the air-raid of the Things with Wings, the control-room in which Frank Morgan is discovered controlling the light and sound effects that make the Wizard. Morgan in fact is the only unaffected trouper in the bunch; the rest either try too hard or are Judy Garland. It isn't that this little slip of a miss spoils the fantasy so much as that her thumping, overgrown gambols are characteristic of its treatment here: when she is merry the house shakes, and everybody gets wet when she is lorn.

I'd much rather talk about *The Adventures of Sherlock Holmes,* which is credited as being "based on" the Gillette play, but which is actually a new creation on its own, written by Edwin Blum and William Drake, produced by Darryl Zanuck. Its plot deals with a master criminal who is getting bored with the business but who elects to postpone his retirement until he sews up Sherlock for good—he's going to steal his head and send it to him COD.

Mr. Holmes is Basil Rathbone, and after two pictures (the first was the *Baskervilles* remake) you can't believe he was really anybody else. Watson is Nigel Bruce, who is not only much more delightful than Watson but much more Watson. His blank confusion, his little triumphs, his earnest wrestle with the mysterious and occasional petulance—none of these is overplayed or minimized to woodenness, and all are played with the added grace of a personal interpretation. Rathbone is capable in both energy or repose without mixing them up, and has that poise in understatement required by the character, *plus* the same actor's reserve of qualities that must be implied and felt beneath any actual statement as such. The two work together as though they had never had such a time in their lives. But in the complications of any mystery, much rests with writers and directors to make their intricacies clear to the audience at the same time that the audience is being kept in darkness and suspense. And in this case it is finely done.

It is one of the unfortunate things of criticism that when the highly complex craftsmanship by which a story is kept well in motion succeeds, there is nothing more complex to say about it than just that. However, there are some very nice effects brought off here—some by means of right timing, some by the use of the setting, some by the use of plot music. But the most effective use of the medium as no other medium could be used comes in the sequence where we see death stalking, slowly, and then faster, in a pair of shapeless trousers shown from the knee down to the horrible false shoe, built up three inches under the sole to resemble a clubfoot, carried awkwardly through the mud and bushes, one, limp, two, limp, etc. It is a device, or gimmick; but it is used with a contextual appreciation of the whole effect which appears only when movies are being made as they should be. As a film, *Holmes* has its own lightness and speed across the screen, and focuses a close and lifting attention. It is not the sort of thing to be considered as a Work of Art: my point is simply that it is an exciting story told with more real movie art per foot than seven reels of anything the intellectual men have been finding good this whole year or more.

20 September 1939

Own-Words-for-Breakfast Department

When I said recently of Darryl Zanuck's *Stanley and Livingstone* that it was so good a picture possibly because Mr. Zanuck had his back turned while his assistant Kenneth Macgowan did the work, both Mr. Macgowan and Philip Dunne of the Zanuck studio came down on me, though with kind words. They said in effect that whatever Zanuck's faults, he didn't have his back turned on a production even when he was asleep; and that my hypothetical crack was therefore ill advised. They were quite right—though I did have the excuse of having walked out on at least twenty Darryl Zanuck specials. There ought to be run as a banner over every film review: the characters (especially writers, cameramen, cutters, directors) appearing in this review are wholly fictitious and not to be confused with any living persons—the best piece of "direction" in the picture might have been suggested by a grip.

I like the idea of the Hollywood boys getting interested enough to pull the critics up short. They do too little of it. I suppose a few years of reading "stunning photography" where it was the location that was stunning, "expert direction" where the writing was foolproof, over and over, makes them feel, What's the use? As Philip Dunne says, "it is almost impossible to tell where one man's contribution stops and another's begins. A reviewer for a trade paper once wrote that 'Donald Ogden Stewart's additional dialogue was sparkling.' You gather that he was able to distinguish between the additional and the ordinary dialogue." And in this particular instance, Kenneth Macgowan points out that Zanuck "happens to have spent more time on the African continent than any except North America, and to have developed an enthusiasm for its life and history which might be compared to the enthusiasm once shown by Stanley and Livingstone." Which shows how far wrong you can be without half trying. My regrets to Mr. Zanuck.

It is another nice thing to know, in regard to the Wiere Brothers I have been blowing a horn for since Kurt Robitschek brought them from London last year, that they were on several vaudeville wheels in this country years ago and in at least three pictures. John Hans Winge of Birmingham, Albama, writes about my discovery: "I saw the three boys the first time in 1930 in Berlin in a stage-show. They had a striking success and were later booked by Mr. Robitschek, who at that time was the owner of the largest Berlin vaudeville theatre." The only one of their American films he can remember was *Wonder Bar*. "They returned to England, but not to their home city of Berlin." Wherever they are, they're all right.

4 October 1939

Mr. Capra Goes Someplace

Frank Capra's *Mr. Smith Goes to Washington* is going to be the big movie explosion of the year, and reviewers are going to think twice and think sourly before they'll want to put it down for the clumsy and irritating thing it is. It is a mixture of tough, factual patter about congressional cloakrooms and pressure groups, and a naïve but shameless hooraw for the American relic—Parson Weems at a flag-raising. It seems just the time for it, just the time of excitement when a barker in good voice could mount the tub, point toward the flag, say ubbuh-ubbah-ubbah and a pluribus union? and the windows would shake. But where all this time is Director Capra?

I'm afraid Mr. Capra began to leave this world at some point during the production of *Mr. Deeds Goes to Town,* his best picture. Among those who admired him from the start I know only Alistair Cooke who called the turn when *Deeds* came out. Writing in England, Cooke confessed to "an uneasy feeling he's on his way out. He's started to make movies about themes instead of people." When *Lost Horizon* appeared, I thought our Mr. Capra was only out to lunch, but Cooke had it. *You Can't Take It with You* in the following year (1938) made it pretty evident that Capra had forgotten about people for good. He had found out about thought and was going up into the clouds to think some. From now on, his continued box-office triumph and the air up there being what they are, he is a sure thing to stay, banking checks, reading *Variety,* and occasionally getting overcast and raining on us. Well, he was a great guy.

Mr. Smith Goes to Washington is the story of how a leader of Boy Rangers was sent to the Senate by the state political machine because he was popular, honest, and dumb. Washington is a shrine to him. So as he gawps around lost for a whole day, throw in thousands of feet of what can only be called a montagasm, buildings, monuments, statues, immortal catchphrases in stone. But before we go any farther, what's the payoff? It is that this priceless boy scout grew up as the son of a small-town editor so staunchly against the interests that they shot him for it under the boy's nose; after which he read American history so widely and fiercely that he knew the Constitution and the cherry tree by heart.

The story goes farther, of course, more than two hours' worth. The boy thinks he falls in love, and then falls in love without thinking so. From these personal relations he learns that he has been a chump. He starts a filibuster (the honest-man-in-court scene Capra has found so successful he won't be without it) in which he says some fine things for liberty and the better world. And it is so harrowing on all concerned that just after he passes out his colleague shoots himself, and the American way is straight again.

Politically, the story is eyewash. The machinery of the Senate and the machinery of how it may be used to advantage is shown better than it ever has been. But the main surviving idea is that one scout leader who knows the Gettysburg Address by heart but wouldn't possibly be hired to mow your lawn can throw passionate faith into the balance and by God we've got a fine free country to live in again.

There are some fine lines and there is a whole magazine of nice types; but the occasional humor is dispersed and the people are embarrassed by just the slugging, unimaginative sort of direction that Capra became famous for avoiding. When the hero is supposed to be made innocent, they write him down an utter fool; when there is supposed to be evil, wickedness triumphs as slick as pushing a button. James Stewart was made fairly ridiculous; Jean Arthur couldn't be; Edward Arnold, Thomas Mitchell, and Eugene Pallette also withstood all such assaults. Claude Rains for once was just right for the part, and Harry Carey was there, fine as ever. But it was everybody for himself, which is a hell of a state of things in movies. The only good sequence was the lovely bit where Miss Arthur and friend got very tight by degrees, and by degrees more reckless and tearful, until they weave up to tell little boy blue that somebody swiped his horn. This seems a case of winning by a lapse; it is like the old Capra, and pretty lonesome.

Ernst Lubitsch has had his ups and downs, since long Before Capra; but there is a thing amateur critics like to call the Lubitsch touch, and whatever that is, he hasn't lost it. His new comedy, *Ninotchka,* started out with what any other comedy director would have ducked away from, a piece of light spoofing that starred Greta Garbo. Lubitsch never had the Capra magic of realizing every last detail as big and right as life; he goes more by steady competence and brilliant flashes. And so *Ninotchka* strikes a wrong note occasionally—nothing serious, but a thing for example like the movie-German accent of a Soviet envoy, or like the weight of too much stationary conversation. But the story gets there, its people are real enough, it has an overall radiance of pleasant but knowing wit.

There is a Soviet commission in Paris to sell some confiscated jewels of a Grand Duchess who also happens to be in Paris. The comrades are human but a bit too simple to be sent on a foreign mission. They are being fed cigarette girls and fast talk enough to imperil the state of the masses when an envoy arrives to supersede and check up on them, a very serious girl comrade with flat heels and no nonsense. That is Miss Garbo, of course, and the combination of Paris in spring and Melvin Douglas in good form goes to work on her with effects which make the balance of the story. Mr. Douglas becomes serious, Miss Garbo is faithful to her mission while blossoming like any girl in love under sordid capitalism, and Miss Ina Claire steps in to raise hell with everybody and give Garbo back to Moscow.

The humor is mostly in the meeting-of-East-and-West variety, no more harmful than Zostchenko, certainly as droll and possibly more up to date. It is the first movie with any airiness at all to discover that Communists are people and may be treated as such in a story. And Greta Garbo is the life of it. Barring the end—and no other was possible short of gloom—her confusion is human, her cause takes a salutary ribbing but is not disgraced. I found her more lovely in the straight-cut clothes of her first scenes than in the later "creations," for while I am strictly antinudist, I should say that a real and commanding beauty is clearest without clutter—all you need on the outside is a stretch of burlap and a bath. But this is comedy and good as such, Miss Garbo moving from the stern to the tipsy with no more effort and no less dignity than she ever showed. Compare hers with the strenuous if veteran performance of Ina Claire, and you will see by contrast something of a natural style in acting which may take hard work to perfect, but never looks like it.

Outside of Lubitsch with the no doubt coordinating touch, this is no one person's triumph—as no one picture should be. It is barbed wire on some aspects of modern life, sometimes with a dry point that is exquisite—the May Day marchers and the solid solemn ranks of Stalin posters. But it is mainly a gay affair, neither heavy with Thought nor absurd with venom; it is partly true and possibly beautiful, but it is certainly good.

1 November 1939

French and Indians

As a film that neither attempts more than it can do nor is satisfied with the trivial, *Port of Shadows* is a pleasure. It was made in France by Marcel Carné; and apart from the thrills and satisfactions of its story, it is one of those things an occasional French film maker does so perfectly: an atmosphere created, a mood unbroken. The scene is Le Havre under a fog, and the lower depths of town at that; but dim lighting and mean walls are not enough in themselves to establish an atmosphere, which is rather a compound of story, its meaning, its people, the scene and tempo of the action, what is said or unsaid, all in the right emphasis.

There are very few things here: a street, a shop, a few angles of the docks, the two rooms of a waterfront deadfall, a bar. But these simplicities, as well as the sustained blacks, grays and fifteen-watt yellows of the setting, are kept from monotony by the shift of interest and the good balance of contrasts. There is even a carnival scene, its brief whirl and tinsel as sad as small carnivals always are, and therefore wholly apt to the meaning. There is aptness in costumes and sets, and the camera work which realizes them. In addition, the picture has the best use (though not recording) of dramatic sound—as opposed to the sound of pistol shots and composer's background—that can be found anywhere outside of Hitchcock. The sad and aimless guitar player behind his empty bar; the pretty chimes on the shop door; and (best) the choir music always flooding from a radio set in the house of murder. From the guitar and the intercutting of the woman's scream and the steamboat whistle, it is clear that M. Carné has studied Hitchcock more than casually. This is nothing against him, for while Hitchcock is the man who can teach them all on the subject of music as an active theatrical force, most of those who have studied how he did what, have neglected to study why.

Port of Shadows is a love story, one of the best. The plot is lively but soon told. An army deserter trying to skip the country; a young girl wiser if not better than she should be, trying to run away from a repulsive but pitifully amorous guardian; the presence of a nicely assorted trio of petty mobsters. The girl meets the soldier, both creatures of knocks and bruises, mutually suspicious at first, and then presently, why not? In less than forty-eight hours the different forces have got mixed up, and write your own conclusion. The conclusion of the picture is that there is a little kindness in the world—not enough to go around and never where you expect to find it—too often unrecognized, but genuine, and when felt as such, beautiful to see: the silly stumblebum, the host of the ginmill, the suicidal painter. The beauty of this picture is partly in this quiet statement of nonspectacular truth, but even more in the steadfast allegiance of each character to his own strength and weakness (no Wallace Beery evil whiskers and heart of gold; no Victor McLaglen transformation). When goodness gets to this surface, it has been a pitched battle, and worth it. Because virtue did not triumph by some flick of the wrist in the scenario department, the majority will find the picture depressing—though with the world as it is, you'd think any story proving there is virtue in it at all would be a token of joy and welcome. Times change, as it is only right they should, but I will take this treatment of love as the sudden hope of heaven, between a roughened man and a scared young woman, before any Romeos or Juliets, even as played in double exposure by Orson Welles.

But the perception and craftsman's skill of story and direction would not be the same without the final eloquence of this group of players, each filling his part and none ambitious to swell beyond it: the occasionals, the character people and the principals. There were Delmont, Aimos, Genin; there was Pierre Brasseur in a difficult mixture of fear and tough bravado; and there was Michel Simon, who managed many effects without giving away to the audience what all concerned suspected him of. As the girl, Michele Morgan was both lovely and secure in the meaning of the part, a little too old for the given age, but one of the few who could establish the fact that a death for love might not be so fantastic after all. The picture's mainspring is of course Jean Gabin, who is a true stalwart—indeed, it would be difficult to imagine the effect of this picture if he had not been there through all its minutes with his projection of strength in immobility, his command of the illusion that crossing a room even to get to the men's room has its meaning and that if he kicks a dog it will be because he loves the mutt. There is something we know no more about than magnets, some inner command, some emanation of qualities that would be destroyed if talked about. There is a feeling of dignity that is more than his own—the dignity of all men—who are after all men and have dignity in some degree whether their surface foibles make fools of them or not. Gabin and all the qualities of the film around him have that perfect eloquence of the thing as perceived, marked down, and brought across to all who have an interest in and hope for the processes of life, as lived.

Drums along the Mohawk is a candy-colored period bit, nice in general but nothing to break your neck getting to. Life in upstate New York during the Revolution. Since John Ford directed it, it is well above the average historical picture, but not up to Mr. Ford's best. There are too many type situations and too many types—ugh-ugh-Indian, hell's-fire army widow, little feller with big jug, etc. And except for the skirmishes, the action is pretty slow.

But when the skirmishes happen there is plenty of fun. It is good to have a lot of Indians milling around in a picture shooting arrows and everything, and now that sound has been added to catch the unearthly rumpus they make, the effect is complete—the audience practically saves that fort with the arms of its seats. Henry Fonda and Claudette Colbert and some good supporting people make very nice going of it; and there is a scattering of handsome picture bits both in action and in the humor of community life. These you can spot as director's work if only because Edna May Oliver is in some of them, and restrained, and restraint is not brought to Miss Oliver until you sit on her head. There are touching things too, and instruction and blood. Perhaps if you can manage to break it only a little bit, you may wish to break your neck getting to see the film after all.

22 November 1939

Fast One

The Roaring Twenties is a great deal more than the melodrama it has been carelessly advertised as, and therefore written down. The story is about some fast bootlegging and gunplay in the high life of prohibition New York, which was quite a time anyway, rich in the kind of motion and things exploding that keep a film alive; and it may be a happy accident, because I do not remember Raoul Walsh for anything very sensational. But there may not be so much accident either, because it is James Cagney's picture and it is the sort of subject James Cagney is likely to find something to say about. At any rate, it has a story to tell and a way to tell it without mumbling or stalling. And that's what we're here for.

The young man comes back from that other war of collective security and what a laugh: he has saved the world but it's somebody else's oyster. No job. On your way, bum, etc. He manages to cut himself in on a little fly bootlegging—a package here, a package there; he organizes a nice little group of boys, and they back trucks up to a government warehouse, take a boat of their own out and load it to the waterline, and presently he's doing all right, with a spot of his own and a place in community life. People who get in his way, he walks on their face with his feet. If you don't see what you want, take it anyway—why kill valuable time asking? He becomes the sort of direct and speedy little gentleman they built the world for.

By this time everybody, knowing Hollywood, is getting braced for the moral. Crime is riding for a fall, correct? Well, Hollywood may have had the story all set for the moral, and arranged for our young friend to go broke and get shot, all very depressing. Crime doesn't pay—except a million dollars at the box office, etc. But the hero went down partly through mooning around after some hardly interesting young heifer (the procreative urge doesn't pay); and partly through the market crash (constitutional finance doesn't pay); partly through loyalty and general square-shooting (virtue is its own reward and serves it right). The point is that Mr. Cagney is the one we pull for, the original golden boy; when he's up we're glad to see it and when he's down finally it's just rotten luck. There isn't any payoff except that this is the way the world is made, and all sorts of people in it.

Somebody—the director, the writer, or both—did some very fine things to keep this story human: just the hint of a feeling rather than the blowing of it in your face like soapsuds, the clasped hands on a table, the single word and turn and cut, the pace of a scene determined by its mood. The songs from those years ("What'll I Do," etc.) were nicely cued in as part of a handsomely worked-out period background. And these would not have been such believable people without the solid presence and actually vivid projection of Humphrey Bogart, Gladys George, Frank McHugh, and Paul Kelly. But apparently it is easy to work at your best in a picture with Cagney, who knows what's what and is even gentle, but more or less takes over. In pictures this goes even farther than the stage phenomenon of a cast raised beyond itself by some great central performance; it loosens things up and gives an actual truth to the cold lines under the white lights.

This story of one aspect of the twenties, the giddy extravagance and iron fist and bad taste in the mouth not far away, is essentially true. But it is more than that in its performance. The movies have not produced any Hamlet parts for us, but they have raised a crop of people whose movie legend and cumulative work are almost of that stature. James Cagney is one of them, and it is hard to say what our impression of the total American character would have been without him. He is all crust and speed and snap on the surface, a gutter-fighter with the grace of dancing, a boy who knows all the answers and won't even wait for them, a very fast one. But underneath, the fable: the quick generosity and hidden sweetness, the antifraud straight-as-a-string dealing, the native humor and the reckless drive—everything everybody would like to be, if he had the time sometime. But always this, always: if as a low type he is wrong, you are going to see why. In spite of writers, directors, and decency legions you are going to see the world and what it does to its people through his subtle understanding of it. And in *The Roaring Twenties* this genuine article has had the chance of his life; he has deliberately done much that a star would refuse to attempt, because hell, he isn't a star, he's an actor; and in this actor's range of life and death he is not only an actor but an intelligence. You do not even have to like that quicksilver personality to see its effect in art here. And if you do appreciate his personality-legend, his face on this screen will haunt your dreams.

6 December 1939

1940

From *GWTW* to *The Bank Dick*

Out to Lunch

I wish to report editorial pressure on me to review the film version of *Gone with the Wind,* from which I have been shrinking ever since the first year of hot gossip over who was to play Clark Gable. The editors don't really care whether it is a good thing for me to see or what line I take on it. What they want is an office guinea pig; they want someone to go sit through that four hours of four million dollars, to see what the shooting's fer—as naturally no one as smart as an editor would subject himself to such a business without visual proof that it won't kill you. So, pressure; memos; unfortunate shifts of conversation at lunch. Wait, I say; let's keep our buttons sewed on. This masterpiece in the common art does not get to the common people for another year. The producers even boast of this fact. So easy does it.

But this does not go down. Read the papers sometime, they say. A sensation. Even to the common people god bless them the film is news. Must be covered. News and other angles get quite a plug; but the real point is still who is going to be the canary in the mine? And when, today? Tomorrow? Be specific; this is serious.

In a minute, I say. Please do not shove: the situation is under control. This mixture of vague compliance and being a known difficult type has held the fort for you readers so far. But under pressure, readers.

Actually there is one reason why *GWTW* is something for a national gander. The reason is $4,000,000. And that is simply all. Of course the book was wildfire in the seller lists, and of course this may be a good and even dramatic version of it. But there have been best-sellers before and dramatic versions before, and actors acting before, costumes, shootings, wigs. And who runs a temperature? Did *The Mystery of Edwin Drood* sell a few copies as a book, and did people act and wave their arms in a movie made from it in these thirties? All right, who produced it for a mere bucket of clams, and when, and at what loss, and who cared? You tell me. As to the living art of movies, I don't review pictures I don't see, but any loose dime you've got will get you a dollar that the

280

only contribution to movie art possible in anything staggering under such demands of hoop and hoorah and the super-spectacular is a new record for running-time in the theater. Good folding dollar bills, if you're the sporting type.

I said the thing is $4,000,000. Now when you have that kind of money sunk in nothing but a flicker and a promise, you've got to light a fire under it, get out in the territory, and talk fast. I should say that the general news, radio, and gossip coverage in this case, and the staging of the premeer in Atlanta, would make P. T. Barnum look like an advance man for Norman Thomas lecture bookings. They handled the blanket so well that their smoke signals now really look like hell burning. And there is something in people you can bank on: they are always happy suckers for a fire engine. But what you use for money is one thing and what you use it for is another; and from where I'm sitting it looks as though a good part of that $4,000,000 was spent toward the end of simply getting it back. Well, it isn't my $4,000,000.

Those with an active interest in the motion picture as an art form, the cause and effect of the good ones and bad ones and especially the different ones, can relax. It used to be you could whip up interest and reviewers with well-timed releases about a budget sheet running to a cool million. Then it was two million; then two-odd, three. Outside of laying more money and press agents along the same line of ordinary drama, there has never been anything very startling to do in pictures—outside of making good pictures. The process of making good pictures, I'm proud to say, is still going on. But not this way.

As I said, the situation is under control. Perfectly. In the line of duty we will have our personally conducted tour through the Clark of Seven Gables. But in a minute.

8 January 1940

When Successful, Try Again

The movie *His Girl Friday* is a remake of *The Front Page* which does no harm and affords some good noisy laughter. It is hard to tell about a new version of an old favorite, especially one of the first actually ripping movies in sound (1931), but I should say that in rewriting it to fit Cary Grant and Rosalind Russell they lost more than one male reporter. Grant can't make the play-acting within a play stick for one minute and in comedy Miss Russell is rapidly developing a tendency to throw her weight around. There are the additions of Ralph Bellamy and Gene Lockhart; but some of the big laugh scenes and much of the conviction of the original have been junked in favor of something they thought up. It's faster and funnier than many newspaper pictures intervening; the main trouble is that when they made *The Front Page* the first time, it stayed made.

The Hunchback of Notre Dame, all expense and care and dramatic possibilities considered, is my candidate for the worst-made class-A film of the year. Charles Laughton is effective as usual; the spectacles are spectacular and the sets are good; the main belfry and mob-scene stuff is so near foolproof that it could be crippled only by a superscrupulous application to ham theatricals. But they went at it scrupulously: a junior Errol Flynn combines the Villon legend, John Reed, and Frank Merriwell; a "gypsy" girl suffers endlessly in what she apparently takes to be the diction of Katharine Cornell; a nice mix-up with *A Tale of Two Cities* flushed a rogues' gallery of types that they made up and photographed in exact character for *A Night in the Bastille* with the Marx Brothers. They practically spelled the final "e" in Sir Cedric Hardwicke with trick lighting effects and conquered Thomas Mitchell long before Alamodo had bounced a rock as big as a coffin off his shoulder like a basketball, making him feel almost too sick to speak his last lines fifteen minutes later. The excitement was exciting when they got to it at last—but the audience was already too limp and damp to rise to anything, except go home. Their main achievement was in using a million dollars' worth of the most complex equipment in the world to prove that those who laugh at the jerky punch-and-judy of *The Vamp* do not laugh last.

22 January 1940

Show for the People

The word that comes in most handily for *The Grapes of Wrath* is magnificent. Movies will probably go on improving and broadening themselves; but in any event, *The Grapes of Wrath* is the most mature picture story that has ever been made, in feeling, in purpose, and in the use of the medium. You can drag out classics (it is often safer not to go back and see them) and you can roll off names in different tongues and times. But this is a best that has no very near comparison to date.

I still don't know how they did it, though its possibility has been latent in Hollywood for years. The story of the Joad family, with its implied story of a migration of thousands of families, is told straight, and told with the sternest care for cause and effect and the condition of society. Not only does Nunnally Johnson's adaptation (he is also assistant producer) refuse any compromise with prettiness or the usual romantic—it actually has the good taste to leave out some incidental fireworks Mr. Steinbeck didn't.

Everything is there as it should be: people dispossessed and shoved around and miserably in want, the fruitgrowers and their armed thugs and snide dodges, men clubbed and the strike broken but the spirit of it living, carrying on in the people. There is no country in the world where such a film of truth could be made today—even made badly, let alone with such a smash that people pack into theaters to see it, and take it away home with them after. This is a thing not only to enjoy but to be proud about.

To get minor flaws out of the way, there was possibly too much of the partial lighting of faces that was in general so effective (it was overdone, for example, on John Carradine as Casy); the starving kids were too plump and glossy; a few of the intercut devices of transition, with road signs, overlaps, etc., were a little trick. But that's all.

The film opens on a shot that strikes the whole mood of the piece like a chord: a half-light, deep, empty space, a road stretching out of sight and a tall young man walking down it, with no other sound but his toneless approaching whistle. Then the truck, another road, the land preacher, the deserted home, and the dust blowing in the wind. Then by candlelight and with faces barely seen, the story of what happened, partly told and partly in flashbacks: the broken countryside. Then outside again, with the dust settling, and suddenly on the edge of the horizon, the lights of a car: the law. Then morning; another road and mean house, and the Joad family at breakfast. It all moves with the simplicity and perfection of a wheel across silk.

When the truck rattles out onto the highway, leaving the open door and the dust blowing forlornly in the wind, there starts a series of great sweeping outdoor shots as beautifully tuned to purpose as anything you've seen (possible exception of Tissé): clouds and space and the endless thrown ribbon of highway, with the truck going off and getting smaller, or coming down into the camera with growing roar and clank, or wheeling around the bend in that illusion of flight of a camera slowly panning to pick up and follow motion. Camps at night, a scene framed in low branches or the darkness around a lamp, fields rolling out in the sun, great pinnacles of rock, and back to the truck itself, and the long road.

Gregg Toland was cameraman, but surely John Ford gets a share of the credit, for he has deliberately forced his subject out into the open, and carries more of his story in long shots than most directors would dare, giving the whole picture a feeling of space and large movement. He works all the way from distances to those tight compositions of two faces, half in the dark: in the tent or the back of the truck or the cab in front (one very striking effect here, in the three set faces seen faintly in the windshield, nothing directly visible but the hand on the wheel). With nothing but the drone of the motor in low, the camera manages the whole story of the Okie camp as it moves down shack after shack, face after face, silent, hostile, and defeated.

Alfred Newman scored the music, but there again it's a good part John Ford music—which is to say almost none of the swelling theme stuff, a snatch of song here and there at night, a wheezy little parlor organ sometimes for the mother-and-son theme, and for the rest the sounds of life—particularly fine here because this life is a cough and sputter and boom of motors up and down the roads. And Ford is not afraid to let silence be eloquent as it should be, or to use it as a background for the poignant train whistle, a mile off at night, for the going-away sequence.

In the production values of costumes, sets, locations, and make-up, the whole thing simply exceeds the imagination. If there is anything more poor, scuffed-out, and plain no-good than these homes, trucks, clothes, and every patched-up detail of equipment; or anything more real in squalor than the Okie camp, the pickers' shacks, etc., I wouldn't know it. Along with it, I suppose, should be put the human properties, the bit players, extras in a crowd, both the overbearing and the downtrodden—all cast and directed as carefully as stars. It suddenly strikes you that there isn't an actor in the show who tries to be dashing or anything but plain folks.

It is Henry Fonda's picture as far as acting goes: he has come a long way in the movies, and here (somewhat as in *Abe Lincoln*) he finds a lank, slow simplicity that comes up from something within him genuinely felt; it is altogether touching and never posed. Jane Darwell is next: her Ma shows an occasional trace of acting but comes out clearly on the whole, a thing of strength and homely beauty. Russell Simpson hasn't much to do as Pa, but I think you will not forget his craggy tragic face, or that of Frank Darien; the young people are what young people should be, and Rose of Sharon is kept in better control than she was in the book (that bucket-of-blood scene of hers at the end is mercifully, and naturally, out, too). Parts also for Charles Grapewin, John Qualen, John Carradine, and others, and they do not fail them.

This is everybody's picture, as a matter of fact—everybody working with one of the world's ace movie directors, which is as it should be. But credit for a lot of courage and a lot of care should go to Darryl Zanuck, who produced it in the teeth of convention and inevitable trouble. If it had turned out to be a floperoo, I tremble for Mr. Z, because those barracuda-teeth he okayed for release are going to nip the tenderest parts of some of our tenderest parties. But the public is *going* to this picture; the nonpolitical awarding groups will put it top of the list for 1940; and the film books of 1950 will put it down as a milestone in the art of the motion picture.

For the rest, what is there to say after 1,000 words?

The picture nears its end when Henry Fonda tells Ma, even though she can't understand it, that he is going away but she can always know where he is—wherever men are hungry, wherever their kids are in rags, wherever people don't have the right to live and be people—and he goes off toward the train whistle, walking up the hill, a dark figure from a distance, seen against the light of the sky. And it ends as they move on down the road again in the cab of the truck, toward twenty days' picking, and Ma snorts at the idea of her being scared. *Her?* She's been scared before, she says, but she's had it knocked out of her. We'll go on, she says. We may get kicked but they can't get rid of us, rich men or not; sometime they won't scare so many of us any more, because we go on, because they can't kill us; we're the people.

And so the people will go to see and hear, and I hope they'll listen to it. Because this is their show, for and by; it is more their show than any show on the face of the earth.

12 February 1940

Steinbeck's Other Vineyard

Of Mice and Men as a book seems to have been written with the stage in mind—scene one, scene two, etc. Therefore it presents a tough problem to any movie maker like Lewis Milestone who would want to do a job faithfully and well, and still fill his screen with the shift of scene and motion possible to his art—and therefore demanded by it. His film version as it stands is something you never expected to see, perhaps. Minus profanity, it is the straight story itself, as poignant and in many visual qualities more actual and vivid. I do not think Burgess Meredith (as George) is quite the type the doctor ordered. Though he does a handsome and intelligent job here, his style is a little too resolutely intense and his idea of rough-and-ready is walking around with your elbows crooked out. Lennie is a very difficult part to make true, and I have never been quite sure that George shouldn't have shot him before the story began; but the combination of the merciless close-up and Lon Chaney, Jr., in the part often reminded me of that wonderful parody in the Elsa Maxwell show where a great hulk stood in the center of a stage littered with corpses and said, "Gosh, George is going to be awful sore!" (Curtain.)

But Mr. Milestone got around it somehow, and you can put *Of Mice and Men* down on the list of the ten best of 1940. Where Steinbeck sketched in the set for A. I; sc. 1, the scenario (adaptation by Eugene Solow) shows the escape and the boxcars and the bus. Later it gets out of the bunkhouse into the life of a very convincing ranch (incidentally, a nice realization of interior and exterior throughout). And the character of the girl, though done I fear to throw the Hays office a fish, was rounded out into a more truly motivating case. In general there was more air in the picture, somehow, and perhaps it was just this, perhaps it was just a matter of getting used to it, that made its problem real without leaving that hint of a gamy aftertaste—Lennie's habit of stroking soft things into a pulp, etc. But one undisputed thing is the life in pictures given it by Mr. Milestone's subtle use of camera accent to shift the scene within the scene, to anticipate, heighten, and release both inward and outward struggle throughout.

It was done with no loss of intensity, in the best faith and with dignity, as a story of friendship and a common poetry of dream, of human landfalls and departures and the dream inevitably in ashes. It was done that way even though the dogged following of the original meant talky sequences that are a bane to pictures and should be to the stage. But the punch was there, and a fine sense of life in the handling and the surrounding characters. Charles Bickford is the man's man of the picture; Bob Steele (from the horse operies) made a swell Curly. Roman Bohnen was good and Leigh Whipper as Crooks was thoroughly fine—the lines about niggers he was not allowed to speak were there in his eloquence and dignity.

To some extent, they and their troubles were real because in such a sensitive comprehension of truth, the air simply would not be right for hamming. The film had a release date preceding that of *The Grapes of Wrath*, but it is too bad they should be thrown into inevitable but needless comparison. *Of Mice and Men* is among the good films of any time, but Lewis Milestone's triumph in it is necessarily that of a watchmaker, whereas John Ford was given the scope of a sundial and all the heavens above it.

Since Margaret Sullavan does something peculiarly basic to me—and I doubt if even the institution of marriage has ever scouted the male idea of some young-girl quality, rare and sweet—I would do well to get down to simple cases on the new picture she's in, *The Shop around the Corner.* And since I think James Stewart is a young American with as broad and unaffected a base in a country's experience and joy as Huck Finn, I can let lame praise of him go by the board too, and get down to business. And since Frank Morgan has been languishing for a part that would bring out not only the surface brilliance of his stop-motion humor, but the depth of feeling and perception beneath it; and since Felix Bressart is a well-seasoned trouper and favorite, and in his absurdities somehow manages to remind you visually of the (somehow) sublime absurdities of Groucho Marx . . . they had better be left out too.

The actual story, involving the family life of a Bucharest leather-goods shop and the romantic parallel of I-love-you-I-hate-you developing from a lonely-hearts correspondence, is sometimes laid on a little bit thick; but it is directed by one of the aces I personally keep up my sleeve always, to keep the wrists warm—Ernst Lubitsch—and so in all fairness he'd better be left out of the discussion too, because his realization of character and treatment of episode are so perennially neat as to become a personal thing with all who take movie genius or the lack of it personally. In fact and in spite of moments when its feeling and fancy are suspect, I am hemmed in on all sides from saying anything about this picture, which is a little honey.

19 February 1940

Attitudes toward Legend

King Vidor's production of *Northwest Passage* (actually only the first part of Kenneth Roberts' book) has a great deal of spaciousness, and some speciousness too. The film is careless in spots and directed with only half a heart in others. When the people were hiding out from some French gunboats in the wilderness, the story called for a powder explosion among them that could have been heard in Quebec; when they took heavy whaleboats overland (and rocks) they didn't bother to use rollers—not so dramatic no doubt, but what's a boat with the bottom torn out? At one point a man puts his rifle down, jumps into a boat without it, and then shows up in the next shot on the other bank with two rifles; at another point they fight across a river only by making a human chain under the most perilous circumstances, but leave behind a squad of Indians who are part of the company again in the next sequence, possibly through some misunderstanding of the origins and use of the Indian rope trick. And the Technicolor gives such fuzzy outlines that you don't know whether it's night, morning, or Spencer Tracy. (Some very fine scenic effects on the long shots, though.)

The directional carelessness shows most in the handling of actors and timing of their speeches—even of their emotions, as in the home thoughts of the wounded Harvard man and the confused peroration. You get the effect of the studied, the too highly pitched, the hollow and uneasy in make-up. The camera's idea of catching a natural muttered aside is to bang it in the face with a close-up; and the shift from despair to triumph at the deserted fort is so pat and hurried as to spoil the climax before it happens.

But *Northwest Passage* is a film worth talking about, for its material is just about the most epic and fascinating in American legend. There were the pioneers surmounting the insurmountable as is their custom; there were the Indian tribes, great hunters and fighters, easy and terrible in their vast uncharted forest; there were those almost as strange among our people, the Indian-hunters, learning from the Indians and speaking their language, hounding them and being hounded. There were the rivers and mountains and the ringing names of outpost stockades, and the great unknown to the north and west of them. Surely we raise few children today—especially in New England and the West—who do not know the words warpath, tomahawk, lodge, pipe of peace, scalp, venison, canoe, as well as they know their own names and with more thrill. Add to that the rum and powderhorn and various alliances and hatreds of Mohawk, French, Redcoats, renegades. Kenneth Roberts has a great knack for building all of this stuff into the immediate verity of fiction, and the movies, with their greater range of effects, could well take his gift and build further.

In this picture the best success is achieved in scenes of mass motion: the trip upriver, the portage of the boats, the desolate silence of the swamps, the surprise attack and massacre—some of it action stuff on the grandest scale. And some of the individual touches are brought out powerfully: the blood-crazed young man is a realization of horror that you will remember in the middle of more than one night; the sudden fights, the desertions—these build to a total effect and so do the costuming and make-up of the people in the increasing haggard wildness of their condition.

But the fact remains that the principal and deciding factor of character itself is ill seated and slips around from motive to melodrama as the situation demands. Spencer Tracy, Robert Young, Walter Brennan, etc., are all right but they have been better and more secure elsewhere; and against such an epic setting they should have been splendid.

Abe Lincoln in Illinois deals with another legend, and one that has had a great play the last year or two—not only the rise in national politics of an endearing figure, but the whole schoolboy's example of homespun greatness, log-cabin virtue, heave-ho on your own bootstraps, and so on. The legend is universally appealing; the picture will appeal to those who like it. I found little to look at in it, though some very fine stuff to listen to—which isn't strange when you remember that many of the big scenes are either history or fable, and that even where quips are apocryphal they have been good enough at the outset to stand up under the wear and tear of some four score and seven years.

Mainly the production lacks the sense of reality that made John Ford's *Young Mr. Lincoln* so vivid and seeming-true. The sets are good, but the camera concentrates on big heads at the expense of surroundings, so that the outdoor shots in particular get that bright and out-of-focus blur of process work. And the surrounding characters, my God. Everybody wants to be an actor except the actors, which principally consist of Raymond Massey in the early scenes and Gene Lockhart throughout (he makes a good and resonant Douglas, especially when they let him go on the big debate sequence). Ruth Gordon studied her part as Mary Todd some, and I don't imagine intended to be funny; but Mary Howard and the young-handsome contingent, the my-land spinster parts and the haw-hawing yokels, arrive at something—not hamming, which implies some kind of conscious seasoning—suggesting a cross between an animated cartoon and a tray of French pastry.

I liked Raymond Massey better than I did in the stage version, and finally believe him to be a sincere and intelligent actor; but the last scenes gave out an empty and studied vocalizing that made the striking resemblance of make-up his soundest creation, and somehow reminded me of the Hollywood extra who had slept in a beard, knee-length coat, and hat for fifteen years but invariably blew up in the third line of the Gettysburg Address.

It may not have been the fault of actors altogether. John Cromwell directed from a well-devised if talky script, but he didn't seem to feel it, or to believe it ever really occurred. Part of the bad words spoken of Hollywood are directly attributable to just such a lack of conviction. The research and costume departments—and the writers too, often—do their painful best to get everything right as something that happened, or at least might have happened. And then a director comes along and says, This is a prestige picture, even artistic, and we got to have everything just right—and then makes it with greater care and expense as though he were staging *The Yeomen of the Guard*. If you want attitudes, a five-gallon hat, famous incidents, and One Nation Indivisible, they're all here. As a picture and as a whole, it just doesn't stick.

4 March 1940

It's a Disney

Walt Disney's *Pinocchio* is a delight and at times will take your breath away, for the limits of the animated cartoon have been blown so wide open that some of the original wonder of pictures—wonder and terror too, as when that train roared up into the camera—is restored. I don't mean it's an epic, even a new outpost. It has the faults of most things designed to instill sweetness into the young by spraying them with it. Take the puppet hero; take the rather ham Jean Hersholt clockmaker. Keep them. Their troubles are not real and their moral lesson is mainly that you should be a *good* boy, and there's a kind fairy in every box of Crackerjack.

The fun is in the adventure and the villains; and these are everywhere and lusty. And the animals. There isn't a snail or puppy-dog's tail that a Disney animator cannot give character and expression to—but always in terms of the animal world as studied with what strikes you over and over again as a tireless application, and love. Every precise ripple of a cat being stroked or bushing its tail out; every detail in the motor habits of fish or sea anemones, or birds, or the common housefly. The goldfish here is a neat take-off on Betty Boop; the fox is really the big bad wolf as John Barrymore, but on the road. And so on.

And so on with backgrounds and the life that goes on in them, recreated with both fancy and scrupulous care: the antique town and clockshop, the sinister gaiety and roller coasters of Pleasure Island, the puppet show, the inside of the whale, the tavern, complete with English host, sinful and ruddy. You would waste a life around pool tables or Kretchmas before you would get the exact feel of cue and the nine-ball clean in the corner pocket (chock) they get here, or the terrific whirl and squat (Hi!) of the Russian puppets. And so on again.

If little has been said of the story, it may be because all these excitements make up for very little story at all: it's a string of adventures in very adventuresome places, and surely the last part with the charging bull whale is as fast action as your digestion will allow. Through here you will find the animated cartoon opening out into a wide and plunging motion it never had the range for till now. And this, plus a watchmaker's care for each hairspring, the bevel of each cog—plus a high sense of color and the unsurpassed design and synchronization of sound—brings the cartoon to a level of perfection that the word cartoon will not cover. We get around the problem of no old word for a new thing by saying, it's a Disney.

It is a technical perfection that has cost, and made back (four times over), more millions than many industries have. But it was not inevitable; underneath this vast and intricate workshop there was always a single attitude toward life and attitude toward work. The Disney studio can name its figure and has the world on a string; but it got into such a position by its straight allegiance to principles—its main sinking fund is by now inexhaustible, and consists of a routine not only of established craftsmanship, but of true invention and a definite approach to the heights of fantasy.

The incongruous always—the little cricket with the big voice, for example. The sudden reduction of the outlandish to the familiar—as when, in the underwater sequence, the cricket notices Pinocchio's anchor rock coated with barnacles, snails, starfish, and what not, and gives it a smart rap with his umbrella: "All right, break it up." *Pinocchio* has a whole marvelous gallery of clocks and music-boxes that do things; it has a heavy who blows a terrific slow smoke ring, catches it absent-mindedly, and dunks it in the coffee. And it has not only details but whole settings—what more natural and never thought of than that the old man in the whale should be sitting on some wreckage fishing, and no luck.

It is a long way from *Steamboat Willie,* it is a longer way from Fleischer and his Ink Bottle, and longer still from that veteran of animated strips: "Ladies, please take off your hats!" But after all it is not for that that we go to see it, I hope. We go as we go to the pictures, to any picture, saying: This is just a part of the diet; you've still got to show me. We stay to laugh, and feel good and finally admire; and we go away to marvel.

The Human Beast, a French film with the usual English titles and atrociously dim photography, is an exciting film to see. Its story is psychologically confused and directed in confusion—that is, you are often not at all sure whether a character is coming or going or a Chinaman, or where you are, or why. It is taken out of a Zola family cycle and its only connection with such a title is that the main character, a locomotive engineer and fine fellow, gets in love with two girls, and strangles them. It's his blood.

Simone Simon is the girl who shrinks from one murder but urges another, takes on an old lover but eventually shies away from her love. The part goes several ways at once, but not Simone Simon, who is a charming young lady and no doubt that is enough.

In the direction of actors and separate scenes Jean Renoir has done another swell job, and for a brilliant piece of filmic emphasis I'll take the long moment where the husband, the maddened cuckold, discovers his wife dead on the floor. No stage gasp or actor's take: Ledoux (who incidentally has been fine throughout) simply stands, his face frozen and the horror growing in his eyes; then the camera cuts behind him as he lurches against the door frame, crying, with the watch, the guilty symbol, dangling from his hand and catching the innocent light gently. And although the story starts and ends nowhere in particular, you aren't cheated, because it has Jean Gabin and the trains.

Gabin is one of the really massive personalities of films: he makes his silences count and his mere presence felt, he has the kind of mind and hand you would count on in tight places, he has both solidity and dash. A natural, perhaps; but you always get that feeling of intelligence, of conscious analysis and selection and the deliberately bold stroke.

And the trains. Put a camera in the cab of a locomotive, watching the immense controls or the flowing landscape or track ahead coming up like thunder, with bridges, tunnels, the inexorable straightaway or the suspense of curves and perilous opening spiderwork of switches; or put a camera in the dispatcher's window as they move out gathering momentum through the intricate yards; or catch them at the terminal, the great engine still and satisfied, huffing and standing and singing like a kettle with steam; get cameras near a railroad and you've got motion and romance before your story starts at all.

11 March 1940

Who's the Doctor?

There is a tendency to confuse intention with full accomplishment which is probably older than the quaint proposition that you shouldn't kick a lady. At any rate, it is as old as I am and was brought into high perfection in our family, where repulsive little brothers were using it like a bolo as soon as they could toddle (*e.g.*, all one of them had to do was be sick with measles and hear me balking at some duty, and yip wanly from the couch, *I'd* do it for you if I *could*, Muvver; and Mother wouldn't know which to do first, kiss him or whop me, and still manage both).

The film *Pasteur* was the do-it-if-I-could play on epic lines; and so nimble and infectious is legend that it will be invoked with awe every time someone with a beard spies a test tube—until some young and leading mind of 1950 decides to investigate what the shooting's for, and sits through its absurd and hollow theatricals for the first time. Of course its theme was noble, and so is that of the worst epic poetry that was ever rejected; and of course it is about the martyrs of medicine. But its vested enemies were safely previous, it wasn't remotely in the line of film advance, and it could not put a finger on John Ford's *Arrowsmith,* which had been made and forgotten years before.

Dr. Ehrlich's Magic Bullet is what brings this up. It is a competent strip of medical biography and thus way above *Pasteur.* It pays much more attention to its essential and fascinating business of cultures and serums and desperate decisions. There is some beautiful work with colored slides and there is a nice avoidance of the tedious in explaining the nearly infinite combinations of dyes and their affinities that a laboratory man is up against. In these things it is a picture to hold the eye.

And in its actors as well. Although Edward G. Robinson has been typed unmercifully, I have always found him an arresting personality and so cannot take part in the surprise currently shown over his being an Actor Too. The part calls for a quiet and steady intensity, and Robinson has it. And there you are. Outside of Ruth Gordon, whose resolute sweetness kept reminding me of the word persimmon, the supporting cast is easy and good—some old standbys and some new, as witness the Basserman performance.

It was all to the good all along the way; but somehow my main impression was that when they got there the cupboard was bare. As a picture it really didn't seem to move. I am very definitely for the truth about medicine, and for pictures that spread that or any other truth; but one need not be a moral playboy to come out frankly and say that a microscope is a microscope and a picture is a picture, and that for a mixture of both with Edward G. Robinson, preference still goes to that quick and entertaining bucket of blood, *The Amazing Dr. Clitterhouse.*

The Fight for Life is about the problems and work of a big-city maternity center. A government agency sponsored it and Pare Lorentz made it—in a mood which must at least have been one of abstraction. For the picture, in spite of a dignified treatment of the most breathtaking experience of the race next to death, left me feeling as though I'd left my coat somewhere.

As to story, it opens on a death in childbirth. Childbearing is quite a problem, and in the next sequence the internes are lectured about it. They are told about an appalling death rate from septicemia, hemorrhage, and what not. In the person of one resolute young man they go forth to bring their art of healing to the people in the fourth-floor rear. The young man is an observer, an assistant, finally a full-fledged doctor. But actually nothing has been achieved at all; we have been told that there is a high rate of mortality in childbirth and that even with doctors on the job some live and some don't.

In the little sideplay of doctors graduating into their profession; in the purely tacked-on allusion to the hopelessness of slum conditions; in the lectures on the need of dispatch, decision, perfect sterilization; in the fight for life at the climax—in all these devices Pare Lorentz has borrowed just that many different techniques for only as long as they served his purpose, following no one through. Thus it is neither an inspiration to doctors *(Arrowsmith)* nor a caution or advice-chart to mothers *(Birth of a Baby)*; neither a story of triumph over disease *(Yellow Jack)* and/or reaction *(Pasteur)* nor a story of a man's salvation *(The Citadel)*. Its climax is thrilling but no true climax, for there is no dramatic reason why this woman should live or die, no true victory or defeat.

This kind of film above all others demands sincerity—and you know without asking that the sincerest purpose here was to get out sixty well-paced minutes of celluloid around a subject that had come up for filming. In that they did a fine job. The slums are as real as living there; the actors are restrained; the people are straight personal-appearance. The handling of the commentary is exceptional and Gruenberg's musical score is a rare blend of quiet effectiveness and original good sense. And the picture knows how to build silence into suspense.

We should not forget at any point that *The Fight for Life* is a groundbreaker in getting things that can't be spoken said well enough so that people will hear. But even with the best charity for those who have to fight for life in films every time they make another, we can realize the distinction: This is a good film; it is not such a good Pare Lorentz film.

25 March 1940

Slight Cases of Marriage

You will not want to miss *The Baker's Wife,* a film comedy made with a great deal of zest by Marcel Pagnol and his company. (If you are in New York, where it is showing at the World Theatre, you had better wait it out a while: with the second hit in its history, the World management has no trouble filling its absurd shoe-box and has promptly swollen up into a mixture of Radio City and police-station courtesy, and while I stepped up with the money in my fist and was grudgingly permitted to pay $1.10 a seat for the 6:15 show which started promptly at 6:35, scolded at the wicket and heckled throughout by staff gossip and slamming doors up in back, only the good Lord knows what happened to the patient cattle who were lining up for the next show on the windy sidewalk outside.)

Underneath the fun it makes with stock French types—the nance priest, the Marquis, the deef old codger, the old maid, the town rowdies—the film has a rather touching story and is curiously able to live up to it. The new baker's wife, whom nobody will believe for a minute, has run off with a fancy shepherd. And the baker, a magnificently inept and uxorious pot of man, is absolutely breaking his big fool heart. His trouble is a matter of heavy humor in some quarters and scandal in others. But the town unites on one proposition soon enough—with his ovens, his fine loaves and brioches, he is the key man of the community, and he is not baking.

On his alternate buffooning and poor weak tears the attention of everybody is focused. For the baker is Raimu, who works before cameras out of some uncanny divination. The word that will come most neatly, if you look for a word for this exposition of the humanities and the lovely in the commonplace, is droll. It is a word of many shadings and that is exactly true of the picture—in fact its one fault is that it is mature beyond its audience, which I suppose cannot be expected to realize how close laughter may be to tears, and consequently to check its nervous and idiot guffaw when the surface horseplay gives suddenly over to true heartbreak. There can be minor objections, of course: the young wife is something out of "Mademoiselle from Armentières" and her seduction is awfully sudden; the regeneration at the end is not too credible; and everybody has a heart of gold. But you can go to see it in confidence; it was made not only with the double understanding of pictures and people but with a robust and contagious tenderness; and if you don't have to find a word for it, you're lucky, because a good picture is like the famous day in June—for all but anthologists and English instructors, it is much better to see than to hear about.

The film made of *The Primrose Path* is all about a sweet thing of a girl whose grandmother is a nightmare, whose father is a dipso, and whose mother takes in gentlemen to support the family. Now the girl, who is Ginger Rogers, runs into a local hotrock in the person of Joel McCrea, who throws a fast line behind the counter of a beanery daytimes and around the tables of the town Bar and Reel at night. She has been a tomboy but this is love, so she cooks up a story about being thrown out of the house and they marry and there are happy days at the beanery.

They could have stopped here and got on with making another picture, and I would have thanked them, for the background and wild life of the home are different and good, the local types are as they should be, the dialogue is fast though occasionally painful, and anybody who would not walk up the side of a brick building to see Ginger Rogers may leave the room. But no, Allan Scott and Gregory La Cava (co-author and producer-director) were going to make a picture of this if they sprained a camera. The boy visits the girl's home, is insulted, leaves, insults the girl when she comes after him, and she leaves. Quite a hideous time all around. Just about the time the story had completely double-crossed everybody in it, the sun came out with an apple in its mouth and everybody had a happy ending, I'll leave you to guess how.

Well, don't cheer, boys, etc. Everybody did the best with what he had to do, but the screenplay at the outset ducked every issue it raised and others too, turning tragedy into a hit-the-coon game and vice versa. As the film seems slated to lay an egg at the general box office, the many enemies of truth in pictures will point to the mere false semblance of its social realism and say nyah, and what this country needs is a good five-cent Errol Flynn.

In the case of *Rebecca,* the effect isn't so bad. Alfred Hitchcock, of course, has always been a man of much more talent than taste, always a little awestruck in the presence of such terms as "psychological study" and "artistic novel," etcetera. I remember once spending an hour in an attempt to steer him, by elaborate, prepared questions, into the admission that his method itself, his practice in melodrama, was sounder drama than many upper-case dramatists; that such a method once extended to an essentially serious or purposeful subject would sweep the field. Mr. Hitchcock rubbed his stomach, beamed, and rumbled, but he wasn't having any. He talked nonsense about art but he was leery of it, somewhat as the grade-school man is forever reverent before the world university.

Rebecca is not really a bad picture, but it is a change in stride and not a healthy one. A wispy and overwrought femininity in it somehow. A boudoir. The first half of the picture just proves that a bright girl who is at home with such words as "lahst" and "conservtreh" could continue to be the lady of a house in which she tripped on every stair and bumped into every butler and slipped on every stretch of floor and dropped her gloves or coffee cup or otherwise made a frightful mess every time a superior domestic appeared. Joan Fontaine, quite lovely as a bride, lived a miniature hell every minute there, and so did I.

After that, things began to go (too late). All this absurd nightmare of helplessness turned out to be mere preparation for an unsuspected angle of murder and mystery and blackmail, and what things fermented beneath the surface of this proud estate in Cornwall. Then Hitchcock's infallible sense of timing and camera effect of suspense opened the window and let some fresh air in. And the cast was right there with him: Judith Anderson, George Sanders, those fine old reliables, Nigel Bruce, C. Aubrey Smith, Reginald Denny, Leo G. Carroll—always just right. Laurence Olivier may be too perfect, and surely he must know how, when he clasps that fine anguished forehead with those fine despairing hands, ladies weep and moan; but he has grace and self-command and the most offhand of elegance, and I like him at it. They could have made the last half first, and then saved the first half for a bit of Guy Fawkes bonfire. Unfortunately they didn't; so the whole thing runs off in fireproof projection booths for two hours and a quarter and the audience burns instead.

8 April 1940

Where Was Moses . . .

You will be hearing quite a lot for quite a while about Herbert Kline's *Lights Out in Europe,* a film about an hour long, of life in England and Poland up to and including the outbreak of the war. War is a very terrible thing for those actually engaged in it. In the excitement of headlines, newscasts, this sunk and that in flames and all, I believe this is not generally realized. The Admiralty will not at a time of stress and national strain, when all good men etcetera—the Admiralty will not trouble itself or you with accounts of the men in the water, the mothers, fathers, sons, and daughters in the burning building. No. This picture about war at the outbreak conveys most strongly the human reluctance to believe in disaster. In fact, the main thing wrong with its content is that it cannot quite believe in the disaster itself. The Polish sequence is both the news scoop of the picture and its climax in horror. But it is inset, so to speak; it is an afterthought.

The main body is the change in British civilian life brought about by the war. Air-raid precautions; evacuation; drills; proper registration; recruiting—all with a happy and willful cheerio or sentimental tear, and all with a mugging face turned to the camera (this is recognized as the documentary man's bane, but is rarely passed so directly over to the audience). In short, *Lights Out in Europe* is supposed to be a study of national psychology at the deadline, and through the movie enthusiasm and limitations of its makers it turns out to be a newsreel pastiche without reference or control: the point of view (England buckling down) is arbitrary, and the true fear and ignorance under the cheerio are not brought up. People whose business is making pictures have to keep their cameras going, naturally. But you can call this a psychological study only if you grant at the outset that the study was conducted largely by inmates.

I haven't told you much about the picture. Well, it *did* scoop a lot of watchful cameras and got into Poland before that tragedy, almost ancient by now, was generally dreamed of. And it does show you England as England prepares to fight for her national life. What a country. It has some very fine music-hall footage, reminiscent of the ineffable Mr. Cohan and the Over There play; and it pictures what you have been reading or guessing about in the reporting of a mother's goodbye to her big son in the infantry or little daughter leaving for her billet on one of the Stately Homes. It shows you the rubber boots getting their first outfit; it shows you Mosley, an absurd and dangerous clown; it shows you in full-face the commentators you have been hearing more often than your own landlady.

For some reason, possibly because we have read about it all before, possibly because we merely grow callous as the horrors mount, this film doesn't have much lift to it. So the English have gas masks and air-raid drill and Chamberlain and their men join the army and their ships steam out into the North Sea. So, just that. The camera, like the mind, balks at the final implication; and the selection and cutting have done nothing to provide springboards for the imagination. I know the film is news and I know it speaks the truth; but I don't know how you're going to get around the fact that it is also slightly dull.

The Biscuit Eater will probably come to you as the second half of a double bill. So my suggestion is that you skip the first feature. It is an out-of-the-way story about bird-dogs, taken mostly on location in Georgia where they raise them, and where a biscuit-eater is a no-good pup who would rather eat than point and goes around when he does point indicating skunks, grasshoppers, and old tin cans. Some have found the story hackneyed but I didn't notice, for the director, Stuart Heisler, has managed to keep it going with a lot of fresh stuff about dogs and people.

Two boys, Billy Lee and Cordell Hickman, get the runt of a thoroughbred litter for their own. They can train him, but keep him out of the way. One is the son of the kennel master on a big estate, which may now be put into horses, leaving the family unemployed. The other is the son of the Negro trainer—and in spite of a few Aunt Jemima fear angles, the relation between them is handled unpretentiously and well. The dog doesn't do right; they have to hide him. But they keep on training him and finally he's big and handsome, and the best in the field trials. Never mind the upshot, a mixture of heartbreak, vindication, and hope. They could have possibly given a more complete account of the training period but there are enough fine miraculous animals competing at the end to make a true dog-lovers' dream. The countryside is fine; the characters are all unassuming and natural enough; and quite outside of the plot there is enough to make a documentary on a profession that is almost an art. After all, you don't see such intelligent faces on the screen every day, and the first feature might have Nelson Eddy, and the dogs don't sing.

News Flash.—Now that *Gone with the Wind* is in the neighborhoods, I can tell you about it as promised. It moves, just as I suspected it would, and it is in color, just as I heard it was, and the Civil War gets very civil indeed and there is a wonderful bonfire and there are also young love and balls and plantations and practically everything. Actually it is two pictures or more: the death of the South and the birth of Vivien Leigh, or more; and Clark Gable managed to be just the size ordered and to shift his gumdrop from side to side with unusual aplomb; and Olivia de Havilland either is a baby or has one or something; and Thomas Mitchell is swell and dies eventually.

As a matter of fact, *Gone with the Wind* stands around on its own foot purely out of size and story complexity. The history it dabbles with is true enough to the mood of a time, a place, a certain position in life; but history gives out by the end of the first picture, and to keep things going in the sequel they shift from period to personal—with some effect but no total success. Scarlett is too many things in too rapid succession; the exact point of her aspirations is confused; there is so much sobbing and color and DeMille display, such a mudbath of theme music, that a clean realization of character or events is out of the question. Their ingenuity in pulling this vast sprawl together was enormous and their public acclaim is deserved. They put enough talent into it to make one good picture—but there they were, up to the neck in four years, four million dollars, four hours' running time. They threw in many good things, and everything else but a towel, and they got them in line and added them all up to one of the world's imposing cancellations.

22 April 1940

Weep No More, My Ladies

The heart of man being fond and somewhat foolish, our better filmers are always rushing to some new kind of snake-oil. The double-feature menace has long been a favorite with them, and now even Dr. Gallup himself is going to get on his horse and find out what the country thinks about it. But movie exhibitors, who do not have to believe earnestly in anything except the iron truth of the day's take, have found repeatedly that as far as pure voting goes their neighborhood may be against double features—but just let them try a single-picture program and there is the same neighborhood, cramming over into their nearest competitor.

The only double feature I've sat through in years is *Gone with the Wind*, but do you know a thing? I find so few of the best people who can take one feature, and walk out and leave the other alone, that I feel like a woodpecker in an oil field. The man who huffs and puffs and casts indignant ballots is very likely the same man who interrupts you to say he'd have liked to see *that* one but couldn't stand its running mate on the bill. No showman is going to add to his rental and halve his turnover if he can help it, so leave it at this: If the people don't want the double feature, there will be no double feature presented to the people, poll or no poll.

But just now there is a new boon: the Neeley bill and its attack on the evil of block-booking. Block-booking. For culture groups and better-film groups and Ladies' This and That, condemning it is like being against sin. One out of ten throwing the weight of the word about may have some idea what it means by now. And possibly one out of every ten with this sketchy knowledge may know the causes and results of the process. But when you come down to what workable new system could be put into practice for the greater glory of pictures, you don't find anyone there at all.

Block-booking is the process by which those whose investments are in making movies ensure the future distribution of them, in such numbers and at such rates as will underwrite the present investment. Those familiar with the history of the industry will know the endless fight between production and distribution; but unfortunately we are not talking of those familiar with the history. Naturally, any powerful combine of exhibitors could quickly become the tail that wagged the dog. Since the movie gold-rush idea of buying or building every theater in the world dropped the bottom out on them, the producers have been devising some other means of keeping distribution under control.

Now there has always been another play of forces within the industry, and that is the holy war waged by the Outs, against the Ins. Very lively acts in that play too, only you should remember that yesterday's Outs are today's Ins, against whom tomorrow's Outs are already pawing the earth and snorting. Today's Outs, in this block-booking business, are the boys with a nice lucrative theater pitch, or with a string of them, who figure they could do all kinds of business if they could make their own program for the year out of the best releases of each producer. Nice work. But enter here the hollow laughter. The companies make the pictures, some 600 a year, and they make them to sell.

So the companies sell in blocks and in advance (blind buying), and if an exhibitor wants a duzer of a money-getter he has to take it in a block of, say, twenty average films. Unlike the publishing business, the movies actually pay off modestly on this run of the mill. But no exhibitor without strong prodding wants the pictures that pay moderately or merely break even. He'd like to run a *Gone with the Wind* every week. He can't make one. He can't say how or when one should be made and would squeal like a pig if the finger were put on him for one-thousandth of the production cost in advance. So the companies simply whip him back into line. If he wants to run the one dream picture in twenty, he is going to run the semi-turkeys as well. He has a certain margin of option in the block: he can refuse a certain number of the pictures that will be the worst poison to his particular audience. He doesn't have to take the block at all, as nobody forces him to show pictures. But he has to get pictures or go out of business. And that is where most of the yelling comes from.

For years now, exhibitors have found that clubs and groups of concerned ladies will listen to his complaints if he says, "I know it's an awful picture, but what can I do? Block-Booking!" Or: "Madam, I would really be proud to run that film but how can I get it? Block-Booking!" Whereas the cold truth is probably that the first made a cozy sum for him and that the second, being a prestige picture, was canceled out by him after seeing from *Variety* that it was laying an egg in the key cities. And never forget that in the timidest art in the world, all it would take to keep a *Grapes of Wrath* or a *Confessions of a Nazi Spy* out of your neighborhood for keeps would be any handful of wild Catholics or half-baked Main Street merchants—if, that is, the exhibitor were free to shiver and cancel a film every time somebody wrote him a letter.

The Neeley bill of course goes into more complicated matters, but the main fact is that its main and vociferous supporters are the independents who want a cut of cake. No exhibitor gives a real hoot whether a picture is good or bad: if it makes money, that's what he's there for and that's how he is going to stay, independent or whatever.

It is going to be said that I am playing stalking horse for the companies, who are on their side busy painting a picture of chaos to come, enterprise stifled, and what not. It is true that if the present system of distribution is broken down there will be one hell of a mess for a while. But that can take care of itself as it always has. My concern is with better pictures, and anyone who says that block-booking has anything to do with the production of better pictures is singing a song.

With the infrequent exception of a prestige item, no company deliberately makes a picture that will lose money, for the exhibitor or anyone else. And no exhibitor I have ever heard of has refused to run an approved film that will make money, no matter if it is the world's absolute worst. And pictures that are merely bad will continue to be made *and* shown so long as the traffic will bear it.

Double bills and block-booking are not at the source of the matter. Directors and their status are. If you really want some improvement, get behind the Directors' Guild. Or at least get to know some directors' names for a change. Whenever one seems to do a good job, write the company a letter, or write your local paper. So weep no more, my ladies, or rather, weep to some effect.

3 June 1940

Hollywood Town

Our Town is not so much a new thing in the movies as it is several kinds of thing done before but now put together and done especially well. Fantasy indeed has reached higher levels before this, strictly within the medium; but the unnatural usually lacks homeliness and warmth, and thanks to the conception and body of Thornton Wilder's play, the picture has these qualities in abundance, and its own air of the unreal and remote, as well.

Not that there is anything very fantastic about it. Frank Craven merely mooches about cuddling the bowl of his pipe and yarning about the folks in town and how they live and you see them one after the other, over the stove or home from school. Sometimes they know they have an audience but most times not. Sometimes you hear them without seeing them; sometimes you hear them without their speaking aloud. The interlocutor sets the time ahead a day, three years, or sets it back, always rambling but shrewd about the business in hand. At the end the story goes off into another dimension altogether—all about the dead and how they must forget the past, standing there in rows, but interminably, until their latest recruit goes back to a day of her youth, where in a rather depressing double-exposure set she learns with heartbreak that every minute of life is precious, and we should live it that way before too late.

The message and resolution of this are too slight and mechanical ever to be far from the mawkish; and in the picture it was done with every care except heed for the passage of time, so that I was relieved to get back to Frank Craven again, saying good-night to the folks. The only other fault I could find is with the rather choppy and stilted cutting of the early sequences of breakfast in the two houses, where the most natural thing in the world to strive for should be the natural and not the trick.

I believe the fine thing about *Our Town* is its recreation of a mood—a town, a people, a region. You can nearly smell things cooking, and feel the night air; you can certainly see as fine a collection of atrocious lamps and bric-à-brac, good heavy pots and dishes, rail fences and front piazzas, a church, a schoolhouse, a Main Street skyscraper of two stories (as of 1903) as you'd find in a museum. More important than this of course are the local habits, as defined and put into everyday action; and especially as put into the mouths of the various local types—mothers and fathers, the doc and Frank Craven (doubling as the druggist himself), several kids, the local editor, the constable, a fine drunken organist and town scandal. It is always very insignificant and everyday stuff, and most delightful because recognized and created as just that.

Our Town as a film was fortunate in the best production all around, and especially in the field of music. Aaron Copland had a better chance than most composers, for the structure of the thing made bridge music appropriate and vital; and he lived up to his possibilities, unobtrusive but behind all, sometimes thin, sometimes antic, sometimes lyric with spring or nostalgia; but always dry. Sam Wood directed and the village characters fell into place naturally with Thomas Mitchell, Beulah Bondi, Fay Bainter, Guy Kibbee, Stuart Erwin, and the rest (check at least part of the direction by how some of these people have so often looked like somebody in a wig). But the most delicate part of the mechanism is saved from maudlin breakdown by the sensitive, human, and intelligent work of William Holden and Martha Scott, as boy and girl—for it is dangerous to attempt the puppy's awkwardness and first sweet dream of these matters, so absurd with the bloom rubbed off. Miss Scott is new to cameras and may be excused a tendency to suppose that before them radiance need be projected half a block. Otherwise they are that boy and that girl in that place.

Some of us will find that our own native part of town was not in it, and all will admit the structural weakness of a story which hints at more things than it is able to tell, and does some of its heaviest talking purely for lack of something to say. Sticks and stones won't break its bones, but this picture is one of those which fools' praise could spoil for you—which would be too bad.

There is some of the best comedy work in *My Favorite Wife,* a sort of nonsense-sequel to *The Awful Truth.* There is also some of the worst plot-making, and Irene Dunne. The story was written by Bella and Samuel Spewack, and I am not going to tell on it; but apart from its being quite impossible, which may be called comic license, it forces its best people to treat each other with an aimless viciousness that even Boris Karloff might hesitate to reveal to his public. And while most of the characters can manage to cover up this bankruptcy of motivation with quips and tumbles, Miss Dunne has apparently become *very* interested in acting and what may be achieved with the Human Voice. So it becomes her field day. She is not one person but seven, and if she is not all seven at once she is several in rapid succession without aid from script or meaning, running the gamut from Little Eva to Gracie Allen, from *The Women* to (by actual count) Amos and Andy. What a lark.

But this is a Garson Kanin picture and to miss it would not be sensible, for Mr. Kanin is already first-string in comedy, and comedy is no steady boarder these last few months. In addition, it shows Cary Grant developing a very pleasant style of male-animal humor, with charm and a distinct sense of where to poise or throw his weight. A good director can bring this sort of thing out, and does here. The Spewacks devised some funny situations and really good lines. And what with the aid of these things and bit players and a better-than-average musical score, Garson Kanin when he could find a good open space piled up his laughs like cordwood, all in a concealed and relentless film artistry that left the Music Hall audience chuckling still and charmed by everything, including the good parts. The best indication of a director's presence is the opening scene in court, where Granville Bates as the Judge has himself a picnic. Only four people, only one room, and it went on quite a time—but so easily you would not realize till afterward that all the heavy exposition of Act I, Scene 1, had run off in it like a shout. There was another courtroom scene near the end, too, though with more people; and there were scenes here and there all the way through, covering the retreat of the story. Such flowers will not bloom unseen, but it's a pity there has to be so damn much desert air around.

17 June 1940

Hits, Errors, Second-Runs

The Ghost Breakers is the kind of silly comedy that a lot of people are going to hear about and see and laugh at. It is humor completely on the gag side and neither its plot nor its people mean a thing. Paulette Goddard has been willed a haunted castle in Cuba. Bob Hope is a radio gossip columnist who gets mixed up in a killing in Miss Goddard's hotel. Disguised as part of her baggage, he accompanies her to the castle; the last part is spook melodrama, with sliding panels, sinister gentlemen, cobwebs, an organ, and a zombie—all of which are finally overcome. I had hoped that once in the comedy mood, they would burlesque the familiar hokum. They didn't. The film is worked over from an old play obviously for the talents of Bob Hope, a very breezy young man with a laugh line. Miss Goddard and almost everybody else are given pretty thankless straight parts; Willie Best runs second to Hope as his colored detainer (stet "d"). See it, but hold out for air cooling.

In the recent picture *Edison the Man,* the MGM staff has got around the problems of dramatizing the essentially untheatrical, choosing or imagining incidents and winnowing through the whole vast pile of fable and achievement to make a continuous and credible story. They made the laboratory work come alive with interest, and from actual machinists to bankers and aldermen, they were able to point up at least some of the forces involved.

As a picture, it is forced to be rather slow-moving and talky—though surely the phonograph incident, the long struggle with the incandescent lamp, the dynamos gone wild at the climax, are sequences of excitement. Also it is a little simple, especially in the direction of humor and human interest; and at times—the telegraphed proposal, the accident of Little Lord Tinkertoy—clumsy or mawkish. They were lucky to have such people as Spencer Tracy, Rita Johnson, Lynne Overman, Charles Coburn, etc., to take the flatness out of it. And Tracy, who was in the middle right through, was especially successful with those difficult bits as the old man. They got the fable down just about as it was told to us. That is, everything purely good and the term "great inventor" construed quite simply as a man who thinks things up out of the air and all by himself.

Notes from a Ten-O'Clock Scholar.—There are always pictures people still mean to see, still in the second- and third-run circuits. Sometimes it is merely because people have not been warned. I should have warned you against *Buck Benny Rides Again*—which is nothing as a picture and almost a libel on Jack Benny's gag-men. The various faint laughter occasioned by this story of a radio comedian who fell in love for no reason that is given in the picture, and went West to prove apparently that he was not the type of man the West was big enough to have a place for, died long before the story . . . . It is too late to review *The Earl of Chicago,* but the film may still be seen by the curious. Directed by

Richard Thorpe and using both Robert Montgomery and an English setting, it caused speculation on whether it would contain overtones of *Night Must Fall.* There aren't very many. Montgomery is sinister and charming; murder and betrayal are dealt with; and at least a third of the film is a very good example of how to get the most out of a given situation. But the story of a gangster who comes gradually to reverence the venerable glories of English butlers and the English House of Lords is much too much to take. In order to give it the bare likelihood necessary for some conclusion, they have had to make their hard guy at once too smart and too dumb to live. Furthermore, Robert Montgomery is not a hard guy whether he laughs through his nose or not. . . . *Torrid Zone* is another that looks like fun, from the outside: action and banana plantations; James Cagney, Pat O'Brien. There is tropical background and there is action. But there is more noise, for Ann Sheridan (shopworn heroine) has a voice like wagon wheels and no remorse, and the dialogue idea is, if it's louder it's funnier. Mainly, this version of Quirt and Flagg belting natives and getting out the fruit sees no reason to believe for a minute in any one of the diverse plot turns it has borrowed. Neither will you.

You-Could-Do-Worse Department.—The Fifth Avenue Playhouse in New York has been running a program of all the Alfred Hitchcock films—that is, the films starting with *The Man Who Knew Too Much* and going up to the time our blessed fat man fell into *Rebecca.* The list as I remember is: *The 39 Steps, Secret Agent, The Lady Vanishes* (these are my three best); *A Woman Alone, A Girl Was Young,* and *Jamaica Inn.* Perhaps other theater managers in towns of any size could be convinced that such a program for a week or two might not be a bad thing in the summer doldrums. It wouldn't hurt to try. The prints are available and I've found that even in New York, where the revivals have been countless, there is always someone who always meant to see this or that one; and (here's the test) always someone else who saw it but is willing to go along again.

Note of No Progress.—Although D. W. Griffith's *Birth of a Nation* is practically a celluloid shrine in American art, the social hopers, busy as ever with line and page of text, have found its ideology to be not ideal and gone to work on it accordingly. Protests. Picket lines. Grave noddings of the head like a roostful of penguins. It doesn't really matter that outside of some magnificent large-action scenes, *The Birth of a Nation* is more like an early primitive than a classic. Theater managers have got into enough trouble so that it has been worth their while to have the old classic cut almost in half and reissued as a sort of March of Time on the Civil War. It does not even matter that no one could conceivably look at the remote puppet-jerkings of this early screen and be influenced in his present thought or action; or that occasional side-of-the-road touches of humor or pathos retain their original illusion while the big heroics and villainies are now good only for students and for laughs. Half of the artistic contribution of this film at least has been cut out in answer to moral pressure. Few intelligent people today certainly would advocate that the Negro should be vilified; but you can imagine how may voices would get hoarse today if it were found that da Vinci had been hung by the neck to a rope made from his canvases, for having shot a spitball at a saint.

22 July 1940

At Your Own Risk

The March of Time is putting out a collection of old newsreels, stock shots and many bridging reenactments that runs the length of a feature picture and tells all in the title: *The Ramparts We Watch*. It is history and also rub-a-dub-dub. There are indications in the early sections that under the corporalship of Mr. Luce time was marching two ways at once, and that there might possibly be two sides to how fast we tossed young fellers into the overseas furnace; but by the end the purpose is pretty well straightened out.

Whatever the purpose, the effect of a thing like this lies in how well it is done. There have been several collections of World War shots that reached a higher emotional rise and climax—back in the days when raising boys to be soldiers was not being done in the better magazines, remember? But its overall coverage of how the country felt and how the Wilson Cabinet and New York streets and ladies' hats and new Packards looked; what people were saying and singing and dancing to; what happened in church and in the schools and town meetings; who was being elected or run out of town—in this recreation of an era it is a handsome thing to see. In spite of the inevitable trace of stiltedness attaching to the people in documentaries who are set doing things as actors without really being actors, the little representative groups of students, gals, doctors, lawyers, politicans, and journalists are put in motion with a nearer approach to things as they were than you find in memory. And the sound division has done a major job of recreation: you will hear every song of those days you can remember, and as many more you've forgotten. (But may I hope that someday some man who scores music will go listen to how a bugle call is played by a bugler, not a second-desk trumpet brought up on the Egmont Overture? It's a lot to ask, but a hope worth hoping, for a good bugler is one of the joys of life and may not be copied.)

Very well, the job is well done. And it touches on the mighty theme of a nation coming to life and to arms. It is stirring. Very well, stirring to what?

Here is where the objections come in, and the question: even granting it is all truth, which it isn't, how much of the whole truth is it? Was the war as easy as that? A few ships, a few shell-bursts, many men marching and some of them rather dirty? A German or two eased off a homeguard committee? Liberty Loans for liberty and not to buy the bag Morgan and Company was holding? Khaki and shoes and guns turned out with a busy will for the boys over there and none of them paper, or backfiring? No disillusion but a few brave tears of a mother? American boys in France saying "Vive la France" and Frenchmen in cabarets saying "Vive Vilson" and nothing, absolutely nothing else to the AEF? Barracks and no slackers, no objectors? No beatings and witch hunts? Really?

The fever, the national will, the whoop and hoorah were all true at the time, no doubt. So was the world square once; so were the lives of men dependent on the will of the little people. Now we know otherwise—or we did yesterday. And to leave out what we have learned, to say for truth what we know was false, to pass over the misery, the stupidity, the greed, the waste and slaughter, is to blow up a great recruiting poster, an invitation to leave your head outside. We may be proud to be America. We may be ready to stand back of it. But these are just the times when we should turn away from any group of cheapjacks using such times and such high and noble emotions for nothing in the world but to sell their stinking little tentshow. I'm afraid this film comes with very good timing, and I know it is done as smooth as oil. But we should have learned by now. If that's what you want, America, take it away.

Osa Johnson wrote an interesting and instructive book about the Martin Johnsons' life and travels, called *I Married Adventure*. The book got a lot of attention and this was unfortunate, because now Mrs. Johnson has been encouraged to make a feature-length picture by the same title. The film sketches in the early trips to the South Seas, the later trips to Africa, and the final Borneo expedition, mostly by use of the old Johnson releases—and this is all to the good, for the animals, natives, and sometimes breathless scenery they brought back for the screen still make a three-ring circus. There are also reenactments, which were probably necessary and necessarily glib; and Mrs. Johnson's most pressing interest in photography and far places is again wrongly indicated to be one of getting her picture taken in them.

But the film has a commentary, and worse a Voice, incessant and relentless and even drowning the eloquent sounds on original location—the standard-announcer species. Which is to say, a constant fever pitch of accent without rhythm and shiftiness without variety, every word a passion and torn to tatters and no word with any meaning in it; it is a race against time won at the start, all haste and no destination, like the mechanical rabbit at the dog races. There is also a musical score. So if the theater is wired for sound, go at your own risk.

5 August 1940

One Thing and Another

The two reasons why you will want to see *The Return of Frank James* are that Fritz Lang directed it and Henry Fonda is in it. Frank was the brother of Jesse, who really wasn't a bad boy but was shot in the back by the Ford brothers. According to the story, Frank comes out of his disguise as a farmer when the Fords are pardoned, and finances his cruise of vengeance by robbing the payroll of the railroad that was actually behind the Fords and had hounded the whole James family (he did it in a considerate way and anyhow the trains probably didn't run on time). But about the time he got near the assassins, Frank met the girl, and you know what that means. The story ends with a trial, a shooting fest in the local stables, and a meaningful look at the girl—who may have been in the wild West but had taken a power of elocution lessons, damn her.

As to the way the picture moves, I think it can be said that it does, because there is a lot of chase and horses and some pretty spirited stuff around frontier towns. I doubt if any character was ever as lily white as that of Frank James here, but that is a present from the Hays office to you, and anyway the part is played by Henry Fonda. Durn if I don't like that boy. I remember the first picture he played in, with about as much expression as an empty paper bag, and now he is playing Abe Lincoln and hardcase heroes and chewing plug-cut— and making everything slow and easy and right. Henry Hull still thinks that character in acting means raising dust from the floorboards; otherwise the support—Jackie Cooper, John Carradine, and a swell station agent—is good. You might as well go see what they're up to.

Our-Boy-Was-Robbed Department.—I've been going back over a lot of the revival films recently, in various holes and corners, and it is a sad fact that the print you see of a picture six months old is not the picture your critic saw in a projection room or your friends saw in the first-run houses. The print rapidly gets dim and sometimes tattered; sometimes the sound-track is chewed up here and there. And sometimes you have the double bad luck to get a theater with cheap or faulty equipment in the vital factors of projection, reproduction, screen. About this I suppose nothing can be done, as the best equipment is an expensive proposition. But it isn't too much to ask that prints be retired when they begin to falter. After all, a movie has paid off long before it gets into this stage, and if companies are going to continue taking in rentals for a picture, they can stand the cost of reprinting. You can't sell for five cents a picture postcard that has been kicked halfway across the country's mails; you can't get list prices for some beat-up phonograph record—why department stores have to knock off up to 50 percent for a little washable dirt on linen or scratches on the sole of a shoe. But the movie public is still dumb enough to set this kind of chiseling down to "bad photography" and so long suffering that they will pay their patient money for damaged goods until some bright exhibitor begins to steal his competitor's patrons by advertising a FRESH PRINT,   or more to the point: YOU CAN ACTUALLY SEE THEIR FACES.

2 September 1940

Hitchcock in Hollywood

Alfred Hitchcock seemed to be fooling around where he didn't belong in his last two pictures (*Jamaica Inn* and *Rebecca*), but in *Foreign Correspondent* the man has done it again. The plot is bare enough, a routine Oppenheimer about an American reporter who gets caught up in international intrigue between peacemakers and warmongers as of about a year ago—the better part of the action lying in Holland and England. But with Hitchcock it isn't ever so much what was done as what it was done with. He has explored the range of the modern story-film farther than any other man; and if you have any interest in the true motion and sweep of pictures, watching that man work is like listening to music.

Taking the picture for what it is, however—basically spy melodrama with more emphasis on keeping going than on where—there are still awkward bits. Joel McCrea is an awkward bit—at least when he figures that the part requires acting. The meeting of the peace society has prominently ham elements; the terrific secret is pretty meaningless; and the speechification is sometimes overdone, especially toward the end. Otherwise it goes like the night mail, from the home office to London to The Hague and a shooting in the rain. Then a wonderful sequence out in the flat country and inside the sinister windmill, the chase to London and the murderous practices uncovered there, evil closing in, the flight in the Clipper, the wreck (this last, with its eerie sensation of being fired upon and magnificent water shots, is one of the big dramatic effects in pictures).

Whatever the framework, a detective story with Hitchcock is no longer a detective story—though he's after the same action and suspense, and gets it. He loves details like a Dutch painter, and crowds his set with them, whether they are the wonderful mechanics of the windmill (a Hitchcock interior if you ever saw one) or the Great Dane lumbering around, or the Lett with the blueplate eyes, or the silly dame, or the local constabulary all speaking Dutch. He loads his set with them without loading down his action; and because everything and everybody aren't direct accessories to the plot, so many mechanical aids, you get the effect of life, which also has its dogs and casual passers-by who are real without having anything to do with any plot you know about. He makes a character out of every extra.

Another of his tricks is to show you the little birdie—*i.e.*, he likes to have a bland face or a sweet old lady personify evil, and the tricky-looking fellow turn out to be a right one all along. Even here he shuffles the types around so there is still no rule-of-thumb, for Mr. Ciannelli and his mobsters are sinister enough, and the scene in the torture room is enough to leave you with the creeps. Another trick is the strange-mechanical, like the reversing windmill, the assassin's camera, the disappearing car. And he likes to scare you with high and precarious places.

Above everything there is a feeling of how to use sound and things and people for suspensive effect that is like a painter's sense of color or like a musician's sense—if you haven't got it you can't buy one, and you can copy every last trick in a Hitchcock picture without having anything but Boris Karloff left. He likes to play with wind and rain, with natural music (as opposed to atmospheric scores, though there is too much of one here) amd a natural background murmur of people talking without the words coming out, of street-noises or machinery or just the wind and rain by themselves. He knows where to set the microphone and camera to catch the effect he has figured out, and with all the devices of this complex art completely under his fingers, you may be sure a person never enters a deserted building or a dark alley without your wondering actively if he will ever come out.

Group scenes too, in action or repose. One of the hardest things film men have had to learn is not to spot one thing out of many by rubbing your nose in it; another, more often achieved, is how to keep a lot of people milling around desperately without the focus getting lost and the end confused.

Add humor. Hitchcock knows suspense should not get too tight, so there is always some absurd side-talk going on, often with edge to it. Robert Benchley is the principal funny man here—though others keep popping up—and the mixture of his feverish ride on the water wagon and his comments on the practice of foreign correspondence is a nice thing to have around. He apparently wrote his own part, and if he didn't have a hand in the general dialogue, somebody did who was good and witty.

In short, if you would like a seminar in how to make a movie travel the lightest and fastest way, in a kind of beauty that is peculiar to movies alone, you can see this once, and then again to see what you missed, and then study it twice. If all you're out for is an evening you'll have that too—or what do you want for 35-75 cents?

In *Lucky Partners* Ginger Rogers has changed her hair but not whatever it is she's got that gets us, and Ronald Colman is as charming and steady as ever, and there are some very nice minor people to see, so we can pay less attention than usual to the story (*and* the title). The story is a Sacha Guitry affair, a pretty thin fantasy: a famous but disillusioned and incognito painter goes halves on a sweepstakes ticket with a girl, and conducts an experiment with her on the winnings. He wants to take her for a platonic spin through the world before she settles down to marry a rather porky insurance chap, to see if this will settle or unsettle her for small-town housewifery. It is as you guess, though after quite a bit of trouble. Lewis Milestone directed, in his first comedy assignment in years, and I wish he had had a better story: steering a course between the Hays office and the laws of probability in bedroom mix-ups, is no man's apple pie, and a thing like the old wishing-well couple in the story will send strong men to the nearest bar. As it is, he gets some good and unusual comedy out of what is there, and a closing scene in court that takes second place only to the juridical opening of *My Favorite Wife*. It may depend on the mood you're in, but this seems one of those comedies with a glow on it.

16 September 1940

For Better, for Worse

It is nearly two months since I reported on the March of Time's *Ramparts We Watch,* during which time there have been several kinds of holdup on the picture's release. But now it is out in New York I'd like to say again it is not one of those things you should care to be a party to. I said before and I don't feel it any less: "To leave out what we have learned, to say for truth what we know was false, to pass over the misery, the stupidity, the greed, the waste and slaughter, is to blow up a great recruiting poster, an invitation to leave your head outside. We may be proud to be America. We may be ready to stand back of it. But these are just the times when we should turn away from any group of cheapjacks using such times and such high and noble emotions for nothing in the world but to sell their stinking little tentshow for money."

It is a relief to find a couple of movies as such around at the second-run houses. It is perfectly safe to see *The Great McGinty,* which is a little different and quite a lot of fun. It has mainly to do with the rise through city politics from soup line to Governor's mansion of a toughie who learns very fast. Unfortunately for him—and to some extent for us—he gets married to a young divorcée with two rather prominent kids. First it's for convenience, and then (surprise) it's for fun, and then she wants him to buck the machine and clean out corruption. He does and they nail him—except that he escapes to tend a very pleasant bar somewhere in the banana country, where he tells the story that makes the picture in flashback.

The picture is out of the ordinary partly because of its delightful and wicked jabs at the various forms of the squeeze, the shakedown, and ballot-stuffing as practiced by a Tammany setup; partly for the way its small matters are handled. Preston Sturges, who both wrote and directed, takes credit for all of this. This is his first directing job and where has he been all our lives? *The Great McGinty* does have its rather soggy moments and occasionally a heavy touch right in the middle of the deftest humor (for example, the Charley Chase tiptoe of the jailbreak, contrasted to the neat steal of the guard's paper and the perfect chairfall). Brian Donlevy is a little given to mugging, but that is more than made up for by Akim Tamiroff as the political boss ("We'll be at the mercy!") and a swell assortment of small parts. Preston Sturges has that sense of the incongruous which makes some of the best gaiety; on the whole he gets more fast doings and laughs packed in here than you've seen in quite a while.

They Drive by Night is also around and worth looking into, especially if you can get up and go when Ida Lupino insists on acting in the later sequences (incidentally, these were a complete and shameless steal from a Bette Davis picture, *Bordertown,* I think). At least half of the film was "suggested" by the Bezzerides novel, *Long Haul,* and in this I wish they had been more suggestible, for the trucking stuff is very good and could have not only made the whole picture but made it better.

Two brothers are wildcatting up and down the West Coast, one jump ahead of the Shylock and always behind on sleep. But they are luckier than most others and get their truck paid for with enough money ahead to buy their own loads and beat the market. But there is still the worst nightmare, of going to sleep and off the road, and this one catches up with them finally—about the middle of the picture. After that, except for some fine work by Alan Hale, you can haul it away: one brother loses an arm and the other gets a good job and starts running away from Ida Lupino.

I don't know why this split in the middle was necessary because there was so much more they could have done with what they were doing. There was a lot of it in the book—going broke on a load of apples, say, and then getting into the market just at the time apples weren't worth dumping off the truck. Or finding no load and having to go back light. All the various fines, fees, and holdups. Breakdowns. It could easily have been worked into the story, because the motion of trucks rolling alone is enough to give the semblance of action, and they had a fine lot of life in the roadside diners and the markets, and for feminine interest they already had Ann Sheridan in the story and a little of her will carry quite a distance.

Well, it's their picture, not mine. George Raft makes a good enough trucker, if not a flexible screen player; Humphrey Bogart has the smaller part, which seems wrong way around. Roscoe Karns is in it for comedy relief, and the odd character bits are good. Joe Breen was looking the other way again on some of this dialogue, which is salty and fast throughout, and it's a relief to hear people talk like people talking. Add a couple of terrific wrecks and a good party. As I was saying, when it is good it is no turkey.

You may soon get a chance to see what somebody else thinks are the great parts of the great picture nobody ever saw—the miles of film Sergei Eisenstein exposed down in Mexico, some thousands of feet of which were released as *Thunder over Mexico* in 1933. Marie Seton has resurrected the original and edited from it about an hour of film that is supposed to follow the master's original idea, under the title *Time in the Sun*. It makes an interesting travelogue with pageantry, social overtones, self-conscious mugging natives, and fine though trick photography (Tissé). It was not taken or edited with imagination and moves heavily when it moves at all. The plain truth of the matter is that Eisenstein went to Mexico for some documentary stuff and there got drunk partly on his own reputation and partly on the million different things that could be photographed if you spent the rest of your life at it on subsidy; and that Upton Sinclair took a villainous drubbing for pulling him away in the end and trying to salvage some of that naïve investment. A way to be a film critic for years was to holler about this rape of great art, though it should have taken no more critical equipment than common sense to see that whatever was cut out, its clumping repetitions and lack of film motion could not have been cut *in*. The greatness of that heavy hoax was never left on the cutting-room floor; it was left where it started—inside a lot of very suggestible but not very good heads.

30 September 1940

Film Ups and Downs

The present remake of *They Knew What They Wanted* gives Garson Kanin another chance to come through with some fine picture making (an Erich Pommer production; screenplay, Robert Ardrey; camera, Harry Stradling; music, Alfred Newman). If you remember, the story goes pretty thoroughly to pieces in the end, and of course since it's a case of a girl getting slightly That Way a great deal of attention has to be spent on putting a halo behind the priest as big as a dishpan, and Charles Laughton is starred and has formerly been known to steal everything in a picture that wasn't nailed down, and Carole Lombard's part is straight-dramatic, which is not the style to which she is accustomed—on the whole it required quite a deal of director's patience and skill, and got it.

Most of the film is simple and touching and funny, just about people: an Italian ranch-owner in the California Valley, dumb but with a heart the size of your hat; a cute trick of a waitress who takes him sight unseen for his money and comes to love him, though a little late, as his foreman has been at her; a padre; a doctor; the natives. It rolls along at its good leisure through some very clever business with Tony's making his heart up for the girl and getting into a correspondence courtship that is no whirlwind on either end, and into worse trouble when he is afraid to send her his picture, and a pretty hilarious first meeting on the ranch, and a marvelously done fiesta, as a climax to which Tony breaks both his fool legs.

You hear a lot about masters at the mob scene, but there is really unbeatable work here in the natural shift and color of many people, first in games and dances, then in horror, then converging on the house as a doctor comes out, many voices in a background pattern of sound, a word here and there, the whole rising then falling away as the people hear the news and go away hushed. There is more drama to this per film foot than in the whole climax of violence, when Tony finds out about his foreman and beats him rather ineffectively; and there is another kind of drama Kanin has done very well, in the quiet after the fiesta, when the boy and girl get together on the attraction-repulsion basis.

But it is about this time that the issue begins to cloud, for they are never quite sure how to get around the character of William Gargan as the foreman, whether he is a villain (the Hays office says so) and just how much, and what to do with him for the rest of the story. They end up by making him 51 percent villain and Miss Lombard resolved *never* to do a thing like that again, and with a hint of expiation but the stern need to go away for the present, and with Tony forgiving but only because he is so *big,* and the halo lighting up desperately like 5,000 watts.

There are some fine things in the last part, words said and actions taken, the sentimental and the gay too; Laughton is fine as the Italo-American, almost letter-perfect and very jocund; Miss Lombard is at her best; and Harry Carey is as wonderful and right as ever—he is cast as the country doctor and damned if I wouldn't let him operate right now, though as he says, "Lady, the things I don't know you could herd like cows." Everyone does the best with what he's got, and there is no truth lost by the way—in fact there is some truth achieved in it that we don't often get. But there are that story uncertainty and that forced ending; and so you have to admit that it wobbles on its pins occasionally at the same time you say that for dialogue, acting, background, and film creation it's a honey.

The Long Voyage Home will hold your interest as a picture, I think, for all its aimlessness and general failure to add up to anything. John Ford and Dudley Nichols made it out of several old O'Neill one-actors, and it runs as a series of incidents in a ship's life, the only one with any particular meaning being the last, in which it is simply shown that sailors are always swearing they're through and shipping over. Three others are adventure pieces: the girls who bring rum into the ship; the sailor who gets killed by the runaway anchor; the sailor falsely suspected of being an enemy in the hysteria of crossing the war zone—this last given a modern touch by Stuka divers and machine guns.

Where the picture excels is in the truth of atmosphere and the kind of tension that is built up in character. Here, in the dark sides of an old tramp at dock, in the foc'sle, the cluttered busy decks, the bows under water, etc., Ford and his camera, Gregg Toland, have an effective use for the half-lighting and dark masses—together with the realism of detail—Ford likes so much. And though this always tends to make it seem more than it really is, it is good background for the work of Thomas Mitchell, Ward Bond, Ian Hunter, John Wayne, Wilfrid Lawson, and the three Abbey Players: Barry Fitzgerald, Arthur Shields, and J. M. Kerrigan. These people make fine things out of parts of it, and indeed make most of the picture, for without their steady talent you would have seen the bare bones of its loose construction, and that it goes nowhere interminably. It is occasionally way overdone but generally true to life, and I suppose we might concentrate on how it would have been worse, rather than on the fact that it should have been better.

21 October 1940

Less Time for Comedy

There will be some to whom a systematic four- or five-year advance build-up on each picture is going to make *The Great Dictator* a disappointment. That will be too bad, because it is a good picture, and this time something new in Chaplin. There will be others, however, who will find the symbiosis of comedy and earnestness an unhappy state of union, detrimental to both; and I think these people will be right. For the world's first funny man to prove that he too can write a *New Republic* editorial, but several years later, is something rather less than the dog who walked on his hind legs, because this is the place in the act where he was supposed to do "dead dog."

Through Mr. Chaplin's characteristic reticence you know what the picture is all about, of course. One Charlie is Hitler; the other is a Jewish barber in Hitler's Germany, an amnesia victim left over from the World War. Paulette Goddard is a Waif. Jack Oakie is a Mussolini briefly, and good while he's there. And both Charlies talk. Everybody knows all about these facts because the secret was guarded so hard for so long.

What nobody suspected is that the Hitler Charlie, the new Charlie of authority, double-talk, and complete confusion, actually steals the show. This was hardly by design. All the old luggage of slapstick and pathos and after-my-laughter-came-tears is in the ghetto sequences, with people being bonged over the head with a skillet and Chaplin with the stick and that crazy-ballet walk of his and the girl being waifed right and left and the Keystone cops in storm-trooper uniforms piling all over the place.

The Great Dictator opens on some pretty dated nonsense in the war zone and the kind of lighting and movie action they used in *Shoulder Arms.* What's new is the acting, the new and different character, a mixture of sharp mimicry and the devices of absurdity. And as we might have expected from the wonderful double-talk song in *Modern Times,* Chaplin is as acute and perfect verbally as he is in pantomime: he has the splenetic and krauty fustian of the German orator as exactly as Hitler himself. When he says "Democracy shtoonk. Liberty shtoonk," he crowds out over his collar to the precise degree, and he never misses an opportunity to go from the normal English of the story into this hortatory gibberish, booting his lieutenants around and scaring the devil out of everybody, including himself. And the old reliable panto at the same time too, so that his version of the Nazi salute is a blend of pomp and monkeyshine that leaves them in the aisles, and his dance with the globe is one of the triumphs of all satiric dancing, for point, grace, and perfection.

The whole thing is worked out with a great deal of care for many effects, some of which are on the gag side, some not. The dictator can never quite get a pen out of the patent inkwell to sign documents with, for example; or he gets tied up in his cape, or the train he is meeting stops at the wrong place (this, the arrival of Napolini of Bacteria, is one of the highlights, together with the review of the troops that follows). On the other side there is great business with affairs of state, the dapper and ominous figure whipping around from audience to conference to portrait sitting, half a minute for each. There is a character called Herring (Henry Daniell) and a character called Garbitsch (Billy Gilbert), who is always demonstrating a new and invincible device that doesn't work—as when the parachute inventor takes off and they watch him crash to the sidewalk below: "Far from perfect," the dictator says incisively. The two dictators end up trying to bluff each other, and we go back to the story of Charlie the barber, which has been going on intermittently.

When this is funny it is funny as always, in the shop, on the street, around the chimney pots, with some of the oldest Chaplin favorites still peeping through. But it is also tragic because a people is being persecuted; these Jews are straight characters, not the old cartoons; and the laughter chokes suddenly and is reluctant to start again. Chaplin likes to pull out all the stops on sentimental passages, but this thing is too near and meaningful. It isn't that a comedian should be denied indignation and kept clowning forever; it is that old thing in all art of the demands of unity, of a complete and sustained mood or tone. He was always a funny figure against the rude world, but the gulf between a kick in the pants and a pogrom is something even his talent for the humorous-pathetic will not cross. And his unrelieved six-minute exhortation to the downtrodden of the world, look up, stand up, etc., is not only a bad case of overwriting but dramatically and even inspirationally futile.

These things must be reported, though that other burning question of whether the satire is actually effective, and to what extent, will get small play here. You could remember that the size of policemen's feet was never seriously affected by all the skylarking of the Keystone lot; but you could also remember that a man's heart being in the right place is a good thing to witness, and that laughter is one of the great and joyous healers of the spirit, whatever the recent crop of solemn buffoons have to say about its social waste. And again as always where there is a Chaplin picture, there is laughter here, warmth and grace too. I think it will do you good, just for what is there, let alone that this is still Chaplin the Great, and growing at his age.

A lot of people don't have time enough for comedy these days, and it is getting so you wince every time someone in a film trifle says the word democracy; it means they are going to pull out with a heavy speech. *Arise, My Love* is the latest to capitalize on the situation in Europe. It is the old girl-reporter framework with angles, such as idealism. Mitchell Leisen did another one of his bright comedy jobs through most of it, and got action in too; the dialogue really jumps; there is a nice boy-girl angle; Claudette Colbert, Ray Milland, and a well-placed cast breeze through it.

But there is that need to milk the headlines, which is not so much a bad thing in itself as a poor excuse for shooting around story complications; and when they start talking with too much feeling and punk poetry about the little fellows in Spain (a safe subject now; when it would have done some good it was too hot to touch), Poland, Norway, France, without really caring a damn or devoting enough of the picture to making it real, it gets embarrassing. This is the story of a condemned Loyalist aviator, pardoned by a ruse, chasing the newspaper career girl to Paris, almost running away home with her, and then going back to fly in Poland. It came to a good enough end in about an hour and a half; but twenty minutes later they were still making speeches and all they needed was the American flag in *The Time of Your Life* and a new arrangement of "The Parade of the Wooden Soldiers." You can save time by getting out when it becomes clear that the boat the two are on is the *Athenia*, by a device heisted from *Cavalcade*, though in this instance the lovers don't die—just the picture. Can I help you with your coat?

4 November 1940

Both Fantasy and Fancy

In a general or show-business way, I think Mr. Walt Disney has made his first mistake. Someone told him about the capital letter in Music, or more specifically someone introduced him to Dr. Leopold Stokowski. This is a wrong-foot start for describing *Fantasia,* which I intend to review here, but I do wish that people who are simply swell in their own right would stop discovering about art and stuff and going swish. First Chaplin learns about the class struggle; now Disney meets the Performing Pole. And it's worse in Disney's case, because his studio has always turned out the most original sound-track in films.

Fantasia as a film for everybody to see and enjoy has as a main weakness an absence of story, of motion, of interest. It takes eight pieces of music, introduces each with a little homey ramble by Deems Taylor, and as we dissolve gratefully from Mr. Taylor we go into what the music may be about or may suggest or in some cases might suggest if you were in a certain state. As a background and continuum for this, there is the noise and motion of an orchestra assembling and tuning up, than which there is nothing more fascinating, nothing more exciting with promise in the world. But over and above this, on some kind of promontory and silhouetted in awful color is Dr. Leopold in a claw-hammer coat, leading with expression that only falls short of balancing a seal on its nose an orchestra which made that part of the sound-track yesterday in shirtsleeves and is at the moment out for a cigarette. I rarely bray aloud in the theater, as this is rude and also may get you into an argument with men who have muscles in their arms, but when Dr. L. yearned out over the strings to the left of him in a passage for horns (which are in the center when they're there at all) and the bedazzlement of color yearned sympathetically from baby-blue to baby-something-else, I released a short one.

Don't get me wrong. I know well enough that this is what the boobs want, and that, strangely enough, it serves to lead them to music sometimes, and that Stokowski is the greatest conductor-showman who ever came down the podium, that he can make a band play and sell it too, being at the same time great and god-awful. It is just too bad that in this picture, made with hope and faith and over two million dollars, dedicated to the principle that music as it was created and as it is released for you is a thing of beauty—it is just a mortal pity that we should have such hollow fakery and that Disney, if not his wise musicians on the staff, should be taken in by it.

And if there is any use knowing what I think of *Fantasia,* don't get me wrong there either. Dull as it is toward the end, ridiculous as it is in the bend of the knee before Art, and taking one thing with another, it is one of the strange and beautiful things that have happened in the world. I probably have a personal bug about music, for I would rather hear a symphony rehearse than catch the stiff-shirt première, and so this background of shadows with the different sections filing in and fussing with their instruments, this bedlam of tuning, rustling, and scraping chairs, is the background of a picture I might have dreamed about. And the screen itself when the music is playing is the only excuse I have ever seen for having eyes and ears at the same time. Some of the screen material is abstract, as in the Bach; some of it is antic, as in the ballets of plant-life, etc., and the Mickey Mouse sketch; some is dramatic and a little of it is less fantasy than nancy-fancy.

It is all done with that bright gift of the imagination that has become such a part of the American household we fall into the habit of taking it for granted, which we never should do, for the Disney bunch not only pioneers the field in cartoon sight and sound but is busy year in, year out with the creation of fable and fabulous things, sometimes repeating but sometimes coming up with something never thought of and not soon forgotten. And you might guess from the lively union of music with image that is the Disney hallmark, that this group of craftsmen would have them a field-day on any such range of pure and program music as is offered here; that for all the "experimental" work that has been done by serious and rather fierce dedicates to art, when the Disney men took this sort of thing up as being necessary in their work, they would leave all the others on a siding way down the track.

The music was beautifully recorded (Stokowski and the full Philadelphia Orchestra), but whether the special reproduction equipment is worth the heavy expense and cumbersomeness I do not know at one hearing. They have whole batteries of speakers to make sound come from everywhere and they have them hooked up directionally. This is still mechanical in effect, and not the illusion of an orchestra it might figure out to be on paper. It was a bold move anyway, and may lead the way to better acoustics, but there has been too much hoorah about it already for what it achieves, and it is serving to hold up distribution endlessly.

There have always been objections to program music, which we need not go into here except to say that most of the curse on it owes less to the type of music than to what fools can make of it. "The Pastoral Symphony" is played sensitively for the mood of the thing; Stravinsky's "Rites of Spring" is made completely over into a pretty frightening story of the creation of the earth and the coming of life; "A Night on Bald Mountain" is another mood piece, this time dark and austere; and the "Nutcracker Suite" was of course a pushover for any Disney fantasy, and lovely. The other things, and there are hundreds, are what you will see as you are in there forgetting about the more didactically elevating side of the show in the general delight and splendor of its passage.

Escape is not a picture I can safely recommend, as the best I can say is that some have approved it but if you are me you won't go. Whatever the truth and suspense of the original story—the American-born son of a German mother rescuing her from a concentration camp through luck, an old family retainer, a

Nazi who weakens for reasons not well built up, and a love affair—is pretty well lost in a script that both dawdles and hammers the obvious (Arch Oboler and Marguerite Roberts), and direction that lacks timing, incisiveness, natural forward motion, and (especially) belief. With Felix Bressart, Conrad Veidt, Albert Basserman, Philip Dorn, etc., and with its grim and exciting subject, it might still have been fine in spite of Robert Taylor and Norma Shearer as ineffective leads. As it is, it takes an hour to get started and makes just another feeble fable from headlines.

25 November 1940

Films, Taken or Left Alone

In the American Spectacle class, O-Pioneers division, *Arizona* is the best I have seen so far, partly because it tries to do its job well, partly because it does not try to do anything else. Its story is that of the wagon trains going westward to settle the new Arizona Territory; of how at the start of the Civil War the Union garrison left Tucson to the desert and the Indians; of how the settlers accepted Confederate protection, and later renounced it with huzzas as the Union forces moved back in. In the films, I suppose, history is as history does at the box office; but the prime motives of new land and holding it, with good men and bad men and a few men with ideals in their eyes, with hardships and danger and heartbreaking setbacks and summary justice—these facts of the great American trek to the West are roughly set forth as background to this story. Since they are simple if breathtaking facts and since there is nothing to be served now by twisting, they seem honest enough.

The foreground has the usual story of romance and rising conflict, with Jean Arthur in long pants and shirt, cleaning up vice and shoving villains around; Warren William holding up well under the strain but obviously conscious that all he needs for a complete set of Basil Rathbone is an English accent; William Holden coming through on his way to California but getting back just when badness has got too fat and insolent even for Miss Arthur, who is by now so much in love she puts on a dress. And the business of freighting goods through Indian country, buying and building and fighting for some kind of law, is woven in all through. Outside of love and natural reprisal, the activating theme is that of belief in the expansion of a new land, its future proud growth and promise of amenity. In the story, this not only motivates but worries quite a few people.

But if the story has places where it buckles, this is neither on history nor on motivation. Jean Arthur for one thing just isn't the type of thing to start a revolution or outface an established bad man. I think Alison Skipworth might do it. For another thing, the local wickedness all stems from a partnership between

Mr. William and Porter Hall. Hall is an actor I delight to watch, but he has to be so poor-grade and sniveling here that you wonder how people with the hardihood to make the passage over the George Washington Bridge could be herded and hogtied by such a naïve bad shot.

For the rest of it, leave them alone, because they are tolerable enough real people, in a real time. Edgar Buchanan as the W. C. Fields judge is good all by himself, but the others for the most part depended on the background set up, the way the story was written for them (Claude Binyon) and worked out through them (Wesley Ruggles and his good camera crew). As this is a Ruggles production, as "art direction" and "set decorations" are credited to Lionel Banks and Frank Tuttle, respectively, I suppose credit for the fine construction of end-of-the-trail wagons, shacks, bars, interiors, and implements rests somewhere between these people and the research department. Matters like this have been tended with such care that part of the illusion is there before it has had a chance, in the theater sense, to be created. But I like to think this picture makes its modest sense less through tossing good De Millions after bad, the warpaths and stampedes, etc., than through getting a director and writer who can make the epic part of it into real and familiar life.

The Seven Sinners is nothing to worry about unless you happen to be in the theater watching it go from fairly good to worse than worse. It collects many of those old charmers of the senses: the South Seas and the legendary rare flower of the waterfront bars; the fleet at anchor and the sailors on the town; curious bad men; natives and outcasts gone native. And Marlene Dietrich. Marlene is still something to see, though her best friend is still her singing voice—a fair voice, with personality and feeling in song—for her acting presence here carries the insistent hint that she knows where the camera is and where the early Mae West prints are buried. She is so many things and so many out of key that you can't help feeling that the director has given her her head because he didn't know what else to do, and that she is bringing it in on a platter.

It is a hokum picture, but with a basis of appeal; and much can be made out of this when properly contrived. But here the main director's contriving falls to Tay Garnett, who apparently figured that a class-A production setup and a chair with his name on the back and an aged-in-the-wood script are what it takes to make a picture. So he lets insignificant details, like why someone should love someone or how any punk lieutenant could pet and flout and bang doors on a captain in his navy, take care of themselves, while he saves up for a scene which reads "They gather round her eagerly," and which he runs up into the storming of the Bastille. The sequence of the last free-for-all in the cabaret might be worth seeing, for it is as far beyond description as it is beyond belief. It is the climax of the picture—which demonstrably thinks it is taking the boobs in with a story of the big things, like romance and renunciation, loyalty, and basic honor—and the biggest thing it sees to do with itself is provide a stunt-man's holiday on top of a working-girl's heartbreak, with all the high technical resources of the modern film called in to magnify the absurd drama of *Rescued from an Eagle's Nest,* the relentless humor of the pie-throw, the pratfall, and the broken back.

You will be enabled to wait for this burnt-cork golconda by virtue of the old standby situations already mentioned, by quirks in the writing, and by the people conscripted for this duty. Marlene of course—if only for what she looks like, especially in attitudes of repose. Oscar Homolka, who in spite of everything comes through as a living intelligence, real in both terror and charm, is a boon to the story, which never explains where or why he does what for which. John Wayne is all right for a part like this; Broderick Crawford is active and good. Billy Gilbert should always be kept to long shots; Mischa Auer had a part that would have been good for laughs if they hadn't discovered it as the business was made up; and the cast in general was more than usually livened by the presence of Vince Barnett, Sam Hinds, Reginald Denny, Albert Dekker, etc. All this detail only to make one point: the director of a picture is still a bigger man than anyone knows, purely because he is the man who brings the line to life. Would anybody like to speculate a pound of flesh on what Lewis Milestone could have done with this story, these people, this atmosphere and its settings? Any takers on what makes the difference between the art of pictures and such a mountain of motorman's glove?

2 December 1940

Make Your Own Movie

Angels Over Broadway was written, produced, and directed by the ex-writer Ben Hecht. It has excitement, fast talk, some knowable people, cynicism, and sentiment. It is different, if you like to think of one Ben Hecht picture as different from another, for the man has a formula no less artificial or more true than any standard problem-plot. Between one evening and the next morning three widely assorted strangers are brought together in a scheme to save a little man from suicide by promoting the money he has been caught embezzling; one is a broken playwright, working for his D.T.; the second is a hard Broadway young man, a part-time steerer for one of the important poker games; the third is a girl who is a good girl but footlight-happy, and mostly stands around.

Open on New York in the rain, a soliloquy by the sharp young man, mostly about the rain, the suckers, his last seven bucks, his next lucky seven, the suckers let it rain on them. Follow him, pick up a sign Engle & Co. and leave him for Engle's office upstairs, where the little man is at the end of his rope, though not literally, as he has chosen the hard way. So cut to one of the bridges. But here the copper on the beat has not yet holed up for the night, so pick up the little man, dazed, wandering into a night spot to spend the time. Everything from here on is either the night club, on-stage at the folded play, or the hotel of the gambling ring, where there is mounting suspense and a free-for-all. Cut to next morning in court; to next morning in a coffee stand; to the street outside for the last scene, in the sunlight. Each of the four has been given a new lease on life, and the young man with the answers and the asphalt heart has been regenerated.

That is the framework of it, and the depth too, and about all it has as motion picture. Ben Hecht is one of the first-rate screenwriters when he is working in Hollywood proper, and under someone else; and you might expect him to have acquired some of the difference between a play and a picture purely by unconscious absorption. But the minute he gets off by himself he has the same old picnic: people begin to talk and things not to happen. Two faces, three faces, interminably, always talking and not always to much purpose. And by "much purpose" I mean that he is not sacrificing a fluid progression in order to get large effects or build characters out of rock: he establishes a man in a certain attitude and then, to get him out of the way of the plot or the plot out of its own way, he stands him on the trap door, and picks up the switch.

Accepting this and not asking for more, you will find the picture pretty good fun, for the talk *is* bright and the various complications well devised—the poker game, in fact, is a first-rate movie sequence all around. Thomas Mitchell as the genial has-been and ham Good Fairy steals the show: the part is juicy, but beyond that he is a character of weight and address and rolling periods with humor and sensitive perception under that. Douglas Fairbanks Jr. does a sustained and sustaining piece of work on a character better realized than conceived: he has a graceful talent, ease, and much wisdom in how to get around. John Qualen was the third person and should be mentioned; Rita Hayworth as the fourth probably shouldn't.

The encouraging thing about a picture like this, with its absence of epic and a cast of thousands, is that it is like a carpenter puttering around in his own shop. Men who can learn the ropes and get into Hecht's position can do as much for movies as anybody; there is still the opportunity for opening windows and letting the air in—a vital thing in this magnificent and terrible industry, even if it is only hot air. If you don't need encouragement but only a way to spend an evening, why that's here too. In movies, if stern yearners would someday realize it, that has to be here too.

So You're Going to Have a Movie, or, One Hundred Hints to Expectant Directors.—There are no funny pictures around to see now; the Marx Brothers are absent, the Wiere Brothers have been lost sight of, the Ritz Brothers should have been. (Those who think that Olsen, Jolson, Johnson, and Cantor are funny men can leave the room.) W. C. Fields is resting on one elbow; Allen, Benny, and Hope are tied up on the air; Rags Raglan has left Forty-second Street and got himself a job; and Chaplin and Disney have made a balloon ascension to upper-case. So as an exercise in the visual arts while we're waiting, make your own comedy sequence, why not.

Characters: three beds, two Marx Brothers, asleep. Also a phone-booth interior, a Dialing Hand, a bedside phone, a large vase or jug. (These are merely properties and do not necessarily resemble any coincidence or appear all at the same time.)

Scene I; Take I. The Dialing Hand drops a nickel into the phone and starts to work dialing. Cut to bedroom: three beds, one, two, three; two Marx Brothers (sleeping), one, two. The phone rings. (We get this from the sound-track.) No motion. Rings again. No change. Rings again. The same: peace, tranquility. Cut back to the phone-booth interior. No peace here. Hand shakes instrument violently to see if nickel will refund. No refund. Goes to pocket and comes back with large coin; drops coin in 25-cent slot. On the sound-track an extra-loud and significant BONG and a jingle. Dissolve into:

Close-up of phone in bedroom, moving back to show three beds, two Marx Brothers (as before), one large vase or jug, preferably about three feet tall, fat and well foliaged with nymphs, branches, and garden produce, on a stand a little above and midway between beds 1 and 2. Or, Marx Brothers 1 and 2. Or just midway. Insert shot of hand in phone-booth dialing last number. Cut back to medium shot, bedroom, showing phone, jug, M. B. number one, asleep.

Phone goes off, but this time *bang*. Not a ring, an explosion, with smoke. It's loaded! It's a disguised revolver like in the camera assassination from *Foreign Correspondent*. It is pointed straight at the vase or other large receptacle, and this now *shatters* like a bomb, taking it big. It's a shambles! Camera moves back out of the smoke and debris a little, shows M. B. number two still asleep, M. B. number one reaching sleepily for phone. Title: "Eh?"

He looks at bed number three (close-up of bed number three, empty); yawns. Title:

"No. No, he's not in yet." Puts phone back, yawns, gets back under covers; long sigh and silence, peace, tranquility.

Camera pans a little, moves in to M. B. number two, who reaches automatically and sleepily out of bed to grope on the floor beside. Brings up another vase or jug, a duplicate. With a tremendous effort but his eyes still shut, he places the new vase or vahz on the wall stand. It's reloaded! He goes back under covers, cuddling pillow; long sigh and silence, peace, tranquility, as we:

Fade slowly, music up on the sound-track, probably "Ave Maria."

I know, but on the screen it might still be funny and it wouldn't have to run more than seventy-five feet. (There must be someone out there, I can hear people breathing.) And next time, operatic tragedy having got as dull on us as comedy has, I will give you the complete scenario of Grace Moore as Little Eva crossing the ice cubes in full bay. I have always wanted to do a vehicle for La Moore, and now I think, things being as slack as they are, I'll run her up a tumbril.

9 December 1940

Philadelphia and Bagdad

To judge whether *The Philadelphia Story* is more effective on the screen than it was on Broadway would be to raise a lot of useless issues, and cloud others. I think the thing to say is that it was originally constructed for the strict tightness of a few sets, and that in remaining faithful to it, the picture's producer (Joe Mankiewicz) had to make some of his successes the hollow victory of just overcoming obstacles. Two things have resulted from this: (1) the play has been opened out into natural shifting scenes, if not actually broadened in effect; (2) the story seems to slow up toward the end, where everything was talk anyway.

A great deal depends, for sense and meaning, on Katharine Hepburn as the central character; and there are things in the range of her personality too delicate and subtle for anything but the close, pliant observation of cameras. Here she is, as I did not find her coming through so clearly before, the high-strung but overpetted thoroughbred who must be broken to be released into the good stride of her nature; and here the breaking is a gradual and visible process at once painful, touching, and funny. You know the story and Philadelphia too, and there is little new to say about the work of Miss Hepburn, whose peculiar dry radiance and intelligence, whose metallic and even mannered voice finding its special beauty, are known if not defined, easity imitated but never reproduced in their final style.

But the story is no mere vehicle; it was not written, picturized, or directed as such. Donald Ogden Stewart is credited with an exceptionally bright job of screenplay writing; George Cukor seems to sit with more authority in his director's chair than he has on many another such occasion of reverential transfer; and to have Cary Grant, James Stewart, Roland Young, Ruth Hussey, and John Halliday posted all about in key positions was a happy thing for all. Grant is perfectly gracious to a thankless part, winning sympathy and belief. Stewart keeps to his level of near-perfection as the impulsive, wrong-moving, ordinary guy, and certainly adds another star to his honor chart for the whole sequence of moonlight and four roses. Young Virginia Weidler has a good part and time for herself.

Having expended so much care to such effect, they might have considered also that it is only brooks in poems that go on forever without somebody's beginning to yawn, scratch, and wonder seriously whether it is the suspense or just his underwear that is climbing. They might have cut out the boob move of the writer proposing at the wedding and right before his own fiancée. They could have gone back through the last third and clipped lines of dialogue all along in the interest of general motion. They could, I suppose, have extended the very funny business at the expense of *Timelife* and its prose-bearing oracular baby-talk—though I wonder whether even the keen edge that is present as it is cuts any of the dull butter that must be out there haw-hawing at the performance and trundling up with a ring in its nose to the same newsstand afterward. But there is nothing served in figuring how to do something after someone has very well proved that it's done already because he did it. Though films like *The Philadelphia Story* do little to advance the art of pictures, they may help convince some of the more discerning among cultural slugabeds that when the movies want to turn their hand to anything, they can turn it. Or, what's he got that I haven't got?

The Thief of Bagdad, an extravaganza in full color, fabulous sets, and processed devices of many wonderful kinds, with something like two years of Alexander Korda's staff work behind it in both England and America, is a picture for children of all ages up to six. Beyond six, to all except cases of retarded development and Swahili who are seeing their first magic-lantern show, its numerous defects will very quickly become apparent. For one thing it runs almost two hours on almost fifteen minutes of story—how the good deposed young king is enabled to save the princess from the bad vizier through the offices of a beggar boy, the princess being first lost, then found, then under spell, the young king being first blinded, then lost, then found, then restored in a mass rescue that is managed by the flying-carpet trick. For another thing, it mixes fairy-tale with a clumsy-footed literalism until both imagination and belief are equally hamstrung. And for a final thing, it so mismanages its actors and their lines and scenes that it seems actually to have deserved the absurd and shallow mugging of John Justin as the young king. Sabu is a delightful kid, and Conrad Veidt is what an evil magician might look like if he had to play in summer stock, but that's about all.

For all its slowness, the thing has excitements, some of them a mile high, in the shape of a marvelous Technicolor city, palaces, temples, canyons, and parades; some of them in mechanical wonders, such as the flying horse, the robot dancer, the genie, and the carpet; some of them, and not many of them at that, in action (the standout scene in the latter department is Sabu's adventure in the enormous goddess). There is also the luminous combination of construction and costuming and the camera work of George Perinal and Osmond Borradaile. But the thing that even children will get vaguely restless over is that here are the means and money to make come true some of the world's stored treasures of the imagination; and here, in all its empty splendor, is a movie walking flatfooted among them without any use of the imagination at all.

23 December 1940

The Old-Fashioned Way

Woolchester Cowperthwaite Fields is among the great one-man shows. He has been able to write his name in lights since before the incandescent bulb was invented, and within his own special province he is still the funniest fraud who ever pitched them into the aisles from laughter. He started with a line of chatter and some balls and cigar boxes, which he juggled with a snore of comment and defiance of the laws of gravity, which quickly established him as a character, which character he gradually filled out to the full limits of burlesque and vaudeville and Follies skits. Since then the movies were invented and a form for them gradually developed. But nobody told him about this new invention; nobody was able. He made movie shorts of course, and they were wonderful; he did skits in feature pictures and they were wonderful too. But movies as something different he never heard of. They grew up and he never found out which shell the pea was under, because he couldn't be bothered: that was just a rival pitch. This way, folks, test your skill, etc.

Biographers of The Incomparable, the Marvel of the Aged in Wood, will, I am sure, find it in the record that he was not only a bad boy in school but they had to change the numbers on the rooms to get him from one grade to the other. And that when he was kidnaped from the upper third at the age of fourteen by a passing minstrel show he was already very unruly and set in his ways. That learning was the other fellow's game, and being a born pitch-man he would never be a sucker for it; but that when he played he played for keeps. That when movies came along he took a look at his first camera and said, Why I can lick that, easiest thing in the world, yes—did you note what I did to them at the Palace by any chance? (You did, eh. . . .) And that even after he had got himself blackballed in every producer's office on the Coast, his firm belief was that any wheeze routine could be extended by gags and names like Throttlebottom to what the rest of the world was beginning to know as a modern film comedy.

He still believes it. His new movie was written by him and mostly directed by him and then stolen by him in the principal part. It is called *The Bank Dick* and it shows Fields in the uniform of a detective and all-round doorman for the local bank (he was given the job as a reward, under the severest misapprehension). He gets into trouble as nobody else can, and gets out the same way; he is the harried man of family and emperor of the world, his address and resource are infinite except when approaching a simple flight of steps, he is fastidious to the high point of using his chaser for a finger bowl, he is dignity with a red nose, and courtly, and he has never truckled to any man, which would naturally not include small boys and his own shadow—which if it ever moves back a step he will make like he is going to wring its neck. He is W. C. Fields, which is a considerable sort of thing to be, and purely a joy to watch. But that is all the movie is about.

When the man is funny he is terrific, but in between the high points—and they are as good in stage device as in line and in character conception—what is the audience doing? The story is makeshift, the other characters are stock types, the only pace discernible is in the distance between drinks or the rhythm of the fleeting seconds it takes Fields to size up trouble coming and duck to hell out. The audience is asleep because this was never made as a picture. It is stiff and static and holds no interest outside of W. C. Fields—you don't care what happens to anybody else, you don't care what the outcome; you forget immediately if there was any. Today there are no one-man shows in good pictures, unless the man is a director, and even then he must have a script and people to work with. Today we ask that even such a genius of character act as W. C. Fields be built-in, and that the structure as a whole amount to something, however light or little.

I hoped once that he would someday be content not to run the whole show in his own way, and let someone write him into and direct him through a story infinitely more absorbing than anything he has ever done. It would be the story of one of the world's deathless fools, a snide and bulbous sort of man who knew the top from the bottom, having been on both; a man who could make a comeback and throw it away and make another, a man getting old and very sick, and still coming back to damn all and do it his way, with his legs weak and his face changed to puffy, still talking through his nose like a bugle, and still touching here and there the springs of human laughter. In this dream story you could even call the character Throttlebottom, though we would know who he is; and though we don't know the end, you could make one that would bring home not only what a joy he has been, to the hearts of his countrymen, but how dear. The end would be that he made a picture called *The Bank Dick* in which he was a good part of his old and indomitable self, and which he was fully himself in writing, directing, acting, and atmosphering in the face of almost everything that ever happened in the movies. He was W. C. Fields in it, the trouper of all troupers once again. And the picture opened in Brooklyn.

In a meeting last week the committee on exceptional photoplays, National Board of Review, voted the following pictures the best of the year: *The Grapes of Wrath, The Great Dictator, Of Mice and Men, Our Town, Fantasia, The Long Voyage Home, Foreign Correspondent, The Biscuit Eater, Gone with the Wind, Rebecca*—in that order. I was sorry *The Shop Around the Corner* and *Pinocchio* did not get on, in place of the last two films, which hardly make the good category, let alone the best; and the order wouldn't be exactly mine. But many elaborate duds and empty pageants that will show on other lists were expunged, and *The Grapes of Wrath* was the best picture of this year and many others.

Picking pictures is an exciting and on the whole harmless sport, but I wish there were some means of counteracting the human error inevitable in the tricks memory and mental revision will play: the picture seen twelve months ago will not be remembered so vividly as the picture released last week—which in turn may not be remembered at all twelve months from now. Or the older one may have already become sainted, which is a damned state of affairs, but it happens. Who will now make a list of the ten best of 1930, and who on the other hand will read it?

30 December 1940

1941

From *Hudson's Bay* to the Legion of Decency

Resurrection without Life

Hudson's Bay is another epic from the pages of history that ends up with no epic quality, two or three dates that cannot be controverted, and little enough of interest. This time we are in on the opening up of the Hudson's Bay fur-trading business, or at least the part played in it by the Canuck trapper, hunter, and guide, Radisson. Getting no cooperation from either the French or English colonial governors, he went, so they say, to the King of England, who gave unofficial sanction to the first company. There has been meanwhile some talk of the forest primeval and the rich places created as all know by *le bon Dieu,* some business of paddling and portaging into the wilderness and trading with the Indians. But there has been too little of this and too much moonshining around with the soul of John Sutton, an exiled English lord who is supposed to be finding himself but could very well have done with a flashlight. Naturally he is in love with a bit of fluff back home, so we take him back home, where the lovely has a brother who is a fop but decides to find himself too.

With all this machinery creaking into motion we pretty well lose sight of the noble red man and the noble beaver. The first Hudson's Bay post is established (the film has no time for how they got a ship in through those treacherous reaches to the north) and fabulous wealth is at hand; but by that time the two English fancies are turning out to be more bounders than a pogo meet. Back to England, where everybody almost hangs, but not quite.

Paul Muni is not just the man for the character of Radisson; he has dignity and command but throws most of it away in popping his eyes and chewing on a French accent—as a trapper he would have scared every fur-bearing animal within ten days' march. Laird Cregar as the big-hearted wild man of the piece and Vincent Price as King Charles were the ones who came off best; the other foremost people were apron-strung by a script that missed the story by making up its own. Radisson is called a rogue and haloed like a saint; the Englishman is called a good fellow and made a heel; most of the red men were lost without a cigar store to stand in front of, and the great virgin Northwest took a lacing

329

every time the plot rounded a corner. There is still sweep to parts of it, and some good rough-and-tumble, some nice quirks of humor in character. But if the picture doesn't care about the dramatic material in front of it, why should you?

It never rains but you get all wet. *Santa Fe Trail* had roughly the same idea as *Hudson's Bay* in going back to dramatic incidents in the development of this continent; the same kindergarten history; the same frosting of the romantic-ridiculous. It is probably more unfortunate in having Errol Flynn to be the young West Pointer who rises to military honors largely by appearing in front of the young lady and mooing woo. But it is less a burlesque of men and motives in that it has to do with the story of John Brown, who is not the picture's hero or quite its villain, and who is therefore allowed the indulgence of a little straight talk.

We start with Brown at the height of his early activities in Kansas and follow him—in the occasional lulls between military balls—to Harpers Ferry and the gallows. The main issues are not clear, but the man is shown as a fanatic and the hammer of God, and some sense of the time's confusion comes through. Raymond Massey gives a measure of dignity to the part and finds possibilities in it that others would have missed. But even if the character had been written into dramatic truth at the center of the picture, I'm afraid those India-rubber eyes and that tendency in enunciation to make like spelling out I. J. FOX FINE FURS in a force-3 breeze would still have got him in the end, and John Brown would still lie a-moldering. The film has some good characters in small parts, even though they are mocked by careless usage; and the one convincing near-principal is Van Heflin as the general focus of villainy.

These pictures of early turbulence are actually getting so slipshod that even their wild-west hoorah makes no sense. Thirty sharpshooters at thirty paces fire thirty rounds into Errol Flynn without spoiling a crease in his trousers (can it be they aren't *trying*—good God!); yet any pretty boy fresh from Senior Year can take a snapshot with an 1860 pistol from a galloping horse over rough country and bring down stone dead anything up to a more expensive character actor at 200 yards. Seasoned guerillas, planning a raid in their home country and in numbers of three-to-one, are routed by a charge in column of four and can't think of anything to do but gallop off and tell the wagons carrying their prize munitions to hurry up a little. Every pistol in a high-spot sequence fires thirty without a reload, but in a defeat scene will shoot two wide misses and then go click. Men besieged in an arsenal use revolvers at long range, rifles for close combat and, wading through piles of looted guns and ammunition all the time, get a click out of old Deerslayer and throw the whole gun at somebody as a last resort. The bare tumult of action for its own sake, so thoroughly learned and developed by the movies, is now walked through with a sort of idiot's sublime trust in the long firearm of coincidence.

This attitude of unconcern in the midst of incompetence is not awful merely because someone thinks it so. It is a picture of the zany-roost, funny and saddening. There they have millions of dollars of technical investment ready to go to work, the greatest craftsmen with their equipment, the highest-paid actors and directors and writers, the infinite engineers. It calls for a bucket of blood, so they send out for bona-fide donors; they get the blood by the washtubful just in case, and they bring it in in a paper bag.

If you have already seen *Northwest Mounted Police* around the neighborhood, this is mostly my fault, or your fault, but partly because the program includes the names of Gary Cooper, Akim Tamiroff, and Lynne Overman—which are good names in a firm, proud hand. But these boys, like everybody else in this spill of splendor, don't get more than close enough to throw the *Evening Gazette* against the back door of history. Any more than reference to history's street address would be hard to find here, as the story winds tighter and tighter in snarls of five lovers, Mounted Police, a Texas Ranger, half-breeds.

Cecil B. DeMille made it completely in Technicolor, and that should be enough or too much. If you think this accredited master of the million-dollar pinwheel could direct traffic, let alone add to the hard-won art of pictures by so much as one stretch of the imagination, this two hours of color, killing, kindness, and magnificent country may be your dish. If you have at any time in your life been more impressed by apartment-house doormen than by Preston Foster as inscriber of pioneer history, commander of men, you will hardly go for it. As a whole, the picture is devastating in its proof that even the tough established past can be as barren a land for the story of men and their real work and women, their indomitable brief victory over oblivion, as the pastry futuramas of any H. G. Wells.

6 January 1941

A Hit and a Miss

Night Train is a picture I can urge you to go see. But I cannot urge anybody to see anything that is playing at the Globe Theatre in New York City. The Globe is one of those Broadway fleatraps which hawk at modest prices the pick of the refuse left in the distributor's bin after every theater exhibitor with any kind of decent pitch has had first, second, and third choice on everything from fair to awful. It has naturally built up its own kind of audience, a trampling, hoarse, and hoodlum pack off the garish sidewalks of what ranks today among the first gutters of the world, Broadway and Seventh, from Fortieth to Fifty-second. Recently the Globe has been in luck, having three first-runs in a row that other houses couldn't handle because of commitments, etc., but that people wanted to see. So it ran its prices up as high as 75 cents and took ads. The reviewers were very generous about the picture and mentioned nothing else.

The Globe was suddenly rolling. But it didn't fix its broken-down seats, it didn't open a window, and it couldn't change its habits or the yawp and scuffle of its regulars. You pay first-class prices to fight for a seat and find the picture starting half an hour later than schedule, part of which waiting time is taken up with a throwaway advertising short, and most of the rest of the time is devoted to sweat and suffocation and being walked over. If you can imagine a Turkish bath in a tight seat with all your clothes on, the steam coming from roiling vats of old underwear, you will know what fusty anachronism is ahead of you. It may, of course, be merely naïve to expect that a reviewer's first duty of kindness is to the audience which supports him, but there's your report.

This *Night Train* is another disciple-of-Hitchcock film, when you get a chance to catch it and a breath of air too. It was directed by Carol Reed, whose *Three on a Week End* was also good but quite different—except for the swell atmosphere of both in an English Coney Island. Even granting that a similarity of subject material could explain a similarity of treatment, and that the two priceless vague sporting toffs from *The Lady Vanishes* (Basil Radford and Naunton Wayne) practically suggest their own parts, still you see devices lifted bodily from the magic fat man's workshop. The opening shot, a long swooping truck; the use of music to cover underground activity; the high mechanical stuff used in the escape; Hitchcock's favorite train with guards and counterguards and messages; the sinister play of light allowed by the oculist—even lines, as when the Englishman abroad drops a newspaper in disgust and almost disbelief, "Why, it's all in German!" The film assimilates these things to its own method, and there would be no use mentioning them if they did not point a future lesson: Hitchcock's devices are effective because they arose out of his inventiveness in achieving a purpose. Used again and again as script stunts, they will become merely familiar, as dull coins as Ruth Roland on the railroad tracks, Pearl White and the buzz saw.

But Carol Reed has learned mainly how to keep a story going in a straight and breathless line, and this is the main thing, giving rise to its own devices. A Czech inventor with a steel-hardening process is whisked away from the Nazis to safety in England, from which he is whisked by the Nazis away to Berlin, from which he is just barely whisked again by one of those dashing young chaps who are the backbone of the empire's Intelligence Service, Rex Harrison this time. The inventor has a daughter, Margaret Lockwood, which fact supplies the excuse for some restrained and very fetching romance and also for the extra-intelligent efforts of the Intelligence. (The Nazi admiralty has Paul von Henreid as opposite number.)

As in all countercounterspy plots, there are gaps in the fabric—such as that a man who can fool the entire foreign headquarters hasn't sense to pick a name from the army register; and there are two or three time-jerks that seem more or less like a lazy-man's out—from Prague to England, for example; from London to Berlin; from twenty miles behind (in a fast, equal chase) to just rounding the last bend. But the action is always well in hand for the purpose of the present, and the present is a magic carpet. The movies have now grown and broadened to where the good men realize that in telling even a fast and furious story you have to have people, and that these people should have some real life of their own and a place to live.

Where *Night Train* automatically becomes one of the best of its kind is in its attention to character all through the minor parts, so that there is no burlesque hero or burlesque villain on the one hand, and no mugging extras on the other. And so slight a sequence as that in English Intelligence headquarters has just the delightful air of how even big things happen in a certain everyday way, without Paul Muni, and life goes on. And we know from memoirs that the German admiralty was that way in wartime once, at least. And the dialogue throughout is both sharp and subtle, gay, understated, and perfectly relevant to what goes on with no jingo and no Beast of Berlin (Sidney Gilliat's and Frank Launder's screenplay). It is all a very nice triumph of skill and maturity in films, and thus a pleasure to have.

Comrade X, if you catch it in the 23-35-cent category on an off evening, is cautiously recommended. It is a burlesque at the expense of the Soviet Union and often funny as such, with some neat lines and a whole library of oldtime movie slapstick. There is also Hedy Lamarr to look at—and unfortunately listen to as well, for her voice is brassy and shrill, and in direction King Vidor's idea of funnier is often simply louder. Oscar Homolka and Vladimir Sokoloff in brief parts take the honors, for Clark Gable and Felix Bressart and the rest are victims of the way the story has grafted spoofing onto some very serious spleen (Ben Hecht did a good part of the screenplay, and Hecht has always tasted bile at the thought of the Comrades). So the painful parts of it come when light comedy takes itself in heavy and bad-tempered earnest. The familiar parts are those where laughter was released purely on its own good conduct, and the funniest I think was the blackout of the pallbearers after the shooting, from dignity with a dirge to something like a scuttle, to complete rout with the coffin bouncing and bursting and the assassin hustling off out of it. This one should have the Marx Brothers and no time for amateur politics: with its appreciation of the chase, the breakaway, and the impossible, it would have been a riot as *A Night in the Kremlin.*

13 January 1941

Odd Ends

In the movie version, *Kitty Foyle* is no longer a study of the white-collar girl. Kitty is poor-Irish and has to work for a living, but she would have had about the same important troubles of the heart if she had been anybody or anywhere else with the same heart design. It is now simply a love story, with social complications, inner debates, good times and bad—and an effective enough working-girl background. It is done with such earnestness as to be slow and talky at times, but since the girl in love is Ginger Rogers, the picture has its truth and beauty too.

As the story goes, Kitty has a romance with a young Philadelphia heirloom, finally marries him but finds the family vault too much to take, and goes back to her job in New York, where she has her baby alone. There has been an interne hanging around and there comes eventually the news of the young heir's remarriage (the Hays office isn't so scared of a divorce as it is of there not being any legal need for one). And as all this has been told in flashback, a sort of debate between Kitty and her conscience, we come in the end back to the question we started on, which of two candidates is she going to leave with this midnight? The ex-interne is one; the heir is the other—he has broken away from his second wife without a divorce but for good. I am sure the girl is more in suspense over the heads and tails of it than you will be, for the two men have been written into the story rather carelessly, and life with either of them looks like much less fun than just being Ginger Rogers.

The film, as written by Dalton Trumbo and Donald Ogden Stewart and directed by Sam Wood, runs some fifteen minutes too long and still manages some of its turns too abruptly. But it is good fun when it is on the lighter side and dextrous in handling the difficulties of the inner voice and the flashback technique. It will be remembered most warmly as appropriate setting for Miss Rogers and the many shades of a character she can make come to life. I've said it too many times, I'm afraid, but it's still true that this girl from the dancing pictures has learned a great deal and divines a great deal more, and still stays just as bright and as sweet as she is, and very high among the screen's first young ladies.

As the movie awards are given this way and that at this end of the year, most of the good pictures get at least some attention. But some interesting things come of it too. Where children had a vote, *Knute Rockne—All American* won out over every picture made especially for kiddies. As a movie, this had some football, but not enough, and a whitewash of saintliness. The best thing it had was a fine, sturdy performance by Pat O'Brien that made you happy for him. Anyway, the lesson is plain: there are still heroes on the earth for children to know about and dream of being, and candy boxes about such a little *darling* as the Thief of Bagdad are most probably made for your old lady (my hero was Christy Mathewson, and to me the name Bagdad is still somehow associated with my father's working pants).

One thing that happened in 1940 was Preston Sturges, who made *The Great McGinty* (released last summer) and *Christmas in July,* which is still in the second-run houses. I should have mentioned *Christmas in July* sooner. It is fairly lightweight but it is more fun than many of the year's prouder efforts in comedy; and it is the work of a director who makes hard things seem like doing it the easy way, rather than vice versa. He apparently did most of it himself, taking the idea of a twenty-a-week chump who can't lose his faith in $25,000 radio contests—he is hoaxed by office merry andrews into believing he has made first prize at last—and working that out with complications and coincidences into a little over an hour of comedy. There's a girl of course; there are neighbors and office workers, managers and employers. There are dejection, elation, heartbreak, and happy ending, in that order. The heartbreak part of it is overdone: too much talk, too easy a reliance on those pitfalls of comedy (1) slapstick to cover mush, (2) mush, and more particularly the type that ends in a ringing plea for little men everywhere, the poor underprivileged little mussels in the shoals.

But that is outline merely. What gives the thing its modest warm charm is the easy way a situation appears and recedes, like the countryside from a train. And for all the weakness you may find in it, what you will see if you wish is a man working in pictures, deftly. The opening sequence is dialogue in the strictest sense of two people talking; but the talk is the good thing of common coin shined up and found anew like a lucky penny; the exposition needs no wheelchair; the play of feeling is gauged and fitted into motion like the escapement of a watch. And Dick Powell is the young man, the hopeful chump in love without a hope chest, and he does not bounce up and down once. Right there at the start of a picture you have it: anyone who can coax, trick, or coerce Dick Powell into being a nice enough and ordinary guy completely free of a sandwich board saying KICK ME must be a man who can work with materials like a cabinetmaker, knowing both what it is and what it should be when finished. A director, in short.

It is of course a very bothersome thing that you can't see Direction in pictures like Dr. Stokowski on the podium ("the smith a mighty man is he with arms like rubber bands"); and that most of the directors who get known by way of the theater marquees are to the craftsmanship of telling a story with people and cameras what the writings of Walter B. Pitkin are to English prose style. But the fact is it not only goes on, it is the most important thing in pictures.

This is probably old stuff to many who go to films for pleasure, but I can't tell about that because they are obviously not the species of bird to be heard in all the chatter of reviewing, reviling, resurrecting-revering, or merely retailing films constantly and everywhere, like rain. The general public becomes articulate only at the box office, but I've reason to believe that among these mute millions you'll find a good lacing of people who know a movie from a milkshake. And it is to them that the good film writers and directors must look, not for the fame, which is commercially calculable, or for the money, which is certainly not cornflakes, but for the appreciation of a job well done. They must be there, though doing the thing for them or speaking of it to them must often seem like talking with your head down a rain barrel.

20 January 1941

Methods of Madness

Go West is a picture full of Marx Brothers in their best style; and it is also something of a revolution, or seems like one in these times, when comedy has gone pretty much to verbal play, plot development, meaning even. This is buffoonery at the expense of all Winnings of the West (you could not call it satire, they're having too much terrifying fun from one minute to the next to be bothered with a consistent edge). Harpo and Chico go out to prospect for gold; Groucho goes out to prospect. They all get involved in a bad-man plot to swindle the Forty-niner and his daughter out of Death Gulch, soon to be railroad right of way, and John Carroll as a Clark Gable young man is involved with the girl, and everybody takes part in a breakdown race to get the deed back to the railroad and close the deal.

Through this the gags run three to the minute, naturally, and it is impossible that you have heard all of them before ("You love your brother, don't you?"–"No, but I got used to him," and "Send for a St. Bernard, I'm snowbound," have been stolen even by Lou Holtz, but there are plenty with the mint-marks left). Harpo as usual plays the harp, this time with a nice wrinkle; Chico plays the piano, as usual but no wrinkle; Groucho plays cigar and obliges in one ensemble number with some blue riffs that must have come from the heart, and in another number does a very hot Black Bottom take-out, with his usual crouch. And of course all the boys run as usual straight up every girl they meet and they meet a lot.

Many things are as before, but in general, here for the first time in years is a picture that goes right back to Keystone, not just because everything is blowing up or breaking down, as God knows it seems to be, but because it was made with an infectious crazy exuberance and a constant flow of invention, and it is done in motion. This isn't so true of the first part, which is more in the hard-working funny-hat manner, but by the time the brothers start to take the Crystal Palace saloon apart, there are always more things happening than you can keep track of. (In a way this is all to the good: some of them are not funny.) The scene where Groucho keeps toasting the flower of Southern womanhood (they're all sisters but he has to toast three separate states: mother lived in a trailer) to cover up the safe-blowing operations in the next room, and presently everybody is either drunk or coming in through several doors with a gun, is imbecility in just the proper key. The musical on-the-trail number that follows is just enough offhand and off-key and weirdly instrumented to take the curse off a musical number; the next sequence at the Indian village starts the laughter in earnest (John Collier will presumably request an injunction); and the final all-in sequence of the race with the train achieves the perfect spontaneous world of madmen. Here individuals are lost in the furioso of the main action with its constant multiplication of gag and device, its speed and explosion balanced by the almost fairyland quality of the train suddenly running after itself in a circle, accompanied by merry-go-round music and the business of catching the brass ring in the nose of the farm bull. This is comedy, for once, with no time for S. N. Behrman; and I shake its hand.

Trail of the Vigilantes is something like *Go West* in having action and also taking sly cuts at the whole action-picture tradition. But it is no such merry shambles as the other and it falls short of satire—in the same way but even shorter. Its failure is one of indecision over what Western wheeze to kid and what to milk for all it's worth in story interest; and instead of Marx Brothers, in at least two main characters it has people. The story is one of a tenderfoot but competent federal agent being sent out where a vigilante ring has been turned into a racket (the word, like the phrase Associated Farmers, is contemporary; the custom is perennial). He is to see what goes, and being Franchot Tone he does, to the mortification of Warren William and the best interests of such honest folk as the father of the farmer's daughter. He has the assistance of Broderick Crawford, who is a solid man to have around, and the open-comedy team of Mischa Auer and Andy Devine. There is a lot of action, hell on horseback, and quite a lot of outdoors sometimes nobly brought up in the cameras. There is everything the director (Allan Dwan) needed, whichever way he took it.

But he made it like the word whichever, somehow without belief either way. The effect is given of someone playing a fairly serious straight part but occasionally introducing cracks in asides, as if to cover up and say "I could be better things." As light amusement it does all right, but it is still amusement in confusion.

Although it isn't usually the case that a poor movie provides enough innocent fun to be worth sitting through to the end, I think this can be said of *Victory,* a picture now on display. It has a Conrad setting and characters at least superficially interesting, and the good performance in villainy of Jerome Cowan and Cedric Hardwicke. There isn't much motion to it, though there is always at its back that mine of fascination, the Conrad East and the curiosties of sin. But as adapted by John Balderston and directed by John Cromwell, it is so jerrybuilt in both detail and general management that it needs something more than its own story to be bearable. And I think you will find this redeeming delight in watching the hollow dramatics of Fredric March and Betty Field, increasingly front and center as the film progresses. Apparently someone played a joke on Mr. March by tipping him off that Heyst was really meant to be a sleepwalker; but however it was managed, there is achieved a combination of amateur theatricals and earnest emptiness of motive and motion that will throw a blanket of reminiscent affection around this solemn, innocent, and exotic buffoonery.

Third Finger, Left Hand is something I forgot to mention at the time of release, and it is hardly memorable. But there are some funny things in it, and an especially funny ending on a train, and if you have not got completely weary of the type of comedy it is, it will do for an off night. The type is the MGM spoof and glitter story of love fighting itself off through curious complications and then fighting itself right back in again. The girl wears a wedding ring to protect her job and other things, and when Melvyn Douglas finds the husband is a myth he is first put out and then the husband himself, and Myrna Loy is the editor of a magazine.

27 January 1941

Handsome Is . . .

Since *High Sierra* seems to meet with some difference of critical opinion, I must caution you that all expressions of praise here are purely coincidental and not to be confused with any living persons. It has faults; but it is fine and exciting and it is a moving picture. It is about a gangster—which, far from putting it in any easy category, is one of the things that make it go so well. The inevitable outcome of the profession of shooting your way places is getting shot yourself, and in this there is an almost perfect nemesis pattern whose state of preservation in movie stories is probably the only gift to pictures conferred by the Decency Code. So when Humphrey Bogart is sprung from a life sentence here in order to take charge of a big underworld project, you need not fear the ending will find him with a radio contract, a cottage, and kids. To keep up with himself as an outlaw from the whole world though living in it, he must go faster and faster toward an end that is precise and inescapable and dramatically right.

Mr. Bogart is a very cool number at his job, but you will not need a recounting of the plot. It is enough that this is one of the rare times a good action story has had naturally within it some of the elements of the fates and the furies which are the material of tragedy, in which death can be neither a bluebird nor a mere pool of blood. Of course the pantywaist moralists will be saying that we are glorifying the gangster again, which will of course be as true a statement of this instance as it would be of whole lashings of the world's art, with its romantic brigands, highwaymen, pirates, dictators, Napoleons, vigilantes, cops and robbers generally. And as little to any purpose.

But no picture may live by its point or civic purpose alone, and this is a picture that lives on the screen. In the middle of it is Humphrey Bogart, whose conception and rock-bound maintenance of the hard-handed, graying, and bitter ex-con is not only one of the finest projections of character in any story of men in action, but the whole vertebrate structure of this one. A good part of the telling time is given to his human side and—particularly in the case of the crippled girl he can help but not marry—is slugged a little too hard. But this is a logical part of his life, and it is his life we must be concerned with. He was not betrayed by the spare few he helped and trusted, and it is absurd to suppose that a man who makes his living with an unlicensed gun may not like dogs or need women.

In the end it is Bogart who makes it true anyway, for there is not one minute in this picture when the intensity of his presence is not felt, or when he is false or foolish. He is a man you are gradually allowed to hear tick and would not monkey with, a man you feel must be obeyed instinctively, and remembered. There are of course the others—good character actors, down to the dog and up to the rather difficult and well done part of Ida Lupino; writing and direction gauged to the stern demands of the true movie (John Huston, W. R. Burnett, Raoul Walsh); and a setting that is as much a tribute to the original conception as to the eloquent, flexible camera setups of Tony Gaudio, with their contained action and high Sierras too.

Except for the tire-patch quality of the crippled-girl theme, and a wet three minutes of putting hearts through the wringer at the end, this is what I should call a film worth exposing negative for, and comes almost as a valedictory, in both dialogue interpolations and its position in a cycle. As I say, it's a divided-response business and perhaps will take more imagination, awe, and pity than you are willing to spare. But like it or not, I'll be damned if you leave before the end or go to sleep; and in the way of movies, that's what I'm talking about.

Word has got around that *Tall, Dark and Handsome* is considerable of a lark, and maybe it is. The idea I got from reading about it is that it kids the killer legend, but this must have been two other pictures, because the only leg they pull on the actual screen here is their own.

It is made as comedy, so much is true. On one side of a serious gang war there is a mob-leader whose erasure of those who disagree with him has made him the terror of the underworld, or so it seems until he falls in love. In love, he schemes to present himself to the pigeon of his choice as a banker and the doting father of children, but ixnay see, because in walks the opposition mob-leader, who is a man not out for laughs, and the truth is out before the girl's own eyes and how could you I hate you oh.

But the bad man being Cesar Romero she can't quite help feeling something ("If only he wasn't a, a *killer!*"). Well, he gets her a job singing in a spot of his and she is of course sensational. But she can't still get over that *killer*. So how is everything squared? Why it comes out by chance that he is the kindest man in the world and has never killed anybody in his life; his supposed victims are kept in a comfortable private jail in the basement while he provides for their bereaved families—he wouldn't hurt a fly. This is the big twist of the picture and not a bad idea, but even if you hadn't seen the earnest straight way they play it you would guess that their eye was not so much on comedy as the Hays office.

There is comedy in the picture, all right: some bright lines and Milton Berle, who was certainly responsible for some of them, and a nice collection of humorous and tender-hearted gorillas, and also a youngster who is reputed to make the Dead End kids look like Freddie Bartholomew—though here again is an example of debasement through typing, for the little man works so hard along the line laid out for him that he is just Peck's Bad Boy with a paint job. This is pretty much fringe, however. Action is one of the central things, and there is a little of it at the end, when the opposition mob-leader who is *not* kind to his mother tries to move in on the girl and erase practically the whole blackboard, but goes to a nasty jail instead.

The other central thing is romance, and gets most of the play. How many old-hat tricks can you remember offhand in the story of the rough diamond and his lovely but timid lovey? All here, all played for straight belief. They mean it, or they try to mean it, and it is just hollow enough and ham enough to be essentially distasteful. Not just bad, you understand—for in writing and direction, casting and incidental invention, it is a thin cut above the awful average—but distasteful, like piety with a stale breath. I know critics are tried and tired men, but there needs to be some law that the fine, complete English word "hilarious" should be limited, like the carrying of a pistol, to those who can prove they both need and can use it.

10 February 1941

They Still Go West

I suppose now that Western Union has been taken care of in a film called *Western Union*, the next turn of the epics-of-enterprise list should definitely be set for Sears, Roebuck, which has certainly waited long enough. (Lydia E. Pinkham could not get past the Hays office these days, and what could you do with the Smith Brothers anyway? Just a couple of beards.) So we start when a young Princeton man named Chuck Sears, distinctly scion, dudes it out into frontier territory where they are trying to discover Chicago ahead of the Indians. At the last outpost in the Last Looks Cabaret, he runs afoul of Dusty Roebuck, who is a shooting spitting man for fair, and the most feared and valuable scout in the region through being able to tie five kinds of knot in the moss on the northeast side of a tree. They fight.

A no-decision battle, of course, but it proves that under his washing up before supper every night, the tenderfoot has a heart of gold and ties the knots in his own shoelaces. They leave the Last Looks arm in arm, or probably would have left it, except the cashier strikes them both at once, though in two separate camera takes. Her name is Femail Order and it quickly turns out that her old man owns the joint and the town and part of the United States Senate, in which it is the stated purpose of his life to discover enough of Chicago so that the Indians can be sent back where they're heading for and this union shall not perish from E. Pluribus.

So for the first third of the picture, the boys cook up elaborate devices by which they shall appear simultaneously from different directions in the same place, which is the icebox of the Senator's mansion, where they can't get at the girl because of their innate good breeding and the Senator, who is always there himself, drawing maps of Lake Michigan with a cold leg of turkey in a way that carries them beyond themselves in spite of themselves.

Into this there should be cut several humorous shots of a catalogue copy-reader whose big laugh line is that he cannot stand Chicago because it makes him ill, and whose fear of Indians is so real he still can't buy a paper at a cigar store, and whose name is Montgomery Ward (for laughs). There will be a bad man too, and there will be an elderly kind counselor who tries to impress on these hotheads the advantage of the instalment plan, which will need a credit department but knock them over for something like 12 percent in the end.

That's all. The girl has an idea that the farflung farmer who buys overalls at $2.98 will pounce like a tiger on the catalogue $2.84 special and not notice the ".17 ea." for the two straps as extra items, and as for the $3.02 de-luxe offer "with button on fly," oh my. So knowing they could not win her until one or the other had counted all forty-eight states, they set out with hearts of flint and an arrow full of quivers and land up somewhere around Cape Girardeau, which is 150 miles down the heap big river from St. Louis but near enough, because the

Chicago boat stops there every Sunday. They are about to, as they say, take Chicago for a loop when one of them stumbles forward to the ground with a warwhoop in his back, which gives the other a chance to swear vengeance and the house-band a chance to come in with a funeral march but a different twist, for through the last chords come the clank-clank of a frontier-picture banjo and a deep steamboat hoot to indicate that the gal was following on the next scheduled arrival, to join with whatever was left and start an institution, preferably mail-order. So the house is established with the name of the valiant dead partner as the other half of the title and the copy-reader running up a catalogue from Art-gum to X-ray, with a two-page color layout for Bells, Wedding and very little time for Suits, Masquerade, Indian.

Western Union does about that with the dramatic material of stringing its wires through Indian territory, from Omaha to Salt Lake City, with Randolph Scott, Robert Young, and Barton McLane as principals, with Virginia Gilmore for love and Slim Summerville for humor, and with others. There is no trace of any coordinating hand in directing, though the fine name of Fritz Lang appears in the credit titles; there is some good Indian warfare and there is some fine camera appreciation of this great countryside (until Technicolor arrives either at a set formalization or at the true thing it is trying to paint, it will do little for the unbelievable drama of pictures but suggest Fanny Farmer). The actual business of surveying and setting up poles, of insulators, wire splicing, keys and batteries, is strained carefully out of the romance and humor and plottery of the story—which reduces itself to the same old guff largely because none connected with it thought of it as anything else. There are wagon-training and Indian-shooting enough to keep your eyes occupied, also one of the most terrific bonfires and a gun battle at the end. It is impossible to know what clichés the director may have prevented, but it is enough and too much to see those he left in solemnly acted out before you. As I started to say, this ancient circus has about as much to do with Western Union as it has with R. H. Macy, and you can have either.

In the foreign department, we have the French original of what Hollywood called *Algiers,* and made a nice action picture out of. Hollywood was probably wise in buying up and holding off *Pépé le Moko,* because the two are so close in script and background that whichever came first would take the edge off the other. (It is clear now that *Algiers* was made from the other even to camera angles.) You will enjoy the French one, I think, for Jean Gabin as Pépé, for the chief of native inspectors, and for the many others. I can't tell now whether the action is a little sluggish or only seems so through familiarity, but the effect is the same—a certain lack of intensity by comparison. But the faulty engineering and clipped jargon will serve to improve your ignorance of French, and the story is one of the true naturals for pictures; and when it comes around it will probably be the best thing to see that week.

17 February 1941

Not All to the Good

I wish Alfred Hitchcock would stick to doing the thing he does better than anybody in the world. *Mr. and Mrs. Smith,* the new Hitchcock film, is American farce comedy and made for nothing but laughs. When comedy was incidental to his story, Hitchcock did well enough with it always; but this time he goes heavy on us, he tries very hard and throws things about. The laughs will be there for some, though they are about as subtle as Moxie billboards, and I doubt that in general your interest or amusement will last as long as the picture.

The story is arch enough to be annoying. You can't have people trying to sleep together unless they are married, so there has to be a wrinkle, and in this case the wrinkle is that Carole Lombard and Robert Montgomery find that the marriage they have been enjoying moderately is void through a legal technicality. Well the boy fools around about that and the girl locks him out, how could he want to do anything so perfectly *nasty,* and the balance of the picture is taken up with the boy trying to get back in, first by bullying, then by pleading, then by stealth. Gene Raymond—in a metamorphosis of both make-up and personality that makes him even agreeable—starts out as his loyal partner but is soon trying to beat his time as the wedge of a triangle, and that must be taken care of too. There are incidental characters. But the emphasis is steadily on the main business, which is not only too loud but faintly repugnant in its occasional leer and innuendo. To be spicy today, Hollywood has to suggest the familiar spectacle of the offensive little model boy of the neighborhood, looking at French postcards behind the barn.

The trouble with *Mr. and Mrs. Smith* is central, and I'm afraid that in all such artificial obstacle races they're licked before they start. The cast is good; at times and in flashes brilliant. There are several funny situations that grow naturally, for instance Mr. Raymond as the perfect gentleman and woefully tight, Charles Halton as the apologetic bringer of bad tidings, Jack Carson in the Turkish bath, the shocking of the home folks, etc. If, like some 50 percent of the ladies in the movie audience, you could manage only to glance at the screen from time to time while keeping up the more important business of talking about something else, I suppose you could miss most of the plot and have some patches of fun as well.

Personal Column is another of the hundred and one absolutely last films to be made in France, as France. Its most noteworthy point is that in it Maurice Chevalier gets tied up in a murder plot, and in the latter stretches plays a straight part—quite nicely too (one of his songs is pretty awful, but the number about "Il pleurait" is terrific). There's a pretty gal in it, Marie Dea, who is employed by the police to answer the newspaper ads a sexual assassin is using to get ladies for his purposes. Some of the business is exciting at times, and frequently it is funny in an open, easy way, well removed from the not-quite-nice-Nellyism of *Mr. and*

Mrs. Smith. But as a whole it is choppy, confused, and low-pressure; and you could only think it was made like a movie if you had never seen one.

Two-on-the-Same-Screen Department. – As to the double bill leading off with *Flight Command,* you had better arrange to see the second feature first. It is *Haunted Honeymoon,* made unpretentiously but neatly from one of the better Dorothy Sayers mysteries, and involving Robert Montgomery and Constance Cummings as a honeymoon couple who have (respectively) sworn off the detection of and writing about crime. So naturally they run smack into a murder, and then get naturally into harness to solve the same old insoluble in a casual, easy manner. The mood of the thing is rather gay and murder is little more than the absorption of fitting together a well-devised puzzle, and on the whole you get the feeling that they are better off breaking in a marriage in this fashion and with this supporting cast than they would be playing *qu'est-ce que tu as que je n'en ai pas.* This one is all right.

Flight Command is the old service story, but at its worst. The regulars don't like the new pilot because he is a rookie, not because he is Robert Taylor, and won't even *speak* to him except insults; and on top of that he is suspected of playing twosy with the Old Man's wife—which, being Robert Taylor, he wouldn't ever. Then presently he is a hero, but after two hours, and now they are all buddies and thick as molasses down in good old Coca Sola with its good old distance from where any of us are sitting. For this one you may wish to stay and watch the really fine sequences establishing the whole dangerous and exciting business of plane maneuver, one of the best of which has a modern carrier sending her roaring brood of chicks off into the wind and away in formation. You may, but it's your own risk.

3 March 1941

Black-and-White Trash

The movie made of *Tobacco Road* and called *Tobacco Road* is not only without edge or purpose, but in several departments is not very well made as a picture. And that is considering it for what it is, not for what someone expected, or predetermined it ought to be, or thought he spied with a finicking eye for similarity and difference. Its story is about a shiftless but lovable old cuss who is about to be thrown off his run-down land by bank foreclosure. Of his enormous family only the youngest boy and girl are left around the house, and when the young lout takes the eye of a greenly widowed evangelist with insurance money enough to bribe him into marriage with a new car, the old sinner sees a way to get his fingers on the rent money. He tries to steal the car and fails, and he and his sad, worn wife are about to go to the poor farm when in steps little Honor Bright, the neighborhood planter's son, with the necessary. End of picture.

The central idea is that the old man loves the land he was born on, though he never scratches it enough to stop an itch; and any further attempt to show the decay of the South and the degenerating effect of submarginal living is blotted out in the byplay necessary to keep such a simple, ancient plot creaking along. There are folky jokes and situations, there is a pretty terrible auto horn, and people occasionally give out on a hymn. The story does move in the sense that one thing happens after another, but the plain fact of the matter is that the only lively thing about the picture is in the purely technical values: good sets effectively lighted, or half-lighted; a triumph in the choice of location; and the fine camera work of Arthur Miller.

The acting is weak when it isn't downright bad, as in the insufferably noisy clowning of William Tracy and the hollow cry-babyism of Ward Bond. Charles Grapewin does a competent "character" part, but as Jeeter Lester he is merely an artful dodger for the minstrel-show time. Marjorie Rambeau, Gene Tierney, and Elizabeth Patterson don't have much to do but don't seem to guess how well off they are; and the rest are merely types. This brings up the strangest thing of all, which is that John Ford should have taken on the job of directing such an idle brummagem, and having taken it on, should allow such vagaries in casting and such sniffling and capering and general hamfat on his own set. The difference between John Ford's bad pictures and his good pictures is so wide that you have to assume he neither knows actors nor how to hold them down, and that he is never sure whether he is working on a good story or not. For all the firm guiding hand that is evident here, about all he did for *Tobacco Road* as a movie fiction was to say "Cut," which is of course the word that is always left out of the finished picture.

Possibly this was a shade above such semi-pleasant futilities as *Banjo on My Knee,* but I wouldn't know. Its conditions are just real enough and implicitly tragic enough to make burlesque of them offensive; while on the other hand it deliberately goes out to milk the tears of your compassion only to whip around behind every other minute and clout you on the backside with a slapstick. So the general effect is one of increasing indignation at the way it makes fools of its people and uses misery for irresponsible merriment. It isn't that tragedy and humor may not exist side by side, but that your respect for each must be forfeited when both are set at each other's throats in some meaningless, perpetual fury of Punch and Judy.

Strawberry Blonde could never have been a thoroughly sound picture because of a pale and self-defeating story. But it could have been a far better thing than it is—in fact it should have been, for it has Jim Cagney in it and some of those isolated situations, either of humor or of tenderness, which can happen to any story and can be lovely. It has some nostalgia to play around with, the chance for good fast talk, and a few gadgets, as for example the correspondence-school dentist, the neighborhood band. But with the heavy slugging in script of Julius and Philip Epstein, with the direction of Raoul Walsh, it never had a chance.

For all the mugging, word chewing, stiff posing, and flouncing that go on, you would think they were trying to register this hatful of threadbare emotions in a camera set up across the river. The combined technical staff seems to have conspired in all this, for reel after reel puts the action against some of the most fraudulent, ill-matched background work since the Dunning process was first tried out in somebody's cellar; they could have done half of it better against a set of painted flats—except that even the simple lighting of faces is a flickery business. What they have succeeded in without trying is to create the weird illusion, in technical and emotional effect, of a play from the eighties run off in its entirety before the camera of the Astoria twenties.

As I said, the story deserves no better, though. The son of the neighborhood's drunk is always studying dentistry and always being kicked around by the neighborhood flash boy, in the matter of money and of girls. Continue with this for a while, with stop-offs for barbershop quartets, black eyes, buggy rides, feminism, and other forms of humor. Then the fancy promoter runs off with the girl, and the next we hear of him he is offering his struggling pal (now married to Another) a marvelous job. This turns out to be a front job for crooked contracting, and when the scandal breaks our hero takes a five-year rap. Having done his full time, Moe the Molar hangs out a shingle in neighborhood after neighborhood with no success until—well guess. Anyway his revenge against the great betrayer consists in an extraction without gas, because he has seen in a flash that success has not made the big man happy, whereas he himself has found happiness—though what he is going to feed it on we do not see before the fade-out.

My point is only that there were at least things that could have been done along the way, and that Cagney does not deserve such treatment whether the story does or not. He is the only point of light in it, and even manages to complete one of his tragic scenes before being hit in the ear again with a bucket of clams (the one after he comes out of prison, hard of face in those poor clothes, and bitter). But light should have some reflection around it, and while George Tobias helps throughout and Miss de Havilland is quite fetching on her first date (and then fetches the same way all through) he might as well be shining inside some horse-drawn ambulance hung with black felt.

10 March 1941

Who Was That Lady . . .?

They are still asking how he does it, for *The Lady Eve* is his third picture in seven months, and one after the other they have been a delight both to exhibitors and to sit through. Part of the answer is that Preston Sturges is a hardworking man with a sense of humor. Another part is that he seems to possess a hex on actors, so that he can use even Dick Powell and Barbara Stanwyck as principals and walk out of the cage unscratched. But most of it is that he has found movies, the rolling camera as a sensitive medium of expression, the vast and frightening range of technical properties as instruments to be used with a craftsman's economy and purpose.

The purpose never amounts to much, or it amounts to a great deal, according to whether you go to the theater to be stern with it or as you read a book, for enjoyment. Mr. Sturges picks his own subjects, writes his own screenplay, and puts on his own show. Thus far his attention has concentrated on the light comedy of modern life, which is a good place to keep it I will be bound; and thus *The Lady Eve* is precisely as inconsequential as any breath of air in muggy weather. It is the story about the lady card-sharper who falls in love with her victim, enlivened by certain complications, such as the variously conflicting interests of Charles Coburn and Eugene Pallette as fathers, Eric Blore, William Demarest, and Melville Cooper, and others. It starts on a boat, gets off halfway through, has itself a houseparty and a honeymoon, and ends on a boat. That is about all except the social message to Our Readers, which is that love is sometimes more damn trouble than measles.

Sturges is already being compared to Capra and Clair, but this is not fair to them. They were masters in film comedy, and they not only set a pace but made it so fast that their names are still the obvious and only ones for loose-mouth comparison. They saw not only the possibilities but the actual achievement in film history of the Mack Sennett type of visual comedy; they had the sense of its spontaneity within themselves; and they came at a time when the crude distortions necessary to the early silents were being refined and the film in general was becoming personalized. They can no more be bracketed than French and Los Angelese, but they were the two outstanding who adapted the old standbys of explosive surprise, camera mobility, and chase to the new intimacy of actual people. And in their four or five best pictures each, they worked always with a delicate sense of when enough was enough. They knew better than anybody how to use funny happenings in a chain like firecrackers, so that one set off another; but they never subscribed to the belief that if a thing is done once and gets a laugh, it will get six more laughs if you do it six times over.

Preston Sturges has an appreciation of slapstick and a feeling for people as they are to be found in life. But he has not yet the discipline to get the good out of a thing and then leave it alone—*vide* the full-length falls of Henry Fonda or the supposed Briticisms of Barbara Stanwyck. The story of *The Lady Eve* is not an original and doesn't need to be, but even spoofing has its logic, and no story can be done justice by an ending that fits it like a Montgomery Ward toupée. The director took on the job of holding Eric Blore down and making a reasonable character out of him, and he did it; he took on the job of animating Barbara Stanwyck, and he succeeded at that. But he tried too much. You see, we are supposed to believe that everybody in the story believes for one entire sequence that Miss Stanwyck resembles Miss Stanwyck but is really an English lady instead. We don't, and as belief begins to fade Miss Stanwyck works harder, and finally what could only have been done by the subtle and personal arts of good mimicry and character projection is abandoned in favor of what is merely raucous.

But such minor flaws and overreachings would not be worth mention in most films, and if you are conscious of them here it is because of the general high level, the easy play of interest, natural comedy, sentiment; the unobtrusive but vital devising of little things, like the contrast of the absurd tender-whistle with the liner's answer, the symbol of rage and frustration as the camera goes from each new disillusionment in Room B, Car 69, to the speed and roar of the engine up front, etc. The lines are what people might say, and in spite of comedy's formalization, most of the things are what people might do. Some of it is slapstick; a little of it is impossible the wrong way; but in general its pleasures come from the characters as found—you could not expect anything different to happen if Henry Fonda were a rich young naturalist and Charles Coburn a gambler with short-wave fingers, and if—as such—they ever should happen to meet. And by whatever means, this Preston Sturges has wrapped you up another package that is neither very big nor very flashy, but the best fun in months.

All you need to know about *Cheers for Miss Bishop* is that it is what you probably feared. *Goodbye, Mr. Chips* was a gentle weep over the honorable senility of a schoolmaster with his lifetime of service behind him, and it was box-office wildfire. So now they'll see if it can be done all over again with a schoolmarm. We start out with a girl no older than Martha Scott at her dewiest, inspired to the ideal of education by the president's address at her commencement, and we go episode by episode through the changing years of her teaching at the university, her problems and heartbreaks and mute heroism, until time and the make-up department have weathered her into something like Ouspenskaya at her chewiest. Any such thing must run off like those old Biblical panoramas on rollers, and *Miss Bishop* (I keep wanting to retitle it *Three Near Beers for Miss Hiccup*) is a smoother job of coping with the endless string of incidents that *Mr. Chips*. The girl has two love affairs that end in no-decision, and she has faithful friends that enliven the action at different times by showing up at the house for a dish of fudge.

The only surprising thing about it is that so many standard devices for squeezing a tear can be crowded into the same few hours—I forget the running time, but attendance from beginning to end left me with the impression of a four-and-a-half-day bivouac. They set out to do a thing and they have done it exactly to taste, and for all I know there may even be inspiration in it for those who will learn respect for the higher education from the fact that a brave little wisp of a girl carries on though her heart is breaking and puts her class in Freshman English through its stern paces of "What is a transitive verb?" and "Give the principal parts of the verb 'strike.' "

17 March 1941

Democracy at the Box Office

Though Frank Capra is still right in the formula he has been holding to for five years now, *Meet John Doe* is at least a promise that he may be coming back to pictures. It is almost a point-for-point replica of *Mr. Smith Goes to Washington,* but some of the old felicity is there again and there are actually comedy sequences in it. I am not holding out too much hope, for today there is nothing Americans so like to be told from the screen as that they are Americans. So why should anybody with a formula and a credit line like skywriting bother with making a swell simple movie as his "production for 1941"?

The John Doe of the story is Capra's familiar and favorite American type, the easy shambling young man, shrewd and confused, rugged, a lovable innocent but don't tread on him—the uncommon common man, in short, with a heart of gold and a limestone fist, and integrity in long fibers. Eyewash, of course, but there is something in it, for a national hero is some sort of national index after all, and it is not so much how miserably short we fall of being an ideal as what ideal we choose to dream of. Anyhow, this young man, a bush-league baseball player with a glass arm, is caught up in a freak stunt for tabloid circulation-building which turns out to be dynamite both ways. As J. Doe, he is supposed to be a social reformer with a deadline for a suicide of protest; as a national news personality, he becomes so arresting and eloquent in his plea for love and understanding—the Sermon on the Mount with a drawl—that miracles are passed and John Doe clubs are formed, and it is presently worth someone's while to own him as political property. It started as fraud but eventually led to the young man's believing his own spiel and wrecking the sinister plans when he found out their anti-democratic aim. Love was a part of it, of course, and there are various clever wrinkles; but the outline is enough.

The fascination of gossip and the awe of prestige make it impossible that the question of what makes a picture should ever have a chance against the question of who. But while the names of Robert Riskin and Frank Capra are behind the production and writing and direction of *John Doe,* I think we can see even behind the names to what is under our noses. The message is that since it is all the little men who truly make the big world, they should live together and hang together, doing away with hate and suspicion and bad-neighborliness. Fine. Ringing. Of course there are present among us oppression and injustice and scorn for all unsung heroes whose names are Moe Million. Too bad; an outrage; something should be done. So the lift of the story comes in the doing, in the rallying to a new simple faith, as people and as Americans, through homely things but as a mighty army under the flag. In this story the powers of darkness are able to check the advance, but the victory in defeat is that there will be advance again.

I have no doubt the authors of such theses believe in them, just as it is easy for a song-writer to believe that God should bless America after he has glanced over the recent sheet-music sales. But sifted in with any such half-thought-out hoorah must be the true motivating conviction that the box office is out there and will be terrific. And that is where the thing begins to crack like Parson Weems's Liberty Bell, for in art there is a certain terrible exaction upon those who would carry their show by arousing people to believe, and it is that any such show must be made out of belief, in good faith and pure earnest, in the whole of belief itself. This rhetoric and mortising of sure-fire device of a success today is its sure betrayal by tomorrow—the flag in a game of charades, the mock prayer at a picnic.

As a picture, it does well the things which have proved highlights before: the tender concern over the little fellers with great faith; the underdog finally getting on his hind legs to tell them off; the regeneration of even a hard-boiled newspaper gal; the final blow-off scene with the nation as audience. But it talks too much to no purpose and in the same spot. The musical score is both arch and heavy (the most undeveloped department in all Hollywood anyway). And one of the saddest things is to find Capra so preoccupied with getting over a message of holy-hokum that he lets in half a dozen of the worst montage transitions— mumming faces, headlines, wheels and whorls—that have been seen in a major effort since the trick first turned stale.

Whether this much of hollowness and prefabrication will spoil the picture for you, I wouldn't know. There are things in it to see. The business of promoting a thesis has distracted Frank Capra's attention from much that he was superb at doing, and he still skips over many of the little fitted pieces which make a story inevitable. But now and then he lingers and you can see the hand of the loving workman bringing out the fine grain—as in the direction of the little crowd around the local mayor when Joe Doe is apprehended, with its naturalness and light spontaneous humor: as in the edge of satire in the management of the radio broadcast; as in the bringing out of homely humorous quirks in John Doe himself; and as always in the timing of a line, its cause and effect, so that it comes out with just force and clarity among the shifting images. But Capra and Riskin now seem content to let good actors fill out a stock part and stop at that, so Edward Arnold, Walter Brennan, Gene Lockhart, J. Farrell McDonald, and several others have nothing more incisive to do than they would in any B picture. Barbara Stanwyck has always needed managing, and apparently got it here, though her idea of a passion is still that it is something to tear to firecrackers. But one man the director did give a chance to and smooth the way for, and that is James Gleason, who made more of this chance than there was in the lines and their meaning. The one scene which came through all these streamlined Fourth of July exercises with true sincerity and eloquence was Gleason's drunken talk in the bar, the one that starts, "I like you, you're gentle. Take me, I've always been hard. Hard. Don't like hard people, you hear?" It was just talk, with business, but he made it his, and it will remain one of the magnificent scenes in pictures.

That leaves only the star, who is so much an American John Doe type you could never say whether he was cast in a part or vice versa—Gary Cooper. It is he who has the human dignity which this two hours of talk is talking about, and talking about; and it seems impossible for him to be quite foolish even in the midst of foolishness. His is the kind of stage presence which needs no special lighting or camera magic; he makes an entrance by opening a door, and immediately you know that someone is in the room. *Meet John Doe* has its humor, inspiration, and interest in uneven degrees; but whether you find it good, fair, or merely endurable depends more on Cooper than on what we know as sound movie making.

24 March 1941

Nothing Happens

With its cast, budget, direction, and general idea, *Rage in Heaven* could have been an exciting movie. It has the case of a refugee from the psychopathic wards who marries and then builds his own madhouse to live in, with jealousy raised to an obsession, and obsession raised to thoughts of murder. It has Robert Montgomery in the kind of baby-face and ancient evil he proved he could do in *Night Must Fall;* and George Sanders and Oscar Homolka too. It has the direction of W. S. Van Dyke, who knows how to keep a sequence fast and clear; the camera of Oliver T. Marsh, who knows where to put his camera and at what time. But it started out with a James Hilton story that was either so loose-woven to start with or so pawed over afterward by the screen adapters (Christopher Isherwood and Robert Thoeren) that nothing happens but the obvious, and that only after a long and confused struggle.

It is one of those stories where everything could have happened, if everything had been in its due and proper place. But there is only one incident of illustration where there should have been twenty (the one incident is the murder of the cat, which just isn't handled to the best dramatic advantage); and the private horrors of a soul, the process of living behind an eternal mask, the growth of frenzy—these are not shown. We are told and can see that the natural course of petty jealousy and disbelief can be twisted and intensified until the only outcome is some unnatural action. But we lack the inevitable factors of the process itself. We see the man in his motion across the screen, but the many events of his life that would justify his death are not seen because not here. Where there should have been interest and partial self-identification, there is only curiosity, and it is unsatisfied.

The actors cannot be blamed for faulty characterization when it is a case of their having been written down as mere vague chumps in the first place. Ingrid Bergman is a pretty miss and energetic, but her accent and demeanor fit ill with the script. She does not get under the surface of the part. Along with Montgomery and Homolka, George Sanders is merely a case of talent hamstrung by obscure and conflicting motives; supposed to be a tower of strength, he is actually no more than a little foolish. So the whole thing goes to pieces, and the only reason for talking of it is the brightness of some of the fragments salvaged here and there, by force of direction, personality, and natural interest.

The Mad Emperor is another of those dark and choppy French films that have moments of a very fine thing but over an hour of something else. The story is one that could have been driven over with high movie effect: Paul the First of Russia, walking with the cruel and captious and unfocused mind of a child through his boudoirs and great halls of state and conferences; his minister plotting to betray him to save the Empire; his officers and mistresses in a nightmare of suspicions and cross-purposes. And there is reserve power in the acting personalities of Harry Baur and Pierre Renoir, among others. But the story is not even thought out, let alone fitted into any distinct line of motion. The technical equipment is movie-medieval, and there has undoubtedly been some fairly brutal censoring; but such deficiencies cannot serve to cover the main deficiency, which is that the producers, scene by scene, knew as little of what was going on as the audience does. There are two big moments nearly at the end, where everything comes clear—or as clear as print and lighting will allow—and the Emperor is seen in his pitiful grandeur. If you go, it must be for such picture pittance only.

Fond-Recollection Department.—I went again to see Hitchcock's *Secret Agent,* and I wonder again why more people don't yell their heads off when theater managers sell them mauled and moldy prints at respectable prices. In many films the wear and tear, dimming and blurring, patching and consequent loss of footage wouldn't matter—but not many films are worth constant playing. In the case of Hitchcock, scenes are crippled and dialogue is broken just where the sequence in its spare economy is achieving its real effect. It is not quite so bad as reading a book with pages out, though in the sense of film rhythm it is worse. And all that has to be done is make a new print from the negative, and all that this requires is some future fair-trade-practices act, and all that this requires is enough intelligent grousing on the part of those who foot the bill. Or are we mice?

Change-in-the-Weather Department. – Everything you read on this page from now until further notice will be coincidental or purely fictitious, as the paper is sending me to Hollwood to see if there is one.* It is the first rough assignment the owners have given me since the premiére of *Gone with the Wind.* But don't get me wrong: I love Sidney Skolsky.

31 March 1941

Nothing to Write Home About

The Sea Wolf is a straight adventure picture with overtones of megalomania and sadism, done in a forthright way with actors, a full-rigged ship, and the big Warner tank stage. The story is among the best adventure fictions, and betters many such in having as its chief character in terror and villainy a man who makes an intellectual hobby of such qualities. It throws a writer, two young and rather tough escaped convicts (boy and girl), a rum-busted doctor, a crew of Warners' best stock plug-uglies, and Barry Fitzgerald into the hands of Wolf Larsen, the hazing master of a death ship, a latter-day pirate schooner. And it rises through beatings, suicide, mutiny, and attempts at escape to its big climax. The writer, the boy, and the girl, who have got adrift and lost in their open boat before the Wolf is struck down, stumble back alongside the schooner in a chance fog to find the captain alone and blind in his ruined ship, malevolent still.

Here in the new version the story is given a $900,000 production. It has the violent direction of Michael Curtiz, who among many qualities is known for his almost daily insistence we should have some moofing with business, and who has achieved some good big mass scenes and tumult. And it has the characters of Edward G. Robinson, Ida Lupino, Barry Fitzgerald, Gene Lockhart, John Garfield, Alexander Knox, and Stanley Ridges. All are good, the first four particularly, and though it is Robinson's picture by definition, he is in there working anyway and making his bulk and bluster seem to mean it. The construction, lighting, and difficult special effects are marvelous for workmanship and resource; and everything is there. But where is the original wonder?

*Ferguson's reports from Hollywood appear at the end of this collection under the title "To the Promissory Land."

Like most of Jack London's fiction itself, the story loses persuasion through careless overpassing of the small but necessary, through overconfidence in the strident no matter how clumsy. For example, you can't hate Larsen enough not to respect him above the vague or purposeless spirits *we* are supposed to admire but *he* had to put up with. John Garfield was made to give out so much and take so little that whatever he got in punches on the nose, he was welcome. The writer shouldn't have been allowed near a duck pond without his mother or agent. The girl talked about despair and the end, but plenty of nice little ladies have lost more on simple Bermuda cruises than she lost here, and certainly with more show of gratitude, not trying to kill themselves all over the footage. That much could be charged to writing, but there are things about direction as well. The final hulk with its lurking madman should have been loaded with terror but was mostly filled with dialogue; the Wolf's return from the dead should have been built up as cold shock, but was telegraphed in advance.

Perhaps the miracles of melodrama belong properly in childhood anyway, or some place where faith is based on simple things, where just to be told is to believe, and have nightmares. And while the movies do wonderfully with illusion, in cases like this their magic—financial and technical resources of such a magnitude as to take your breath away and leave no hat check—is all expended on making near-reality out of the actual. But true illusion demands participation always; and the plain fact is, they have carried your imagination so far in a litter that it has gone to sleep, and will yawn instead of function. Their indoor ocean is just about everything marvelous but an ocean—and in the same way you will find their sea wolf interesting and want to pat its head.

On Miss Durbin's latest lifesaver for Universal Pictures I am killing myself with gags about how *Nice Girl?* tolls the little knell of parting Deanna, but I'll be all right in a minute. The film isn't important but it is one of those things that have nice things in them and a promise, and then practically spit in the eye of human nature merely for a plot twist or the lack of it. Also it is the end of Deanna Durbin as papoose, which may possibly be the end of her serious contentions to Bette Davis, for her face in the camera setups of this first grown-up stage has little more modeling or character than a corsage of mushrooms, and her acting range is what is chalked on the floor so she won't get out of focus. The story has her in love with a dope without her knowing it, or his either, and rebelling against the nonromance of her home life as young girls will every time, the silly dears. Franchot Tone comes from the city just to look in, and she decides that is for her and connives to get back to town with him and into pajamas (as the silly dears won't, my friends can tell you).

Up to here it has been quite human and nice, because what are people going to do with themselves anyway, and Robert Benchley as the father has made a well-disordered home out of all this going on around, and in town Franchot is half polite, half humorous, as one would wish to be for the sake of the story—and then we have our tantrums. Youth sees what a fool it has been and rushes back home, ki-yi, ki-yi, and proceeds to its final happy triumph by a process of being strictly venomous to everyone. As some have speculated, the question-mark after the title may be more than the snide device it certainly is fundamentally. Universal is wondering what to do with Deanna, now she has out-distanced the quintuplets, make her a nice girl? They'd better.

I can't speak with much authority, here in the center of the film industry, because the only pictures being shown to the natives are pictures long gone from New York, so nice to have seen them. But from my first sneak preview I should say that the Hollywood audience is a heartening one to try pictures out on for the same reason that producers' stooges are good men to try producers' jokes out on: they double up well before the punch line and Oh it's *murder*, Chief. At the showing of *Repent at Leisure,* directed by Frank Woodruff for RKO, they laughed and laughed, and they couldn't have all been the producer's mother because his mother and staff left at the end and the feature came on and they laughed and laughed again.

Repent at Leisure has some sharp angles to it but the story of the depart-ment-store owner's daughter (Wendy Barrie) and the nontraveling salesman she marries (Kent Taylor) is just one more suddenly-necessary-husband-and-baby situation. Movie writers are hard put to it these days to concoct something that is (1) national defense, (2) no offense to anyone, and so an affair like this gets into a B-producer's schedule almost automatically. To keep the plot going the young fellow has to make himself quite unbearable, but there is a certain comedy life throughout, and if you're passing time waiting for the first feature, you can at least use it for comparisons and for a textbook on how to write nothing much.

28 April 1941

Safari, So Good

The Road to Zanzibar is purely a gag picture, in the main conception and in every inch of the way; and it is the funniest thing I have seen on the screen in years. Years. So many comedies now feel the need for a theme and a near-meaning, like have a good laugh and win a set of dishes too, or, uneasy lies the clown that wears a head. And so many of the few pictures made in the old free-comedy way never attain a minute of freedom from the laborious antic of a script that must be followed word-for-word by a group with an honorable train-ing in old japes, willingness to the point of violence, and no idea of humor. But here is one that exists in a ponderously difficult medium and still has the free and happy air of the spontaneous, the best vein, the laughter shared and mounting.

There is nothing new here in the movie form. (The effect of commenting on the picture as from outside, the old breakthrough of the footlights, is merely given a little more imaginative play than usual; and the true phenomenon of it belongs to show business in general: two comedians without straight men happy in playing two straight men in search of a comic.) It is a Victor Schertzinger production for Paramount; it is done with care and overall good timing, with the best professional set-work, lighting, scoring, and photography in the world. They started with the idea of combining Bing Crosby and Bob Hope as two young Americans from the carnival time who can't agree through the story whether they are really stranded in Africa or about to take the continent over for 3 percent against the gross. Their problem is complicated by the police, two Brooklyn girls on safari, hostile natives, a couple of musical numbers, and some stock shots Mrs. Martin Johnson brought back alive. This much might have been just a setting for Laurel and Hardy, or the track without the race.

Bob Hope is supposed to employ so many gag-men they are organizing a union, but anyway he selects the best and puts them over as a bright natural, the acknowledged master of the delayed take, a comic with the grace and surprise in action of eccentric dancing and a foolish innocence of face through which he can crack out a line like a mule skinner. And Bing Crosby, an increasingly valuable movie property but indexed as a Voice, is already known in the radio and recording studios as Old Unbreakable, never bothered and never at a loss (when the drummer on his program dropped half his hardware in the middle of a key number, Bing just said like smoking a pipe in slippers, "Hold the phone, there's been a nasty accident" and carried over with laughter). Besides that, I believe him to be the first artist in popular expression today—not just slang for its newness or to be different, but the kind of speech that is a kind of folk poetry, with its words of concision, edge, and cocky elegance fitted to speech rhythms, so that they may run free to the point, musical and easy.

And so when these two came to *Zanzibar* they were hot and they were ready. Every bit of business led them to a new one, every new one led to some more new lines, and the laugh they found there set them off again. The film wasn't in work three days before the word went out that the two boys had taken over and were killing everybody including themselves. Just give them the general idea and show them where the audience is sitting, that's all they need. The laughs engendered are so many and near between that for once they can dispense with that frost on every blossom: But will the vast public understand what you *mean?* So for once two characters from show business are allowed to talk in character, and the public will get it as it will get anything it likes.

As to the word "gag" —and incidentally the process on which this show depends—I think it should be clear that the term applies to "any device intended to elicit laughter, usually superimposed on the main body of proceedings." It may be largely verbal—as when the boys are surrounded by hostile black men hideous with war paint, and try to act like nothing has happened: "Why, hello there," Bing says, advancing cheerily,"Who's got the dice?" It may be half and half, as when Hope is presented to a skeleton and shakes its hand absentmindedly, murmuring: "Don't bother to get up." It may be action, a reversal in business, as in the wrestling bout with the gorilla, which Bing is able to distract by holding a lighted match through the bars (the gorilla can't resist dropping Hope and running over to blow it out), and then when Hope gets going and begins to take falls out of the gorilla he rushes over in sweat and confusion to blow the match out himself (sudden realization: "Did *I* do that?"). All they have to know is that Hope as the one called Fearless is scheduled to wrestle with a bear, a python, an octopus, as the newest Sensational Idea of his partner, and that the prop department has set up an enormous live octopus in a glass case, and they go to work on the thing for laughs (while Fearless is wrestling single-handed with the damn fish, what are those other six arms going to be doing, knitting sweaters?) until time to throw it away. They buy a fake diamond mine and sell it, later two fake maidens in distress and can't give them away, and are always one jump behind the sheriff, or local eight ball. But always talking fast.

Dorothy Lamour and Una Merkel are in the picture but have little to do, and that little is written and directed in such a set way that you know what window the breeze is coming through. The merriment here is so knowing, veteran, and kindly, so irreverent of all things encountered and straightway forgot, so happily infectious within its own strict demands of trouping, that Stark Young might see it and forgive my allusion to his own *commedia dell' arte.* The boys are two zanies with the bit in their teeth and running away with everything not nailed down, and still kicking up new capers to their own continual surprise, like pulling the rabbit out of the hat and having to stuff it back out of sight because the damn thing already had a hat on.

5 May 1941

Chain-Store Daisy

The Devil and Miss Jones is a picture that provides a nice evening of entertainment for a number of good reasons, and then for some mysterious but bad reasons blows up in its own face. I don't get it. Its story has to do with the labor situation in a department store, and the general feeling among Hollywood producers is that monkeying around with labor even enough to spell the word out is like throwing rocks at a stranded mine. But they had started on the subject, and for the particular case had treated it well enough if innocuously; the line of the story was clear and all in order. Yet at the end, for which everybody is waiting and in which an honorable resolution of difficulties could have been very easily achieved without barricades, the whole tone and treatment change and the story does a sudden shuffle-off in blackface.

Frank Ross and Norman Krasna (also the screenplay writer) produced it as a vehicle for Jean Arthur (Mrs. Frank Ross); Sam Wood directed, and the support includes Charles Coburn, Edmund Gwenn, and Spring Byington as veterans, Robert Cummings as a young live-wire who occasionally short-circuits. The owner of a department store gets the idea of checking up on the employees who have been organizing a union, and is able to get himself taken on as a salesman in slippers. Of course he immediately gets interested in the young people of the shoe department, who befriend him, and particularly interested in the floor-walker, the manager, etc., who gives him the usual booting around. He still can't see the young organizer, Jean Arthur's boy friend, but give him time. There is a Coney Island party at which he learns a bit, and when he loses his locker key and is picked up as a suspicious character in a bathing suit, he learns the Bill of Rights can be a helpful thing to have around. Thrown in with this is his loss of a very expensive dyspepsia through the simple life (this is known as a piece of the roof) and his crusty bachelor's yen for one of the salesladies. No harm done.

Up to now it has made sense and fun too, quite a mature job of working an idea into lines and action, working out the different angles so that the whole is a story. You will not expect a sobersides analysis of trade unionism in a comedy, but you do not ordinarily expect the little highlights of sympathetic treatment along this way, the firings, the Macy plan of layoff, the fear of company spies, the young organizer with his losing minority. The stuff is treated lightly but in a kindly way, and since it was written with movie intelligence and directed with taste, there is quite a pleasant time.

I think where it first begins to go writer-wild is in having the young fellow go off from the beach in a mixture of despair and huff (he has been a pretty juvenile sort of organizer anyway, not to say unaffiliated), for the story continues with its good touches for a while, but the end is gathering. There is a finely devised scene where Jean Arthur, getting off the subway with the doors closing behind, suddenly knows what the card meant that she has read and thrown away in her distraction; there are a few high moments in the store. Then everything begins to jerk and clank around like Stuff and Guff on a Saturday-night laughing jag, everybody except the people you really hope to see licked arrives at a burlesque directors' meeting, there is some comic-strip foolishness, and the happy ending is rushed in before it has had time to dress.

Jean Arthur has done a really first-rate job with a part made for her; she can be at once astringent and appealing, brash, tender, and gay. Charles Coburn always seems as though the part were made for him, as though he were there and not even thinking of acting—which of course demands the best and only true thinking about acting. Yet in that last riptide of risibles everyone bobs around with the identity and meaning of a cork, and is lost in the confusion. I still don't get it, but would suggest that it is dangerous business to tamper with burning subjects when you do not burn about them, and when the subject of Labor in particular still afflicts the most orgulous interests with what we might call the Hollywood hop.

I shall be very late to class with a report on *Citizen Kane.* For one thing, the film is opening in Los Angeles several days after it has opened in New York and other key cities, as that is the way they do things out here. For another, I missed the West Coast press showing by not getting out here in time, and the New York previews by getting away too early. And then another of the peculiar things that have been happening to this opus took place: RKO (the reluctant distributor) and/or the Welles outfit, who had been showing the picture like mad and hired a whole theater for the trade preview, suddenly locked it away in bond, and for the last month even its own mother couldn't see it. *Variety* gave as a reason that the studio found, to its dismay, the picture being run off in projection rooms before just the film-colony people it hoped to nick for the high prices of the initial two-a-day run. RKO just says unbreakable contractual agreements, being both vague and very nice about it.

Citizen Kane is an advance-curiosity picture, not by accident. When Orson Welles needs a press agent, that is something; and when W. R. Hearst throws all his formidable power into annihilating a work or person, that is something too, and probably means it (or he) will be an inevitable and sweeping success. Add to that the facts of Welles's being already a combination boy wonder and one-man-band; of the straw-man battle's being joined as between Welles of the theater art and the jealous moguls of the movie; of lullabys for laymen about technical innovations, canons defied, and barriers burned away. Finally it becomes sight unseen the kind of picture most eagerly awaited by those who at no other time show the slightest interest in the art of films. Sink or swim, it is assured more cultural memorability in advance of showing than anything since Eisenstein's mighty fizzle in Old Mexico.

How good a film *Citizen Kane* is in terms of telling a story and carrying its mood with lights and the delicate electric camera will depend on how good a film it is, in the end if not the beginning. Out here, the good directors, writers, and cameramen—which is to say the men who know most about the movie art, having worked up through and with it an average of fifteen to twenty years—anticipate it with interest, perhaps an occasional twinkle of amusement, and no rancor. That's about the way it looks, still locked away in the cans, but perhaps this time you hadn't better wait for baby.

12 May 1941

Grade-A Glycerine

Penny Serenade is frankly a weeper, but it is not quite like any other film I can think of. It has no preachment in the *Over the Hill* tradition; it has not the ambitious glucose of *Mr. Chips;* it is not revolutionary in a picture sense, and I cannot imagine its material being put on in a play. It needs only three or four characters for most of the telling and its idea is simply that of a young couple who can't have a baby and so adopt one which becomes the center and anchor of their lives, and dies at six. What now keeps them from going completely to pieces is that they are able to adopt another—and that is all of it. An errant subtheme could have been strengthened with good effect, I think, in the steadying down of the young newspaperman-husband by marriage, tragedy, and life with the kid; but this is not sufficiently worked into the texture to figure in the end. It remains a picture of the early years of marriage as they pass over so many a thousand Mr. and Mrs., so ordinary as to be terribly difficult to do.

Any other combination of talents could have ruined *Penny Serenade.* Morrie Ryskind did the screenplay; George Stevens directed it; and it seems to have worked out as one of those happy director-writer teams so vital in movies. For all the lack of action in the strictest sense, you will notice whole sections here where narration has been devised purely for the camera—which as the first and loveliest instrument in this whole orchestra is too often neglected. Frequently they do a whole scene without talk, and at one point they set up to catch the mood of a leavetaking from down the stairs and through the banisters, catching only the lower third of the full-length picture above. But the main jobs of a director on such an assignment are to keep the mood clean and firm, sequence by sequence, as he is working it out on the spot and cutting afterward; and to get the best out of his actors. It is tribute to Stevens as much as to the principals that they have never turned in such a performance before.

Irene Dunne has been growing through good directors in successive films, and is now one of the very few gals who could sustain a part like this (I could wish the early scenes of her desire for babies and stuff had been shaded off just a little in the script: there is no abstract thing so noble that it cannot be made to seem personally selfish and rubbed in). And Cary Grant is thoroughly good, in some ways to the point of surprise, for there are not only that easy swing and hint of the devil in him, but faith and passion expressed, the character held together where it might so easily have fallen into the component parts of the too good, the silly, etc. His scene with the judge is one of the rightly moving things in the picture. Edgar Buchanan is the darling boy though, and runs quietly away with every scene he is in, simply by the depth of his reality as the stumbling, kindly friend of the family, absurdly thick-fingered and ill-at-ease in everything but the delicate operations of the pressroom or washing the baby or patching troubles or cooking. It is what is known as a juicy part and usually squeezed like an orange, till it means nothing; here it is done with the right balance of humor, loyalty, and love, and you will not forget Edgar Buchanan.

There remain story flaws: it is unlikely a by-line foreign correspondent could never get himself another job on papers after quitting once; it is never explained what the folks did for a living after it was established they didn't have one, or how the loyal friend could have lived while sticking around; and the near breakup at the end is neither sufficiently prepared for nor convincingly averted. There remains the final business of music, which figures quite nicely in the device of cutting back to the main story through records of the old songs, and never crowds the action. As for general mounting, this is class-A, but there is still to be said that processing and painted backings, however marvelous, are still not the air of outdoors, and there must always be a jarring difference between the acceptance of illusion and the perception of faking.

This is a picture not spectacular for any one thing, and yet the fact of its unassuming humanity, of its direct appeal without other aids, is something in the way of pictures growing up after all; for to make something out of very little, and that so near at hand, is one of the tests of artistry.

Cameras-Rolling Department.—In greater Los Angeles it is pretty true that wherever you may live, you have to travel more miles to see a movie that is already produced than one still producing. Also it is true that there is a much better chance of seeing pictures through the courtesy of those who actually make them than through the red tape and suspicious run-around which starts once the film has left the cutting room for the mercies of those who make nothing. At any rate, I have little to report on this week, except for what you will be seeing through the summer and fall. Looks pretty hopeful for you, too. Lewis Milestone has finished a comedy [*My Life with Caroline*] with angles that look very delightful so far. John Van Druten and Arnold Belgard wrote the screenplay; Milestone—now a producing unit by himself—got his own art director, Ronald Colman, and a new (perhaps) star, Anna Lee; and he went to work in a field too few realize his genius in, fun without foolishness, gaiety with the full command of the art of pictures.

Fritz Lang has just finished for Twentieth-Century-Fox a movie *(Man Hunt)* that may well run away with the year. It is based on the novel *Rogue Male,* and it is made with such care for scenic depth and suspense both, that I shouldn't be surprised at anything: critics even will be leafing back through the files to see who made *M.* And Anatole Litvak has washed up the film version of *The Gentle People,* another picture that will be loaded with atmosphere, and be found true and handsome.

From what I have seen of Alfred Hitchcock's *Before the Law* [*Suspicion*] , our fat man has got himself the kind of thing he wants to do again, and can do with such swift and subtle play of terror. And Garson Kanin, the young fireball from Broadway who came out here and made good better, is well along in a Ginger Rogers picture [*Tom, Dick and Harry*] that will be fairly strange and lovely as usual, and no doubt heard of long after it has passed over the brimming box office and our Mr. K is a private in the army, which he joins as of 1 June (Burgess Meredith is in the picture: plug, as requested).

These aren't all the names and this isn't more than a fraction of what is going on, but it looks pretty good from where I sit. More summer forecasts next time.

19 May 1941

Cameras-Rolling Department

William Wyler had a curious break. He and Philip Dunne (writer) worked three months on a preparation of *How Green Was My Valley,* to which Twentieth-Century-Fox was giving its productional all. Then because of commitments and weather and star availability, he had to release the picture to John Ford, who is about to start work on it. Wyler himself, one of the best men in the business, is already shooting on *The Little Foxes,* which looks like another to wait for. Preston Sturges is going into work with a new picture. John Brahm has had poor breaks in this country so far but is remembered, and he is starting now on some story that may mean nothing but on a Fox contract, which under the new policy there may mean quite a lot. Otto Brower has had a picture on location in the Middle West for weeks and something ought to come of that. The most recent crop of emigrés is settling down. Julien Duvivier is starting a picture. Jean Gabin is filling John O'Hara with hope for the picture they have both been assigned to and John is cooking up. And so on.

I suppose we may not expect anything like a renaissance for any scheduled time: the pictures will come out as the good things always come out, scattered here and there through the dull season. But it does seem that a better time is in store, if blubber-mouth fools can be prevented from turning the accumulated art of movies into the new meloroll fad of goody-here's-a-war-and-the-last-one-in's-a-dirty-word (the hysteria is already high enough so that one director who happens to be an active and accredited reserve officer dare not point out the technical error of drafting him as a private for a year or forever, and so packs his bag and holds his peace). The men who make pictures are getting more of a chance to make them; it may be accident or it may be the gradual advance into some say-so of an art form's indispensable talent. One takes one's pick and one hopes one's hope. From where I am it looks like a better year for movies, holding a fine promise and a damnable if.

26 May 1941

Citizen Welles

Citizen Kane can be approached in several ways: as a film, as an event, as a topic of the times, etc. The outline of the story is simplicity itself, almost like saying, "Once upon a time there was a man of whom certain things are remembered." But its presentation is managed in complex ways and its conclusions are so vague with the shadows of meaning that it is easy to read almost anything into it, including what was actually put there. The things to be said are that it is the boldest free hand stroke in a major screen production since Griffith and Bitzer were running wild to unshackle the camera; that it has the excitement of all surprises without stirring emotions much more enduring; and that in the line of the narrative film, as developed in all countries but most highly on the West Coast of America, it holds no great place.

The picture starts right in with the death of Citizen Kane alone with his crates of priceless art treasures in his fabulous castle on a mountain, where he has ruled for a time at least a miniature of the world. He said a thing when he died and the March of Time wants to make a story out of it, so we start combing the file of old acquaintance, with episode by episode told in flashbacks, and eventually we get the answer through the efforts of the inquiring reporter, who tracks down documents, the man's oldest friend, his newspaper manager, the girl, the butler of the castle. Some of the points are made by the people questioned; some are made in what there is of story as it moves over the years from back to front; but the main point is that Citizen Kane wanted love from the world and went to most of his fantastic extremes to get it, yet never had any love of his own to give. And the thing the searchers have been after, the dying apostrophe which assumes the importance of a mystery-story clue in the last sequence, develops as no more than a memory of the self of his childhood.

There has been so much snarling and blowing on the subject of what this picture is about that it won't hurt to clear the issue: most of the surface facts parallel incidents in the career of one W. R. Hearst; some traits are borrowed from other figures; some are pure ad-libbing. But any resemblance is distinctly coincidental; I could, and would if the editor were not afraid of libel, give you quite a list of Hearst's undesirable characteristics not possessed by Kane. As for the importance of the figure as an element of society, I don't think you can make that stick either. Kane started a war to get circulation for his paper; we hear in casual reference that he is a yellow journalist, and we see in a three-for-a-nickel montage clip that he fought graft and some corrupt trusts; there is a prophecy, not followed up, that when the workingman becomes organized labor he will not love the workingman; he is interviewed by the press and makes wild statements with gravity; when anyone gets in his way he calls him an anarchist. Otherwise his troubles are personal, and his death is that of a domineering and lonely man, known to all for his money, loved by none. The only possible moral of the picture is, don't be that way or you'll be sorry.

Beyond the facts of the career there is the man himself, and this man is Orson Welles, young, older, middle-aged, and in the last decrepit years, dominant throughout. Here perhaps, not so much spoken as expressed in the figure and bearing, is the ruthless force, the self-will, the restless-acquisitive that we feel the story should express if it is to tell of these things at all. This man in these circumstances should be our twentieth-century brand of a figure out of Gustavus Myers: he did not roll up that fortune to start with, but he is no second generation gone to seed, for he turned the nonworking capital into influence and public excitement and a sort of twisted splendor. It is as though Welles, as the man who conceived and produced this film story, had little enough grasp of the issues involved; but Welles as the actor somehow managed, by the genius that is in actors when they have it, to be more of the thing than he could realize. His presence in the picture is always a vital thing, an object of fascination to the beholder. In fact, without him the picture would have fallen all into its various component pieces of effect, allusion, and display. He is the big part and no one will say he is not worth it.

Of his actors, you can say that there are good jobs done and also that there are better ones still to be done. Dorothy Comingore is forced to be too shrill as the shrill wife (the audience ear will absorb only so much) and too ham as the opera singer (subtlety never hurt anyone, and those of us who aren't gaping yokels are not alone, Mr. Orson Citizen). Joseph Cotten had a part that was possibly short on savor because when he was with the great man he had to be something of a chump and when he was talking of him afterward he had to be something of a Mr. Chips, with twinkle and lip-smacking. Ray Collins did a good piece of work with a stock part, and so did all the other stock parts; but to me the man to remember was Everett Sloane, who seemed to understand and seemed to represent it, the little man with the big mind, the projection without the face motion and flapping of arms. You may be surprised when you take the film apart, and find that his relations to any analysis of Kane were as much as anything else the things that made him real.

Now I believe we can look at the picture, and of course we have been told to wait for that. The picture. The new art. The camera unbound. The picture is very exciting to anyone who gets excited about how things can be done in the movies; and the many places where it takes off like the Wright brothers should be credited to Welles first and his cameraman second (Herman J. Mankiewicz as writing collaborator should come in too). The Kubla Khan setting, the electioneering stage, the end of the rough-cut in the Marsh of Thyme projection room, the kid outside the window in the legacy scene, the opera stage, the dramatics of the review copy on opening night—the whole idea of a man in these attitudes must be credited to Welles himself.

And in these things there is no doubt the picture is dramatic. But what goes on between the dramatic high points, the story? No. What goes on is talk and moie talk. And while the stage may stand for this, the movies don't. And where a cameraman like Gregg Toland can be every sort of help to a director, in showing him what will pick up, in getting this effect or that, in achieving some lifting trick the guy has thought up, the cameraman still can't teach him how to shoot and cut a picture, even if he knows how himself. It is a thing that takes years and practice to learn. And its main problem always is story, story, story—or, How can we do it to them so they don't know beforehand that it's being done? Low-key photography won't help, except in the case of critics. Crane shots and pan shots, funny angles like showing the guy as though you are lying down at his feet, or moving in over him on the wings of an angel, won't help. Partial lighting won't help, or even blacking out a face or figure won't help, though it may keep people puzzled. Tricks and symbols never really come to much. The real art of movies concentrates on getting the right story and the right actors, the right kind of production and then smoothing everything out. And after that, in figuring how each idea can be made true, how each action can be made to happen, how you cut and reverse-camera and remake each minute of action, and run it into a line afterward, like the motion in the ocean. Does this picture do this? See some future issue when I have the time to say it doesn't, quite. Right now I have to hurry to catch a boat back to New York.

2 June 1941

Not So Good

Major Barbara is not just another movie for two reasons, both good: (1) it was made from a play by G. B. Shaw; (2) it is not, in the best use of the word, a movie. To get briefly through the this-and-that, it was made to follow up *Pygmalion,* by Gabriel Pascal in England, and is released here through United Artists. Shaw is supposed to have supplied additional dialogue where needed, and the production contains Wendy Hiller, Rex Harrison, Robert Morley, Robert Newton, and Emlyn Williams. It represents a sort of culture-by-contact, in that many who wouldn't know the name Shaw learn that there is a name Shaw in England; it runs almost two hours and I'm afraid it's a bore.

G. B. Shaw has always been a delight to me, and surely he is the dean of all intellectual showmen in this language. There isn't a play he has written that doesn't make good reading in some way or other, if only the preface, and his remarks to the press, footnotes to Frank Harris, and business letters make up a spry literature all their own. But I doubt if the theater ever occurred to him as anything but a dinner table at which—by the theater's arresting glow of lights and actors—you would listen to his ideas, or else. One of the few consistently brilliant minds in writing, whether in advanced theories or in tosh, and a shrewd hand at all the devices (a literary M. C.), he has had no time for that deep and different thing of the true theater which goes beyond words—because he wanted to talk.

Major Barbara may serve today as a comment on the idea that art should have significance sticking out all over it like cloves in a ham first, and the ham after if practicable. It is a play about religious hypocrisy; it says nothing that is untrue and was probably very daring in the early years of the century. But when you take the "about" part away, as the years have taken it, what have you left, outside of a boy-girl movie situation in which neither means much to us? The idea carried it once, the idea and everybody on the stage talking on and on about it. But now the kind of people who will be shocked and still like it can see only platitude; the kind of people who report shocks to the Hays office can stay away, and the people who wait for something real to happen are still waiting when the lights go up.

In the film as it goes from this point to that point, you will see the story of a girl who met a boy. He did something with Greek and she was dedicated to the Salvation Army or something, though her father had everything. She is working with the purest faith and energy to save souls, several of which are character actors in the story, and so naturally he gets involved in that business and incidents happen and are discussed. The final switch is brought about when the girl, Major Barbara, finds that the dirty munitions money of her father is perfectly acceptable to her superiors in this cause of regeneration, and afterward that the workingmen in the old man's business are happier and more useful as citizens in its benefits, as a going institution, than those she has been concerned with. There have been comments and comedy interludes, but the framework is what you remember in a vague and unsatisfactory way. It was never written as a movie, or directed with any skill for building a hundred little things securely into one effective thing, and leading each thing into another, and holding all together. As a transcript of an early Shaw play it is all right enough. As something aimed at the kind of life and power we have come to expect of a good movie, it just isn't there, it dies on its own clubfeet.

There is no reason why the movies should stop making bad musical comedies so long as bad musical comedies make money in buckets, so the only squawk on *The Great American Broadcast* is that its standard ingredients for success in this field could have been shaped together for fair entertainment, as well. It is another of the Twentieth-Century-Fox series of Only Yesterday in Tinpan Alley and uses everything in the formula: the ups and downs of love in show business (radio, this time), specialty acts, songs, wisecracks, blows, background music with old tunes, and what we might call a Spitalny Finale. As usual, the story is only an excuse for introducing these baubles; but at the same time, and also as usual, the story manages to do a lot of shoving around and by the end has got half the emphasis all to itself.

At first they thought of doing an authentic history of radio as entertainment and imported a prominent studio engineer from the early days as adviser. Well, this gentleman worked up a lot of material, but this was too technical and dull, so they put a writer on with him and the two worked up one or more treatments, but these were technical and not bright enough. So apparently they said to hell with it and threw the stuff into the customary mill, with credits for four writers but nothing more from the engineer, or from history. So Jack Oakie meets John Payne in a fight and they meet Alice Faye. Jack loves Alice but she doesn't love him. Alice *hates* John but soon they are making with kisses, so Jack hates John. Cesar Romero loves Alice but she marries John and nobody loves Cesar, but Jack goes to work for him. Then Alice goes to Cesar on a technical matter and John hates Alice and leaves the country. Alice and Cesar are going to Reno, off with the old and on with the new, so Jack hates Cesar and manages to get hold of John. Jack wants to help John and now loves him, so they fight. Cesar goes away and Alice and John fight. Then they kiss. Then it says the end.

Along this way we meet incidents from the early hard times and later triumphs of broadcasting, and these furnish interesting background—fairly authentic though telescoped and sometimes shuffled for the story. At one point we see actual and exciting news-clips of the Dempsey-Willard fight in Toledo (and of the many blows struck throughout the picture, these are the only ones with any grace of meaning). The songs are pleasant, the Nicholas Brothers do a terrific act, the Ink Spots are there if you like them, and the Wiere Brothers go through their beautiful drollery again—it is worth a picture to see them, though they are no good in the first close-up chorus, and some of their magic is lost in the camera, having been designed for the set conditions of the stage. The rest of the picture is Jack Oakie, who is the solid fellow and clown throughout. He is not lovely; he might be found vulgar, dear dear; but he has energy and good humor in abundance, and he was the only one there who seemed to be having fun.

Archie Mayo directed, sometimes with a very heavy hand, not helping much with a script which has about the general sense I have indicated, plus a constant treatment of particulars—lines and character play—that is about as light in getting off the ground as a dead fish. The picture had the best auspices in production, scoring, art work, camera (some of these departments being well above any mere class A), but in the two factors which finally give a movie life—writing and direction—it is shabby and it is sad. We ought to say it is pure criminal waste, I suppose. But we can't, because it is not waste so long as yahoos swarm to it, bringing in their money two and threefold. For this is the money that makes possible these elaborately skilled departments of craftsmanship, establishing them as a sort of fund in trust, to be drawn upon equally for the bad and for the good when it comes along.

9 June 1941

Welles and His Wonders: II

To make any sense about technical innovations in any one movie, one should, in an ideal state at least, have some idea of the general technique of making every movie. Before coming to the wonders of *Citizen Kane,* therefore, we will just run over a few fundamentals (we will, that is, if anyone is still around when these wandering messages of mine catch up with themselves).

The first thing necessary to a movie is a story, and the first thing necessary to stories for the screen is a writer who understands the screen and works along the line the director will take later, preferably with the director. But the most important thing in the technique of a motion picture—and here director and writer are in varying degrees interdependent—is its construction shot by shot, not for the effect or punch line of any one fragment, but for such devising and spacing as avoid monotony, hold the interest, and lead easily from one thing into another, *the devices for illusion being always and necessarily hidden in the natural emergence of the illusion itself.* One scene may be broken down into six or twenty camera positions, yet these shifts you are not conscious of: you follow the actor across the room and pick him up coming through the door; you may not see him when he is speaking; you may see only his face when someone else is speaking; he turns to look through a window and suddenly you are looking out the window. These are the smallest things, but they make for pace and variety—which will be the biggest things before you are through.

A scene is made, another to fit with it; there may be interscenes, or long shots covering action, establishing atmosphere; later there will be inserts, titles, the transitional devices of trick or straight cutting, dissolves, montages. At the end of maybe five, maybe ten days' work you will have a sequence, that is, an essential incident in the story carried through from start to finish. And the next sequence should take up without jar, without confusion, and lead on again, shot by shot and scene by scene, in the right way of the story. Finally when all the sequences have been made and assembled in a rough-cut, you must study over and over this familiar work of weeks to inquire whether what you put in it is there, to study it for continuity of mood, for how well the sequences match and balance—and for where to cut, where to remake. Does it move, does it complete its circle, do characters and ideas and the express meaning come alive in action? Maybe you've got a picture, but it won't be by chance.

It is true that of all the arts, movies are farthest from being one-man shows. Actors are the most important in the public eye, and indeed they are the dramatic exposition, the writing hand, of stories on the screen; without good ones you are lost. The music and scenic departments are important, and the cutting room is the watchtower of unsung heroes who have brought a thousand bungling messes out of the hopeless into something that at least moves and has coherence. Technically, the most indispensable is the cameraman, with his crew of assistants and batteries of lights; he is a high man indeed. But it is also true that without writing and direction of intelligence, taste, and actual mastery of the craft, you just won't get a picture that is a good picture. It comes down to this: writer and director (much more the director) tell a story in movie terms, and the way they do it is the prime technique of pictures.

Citizen Kane in its story uses the cut-back method—which is convenient but has its drawbacks in the constant interruption of a steady line; it is quite common and I wish it were less so. For dramatic action, it shows its one big character in four main situations, supplemented by newsreel interludes here and there. This makes a pretty weak structure dramatically, so it has to be surrounded with a great deal of stationary talk, as Kane is described, analyzed, asked about, remembered, talked into existence and practically out of it. This is different from many good movies but it is not new, technically or otherwise. The mood is established or heightened by an occasional symbol: the sled and the falling-snow toy, the curtain-warning light on the stage, the bird screaming in escape, etc. Symbols are a dime a dozen and justify their use in the result achieved. I thought the fading light filament and dying sound-track at the end of the singer's career very effective; also the opening and close on the iron fence around the castle. The smoke rising to heaven at the end was trite to start with and dragged out absurdly.

As you can see, there is nothing startling in these component parts. The outstanding technical effect in the picture is in the conception of settings and the use of the camera. Gregg Toland is a trained cameraman and ace-high in his profession, and it is apparent that Welles himself was fascinated most of all by this department in movies—that many of the things done were first sketched in with the bold freehand of his dramatic imagination. (It shouldn't be forgotten that a screen-mood is more than just "photography," that it results from the collaboration, in this order, of director, cameraman, art director.)

The camera here loves deep perspectives, long rooms, rooms seen through doors and giving onto rooms through other doors, rooms lengthened out by low ceilings or made immense by high-angle shots where the ceiling seems to be the sky. Figures are widely spaced down this perspective, moving far off at will, yet kept in focus. The camera loves partial lighting or underlighting, with faces or figures blacked out, features emphasized or thrown into shadow, with one point of high light in an area of gloom or foreground figures black against brightness, with the key shifting according to mood, with every scene modeled for special effects with light batteries of varying function and power, gobos, barndoors, screens, and what not. These things are all written into the accomplished cameraman's book. There is nothing newer about shooting into lights than shooting into the sun, but there is, I suppose, something new in having the whole book thrown at you at once. Certainly there has not been such use of darkness in masses since the Russians, who simply didn't have any lights.

Sometimes all this is fine and really does the job it is put to. Along with the wide action range, it is a relief from too much closeness and light, an effect of stretching. But at other times it appears just willful dabbling: figures are in the dark for no reason—reading without the light to see, for example; or they are kept in darkness right among other clearly lighted figures (the idea is supposed to be that this shows they aren't important; the effect is to draw attention to them, as being maybe the Masked Marvel). Half real and half fish, as in the case of mermaids, is always a thing to cause vague frustration; and too often here it seems as though they were working up a feeling of omen just for the ride.

This camera also likes many of the angles so thoroughly kicked around by the experimental films—floor shots, especially, where the camera gives figures height and takes away width, makes them ominous, or at least portentous in their motions. Crane shots, too, some of them breathtaking as you move down and forward from heights or rise straight up—some of them overdone, as in the last Cook's tour of Kane's boxed accumulations. Add undercranking, to make the people in the "newsreel" clips jerk and scuttle. Add mirrors. And add the usual working tools of long, medium, and two-shots, close-ups, dolly shots, panoramas.

In the cutting there are several things noticeable. One is the long easy sweep you can get when a scene of action is covered in one long-range setup. Another lies partly in the method of treatment and partly in lack of care, and that is the time-and-place confusion which arises when you go smack from the first two-thirds of a sentence to the last third of the same sentence, spoken elsewhere years later. This is done time and again, and you might call it jump-cutting or you might call it the old shell game as far as the audience is concerned.

Another thing about the cutting that goes altogether to the fault of direction is the monotony and amateurism of handling simple dialogue. Over and over there are the two faces talking, talk, talk, talk, then close-up of the right speaker asking, then close-up of the left speaker answering, then back to two. Outside of getting your name in large letters, being a director consists exactly in knowing how to break this up, to keep interest shifting, to stress the *reaction* to a line more sharply than the face saying it. This is what gives a picture life, and it isn't done by camera ructions, however clever.

Orson Welles was naturally entranced with the marvelous things the moving camera could do for him; and while much has resulted from this preoccupation, I think his neglect of what the camera could do *to* him is the main reason why the picture somehow leaves you cold even while your mouth is still open at its excitements. There may have been the heart and belief to put into it, but there wasn't the time to learn how this might be done, or much regard for any such humdrum skill. I'll tell you about a picture which was the story of a man's life told by the cut-back method after his death, and which had the real life in it, the skill and the heart too. It was *A Man to Remember,* made in a little over two weeks for a little over $100,000 by an ex-Broadway director who was learning about pictures the hard way, and his name was Garson Kanin. And if you want to read into a story some comment on the modern man of predacious industrial power, how he got that way and what it did to him, I'll remind you of a film that told the story and made it stick, its people full-length and alive. It was made some five years ago for Sam Goldwyn and called *Come and Get It,* and the better part of its direction was done by William Wyler.

As for the contributing departments in *Citizen Kane,* Bernard Herrman's music is an active aid; the sets are made right, both for the fantastic and for use or living; it is an all-round class-A production. But the most effective things in it are the creation of Orson Welles's drawing board, not only in whole story ideas but in plausible and adult dialogue (witty, sardonic, knowledgeable), the impression of life as it actually goes on in the big world, the ready dramatic vigor. You remember things like the kid in the snow outside the window as the hard business is transacted within; the newspaper office at night; the understatement of successive breakfasts in Kane's first marriage; the wonderful campaign-hall scene; the opera-opening (there was too much ham in some of this); the trick approach through the night-club skylight and ensuing scenes; the newsreel projection-room conference as a sendoff for the story; and the newsreels themselves—excellent naturalism here.

This stuff is fine theater, technically or any other way, and along with them the film is exciting for the recklessness of its independence, even if it seems to have little to be free *for.* There is surely nothing against it as a dramatic venture that it is no advance in screen technique at all, but a retrogression. The movies could use Orson Welles. But so could Orson Welles use the movies, that is, if he wants to make pictures. Hollywood is a great field for fanfare, but it is also a field in which even Genius has to do it the hard way; and *Citizen Kane* rather makes me doubt that Orson Welles really wants to make pictures.

16 June 1941

Fritz Lang and Company

We should try to forget that the picture *Man Hunt* was made from the book *Rogue Male.* No good ever came out of comparisons yet, except they were made responsibly for purposes of clarifying points, gauging effects, etc., and in this case Dudley Nichols and Fritz Lang as writer and director were faced with the problem of taking material that had a great deal to do with mental states and reworking it into terms of action.

Man Hunt starts out with a dilettante English sportsman who has got bored with animals as big game, and come to within five hundred odd yards of the Führer's country place in Germany. He does not believe he is going to shoot: just wants to prove he can do it, and hold that man steady in his sight telescope. But the Gestapo surprises him, and then goes to work. (Objection number one: there might have been more stalk and less talk afterward, for as it is, the game seems too easy and the point is not fairly made.)

There are the torture, with no results, the Gestapo's reconsideration and decision to frame an accident, their failure to make the accident hard enough, and the chase through Germany, onto an English ship and into England. He meets a cockney girl who helps him evade the several German agents on his heels, which means he is to have more than a personal motive in doing the enemy in. As in the book, he is gradually learning anyway that there was a subconscious feeling deeper than stalking for sport behind his venture, that these people and their methods are repugnant to him as a decent free person. So when he has killed one of the agents and got clear of London, and word comes that the girl has been captured and killed by the other side, he is ready to try it again in deadly earnest, without failing again.

Meanwhile they have got him holed up in the cave where he has been hiding somewhere in the English countryside, and the Gestapo man in charge of operations proceeds with his final piece of chicanery, is denounced once and for all and finally tricked, and the end of the picture comes when our man gets into active service at the outbreak of war, and bails out of a British plane once more into German hunting territory. (Objection number two: as the climax sequence of the picture, this should have been built up more, led into more firmly and carried out with less haste. They had a wonderful set for the approach to the cave and the cave itself, but we are suddenly in the middle of it without more preparation than a dissolve or two, and all the fine suspense the book achieved in the minute preparations, first for concealment, then for escape, is passed over here. The picture is overlength at least ten minutes, but the thing to have sacrificed was the earlier talk.)

It is Fritz Lang's picture, of course, his first good chance in several years to get a script with something to it and a writer on it. He had about the best in the way of cameraman, art direction, scoring, and cutting; but I think without knowing any of this, or who he was himself, you would sense the creative presence there of an artist in the medium. Lang gets depth in every scene he makes; he is a careful and thorough man with detail; and his first concern is with the rightness and immediacy of each fragment as it appears to you, makes its impression, leads you along with each incident of the story, and projects the imagination beyond into things to come. He is one of the best men with the feeling of crowds, with life going on around the particular action, that is. He is vigilant in his use of actors to make the scene itself more important than any one line or reaction, so that camera lighting, and background give shape to action and meaning to a situation. It would make good gossip to say that he breaks every slight maneuver down into its component parts with step-by-step diagram of A here, B there, camera here, and X crossing; but that is only a surface indication of the main thing, which is that he knows pictures, he thinks in terms of how to make them achieve the truth of life and the excitement of movement.

Walter Pidgeon and George Sanders are the two principal acting people, and good use was made of John Carradine as the deadly pursuer. Joan Bennett is not a perfect cockney by any means, but there was a sweetness to the interlude with her which helped keep desperate deeds on a plane of living, and the writing, acting, and direction of her leavetaking made a very nice original bit (the girl in the book, as you remember, was all in the mind, and rather dragged in). There were others, each in his place. But more than many films, this was a writer-director proposition; its strength and weakness lie finally in those departments. Its weakness is that as melodrama it is uneven, there is just something off-balance in its progression, there is a sense when you have got to a big event that the event is not big enough. Its strength is that it is made with such care and polish that it does not seem melodrama, that it seems true. And in its manipulation of these dark and intent forces on a checkerboard, it manages to take your breath away. There is an actual vividness about it that makes you wish it could somehow come out more penetrating and terrible.

Mickey Churchmouse Department.—It is unfortunate that of all the studios in Hollywood, it should be Walt Disney's where the workers had to go on strike. But it is not surprising. Disney himself is a charming fellow; he has the gift of getting his workers to like him and contribute with democratic freedom to whatever they are all engaged on; he is sending out good pictures and bringing good millions back; and he is operating what is by Hollywood standards a sweatshop. The idea out toward Burbank is that cartoons marketed at class-A Hollywood prices are not to be made by anything like Hollywood wage scales. The Disney studio has all the easy informality of a New York department store—girls coming in with a college and art-school background do a good racking six days of work for sixteen or seventeen lousy dollars a week, with efficiency checker-uppers and rest-room watchers and with one of the more notorious speed-up systems operating as in any factory. Above the fact that Disney is getting fifty to a hundred skilled craftsmen for the weekly price of one Hollywood bum with a profile, is the way that you can hear in his commissary someone say with awe: "Oh, that's one of the *big* guys, gets three or three-five." And they do not mean $3,500, which is what this would mean on any major lot unless it were for laughs: $350 is a rising man, strictly élite of type. Well the hundreds working, élite or not, have apparently gone out to wake up Mr. Disney. The man must be sleeping to think he can be the magician who makes ten million children laugh and wonder, and at the same time employ the hands of men who can't be sure the kids of their own will have the good clothes to go to school.

23 June 1941

Behind the Camera: Lang

In Hollywood, as I guess anywhere else, it is not enough to be just a director: you must be a smart director. Making movies is such an expensive business that you have to get signed up with a studio to make them in, negotiate some kind of backing and tie-up, and learn enough of production cost to keep within reasonable budget requirements. You can't sit around waiting for a story you like to come and curl up in your lap; you can't go bang into your work without considering the attitude to the work of dozens of others engaged on it, writers, actors, technicians. Above everything you must consider your own standing and what things will make or break it, for this prestige is your main bargaining point, and it is with this you will be able to get your way when necessary. And for a while in Hollywood it looked as though Fritz Lang were not being smart.

He came over with a full-grown European reputation seven years ago. He had just completed *Liliom* abroad and it was a pretty awful picture, but it got a lot of solemn attention because the director of *M, Metropolis, Mabuse,* etc., had made it. I don't know the exact details on the first years in Hollywood, and they probably weren't important, but they built up a general picture of Fritz Lang that it was not good for a director to have. He was a Prussian with a monocle; he treated his actors like a Prussian with a monocle, and he had tantrums; he would fuss around until he had run up a month's expense for a week of actual footage; he only wanted to make what he wanted to make and what *had* he made? The picture *M* can still be seen, but did he think he could live on that forever? He had as a matter of fact made *Fury* (1936), with some of the most terrific stuff ever in pictures; but in around three years following he had completed two weak films, and the word was out. However that may have been, you will not find traces of it today: the man is making pictures, in what seems to be the right way.

Fritz Lang is a fairly heavyset man with a prominent nose, quick, boring eyes, hair just on the edge of bushy and receding only a little, brushed straight back, and a toed-out walk that would be a shuffle if it were not so nervous and purposeful. He is fifty-one and looks a good forty. Probably the first noticeable thing is the accent in the speech, but while this is prominent, it is no heavy thing of kraut, as he has assimilated English in its best racy forms, is voluble, at ease in the colloquial, sometimes barbed, and sometimes profane. He makes also with jokes and puns and will chuckle when you tell him they stink, which sometimes they don't. This is about as true of him when he is hopping and fussing around the set as when he is on his couch at the office, which always has the windows closed through some theory of his that fresh air will be the death of somebody yet. Or when he is relaxing in New York and has the monocle on, *i.e.*, times of a social nature (the monocle is made of plate glass and gives him the effect of a walleye in a waxworks, which might be terrifying to some and thus have contributed to the legend). He is one of the few men who can concentrate furiously and then leave it alone—as, for example, when he is doing a mob scene with extras, storming in and out and around them and the actors and the grips and generally killing himself over some main point of action, and comes over between takes to sit down: "There. Now what is this about this God-damn Hitler in Greece, eh?"

He is a careful, careful man, which means that scenes will be done over until they are right, until they are the way he saw them back when he was working on the story and working out diagrams for it. But he works while others are resting and then when they are working he is right there within two feet of their nose, working with them, coaching and coaxing and explaining even as the cameras are taking it (that part of the sound-track has to be cut out: they must love him in the recording room). And he doesn't delegate the handling of groups to an assistant but does the running himself—which is one way and about the only way to get such mob-violence scenes as he got in *Fury*, if you don't weaken. And one afternoon I saw him, washing up a subway chase sequence in the last picture, when one of the crew had dumped a heavy candy-purveyor onto his foot, breaking two toes. He took it, he didn't even grouse, and the rest of the afternoon he did his hobbling and hopping up and down the set with a cane, a rough bandage, and an old slipper on that foot, bent over but getting his scenes in like hay before the rain and making a fine spectacle for the others, who said he was now even walking with a thick accent (he really looked something like the crochety passion of the doctor in *Caligari*), and still all he said when he came to sit down during a new setup and feel his toes speculatively was, "Now, you tell me: what are you going to do with the damn critics?" The legend of the terrible Prussian was not to be found on that set.

He is a strange man from any angle. Born in Vienna, educated at the Realschule there, first studying to be an architect, later studying painting in Munich and Paris. He went into the war as an Austrian officer. His record was three wounds and four decorations, but his stories are better. That poor old Austrian army of ours, he says, chuckling to think they were nearly as bad as the Italians. Many things they did and didn't do, but in the mellow distance, a thing that makes the best telling is one like the time the Austrians were in some holding position and so short of ammunition that they only fired three salvos from every other battery at nine every morning, to keep the franchise. It was all very peaceful until the Italians angered them by hanging out an impudent and enormous sign: Tomorrow, Tuesday, 24, please fire three salvos 10:15 not 9. They passed the word all around the batteries and got up all the advance ammunition for the week on every battery, and waited until 10:15 and blew the roof completely off with an all-out barrage. They really meant it. When all the advance ammunition was gone and they'd pulled the cotton out of their ears, they looked over to see the devastation, and were naturally a little slow in getting the sign, rising, neatly lettered, over the front-line trenches. The Italians had meant it too: they were in for an inspection from the commanding colonel and had plotted him for front-line position some time between ten and ten-thirty. And the new sign read: "Thanks, friends; colonel critical, maybe dead."

But those years were not so happy in their day-to-day passage, or the years afterward. Fritz Lang has been in several revolutions, always on the side of the new order until the new order meant the Hitler idea. Four revolutions, he says, but it was in between and around revolutions that he became the man you have heard of. There will be time for more of this part later.

30 June 1941

Fritz Lang, Continued

One of the times he was in a hospital, as a result of things in the World War he does not talk about, Lang thought he would help his convalescence by writing stories. What could he lose? And here comes a factor that neither he nor any other of the old-line first-class men can explain, putting words down in the open. When the movies were just a clumsy struggling art everywhere, there were men everywhere who knew somehow that work in this form was the work they wanted to do. Some of the stories of Lang's convalescence were scenarios, ideas for movies. So when the peace came and his last wound was healed up, when other intellectuals were spending their time being very much so and Bohemian if nothing else, he went to where he could get his chance in making movies. At the time he went there, it was Berlin, where Erich Pommer was reorganizing the German film industry. Pommer seems to have been the first big producer with an eye for talent, and idea of how to let it express itself, and it was his backing if nothing else that opened the way to a good-sized fraction of men who have made film history.

Lang went to work as a director, after learning some of the techniques of the business, and he made some pictures that are still talked about. *The Weary Death* in 1921. After that *Dr. Mabuse.* After that *The Niebelungs.* After that *Metropolis.* He made a lot of pictures and in the impressionistic, half-terroristic movies of postwar Germany, he was one of the five or six big names. We did not know of him over here, but he was not worrying about that. He made *The Spy* and *The Girl in the Mirror,* and then in 1933 he made *M,* which was so terrible and exciting that it spread to here and was talked of here.

But Fritz Lang, in his growth as artist, has also had growth as a man. When the war came, it was up to him to fight and he accepted it. After the war there were movements stirring against things which weren't right, and these things were matters he had been thinking about. So he backed the revolutions in

Germany. He was active. I doubt he was ever by nature a fighter, but when the battle was joined across the deceptive peaceful fields or in the clamoring streets, he was there, one way or another. That was outside his art, which was his way of life, and it was only right. He did not make propaganda, so far as I can find; he made pictures when the fighting stopped.

It was in his time that the great German production firm of UFA was started, under Pommer. It was a time when movie directors of weight and talent were bringing the strange corners of human existence to the screen, in the German films. Everybody was learning about the possibilities of movies everywhere, and in Germany in those days they were on top of the world for the thing they were doing, but even there the best men were learning the slow and hard way, from their mistakes, that is. *M* went around the world as the best thing of its kind, and the best thing for Fritz Lang was that it aroused excitement in America. For about the time it was to be released he found himself in his last revolution, and this time it was not so much a revolution as a stand against the upstart Adolf Hitler. After the victory of something like that, he left his country for good, along with all the other good movie workers, one by one. Hitler and *M* are why we have Lang today.

You would of course wish to know what he thinks in such times. He is for war now, war anyway, for fighting and defeating, and while I am against his position, I must respect it, for I know that if tattoo sounds and age limits are to be got around, he will be there, hobbling and hopping and formidable with his monocle. But above that he is for people, for the working people and the people who do not have it generally. It may be strange, coming from a room in the Waldorf Towers in New York, but what he says there I deem enough to put him on the side of the good men, for I know that there are many things he has thrown away and will throw again, on the same old losing side, which is the right side.

He is worried about his pictures: do they do anything? Well, I say, when they're good, yes. But is it anything worthwhile? Well, knowing his record in Hollywood and in the world, I have to say yes again. Because he thinks the way I think: if you can make something that people will want to see because it's enjoyable and not a duty, and still put in something people should know, they will learn easily, in the midst of their pleasure, to know it. Do you think the lynching scenes in *Fury* were only melodrama, God damn? he asks. And I have to say as thousands must who saw them, No, they were the real thing and made the heart turn over—it was a very fine thing to have made them. Mm, he says, in that story I thought it could be done, but I don't know. Worrying over his new picture (*Man Hunt*) he says, Is it enough I should put in here a thing against Hitler, is that the way I can do it? About that I don't know, except to say that what is in your heart when you are doing a thing with your whole heart in it will be right somehow. I only know that he is a good man who has mastered a craft so few people understand. He can still make a turkey but he cannot make anything that is wrong for people, or vicious. But this cannot be said.

Fritz Lang may have learned a great deal of what he knows from his schooling in formal art, painting, and architecture. But he had to approach it with that knowledge under his hat and humility in his heart, because this is the strangest art ever, the newest and widest. Anyway what he learned under Pommer and with the directors of that group was a feeling for scenes, for the thing to be made real and effective, for the care to be taken in each detail, *not* for the detail's sake but for the final expression as from behind the screen forward into the audience. He learned to build suspense, to mount horror, to make the simple things true by use of actors and lights and camera, sets and cutting, by use of the movie as a thing to be taken by itself.

As I said last week, he got into a hole in Hollywood; he was making pictures that weren't much and that he didn't believe to be much, or he wasn't making pictures at all. But he pulled himself together, took a major contract, made a picture like *Western Union* so he could make a picture like *Man Hunt,* and is already busy on another assignment he wanted. He learned to take a step back so he could take two ahead; he learned to cut time off the production schedule, to wangle the actors he would need. No one could say that he hadn't got over the foreign hurdle into the atmosphere of American people and towns in *Fury,* but I think he *feels* more at ease now in the American film tempo. He is as spry as ever; his province is, one way or another, what is going on in the world; he keeps busy and seems happy.

7 July 1941

Garson's Guard

Garson Kanin wouldn't say anything much when he was working on the picture. "Oh, it will be a sort of cute story, I guess. Who's going over to Lucey's for some drinking fluid?" Kanin likes to fight something through and get something done that is not considered do-able, but he was low-rating his *Tom, Dick and Harry* nevertheless. It is what is known technically as a honey of a picture. On the surface it is little or nothing; under the surface it is little or nothing. But from the way it was devised and made it has a sweetness of its own, a foolish but endearing truth.

It is a Ginger Rogers picture and sensibly exploited as such. But while it is true that with almost any other acting lady the central part would have faded and frayed, exploitation has nothing whatever to do with any sense of values in the world: the only true thing to say is that here is a piece of light-comedy writing through which a group of actors move in natural and happy ease, the whole thing being made actual through one man's taste, judgment, and willing ear, cheerful spirits, and shrewd theater knowledge.

Paul Jarrico's story has for its only basis the problem of the young working girl, a shrewd enough number to take care of herself with some to spare, but a pushover for the romantic things about romance. She is proposed to by three men in fairly rapid succession, the go-getter, the happy-go-lucky-go-flat-broke, the young heir. She naturally accepts them all and comes to like them, but the rich one is the only one she was aiming at, and really trying. Still, it is a problem to choose just one with all three right there waiting. So she finally hares off with the one you'd expect, though there was a bad minute for a moment. I told you it was nothing.

But while the conflict is basically old, Jarrico never gave it a wink of sleep from beginning to end. There is the business of a girl's dreams done in the fantasy of cartoons. (For once in a hundred, Vernon Walker's special effects were special and effective.) There is one lover played neatly against another, those two against the third, then all three tossed in the same blanket. There is the quickening realism of the switchboard and its possibilities. There are the brat of a sister; Betty Breckenridge parlaying a bit part into a neat performance; Phil Silvers as the friendless good-humor man; even Sidney Skolsky in a magnificent interpretation of seven words all different. What with cars, planes, streets, rooms, and bowling alleys, there is a good sense of motion though it is essentially a dialogue plot. And part of the smooth running may be credited to the work of the several writers and assistants we may call Garson's Guard, though they are not billed as such, when billed at all.

There is a quality of the pleasantly absurd in understatement and the offhand, as in the afterthought of the two on the newest successful suitor: "Nice-looking fellah."—"Yeah, uh huh. . . . " Or the father's switch from the shotgun when he finds the prospective cad is a millionaire instead, "What's she going to do about *shoes*, hurry up!" This has its sure effect on the audience, making the picture a thing of steady good humor rather than of scattered guffaws (the two places where they were stretching for laughs, the bowling-alley header and an ancient play on the word democratic, are out of key).

Probably more important, certainly more difficult to achieve, is a sustained matching of the gentle charm of fairy-tales with an everyday realism, so that people are delighted to identify themselves with the automobile salesman's prospect, the air of the family's living room after supper, the girl out of her depth in the bright life. There could be no better devising for such a film than that opening on a movie audience, far romance carried away from the screen to the ice-cream parlor afterward and into the humdrum of tomorrow's job. It is a definition of the word economy, it is a whole course in setting the mood with one chord. Then the single touch to show the boys have been waiting on those steps a long long time, one wanting to say something hateful but finding a frog in his throat as big as a pillow. The overlapping dialogue, especially as worked out by Miss Rogers and Meredith, is a release of the strained in itself—one talking and coming over clearly, the other following, anticipating, still objecting, the silly mumble and cross-purpose of all human exchange. Everything is done with such appreciation of the delicate fabric they were working in that there is nothing more natural than that someone should go off into dream fragments at any time.

This was in the writing and direction. But it is brought over most clearly to us with the people we see. With the one exception of Alan Marshall, who could be called a stick of wood except that he bends and opens the mouth, the cast seems to have been living there all its life. The good lord knows where she gets it, but Ginger Rogers has got every range of the working-girl character and a direct projection far ahead of the lines themselves; as I'm afraid I've said too many times, she has learned more of the right things faster than any actress today, and is still at it. George Murphy is exactly it for a part that could so easily have run off into the heavy-stupid or vice versa. But the center of the frame belongs naturally to Miss Rogers and Burgess Meredith, who has never been quite so brash and yet appealing without a false note, the perfect Little Man, happy for nothing, wistful and right underneath and friends with the world. ("I don't believe in this every-man-for-himself: I get *lonesome*.") The best sequence in the picture and one of the best anywhere, for fun and poetry and all in proper ascension and beautiful timing, is his first date with the girl on a dollar-eighty, the walk home, the front steps in summer, these foolish things, etc. Garson's Guard in fact might as well include everybody on those sets, for that is the kind of thing it is, with the bloom on it. (P.S. You can't ad-lib bloom: the feeling must be there, and care too.)

There are a few weak points. Monkeyshines with the credit titles are getting out of control these days. Music as mimicry of voice or action is not good scoring; otherwise Roy Webb's background carries along. One special effect could have been spared us: the dissolve through a whirling image, which belongs in a Grantland Rice Sportlight. And the ending is just a little too abrupt; it has the necessary surprise, or punch, but it is not quite led up to, and sends them away on a somewhat lower note.

Of course it is true that our eaters of raw meat will be impatient with such frivolous verities as a young girl's dream of life, for these are times when we must be up and acting just as soon as ever we can get out of the swivel chair, in just a minute. But it was finished under Citizen Kanin's temporary deferment of induction into the actual armed, or nonswivel forces—which I believe will enjoy such a show thoroughly wherever they may find themselves. And it is foot by foot the best-made picture of this year, if that means anything.

28 July 1941

The Sober Truth

As a picture *The Stars Look Down* has already had an uneasy time. It was made in England and finished at least a year and a half ago. But it concerned mining problems; it was dark in mood and slow in pace; and its owner, MGM, didn't know what to do with it. But now with the rival and similar *How Green Was My Valley* actually in work they couldn't sit on their hands forever, so a campaign was started—"the stars look up to *The Stars Look Down*," the stars being such deepwater critics as Clark Gable, Hedy Lamarr, Robert Taylor, Norma Shearer, and other MGM properties, and their opinion being that here was Art, but a whole museum. Then the film was opened in New York City, the Criterion Theatre bowing and saying, Honored, Overwhelmed, in the ads, as it had little choice but do, poor chick, being on what is known as the wastebasket circuit and used to limping along with the screams and gunshots of a double bill without the feature.

It was a tough film to exploit, but I can't help feeling that matters are only made worse when people supposed to know their business make such an obvious business of saying, "Whoo, whoo, we've got the jitters, haven't you?" It is called a critics' picture and everybody says *uh*-oh, including the critics, and exhibitors all over the country book the film into the nearest competitor's house in their prayers. The thing is to act like nothing has happened, especially if your money-loser has the luck to be a good picture, for in this trade there are more sheep than wolves. And now look. Even in the 1,600-seat Criterion, *The Stars Look Down* actually grossed $13,000 against the $10,000 of a regular-campaign feature on a concurrent first week in MGM's own showcase up the street, the higher-scale, 4,500-seat Capitol. Exploitation, they call it; movie-wise, they say. Give a good dog a bad name and call a turkey *Juarez;* I don't get it.

The Stars Look Down is a solid piece of work, and it was not an easy picture to make. Its story is so plain and its scope for play of character so narrow that to achieve the final, all-carrying sweep of such a theme and its forces realized in art, it would have taken some mastery in film technique beyond story, and the detail work around this character or that—something like the massed effects in intricate motion of Pudovkin or the sustained tension of a crowding and oppressive darkness you can still experience in Pabst's *Kamerad-schaft*. One of the fighting Welsh miners has a son who comes back from school to take his place among the men after he has been jailed and the strike crippled. The strike is a local affair, brought against an owner who is working a murderous condemned shaft, and the local agitators do not have the support of their union.

There is a local smooth chap who works with the owner and any local young women not nailed down; there is a local young woman who wheedles the boy into leaving the university for her. She is the one who nearly destroys him, for she is no better than willful bitch enough to tangle him up with the smooth chap (he had been there before) at a time when the union still had time to avert the cave-in, which is the climax of the picture, its tragedy, but also its justification of the good fight and therefore note of hope.

A few people from the rich and poor of the neighborhood come into the story as far as the edge. Otherwise it is this triangle affair widened out by selfishness on one side and high aspiration on the other to the rising question of miners' lives and poor rewards. It is done soberly and with exact detail; its settings are somber and fine; it is even more unrelieved than it needs to be in its steadfast progression. But its outcome is at once so inevitable but simple, tragic but forever in arriving, that a dramatic tension has been lost and with it a certain dramatic meaning.

Still, it is an enduring sort of piece, and this effect is made possible by the easy realism of home life and speech in writing and direction, the good forthright work of the cast. Carol Reed proved more by it than that he is a good director, for it is good in quite different ways than his others; J. B. Williams took the script from A. J. Cronin's adaptation of his novel. Michael Redgrave is the young man, Margaret Lockwood the girl, Emlyn Williams the smooth number, and there are a lot of others filling in with craggy speech and faces, Nancy Price, Cecil Parker, Milton Rosmer, Edward Rigby. The picture, in fact, would not have been what it is with another cast, for its sense of vitality, of the thing being so because it happened, of trouble being real and always close behind, travels on their shoulders. Except for a trick or two and the bloody rumpus of angels at the end, it is a picture you can sit through with profit and without squirming—and should therefore rally round.

The pictures that Rey Scott took during his travels in China under the war make a certain illustration of both today's headlines and tomorrow's hope. They have been put together under the title *Ku Kan*. Scott started in South China, went over the Burma road to Chungking, and went on north from there to the boundary provinces, almost to Tibet. He went by truck, by pony, by plane, by boat. He covered a staggering amount of territory and he also covered the activities of China in her fight to keep men provisioned and equipped in the field, to keep roads open, to rebuild bombed cities, repatriate orphans. He got thousands of faces, hundreds of varied landscapes; in many cases he brought back the inaccessible and seldom seen.

The picture is not set up as a travelogue, however. It comes to a designed climax in the photographed bombing of Chungking, but otherwise is intended to be more inspirational, a tribute to China's democracy, than anything else. Granted the hazards under which it was taken, it is a pretty poor technical job even for a home movie. You can leave out of it the unsteady and often dim camera work and the color, which is simply atrocious, but you can't give it a grade of any kind for its choice of key situation, its overfootage of self-conscious grinning faces, its constant failure to complete the action and thus the meaning, its heavy repetition and heavier Mr. Scott, cavorting. The amateur's look-at-me-I'm-taking-your-picture robs the people shown of the natural dignity of their life; there are long stretches of the dull unnecessary. Mr. Scott brings back a record of importance. But I submit that it is of equal importance for those who have something to say to pay some heed to the art of saying it. Various credits for continuity and editing are sprinkled around, but the credit titles are as far as any traces of the shaping process go. The thing is so vivid in material that it is more of a shame than usual its possibilities were just never realized in a picture way.

11 August 1941

The Man in the Movies

If you will hold onto your hats going around this corner I will say that Sam Goldwyn's screen version of *The Little Foxes* is one of the really beautiful jobs in the whole range of movie making, and that includes any time or place or name. And speaking of names, we might try to remember sometimes that for every fifty bonehead jokes ascribed to Goldwyn, there is a Goldwyn picture. And the picture is not his first, or his fifteenth either, and you will club your wits a good bit before you will turn up a producer, any time or place, with such a steady record of fine jobs behind him.

It was William Wyler who actually made the picture, of course; Wyler as director of the people and the material before him, especially the very good material provided by the script makers: Dorothy Parker, Alan Campbell, and Arthur Kober working on Lillian Hellman's screenplay of her original. William Wyler as assisted by the finest technicians anywhere in the art of set building, by the camera work of Gregg Toland, who is back again from Orson Welles to the true art of picture making, at which he is one of the first men. But above all, as it must be in films, William Wyler. There are director-proof scripts written and there are director-proof actors; but these show their heads only in the full of the blue moon and they do not result in a picture like *The Little Foxes*. When he is good, as he should be, and given the chance, as he should be, the director is the man in the movies; and William Wyler—brought here by Jesse Lasky as an outlander kid, going to the Coast as general chore boy, working up as an assistant on the old Westerns—is one of the men, his name a better guarantee than all the titles and the stars.

If it can be put briefly at all: the story is the same, but the possible implications of a speech downstage, center, have been made probable in the life of a community as we see it; they have been prepared for earlier, and are followed through; their meaning has become a part of our unconscious acceptance. It is true that afterthought still raises its puzzles: everything seems to come even but what is the end in fate of Birdie, once her dramatic purpose has been served? Is this nest of evil to be taken as a thing pointing backward toward a superior past, ahead to heavier darkness, to some state of grace? At one time or another, as it serves the purpose of story, each of these still seems to be alternately inevitable or impossible; and in terms of dramatic truth, it is still a case of the Furies themselves in a dogfight, ending with a bitter truce and no hope for the race.

But afterthought is never the dramatic experience, and that experience is one of clear and mounting power. There is the atmosphere of pleasant rooms and sunlight, and a sort of graciousness in the externals of living as sweet and recurrent as an old tune. And in the middle of it, the acid and metal, the terrible pattern, the banking and bonding and percenting knavery of hearts hard enough to hold money and make it work, so that the only horror is in setting dollar against dollar—call it the ethics of business, in a distillation of the very worst. You know the story or you don't need to know it until you see it. The point is in its translation from concepts into picture, into developing every possibility so that this thing may be seen, the good and weak holding out against the wicked in their strength.

It is done through the characters of Bette Davis, Herbert Marshall, Teresa Wright, and Richard Carlson, with Patricia Collinge, Charles Dingle, Carlton Reid, Dan Duryea, and John Marriott from the Broadway cast. It is in fact done with everybody who appears in it, for I do not remember a bad performance, or anything that seemed like a performance as spoken with emphasis; and the written-in parts for the Negroes of the town were in that rare balance of the humor and dignity that so many pictures and plays (including the Broadway original) try for without achieving more than a Tom-show. Bette Davis is probably in the best role of her life here, and seems born to it. The tricks with the hands and the hyperthyroid are not necessary, and she discards them. She is there as a central figure, she maintains that perfect truth which makes the figure perfectly terrible; she is working along her own special line, but that line becomes the picture for its duration, and if any actress has done better you will have to read about it in memoirs.

Herbert Marshall hereby cancels out any part he has ever played: as the acute cardiac and man of gentleness he is actually grand, and I do not believe there is a dry eye in the audience to see him go. I do not believe either that we have seen so sensitive and wise a young girl as Teresa Wright for a long time, and in the picture version her youth and wonder become important for more reasons than that of providing a play without an ending with an ending. She is sweet and bewildered and she has the instinct for the actor's belief, so that even then, even so young and foolish, she moves with the unaffected serenity of that many years. The two brothers and the nephew are as they should be, solid pieces well joined in the structure—always with special credit to Dan Duryea, who makes an arrogance of sniveling, with both praise and a question mark for Patricia Collinge, whose Birdie is wonderful in some scenes and in others seems overwritten, too fluttery, too emphatic for the simple goodness that is supposed to be in her.

But we come back to the director again. By his patience, by his sort of omniscience in the matter of what detail will blend with the overall effect still in his mind, by the confidence he inspires even—by the knowledge on the part of an actor that this is a man who will not only tolerate but encourage good work—he has used these people to the ends of his picture. He needs them; he is lost without them. But they are lost without him, and if he is not a really high man at his work, with all its implications of patience and guidance and general finish, they may show but not to the best advantage. Just take one scene, a minor thing too. Herbert Marshall has come out to lean his weak fury against the banister, Bette Davis has come home from the battle-line, entering from the door across the space below, preoccupied and busy with gloves and stuff, to take five steps, six, seven (we know he is there, we are waiting) and another step and, *stop*. The dramatic part of the scene lifts up like a full chord in the orchestra, and we think, it is this woman who has looked up with her hard nervous eyes to find this object of hate. But it is actually the man who devised this much, to put her in the center of the screen, to warn us in advance, to give us that sense of an even count up to the point of collision, and then, seven, eight, collision. And that man is the director; it is in a picture like this that you can see him at work.

1 September 1941

In the Army, Aren't We All

The only shred of truth in the wild and already rather laughable charges against Hollywood recently made in Washington is that with the rising general interest in the war abroad and the Hitler specter, the producers have made a few tentative excursions into these fields of interest. It is along the ancient line of their practice—be topical when it doesn't hurt—and if we go shrieking to war again, we may expect to find them shrieking their heads off right along with us, and cleaning up. But we may not expect to find them taking any long leads off second, in war or in anything else.

Sergeant York is a case in point. It is about the army and arming in a time when people damn well *have* to think about the army. The film is actually not so bad as could be expected. It is a stunt picture to start with, and the publicity people have blown the roof off with the story of the authenticity of the authentic, etc. Like Lindbergh, also like Dr. Johnson's dog, York did something unusual enough to make the press wires and the easy imagination of newspaper readers. He captured a number of Germans single-handed, nothing wrong with that. But the thing got out of focus and seemed a big thing about the war, which it did nothing toward winning, which was too enormous a shambles to be expressed in any one act or gesture, and which made far greater demands in the way of day-in-day-out heroism.

Anyhow, the picture people got hold of York, got the details of his story, and ran him up into a spectacle. The war itself plays a minor part in the film, almost half of which is taken up with the troubles of a poor young farmer off in the hills of Tennessee. Where this part is homely and direct in its treatment of outpost living, it is good, it is leisurely and enjoyable (much of its solidity is based in the characters of Gary Cooper and of Margaret Wycherly, the fighting mother). Where it goes into York's first conversion from hoodlumism to shouting hallelujah it is just sticky enough to get uncomfortable, and where York gets his second conversion—from a religious pacifism to militancy in defense of the American land—it has got mystically out of hand. The first part of the military phase is humorous and exciting, starting with camp life (particular mention for Stanley Ridges and George Tobias), and ending on the high dramatic note of the battle and the capture.

After that it is nothing but a memorial screed, with accounts of each decoration, each triumphal parade, each headline, etc., on and on, with the war receding into a happy backdrop and all the dead men underground. There is parallelism, of course—1917 and 1941—but it is not stressed; and mainly standing out at the end is the typical-American figure of Gary Cooper, whom we know. The keynote is patriotism, but they've been trying to get York to let the picture be made since the end of the last war, and I hardly think the effect is any different from that of a parade, with colors and a band: it is stirring and it is too long; there are too many holdups and too many people out of step, and your residue of opinion on the matter is that it will be nice to get home and get your shoes off.

Dive Bomber will be a design for whooping it up only to the uninitiated. Warner Brothers have been making a picture about every possible branch of the armed services ever since *What Price Glory?* About every fifth time, I pick one up to see if they have changed the formula. They haven't.

Dive Bomber borrows slightly from the Paul Muni Science Series in that the hero is a flight surgeon, worrying about the prevention of temporary blackout and high-altitude sickness. Otherwise it is the same old pudding of thrill in maneuvers (the too few intercuttings of planes in formation are fine) and the impossible in personal relations. Everybody is simply poisonous to everybody else for no discoverable reason; officers with two or three full stripes go barking at each other for reels like so many Dead End kids; and then suddenly—that is, suddenly after two hours—everybody has either died heroically or loves everybody else and is a fine chap, and Errol Flynn hasn't even been very brave. (The girl is kept in the background but still serves as another thin excuse for people to spit in each other's eye.) If any investigation is necessary, there might be a committee set up to inquire why such incompetence in both the psychology and the art of both writing and direction should be allowed to make pretty fools out of any body of men working anywhere in any cause, peace or war.

A word on Technicolor. *Dive Bomber* is made in Technicolor. I haven't heard many dissenting voices, and I hesitate to throw in with the stick-in-the-muds who thought sound pictures were doomed; but for telling a story, for balancing picture values, for bringing the point into focus and the many points into a line, I think Technicolor stinks. It is no more natural than a picture postcard of Old Orchard Beach, *circa* 1912; it muddies up every scene of action by throwing everything with a blob of color on it square into the dramatic foreground; it gives dim outlines wherever a sharp edge is essential; and it so distorts anything but sky and distance that the grim efficiency of men in a flying field is made to look like chocolate soldiers playing with a box of candy. A painter can be color-mad, but will still keep the thing in his own design. Before the camera, as highly as it has been developed today, color simply takes control and runs away with the show. Color in pictures is here to stay, all right. They can make a picture like *Dive Bomber* out of anything they want to, including mud pies, and we should be willing to wait for it to straighten itself out—a process that is not hurried so long as there are so many people of moderate good taste in other things who still give glad little cries every time a dramatic background lights up like Christmas. But we should regret and damn its daubed encroachment on the full effect of anything that might be called a good picture.

29 September 1941

Movie-Goer Blues

The Birth of the Blues was a good idea for a picture story, but since it was to be about music it had to be treated as a musical, and apparently when you start a musical production you throw story values out the window in the first place. The proposition here is that something like the first popularity of the Dixieland Band and the new jazz be made into a fiction using various characters and speaking of certain aspects of musical development. With the natural dramatic license in the way of remoteness from the difficult and scattered facts, the simplification and avoidance of essential but monotonous detail, the pointing up of effects beyond their relative importance, this could still make a sound tale, as such things go. But there is too strong a pattern in the inherited tradition of the vaudeville and burlesque turn, the revue, stage musicals, and previous movie extravaganzas. You get the face of even a mild and amiable truth; you see that the schedule calls for numbers and specialties and a band; and you grab for the burnt cork to draw a mustache on it, blacken a couple of front teeth or an eye, and put a pipe in its mouth.

The picture has the musical and supervisional talents of Victor Schertzinger; it has Brian Donlevy and Mary Martin (but alas); and two absolutely top men, each in his field of music: Bing Crosby and Jack Teagarden. And the story keeps more or less in motion: the early struggles of the band, the first success in a cabaret and the complications that follow because the spot is run by ominous characters, and—along another line—because among the two men and the girl everybody thinks everybody loves somebody else right up to the end. There is some good atmosphere stuff, several choruses and reprises of tunes like "Memphis Blues," "Melancholy Baby" (anachronism, but done very nicely), and "St. Louis Blues" (done with choirs and pathos as thick as molasses, awful).

For awhile there is a little fun with the gangsters, who are soon allowed to get out of key—though never so much out as the idea that Dixieland playing made its first one-shot success through the voice and figure of Miss Martin, who wiggles both. Rochester has some good things to do, some bad. There is a girl child whom everybody has to adore for some reason which is closer to the fact that Paramount is stuck with her contract than to anything else. And a fight or two. Teagarden gets a few lines, looks a little nervous, and is allowed to do a few introductions and backgrounds (but keep it way down: actors working).

Probably the trouble with all such attempts is that musicians have spent their lives learning one thing, actors another; and with the exception of Bing Crosby, a natural, they never mix jobs well enough to take off the curse of falsity and strain. But in anything like the *The Birth of the Blues* this is just surmise: here the writers and director were following a pattern, not only in outline but in treatment, that is false as hell to start with. Their good effects come in patches, and the total effect is first pleasant, then depressing. Its patches are quite a bit above the average and so I'd go to see it anyway; but you have to be that way.

One of the phenomena of movie success in the last few years has been the institution known as the Hardy Family. MGM has gotten around ten pictures out of it in three and a half years, and it is a gold mine. But unlike the Bobbsey Twins cycle for kiddies, it can't go on forever, and it can never quite stand still either. The adults in the cast remain the same, more or less, but the interest is in the kids, who in actual life grow up. As the movie people have always found to their sorrow, you get a million-dollar property with golden curls and first thing you know the little stinker is giving with a bass voice. And even when you can keep them looking cute and young, there are always the Hollywood gossip reports of haring around in night clubs and fast cars, and what can you do about innocence in a pinafore when Deanna Durbin decides she is going to get herself married?

So the Hardy Family—the only such group I can remember—has had to keep scratching, and as a result there was some rather nice stuff in the earlier pictures, on the subject of growing pains, etc. And this fall Mickey Rooney must enter college. (Already this summer Lewis Stone had to warn Rooney that certain women did certain things, which brought distress to some of the goodie groups.) But the only reason for bringing the subject up now is a report in *Variety* that I fancy very much: MGM has completed the important early groundwork for a new one: *Andy Hardy Meets Dr. Kildare.*

Dr. Kildare is one of what you might call the static series, of which scores flourish a while and then peter out for lack of sustaining interest. It is so easy, with the same adult characters, to go on making carbons of the first success, that they go on making carbons. Only Westerns and detective stories can get away with it indefinitely, it seems: the Lone Ranger, the Saint, Mr. Moto, Charlie Chan (even the death of their lead character didn't prevent them from making twenty Chans or so). And *Dr. Kildare's Wedding Day* showed a weakening that alarmed the company. The doctor's bride, apparently, had to be pulled from the series for bigger things, and so in the "wedding" picture they ran a truck over her before she made the altar. Now we can expect little development until the doctor's next landmark in picture titles, the less dramatic state of contemplation and completed wisdom which will be called *Dr. Kildare's Mental Pause.* Anyway, they are going to see if one can shore up the other.

The more I think of the idea, the more I like it. Mickey Rooney's latest, *Life Begins for Andy Hardy,* showed him as completely out of hand. I liked him as a frank and noisy kid, but he is growing up in the story without dropping any noisy-kid mannerisms. By this time it is plain mugging and it is not cute, and the story itself has got away from the moderately natural in family troubles (middle-class, small-town) which gave charm to its simplicity in the beginning. Now it is merely simple and almost offensive. MGM owns both Kildare and Hardy; it could naturally not be coaxed into mergers off its own lot. But I can by now think of some nice ones. Andy Hardy Meets the Dracula Group, or Andy Hardy Meets the Masked Avenger.

In reviewing *Tom, Dick and Harry,* I used the term "Garson's Guard" in a loose and foolish way to designate the people who did some of the worrying on the stages and over the rushes. If this confused anybody about Paul Jarrico's true worth as the author of the screenplay except Jarrico (the rat), I'm mortified. It was a sweet little job.

6 October 1941

Some Pictures Move

The Maltese Falcon is the first crime melodrama with finish, speed, and bang to come along in what seems ages, and since its pattern is one of the best things Hollywood does, we have been missing it. It is the old Dashiell Hammett book, written back in the days when you could turn out a story and leave it at that, without any characters joining the army, fleeing as refugees or reforming bad boys, men, or women. It is hokum, all right—about a historic image so costly with gold and jewels that people follow it all over the world, plotting to get it away from other people similarly employed, the various forces finally converging in the territory of Sam Spade, a detective. But John Huston has written the screenplay and directed the picture so that a fast pace and direct, vigorous approach give a surface meaning to each situation as it follows another.

The story is one of the few cases where they have their cake and eat it too, for the detective *is* in love with the mystery woman, and she *might* turn out in the end to be another case of (a) innocence wronged, (b) the most trusted agent of the United States government. But she doesn't, and he sends her up for twenty years. There is bound to be a little confusion in this, for an audience likes to know where it stands, and neither Mary Astor's lines nor her abilities above them quite get over the difficulty of seeming black and then seeming white, and being both all along.

Scene by scene, the picture has many good services—first of all those of the director, who has a genuine sense of suggestion and picture motion. Peter Lorre is never dull though much too often typed. There are Ward Bond, Barton MacLane, Gladys George, and Jerome Cowan, but the key man in the supporting cast is Sydney Greenstreet, who does a marvelous and veteran creation, solid in the center of each scene, as the genial and menacing fat man. There is character in the picture and this, as well as the swift succession of its contrived excitements and very shrewd dialogue, is what gives the temporary but sufficient meaning required by its violent fantasy.

And outside of the writer-director, the chief character influence in the story is Humphrey Bogart, a man of explosive action in an iron mask. He is not a villain here, though a pretty hard type; but it doesn't make any difference: he has some of that magnetism you can feel through the screen; he is a villain with appeal. He has a good part here, a steady outlet for that authority and decision and hard level talk of his. But he fills it without trying and you're with him.

It is pleasant to see a French picture again, though *The Man Who Seeks the Truth* was obviously not rushed over here when it was made a couple of years ago because of weaknesses in general construction, and lack of much excitement. It is the story of a banker who was a cuckold and general butt of friends and relatives, but who hit upon the trick of pretending sudden deafness, and thus found them all out as they took advantage of him openly, and told them all off. The trick and the way it is handled turn up some good humorous stuff, the banker is made a likable character, and though the situations of betrayal and ingratitude are the kind of thing worn thin with ancient use, the thing has a certain homeliness and edge.

Very few of the French directors, however, have learned the meaning of the words continuity and motion in connection with turning out pictures. They have been more advanced in the adult subjects they could choose, the way of treating them, and they have been content to rest on that: in a picture sense most of them have been making primitives for years. *The Man Who Seeks the Truth* is poorly lighted and badly recorded, but worse than that it is so abruptly chopped up into a stage-set (speech) and then another unrelated and mystifying stage-set (speech) that there is none of that clarity and flow that are one of the joys of pictures. Actually, pictures are so immediate in their nearness and rapidity of transition that they may not depend on the audience contribution—suspension of disbelief, imagination, etc.—of the slower stage. When there is no clear lead from both the time and place of one scene over into those factors in the next, the audience spends most of its time not truly participating, but figuring. As a show, this one is still worth it, for the story qualities mentioned, and for Raimu, whose central performance is one of those substantial delights of the theater.

The only thing to know about the film *Tanks a Million*—outside of that it is comedy so far short of funny as to be embarrassing—is that it represents a new try in pictures, as to type and length. Hal Roach has got the idea of blowing up the usual two-reel comedy short into something under an hour, for the second half of a double bill, taking little more expense and devising than is needed for the usual short, which is practically a throwaway. *Tanks a Million* is the first of these streamlined features, and was considered good enough in its own right to be played into a single bill at the Criterion Theatre in New York, where it drew a kind of yokel laughter. One should be interested in any screen venture which scales down the deadly overlength of pictures as they are generally run up today. But there is no hope in Hal Roach, who cashes in on the idea of national-defense effort by assuming that the officers of our armed forces are still as good for laughs as the antique kick-in-the-pants-and-cut-to-chase of the Keystone cops.

20 October 1941

Two for the Show

Every time you think the Disney studio can't do any more because they have done everything, they turn around and do it again, the new and never dreamed of, the thing lovely and touching and gay. *Dumbo* is the new feature-length film, and I believe you could see it four times anyway, for there is much in it of frank and open laughter, there is much in it so high of fancy that you will not assimilate everything the first two times—and like everything done by the people of that organization, quick as their sympathy and understanding for the animals of their eternal fables have to be, there is something of sweetness and quick feeling that is often close to tears.

The idea was a natural, taken from a book: a baby elephant in a circus who is always in trouble and has ears so big he is considered a freak. His mother elephant is called mad and put in irons because she tears the place up a little in his defense, and so he is practically an orphan and, much worse, made a clown in the show. It is as simple as that, and unless such simplicities put a match to the imagination, as they invariably seem to do to the Disney staff, you had better leave the story as it would come out on paper alone. The thing is done with expressions, with incidents arising from character and the general nature of things, and with a constant improvisation that is not only an endless wonder but the first, perhaps the only, machinery for true fable of our time.

More than ever in this picture, Disney is bringing in the distinctive human element, while still remaining in the background of the cartoon. The voices are those not of specialized sound men but of character actors; the facial cast of an elephant here, a tiger there, is closer to someone known; the comment on human affairs is very busy and sharp. Those boys are always moving forward in experiment: there is a difference here, and more edge. (Strangely enough, they have taken cognizance of the terrors of *Snow White,* and those who make it their business to see that children eat their cereal and don't have too good a time pronounce this one free of any evil, while admitting its excitement.) The one other noticeable advance in cartoon technique is a bold stepping out in the field of deliberate fantasy, as tied into the story by dream, by the imagined image, by a hangover even. Whatever you wish to call it, I say that nothing, not even *Alice in Wonderland,* has turned nonsense into such strictly sensible beauty as the sequence of the pink-elephant dance; I have never seen anything to approach it and neither have you, because there hasn't been anything. And the children will like it as they like *The Jungle Books*—it is made for them as well as for us; and they will like it and go through the skies with it as they never could with the legend of Pegasus, taught in school. The highest and most rare of experimentation has been brought by the iron rule of movies-to-please-the-public to the lowest common denominator, has been tried and justified, and is still so far out ahead of any crackpot artist who thought of wiring geranium pots onto the second-floor windows of the Museum of Modern Art, for the music of rhythm and the astounding creations of the human mind, that you feel what a child must feel before any crackpot artist. All I can say is that there were between twelve and twenty of us looking at another Disney, and that we had all of us been looking at pictures in a way of amateur professionalism for years, and we were none of us, for once, either very vocal or very coherent. It is one of the lovely things, a proof of pictures.

There is one more thing to notice and that is the harmless nature of the fun, the comedy without malice. The black-crow chorus, for example, might seem to be straight out of Octavus Roy Cohen, but that is only seeming and the truth of it is finally that the thing is done with such affection that even its close and clever take-off leaves you with the appreciation of something done for the love of it only. I have done a little hollering on the score of the Disney sound effects and music being the best that have been put to the use of pictures, and I see no reason to discontinue. *Dumbo* ends in almost a blaze of music and the chances are you will come away from it singing with the crow choir: "I done been seen 'bout most everything." And that sums it up: you have done been—until next time.

The story of *The Remarkable Mr. Kipps* is one of those satires involving a good man being made a fool of that are insistent enough to be painful, and that now seem dated more in the manner of treatment than in subject matter. And Carol Reed's movie from the old Wells novel (made in England for Twentieth Century-Fox release here) fails to be thoroughly enjoyable through just such considerations. It was made to follow the original idea carefully and too carefully. When the young draper's clerk suddenly inherits an estate, there follows an unremitting series of incidents in which he is played for the most painful kind of chump by a set of the most flagrant kind of snobs. You are not given any relief, or any sense of conflict either, and condescension and conniving are laid on so thick by the various actors selected to represent types that you fall from hoping he will slap *somebody's* face to the resigned belief that he has not actually the native good sense and dignity to take him out of the idiot class into anything worth all this fictional fuss and labor.

If the characters to be exposed had been held to the subtlety of understatement, some of the curse might have been removed. And the ending of the picture on the other hand is such an understatement of any point made as to be simply inconclusive. Otherwise, it is a well-made yarn, shrewd in little things, blessed in its profusion of such odds and ends as details from life, from character, from customs and period. The good English directors, the conscientious and humane people, have fine things to give us in the way of solid natural backgrounds and character parts. The actors, of course, fortuitously escape the worn familiarity of our Hollywood types bobbing up picture after picture—they only correspond to our Walter Brennans and Slim Summervilles and Warren Hymers and Gene Lockharts.

In any event, it is the people and the way they are built solidly into their world that matter here. Michael Redgrave throws away all chances to be dashing in recreating the chump; Arthur Roscoe has a perfectly gorgeous time as the unreliable cockney theater buff; Diana Wynyard is the girl of the story. It is one of those things that clicks into its place without trying to go above it, and it seems a pity to waste such work in production on material, whether or not it is supposed by the foolish to be classic, on stuff so poor.

27 October 1941

Happy Endings

Show people have a word that is to them a final work, "sordid." If a picture is "sordid," they say—meaning if it is about the less fortunate or less admirable types of character—the public will not care for it. In a loose and very general way the rule might hold good, but it makes an absurd yardstick to measure any one picture by and it can only too easily be turned into a club to beat producers, writers, and directors over the head with. The truth is that if a picture is well and soundly made and has the indispensables of interest and action, it can be "sordid" or anything else and let all prophetic crows be damned. *The Little Foxes* has about as much concentrated evil in main story and main characters as the films have ever tackeled; and *The Little Foxes* is one of the three leading pictures in the current nationwide box office.

Now comes Alfred Hitchcock with one of the better-known murder stories, a clever study in the abnormal and vicious under a cloak of charm. The book was called *Before the Fact,* but they had to change the title of the movie to the much lamer one of *Suspicion,* for the reason that there is no longer actually any fact. The book itself is too slow, talky, and undercharacterized for my taste, but the very capacities for speed, suspense, and actual people of the films could have been used to turn it into an exciting picture. Well, they weren't. The show runs an hour and three-quarters and the suspense gets less and less. Hitchcock had planned to keep both the girl in the story and the audience guessing right up to the last minute, and get away from the "sordid" at the last minute by having everything happily explained. On paper it still looks like a good idea; on film it simply breaks down, first through the nature of things and second through the film's lapses.

It is about an irresponsible young Englishman, plausible, lovable even, but with a complete innocence of scruple and a terrible need for betting-money. And I think where it breaks down in the nature of things is that if this young man turns out to be no more than what he appears to be on the surface all along, what have you got? Cary Grant. He is a nice chap, and despite what Joan Fontaine is supposed to dread about him, you cannot but go on believing that he is just a nice chap. This transfers the center of interest to the suspicions of his wife, which are so admittedly ill-founded as to make her a pretty negative type at best. So nothing happens except that a quick twist at the end explains everything to her satisfaction, if not the audience's.

The film is well cast all down the line. Cary Grant in particular is just right for that part; the picture's most successful figure is Nigel Bruce as Beaky, which is simply the case of a grand trouper having a grand time building up a part out of what in the original was very little. As a matter of fact, one of the reasons the original wasn't followed closely enough to achieve the original effect is that as human beings—which even actors are when they're good—it is hard to achieve the grim monotony of the book, which deals with a submoral scoundrel, a tidy and vapid wife, and a near-cretin from the public schools.

In every way save that of speed and form the production is a glossy, and done with a very shrewd eye for bringing out the inner conflict as it was redesigned. You do not say it was poor so much as that it was a disappointment, which is praise of a sort. The thing as it should have been to make sense, with certainty and horror mounting together, and faster, was not attempted— apparently because Hitchcock let an old and shaky attitude scare him into thinking more of his box office than of his story logic and picture effect. He is a wise enough man in films to know better, a big enough name in films to dare more and get away with it. Every film maker with his wits about him knows the constant demand for compromise and how to accede to it gracefully; but he should know even more what can and what can't be sacrificed if he is to make good pictures. Men with their eye on the box office soon find that they can maintain fame and income without making good pictures, and presently are not making them, and finally cannot.

There is nobody who makes bad comedies more funny than W. C. Fields—who is responsible for making them bad in the first place. *Never Give a Sucker an Even Break* is his newest and written by himself. It should have been about the life among carnival barkers and pitchmen that its title celebrates, or it should have been about something. Instead it is just an old-time farce showing Fields as a broken-down movie hack outlining a plot to a producer and acting out the plot through the main part of the picture. Young Gloria Jean is a sort of Deanna Durbin singer and heart interest; Fields is her uncle and although she is a cute kid I should say it generally serves her right.

There are other people scattered through the story, very scattered, and the irony of their situation is that most of what little work they do in the picture leaves you impatient for the solo appearance of the very man responsible for the dull absurdity of the state they find themselves in.

However, my sermon on the obsolescence of the movie comedy as a one-man series of turns is beginning to bore me too, and Fields of course has listened to no one since someone told him there wasn't any fire in Chicago. He is one of the natural funny men, against all odds and comers, and you could as soon reform him into pictures as you could get him on a diet of vegetable juices—probably with a result as fatal. Once again disaster is his friend; once again the forces of gravity and public opinion are against him, little recking that he is their master, at least of ceremonies. His nose is still red but unbloody, he still finds the rich and awful widow by the middle of the picture, he has still about him that majesty of place and breeding which turns the point of any blade save his own; he is still the gay dog with the old tricks—the business with the feet, the stick, the plug hat, the reflective but sonorous aside, the topper, nasal and triumphant, with which the entire architecture of the forces for order is toppled at least once in every picture. He is usually down but he is never right, and yet there is in him a kind of humor so deeply seated that familiarity becomes somehow a further extension of our delight in this figure that is already American legend, having built itself up by giving itself away. If there was ever a great clown in this time of changeover from the beer and music-hall to the universal distribution of radio and films, I would say it was in the person and the character and the undying if corny gusto of Bill Fields, who moved mountains until they fell on him, and then brushed himself off and looked around for more.

10 November 1941

Valley with Shadows

How Green Was My Valley is the kind of material the movies are always banking on to answer the demand always being made on them: Why don't you *do* something? It is the picture from the book by Richard Llewellyn, made with great expense and great care and with every intention of fidelity. It is a good job, going into life for both hard times and good times, for sorrow and the fresh gust of laughter alike. But just as the book sprawled, so the story sprawls here, and it seems that too much of the craft of films has had to be deployed in the overcoming of factors that are not essentially film stuff. The full force of a picture, that is to say, is not here in full force.

The story starts with an I-remember-I-remember from the man who is now grown, now leaving his native valley in the coal deposits of Wales; the camera goes under his words and back to the town and house where he was a boy, the youngest son of a family of proud miners. And it is from the life of this family as a center that the episodes of the story proceed, with an occasional comment or bridging from the narrator. The boy is growing up as the inevitable forces of modern industrialism are growing up and the pleasant, respectable life of the community is growing down. Wages are cut and cut again, and the young men, including the sons of the family, are urgent for union and a strike in self-defense. But to the old man, the rock of ages among the hard-working, good-living people of that town, such talk flies in the face of his father and his grandfather, and thus of God.

The strike is settled after hard months (the full meaning of hunger and fear in so bleak a condition has been better handled in other pictures); and already there are men in the valley who will never find a day's work in it again. Meanwhile the emphasis of the narrative has been shifting to other matters of family life. One of the sons is married and then killed in the mine. The daughter is in love with the young parson, and since he has married the Church, she takes a miserable fop instead. Later there is a baseless but crushing scandal, for the village is running down below the clean honest dirt of coal-dust these times. The parson is both tutor and guardian angel to the boy, who is finally old enough to go to school and get his lumps, and who breaks his father's heart because he would rather go into the mines than the university. And at the end of this two hours in the theater, there is a mine explosion in which the old man dies.

Too long and too various. The trouble is not with the fine things in this sincere piece of work, but with the structure holding them. Just as he did in *The Long Voyage Home*, John Ford has been willing to take on a weak continuity for the sake of the rich stuff he can get out of the separate parts, in atmosphere, character, situation. And continuity by any dramatic standard is not an empty word, a formula for the well pressed and trivial. It signifies that cumulative power of a story, of a statement of conflict, when it progresses from its elected point to its stern, inevitable end. Neither is unity merely another word for reviewers to use like a crutch. For the effect alone there should be a steady and observable purpose, and all the intrusions of the extraneous and absurd, as from life, should be made to work for this purpose, becoming genuinely a part of it, for it is truer in the theater than in early colonies that those who do not work shall not finally eat.

But this is a John Ford picture, and nobody who can learn about movies will suppose that Ford will get a story he likes and not have enough say as to writers and actors so that things can't happen. Ford got Philip Dunne to make a movie script out of *How Green Was My Valley,* and the book was gradually adapted and smoothed out so that there would be no jar in transition between the living room and the high street to the town's center, yet so there would remain the roughness of working hands and people living as their fathers had lived, all in its natural simplicity through the delicate prism of the form's technical demand. Working in a major studio, the director had the best resources of the art and music departments at his command, the most likely actors available. He had him a Welsh village built among the hills of California; and when against this impeccable reproduction there was a scene to be played in the heart of things, he had his writer to dig it out and gauge it for motion, and he had the people who knew how to understand him and whom he knew when to leave alone.

Among the towering figures of theatrical presentation there will from now on be Donald Crisp as the father, as low but essential in his society as a cornerstone, in his home life the despot first, with the benevolence never acknowledged but forever lurking after. As the kid of the family, Roddy MacDowell gets a lot of play, and is no more pretentious than actual boys are (though possibly a little more soulful, wistful, wide-eyed). There are good people all through the cast, almost none of them speaking with a Welsh tongue, and there is above them and against Donald Crisp the chunky and dynamic figure of Sara Allgood as the wife, capable as always in the sharp back of her hand and anchored bulk of her conviction. But it is Donald Crisp's picture when all the results are in. In the story it is his family, to command and to stand for, and by his majestic simplicity in the fine things of an actor's projection, he manages to command as well the sympathy and understanding of those who look at the screen to see a man in his trouble. His part is not easily compared with other parts because it has its own solidity in special character. It has pathos with no quarter asked, it has ancient authority, and it has the play all through of delicacies roughly hidden, of sentiment and shrewd humor, as though you had covered over with rubble and found again some fine and twenty-jewel mechanism.

The picture as a whole is nothing so much as a return to the gone days of boyhood in their proper setting, with the family bickering and eating its healthy fill under the big and final fellow at the head of the table. And if Donald Crisp and the others bring the reality of life out of these scenes—too nearly perfect in the reproduction and not nearly perfect enough in even the illusion of Art Miller's camera work—it is because they were worked over by men who had an abiding interest in people. The deepest things in the picture are the incidental things, but they are thoroughly realized, they are vivid to us, and John Ford did not leave them there by chance. He and his people had something, and they knew it, and believing that what they had was good, they made it so.

1 December 1941

Forgotten or Forgettable

The New York State Board of Censors, learning nothing and forgetting nothing, has recently been kicked around quite satisfactorily for its action in barring the film *The Forgotten Village*. The board seems to have no friends on the press, which in the movie departments was almost unanimously happy over the outcome; I have never heard of any audience demonstration in its behalf, or against any public matter on which it had been overruled; and this is the second prominent case on which it was flatly told to go home by the Board of Regents.

The Forgotten Village is out-of-the-way, but not an extraordinary film. With John Steinbeck to provide the script, Herbert Kline took a small company down to a buried Mexican agricultural village, not yet touched by modern sanitation and state health. There they got the natives used to them and easy before the camera, and got them to working naturally in what seems a mixture of native life and the acting out of the simple pageant of the film's framework in story.

In the story, the Mexican village is subjected to a plague, arising from foul water supply. In the main family taken for consideration, the boy's brother dies, his mother has a premature childbirth, and his sister is taken sick. Going to the schoolteacher, he is told that what is needed is a doctor from the rural health-service organization. It is impossible to get the townspeople to agree to this, of course, so the boy goes off to the city in secret and alone. When the doctor comes, there is nothing he can do; the town is against him like a wall, and led by the old hokey-pokey witchwife is soon violent enough to chase him out. The boy is outlawed from his people and from his own family; but the note of hope is that as he goes to the city to study medicine himself, he will acquire that which his people need most, knowledge and skill in the new ways.

Mixed in with this, as you can imagine, are community scenes, the customs of the country, the way both of living and believing. It is all done with a stern avoidance of the brilliant in effects, and no hint of the picturesque; but there is a commensurate gain in the dignity of people; in the rightness—within the narrow bounds of their primitive training and poverty—of such a code of life. They are not emotionally expressive but they are not camera-conscious or silly, and much of the thing has the illusion of having been taken without their knowing it.

Technically, the film is not strong on dramatic appeal, and occasionally falls down on the time sense (*i.e.,* some actions spaced well apart in the life they represent pile into one another with nothing more than a cut and a jolt). Hanns Eisler's musical score is fundamentally right for this subdued type of story in this place, but seems rather thin and stringy, and not too germane to a simple but singing people. Probably the best thing is the absence of the usual announcer's hollow passions in the narrative tying it together. (Burgess Meredith is the Voice here.) What the film as a whole sets out to do is pretty minor, remote, and without much call for emphasis. But in what it does it is a good and honest job.

Swamp Water is so bad it's terrific. (Dudley Nichols takes discredit for the screenplay.) What the good actors say here cannot be held against them: Walter Huston, Walter Brennan, Eugene Pallette, John Carradine, Anne Baxter, Dana Andrews. But the hasty and absurd melodrama of the story is not to be excused in anybody writing later than the nineties; or in the direction of Jean Renoir.

Since the subject of the piece is the life of poor whites in the Georgia swamps, a Frenchman could be forgiven some of the awkwardness on grounds of the strangeness and bafflement of local custom and another language. But no more than 10 percent. How many directors and writers are familiar with the Georgia swamps anyway? Renoir is a man whose work has been spotty: if he had a solid story and solid natural actors to understand and walk through it, he could make a good picture, and no one could say whether it hadn't been director-proof in the first place *(Grand Illusion)*. If he had no more than was given him in a poor script, he could turn out a howling bore *(Madame Bovary)*. And now in the present picture he is so far from any appreciation of pace or motion, the illusion of even fragmentary sense or reality, that the more perceptive are going to withdraw from the chorus, "Hollywood has ruined another great man," and begin a little revision of what has up to now been almost uncontested law: if a Frenchman can get out two films that will merely fit on the projector sprockets, he becomes automatically the Great French Director. You don't easily get to be a Great Director in Hollywood, but if you learn the job the way it should be learned, you can get to be a damn good one. Which is a different thing.

8 December 1941

Bright Hokum

Serious people naturally want Miss Greta Garbo to be serious. She ought to go with the guy that brung her, that is. Serious people also want W. C. Fields to go on being funny. Serious people object with high contempt to what they call Hollywood typing, and then turn around and issue the exact sounds that make shrewd movie producers keep as many actors as possible in as nearly the same part as possible, to keep the paying dumb public from squinting and shuffling its feet. Serious people of the kind I mean feel themselves above the dumb public, but cannot be differentiated in the matter of squinting and shuffling feet. Do I like serious people of the kind I mean? I do not.

Working in the glamor mill of pictures for over fifteen years, Greta Garbo is still the most glamorous woman in the world. But she likes comedy and has a nice dry talent for it, and I suppose is fed up with being a tragic order of smorgasbord all her life. She was a brilliant success in *Ninotchka* and allowed to be such by special dispensation from even the serious. That was an Ernst Lubitsch production, but the reason for its felicity was neither Lubitsch nor Miss Garbo herself in the main; the reason was an absolutely stunning screenplay by Charles Brackett and Billy Wilder and Walter Reisch, as you can discover from reading it in the modified published form.

Now Miss Garbo is seen in another comedy, but with the direction of George Cukor, who is apparently a director careful to the point of elegance but always at the mercy of what the boys have cooked up for script. Since he is in the pleasant, easy latitudes of the top-budget "A" group, he can take his time in following the tortuosities of a script that wastes the audience's. If a writer lugs his uncle's wife into the story for no other purpose than that of padding out the chore of his contract, Mr. Cukor will apparently be patient and even elegant on the job of importing the writer's uncle's wife. The writers of *Two-Faced Woman* were Samuel Behrman, Salka Viertel, and George Oppenheimer, and occasionally they seemed tired. At such points the director yawned himself, out of carefulness, elegance, and politeness. So how did Miss Garbo know what was left on the cutting-room floor and what unfortunately wasn't, or how the strips of all the tiresome takes and retakes of the long day's work fitted together after all the weeks of production?

This brings us back to another fact in pictures deplored and abetted by the serious people: the star system. It is not only a letdown that the tragic Miss Garbo should work in a comedy, but they must say: "In the last Garbo picture," or "For a Garbo picture this is etcetera." Such a flexible and lovely star is important, true. Without her this would be very little, true. But how are we ever going to understand about pictures if we go blindly around like the autograph dopes thinking of the star as the living image, responsible for all refractions? Your production and camera in a major-studio job will probably be good, or at least acceptable. But among the prime matters of script and direction and acting, the second depends on the first (and *vice versa*), and the third depends on both. A little less nonsense from the serious, please. Or, act your age.

The idea of the story is the old mistaken-identity situation, principally as modified into the form of *The Guardsman:* that is, a proper girl who has been neglected by her husband goes gunning for him in the role of her twin sister, the family blacksheep and a very available type. She is lucky in the matter of assistance from friends and coincidence, and the rather giddy husband falls with a thoroughness that shocks her. But she hangs on and after some extremely cross-purposes toward the end apparently gets everything straightened out for both of them—though which of the characters she is now going to have her new married bliss as, is left up to the audience, since the man seems to go impartially for both.

It is the kind of thing whose success depends on a light touch, humor in and between the lines, and considerable invention. The invention is there, in both situations and the little touches that surprise laughter and divert attention from improbability. As for lines, it is the wittiest set of them in one picture I have heard in a long time (and the writers probably deserve credit beyond them for the absurd in pictorial device, also neatly realized). But the light touch presses rather heavily on you in terms of needless length and a certain grim emphasis in prosecuting minor affairs. It runs a little over an hour and a half, but the time seems longer because sequence after sequence has hung on after the idea is thoroughly clear and worked out: Garbo and the burlesque conga, Garbo as heavy siren, Garbo drunk, etc. And some of the comedy, especially in the skiing scenes, is broadened to the point of slapstick.

It is pretty much a one-woman picture (Melvyn Douglas, Roland Young, and Constance Bennett have parts), and thus hard to keep fresh and sprightly as comedy. But the woman is in herself a pleasure to watch and never monotonous. More important in comedy: in spite of defects, the laughs keep coming. Unless you are determined to be grumpy you will probably enjoy it.

15 December 1941

The Legion Rides Again

Comes again the question of movie censorship. Depending on where you live (Boston, Philadelphia, Cleveland, Providence, Rochester, Albany), you will have heard the Catholic Legion getting into action on the film *Two-Faced Woman*. In some places they have got if officially banned. In all places they have got the producers so scared they are reported as willing to withdraw, cut, and reshoot, if only the picture can be taken off the "objectionable" list. I don't think the Catholic Legion wants a few objectionable things taken out so much as it wants an issue.

Let me start at the beginning. Years ago when the Legion of Decency and I were both starting, a wise old editor said, "Write an editorial saying that this is just another transient reform wave. These people," he said, "are a simple case of psychological maladjustment, meaning nothing. I have seen it come and go a hundred times in my career. Say that it hardly merits the attention of intelligent people," he said wearily, and went back to his work as a signal that I should get on with mine. When I began to grow up I quickly discovered that forces for evil were actually working and winning out in this matter, that the uneasy and itching element in the Catholic minority had got control of the Catholic machinery and its organized effect on national publicity, that they had stampeded the Protestants and all other Better Breakfast Food groups, and had captured the movies. Or that was what they thought. What a couple of faceless scrubs named Will Hays and Joe Breen thought was that they had captured the Catholic Legion, and cut themselves as big a piece of pie in Hollywood as anyone had who'd been playing the racket through all the years, and winning. Whoever captured whom, the Hays Office was a tyrant to producers with money to invest and flesh to quiver at every alarm.

And the Hays nix on any matter of truth is a part of film history. On the actual things that are actually made, the office can be lenient, in proportion to the producer's investment of course. But its influence on what can be taken up as a subject, what can be written into a movie script, what can be made with cameras, is insidious and final. To give one modern example: why wasn't the scenario of Vincent Sheean's *Personal History* ever advanced farther than the shelf by the producer—Walter Wanger, the press agents' College Man—when the movie minds judged it ready to go? Could it be that the movie liberal had done a straight liberal, or somersault for the money, when the Hays Office had refused to commit itself until the picture was made? Between you and me, it damn well could.

Could it be that Garson Kanin had to fight every last point of the story of *They Knew What They Wanted* with his own studio as it quaked under the Hays Office? Could be, possibly. That he finally made the picture his own way is only an illustration of a lousy state of affairs. In any such state, watched over by such an organization of orgulence and stealth, the man who comes through must come through with a belief in his heart like barricades. And so it has been possible for men whose talents ran counter to the industry and also to the Hays Office that it made possible, to beat down narrow prejudice and to give us the event as it truly happened. But as the gap was opened, gag men rushed in, and flooded the public again with plays on words and plays on situations which were no more than the sly echo of the jaded laughter of burlesque. I mean that the Hays Office has been more concerned with such delicate subjects as the condition of workingmen, poor men, the never rewarded salesmen and farmers, than it has been with the indelicate and essentially useless and unmeaningful gag about a husband sleeping with his wife.

Many things have been allowed and passed over with a sort of bought tolerance. But many things have died in the initial stage before you ever heard about them. And many things have been crippled after the project was under way. And in such cases, who is to say which is which? The public decides, finally, and we are the public. If we have allowed such power-loving people as Will Hays and Joe Breen and Hays's earnest stooge Martin P. Quigley—if we have allowed them to take over, we deserve what happened. By being fed a few bleeding hearts for appearances' sake, the major companies have been able to get away with more and more doubtful cracks and sly situations—never to the advantage of pictures at large, but always to the spicing up of some stale wind of plot. With the very few exceptions of men of courage and conviction, the producers have simply used the term "better," in connection with pictures, as the Catholic Legion has used it, and they have been satisfied to seek no further but connive with the complacence of the Hays Office in getting this or that faint saving tract of smut certified and onto the screens of the nation. Breen has got himself a fat and handsome job at RKO and maybe someday they will pension Hays off as sheriff or circus press agent or something. No matter for them.

The question is, now that they have made their pile and had their day of dictator's glory, who is going to take over this new awakening of the Catholic Legion, and ride it to our loss? *Variety* reports that in cities where the double-intention gags of *Two-Faced Woman* have drawn a blast from the clergy, the picture is doing double business. This would be a fitting outcome but it would be unfortunate even if it could last, which it can't. When any work of art is cried up as salacious, it gets around to the psychotic types who are the mere obverse of the censors, if they aren't the censors themselves. And any work of art that consciously stirs up such a cry or plays to these types, is just that much farther from art itself and from the general good. What we want to know, the majority of us, is what mangy assortment of tails is trying to wag this majority dog. I have seen the Catholic ladies at screenings and I can report that they compose a congregation of horrors that no good Catholic would have any business with if he had any business at all. Yet they are part of the organization that is going to tell us what we may see for the next ten years. There is no need ever for a religious war. In a nation already at war there is no room for interfactional bickering. But the Catholic Legion has proved itself, in the movies, an enemy of the spacious truth, an actual abettor of petty filth—that is, the dirt you can get away with for an extra dollar, and never mind that it never came out of the honest earth. If you are a good Catholic you will not take this amiss, and could not do so with integrity. If you are a good Catholic you will know that for the sake of the country if not your own, it is time to clean your stables.

22 December 1941

1942

From *You're in the Army Now* to *Kings Row*

The Flag for a Gag

For more than a year now the movies have been growing hotter and hotter on the idea of using our armed forces for story material, preferably in comedy, for there is hardly a Hollywood zany who has not recently spent more time in uniform than the average man actually in the camps. The thing has gone so far back into the stale past for its method of topical treatment as to become a new thing. Already there are cases on record where an army comedy has had to be withheld from release in South America, despite loss of revenue. Audiences there would get a wrong and contemptuous view of our military, it was decided. People there just wouldn't understand things in the light of our Yankee sense of humor. Neither do I.

The pattern on this type of picture is already frozen, recent as it is. All the clichés of the rookie and his first issue of clothing, the hazing sergeant and the spud pile and the officer's daughter, are there—all advancing in about the same order through predicament into catastrophe, like a recurrent nightmare of impotence, until at the last moment the unwitting comic saves two divisions and four staff officers' faces, and is made at least a lieutenant before his year is up. And the pattern is given a treatment which openly shuns all subtlety and sense, and tries only to out-Sennett Sennett. But the catch is this, and it is a catch as big as a harbor mudscoop: the wild slapstick of early screen comedy stuck to a pattern only in the certain routines it developed. Beyond a situation and a routine for cutting away from it, anything could happen, anything *had* to happen. And it did. The early companies were forced to improvise and to be good at it to stay in the running; but you cannot copy improvisation from a projection room. And even more important: you can't transpose from a stylized medium of pantomime (just outside Punch and Judy) into the highly developed realism of the modern talking film, without looking like Grandma with her toenails painted and a halter top.

That is for the treatment of material. As for the material itself, no army or navy life has ever been conceived with such careless vulgarity and absence of any life or any essential humor. And now in the latest picture of this curious assembly line, one good comic and one priceless comic are both submerged beyond recognizability, as much by this dull copy of a story as by the brute lack of imagination with which it is mauled around. The picture is *You're in the Army Now,* the comics are Jimmy Durante and Phil Silvers, the authors are Paul Gerard Smith and George Beatty, the director is Lewis Seiler.

There are a few new sketches in this one, mostly to frame the talents of Jimmy Durante, but otherwise it is a shameless copy of *Tanks a Million,* which was just another synthetic itself. When you add the abetted mugging of Col. Donald McBride and Sgt. Joseph Sawyer, you will not need any more. Durante gets an occasional opportunity to murder the language and the laws of vocal harmony, but in general has nothing to do that couldn't have been played by a punching bag in mating time.

It isn't this one picture, but this whole tendency. And there wouldn't be a tendency if it didn't pay in audience approval. And what in God's name are we as a nation and an audience thinking of, at this time? Levity will not die and has not in the toughest times—at least among those who found their duty to lie where it was toughest; and there was no armed outfit that would not laugh at a shrewd service story, or joke, or picture. But this stuff is not shrewd, and it furthermore seems to assure those who prefer to stay in their safe comfortable skins and bang hands and hiss like anything for their patriotism, that life in the army is a joke, with pratfalls and no meaning.

Who is laughing out there? Whoever it is, he is making a fine profit out of these ventures for some producer who is producing them for that reason alone. It does seem that only the sly and profit-taking ones among us are as yet truly awake to the possibilities of hardship and peril for millions who never asked this fate for anybody, let alone made a career of it. There are as yet too many of us who pull an important long face over the morning's headlines, twinge only enough in sudden remote fear to tighten up the belt on somebody else's belly while laying in canned goods and contracts and bags of sugar and Washington pay checks for our own, and then guffaw at night in the theater to pay a fiddler who is callous enough in commercialism and lacking enough in any art, to be at this time an obscenity.

It is a relief at such a time of whoop-it-up and strenuous work with the flag by those who do not follow it, to come to a film like *Sundown,* a fast-moving if familiar story of the white man in the dark continent of Africa. But not altogether a relief. Naturally the theme is more contemporary than *Beau Geste,* and so the English in this outpost are no longer trying to save Kenya from itself by keeping it for themselves: they are on the trail of a plot to bring the uneasy natives of the continent under Nazi domination. And actually, the story has more point this way. But you will find tacked on at the end a long, muddled, and incongruous statement about onward Christian soldiers.

For the most part, you will have seen most of the action of this picture before: the few white men, the circle of natives, the tight little spot with its taut nerves in this mysterious immensity of jungle, rock, sand, and hills; the routine of outpost life, the intrusion of a beautiful woman and a human snake; the rumors and war drums and the sinister mechanism of a secret passage and the absolute stronghold in a hidden valley, two against hundreds, etc.

But in spite of its rather frequent absurdity, *Sundown* has that trick of illusion, of using the fast and faraway for the maximum of breathlessness possible, which pictures have developed into one of their best and unique resources. Henry Hathaway directed to this end, Charles Lang made some handsome photography out of it, Barre Lyndon adapted the story from some of his own stuff. But the divide between partial acceptance and the rejection of the absurd was crossed with the help of actors, who could carry many of the weak lines and instances on their own backs. George Sanders, Bruce Cabot, Joseph Calleia (poorly typed in writing and direction), Harry Carey, Reginald Gardiner, etc. People like that, under fast enough direction and the looming of the unknown, can put meaning in where meaning isn't (Gene Tierney as a strong desert figure is strictly a mirage). It is the people and the way the thing is handled that pulls this story up by the bootstraps out of its adventure-thriller quality as writing. You can thank them when you are through.

5 January 1942

Let Who Will Be Clever

In recent years there have been many who would define a comedy as anything with Bob Hope in it. For a longer time there has been a smaller band who say it is anything with Victor Moore in it. Both Hope and Moore are in the screen version of *Louisiana Purchase,* which is therefore going to make a lot of people happy. But if the picture is more pleasant and less strenuous than most of its type, credit must also be given to the fact that it is a musical comedy with a book, which it follows.

There isn't much point and almost no edge to its spoofing of the New Orleans graft ring, which is here trying to hide from the muckraking Northern Senator behind a young man who is sly but not evil, and delegated by the bosses to avert the rap or take it. It would have been livelier with more point and a lot less of Vera Zorina (a comedy is also something without Vera Zorina in it); but what holds it together is the conception and character of Victor Moore, a Coolidge with likable qualities and a sense of humor. He is full of a childish delight in and surprise at the strange things in the world, and both elements communicate themselves to the audience; but he is also somehow about as easily roped and tied down as the ranking bull alligator in any swamp, though he spends most of the picture blundering out of one trap and into another.

In the comedy of situation and comeback, Bob Hope is as nimble and engaging as ever. I do not find, as some have, that he is here eclipsed; he is at times gracefully playing the straight foil called for in the script, but he is around the place like quicksilver, and that instantaneous trick of projection of his never has to beg favors of your attention. He does one routine all by himself, Woman Getting into a Girdle, and he has lines scattered around from here to there, some of them the ad-libs with the special reference he likes so much. (He has talked the Senate to sleep and notices it suddenly. Ho hum, back to vaudeville, he says, clapping his hands loudly and making with animation.) The rest of the cast is pretty lean dramatic pickings. Frank Albertson and Raymond Walburn are far enough from their potential level in comedy or realism to suggest that, as far as character went, Irving Cummings just stuck to directing the show for pace and color and let the rest go.

Since the film is in Technicolor, people are sometimes a little hard to see; the single big spectacle scene of the New Orleans Mardi Gras has a note of lavishness and abandon something like the Woolworth candy counter. But instead of adding seven completely new songs, they have even cut some of the vocal numbers of the play down to background music. In short, what emerges is not so much a machine musical as a not very clever comedy of errors giving scope to the talents of Mr. Hope and Mr. Moore, and for once giving them some reason for being there.

In the picturizing of *The Man Who Came to Dinner,* fidelity to the original is definitely a handicap. The picture is too long, too stuffy in its talk-talk and one main set, and in many respects just poorly done. In direction (William Keighley) it is often a case of overemphasis—big takes, exaggerated confusion, too much noise.

It isn't hard to see why. Monty Woolley is in a central part he considers his own property, and while he manages all the attention-getting and point of the veteran stage man, he creates a character at once ill-defined and pushed outward with the emphasis of burlesque. These popping consonants, this practiced roar, this sarcasm without inner compulsion and ranting without the fire of rage—these are possibly necessary where there are people to be tickled in the back row, where motion needs overemphasis to keep the front rows awake, and where an actor has been so long in the same routine that he has felt it go stale and slipped into making it louder and busier, hence funnier. The camera eye picks this all up, shows relentlessly where it is false, and literally throws it at your head, back row or front.

Billie Burke has a fluttery personality that needs great restraint, and had so little here as to be painful. Jimmy Durante, in a short routine, is of course the sworn enemy of all restraint, does not need it in his business, and gets the most honest laughs of all. Bette Davis is the one cool presence of the affair and the only thoroughly sympathetic of the main characters. (If Ann Sheridan knew that her part was practically molded around Ann Sheridan, then her part was good work too, and is anyway venomous.)

You will like this in measures to your tastes in the matter of simply poisonous people thrown against defenseless local yokels. To be successful completely, it has to be very brittle, fast, and brilliant. It is not. There are plenty of laughs; the situation is essentially humorous as a concept; and the satire on the literary and amusement world is there, if rough and ready. But many of the withering witticisms are just loud noise, many of the finer comments of sophistication are about as delicate as a slapstick, and meanness for meanness' sake is always interesting as a study but always leaves a little nagging aftertaste in laughter. It is on the whole a better than average show, so you can do like Woollcott: laugh at it and also nickname it Repulsive.

Quiet Wedding is English, all plot in the most set drawing-room manner, and comedy, and English. I haven't seen one like it for years but recognize it instantly, for its approach and style, its bag of chestnuts and improbabilities. In design it is genial and human and full of the quirks by which people live and on which they bark their shins; but in treatment (Anthony Asquith), it is as stiffly overdressed and determined to be larky as your first masquerade ball. In between this film and the sad string of them that was coming over around 1934-35, there have been many developments in the English story films, whose complacence in the lack of technique was first broken through by Hitchcock and later by the young men who followed—all of whom have been brilliant in incidental humor, whether they were making a thriller or something about the West Riding. But now back to fun for fun's sake, with that note of forcing, with that innocence of crucial point and timing, with everybody a little embarrassed.

This one turns on the point of a sensitive girl's reaction to the barbaric row staged by family and friends in preparation for her bridal night. Well taken, but not enough for a whole screen story without much devising and character—and so they push the second around to cover up deficiencies in the first, until a pretty like Margaret Lockwood is merely pettish and the droll cousins, etc., are lost in an arbitrary uproar. Fair at best.

12 January 1942

The Measure of Comedy

A man with a fresh idea and the way of realizing it is a happy addition to pictures. Preston Sturges is one of these people (writer-director), and in the last couple of years he has made enough stir all by himself to be considered a sort of grown-up Orson Welles—and has relied more on his pictures than his press agent at that. He got a little tired of the reviewers' stereotype about what wonders he did in the low-budget field, so he thought himself up a high-budget picture to discomfit them. He calls it *Sullivan's Travels,* and just to show you what absurd things show business is up against, *Variety* comes out with some pretty serious speculations on the title: can clever exploitation do away with the possibility that people will think it is a remake of *Gulliver's Travels,* and a cartoon, and stay away? Heavy lies the head, etc.

As a picture, *Sullivan's Travels* is from fair to good, going from witty banter to the present crude renascence of the Mack Sennett pratfall, from high talk about humanity to the bazzoom of Veronica Lake, from brutality to a *Green Pastures* production number. But as an idea it is both original and cute, and handled with a good rasp of satire. A successful director who is young and college and reads books, pounds on the desk and says he is going to make a picture about world trouble, a picture for and from the heart. When they try to head him off with a now-now and other soothing noises, ending with the true fact that he doesn't know what trouble is, let alone whether people who are in it want to see it on the screen, he ties them up by saying he will be a hobo himself and find out. When the studio decides to make this experiment a press-agent's dream, he ducks the pursuing bus-load from Publicity. Then he meets a girl, strictly on the town; then after a while the experiment has been completed and things have got romantic, and just when you are saying End of Picture (though its completed length is admirably an hour and a half), he gets knocked over the head, slapped into a Southern chain gang for scuffling in a railroad yard, and is reported dead back home through a case of mistaken identity.

You will see how it comes out, and quite neatly too; but the idea is that he has learned through observation of real hardship that comedy may not be anything so much, but it is all some poor devils have—when they can get it. He will make another comedy. It is just an idea but it is a clever idea and it is worked up into a story with suspense, odd situations, and a lot of crackle in the lines. It seems to have been a lot of fun to make, and it had some pretty good support from Joel McCrea as the half-serious and half-foolish but wholly likable young man.

Where it falls down—whether you go for slapstick the size of a whaleboat oar or not—is in the fact that Preston Sturges is a shrewder writer than he has become a director. The dialogue is intelligent and usually logical; the structure is good. But when he wants fun in a swimming pool, no less than four people have to fall or be pushed in; when he indicates laughter he has to break your eardrums; when he wants squalor he ties it around your neck with a bowknot—in fact when he wants anything at all in visual effect he does himself the rather serious disservice of talking down to the public as a bunch of mugs, making too much noise and too little connection with the sustained mood of true-to-life. I do not know why it is, but one after the other every man who has what we could call partial intelligence seems to carry it with him into the field of entertainment as a mixture of snobbism and a self-consciousness. That is, he approaches a piece of crude horseplay with a professed and knowing scorn for just the kind of thing the dumb sods want, and a secret admiration for it as an instrument of laughter. If the final thing has more anxious violence than humor, who is the sod after all?

The truly funny man in this business of presentation is either the complete intelligence, human and urbane, or the complete zany. And neither of these ever confuses the surface fool's guffaw with that nice mixture of belief and delight which is the final measure of comedy. Nor does either make the fatal showman's mistake of insulting his audience by talking down to it. The partial intelligence is a dangerous thing: being intelligence, it gives the reviewers something to review about; but being timid, it sets up a defense against its own unsureness of taste by blaming a sluggish public. Actually, you only get what you ask for. The public is sluggish. But it has a potential of appreciation that has been proved again and again, and its active participation in mirth can only be heightened by those men who give the best of themselves to the work they are doing, whatever it may be called, without shame.

26 January 1942

The Case of the Critics

I have been on this pitch for quite a long time, and now I should like to inquire why we as the nation that produces the movies should never have developed any sound school of movie criticism. That we haven't is obvious; read your papers. Why we haven't is probably owing to the ineradicable ignorance in theatricals of the ordinary writing hack, and to the fact that the ordinary reviewer on a newspaper or magazine is traditionally an amiable chump who has been kicked upstairs. In the deep-water magazines he may be a promising fellow who is working up to be a paid critic of the Drama or Literature, but if he has the slightest conception of how movies are made and why, he will probably be given a job doing something else.

I got a job as film critic late in 1933. It wasn't because I knew anything about films but because I was a sort of utility writer, and it was like hiring a ball player on the farm system of the big league. In spite of that, I learned very quickly that movies were one of the biggest things that had happened to the country of America. They had not only great possibilities but they had life, and what they accomplished was more in the talk of anyone you could meet than the works of any other art form.

The time 1933 wasn't a very good time for movies. On the level of the lofty brow you weren't allowed to notice anything unless it came from abroad or had been made in the nostalgic days of the silent film, or were otherwise permitted the allusion to a body of knowledge not commonly shared and having little enough to do with pictures.

We had had Gilbert Seldes to carry the banner for the vulgar arts, and we had had Pare Lorentz as a working critic soon to turn producer. We had had precious little else. In 1933 the air was full of noisy people who had figured that if you weren't a writer the surest way to become one was to join a Writers' Group or the *New Masses,* and that meant in film reviewing that Jesus Christ walked on the waters seven shows a day at the old Cameo, and even such a highbrow moneybags as Lincoln of the Filene Kirsteins could go off from a party in a huff just because you didn't properly like Sergei Eisenstein.

It was a pretty tough time, with that perennial Junior, Richard Watts, trying to be Mr. Watts of the Dramah Patch and William Troy trying to be William Troy, and the whole thing boiling down to who had read the most books in a foreign language, could refer thereto and quote therefrom. There was a great rush for words like *régisseur* and *montage* and almost no appreciation of the movies that people after all see, and while Mr. Watts went up into the theater section he had openly envied all along, and Mr. Troy got cross enough to be retired to heaven, and Mr. Kirstein sulked away into the ballet, and André Sennwald (the only promisingly honest one of the first-line newspaper reviewers) murdered himself, there was no change for the better.

Some of the stuffier attitudes disappeared from writing about the movies, and there was a tendency to take films for what they were and with some respect; but there was still no atmosphere for breeding critics. Frank Nugent is the last young man I remember to get a job in a leading position as movie reviewer, and after becoming too proud of his wisecracks for the good of his work, he was bought off with a Hollywood contract and has not been heard from since. Cecelia Ager took over the first-string job when *PM* started up, but she had been best in her incidental remarks in *Variety* and never seemed to get used to the full-time business of reviewing the whole picture. Outside of an occasional visiting professor from abroad, I do not think of anybody else who has made any splash at all.

I wonder if it isn't the movies themselves who are responsible. There are plenty of younger people growing up to whom the films are so natural that they do not have to play the snob about them. Bright people too, who can tell you what makes a screen story tick. But the movies themselves are not interested in having able criticism. They are suspicious of it and shy violently when its presence is suspected. Somehow or other they have not only asked for but got the reviewing attitude that makes a little chat go a long way, usually in the direction of publicity handouts, which tells its following what the story is and who's in it, and then hands down a decision as temperate as possible and as devoid of any clear scale of values.

It is the job of the trade magazines to estimate whether a picture will make money for its producer or not, and this the trade magazines do when they are not outright venal. But the critics, who are supposed to do something more and indeed can't even do this much competently, are stampeded time after time by the mere word of the company that it has got something, or figure they have burned their fingers the first time some movie salesman or dissident reader jumps them for "destructive criticism." Whether the critics can make a picture or whether a picture can make the critics is an argument as old and fruitless as the chicken-or-the-egg; but a lot of lusty shouts are what the companies want, what they often spend absurd sums of money in ensuring, and that is what they get.

Perhaps they deserve it, but the public doesn't. More people go to good and bad movies than read good and bad books, and surely the top layer of this vast audience is as discriminating of taste and exacting of standards as the top layer of the reading public. Yet if you were to write in a big-circulation magazine with anything like the direct estimate of the better book reviewers there would be a howl and a tearing of hair that would make you think the Japanese had landed in force. Hollywood has been able to insist that the whole of its public is feeble enough in the head to admire practically anything on celluloid so long as nobody meanly spoils the show by suggesting that as an actor Errol Flynn is about as expressive as the leg of a chair, or that even a million dollars can be wrong and not art. Consequently film criticism is obediently dull and uninformative, and surely unworthy of so lively and immanent a subject. We started out by paying the movies no respect, and now we lag behind them and are taken into camp. The respect is now there but it is a poor thing and it is paid rather to the wishes of the men who merely sell them for profit rather than to the movies themselves.

2 February 1942

More Sound Than Fury

Woman of the Year is a film you will want to see for the good things in it, and also wring your hands for the bad. It has an engaging quality deriving from its personalities, but where direction and writing are concerned, it is static and often ham, it is at least twenty minutes too long for the motion it carries. And the motion is too little for a picture, because the thing was conceived as two people making a great many long statements at each other.

Tangling by chance with a sportswriter on the paper for which she is a sort of Dorothy Thompson, only young and beautiful, the girl falls in love and marries the fellow, and the rest of the story is devoted to showing how her busy little international hysterias shove him out of sight and make him miserable. He must be a patient, patient man in this story, because when George Stevens directs a sequence showing somebody being booted around, somebody is booted around. Much of this is relieved by the fact that the lady columnist has a convincing routine of being lovely, tender, and seductive for him those rare times when he is ready to blow up, and by the fact that while patient, he is no dope; he has quite a few short right jabs of comment to deliver on his own.

Finally enough is too much; he stops her play with the adopted refugee kid, and leaves. This, we are to suppose, is the start of weaning her from the teletype and cable offices; it is also the start of one of the most unforgivably long marriage ceremonies (when George Stevens marries a couple, they aren't going to pick the lock), and one of the most embarassing sequences of Mrs.-Newlywed-in-Kitchen since whatever was the worst of the Charley Chase shorts. These are the troubles of it: there is something good, even very high and sweet, and then there is something off key or out of possibility, or there is too much of something either in the way of relentless pursuit of it or of stepping it up to stridency. Or there is that crude lack of point and taste of which any is too much.

The problem is a nice one to play around with, an original but done too much in the hackneyed pattern of newspaperman, newspaper woman. It has plenty of edge in the exposition, and it has some of the nicest wit in dialogue—lines right out of the free speech of those who can land on both feet talking, the natural in humor and sarcasm. But I suppose it starts to lose ground when the audience perceives that such a fine type of man would never go all the way down the line for such a uselessly preeminent bitch, and it leaves its doubt afterward how even patience and understanding could reform such an ingrained case of meddlesome tuft-hunting in one lifetime, let alone the last ten minutes.

Katharine Hepburn wouldn't win a screen-test for pretties, yet she has that rare quality of composing all the lines of her face and figure, sense and feeling, into a pattern that is seen and felt as a thing of beauty. And she has never before been able to condense into one performance so much of this almost outrageous challenge and appeal, deliberate affectation and genuine, delightful ease. She is set a little off-center by the writing and direction (she has to do four things at once instead of two; she has to speak ten languages like a native, which no girl with hair and nails like that to take care of would ever be able to spare the time for). But when she has her good scenes of being bright or tender or passionate or wicked, the hip (etc.) shakers of 1942 will have to shake plenty to come near her claim for the most seductive woman of the year.

The man-as-a-rock in this story is Spencer Tracy. He has that poise and self-security that might pass as "just being natural" until you try it on the stage for yourself. And in *Woman of the Year* he blunts or turns aside any tin knife of the ludicrous that the situation may have pointed against him, simply by virtue of a steady intelligence, a cagey grasp of stage motion and effects, and something profound in the way of kindness and knowingness and cheer that needs no flurry of business for its projection, since it is received all around with the immediacy of air waves, and that, being profound, can never be made silly.

Kings Row is an unusual movie, not for anything technically, but for its material and the relatively straight treatment of it. It is taken from the novel by Henry Bellamann, a study of certain relations and violences in American small-town life, especially as felt in the youth and growing-older of the generation 1880. Sam Wood and his screenwriter, Casey Robinson, have succeeded in graying up some of the blacks, and certainly both their ending and the prominence given four young maidens are a detraction of excitement from the actual business. But two of the key families are afflicted by forms of madness; there are murder, suicide, mutilation, sadism (though lightly), and two plans of false commitment to institutions for the insane. It is true that the public will take anything in the way of blood and horror so long as the form is melodrama. But this is not handled for melodrama but for real, seriously and conscientiously.

The faults of *Kings Row* are length (two hours and seven minutes); the casting in a lead part of Robert Cummings, a harmless nice boy with a permanent; and that curse and damn it in all pictures, talk, and then some talk, and after that we'll have some talk. Naturally people talk, you can't stop them. But when the points of a story on the screen have to be made by a head that fills it, telling all about what happened, what is going to happen, what ought to happen; and when as in this case you get a hundred feet of Madame Ouspenskaya mugging without the relief of one camera shift, and then two hundred feet of Mr. Cummings struggling with blown-up lines and threadbare quotations; and when in particular a great deal of this flood of words holds no advancement whatsoever either to the plot or to world knowledge, beauty, or light—why then you know that someone is not making pictures but has got too many wrong ideas about too many bad books.

It was Sam Wood who should have cut this down. He has a talent that not many have, and he has feeling; but he is simply not easy in pictures yet. In spite of overlength, his film has a nice apportionment of dramatic qualities. In spite of times when emotion is merely burlesqued by poor timing or lack of depth, he gets an overall sense of people in trouble and in life, and some of his situations are contrived beautifully enough so that there is no awareness of contrivance—the mood is established and carries on from there. The best treatments were of Claude Rains as the counselor and tragic father, of Betty Field as the girl in love and terrified of her own insanity; of Charles Coburn as the fanatic doctor; and of the boy and the girl from opposite sides of the railroad tracks (Ronald Reagan who is good and no surprise, and Ann Sheridan who is both).

There is also a feeling of likelihood and of truth to the time and place that is never a coincidence, and not brought about by skill alone. To condense what happens in such a case: a man can drive up in a buggy and it isn't good for a laugh. The interiors are well studied and there are many subtle touches in using them to effect. (The exteriors are so poorly lighted and blended as to make you think of the old vaudeville Main Street front drop, and demand before it is too late that for outdoor shots certain studios get the hell outdoors once, so they will remember what it looks like.)

Erich Korngold's music is good and occasionally striking, and it also occasionally seems he thinks *he's* making the picture. I liked Ernest Cossart and Pat Moriarty and their shanty-Irish house. In fact I liked the picture. It is recommended as a yes-and-no affair, with me leaning on the yes.

16 February 1942

3

TO THE
PROMISSORY
LAND

"NY to LA"

Every week in *Variety* you will find two boxes of names, twenty or thirty names of show people to the box. One list is headed "LA to NY," and those are the arrivals; the other is the one of departures, "NY to LA." All year long, back and forth across the country, the people shuttle between the capital of the films and the capital of almost everything else. Those who aren't buying a car in the East because it's much cheaper, and driving out, go West in two ways (1) plane, (2) rail. To one who was ever moved by the far mumbled poetry of the train caller, " . . . Albany and the West," there will be no joining the airplane crowd when the chance comes. What is there up in a plane? A lot of air. And the Twentieth Century Limited goes to Albany and the West.

Every day of the year the Twentieth Century out of New York makes up in the Mott Haven yards and is brought down to Grand Central thirty minutes before traintime, stocked with food and fuel, beds made and rooms ready, to wait quietly beside its red carpet with that mysterious air of power and destiny trains always have in their dim stations. Every night at six sharp, with its passengers sorted and shuffled and hustled aboard and good-bye good-bye good-bye, the engine picks its long string of cars up as gently as a cat and moves out over the switches, gathering its speed past the swarming commuter trains in the underground maze, rolling through the usual jerk and halt of 125th Street as though on a billiard table, and when the blocks are clear ahead settling into the pull up the high main line to Harmon. At Harmon, all steam and floodlights and engines released or ready and waiting, and other wonderful things, there is a leaning back and slowing to a first stop hardly noticed in the diners, the lounge and observation cars, the trim quiet rooms, compartments, suites; but at Harmon the rightful steam engine for this train backs into the coupling, the Hudson-type locomotive with driving wheels over your head, with all the hot shining roar and promise of all the steam engines ever dreamed of; and in less than four minutes and with no jar, the station is gathering speed backward and the train is picking up again on the long way, cuffing small towns aside too quickly for you to read

All of the articles in this section are from *The New Republic*, 1941.

the names on the station signs, and grudging more than the few minutes for mail at Albany, Syracuse, Buffalo. And the West.

It gets late up around Buffalo, and the after-section of the observation car has the lights out, so that there is nothing but curved glass between the soft chair and the running iron of the track down its maze of signal lights, nothing inside but the glow of a cigarette and the big speedometer on the forward wall, with its deliberate needle swinging up to eighty when The Man is seven seconds behind or holding at seventy-five when he is even, or dropping down to thirty-five, twenty-five, twenty as he goes through a coaling stop for all the lesser trains. Around Buffalo, the night is full of trains, passing on the down track in a 150-mile-an-hour flash and blur. The conductor is sitting back there, winking with his flashlight as we pass the lonely men in the signal towers and watching their cheery answer a mile and two miles down the track; he calls off the trains passing and those coming up behind. The Pacemaker is up ahead; #27 and the Wolverine and later #19 are following us in. And the blurs we see, or rather feel as they pass, are the opposite numbers to these specials and will pass them just as we will catch our own opposite number, the Twentieth Century out of Chicago, just clearing Buffalo—all the trains in the night, the freights too, the long manifests. It is late and the lights are out in the houses, no crowds wait in the stations, and there are few cars where roads follow the tracks. But it seems as if the whole country were busy at some monstrous and endless game of puss-in-the-corner, and you get into a bed that will be remade and ready again by four of the next afternoon, waiting in Chicago for the next restless American, bound for New York and his next morning's breakfast.

Skip Chicago: it is a rather sad and very dusty place, full of ruins and sudden wind. But the crack train leaves from the Dearborn Station there in the evening, #17, lv. Chicago Tues. & Sat. PM 7:15. That is the Superchief, the streamliner, the mile-eater over the mountains and across the big states. Its long cars fit smoothly together and are done in silver like the gates of heaven, with an engine half a block long to match. Abandon thoughts of smoothness, however: the cars are an older and more rattly model than those of the Century, and you are not long under way before you know that the Santa Fe roadbed—the home of the Superduper—was probably built by Errol Flynn, as the movie suggested, and out of old washboards. For time, distance, and natural obstacles encountered, I suppose this is our national crack train, but its full speed is often something like traveling a hundred miles an hour on a pogo stick.

The first night out of Chicago it is all black outside and whole areas of history and legend hang on the thumbtack of a rare station sign caught through the window. All night across Illinois and Missouri, across the rivers and cutting the corner of Iowa, rattling down and across the whole state of Kansas all night. This is the straight and fast part of the run, and you wake up in Colorado fourteen hours after leaving, a great leap in the dark.

The Colorado part of it, in the early spring and in the sunshine, is the nicest morning, because the train is getting into the mountains, doubling around on itself and hugging the rock walls, and there is a dazzle of snow. Up to the high point of the line, the Raton tunnel at 7,600 feet, and into New Mexico by lunchtime, and then down the crazy single track and climbing and twisting again for hours, and into Albuquerque and the late afternoon heat. There is nothing like the state of New Mexico; and its sullen reds and immovable distances are outside the windows until the sun goes down; they will not leave you alone with a book.

This is the late afternoon for passing—the Chief, El Capitan, the Superchief, all eastbound—but there is no swarming of trains out here, and we pass the others waiting for us by appointment along the rare stretches of double track. The train has worked twice as hard the second thirteen or fourteen hours to gain a third of the distance of the first, and pulling upgrade again toward Flagstaff late that night, the whistle for the towns ahead seems tired and a little cross. The club car and lounge and observation cars are deserted (the three movie stars yawned and went off to bed early, which made a clean sweep of everything). The doors up and down the train are closed and the curtains drawn; the lights streaking along the ballast beside the track are winking out; there is nothing but Arizona beside the window, gray and jagged under a bright moon. The only difference is in whether the engine is going upgrade, suddenly fantastic in the moonlight as it doubles the curve, or going down the other side, rocking and roaring. The gray is always the same, with a touch of green and unreal in it like something from *Fantasia*. There are many airplane beacons through here, swinging over the horizon ahead and behind and giving the effect among those arid hills of lighthouses along a coastline of shoals. But it goes on hour after hour, the limitless monotony too heavy for heavy sleep after you have been watching for hours, and you rouse up several times to look out and see it still there and the same. This night, trains and motion are unreal and there is only the placid vastness of a continent, impervious to the scratch in its side of all attempts at coast to coast, and time sleeps. All this speed and thunder falls gradually into its temporal perspective, and America takes your breath away at last.

You waken in the sun to find the main streets of towns looking in at you: orange orchards and growth everywhere so lush that plants learn no fear of trains and brush along the sides on a wide curve. Easily downhill through the California groves into Los Angeles, and that stillness of the end of the run, never believable at once, and you step out into a sun you have gained three hours on in three days. The Los Angeles station is all straight wide walks and curves, clean walls and air. It is a little like a cake run up by Sutter's for an Italian wedding, but it is also probably the most sweet and restful terminal in the world.

Otherwise coming in is like coming into any other big town: there are streets, taxis, drugstores, Wrigley signs, and natives going about their business. You should not expect to find Cecil B. DeMille directing traffic—though that would not be a bad idea. This is the town where millions are squandered and movies made, of course, but the main thing is that people live here and have things to do, and babies, and it is they and their cars that are in the streets their houses make, it is to them that the radios, billboards, and papers at the corner stand appeal in the common language to drink Coca-Cola and smoke Chesterfields and demand Esso. Spyros Skouras we are here—but there is nothing so strange. We speak the language and know the folks; being Americans, we have been here before.

Hollywood Is a State of Mind.—Of any place it is best to expect nothing, having believed nothing; and there can hardly be a place in the world of which this is more true than it is of Hollywood. Hollywood is a state of mind—but whose? Where did he get it? What's he selling? Who insulted him or gave him the key to Ciro's or failed to recognize him or gave him a hotfoot? If it's Niven Busch writing a comprehensive study of Darryl Zanuck for that comprehensive magazine *Life,* does anybody check up on how many more screen originals Mr. Busch will sell Mr. Zanuck for the coming year? What visiting reviewers were tossed parties; what reviewer too big for his shoes got what he thought was a contract to take over production and then tossed in a blanket? What austere poets and lowly clowns, what raft of ever-vocal literary tourists, have come through to turn over a few odd rocks and report Hollywood to the world?

Every new soul coming in actually brings his own Hollywood with him. Since it is a rather vast place, of many different levels, he can usually manage to keep it, too. There are special reasons. People bring many wide-eyed expectations when they first come to New York, but they never dream of asking New York to be *them:* when the expectation patently doesn't fit, they simply change it. Nobody could spend a week in New York at the house of friends—maybe a Greenwich Village trap, maybe the home of a publisher, maybe folks in Jackson Heights or Brooklyn or Rahway—and write a solemn, thumping article, "The Real New York," and expect to get out with his skin. But Los Angeles as it is today is still raw and recent; and its movie industry has been only too willing to build it up as the place where you can't believe what you see.

The days of look-at-me-I'm-a-legitimate-crazy are as dead out there as Minetta Street bohemia, but they were sold at the time, and oversold. They made publicity of a sort, but they made better copy. And since Hollywood is actually the state of mind of the whole country peering at and reading about it, you might say that copy made it what it isn't today, a great incessant flood of millions of words a year. Most of it is boob writing; most of it is just plain made-up and badly; an influential fraction has been worked up by deep brows in search of something beneath them. It is nonsense. But it has spread out through the nation with its effect, and spread back again to the town itself, with subtle irony. In Los Angeles you will find people who understand and secretly love the place keeping up a front of jibes about it, as the thing expected of anybody who knows. And surely there is nothing more pathetic than the Hollywood intellectual who is positively voracious for the life of the highbrow magazines, having come as near the actual literary racket as rejection slips will allow, and who must show at any expense that the thing is so vulgar to him he can't even *spit*.

To people back in the country, focusing attention or at least honest curiosity on this second American capital of the arts, there must still be a few puzzling things about the whole business. What and where is Hollywood, exactly, and how much is it different from anything known in everyday living? Due partly to circumstance and partly to clever work on the part of the Chamber of Commerce, Hollywood is generically the state of making movies—not only in the imagination of the rest of the country but right on the spot, where the term "that's Hollywood for you" is about as vague, philosophical, and ironic as the old *c'est la guerre,* and may be applied equally to news that the girl got married and then had the baby afterward as to word that some column cutup had rolled his car into the lobby of a hotel only to find it was a filling station after all.

Exactly and geographically, Hollywood is one of the several suburbs that make up the city of Los Angeles, and Los Angeles is the place that has been summed up as seven suburbs in search of a city. Some of the centers of amusement, victualizing, and hurrah are located in the area of Hollywood proper; a lot more are not. The corner made by Hollywood Boulevard and Vine Street, where celebrities and hot events are usually observed by columnists, looks on an average night something like Times Square by daylight, being frequented by actors out of work, tourists, the usual local types, and columnists. Some of the major studios are also in Hollywood; but it is no more a production center than an amusement center, for the outfits of Fox, MGM, Warners, Universal, and Disney are scattered all to hell out from any center at all. Los Angeles is the place as a whole, but since we have to have some word for it, we can refer to it as Hollywood when we mean the place where movies are made.

Even statistically, the town is not quite like anything else. I suppose if you took all of Manhattan and called it Downtown Los Angeles, and then distributed the bulk of the active city life around through Westchester, southern Connecticut, Long Island, lower New York State, and the east Jersey shore, you would have part of the idea. Except that everything is contiguous, there is no clean sense of passage *through* (there is a godly clear sense of passage itself, as everything is quite a long way from everything else); and the words suburb and commuting are not heard, save possibly in colorful invective. In its present size it is a city made by the movies, those who work in them, those who work to support those who work in them, and so on down the line. And the movies are all over the place, in this suburb, in that suburb. The suburbs have simply taken it away and become the city.

It is one of the powerfully big cities by now. The Los Angeles telephone book is about the size of the Manhattan directory; the total population is whatever the figures show. And for length and width there is nothing anywhere like it, in terms of solid square miles of streets and houses, streets and houses, stores and theaters and then more blocks of houses, all built up and kept up, owned and cared for. The chance for parking anywhere is better than in any big city, because there is always a lot that was held for a higher price until the boom had passed over into the next section; but always you have this feeling of even, steady knitting, loose for comfort but no stitches dropped. And it goes on everywhere, every day, and quick, so that if you catch an empty corner and a cinder in your eye at the same time, you will be an anachronism by the time you get seeing clearly again, because fourteen lath-and-plasterers have got the first story of a house up there and knocked off to have a drink with the first tenant.

And that is about all you see at once, the whole place lying clean and limitless in the sun. To the north are the hills; westward, miles out Wilshire Boulevard to Santa Monica, is the sea; and all the rest is this fantastic gridwork of wide, fast boulevards and wild, fast traffic—almost no electric cars, few buses, almost no cops. The houses line street after street, clean and white, set back on their lawns, half-concealed by trees, flowers, shrubwork. It is a semitropical city and the architecture by now is pleasantly worked into the climate and the romping vegetation (you never saw a city with so many trees, palms, elms, larch, maple—anything that could be stuck in the ground along what was once a "development" but presently became shady accustomed streets). The jokes about Hollywood monstrosities are as dated as the monstrosities themselves— which, like Grauman's Chinese Theatre, are lulus when you still find them, like a nightmare in a box of mirrors. Most of the buildings of today are simple, effective, airy, and often beautiful, stores and houses alike; and if you are out for laughs there are always the gas stations, cathedrals in many different languages.

Living there is of course a different matter and will come, like everything in its place, later.

14 July 1941

Hollywood Will Fool You If You Don't Watch Out

(Didn't It?)

Living in Hollywood is not what anybody expected, and I imagine a figurable percentage of the now more or less permanent citizens once came out there to do six months holding their nose and banking the money, and then get to hell out. The stars live on a plane of fantasy; the studios are enormous, busy, and almost threatening; the complete key to this maze of streets and sprawl of distances is simply beyond grasp. The first sense of isolation deepens as you look through the town's newspapers, in which any resemblance to living characters seems largely coincidental; find all the familiar weeklies on the stand, but all talking about the dead week before; and begin to realize fully that first-class mail to the East is a four, or five-day proposition and airmail-special the only direct way of communication.

These things all wait there on the immediate surface, especially the homes of the stars. And then the traffic. The first thing you learn in the greater Los Angeles district is never cross the street in an automobile; you are no match for drivers here; forget it and don't look for traffic cops either. Everybody owns a car, but there is nothing like what is known in New York as traffic; everybody picks up to thirty or forty on the light and hums along in three lanes at a good clip. The trouble is that it isn't a matter of driving but a sort of mutual contest of Coney Island tumblebug: looking in the mirror is a chump's game and so is waiting for an opening if you decide to turn left against traffic. Just whip out a hand-signal and give it the hard right or left, and listen to see what happens.

On your daily score card, a near-one only counts four and a squeal of brakes and hot smell of rubber even less. A squeal is from one to three depending on whether the other guy (1) didn't have a chance to see you, (2) was obeying a light, (3) turned over. High scores from seven to ten you have to read about in the papers next morning. Seven is a stretcher case; eight is a stretcher case involving three or more cars; nine is for fatals; ten is for fatals involving (a) two other cars, (b) one other car with a party of at least four—very tricky to achieve because in either (a) or (b) the fatal must be absolutely across the board. Pedestrians not registered at Central Casting do not count anything; press agents county twenty-five even if you have to chase them up a flight of stairs. Louella Parsons would count a hundred, or would if she could. But it is the steady average of small numbers that fills out the weekly total, the brake-squeals, near-ones, sidewalk hops, and full stops with locked bumpers. These are what scare you away from touching the wheel of a car. Yet you cannot be in the town without one. You should live so, and you do.

It is when you actually look for a place to stay that you begin to dig in under the climate and glamor and other nonsense. After the East, Los Angeles is simple living, for there is no such thing as moving day, there is little talk of leases, and not only single, double, and triple apartments come furnished, but whole houses—not hotel furniture either: the stuff is clean, comfortable, fairly new, and often in excellent taste. Rents, good Lord. You find people living in a house with lawn and trees looking in the windows at less than it would cost for one room in central Manhattan.

Add on to this the fact that going anywhere is simply a matter of backing out the car and going, quickly though of course at some risk to neck and fenders, and you begin to get an idea. I mean for groceries, for clothes, for fun, or for dinner. And except in the center of Los Angeles, which is one of the places in the world to avoid, arriving is simply a matter of pulling up to the curb or into the parking space, and getting out.

The free life of the automobile is well illustrated in the big drive-ins, which are all over the place, and account for a large majority of the whole town's restaurant business. The proposition is an easy-money dream, for the overhead is comparatively marbles, the car-hops do all the work and carry all responsibility of collection, and are so ill-paid that even Los Angeles has become mildly interested in a labor problem for once, and put pressure on the several large-scale operators. (Good restaurants, incidentally, are few and scattered and likely to be either jammed or ridiculous as to price; and Eastern quality in beef and seafood is no more than approximated even when ballyhooed and marked up accordingly.)

And the markets. They are like the central open-air markets of tropical cities, only clean; and they too are all around. It is not a city for small shops. There is at least one chain of enormous ones, and there are independents at every excuse. The idea is that a chap leases a block, puts up a low building with counters, booths, etc., and sits back while concessionaires in everything from drugs, liquor, household implements, and toilet supplies to pastry, meats, delicatessen, vegetables, fruit, and groceries in a staggering range of all brands, do the business, on a basis of so much guaranteed and a certain percentage against the gross. That is another very pleasant way to make a dollar, as the general idea is self-service and no delivery, and most of the concessions manage to turn it over like hay in the sun.

The general quality is good in nearly everything, simply because such a large number of people per capita have money in folding amounts, and can make possible a large turnover in goods which most communities restrict to a small and special store. But if you think money flutters in the air like little birds, store-owners can prove you crazy. The populace is not taciturn—in fact it is a genial people after the brusque shoving of other big cities—but it will go a mile and stand an hour for almost any kind of handout and keep its pockets sewed. It is used to paying a nickel for its peculiar newspapers, but if you opened up with an extra-quality ice-cream cone for *six* cents, you would go broke unless there were some new angle, such as an American flag waving in the center.

Market and gas-station openings are impressive events, with an exact and solemn duplication of the rites of premeer. The entrepreneur wangles an "appearance" from a couple of character actors some friend holds notes on—maybe even a dim star. He gives away various novel objects to all who appear, advertising the occasion with banners and multiple searchlight fingers in the evening sky. Thousands gather, literally thousands on a good bright opening. They stand around like Indians; they listen carefully to the spiels; they procure their throwaway cake of soap with the noisemaker in it; and next day they are back in Ralph's five blocks away, where they are accustomed to do their shopping. The grandeur of the premeer is so far and thoroughly burlesqued that a hardened soul merely glances at a battery of lights playing over the heavens downtown and shrugs. Probably someone opening a new pushcart.

There is also the general cleanness of the whole setup—not just the visual effect of white houses, foliage, easy streets, but the actual absence from the air of dust, soot, and general city corruption. There are no factories big enough or near enough to send up a smudge; there is very little coal burned anywhere; the air is pure and that's all there is to it. At least 25 percent of the nervous attrition of living in a city of any size at all is here eliminated.

It is how you are going to make a living that kills you—that and what you are going to do with yourself, also with whom. To take the last point first, it seems a late date to establish the fact that people in any free and sufficiently varied community gradually find their own level; that there are thousands of levels in human geology; that coffee grounds, sugar, and old cigar ashes can hardly blame the cup for finding themselves muddy in the bottom of it. Yet in the literature of Hollywood as it Really Is, you may find the life judged more by what fakers or fools a man has freely chosen to consort with than by what horrid types have bruised his sensibilities or his toes. The truth is that it is as possible to live in Hollywood quietly, sanely, and pleasantly occupied with whatever it is you do, as it is in New York, which is the best city I know.

For working in the actual movies, I should have thought anybody could say without going there that you are a headstrong type to try it. Surely no one who has had to work up into the organized racket of any of the arts should ever forget the disheartening mixture of push and front, competition, injustice, academic lethargy, payments deferred and concessions demanded, press agentry, and crass commercialism that rules the field if not its few good men. And for all the talk you have heard, you can give odds and make a pleasant sum of money betting that there is not a practice in Hollywood which cannot be matched in precise kind with procedures from the world of literature, music, and that strange downtown Luna Park referred to affectionately as the Theater. (I will undertake to cover moderate amounts on the literary game myself with cries of glee, and I'm not just talking about the pulps, slicks, or fly-by-night publishing outfits either. If an activity is to be damned by its patent knaves and incompetents, just give me a piece of the field of literature and get your money on the line.)

With Hollywood the difference is a matter of degree—or at best an occasional new wrinkle in a very old pair of pants. The movies take in and squander billions of dollars, wherefore everything is magnified a hundred to a thousand times over the exactly comparable factor in the snide or stupid relations of some two-for-a-nickel publisher with what passes as a big name in his puddle. And the difference between up and down is dizzying, quicker and sharper with uncertainty. It is a fearful, complex scramble, and anyone who would enter into it with some knowledge of the game and the sole purpose of honest achievement in it, is a brash fellow indeed. Unfortunately for the health of movies, next to none of those attracted by the lush money bait have any conception of picture fundamentals—but we come to that later, as a technical field in itself. We are just talking generally about those who work in Hollywood, and what character they give the place.

You would not have to meet any of them to observe their influence on the town. It is more deep and important than Shangri-La swimming pools and premeers and that salvage from the garbage pails of the too-rich put on the syndicate wires by, say, Hedda Hopper. What comes over you very quickly and comes to stay is that for its size Hollywood is about the smallest town in the country. In the first place, you will never find a city in which there is so much luxury and so little time to enjoy it, per capita, per average day. The whole town focuses directly or indirectly on the studios, and the studios start work at 9 A.M. or even before. And they work through to six, seven, nine at night. And they work a six-day week: they never heard of Saturday. The difference between this and any other working community where people get tired and guard dearly the hours of sleep to refresh them again, is that the four-figure men themselves are bound to the iron routine, usually tighter than the others. In short, what would be the leisure class in any other such gold-plated center of privilege is actually working almost day and night, and productively, and must to preserve its status.

A drive up Sunset Boulevard and out toward the ocean will reveal very little of what goes on inside the stately homes of film America. This actor, producer, director—agent even—might as well for long periods be living on the set or in his office. When pictures are shooting, the highest-paid men around them have a harder time even than the technicians, whose eye must be clear and hand steady nearly as soon as the sun is up.

The producer and his assistant, his director and assistant, his stars and writers and various special men, must put in a good eight hours of work at the very inside, just to keep the franchise. Director, producer, stars, and wise writers will probably use part of their lunch hour, or stay after work, to look at the last day's rushes. Producer, director, writers, actors, and others are often around the last thing to see about the next day's camera setups, the script, costumes, what not. And when they go to their homes, dead beat, there are still the endless phone calls, new contingencies brought in, old problems recast ("Chief, we can't have Taylor until after lunch tomorrow: publicity got the front office to release him for some damn bundles or something."—"Manny, I still don't feel that renunciation where she gives up the guy. *You* know how to do it: give me some more *feeling* in that dialogue on page 32—run it over with you at breakfast, right?"). And the stars and their agents and gossip columnists and other stooges may wish to be home in bed but must meet this or that, settle these or wangle those. And the good Lord won't hold back that next dawn breaking any more than the release dates of Louis B. Mayer.

So Hollywood is the world's first squirrel cage. To keep your nose above water, *i.e.,* in the leisure class, you work like hell.

So Hollywood's habits reflect it. The people who have the kind of money to make night out of day, keeping the bars and clubs and gambling setups and general whoopee going, until breakfast comes before bed, just can't afford the time here. The sober working people, as always, have their six-o'clock supper and modest gala at the movies or the evening beach resorts, and stretch and yawn and take their shoes off, and turn in. Even in the desperate poor mill and mine towns, the relief sections of New York, the waterfronts everywhere, there may be a roaring time of a Saturday night. But in Hollywood you may drive up and down and around, no later than midnight of this Saturday blessing of sleepover, and find nothing but the lights winking out, the late drugstore keepers yawning, the cars in the wide boulevards scuttling home as intent and grim as Dobbin to the stable. The town curfew is 2 A.M., and that is the legal limit for selling anything alcoholic. But the town goes to bed rather much before then, and I doubt there could be enough fellows charging around for one more to wet their whistle, to make it worth any tavern's while to stay open.

Partially depending on what has made valuable publicity, the town has had times of shocking ill repute and times of such qualities of purity that you could take your own sister there and have her around your neck every minute, and times when either was as optional as hot and cold in the shower. At present, I imagine as much sin gets itself done there as would be the case in any average community, but sin doesn't run for mayor. It is just now a reform town, and public debauch is held in such municipal disesteem that on certain nights all seven cars of the radio patrol are out surprising every driver through some undesignated intersection to see if he has lights, a license, and no liquor on his breath. And in this department, the fix is almost impossible: the cops are genial, even courtly, and is your stay here proving pleasant? Happen to know my friend so-and-so at Paramount? But they keep writing. For a while the drive-ins were dens of orgy-porgy, in that the kids could relax in their parked cars and order drinks, and act on them in a mild way. But they slapped on a law that if you drank liquor, you drank it sitting at a table—to which the barmen enlisted in this cause of morals slapped on a rider that if a chair were attached to a bar by a chain or patent swivel, the bar became a table; and everybody is happy but not too much.

My friends among the sociologists report that you cannot find a house, not even a respectable call house, not even by asking a cop or folding and unfolding bills in front of a late hackie. The town is simply closed. Some investigators have got telephone numbers, but discover that even the few hardy scofflaws have to keep a gypsy routine, and numbers are obsolete within a week and sometimes two days. They say it is not a happy town for sociologists.

Other investigators report that there is a unique tendency for the kids to learn very young, and fast, so that a normal subject of between-classes chatter on the lawn in front of Fairfax High is how your slide came out. This may of course be just the climate. Gambling on the open-house scale of vacation places like Miami doesn't seem to have any place in the scheme either, though the studios are always unhappy over the fact that as soon as the football season is over it is almost time for another racing season, and everybody with a desk and a blotter to hide forms under has little time for anything but a shrewd way to lose an honest dollar for the duration, including the efficiency experts (one studio found such a terrific jump in telephone bills one season that it put all studio calls through a checking board, which meant that hundreds of sufferers had to switch to wiring their bookies).

It is possible to live as fast as you want; but the town it-self has none of the color of big-city evil in all these surface matters. It is a hardworking and even a dull place—and I suppose the reason this is not all matter of fact and a thing to be accepted, is just that matters of fact are not what America looks for when it turns the page to Hollywood Highlights, or, Backstairs in the Witches' Castle. There are plenty of crazy things going on all right, and we will be into them presently. But this much is all you need see if being in Los Angeles is merely a matter of going about your own damned business.

4 August 1941

The Man Who Invented Hollywood

"Oh, Bertie," the producer said, calling to a fellow in a quiet purple sport coat he had picked out of the people milling back and forth past the Royal, or producer's, alcove in the commissary. The fellow waved and came over. He was wearing a loose-knotted silk scarf to match, some kind of orange mixture. "Bertie, I wonder if I could usurp upon you for a minute of your time."

"Why not," Bertie said, was introduced to the other two of us, and sat down.

"My stomach, picture such a way to live," the producer said, picking vindictively with his fork at a vegetable salad in front of him. "But from a nervous wreck; you should hear my doctor, Bertie. A talker."

"A vegetable salad," Bertie said.

The producer picked up a Rye Krispy, started to put it in his mouth, then tossed it back onto the plate in disgust. "And relatives. I could count twenty of them for you. Worries? Bertie, you have a pleasant life; do not ever become a producer two days behind on schedule, Bertie. What was I saying?"

"Maybe that Hays Office item came through?" Bertie said.

"Exactly, the Office. We get no okay on the word 'guts,' they don't care if it was in the Prime Minister's speech, all the papers, they don't have any interest we take it letter for letter from the Bible. Bertie, we got to have a double for that word, I look squarely up to you on it, Bertie."

"Synonym, eh?" Bertie said, and covered his eyes with one hand.

"I tried to give it to them fast, Bertie. But it's out; we got to rewrite in that scene by tomorrow because Stage Four is. . . ." The producer broke off as a waitress came up. "Here, Sadie, you can take away the bottom of the garden here, before I become sick. Bring me a glass of milk," the producer said. He was giving it the hemlock-cup routine, as my friend pointed out. But afterward. My friend had come to lunch because he thought SK maybe had something cooking for him.

431

"A tough one, SK," Bertie said, taking his hand away from his head long enough to shake it.

My friend suggested three synonyms in rapid succession. The producer made no acknowledgment but kept a weary eye on Bertie and waited for his milk. He was the man who might have something cooking.

"Tell you what," Bertie finally said. "I'll take it over to my office and kick it around. Call you back five at the latest—it's a tough one, strictly a phaseroo, but we'll work around it yet."

"Okay," SK said, "terrific." His milk came and he drank it listlessly.

"You see that guy, that writer?" my friend said when he had left the producer to his production afterward. "Get him, will you. He should be spending the afternoon working on a synonym for the word guts—that son of a bitch is on the payroll for two-five, *two-five*." SK hadn't had anything cooking after all. A crime, it stinks but with a sound-track. "But in *Technicolor*," my friend said, and we began figuring roughly what it was going to cost the company for a rewrite around the word guts, which had also probably taken a third of a day to write in in the first place. A third of a day, not including lunch hour and producer's stomach, or indigestion, on the time of a $2,500-a-week writer. One-third of one-sixth of two-thousand-five. That, we agreed, is Hollywood for you.

And in a sense it is Hollywood for you. It is always there, not a thing of invented slander because the inventors are never rich enough in imagination. I call it the work of the man who invented Hollywood, though actually his patent is only that he lives there in a sort of crazy legend. He gives out with the Hollywood time of day, but he is in a relative minority and while he may be considered a peculiar and flamboyant type of yeast, he is not even a slice of the whole loaf of pictures. What he does is simply better gossip than gossip of work done, a hard day put in, and home for supper. What he does may be fantastic, shrewd, or stupid in brass; but it is a mark to shoot at, and in any industry so raw and vast and suddenly full of beans, he sets a style.

It is Hollywood all right, or the part of Hollywood that is show business—which originally came from somewhere else. Show business has always had its own secret fast talk and methods of practice and high pressure, and it is still unknown country to nearly every innocent who sits out front, or maybe even gets backstage afterward and reads Leonard Lyons on what certainly never happened at Sardi's (his scout picked it up in Walgreen's basement), or maybe even reads *Variety* thinking how quaintly. A few writers like John O'Hara get into the thing and manage to bring it back as it is for stories, and then even the large-bore intellects read what is written there and come up with various startling interpretations of the subconscious.

But Hollywood is a part of show business grown immense above all others and precedents. And the talk of its back stairs is already nationwide copy. The town is always rocking with accounts of so-and-so speaking to such-and-such and the great sounding board of a thousand typewriters sends as much of it out to the land as will bear print, which is unfortunately only a part of it even when it is true. The bulk of it travels by uncensored grapevine, in club cars and across coffeepot counters, so that a fellow who got on the Chief for Chicago just as the really big scandal of the last year was in its first morning of being whispered, was asked in Chicago, a day later in New Orleans, a day later in Miami, by porters and cabdrivers and friends and airport help, always behind a hand, almost with a wink, a nudge: Look, on the level, just *how* did he. . . . While back on the Coast, to bring the story full circle, the executives of the studio concerned fired the guy the morning after it "happened" and wrote him back on the books hastily in the afternoon when his secretary uncovered the damaging fact that he had actually been in New York on business the whole week.

Writers and directors, the good hard-working kind, don't know whether to laugh or cry; but the story usually ends up by being funny. The story is about the newest effrontery, the latest bucket of gall to be poured on; and to live any time at all in the Hollywood legend it must have that true fantasy which is only achieved when the absurd and impossible is surprised in life. The man concerned isn't Sam Goldwyn, though Goldwyn is a name to put on the syndicate wires for any joke in broken English, just as Mae West naturally appears as the heroine of any story with a bosom in it. You don't ever quite know who he is. It is because as a collective personality he is always mysterious and just around some other corner—you hear more about him than you ever see. He is the producer who shows his new house, rapping with both authority and pride on the expensive wood of each reproduction: "Imitation, get it? Strictly a phony." He is the writer out of work who gets insulted by a friend's offer to get him a thousand a week, he is a one-five man by definition, a friend shouldn't talk so. So the friend tells him hold the wire, he'll see what he can do and finally comes back on the phone almost gleeful: if the writer will come to the studio right now, it will be fixed for $1,250, just hustle right over. "What?" the writer screams. "You're asking me I should come to a lousy studio and get locked out of my *room*?"

Or: The writer knew the producer was touchy even for a producer, and the picture just screened for him was so awful there was nothing to say, so he circled the yes-men around the producer as the lights came up and ducked out without saying anything. Next day he was cut dead in the commissary, but dead. This would have been a little funny only he worked for the guy, so he waited a week and got an audience.

"Look, Chief, isn't my work all right, what's with all this air cooling I get?"

The producer looked out the window, but the picture was already a week old and part of the past, so he was merely sad. "Larry, I screen a picture, you show no manners. Even a dog would bark to get out the door, not you."

"Well, Chief, what can I do? I just didn't *like* the picture."

The producer started to pound the desk and then went back to looking Old Patron Betrayed again. "Larry," he said, "the very least, you could have *told* me you liked it." And he wasn't fooling.

Or he isn't anybody but just a general state of affairs, such as the red warning balloon someone sold Twentieth Century-Fox, and how it would cost a fortune to maintain but would keep planes away from the area where their motor noise would be ruinous to sound-track, and how from then until this minute every plane that got in the air within a fifty-mile radius would first come roaring over to see what the hell the thing was and then begin to use it as a pylon. Or such as the state of affairs sneak previews were getting into. Producers claimed that rival studios would inevitably hear of such a christening and pack the house with the aunts, nephews, and kitchen help of everybody on their payroll all loaded up with a blank pan for the laugh lines and snickers for the climax. This didn't affect the public and couldn't change the picture, but it could affect the hell out of all the critics the studio had brought over to write about it next morning.

There are individuals whose career in the industry is established, even honored, and their gall expected. It is like in a serial really, because the last affair hasn't been talked out before they have done another successful impersonation under a new and undreamed-of set of circumstances. The best one I know of for illustration is the main component of Budd Schulberg's story about What Makes Sammy Glick. In the book he is not called by name and is at the best a suggestion for horror sequences, but never mind the formalities, he hops right over to Schulberg's producer before the ink is dry and says, "This guy should not live, he is an insult to the integrity of the industry and a stinkaroo." The producer has not read the book. He tells Jerry Wald he will not have his interrogatives abbreviated or his rights transfixed. I can only carry the story to the point where I was on this producer's lot one day on other business and at the finish of it thought I would drop around again and pass a civil time of day with Schulberg, why not. "I'm mixed up, I guess," I told the girl in the cubbyhole at writers' row, "I thought this was Mr. Schulberg's office." "You are only half mixed up," the girl said. "This used to be the office of a Mr. Budd Schulberg. Last week, I think."

There is also the man whose name is on more credit cards than any five writers, everybody knows the name, perhaps it is even mentioned here. When he was a working writer he caught one snag in a meteoric career, and that was when he was thrown a sequence of the scenario he had submitted and told to rewrite it that afternoon. Rewrite? My God, where was his ghost? He tried to find the man by phoning everywhere from Burbank to Culver City; he called all the Brown Derbies, he had him paged at swimming pools and tennis courts, like at the

Beverly Hills. He finally got in his car and made a door-to-door canvass. I suppose it makes a happy ending that he found him, but anyway he did and got the writing rewritten, and today he is writing what seems to be an average of fourteen pictures at the same time. The topper to every new story about him is of course that he got his start doing a radio column in New York, and that was ghost-written too.

There is a writer less colossal but more colorful, you can keep a roomful of people remembering about him until two any morning, and no repeats. His scrapes are more human but unfortunately less printable—like the one ending "My God I've killed her"—and of a nature others could not know if he didn't go around telling them on himself in wonderment and for sympathy. He is the ghosted writer who stops them all (and you can check his credit titles in *Film Daily Year Book*). He got out there and was doing all right, and he got sick of picking up a phone every time he wanted to tell the ghost what the producer wanted now, so he just brought him into the studio and planted him at a desk. Took him right into story conferences, bland as a pigeon. The producer said, What the hell is that dog doing at my story conference? and the writer just said, Why he's my *ghost*, I need him handy. Okay, the producer said, if he's turning out those B's we're making, I'll hire *him*. Can't, the writer said. I got him under contract. Well do you know, he had. When the producer had got his toupée straightened out again he said finish this picture and get off my set; and the writer merely shrugged and said he'd sell them somewhere else, okay, okay. And do you know, he made three more pictures hand running for that producer, with the ghost right in there at every conference, saving time like anything, and he's still merrily at it. He's safe from everything but the Los Angeles traffic.

Whoever he is, he is the man people want to hear about. He is a man from show business gone wild on the fat margin of millions being in it; and he gives the show-business part of Hollywood its flavor; it is somewhat in his clipped and extravagant language that everybody speaks, thinks even. He will appear all through the picture without ever being one of its true key figures. He is as good for a book as he is for a chapter, and for pure yarning even better. Perhaps that has been the trouble all along. He is a very small part of what you see on the screen, but Hollywood is his town because he has put a good part of it in his pockets; and I will continue with him next time.

18 August 1941

Hollywood Is More So

Hollywood is a part of show business and acts like show business, though probably more so. It talks a special kind of language and talks fast. I believe the general level of aimless ragging, gossip, and pointed storytelling is higher than it is in life generally; but I could advance no special reason except that talk seems to jump more where life has a faster pace, is more precarious with ups and downs, demanding quick wits for existence—and especially where there is a shared body of salty allusion in the complex technical details of the profession. (Remember the story of the vaudeville actor whose mother had died and the friend was fumbling with condolences? I thought I'd wait until after it was over, the friend said; I saw you in front of the Palace and you seemed to be taking it pretty hard. Oh, in front of the *Palace,* the actor said. You should have caught me at Woodlawn.)

You can sit around anywhere and the boys won't fail you, on the set or in between at lunch. A couple of writers descend upon another. "Do you think he really asked for pink when he bought that shirt?"

"He really got pink, all right."

"Listen. I call this just a trailer for a Borris Morros shirt, ever see one? This is just a trailer."

"It must have been made before Technicolor. How can you write in a shirt like that?"

"Isn't this our own free company?"

(Chorus) "This is our own free company, how can anyone grumble?" (After which turn of conversation, the talk unfortunately has to be deleted.)

There is the fellow who calls up a hard-working man. Has a sure-fire story idea for him. The story is called *Four Brothers,* absolutely a new wrinkle: there are four brothers and when they are little they take a solemn vow that when they grow up they will band together from anywhere at an instant's notice and protect their dear mother. Here the working man breaks in, yelling as he was expected to: What are you doing to my time? That is a turkey and it is dead.

436

One moment of your time, the other says. These four brothers grow up (just a moment, I'm only roughing it in) and they do *not* take care of their dear old mother, to hell with her. Should we go ahead with it?

Or take the producer who called in two writers and said he had a swell idea for his next picture, let's get to work on it. It is going to be about the army, everybody is now interested in the army. It will be very hot. For a title I got *Tomorrow's Generals*. Okay, the writers said, what's the idea for the picture? The producer looked at them shaking his head. Didn't I just give you the idea, boys? It makes a swell script, what's wrong?

It is the same with the fine crews on the sets, people remembering for others the time the tame tiger got loose on stage fourteen and sent everybody climbing up the parallels, and it turned out to be some kind of climbing tiger and I think was only deterred by someone's dropping a 2,000-watt arc in its face, wires and all; or the time the black-snake got too curious and dropped into the wind machine; or (a favorite at RKO) don't leave that dolly outside the door while you're shifting the camera, Paramount will be over the back fence and cabbage it. Or over in the semi-dark of a stage where they are dressing a huge outdoor set, with real trees, a low hill built up, a pond with a summer-house—and all around two sides a painted backing of unbleached muslin, sized on the reverse, stretching up into the shadows without a wrinkle.

The old-timer they call Blackie is working on this—part of it is ocean and part rolling land, and this much is already completed. He is now painting in trees and highlights, working on wheeled platforms and high stepladders. "Look at him," one of the men says, seeing people looking at him as indeed they might be, for he sweeps down delicate willow branches with no stencil and a number-thirty house-painter's brush, sure and swiftly. "A loafer. Might as well save the lights—will you take a hinge at the black he is putting on there?"

Blackie looks down, dipping his brush. "Again," he says, and nods sadly. "We had it all out last year; now again."

"Either it's black or it's so light the camera won't pick up," the man says. "The picture will lose money."

Blackie paints three feet of foliage and looks over to where the man is working at some shrubs, wiring flowers to them. "Well look at what he is doing now," Blackie says. "What is it, magnolias? Magnolias, he's putting them onto them god-damn scrub oaks. This is no life for an honest man, I shouldn't of come."

Everything seems leisurely, but only seems so. A rosebush is grown across the front of the main house as you watch, and blossoms into a couple of hundred crepe flowers, for the men talk with their mouths, not their hands. It will be quiet, too, for a half-hour, each one seemingly alone with his serious game of landscaping as trucks back through the big doors of stage five filled with bushes and branches and whole trees, and the working lights look down from the high parallels.

Then it will start up again, the endless reminiscence and jibing of the workshop. "I knew a guy hung bananas on one of these here big rosebushes," one of them says. "He had the bananas anyway and he was dressing the set."

"Who did? You're crazy," Blackie calls over.

"It was some kind of a bush; he had grapefruits too. That was Wheelwright and we were—"

"Oh, Wheelwright," Blackie says. "Say no more. Wheelwright is enough," he says and climbs down to look at his tree.

"Had about five crates of fruit and one orange tree," the man goes on, "so when we wire on the oranges we put on apples. I tried to stop him but he put grapefruits too. Then he put the bananas on this big old bush we had. Maybe it wasn't a rosebush."

"Wheelwright," Blackie says, and spits. "Nature's nobleman: he'd do anything. Put an ad in the papers for art-school kids. Use their sketches, teach them the business as if he knew it, never pay them. Wheelwright. Now what the hell are you doing with that wisteria? Putting it in the middle of the cement walk? It's no life here."

It is not funny when you get shoved around or squeezed out by some broken-down brass front like the special yes-man for Mister Zee, whose main chore to get his name in credit titles is a routine of laughing for which words are inadequate. Mister Zee has brought a pall of gloom over the story conference by saying (with a pause), Hm, very warm for May. Somebody has got to laugh here, and the yes-man comes on: first the look of disbelief, then the wind-up and spasm and *blast* of laughter, the doubling down to his right leg and then up to slap it, the helpless gasp and appeal to the company and pointing with repeated full-shoulder motion, "But *get* that guy!" The subsiding shake and wiping of eyes. He's in. And too many people are shoved and squeezed by just such. The humor of the situations they get into with the kind of assignments they have to take when they can get them is wry at best.

There is a producer I love, at a distance. He has an idea that if he can promote $400, a script, and a pocket kodak, he can make a picture in a barn somewhere. So he calls up Benny to come down to the packing case which is an office because there are paper clips on the desk. He wants a remake of Rex Beach's *The Ne'er-Do-Well,* which impressed him strongly in his youth. It was about the construction of the Panama Canal and very hot stuff at the time it came out, which was the time of the construction of the Panama Canal (for those days it was probably a rich man's *For Whom the Bell Tolls*). I want you to modernize, Benny, he said, pronouncing the first syllable of the word like the name Moe. And we got to leave these politics out, you are a smart writer. Moe-dernize is the word. So Benny thought fast and said, it can't be Panama then. Let's make it something like—how about the sugar plantations in Hawaii?

We open on sugar cane, the cutting, hauling to mill, grinding, juice, sugar, all that color stuff. No politics, but native, see it?

The producer began to get the vivid picture of the sugar cane being picked off the palm trees in the colorful tropics and said terrific. Moe-dernize it, that is the angle. And no politics.

Well Benny did the script with another fellow, jiggered the story all around, and fitted it out for recommissioning. Turned it in. Waited.

But when Benny was called in a few days later, the producer was shaking his head. Uh-uh. Somehow, Benny, you've lost the *flavor* of it. The flavor doesn't hit me. This scene here, this . . . . His voice trailed off and he shuffled pages and finally came out with it. The scene he had read, or had read *to* him more likely, wasn't even like in the book. The original flavor. . . .

So Benny went back over the points for him, giving them to him slowly: (1) the scene referred to was politics, which had to be out; (2) it couldn't be about building a canal because they didn't have one in Hawaii; (3) it couldn't be Panama because there wasn't anything there *but* canal.

I'll think over what you say, said the producer.

Next day he called the writer in and he had the answer worked out. Maybe you better just forget about it, Benny, he said. I see what's your difficulty for what I had in mind, Benny, he said in a kindly way. You made the mistake working too close to the book.

And sometimes a big producer can manage to remain powerless because he wants to remain powerful, and someone is putting the heat on from outside. This one is quite a sparkplug of a producer and he likes liberal things now and then, or likes to think about them, because only look, he went to a college. He has bought a book that is high in contemporary esteem and best-seller lists, and has put a young man of talent and intelligence to work on it (the young man up to now has mostly been working either on horrors or for the shelf). The script is worked over carefully, to get some meaning out of it and keep it a picture, by him and as I remember others: they look it all over finally and they have something. The producer looks it all over and says, boys, you have really got something. Now we'll just get the Hays Office, a routine matter. . . . Into production immediately in time for the oscars.

But hm, what is this? The Office is acting a little strangely, and cannot guarantee an okay until the picture is made and screened before it in the usual way. Perhaps there is a hint? Or perhaps. Well some expense, producing a picture. And if. And the script goes on the shelf. And that is all of the episode period.

Or there is the frequent happening that can happen to anybody: the fellow who made a good picture, the front office got scared, the salesmen and exhibitors got scared. The picture was hush-hushed, released but as though from a stretch in Dannemora, and so there runs a scare and shrinking away through the press departments and critics (you can for the most part shake them all up in a hat and I wish you would). And later when the fellow's name comes up, so do the eyebrows, and they say sure, sure, nice fellow but what's he *made*?

This leads into another thing that should be said before we wind up with the more striking trivia that can be used to set picture making apart as a sequence in waxworks. Human nature works out the same way in Hollywood that it works out anywhere else, but it works out under a peculiar pressure that is not usually felt outside of the various hidden communities of show business. Wherever people are succeeding and failing in the same breath, there is always an air of impermanence in relations, and your bosom friend of today may forget the name by tomorrow—on the other hand, you may do some fast forgetting yourself, because he may be broke. Hollywood as a society is just about completely made up of success and failure, and the whirl is so giddy that the question "Where are you working now?" may be taken as just the inspection through the peepholes of the old speak, as meaning, *"Are* you working?" In all such frank struggles for existence, the main rule is never kick a man when he is up.

So if you are out of work and represent no proud and potent interests, if you need something or are lost, don't look back to people you may have been glad to know when you knew them when. The streets are lined with chaps who could buttonhole you and say, "You see that big high-blood-pressure getting out of the new Packard there? We were like *that* for three years; I boarded him. But did you catch him passing me a full eighteen inches away? See me? Listen, he'll see me *strictly* if I drop on his head from a six-story window, not until. And what will it be then? It will be. Why, Eddie, you rat, I been trying to get you for *two weeks* like crazy, well, be seeing you around, sweetheart—and he will duck into the car, me laying there."

Never mistake that hovering over the whole town, though not so evident in the pleasant air as the satires make out, is a special type of fear, a compound of being got wrong, of laying two eggs in the same basket, of slipping back and down and out. It isn't fairyland but it is that dangerous place where fairyland is on a production line at a cost of billions of dollars, and where all the concealable petty struggling of a quieter life is stepped up in speed, time, and tonal volume. Good people can abound in this atmosphere of a desperate need for front, as much as they can abound anywhere. But here the pressure and the danger are so constantly at elbow that the climbers and bogus biggies are carried beyond themselves to become people of outlandish shapes and menace.

8 September 1941

Before the Cameras Roll

The worst things that happen in pictures happen previous to the first day of actual shooting, usually. In many cases they happen before the story is considered and bought. Yet these things are vital in the art of making pictures, and though they may be improved, I know of no happy state where they may be eliminated, just in the nature of things.

In the book of How to Make a Picture, item one is, first get an audience. To get and hold a body of followers large enough to support this fabulous expense in production is the prime moving force of the whole industry, however clumsy its lunges and however many times it cuts its own throat out of jealousy and meanness. Audience support is the one reason for the emergence of men with talent and push enough to go against the current (you'd never have heard of them in a closed subsidy); it is responsible for both the best and the worst, and I do not know how many thousands of times someone has said, as I have heard them: I made that one so I could make them give me this one. At the same time it has been a powerful brake on the tendency of all art toward obscure faddism; American writers and directors have had to learn to do it the hard way, and it is the way they have learned to tell stories with a camera and a pair of cutting scissors which has come to lead the world, to influence the technique of even the best film making everywhere.

But that is all in the what-I-think-about-the-moon realm of picture making. The audience is there. It is always there. It is there now in such a steady multiple vigor that anybody with a brass voice and craft enough to promote one or two thousand can make the world's worst picture and get away with it (the world's worst picture either will never be made or is made every second Monday after the first Tuesday). But to understand the relationship between those who pay their money to see, and those who make, buy, sell, distribute, and exhibit, you will have to be familiar with the subject or read some of the books in its endless library: this is not the class for beginners, and there is not space here for a subject so wide and intricate. The point is that any understanding of the making

441

of any single picture demands this background of for-whom and to-what-end—as who in civilization would listen to his mouth clapping up and down on the subject of Shakespeare and think himself a critic if he had never so much as heard of the terms Elizabethan, Renaissance, Globe, Holinshed, buskin, blank verse? We must simply remember that when the act of creation involves a thousand people and a million dollars, and wonders of science too deep to see, there must be some kind of monumental and sometimes monstrous plant set up to manufacture and purvey this entertainment for millions.

The plant is Hollywood as a center with lines running out over the world, and the second chapter in the book is: To make a picture you have to have the backing *and* equipment. Now in most cases, the backing comes from one of the major or minor established companies. Not because it comes more readily, and certainly not because it will give you any scope to work in, but because these companies control the channels of distribution—you want to make a picture but you want it to be seen too, don't you? There is a long history of seesaw and confusion in this struggle for the upper hand as between the man who shows and the man who makes the shows. Great companies have swallowed up minor companies by buying up theater chains, *i.e.*, the means of their expansion and their competitors' dwindling revenue; great companies have then staggered under the load and gone down. Great chain owners have tried to dominate the companies, bought them or starved them out, and then failed because they had dried up the very thing they were selling at its source. Men like William Fox, not essentially a picture man, have grown to giant size in the field of build-and-buy-and-produce-for-it, and then been chivvied out by the bankers. The bankers have seen those billions lying around and got in to pick them up, only to discover that their brusque pirate's idea of how to run a picture studio left out the ingredient of how pictures could be made. In the long and varied contest, it is always the working producers who win out in the end. Individuals among them are constantly losing their shirts, but those who make pictures and know pictures must have the final say, as a whole. They are the geese who lay those golden eggs; bankers, exhibitors, distributors, operators, and the like can lay eggs only in the figurative sense. So helpless are they, one after the other, that you take as accepted such facts as that little Shirley Temple alone saved the farflung glory of Twentieth Century-Fox; that Deanna Durbin, also alone, kept Universal off the bread line.

The golden egg itself, of course, is the patents racket. So much costly and marvelous equipment is necessary in the processes of building cameras, making sound and color, that it was impossible the original small inventors or owners should not be bought or buried, until some powerful and unscrupulous monopoly like the American Telephone and Telegraph Company controlled or tied up all the patents being used in some important process or other, and naturally will never sell anything outright because the lease is so rich, beyond fable. Or that an outfit like Electrical Research Products Incorporated should not only control patents but own studios and lend money and generally be the people you have to see, always at your cost. There is du Pont too. There is Eastman. Names fill the sky like buzzards.

The best analysis of these financial, and all-powerful, ends of the business will probably be Leo Rosten's forthcoming book, though from what very little I know of it, it will not have understanding of the philosophy of showmanship, which has no philosopher. The best book on the movie man as operator is still *Upton Sinclair Presents William Fox*—an amazing book but again deficient in knowledge of movies, their cause and effect. For the strange rank growth of the industry in general through the early days, the book is Terry Ramsaye's *Million and One Nights,* if you can read it and remember that Ramsaye is on the whole a journalist whose feet hurt and that he works today as the right hand of the practically unspeakable Martin Quigley. Thousands have fussed and fumed, but I doubt anything else has been written with much pertinence to the forbidding factual mountain of make and sell, buy and beat the drum.

To go back to where we came from, you *can* go to one of the picture-loan promoters and prove to his satisfaction that you have an idea for a picture which will sell, and get financing. In that case you rent a studio and equipment at exorbitant cost, and make the picture, hiring your writers, director, actors, and so forth. And then you get into the problem of what a picture is, what it takes.

The picture always starts at the beginning, which is (1) a writer's idea, (2) a successful book or play if you can buy it, (3) in some other studio. The toughest on the writer, and often on the public, is when the idea comes from a producer and is therefore not an idea—such not being his business—but an impulse. Budd Schulberg has written in these very pages how he and Scott Fitzgerald were sent by Walter Wanger to Hanover to cook up a story "around" Dartmouth simply because Walter Wanger went to Dartmouth and hasn't got out from under it yet. You didn't think that was an exception? Or the story I told last time about the producer who had an idea which boiled down to the title *Tomorrow's Generals.* Or the big-company executive who says, there's a lot of interest in the Lindbergh kidnaping, and it's safe by now, only it can't be Lindbergh and it can't be a kidnaping. Or the company which says, we are due for an ice-carnival picture, or a Colbert picture, or a nongangster picture, or something like an Abbot and Costello, or something like what the hell is the name of that musical Fox is cleaning up on, or a period picture—everybody's still hot for the Civil War after *Gone with the Wind.*

On the whole it is the writer who takes the big rap. Stuff is shoved at him which should never even be considered for pictures, yet he must make a screenplay out of it because the company has money tied up in it and he is tied up with the company, just for the living. It will be done and will go out under his name, and I think it was Sidney Skolsky who broke the story about two writers coming home from work at Republic, one saying: *"You* take the credit title on this one; I had to take it last time." Or the writer shapes up a good screenplay and then has one to five expensive names called in to jigger it all out of true. Or he does some good work and everybody says that is really good work, and the picture is never made, and two months later the same everybodies are saying, Yes, I know, but I don't seem to remember the name.

Whatever the actual genesis, the picture has to start with a writer. If he has an idea of his own, fine, he will sell it as an original and maybe clean up by doing what is called the treatment on salary. But most of the time he has no time for ideas of his own. The company wants a Western, a South Sea Islands, a Hedy Lamarr, or some damn thing. It's a book or a play or a magazine series the company has on the shelf; it has to be done to write off a book loss that would worry the bankers; and it may have to be stretched to include a big deathbed sequence in the gutter at Tia Juana because Paramount has just finished with a whole Mexican street and square they built, and have it uneasy on their hands; or it may have to have a sea episode, to make use of the white-elephant tank and enormous ship models Korda has on his hands over at General Service.

You have a picture cooking, and you have a producer. You have to have a producer because that is the movies' middleman. He takes care of promoting the money, hiring the sound stages, the director, the actors; figuring costs and time elements, getting the thing cut and sound-tracked, ready and distributed. The producer may work in one of three ways. He may be a freelance, completely freelance, trusting in his own judgment to make a picture in the expectation that it will be good enough to force the big chains to buy and show it. He may be a semi-free-lance, a man who has got his own unit, and his own say in everything (the everything is a pipe dream) on a major lot. He may be just a yes-man to the executive in charge of production—and that is what he usually is. But in the present setup he is there, taking the responsibility for smash or flop; and the present setup is not considered all to the good by the men who make pictures, more and more of whom are taking over the producer's job themselves, demanding: Give the movies back to us, the movie makers.

The independent producer is up against long odds. He may move in on, say, RKO. He has his own writers, director. But wait. It is very hard to tell where the equipment you are renting stops: you rent the carpenters, grips, gaffers, cameramen, sound men; why aren't you renting the chiefs of these departments? The director-producer either spends valuable days fighting it out with the front office or uses the company men. He may be somebody like Sam Goldwyn, who has a name that will strike anybody to silence, but even after his picture has been made, he has to fight United Artists on the way it is released, delayed, and generally hamstrung.

Or he may be a producer who is making a picture for one of the majors, and finds that although he has signed his director and stars, as of now, as of high salaries starting today, he has a rather weird time getting the stages and the general go-ahead from the company anxious to produce his production. What goes? After a while of negotiations he finds out. The producer has his own female lead signed up; the company does not mention her. After a few days of objecting to the story or the Toronto sequence the company calls him up, surprise! With envy and with wonder it says, Why you lucky dog, you, we've *got* it. Are you lucky? Listen, get this: we just found we haven't a lead spot for May Bonnet, and, get this, you can have her! Jesus what a lucky guy. May Bonnet!

So he guessed it all along. May Bonnet is the cow this company signed a contract of $60,000 for two pictures and wants to pull out of making the second with, the first was so sad. They were stuck with her and they were doing the holdup on the producer who wanted to make a picture for them. And the final arrangement, the producer knowing necessity when he saw it, was that he bought the remainder of May Bonnet's contract for $30,000, tore it up, and told her to go back to her telephone and stay there, all alone, and found stages available for his picture with his own lead, and enough red ink to write the three-o into the budget.

But when a picture is started, many departments get to work, outside of the producer with his balances and arrangements, the writer and director dreaming up the story they are to tell (if the director is a fair name and not on the Metro or Warners' payroll—which is to say, lucky). The research department gets the script, and looks up the likeness with wonderful pertinacity and skill. The art department gets the green light and the art director delegates his draftsmen, painters, model builders, and curators to work up a rough draft, scene by scene, and then practically the whole picture in drawings, in miniatures, in paintings and models. These men build the thing you see, and change it as the camera requires; but it is always the art director himself who has laid it out, it is his department that has sketched out and painted in the things you see, from beautiful to bum. You have to have an art director, if only because he is the man who sees it in advance and starts the wheels moving for its realization.

Then there is sound, and with sound comes the musical director, who works after the picture has been made. He is a vital man in a picture's effect—at least he is when he is good enough and given any freedom; but like the cutters and special-effects men, he is not at work until after the cameras start rolling. You have to catch him later.

22 September 1941

The Lights Look Down

Making pictures is one of the most monotonous and exacting jobs in the world, and it is hard to realize from the glib images of the screen what persistent slow endeavor has built up bit by bit to any simple minute of action. Inside Warners' sound stage 21, the largest on a lot that advertises itself outside as the largest in the world, the air is dark with gloomy, remote shadows here, overbright there. The thing is somewhat the shape and size of an airplane hangar, but it is also something like a building going up, for high overhead run the catwalks, or parallels, with their batteries of spotlights; and above them, all around, runs a second tier, with ladders and cables going up and down—cables run all over the set in mazes like jungle growth, from the size of telephone wires to flexible rubber mains as big as garden hoses, giving light and rolling cameras and picking up sound. At the near end is a section of street front, with two stores and an alley. The stores are solidly built, one of them two rooms deep, and exactly as old and weathered and ready for business as any fish store along the waterfront. This is one of the sets for *The Gentle People,* which is going to cost around $750,000 with no money wasted.

Along half of one side, her masts rising out of sight into the gloom above the catwalks, there is a full-sized and full-rigged ship, complete and perfect in detail. It is the ship they used for *The Sea Wolf,* and they are leaving her there a while because it is going to take time and thousands to get her out, and meanwhile something might come up. *The Gentle People,* for example, is waterfront, so they're shooting some of the scenes with her forepeak and bowsprit for background. The entire wall down that side is painted a flat dull black, and so is the far end: the cameras shooting across from any of the angles needed will pick up only distance. But the thing that really fills the stage and chills the air is the Warner tank, which is perhaps two-thirds of it. A raised dock goes part way down the near side, with sound, heavy piles along the edge and ladders going down to a landing stage a foot or so above the water—only three feet deep, but colored to look like harbor water, green and sluggish. Various

446

small boats are tied up behind the dock and out of sight. The boat at the landing stage under the lights is the sturdy but weather-beaten fishing boat used by the Gentle People. Part of all this is the standing equipment for that stage, but a good deal has been run up for this one picture. And all the work has been done on it before the story even went into production.

On this afternoon they are setting up for a retake of one of the earlier scenes someone wasn't satisfied with, and have been at it probably an hour already. The dock and the landing stage swarm with grips and electricians, cameramen, assistants; and voices float down from the catwalks. There is a man on the bowsprit of the ship; there are men on stages rising above the water, adjusting junior spots, reflectors, barndoors; there are two or three men in high rubber pants pushing about through the water. Behind this the actors are hanging around waiting for the setup; the director is there; the script girl and make-up people are there. Some carpenters are puttering with a new staging. It is a strange scene of seeming incoordination and idleness, and actual complex bustle.

Just now the place is dominated by the thick unreal voice of the lighting director, the head gaffer, who gives his orders into a hand microphone as lights rise, fall, swing or go out, one by one or in batteries. Three stand-ins hold their places forever as the number-one arc is taken back a foot, as the big junior is blinkered to hit the edge of the landing ("Keep it off her face, Gleason"), as a light is brought up behind the dock in a punt and trained across under it to put an outline around the piles. The center of action is surrounded by a forest of these intent bulbous heads on their adjustable iron stalks, looking mutely into the glow they make, like the men from Mars.

And above, from all sides, looking down across varying distances of shadow, the numbered arcs and rifles, moving slowly to the hollow amplifier-voice which fills the air directing them, on and on. "A little to your right, Burwick—or who's up there?"—"Cut in 22. Now 14, 6. All right, all your arcs, up there."—"Eddie, turn yours up a little. Another turn. No, make it hotter. Okay."—"Steve! Where's Steve? Push yours up about a foot and take a filter out, can you make it?"

Below the dock on the landing-stage level, the camera rests on its dolly, a focus of many cables and needing three or four men around to push and clear everything as it moves smoothly in or back on thick rubber tires along a metal track laid down for it. Even with a blimp hooding its real mysteries, it looks as complicated as the cab of a locomotive. A figure huddled in a topcoat is in the seat, looking occasionally through the finder and motioning to the lighting director; his hair is very black and when one of the electricians calls down directly, "How's this, Jimmie?" his voice in answer has just a trace of high singsong. What he has seen through his camera you have seen since you have seen pictures, and now you see himself, patient and exacting and in a topcoat, James Wong Howe. He is one of the aces, hard to get and invaluable on a picture like this, which is going to depend very much on atmosphere; and he knows it and will sit there immovable until every shadow has been painted in or erased or tinted to suit his precise liking. The unpracticed eye sees no change as these lights come in or shift or burn hotter, gets no sense of values from apparently aimless units looking off across the general pattern, which is something like what a wheel with irregular spokes would look like if it were a globe instead. But through all this laborious process figures are being outlined and faces made clear but natural, and the surrounding air is being given life and density. Mr. Howe will say all right when he is ready.

The man on the jib of the *Sea Wolf* has not moved. The people at ease in the chairs around the back are still talking or studying a script. The Negro service man is still playing a game of toss with one of the grips in front of the fish store and people stop to rag him. ("What time did you get back?"—"Never *did* get back! Ho. ho.") The men in rubber pants wade slowly about in the water, keeping it churned up and snagging odd remnants out of camera sight.

"Number one," says the voice. "Now two," and from high up somewhere two cans of fog let out spurts of vapor, which billow slowly into layers in the air. "Now down and to your left, Mac," the voice says, and the man on the jib boom finally moves, and sends a stream of fog from his can directly down to the water and across the camera field. "Save it," says the voice, and the fog stops coming, and the billows and layers of what has been sent out merge slowly in the air, which is now being set softly in motion by two giant noiseless fans turning slowly, one at the water's edge, one trained down from the dock above. Jimmie looks through his finder and says something to the lighting director, and the voice picks up again: "Al, can you bring that junior. . . ."

The fog is turned on and off two or three times, and the lights move and black out in their inscrutable purpose; and then apparently Mr. Wong Howe says all right, because instead of stand-ins there are actors in the three positions of the scene. Ida Lupino on the stairs to the landing stage; Thomas Mitchell looking up at her; John Qualen in the boat. And now there is a gray-haired gentleman looking through the camera finder, Anatole Litvak, director. It will not be one of those scenes that are made on the first take, because he knows the camera too; he wants that lighted mobility of expression and density of air too, and nobody is through work until he is satisfied on every detail and says "Make it." With Jimmie and Litvak on the same picture you do not make ten camera setups a day, let the front office yell its head off. But you may—and it is always a pure gamble, with odds on that extra sense of the good artist—you may get a color and depth and feeling of immediate happening that will be just the mysterious extra quantity which will bring a picture back to haunt people as they lay them down to sleep, and also finally bring glory to the front office which will make it healthier and wealthier, but no more wise.

The actors hold their positions now. The camera moves in and back, and there are conferences. Overhead on its boom the microphone swings from side to side and runs silently out and back as the center of dialogue shifts. They try it once, the scene opening with Mitchell talking up to Lupino, turning, talking to Qualen, who talks. Then Mitchell to Lupino and her exit; then Mitchell to Qualen. Then with the lights again, with the camera, with conferences. Then, "Places! Places, please." More work with the finders. The fog is dying again so One and Two and the Man on the Boom are called to, and now there is a man with a little fog pot and a fan just to the left of the camera, to send it wisping across the scene. Then again. Mitchell to Lupino, to Qualen (and at the phrase, "That's what they are, swordfishes!" the camera moves noiselessly back to include the three in medium shot; the microphone boom reaches noiselessly out overhead to catch the Mitchell-Qualen) and again the conferences, the changes, the actors quiet in their places, and in the interim the voice ("Save your arcs") to the big eyes around the parallels. Four or five times with the same lines, no perceptible change.

Then the fog is brought out for good, one of the men in rubber pants comes up close but out of sight to move the water and let it slop and ripple against the boat and pilings, and all the big lights hit up and the man with the slate, Scene 243, Take 1, holds it in front of the camera, and this time the camera is really rolling. A bell rings, the endless gossip in dim corners hushes as various grips and assistants on the way to advancement pass back a sharp *Tsht!* The director, now on a high stool, calls out "Action!" and Thomas Mitchell's voice comes up in the old line just as if he'd thought of it: "Now that's no way to be talking about a boy like Tommy."

The camera rolls back, the boom moves out, the water ripples gently, and the only one now to make a move outside the lighted circle is the man with the little fog can and the fan. "Cut," the director says, and after a minute Jimmie says, "Miss Lupino, please?" and the girl comes to her original position on the ladder, and Jimmie turns a handle and looks, and Litvak moves up and looks, and nods, and goes back to the stool. "Places!" he calls as the second assistant holds the slate, Scene 243, Take 2, up for the camera and jumps back on the dolly as it moves in. The bell rings. People say *Tsht!* and through the easy rolling fog the lights look down and up and across with their hot steady thousand eyes, and Thomas Mitchell, again, starts, "Now that's no way to be talking about a boy like Tommy," and the sixty-odd people around look across and down, as fixed and impersonal as the lights.

Take 3, Take 4, Take 5. With time out for more changes, more fog, with the same lines, the same business, the same page of script, and all the thousands of cubic feet of air waiting, being lighted and colored and filled with sound, but waiting. (All the grips and most of the electricians waiting now, as actors, and cameramen, the director and his assistant and his script girl had waited.) Then through it for the last time and the voice comes up again, "Save it!" and the main lights blink off, and the director holds the actors long enough to get places marked out for the next seven lines to follow in the next setup, to come. And Mr. Howe leaves his seat to stretch and pass the topcoat up to someone on the dock above, and the camera looks vacantly straight ahead, its record of these things safely within. Grips and electricians are already swarming over stages and equipment, because the following four lines will need forty different angles; and in the back the service man tosses the improvised ball to someone, agreeable as ever and gay with laughter, "Ho ho, I guess you wasn't on location *that* day either."

The next scene will be a new scene, not just a remake of a scene already worked out like this one, and so the same thing will go on all over again but with even more time for experiment, until Mr. Litvak breaks for the day around five, and goes wearily up to the projection room for rushes on what the camera held as its secret when he finished the work of the day before. And when tomorrow at five he goes up to see what was caught today, and approves the take and attends to its cutting. And when, later when the picture is done and he has seen all the takes as joined together in a director's rough-cut, and the rough-cut has gone to the various departments for the additional sound of music or whistles or traffic, for the splicing in of transition material and printed titles, the little close-ups on numbers and signs and turning calendars, hands writing and what not, and the whole business has gone to the company cutter for final working into line, and a master print made and approved, and duplicates sent to the exchanges and from there to your neighborhood house, you might see it and miss this whole afternoon if your eyes are tired and you look away from the screen a moment and then rub them.

The scene will run no longer than 150 feet, a little over a minute and a half. In its proper continuity it may be foolish; certainly it says nothing and does nothing by itself. But in forgetting it and all the other millions of minute-and-a-half setups, you should not forget that here into it went all the bewildering skill and loving care of miniaturists and watchmakers, moving on their spiderwork of stagings and ladders in that enormous cavern by the hour (and time and a half for overtime) to make everything as truly real as the frailties of writers and actors and directors will allow—in the day's duty to make everything within the experience of man come to life at the proper bidding.

13 October 1941

Hollywood Footnote

I have been doing some articles about Hollywood, always with the feeling that the limitations of space and/or journalism leave half of everything unsaid, or the wrong thing emphasized. The leftover footnotes are already enough to start a Ph.D. thesis, but already time on such a project is drawing to a close. One note is the matter of the shape of Hollywood as it is modeled with the liberal, or uplift, brassière. In this picture all the underpaid or otherwise dissatisfied are good; all the overpaid are evil. The actual work of pictures and the hopes of people who wish to make them well are left out as being dull copy, or at least not an invitation to the emotions of wishfuls and chumps. The copy that results is salable, and so printed; and it gets little or no attention from the only people who need encouragement or reprimand.

When I was on the Coast I saw an article in the *Nation*. It had a Hollywood dateline, but it was written precisely for the *Nation*. It was a piece on extras; it gave out statistics long established; it gave the usual half of the picture any editorial writer can run up from the usual handouts. But did it do anything in Hollywood, dateline and all? And where is the other half that should match it, and make it a recognizable picture of the actual problem? And who cares, finally?

The Hollywood bureaucracy is an inhuman and absurd machine second only to that of the various bureaus in Washington, no doubt about that. But there is one problem the extras have in general. The problem is themselves. In general they constitute no class of agriculturally or industrially dispossessed; they are not victims of geographical disaster; they are not skilled workers pre-empted by the Machine. They have converged on the town in swarms, attracted by the smell of easy money—which some of them have enjoyed in former times and latterly fallen out of. (And strangely, it is this latter class of extra that seems the best and quietest worker.)

But the main trouble with them in common is a lack of ambition, of willingness, of worth in the thing they are doing. Despite what the Screen

Actors' Guild and Central Casting have done to regularize, limit, raise the basic minimum, the thousands still on register cannot get enough work to keep them adequately paid. This is always pointed out and duly bled over, without of course any concrete aid to the extras whatsoever. It is not pointed out that their pay when they work is three to thirty times that of unskilled labor anywhere in the world, starting with a basic minimum of $10.50 a day. From their behavior on the set and from the reports of directors—many of whom are people of as good will as you or I at the very least—I get the idea that by and large they are not the type of people who feel any need to try to do what little is asked of them. They are complacent in bungling, often sullen, sometimes vicious. The idea seems to be that the world owes them a living, and furniture to scratch their matches on.

Their eternal soldiering, remember, never works out against the Oppressors. The willfulness or incompetence of extras mainly presses on the people who are trying to make the pictures, and working hard. They will deliberately louse up a scene toward the end of a day that started at seven or eight in the morning for a company of more than a hundred weary people, simply to push the production into overtime checks for themselves. They will be rehearsed one by one until the whole scene is foolproof, and then on the final take fall to muddling and muttering when they should be still, passing in lockstep when they should be a subway crowd, never alert to anything save a request made on them that could be called an imposition by the book, and charged for as such. As for their answer to the main union framework, which has benefited them, they will cross any line or undercut any category, given the chance.

This is the more glaring in an industry where even the least of the technicians crowding the lot (many of whom are on a week-to-week basis and often unjustly out, or "between pictures") are quick, resourceful, and sunny of humor to a point not found elsewhere. The Directors' Union has taken the problem up openly and probably will again, for while a director in his position and salary bracket may seem like a man on velvet, actually he is a fifteen-hours-a-day, seven-days-a-week man, and all overage in time and expense on the thing he is trying to make is eventually rendered out of his hide. He may also be a Simon Legree or a brass-tongue idiot, but the extra mob makes no distinction either way. (I have seen a good man and a world name in pictures hobbling all afternoon on a broken foot to get them ranged up for a short action take, only to have them mill listlessly into one blowup after another. I've seen a couple of them wait until the camera was rolling to refuse a turn of the head in a scene, purely for the chance of sticking up for more money a director who is known everywhere for his underdog sympathies and who booted them off his set and hired two $50 bit-players instead.)

Of course there are good extras, eager, pleasant, shamefully at the mercy of the rent bill on one hand and no-work-today on the other. If they could be winnowed out by assistant directors, and saved for use, that would give their union a bargaining point. And it would give them more chance to raise themselves out of a rut any good man would get clear of even if it killed him. It would be nice if the Hollywood-dateline writer could make extras as well as readers live in this dream of calling by name for the good extras, or people who would at least try. But unfortunately there is the fact that these very extras' good friends would trip them on their faces at the first opportunity, and there is the fact that Central Casting will be happy to supply named extras—as $25 *actors.*

Extras are a problem not only to themselves but to the unions set up for their betterment. They are a city or a jungle, and the laws of the city rule their actions as a group, and as individuals, and regulate their struggle for work and pay and bread. Their lunging and fickle bulk can be, and is, employed to vitiate the Academy Awards (a subject for a footnote in itself, presently). But their status is simply not that of the legitimately destitute, and their never-ending locust descent on the town where movies are made is never retarded by the reticence of both Left and Right on the subject of any such problem so real to the movie makers. If we are interested in these, the actively good people of Hollywood, we should understand their position and the conditions they work under; if our interest in movies goes no farther than the bleeding heart at space rates, what the hell are we doing here anyway?

17 November 1941

Land of Dreams, and Nightmares

To a sizable bulk of our population, Hollywood is where you go when you die, if you're good. To some of our more impatient critics, Hollywood is where you die if you go there. It is a most complex place to report on, and in this series of articles I have surely not even brushed a good third of the business of picture making, in one respect or another. There are territories left out. There are the endless score sheets in composer's row and the always last-minute hustle over there to get the music out after the film has been made and cut—to get it broken down, sequence by sequence and scene by scene, each shift of mood, place, or action timed to the second and written in on a rehearsed master sheet, with its demand of music to fit and get it up, where is it, why not. There are the overtime sessions on the recording stage, when the score has been written, arrangements made, and the band tired in shirtsleeves and the director looking at his watch, looking at the control-room, waiting for the film to flash on the screen preceded by the metronome beat and numbers shifting with it: 7, 6, 5, 4, 3, 2, *and* in, the men in the band with their single earphone apiece getting the exact tempo for that stretch of action, and then that little stretch of music played once and played again, rephrased here or there and played over, all for just, say, the bridge into a song in a musical, for a strain under the credit titles of the film, for the establishment of a new mood, whether of snow or of city traffic. And the composer sweating, watching his men and the inexorable numbers on the screen, watching the score and the clamped-down faces in the control-room.

And there is the quiet and incomprehensible activity of the art department, with its draftsmen and painters and model builders, filling room after room with scheme and replica, running up a coal mine or a wooded hill in the time it would take you to describe it, establishing the key of a scene with charcoal, crayon, watercolor, scaling a point of action down to inches so that the director may study his moves even as the set is being built. The art department starts as soon as a script has been decided on, and it makes so much of the picture in stills and models that its work for any one show could be made a traveling exhibit, of craftsmanship and care and feeling, too, a background for motion, almost alive in itself.

Following these specifications, there are the veterans on the sets, running you up a house or a tree, a gravel drive or a pasture slope, as neat in each case as you please. They are here today, before they or anybody knows what the picture is about, busy with saw and hammers and guy wires to the tying-off position on the parallels, with paint and shrubbery and paper flowers; tomorrow, when the cameras and lights roll up to look at the first scene, over and over, they are gone, leaving their portion of a city or a canyon ready and solid behind them. No amateur who has ever tried to saw an angle without a mitrebox will fail to delight in this fairyland carpentry where men build only for the illusion but with the speed of illusion. A seat is too low for the effect desired, but cannot be mounted on a box that would show in the camera: within twenty minutes the cushion has been taken off and a wooden riser built and fitted to its curves, stained and secured in place, ready. A door has to open without human aid, and in ten minutes a heavy thread is run out and over a pulley and back, and painted dull black so the camera won't pick it up. A director wants a shot from floor level, and before you know it they have sawed through the planking and established a base for the camera on its dolly three feet below. If you have any idea of what you want, all you have to do is ask them.

Of course there are the actors. They are important in pictures, but by the process of identification are made much more important than they should be. Actually they are at the mercy of the story they are put in, the director who uses them to tell it, and in a lesser but still important way they are at the mercy of costume designers, cameramen, etc. But they are the part of Hollywood on which speculation and gossip focuses most brilliantly, and their contribution to the art of pictures is immediately visible to all. Pictures demand of them, first, that they should have that quality which stands up under the camera eye and lives to project itself out from the shadows of the screen into the imagination of an audience; second, that they have a bounty of patience, of willingness before instruction, above all, of a hardihood of imagination and belief in the fragment that must be run over and over until it is natural and right. You know all about them, or less than nothing about them, by the evergreen lifestories in every kind of journal using movable type. A lot of them are just tired stage actors, doing it the easy way; but some of them are developed for and by the movies, and some of them are very good people. Alongside the flat braveries of Errol Flynn you must put Gary Cooper, to be fair. And you will not forget, I hope, the lank, eager, common-man sweetness of Henry Fonda, whose Abe Lincoln was so high and far above the studied caricature of Raymond Massey that it is not to talk. Sometimes in the movies the free and honest is released as it is nowhere else, needing only a shrewd director and a sensible story; and for every foolish star, exploded into a million dollars by virtue of the public thirst for new personality and new types of brassière, you will find someone plugging along, believing in the thing, worrying over it, trying to do it the best way. They are rarely bright copy but they are there, the movies in their general faceless all-inclusive way having made them because they need them.

The scoring of music is something the movies have not developed to a point where they know what to do about it, and certainly the question is still one of the most difficult, to the composers as well as to the audience. Fanfares, heavy orchestration, lack of imagination obtrude on almost any film story you think of, yet anything in the way of delicacy and restraint is ruled out of most productions on the ground of lack of appeal. Normally intended to underline or even set up a mood, music often comes to have the opposite effect of diverting the attention if not actually pouring over the edge of dramatic necessity into its own puddle of splendor. Composers wrestle sometimes with the demands of the form, but they are too often cut down by some chump from the front office, if not in intention then in the matter of budget, because the front office either knows what it likes or what the whole world likes, as represented of course by some blowsy homebody of a wife.

And there is so little chance of a progressive, continuous, and memorable composition in furnishing chords now for a hurricane and next minute for Nelson Eddy, that the boys all too quickly find the easiest course to be that of swimming with the current, giving the boobs what they want, and overloading the microphone at every point of European action by sitting the brass section for the 1812 Overture no more than ten feet away from it. And if a composer does get a score he fancies he can work on in an original way, who is to blame him for pushing the music at the expense of theater continuity, using the main business of the picture itself as an excuse or suggestion for his themal development, until sometimes a country garden takes on the aspect of a mixture of a Legion convention and the Albert Hall.

Nobody has sufficiently explored this field, though Oscar Levant and Virgil Thomson have dropped a few pertinent and acid notes by the way; nobody has been allowed to; and though no action can seem to happen in its natural silence any more (Fritz Lang got the reputation of reverting to the UFA days of the silents when he took scenes in *Man Hunt* with nothing but the breathing of people and the trickle of water, as they should exactly be heard for the full effect), most of the picture makers accept as incessant that which should be incidental. There is no near-remedy or answer. We cannot get decent scoring of pictures until we somehow breed a type of man who will have the enormous background and training of a good musician, plus the understanding and appreciation of the film at large.

There are also the nicest people in the world, all the people on the set from actual manual labor to script girls, who make the majority, the majority you have to depend on for pictures if not glamor. It is the place they live and work in, and what if crazy things happen in the papers or even actually? They have their homes, they head out for them at the end of the hard day for supper. Maybe they go to a movie, though it is not a movie-mad town and the audiences you find in theaters are a cross between the very wise ("Look at him faking that one, with the tree; the dope forgets it's an elm to start with, look at him, and what's he making a week?") and the unalert or dumb. Most of the technicians have made or seriously wish to make a profession or trade out of it, as you would with machine-tool making or draftsmanship. In it they are happy, and their carefree wisdom in the midst of bewilderment is contagious—I believe it is the main thing, above the money, which makes the long day on the set tolerable. I've said how efficient they are, how unobtrusive in their steady realization of the miracle in such matters as device, weight, time, speed. Hollywood has built up a new ideal in craftsmanship, where to speak a mean word or to be discourteous to the most obvious dope of a stranger, would be an ill thing.

The cameramen there is no space for in any such brief report on an industry so highly technical and ramified. Their mystery is well preserved if only because they have learned the values and intricate means of reproduction of the still camera while appreciating and absorbing the principles of motion, of running emphasis, contrasting moods of fiction. It is said about them simply and finally that you may prefer one man's style to another's, you may have people you do or don't like to work with, but you can't work on an "A" picture and get an "A" cameraman who isn't a veteran in his art, who doesn't know more about what you think you're doing than you do, and who won't turn you in just as good a picture as you are able to see in your mind and pass on to him in the way of communication.

It is always pleasant to speculate about what Hollywood Needs Most, and indeed one of the trade magazines makes a yearly feature out of inviting several hundred film reviewers to tell what is wrong and what they think ought to be done. With the industry set up as it is, catering successfully to millions at a profit of millions, there is little to be hoped for in the way of easy miracles, and what energy is at the disposal of reform movements is almost invariably misled, being misinformed in the first place (the most recent large example is the fuss about block-booking: block-booking was done away with and now the very exhibitors who kept the howl going don't like the result; and as for any change in the quality of pictures, don't ask).

The best thing to hope for is a complete shakeup, some basic shock in the financial relation of pictures to public. It would not be an easy cure for anybody and it certainly wouldn't be complete. But it could achieve what you could never get by asking: the low-budget picture as a general rule, and the low-budget picture means junking expensive stars and fantastic story costs. It also means—if it is low enough and imperative enough—the return of ingenuity to the films. The films were in the hardiest period of their growth when directors had to scrabble and make-do under severe handicaps, when they couldn't employ five or six Name writers of no talent but great salary potential, when they weren't carrying the load of a so-called producer whose salary for six months, let alone his bungling, exceeded the necessary cost of the picture. Now and again someone makes a small picture that is also a good one, and he doubles his cost with ease. But the man is running counter to the industry as it normally operates today, and he is retired soon enough from competition by being given a fat job with one of the majors as assistant something in charge of something.

The immediate hope is that the men who are getting a bellyful of the machine setup, who know a story when they see one and how to go about making a film from it, will get the resolution and the money to come forward with the old United Artists idea, now in decay. They would be directors and director's writers (as opposed to such blown-up nonentities in film as, say, James Hilton or Phil Stong). They would take less money and take more time, and if there were only four or five of them they would turn out a half-dozen moderately good pictures a year. The pictures would be distributed, for only the most ferocious boycott can hold its own with eternal and insistent demand of theater operators for product, for the thing their neighborhood and all the neighborhoods will lay down their coins to see, whether it has been advertised and premièred or not. There isn't a good director or a good writer in Hollywood who doesn't tear his hair over what the front office has done to his story now, and more because of this than because of the nature of things, the front offices will eventually have to take a back seat. They can't make pictures, and that's the size of it. They can throw millions around and they can draw lackeys like flies, but they can't make the pictures, and without pictures they die. I should not be surprised if there were not going on right now, slowly and with no concerted front, something like the managerial revolution in films. With so many private and expensive egos charging around in their own interests, you can never be sure of any common result; but even without concerted action you can hear a general and rising demand: give the movies back to the people who make them.

24 November 1941

Index of Names

Index of Films and Reviews

(Directors of films given major review attention are included following the titles.)

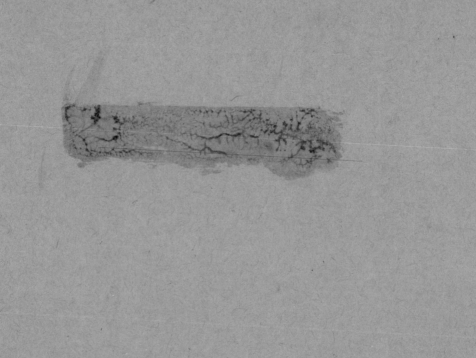